SURVIVOR'S GUIDE TO

THE LEGAL ENVIRONMENT

JOHN ADAMSON

SOUTH-WESTERN

TM

THOMSON LEARNING

Australia • Canada • Mexico • Singapore • Spain • United Kingdom • United States

Survivor's Guide to the Legal Environment
by John Adamson

Vice President/Executive Publisher: Dave Shaut
Team Leader: Karen Schmohe
Executive Editor: Eve Lewis
Project Manager: Enid Nagel
Production Manager: Patricia Matthews Boies
Editor: Darrell E. Frye
Executive Marketing Manager: Carol Volz
Channel Manager: Chris L. McNamee
Marketing Coordinator: Lori Pegg
Manufacturing Coordinator: Kevin L. Kluck
Art and Design Coordinator: Tippy McIntosh
Cover Design: Paul Neff
Internal Design and Composition: settingPace
Editorial Assistant: Stephanie L. White
Production Assistant: Nancy Stamper
Printer: Van Hoffmann Graphics, Eldridge, IA

About the Author

John Adamson is Assistant Professor of Business and Law in the Department of Finance and General Business at Southwest Missouri State University. Adamson received a B.S. from the U.S. Military Academy at West Point, NY; an M.A. from Georgetown University, and an M.B.A. and J.D. from the University of Virginia at Charlottesville. A decorated, disabled veteran and current mayor and school board member of Miller, MO, Adamson is author of numerous business law publications, with a concentration on environmental law.

YOUR COURSE PLANNING JUST GOT EASIER!

The *Survivor's Guide to the Legal Environment* is a text like no other! Designed for professionals and managers who need to know the basics, this text will guide you through the world of the legal environment. Using a conversational style, *Survivor's Guide to the Legal Environment* provides the most current topics and issues in the law in an easy to understand manner.

Looking for other career-enhancement titles for today's professional? Explore these additional Survivor's Guides from South-Western!

Survivor's Guide to Finance
by Bergeron

Finance is the universal language of business! *Survivor's Guide to Finance* makes financial decision-making clear and concise to managers of all levels. Users with no formal training in accounting or finance will find this book as a solid source of financial understanding.

Text/CD Package   0-538-72517-6

Survivor's Guide to Small Business
by Townsley

Designed for the entrepreneur, *Survivor's Guide to Small Business* emphasizes practical and useful information for starting a business. the content is comprehensive and universal and features the most current technology resources.

Text/CD Package   0-538-72573-7

Survivor's Guide to Technical Writing
by Ingre

A comprehensive, easy-to-use guide for key workplace communication skills is found in the *Survivor's Guide to Technical Writing*. Integrating the most current technology, this book reflects the most current topics and issues in technical communication.

Text/CD Package   0-538-72578-8

SOUTH-WESTERN
™
THOMSON LEARNING

Join us on the Internet at www.swep.com

HOW TO USE THIS BOOK

Survivor's Guide to the Legal Environment is intended to provide you with a thorough basic working knowledge of the law and to train you to observe both potential and actual events from a legal perspective. These two goals are especially pursued in Unit 1, which includes materials on ethics, the legal system, torts, and the criminal law. In short, Unit 1 provides you with the background in the law that every person should have, but typically does not.

The focus in the remaining units narrows to the study of traditional business law topics. These topics appear in general order of importance to a business person. Materials on contracts, sales, negotiable instruments (checks, notes, and drafts), debtor-creditor relationships, forms of business organization, employment, property, and insurance are presented in a straightforward way with plenty of examples to ensure understanding and confidence in application.

In addition to merely presenting the existing laws, the text conveys the logic behind them as well. Where inconsistencies and gaps in the law appear, they are openly noted. This book is intended not only to help you understand the law, but, more importantly, to learn from the wisdom and mistakes of others.

CHARTS AND TABLES Throughout the text charts and tables provide a quick overview of the material for review.

HYPOTHETICAL CASES A generous supply of hypothetical (and, sometimes entertaining) cases within the chapters provides understandable applications of legal concepts.

TECHNOLOGY INSIGHTS Features highlighting the impact that new technology has on the law are given for each unit. The Technology Insights features cover the topics of facial mapping, computer simulations, high-tech gadgets, counterfeiting, medical technology, stem cell research, intellectual property and Napster, and surveillance cameras.

END-OF-CHAPTER EXERCISES Each chapter ends with materials to help you review the chapter concepts and assess the strength of your knowledge. Your knowledge of legal terms is assessed in Use Legal Terms. Test Your Reading assesses your retention of the facts. Your critical thinking skills and ability to apply the law are measured in Think Critically About Evidence.

REAL-WORLD CASES The Real-World Cases at the end of the chapters have been selected for their involving nature and their potential to both integrate and project the law. Therefore, often there is no one "right" answer to the questions that follow the cases.

STUDENT CD The CD packaged with your textbook contains documents that enhance your knowledge of the law in general, and business law, in particular. You will refer to the U.S. Constitution and Declaration of Independence in your study of Unit 1. Excerpted text from the Uniform Commercial Code (UCC) is provided as a reference in your study of specific business laws. The Uniform Partnership Act (UPA) and the Revised Uniform Limited Partnership Act (RULPA) is provided for your study of business organizations. Lastly, additional Insight Features are provided on a variety of topics of interest, including legal research, choosing an attorney, compensating an attorney, how to become an attorney, and how case decisions are reported.

STUDY GUIDE A good review of each chapter is provided in a separate *Study Guide.* For each chapter in the textbook, a chapter outline is provided, followed by a series of True-False, Multiple Choice, and Short Essay questions. This guide is especially recommended to help you prepare for tests.

INSTRUCTOR'S RESOURCE CD Provided on the CD to support the text is an *Instructor's Manual* that supplies solutions to all end-of-chapter questions and cases. This CD also includes PowerPoint slides to help instructors present the text material in class.

EXAMVIEW® PRO CD Provides an electronic test bank for each chapter to allow instructors to customize the testing program, edit questions, and create different versions of the same test.

REVIEWERS

Joseph Allegretti
Professor, Business Law
Loudonville, NY

Nanci G. Brady
Instructor, Business Department
Hagerstown, MD

Debra Welch Keener
Campus Coordinator & Instructor, Paralegal Program
San Antonio, TX

Steven C. Kempisty, Esq.
Coordinator of Paralegal Studies
Syracuse, NY

Gerald M. Rogers, J.D.
Professor, Paralegal Program Director
Westminster, CO

Jeffrey S. Rubel
Program Director, Paralegal Technology
Batavia, OH

TABLE OF CONTENTS

UNIT 1

The Essentials of Legal Survival: Foundations of the Law

CHAPTERS

CHAPTER 1

How the Legal System Developed

GOALS

- ◆   Learn what the law is and what it is not
- ◆   Understand the ethical foundations of the legal system
- ◆   Know some fundamental principles of the law

What Is the Law?

A "simple" case to test your wisdom:

> Then came two women . . . before King Solomon.
>
> And the first woman said, O my lord, I and this woman live in the same house; and I was delivered of a child with her in the house.
>
> And it came to pass the third day after that I was delivered, that this woman was delivered also; and we were together: there was no stranger with us in the house, save we two in the house.
>
> And this woman's child died in the night; because she overlaid it [smothered the child with her body].
>
> And she arose at midnight, and took my son from beside me, while thine handmaid slept, and laid it in her bosom, and laid her dead child in my bosom.
>
> And when I rose in the morning to give my child suck, behold it was dead: but when I had considered it in the morning, behold it was not my son, which I did bear. And the other woman said: Nay, but the living is my son, and the dead is thy son.

And the women spoke no more save each to demand the child for
herself; but those in the king's court that day shook their heads saying,
"No greater test of wisdom shall befall Solomon. What judgment will
he render?"

What judgment would you render? Before you decide, consider the following
questions: Why is the king responsible for deciding this case? What possible remedies to the situation can the king choose from? Can the king decide not to decide?
Which remedy would you choose? Why? For King Solomon's decision, read on.

Why Study the Law?

You and other business-oriented people must deal with the law every day. You may
meet it firsthand, in the form of a highway patrol officer personalizing a ticket for
you. You may feel its watchful eye on you as it regulates your workplace, product,
and profit. Your response to it may be frustration, resentment, or gratitude,
depending on the circumstances. Regardless, you must realize that the law maintains a stable environment within which business can flourish. Without the law,
you would have to contend with a level of chaos that would make profitable trade
unlikely, if not impossible. Because of all this, knowledge of the law and how it
works is crucial to your success. As a first step in acquiring that knowledge, you
need to realize exactly what the law is.

Frankly, however, over the centuries there have been as many answers to the
question "What is law?" as there have been people who asked it. The answers
varied so much because each answer was a product of the background and insight
of the person who framed it. Although philosophers such as Aristotle and Hobbes
set down formal definitions, you can be certain that the common people of their
times had their own practical definitions. For the purposes of this book on business law, we need to favor the approach of the common people and pick a definition that is both accurate and practical.

Definition of Law

For our purposes, therefore, the **law** is best defined as the rules of conduct that a
central political authority will enforce. To be sure, we all obey many rules that lack
the force of law. Religions suggest their codes of conduct to us, our communities
and ethnic heritages have their customs, and even our social groups tell us what
behaviors and styles are acceptable. However, all of these lack the power to
imprison or fine to enforce their rules. That power is what sets the law apart.

Definition of Business Law

The first part of this book is meant to give you a background in the law in general.
Then, from Chapter 7 on, we will concentrate on business law, the aspect of the
law that you doubtless expect to study in detail in this book. **Business law** is the
relatively specific group of laws that regulates the establishment, operation, and

termination of commercial enterprises. Don't skimp on your study of these first chapters, however. If you don't have the background that Chapters 1–6 are meant to give you, relying on a knowledge of the law obtained without them will be as dangerous as walking on thin ice over the waters of a deep, fast current.

Development of U.S. Laws and Legal System

Although the historical and ethnic backgrounds of the citizens of the United States are diverse, the roots of the vast majority of our laws and legal systems lie in England. There, over the course of centuries, the power to make, interpret, and apply the law was slowly transferred from the monarchy to legal institutions similar to those of the U.S. So, for a better understanding of how the law works today, we have to go back to the middle of the 12th century.

Courts of Law and the Appellate Court System

At that time, almost a century after their conquest of England, the Normans remained culturally separate from the people they conquered. The Norman king, worried about the potential danger that this division posed to his rule, sought to bring about unity. As one means of achieving this end, he set up a system of circuit riding judges, selected from the Norman nobility. These judges would ride from village to village along a particular "circuit." Using the power the king had given them, they would make decisions that settled disputes among the people.

The power to settle disputes had always been held by monarchs. Throughout history, a king or queen who held "court" was not conducting a social event but making the nitty-gritty decisions that kept his or her realm together. If a king decided wisely and fairly, his power and reputation grew. If he decided poorly and with obvious favoritism, he created long-standing grudges that often came back to haunt him in the form of revolt. In the case that begins this chapter, King Solomon followed the path of wisdom and fairness, as follows:

> And the king said, "Divide the living child in two, and give half to the one, and half to the other."
>
> Then spake the woman who was the living child's real mother, for her bowels yearned upon her son, "Oh my lord, give her the living child and in no wise slay it.
>
> But the mother of the dead child said, "Let it [the living baby] be neither hers nor mine. Divide it with the sword."
>
> Then the king answered and said, "Give her [the woman who did not want the surviving baby slain] the living child, and in no wise slay it: she is the mother thereof."

And all Israel heard of the judgment which the king had judged; and they feared the king.

So it was very important to the king of England that his judges act wisely when they held **courts of law**. These courts were formal proceedings in which the judges were to apply powers that the king had given them to resolve the disputes of the people. To be as certain as possible that his judges decided cases justly, the king of England created a system of **appellate courts**. These higher courts were established to maintain fairness and uniformity in the decisions reached in the lower courts.

Individuals disgruntled with the decisions reached in a court presided over by a circuit riding judge could appeal to a higher court for review. In such cases, the appellate court would determine whether the lower court had acted properly. The king formed the appellate courts by having the circuit riding judges return to London for approximately half of each year and sit together in groups to hear cases brought on appeal. The highest of these appellate courts became known as the King's (or Queen's) Bench.

Origin of the Jury and The Use of Precedent

However, just having a reasonably fair structure for resolving disputes did not ensure that the Norman and older English cultures would draw together as one. To achieve that result within the legal system, the king had to utilize other devices. To explain these devices, we need to follow a sample case through the system that the king set up.

It is late summer and James of Northshire, a farmer and apple-grower, is taking his produce to London in his oxcart. It is the first time he has made the trip, and he has been on the road for two days. Worried that his goods might spoil, James is in a bit of a rush. As he approaches a four-way intersection, he sees another cart that could enter the intersection from his right at the same time that his oxcart will. Does James rein in his ox, which is lumbering along at maximum speed? No, because he knows it is the custom around his home town of Northshire for the right-of-way at an intersection to go to the person on the left. He is that person, so on rumbles his cart. To James's surprise, the driver of the other cart, Ben of the Walnut Grove, does not rein in either. As a consequence, both carts collide in the middle of the intersection. James and Ben are injured, their property is destroyed, and James's ox is gored.

Upon hearing that a circuit riding judge is coming to the nearby town of Binghamton. James decides to bring a case against Ben. When the judge arrives and opens court, James appears before him, accuses Ben of being careless in not allowing him the right-of-way, and asks the court to have Ben pay for the damage. To James's surprise, Ben appears and accuses him of being the careless one and asks that he pay instead.

The Norman judge hears the case but is unable to decide it fairly because he does not know the custom of the region as to who has the right-of-way at an intersection. To find out, he inquires of several local citizens as to whom, in fact, would be to blame for the crash according to the commonly held rules of the road. These citizens advise him that, as in this area the right-of-way goes to the person on the right, James was to blame. The judge then enters a judgment that, as the customary or common law of the area grants the right-of-way to the person on the right, James was, in fact, to blame and owes Ben damages in the form of an amount of money equal to Ben's loss.

James is angered by the decision because he knows that if the judge had asked Northshire citizens instead of Binghamton citizens the same question, he would have won the case. He, therefore, decides to appeal.

Four months later, in London, James' and Ben's case is heard on appeal before the King's Bench, the highest court in the land. The judges, just back from riding circuit throughout the realm, consider whether as a matter of law for the entire kingdom the right-of-way should go to the person on the left or to the person on the right. Drawing on their experiences on circuit with the customs of the kingdom's various regions, they determine that in most areas the right-of-way should go to the person on the left.

The court then announces its decision:

> In the case of *James of Northshire* v. *Ben of the Walnut Grove* and from this day forward in the realm, we have determined that as a matter of law the right-of-way shall fall to the person on the left. Consequently, the decision in the lower court is overturned, and we direct that the lower court reconsider the case to determine the amount of damages to be paid to James of Northshire.

A few months later, when the circuit judge again returned to Binghamton, the court determined how much money Ben was to pay James. The long-term significance of the case was that, after the final decision on appeal, it became law throughout the nation that the right-of-way belonged to the person on the left. If a lower court decided differently, the person who lost could always appeal and have the decision overturned because the **precedent** or rule of law to be applied to this particular legal issue had been set in the case of *James of Northshire* v. *Ben of the Walnut Grove*. The policy of enforcing such established precedents so as to ensure fairness to all similarly situated parties is known as **stare decisis**. More details about the workings of the appellate courts within our state and federal court systems are contained in Chapters 3 and 4.

As you probably suspected, the panel of citizens on which the Norman judge relied to interpret the local customs evolved into what we know as the **jury**. Today the jury fills that same role of assessing evidence and advising the judge on the actual facts of the case. The judge's job is to identify and apply the appropriate law so as to ensure that the trial is conducted properly. In particular, the judge must determine what evidence the jury should hear (excluding hearsay, for example), ensure that proper legal procedure is followed, and, using the facts provided by the jury, reach a judgment in the case. This division of labor in the courtroom (i.e., the jury determines the facts, the judge determines and applies the law) is vital to the common law system.

In the *James of Northshire* v. *Ben of the Walnut Grove* case, the judges ultimately determined the law to be that in England the right-of-way at intersections belongs to the person on the left. Since the facts, as determined by the jury, were that James had been on Ben's left and that Ben's failure to yield the right-of-way had resulted in the infliction of a certain amount of damages on James, the judge ruled that by law Ben must pay James that amount.

Development of Courts of Equity

As is often the case when an authority tries to treat everyone fairly through a detailed system of regulation, the rules of the king's courts of law became more and more inflexible. Thus, as the body of laws grew, the king's courts became prisoners of their own legal system. Unless everything was done just as it had been done before, these courts could accomplish nothing. As a consequence, many problems arose for which the courts of law simply could not provide a remedy. For example, if your cattle were watered solely from one stream and your neighbor dammed it up, you would have to wait until your cattle died and then sue for the damages that the law would provide. Such situations led to great waste. However, if you had the ear of the king, you could simply complain to him, and he would order the dam torn down. Few, of course, were in a position to plead for such an order.

In response to problems that the courts of law could not solve, the king created a new system of courts called the **courts of equity**. To these courts he gave some of his own power to issue orders. Within bounds, these courts could fashion a remedy unavailable to the courts of law and then issue an order to enforce that remedy on the parties involved. Although separate for centuries in England, courts of equity and courts of law have been merged in the great majority of states in the U.S. Thus, you can now seek damages or, if that remedy is not satisfactory, a court order to remedy your problem, all from the same court. Remedies will be discussed further in Chapters 6 and 12.

This system that the king of England set up centuries ago ultimately molded English culture by producing a uniform common law for all of England. This **common law** was based on the customs practiced by most of the realm's people and was applicable to all of its subjects. Building on success, all but one of our states have adopted the English common law system. (Louisiana's law is based on the French legal system due to that state's historic heritage.)

Ethics and the Growth of Law

Although you may never formally study the **ethical systems** we use, these codes of conduct exert a great deal of influence over your behavior. This influence is reflected in society's customs and, ultimately, because the common law is based on customary ways of behaving, in its laws.

The Judeo-Christian Ethical System

Judeo-Christian ethics are well known in this country. This ethical system requires that in dealing with other human beings, a person behave in certain ways regardless of the consequences. "Thou shalt not steal" is not qualified by "unless your children will starve if you do not steal and the person you are stealing from is rich and fat." Because of this approach, our laws punish the Robin Hoods who steal to save the poor as harshly as it punishes thieves who steal only for their own advantage.

A person who follows the Judeo-Christian ethical system is called on to love others, to honor his or her mother and father, to refrain from killing, and to work hard in order to be able to help others rather than to satisfy personal greed. Such a person is to do all of this without consideration of worldly consequences but with an eye to a heavenly reward. Our legal system reflects the Judeo-Christian ethical system in part by making crimes out of certain acts that violate its standards, such as theft and murder.

Egoism

An ethical system that contrasts sharply with the Judeo-Christian system is egoism. Under the system of **egoism**, a person's actions are determined by their consequences for his or her self-interest. Many laws take into account the fact that people are strongly motivated by the greed of egoism instead of the altruism of Judeo-Christian ethics. For example, our tax laws provide tax relief (popularly called "loopholes") for those who tailor their investments or other behavioral patterns in a certain way.

The two main types of egoism are hedonism and psychological egoism. Under **hedonism** a person acts to satisfy or please his or her senses of taste, touch, smell, sight, and hearing. In the alternative, under **psychological egoism** a person acts primarily because of the impact that her or his behavior will have on others. Buying expensive cars or fashions to attract the esteem or envy of others is an example of behavior sparked by psychological egoism.

Utilitarianism

Another ethical system that emphasizes worldly consequences in judging behavior is **utilitarianism**. Under this system an action is proper if it produces the greatest good for the greatest number of those people affected by it. In the law utilitarian analysis can lead both to programs mandating public education and to programs that ignore the educational requirements of minorities, such as persons of certain ethnic backgrounds and the handicapped.

Other Ethical Systems

Finally, there are ethical systems that, like the Judeo-Christian system, do not analyze an action by its worldly consequences. The most notable of these is **Kantian ethics**. This system was developed by Immanuel Kant in the late 1700s. It concluded that every potential action should be analyzed to see whether the principle behind it could be made a universal law without producing an illogical or self-defeating situation. For example, let us say that we are considering falsely yelling "Fire" in a crowded restaurant. The underlying principle here is whether or not freedom of speech should be an absolute right. If it were an absolute right no speech would be believable or reliable. No matter what you say, no one would believe it. This would make freedom of speech useless. Therefore, absolute freedom of speech is self-defeating and should not be permitted.

All of the ethical systems discussed above have affected and continue to affect the development and application of our laws. As with historical developments, changes in our ethical standards cause the law to follow suit and change accordingly.

Jurisprudence

Philosophers who study such evolution in the law explain the changes by using either of two schools of legal philosophy. (A term that you may hear in place of the term legal philosophy is **jurisprudence**.) Aristotle and Aquinas, for example, saw the law as moving toward the achievement of a super-ethical moral standard higher than any that humans in their current state could determine or generate. They were adherents of the **natural law** school, which believes that an ideal legal system was implanted in the reason of human beings before they were ruined by passion, greed, and so forth. Other philosophers, in reaction to such views, saw the law as developing according to a nation's historical experiences. These philosophers adhered to the **historical school** of legal philosophy.

Philosophical differences on why the law changes will always be with us. Therefore in the next chapter, we turn our attention to the more important questions of how legal change occurs and what institutions bring it about.

 ## Technology Insights

NAPSTER

Music copyright violations, once limited to high-profile music-trading sites such as NAPSTER, have spread throughout the Internet. The Recording Industry Association of America (RIAA) recently was quoted as saying that it notified almost 5,000 web sites that they were in violation of the copyright law due to pirating of songs. A recent report estimated that the recording industry will lose more than $3 billion dollars of potential revenues by the year 2005 due to this practice. NAPSTER, meanwhile, announced that it will become a subscription service. Lawsuits against the trading site persist, however.

Think Critically   How do you balance the competing interests here? Should the basic freedom of the Internet (exchanging files) be infringed so that the profits of a lucrative industry can remain strong? Should the hard work of recording artists go unrewarded due to Internet pirates? What are the ethical issues and choices involved here? How would you resolve them?

Chapter Review

USE LEGAL TERMS

Fill in the blanks with the appropriate term. Some terms may not be used.

appellate courts	hedonism	natural law
business law	historical school	precedent
common law	Judeo-Christian ethics	psychological egoism
courts of equity	jurisprudence	stare decisis
courts of law	jury	utilitarianism
egoism	Kantian ethics	
ethical systems	law	

1. The ___?___ has the responsibility of determining the facts of a case.
2. Barton Stonely, voted most likely loser by his high school class of 1992, turned to me one day and said, "Why'd I buy a Porsche 911, you ask? I'll tell you why. It makes people think you have money." Considering ethical systems, in buying the Porsche, Stonely was acting out his ___?___.
3. ___?___ requires the use of established precedents to decide current cases.
4. As our legal system was developing, damages as a remedy were available in courts of law. Alternatively, however, a court order to cease doing something or to do it was available in the ___?___.
5. ___?___ philosophers thought that the best legal system was hidden in the hearts of human beings unaffected by the corruption of the world.
6. The greatest good for the greatest number is the principle of the ethical system called ___?___.
7. "In our area the first vehicle to reach the four-way-stop intersection goes first, regardless of whether that vehicle is going straight, left, or right" is an example of a customary or ___?___.

TEST YOUR READING

8. Why are law and the legal system so important to business and profitable trade?
9. What is the difference between customs and the law?
10. What is business law?
11. What is the difference between the courts of law and the courts of equity?
12. What are the functions of the jury in today's courts?
13. What is meant by stare decisis?
14. What is the basis for the common law?

15. Why should we punish a person who, in a moment of extreme need, steals to feed his starving child while we do not punish a person who kills in self-defense?

16. According to Kant, how should your potential actions be analyzed?

17. What does jurisprudence mean?

THINK CRITICALLY ABOUT EVIDENCE

18. According to the chapter material, which of the following should be considered law?
    a. The Old Testament's prohibition, "Thou shalt not kill."
    b. A sign on the shoulder of the state highway that reads, "$50 to $500 fine for littering."
    c. A 20-mph speed zone near a grade school.

19. The courtrooms of this country still maintain the division of labor that was set in the English system, in which the judge decides the law to be applied and the jury decides the facts of the case. In some cases, however, a jury is either not required or not requested. In such cases, the judge determines the facts by evaluating the evidence. Can you think of reasons why a defendant in a criminal case, for example, would not request a jury?

20. If, after the case of *James of Northshire* v. *Ben of the Walnut Grove* was decided on appeal before the King's Bench, another case involving right-of-way at an intersection came before the Binghamton court. How would that case be decided?
    a. In favor of the person on the right, as the customs of the region have not had time to change.
    b. In favor of the person on the left, as that is now the law.
    c. In favor of the person on the left unless the other person can prove that she or he has not heard of the King's Bench decision.

21. You are late for work for the third time in the last two weeks. Ahead of you on the four-lane divided highway, a station wagon brushes up against the concrete median. It swerves sharply across the lanes of traffic and slams into a light pole on the right hand side of the road. The force of the impact carries it over the shoulder and out of sight. Other drivers ignore the situation and go on. You are coming up to the accident site. How would you react if you subscribed to the utilitarian ethic? To the Judeo-Christian ethic? To the hedonistic ethic?

REAL-WORLD CASE
Marvin v. Marvin
Supreme Court of California
134 Cal. Rptr. (California Reporter) 815 (1976)

Read through this actual case study on how the common law continues to develop in response to society's needs in modern day America.

Actor Lee Marvin, famous for his movie roles in *The Dirty Dozen* and *Cat Ballou*, lived with Michelle Triola for several years. After their relationship ended, Ms. Triola sued Mr. Marvin for what she claimed was her share of the income and property he received during the time they were cohabiting. She claimed that she and Mr. Marvin had made an express agreement to that effect and that, as a consequence of the agreement, she had given up a promising career as an actress to be a homemaker and companion to him. The lower court threw the case out by ruling that the state's Family Law Act (which set down how to become married and the rights of the marital partners) did not allow the enforcement of such private agreements. This left all the property with Mr. Marvin. The case was appealed to the Supreme Court of California.

Justice Tobriner wrote this deciding opinion in the case:

During the past 15 years, there has been a substantial increase in the number of couples living together without marrying. Such nonmarital relationships lead to legal controversy when one partner dies or the couple separates.

We conclude: (1) The provisions of the Family Law Act do not govern the distribution of property acquired during a nonmarital relationship. Such a relationship remains subject solely to judicial decision. (2) The courts should enforce express contracts between nonmarital partners except to the extent that the contract is explicitly founded on the consideration of meretricious sexual services.

Defendant (Lee Marvin) first and principally relies on the contention that the alleged contract is so closely related to the supposed "immoral" character of the relationship between plaintiff and himself that the enforcement of the contract would violate public policy. He points to cases asserting that a contract between nonmarital partners is unenforceable if it is "involved in" an illicit relationship . . . or made in contemplation of such a relationship. A review of the numerous California decisions concerning contracts between nonmarital partners, however, reveals that the courts have not employed such broad and uncertain standards to strike down contracts. The decisions instead disclose a narrower and more precise standard: a contract between nonmarital partners is unenforceable only to the extent that it explicitly rests upon the immoral and illicit consideration of meretricious sexual services.

In summary, we base our opinion on the principle that adults who voluntarily live together and engage in sexual relations are nonetheless as competent as any other persons to contract respecting their earnings and property rights. Of course, they cannot lawfully contract to pay for the performance of sexual services, for such a contract is, in essence, an agreement for prostitution and unlawful for that reason. But they may agree to pool their earnings and to hold all property acquired during the relationship in accord with the law governing community property; conversely, they may agree that each partner's earnings and the property acquired from those earnings remain the separate property of the earning partner. So long as the agreement does not rest upon illicit meretricious consideration, the parties may order their economic affairs as they choose, and no policy precludes the courts from enforcing such agreements.

In the present instance, plaintiff alleges that the parties agreed to pool their earnings, that they contracted to share equally in all property acquired, and that defendant agreed to support plaintiff. The terms of the contract as alleged do not rest upon any unlawful consideration. We therefore conclude that the complaint furnishes a suitable basis upon which the trial court can render declaratory relief. The trial court consequently erred in granting defendant's motion for judgment on the pleadings.

Think Critically

1. What is the basis for the court's decision to uphold contracts between unmarried consenting adults such as the one at issue in this case?
2. Does this decision mean that Ms. Triola will receive one-half of the property in question?
3. Could two or more parties of the same sex enter into such a contract according to the precedent established in this case?
4. Which of the following ethical systems does this decision reflect most closely—the Judeo-Christian system, the utilitarian system, the Kantian system, or the egoistic system? Why?

CHAPTER 2

How Laws Are Made

GOALS

- ◆ Recognize the source of lawmaking power in a democracy
- ◆ Know the process by which laws are made
- ◆ Understand the need for and purposes of administrative agencies

Where Does the Power to Make Laws Come From?

The People

In a democracy, the ultimate lawmaking power is in the hands of the people who are governed by the laws that are made. However, the ways in which this power is transferred to an authority willing to put it into use vary greatly.

In some societies other than the U.S., the people allow the power to be seized or to reside in a dictator or monarch simply because they are unwilling or unable to pay the price of recapturing it. In societies like the U.S., however, the people jealously guard the power with their very lives and only sparingly yield control over themselves to a central authority. For the latter, Patrick Henry, a leader of the American Revolution, put it best:

Why stand we here idle?

What is it that gentlemen wish?

What would they have?

Is life so dear, or peace so sweet, as to be purchased at the price of chains and slavery.

Forbid it, Almighty God!

I know not what course others may take, but as for me,

give me liberty, or give me death.

Address to the Virginia Convention, 1775

A Constitution

Regardless of their origin or current form, most governments today legitimize their powers by a constitution. That **constitution**, however achieved, then becomes the fundamental law of the land. It is important to note that even the federal Constitution of the United States was written by a constitutional convention composed of appointed rather than elected delegates, and ratified by the state legislatures rather than by a direct vote of the people.

The text of this document and the laws and judicial rulings that interpret and apply it are known as **constitutional law**. Whenever there is a conflict between the federal Constitution and federal law, for example, the federal Constitution prevails. In the same manner, all federal law, including the federal Constitution, preempts or supersedes directly conflicting state laws and state constitutional passages. The states agreed to this by ratifying the federal Constitution, which in Article VI, Clause 2, provides that the Constitution itself as well as the laws and treaties of the federal government "shall be the supreme Law of the Land, and the Judges in every State shall be bound thereby." Given the volume and scope of federal laws, the constraints placed on state laws and actions by this "supremacy clause" of the Constitution are numerous. To see how this clause works in practice, read the case at the end of the chapter. It involves a lawsuit by the estate of Karen Silkwood (remember the movie *Silkwood*?) against Kerr-McGee, her employer at a nuclear power plant.

The Branches of Government

The structure of government and the allocation of powers embodied in the U.S. Constitution reflect the application of several principles thought to be vital to the continued freedom of the people. Chief among those principles are separation of powers and checks and balances. In accordance with the former, the power to make laws is given to the **legislative branch** (Article I, Sections 1 and 8). The powers to investigate violations and prosecute alleged violators are given to the **executive branch** (Article II, Section 1). Finally, the powers to conduct **trials**, or formal proceedings for the examination and determination of legal issues, and pronounce judgment are placed with the **judicial branch** (Article III, Sections 1 and 2).

This separation of powers is enhanced by allowing each governmental branch to check or balance out the potential misuse of power by another branch. For example, the judicial branch can declare invalid the laws passed by the legislative branch or can declare void executive actions, such as the use of improperly collected evidence in the prosecution of a criminal law case. By the same token, the

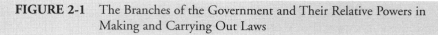

FIGURE 2-1   The Branches of the Government and Their Relative Powers in Making and Carrying Out Laws

Legislative ——————▶ Makes the laws

Executive ——————▶ Investigates and prosecutes alleged violators

Judicial ——————▶ Sits in judgment of alleged violators

very composition of the judicial branch is left to the legislative branch by Article III of the Constitution. As a significant example of this consider that the U.S. Supreme Court was not even created until Congress decided to pass the Federal Judiciary Act, more than six months after the Constitution went into effect.

In a manner similar to that of the federal Constitution, the various state constitutions create and empower the various branches of state government. On the state level, legislatures make the laws. Those laws must be within the guidelines established by the constitution of the given state. The governors and the rest of the executive branch of the state are charged with carrying out the laws. The state courts judge and sentence violators. Finally, the ultimate authority to interpret the state constitution is left to the highest state court, be it named a "supreme court" or a "court of appeals."

How Is the Lawmaking Power Exercised and Applied?

It is important to consider that in making laws in a free society, we must begin with the idea that all behavior is permissible unless it has been made illegal. The opposite approach, that all behavior is impermissible until the authorities specifically allow it, is both frightening and, as shown by the recent break-up of the communist bloc, self-defeating.

The amount of wisdom displayed in choosing what behavior to outlaw and what behavior to encourage is the measure of a democracy. In the U.S., such choices usually take the form of legislatively created laws called **statutes**. Care in drafting, interpreting, and applying specific statutes, especially those making certain behavior illegal, is vital to maintaining freedom. The various branches of the federal and state governments must act in partnership to wisely create and fairly enforce such statutes.

The Creation of a Statute by Congress or a State Legislature

To see what this idea of partnership entails, let's consider an example at the state level. Suppose that for several months the legislators have been receiving reports from voters around the state about break-ins into homes at night while the occupants are asleep. Money and other property have been stolen, people have been injured or killed when they walked in on the intruders, and some homes have even been set afire.

To help stop this wave of violence against people when they are so vulnerable, the legislature creates or **drafts** a statute that makes the specific act involved an offense against the public good. The commission of such an act is then punishable by the government. In other words, the lawmakers define the act as a **crime**. Because there are already statutes that make it illegal to steal, to do physical harm to individuals, and to set fire to structures under such conditions, the legislature realizes that to be effective the penalty for this crime must be more severe.

As a consequence, the legislature creates the crime of **burglary** and defines it as "the breaking and entering of the dwelling house of another at night with the intent to commit a felony therein." ("Felony" is a more serious crime and penalized more severely than most other crimes. It is defined in full in Chapter 5.)

Because of the scrutiny it will receive from the courts, the wording of the statute creating the crime of burglary is extremely important. State legislatures and Congress occasionally make glaring mistakes in the drafting of statutes. In the situation we're considering, however, the statute seems well drafted and clear on its face. The legislature has done its part. Now the statute must stand the test of real life.

A week after the statute goes into effect, in a small town in the southwestern part of the state, Aristottel B. Nasty, who was just released from the state penitentiary after serving three years for grand theft, is stopped at 3 A.M. while driving a brand-new, $3,500 lawn mower down a back street. The lawn mower has been hot-wired. As Aristottel is assuring the police officer who pulled him over that he has gone straight and is now mowing yards for a living (even after dark, there being an enormous demand for his services), a report over the police radio announces the theft of just such a lawn mower from the garage of a nearby home. Aristottel is arrested.

The Utilization of the Statute by a Prosecutor

The next day the state prosecutor, Euwell Burn, reviews the evidence and decides to charge Aristottel with burglary under the new statute rather than the lesser offenses of larceny or breaking and entering. Burn is certain that a conviction of a repeat offender and the greater length of sentence likely to be awarded by the court under the more severe guidelines for burglary sentences will let others know not to attempt similar crimes.

The Application and Review of the Statute by the Courts

At Trial   At the trial the prosecutor is able to prove that a lock on the closed front door of the home was broken to allow access to the garage, that the break-in occurred at night, and that a felony—the theft of the $3,500 lawn mower—was committed afterwards. The police officer then testifies that Aristottel was apprehended less than 15 minutes later as he proudly guided the same lawn mower along a darkened suburban street. The only problem for Prosecutor Burn comes when Aristottel's attorney, public defender Ann Issu, claims that a garage is not a "dwelling house," and therefore Aristottel is not guilty. She puts into evidence the fact that the garage was built onto the side of the house years after the house itself had been constructed and that it was intended for storage and not as a dwelling place. Prosecutor Burn replies that extra rooms and closets for storage added to a dwelling house are protected by the burglary statute. Just because an area is labeled a garage does not mean that it should not be protected in the same way as these are.

On Appeal   The trial judge decides in favor of the prosecutor's interpretation of the law. Aristottel is found guilty and sentenced to 20 years without the possibility of parole for the first 10. Aristottel appeals the guilty verdict, maintaining that the judge erred in ruling in favor of Burn's interpretation of what a "dwelling house" includes. Five months later, the case is argued before the state court of appeals. Two more months pass before the court of appeals issues its ruling. In the opinion of the judge writing for the majority of that court, a garage is held to be a part of a dwelling house if it is permanently attached to the house. If, instead, a garage is freestanding, it is not part of a dwelling house. As the garage in the case was attached to the house, Aristottel's conviction is upheld. Shortly thereafter he tries to appeal to the state supreme court, but that body declines to hear the case. Aristottel is then committed to the state penitentiary to serve his time.

If the prosecutor had lost his argument over what a dwelling house was, Aristottel would have been set free and could not have been tried again on charges arising out of the incident. Instead, the prosecutor, acting as part of the executive branch, properly investigated the case and brought it to trial. Then the courts interpreted and applied the statute to reach a fair result. The appellate court decision in the case helped by establishing a precedent that clarified the definition of burglary.

Through procedures similar to those used in this case involving burglary, repeated over and over again, the branches of a state or federal government play their roles in creating, defining and enforcing laws.

Laws Made by Administrative Agencies

As the pace and complexity of life in this country increased, the ability of the federal government or state governments to make timely and proper laws regulating commerce declined markedly. This was especially true for the federal government. It had been given the responsibility in Article I, Section 8, of the U.S. Constitution for regulating **interstate commerce**, or trade and other commercial intercourse between or among the states. For example, it took more than 30 years for the federal government to recognize the problems posed by the "trusts" which nearly monopolized the markets for oil, sugar, and even whiskey. It then took almost two more decades to pass and apply corrective legislation. By that time, a vast consolidation of economic power in a very few hands had occurred that even today has not been undone. Many experts have identified this consolidation as one of the main factors in causing the Great Depression of the 1930s.

The Rationale for Empowering Agencies

As a reaction to that depression and, by implication, to the failure of Congress to properly regulate interstate commerce, that body created a large number of federal administrative agencies to act for it. Congress delegated to each of these agencies the power to regulate a specific area of interstate commerce. The expert staff of each agency was expected to respond to developing problems with great speed and accuracy. This response has most often been in the form of making and enforcing rules and regulations.

An obstacle to Congress's use of agencies quickly developed, however. Up to the time of the Great Depression the U.S. Supreme Court saw interstate commerce as being only commerce that actually flowed across state lines, such as a shipment of tires from an Illinois manufacturer to a Michigan auto plant. All other domestic commerce was considered **intrastate commerce**, conducted wholly within one state. The Constitution left the regulation of intrastate commerce to the individual states. Unfortunately, this division of labor produced uneven and often ineffective regulation.

The degree of uniform regulation that the new federal agencies felt necessary to counter the problems of the economy caused them to interfere in what had been previously defined as intrastate commerce. This in turn resulted in the U.S. Supreme Court's holding that many of the agencies and their activities were unconstitutional. Finally, in 1937, the Supreme Court changed its mind and, in cases involving Social Security and minimum wages for women and children, yielded to pressure and allowed *interstate commerce* to be redefined to include not just goods actually transported over state lines but any activity within the states that might affect such commerce.

This redefinition greatly enlarged the job of the federal government and had the long-term effect of even more agencies being created at the federal level. In addition, the Supreme Court has since held that the rules and regulations passed by an agency acting with the powers Congress delegated to it have the force and effect of federal law. As a consequence, the regulation of our economy by agencies has probably worked a greater change in the way we live than did the Declaration of Independence or the Constitution.

The Interstate Commerce Commission, the Food and Drug Administration, the Federal Trade Commission, the Securities and Exchange Commission, the National Labor Relations Board, the Federal Communications Commission, the Environmental Protection Agency, the Consumer Product Safety Commission, the Equal Employment Opportunity Commission, and many other agencies are the result. (The areas of responsibility of these agencies are covered near the end of Chapter 3.) Many of the state governments have since followed the federal government's example by setting up their own extensive system of agencies.

The Extent of an Agency's Lawmaking Power

Significantly, the courts have held that the rules and regulations made by agencies have the force of law. Thus, our body of laws is being constantly added to, not only by Congress and the state legislatures, but also by the multitude of state and federal agencies exercising the legislative powers delegated to them. Note that all federal laws, even those made by agencies, are constitutionally supreme when in conflict with state laws.

Chapter Review

USE LEGAL TERMS

Fill in the blanks with the appropriate term. Some terms may not be used.

burglary	draft	judicial branch
constitution	executive branch	legislative branch
constitutional law	interstate commerce	statutes
crime	intrastate commerce	trials

1. A lawmaking body will create or ___?___ a statute.
2. The power to investigate and prosecute violations of statutes belongs to the ___?___ of government.
3. The power to judge and sentence violators of statutes belongs to the ___?___ of government.
4. Under the U.S. Constitution the federal government has the power to regulate ___?___ commerce.
5. The fundamental law of the land is the ___?___.
6. A(n) ___?___ is an offense against the public good that is punishable by the government.
7. Formal proceedings known as ___?___ are conducted for the examination and determination of legal issues.

TEST YOUR READING

8. What are the functions of the legislative, executive and judicial branches of the U.S. government?
9. Who has the ultimate authority to interpret the constitutions of the states and the federal government?
10. What is a crime?
11. Who defines what behavior is considered criminal?
12. If the appellate court in the Nasty trial had decided that the garage was not a part of the dwelling house, what do you think would have happened to Nasty?
13. What is the difference between the original definition of interstate commerce and the one currently in use?
14. What is the difference between interstate and intrastate commerce today?
15. In a conflict of laws between a federal agency's rules and a state constitution, which one would most likely prevail?

THINK CRITICALLY ABOUT EVIDENCE

16. According to Article II, Section 2, of the U.S. Constitution, the president, with the concurrence of two-thirds of the Senate, has the power to make treaties binding the United States. Do these treaties have the force of law within this country? If so, should they be superior to state laws?

17. In the case involving Aristottel B. Nasty, assume that instead of being arrested escaping on a lawn mower, he was caught by the security guard when he tried to leave an apartment building with a solid gold canary cage hidden under his overcoat. The cage and the rare cockatoo inside it, whose whistling Aristottel could not stop, had just been taken from an apartment in the building. The incident occurred at night, and there was evidence of breaking and forced entry.

   a. Assume that you are prosecutor Burn. What issues are crucial to you if you are going to charge Aristottel with burglary in this case? What arguments will you make before the court to support your position on those issues?

   b. Assume that you are public defender Issu. What arguments will you make in defending Aristottel from the burglary charge?

18. Assume that you are an attorney and have just been appointed prosecutor for your area. Since high school, you have dreamed of going into politics. Now your name is going to be in the news frequently and you will become widely known for your success or failure at your job. There are two strategies that you can choose as prosecutor: (1)To prosecute violators to the fullest extent of the law, perhaps breaking new ground in applying statutes to criminal behavior, but also running the risk of losing high-visibility cases; or (2) to prosecute only cases in which you are sure of victory and to plea-bargain away the cases that you might lose. The latter choice would produce an extremely high conviction rate that you could boast of in your political advertising. Which strategy would you choose, and why?

19. In the last 20 years, the area of consumer electronics has grown phenomenally. With that growth have come myriad legal problems, such as copyright violations from rerecorded audiotapes and videotapes, pirated computer programs, and photocopied books; patent violations from shared hardware; and antitrust problems associated with cable access. Should the government create an agency to regulate consumer electronics? What are the advantages and disadvantages of this course of action? If such an agency were created, how should the empowering statute be phrased? What alternatives are there to this course of action?

20. In late 1991, a California state lawmaker proposed that more than 25 of the state's 50-plus counties form a new state, Northern California. The lawmaker made this proposal because many citizens of these counties were angered over the state government's orders that the counties be responsible for providing

health and welfare services to their citizenry. However, although mandating that the counties make these services available, the state did not provide the money to pay for them. Instead, it gave the counties the power to finance any resulting budget shortfalls by raising taxes. For many decades, being a part of the state of California had made the same 25 counties vulnerable to state programs that used their resources, mainly water, to support the growing southern region of the state, a region that dominated the state government due to its large population. What document(s) would determine the right of the 25 counties to secede from the state of California and form their own state? What part of the California government would have primary responsibility for interpreting such document(s) to decide the issue? Consider that the Declaration of Independence reads in part:

"But when a long train of abuses and usurpations, pursuing invariably the same object, evinces a design to reduce them [the people] under absolute Despotism, it is their right, it is their duty, to throw off such Government, and to provide new Guards for their future security." Does this attitude of our country's founders justify the secession of "Northern California"?

REAL-WORLD CASE

Silkwood v. *Kerr-McGee Corporation*
U.S. Supreme Court
464 U.S. 238

Read this actual case involving a potential conflict of federal law with Oklahoma state law in conjunction with Karen Silkwood's alleged plutonium contamination.

Acting for the estate of his deceased daughter, Bill Silkwood brought a successful lawsuit against her former employer, Kerr-McGee. The lawsuit was to recover for injuries to Karen Silkwood from plutonium poisoning sustained as a result of her employment at the Kerr-McGee plutonium fuel production facility near Crescent, Oklahoma. Kerr-McGee appealed the $10 million jury award in favor of Karen's estate.

The appeal maintained that the facility was regulated by the federal Nuclear Regulatory Commission (NRC). As a consequence, Kerr-McGee believed that the Oklahoma laws under which the $10 million recovery was allowed were preempted by the NRC's rules and regulations. Neither these rules and regulations nor the empowering congressional statute of the NRC contained anything on the subject of recovery by a private person injured by violation of NRC standards.

The appeal was ultimately decided by the U.S. Supreme Court, in 1984. In its opinion the Court noted that Congress had probably omitted any mention of judicial recourse for persons injured in situations such as Silkwood's because it considered those parties free to bring lawsuits under state law. It then stated:

Preemption should not be judged on the basis that the Federal Government has so completely occupied the field of safety that state remedies are foreclosed, but on whether there is an irreconcilable conflict between the federal and state standards or whether the imposition of a State standard in a damages action would frustrate the objectives of the federal law. We perceive no such conflict or frustration in the circumstances of this case . . . .

We conclude that the award of . . . damages in this case is not preempted by federal law.

Think Critically

1. Who won?
2. Would a provision in the Oklahoma state constitution allowing such lawsuits supersede an NRC rule that prohibited them?
3. Are you personally comfortable with the balance of power between the federal and state governments? If not, can you think of any way to improve the situation?

CHAPTER 3

The Federal Legal System

GOALS

- ◆ Understand the powers of the various federal courts
- ◆ Know the jurisdictions of the federal administrative agencies
- ◆ Evaluate the relationship between the federal agencies and the federal courts

Powers of the Federal Courts

A court system must decide two basic types of cases. The first type is the **civil case**. In such a case private citizens resolve disputes by placing them before the courts in the form of lawsuits. Over the years, we have come to realize how vital it is to have these issues resolved in court rather than through personal revenge. As a consequence, the right to bring such cases has been expanded even to the point of giving businesses and governmental bodies such as agencies the right to do so.

The second type of case that courts must decide is the **criminal case**. Such a case involves an offense against society as defined in its law code. Note that because the offense is considered as having been committed against society, the actual victim or victims do not have the power to decide whether or not to prosecute those accused of it. That decision belongs to the attorney general, the district attorney, or the local prosecutor, depending on the nature of the case. The court procedures used in resolving criminal and civil cases will be discussed in Chapters 5 and 6, respectively.

Source of the Federal Courts' Powers

Through Article III of the U.S. Constitution, the people of this country gave the power to judge some criminal and civil matters to a system of federal courts:

Section 1. The judicial Power of the United States shall be vested in one supreme Court, and in such inferior Courts as the Congress may from time to time ordain and establish.

Because the country did not have a supreme court under the Articles of Confederation, some citizens thought that one was not needed under the Constitution. As a result, it wasn't until nearly six months after George Washington's inauguration as the first U.S. president that Congress passed the Federal Judiciary Act. This act "ordained and established" the U.S. Supreme Court (USSC) and the circuit courts of appeal. Approximately a century later Congress acted in a similar fashion by creating the federal district courts. Certain specialized courts, such as those concerned primarily with tax and bankruptcy matters, have also been created as the need for them has arisen. Refer to Figure 3-1 below as you work your way through the following description of the federal judicial system.

Currently there are three levels of federal courts with what, for the federal system, approximates general jurisdiction. **Jurisdiction** means the power to hear and decide cases. A court with general jurisdiction can hear almost any kind of

FIGURE 3-1   The Federal Court System

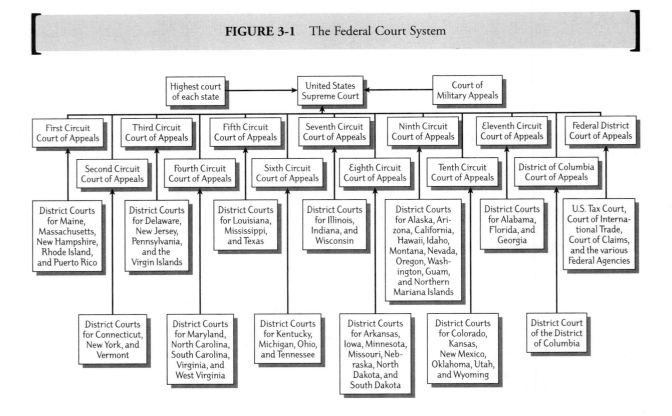

Arrows denote appellate routes. Federal bankruptcy courts take their appeals to the court of appeals with jurisdiction over their state.

case. A court with special jurisdiction, such as the U.S. Tax Court, hears only a specific type of case.

The lowest federal court with general jurisdiction is the U.S. district court. It is the trial court of the federal system. A **trial court** is basically a court in which a case is heard for the first time. The power to determine the facts of the matter and to make the initial determination of the law that is to be used in deciding such a case is called **original jurisdiction**. The district courts have that power for the federal system.

A Federal District Court's Original Jurisdiction

In general, district courts have original jurisdiction over (a) "federal questions," which are cases that arise under the Constitution, U.S. law, and U.S. treaties; and (b) lawsuits between parties with "diversity of citizenship." Such diversity requires that the case be between citizens of different states or between a U.S. citizen and a foreign nation or between a U.S. citizen and a citizen of a foreign nation. In the lawsuits in the "b" category referred to above, more than $75,000 has to be in dispute or the district courts will not handle the case. Instead the case will be assigned to a state court with appropriate jurisdiction.

Hypothetical Case

Luce Wheel, a resident of Colorado, was on vacation in Missouri when his car was hit broadside by a truck driven by Phlat Tire, a farmer from Sikeston, Missouri. Wheel was injured and his car destroyed. His damages totaled more than $130,000. Could he sue Tire in federal court? If his damages were only $74,999, could he do so?

Jurisdiction of Federal Courts of Appeal

The federal courts of appeal have appellate jurisdiction over the district courts, certain specialized federal courts, and many federal administrative agencies. **Appellate jurisdiction** is the power to review cases for errors of law. Such power is exercised when the result of a case in a lower court is appealed by one or more of the parties to the case. It is important to understand that appellate courts do not accept any new evidence or call witnesses. Instead, to reach a decision they may review the **transcript**, which is a verbatim record of what went on at trial, and the written and oral arguments of the opposing attorneys. No appellate court, not even the U.S. Supreme Court, can change the factual determinations of a jury. However, if the appellate court detects significant errors in the original trial, it can order that a new trial be conducted. Thereby a new determination of facts would be made by a new jury.

There are 13 federal courts of appeal. Twelve of these are circuit courts, each of which is responsible for an assigned geographic area. The thirteenth is dedicated to the "Federal Circuit." As such, it handles patent and claims cases appealed out of the district courts as well as appeals from specialized federal courts and from such bodies as the Court of International Trade and the International Trade Commission.

Jurisdiction of U.S. Supreme Court

The U.S. Supreme Court has both original and appellate jurisdiction. Although far less frequently used than its appellate jurisdiction, its original jurisdiction according to the Constitution is over "Cases affecting Ambassadors, other public Ministers and Consuls and those in which a State shall be Party."

The most indispensable function of the U.S. Supreme Court is the application of its appellate jurisdiction. This jurisdiction is exercised over cases on appeal from the U.S. courts of appeal or from the highest courts of the various states. If, after a cursory review, the Supreme Court believes that a case contains a constitutional issue sufficiently important to be decided, it will issue a **writ of certiorari** to the last court that heard the case. This "writ" or order compels the lower court to turn over the record of the case to the Supreme Court for review. Note that the USSC's appellate jurisdiction over state supreme court cases is limited to those in which a federal law has been invalidated or whose issues center on the U.S. Constitution. The decisions of the USSC that interpret or apply the Constitution are final and can only be overturned by the USSC itself or by a constitutional amendment. Without the USSC's role as the ultimate interpreter of the Constitution, the U.S. system of government could not survive.

Jurisdiction of the Federal Administrative Agencies

As important as the courts are, the many regulatory agencies at the federal level are just as vital, if not more so. As mentioned in the preceding chapter, Congress delegated to each agency the power to regulate a specific area. The areas assigned to many of the major federal agencies are listed in Figure 3-2. For example, in the Act of Congress that created it, the Federal Trade Commission (FTC) was given the broad power to "prevent persons, partnerships, or corporations from using unfair methods of competition in or affecting commerce and [from using] unfair or deceptive acts or practices in or affecting commerce."

Congress left it up to the newly formed FTC to set down rules and regulations that specifically defined what these methods, acts, and practices were. The FTC, like other federal agencies, was also given the power to investigate and prosecute violators in proceedings in which the agency personnel act as the equivalent of judge and jury. In effect, the executive, legislative, and judicial powers of government, which are usually held separately under the checks and balances system of the Constitution, were all given to the FTC in the interest of expediency.

Although this consolidation of powers may result in some abuses, appeals can be taken from initial agency decisions. Generally, however, these appeals do not go before a federal court until they have made their way through regional and national agency review boards. Such a process can take years. Finally, recall that the federal courts of appeal handle such appeals, not the federal district courts.

FIGURE 3-2   Problem Areas and Which Agencies to Contact for Help at the Federal Level

Problem Area	Agency	Acronym
Air pollution	Environmental Protection Agency	EPA
Air travel	Federal Aviation Administration	FAA
Bank robbery	Federal Bureau of Investigation	FBI
Chemical spill	Environmental Protection Agency	EPA
Civil rights violations	Commission on Civil Rights	CCR
Consumer goods	Consumer Product Safety Commission	CPSC
Cosmetics quality	Food and Drug Administration	FDA
Drug quality	Food and Drug Administration	FDA
Drug trafficking	Drug Enforcement Agency	DEA
Espionage	Federal Bureau of Investigation	FBI
False advertising	Federal Trade Commission	FTC
Federal law violations	Federal Bureau of Investigation	FBI
Food quality	Food and Drug Administration	FDA
Hazardous wastes	Environmental Protection Agency	EPA
Job discrimination	Equal Employment Opportunity Commission	EEOC
Job safety	Occupational Safety and Health Administration	OSHA
Kidnapping	Federal Bureau of Investigation	FBI
Mail fraud	United States Postal Service	USPS
Shipments of goods	Interstate Commerce Commission	ICC
Stocks and bonds	Securities and Exchange Commission	SEC
Unions	National Labor Relations Board	NLRB
Water pollution	Environmental Protection Agency	EPA

Court Review of Agency Decisions

Because of the high degree of expertise possessed by agency personnel and because of the heavy caseloads of the courts of appeal, court reviews of agency decisions are generally limited to three areas.

Due Process

First, the reviewing Court of Appeals checks to be sure that **due process** has been given to the parties involved. Due process entails several procedural steps:

◆   Notifying involved parties of the agency's intended action, such as the making of rules or the bringing of charges
◆   Notifying of the time, date, and place of the upcoming hearing at which the agency's intended action is to be considered

♦ Providing parties with an opportunity to appear at the proceeding to present evidence or, if the hearing is prosecutorial in nature, confront witnesses, and otherwise defend themselves

Decisions within Agency Powers

Second, the court checks to make sure that the action causing the appeal is within the powers of the agency as granted by Congress. As noted, these grants of power are usually quite broad and ambiguous. Therefore, it is difficult to prove that most actions exceed an agency's powers.

Decisions Not Arbitrary and Capricious

Finally, the court reviews the record of the agency proceedings to ensure that the agency has not acted in an arbitrary or capricious fashion. In other words, the court checks to be sure that there is a reliable basis in the record for the agency action.

If the agency action passes the three tests—due process, within the agency's powers, and not arbitrary and capricious—and the great majority of agency actions do, the action stands. Of course, there are still the alternatives of appealing to the U.S. Supreme Court or of getting Congress to change the statute that empowered the agency. However, these alternatives are seldom successful.

Chapter Review

USE LEGAL TERMS

Fill in the blanks with the appropriate term. Some terms may not be used.

appellate jurisdiction	due process	trial court
civil case	jurisdiction	transcript
criminal case	original jurisdiction	writ of certiorari

1. Required of the federal government in the Fifth Amendment to the Constitution and of the state governments in the Fourteenth Amendment, this protection against governmental power requires at a minimum notice and a hearing before a person is deprived of "life, liberty, or property." It is referred to as _____?_____ of law.

2. A(n) _____?_____ case is brought to prosecute a violation of the state or federal law code.

3. Required for any appeal, the verbatim (word for word) record of what went on at a trial is called a(n) _____?_____.

4. The verbatim record mentioned in Question 3 is a record of the proceedings in a court exercising _____?_____ over the case.

5. A(n) _____?_____ hears a case for the first time.

6. The power to hear and decide cases is termed _____?_____.

7. In a(n) _____?_____, private citizens resolve disputes by placing them before the courts in the form of lawsuits.

8. The district courts have _____?_____ for the federal system.

9. If the court believes that a case contains a constitutional issue sufficiently important to be decided, it will issue a(n) _____?_____ to the last court that heard the case.

TEST YOUR READING

10. What types of jurisdiction are the following federal courts empowered to exercise?
    a. U.S. District Courts
    b. U.S. Courts of Appeal
    c. U.S. Supreme Court

11. What federal agency would you contact in the following matters?
    a. You suspect a local business is dumping toxic waste into a nearby stream.
    b. The packaged meat you bought at the supermarket has foreign material in it.
    c. A stockbroker has sold you 1,000 shares in a non-existent company.
12. What is required for "due process" in agency actions?

THINK CRITICALLY ABOUT EVIDENCE

13. Decide which of the following would result in a criminal case and which would result in a civil case:
    a. Lou Serre is clocked at 73 mph by a patrol officer on an interstate highway where the speed limit is 55 mph.
    b. As he pulls over, Lou accidentally runs into the front fender of the brand-new patrol car, spilling hot coffee onto the patrol officer's lap.
    c. The impact of the collision knocks off Lou's back right hubcap, causing the kilo of cocaine he had cleverly stashed there to fall onto the roadway in full view of the patrol officer.
    d. Lou's attorney forgets about Lou's case and fails to appear to earn the $5,000 fee Lou has already paid him.
14. Which of the following cases would fall under the original jurisdiction of the U.S. district courts?
    a. A car accident involves a driver from Arkansas and another from Missouri. Damage claims from the accident exceed $140,000.
    b. A state supreme court strikes down a federal law.
    c. A Los Angeles man sues a citizen of Taiwan for violation of a contract worth more than $40,000.
    d. A Florida woman claims that, according to federal law, her employer is guilty of sex discrimination and she consequently seeks $30,000 in damages.
15. The sheer volume of cases that the U.S. Supreme Court must administer borders on the overwhelming. Between 6,000 and 10,000 cases come before the Court each year. Each of these cases must be reviewed to see whether it contains issues that the USSC should resolve. More than 500 of the cases are then presented to the Court for its consideration. Most of them require detailed study and research before they can be decided. Lengthy written discussions of the complex legal issues in each case must be read, and often oral arguments by the representatives of the opposing parties must be heard as well. As a result, the USSC's ability to render decisions of the necessary quality has been placed in question. Suggestions on ways to reduce its oppressive workload include:

a. Putting a court in between the courts of appeals and the USSC

b. Increasing the number of justices (which has been as high as ten and as low as five) over the nine currently on the Court

c. Increasing emphasis on alternative means of dispute resolution

Which of these suggestions, if any, would you recommend? Why or why not?

16. Do you think Congress is justified in delegating so much of its regulatory power to administrative agencies such as the FTC? Why can't Congress do the job itself?

17. Finally, consider the Death of Commercial TV:

The voice ripped the dream apart. The South Seas island, white sands, beaches beyond compare, and very, very friendly natives yielded to reality. You awoke and sat up on the couch. Pat, your best friend, was shrieking in your ear. "They've stopped WrestleBania XV. I can't believe it. Just as John ('Sears') Tower was about to use his 'coma clamp' to beat the Burbank Tank, they announced that network commercial TV was being banned by the FTC. Then they put on the test pattern."

Pat stands up and points at you. "You're taking the law class. How could they do that? How do we stop them?"

You shake your head. Since starting school, what with working and all, you haven't kept up with your sleep, much less the news. You promise Pat that you'll hit the library and research the whole thing as soon as possible. Just then the TV comes back to life with a syndicated children's show from the 50s. "Who's Princess SummerFall/WinterSpring?" Pat asks.

Later that evening, you enter the periodical section of the library and grab a newsmagazine. Its cover story is on the FTC action. Evidently, some months ago the agency decided to hold hearings to determine whether or not advertising on network television was an unfair method of competition under Section 5 of the FTC Act. To do so, it provided direct notice of the hearings by mail to all interested and concerned parties that it could identify. It also published notices of the hearings in newspapers, magazines, federal journals, and the Internet. Anyone could appear and offer evidence. The hearings were held around the country. According to the magazine, the major TV networks hired expert witnesses, economists, and financial analysts to appear. These witnesses argued that TV fostered competition and offered vast amounts of statistical data to support their position. Professional sports figures, the heads of America's largest corporations, and leaders of the major political parties appeared in support of commercial TV. But you also read that a small group of academics presented contrary evidence. They maintained that the high cost of ads on network TV kept many small companies from using it and that American culture had been skewed as a result. Regional breweries, bakeries, dairies, and restaurants and countless other regional concerns with quality products had been forced out of business due to the financial ability of only the largest corporations to use TV advertising. Real diversity in America had been franchised out of existence. School systems had been altered to foster the athletes and cheerleaders idolized on network TV rather than the engineers and scientists the country needed. The political process itself had been laid open to subversion as politicians sought the favor of the large contributors whose money could finance the intense TV campaigns necessary for election. The academics also documented their claims with statistical data. At the conclusion of the hearings, the FTC official in charge issued her findings. Her main factual determination was that commercial TV in its current form was an unfair method of competition. She then issued a cease and desist order directing the commercial networks to stop operating. Soap operas, professional sporting events, and Saturday morning TV were all to be replaced by locally originated and supportable shows and live talent presentations.

Your mind reels as you think of what you can tell Pat. To help you in that regard, consider the following questions:

a.   What is the appellate route that must be taken if the decision is appealed?

b.   If the appeal reaches the courts, which court will handle it first?

c.   What standards of review will the courts use?

d.   Given the facts of this case, is the decision likely to be overturned?

e.   If the courts allow the decision to stand, do the networks have any further recourse?

REAL-WORLD CASE
National Collegiate Athletic Association v. *Jerry Tarkanian*
109 Supreme Court Reporter 454

Consider the importance of the guarantee of due process in a case involving big-time college basketball and a very well paid coach.

Coach Tarkanian took over a mediocre basketball program at the University of Nevada at Las Vegas. Within four years his team was in the "Final Four" of the NCAA Tourney. His salary bordered on the fabulous. In lieu of the approximately $53,000 per year he would have made as a tenured professor, "Tark the Shark" had a contract for $125,000 and 10 percent of the net proceeds received by the university from its team's participation in NCAA postseason events as well as fees from endorsements, camps, clinics, newspaper columns, and his own radio and TV shows. Then the NCAA struck. After a lengthy investigation, it detailed 38 violations of its rules by UNLV personnel, mainly concerning player recruitment; 10 of the violations involved Coach Tarkanian. The NCAA placed UNLV on probation for two years, which meant that its basketball team could not appear on TV or in postseason games. The NCAA also required UNLV to show cause why it should not be further disciplined for not removing Tarkanian from its program during the probationary period. Ultimately, UNLV responded to this threat by doing just that. Faced with a drastic cut in salary, Coach Tarkanian brought suit, alleging that his disciplining was an action of the state government and that his right to due process guaranteed under the Fourteenth Amendment of the U.S. Constitution had been denied him because the university administration had accepted the NCAA determination without giving him notice and a hearing. The university and the NCAA responded that no such due process was required as the NCAA was a private body and therefore not subject to the requirements of the Fourteenth Amendment. When the Nevada Supreme Court rejected this view, the NCAA appealed to the U.S. Supreme Court.

In a 5-4 decision, the Supreme Court concluded as follows:

> Embedded in the Fourteenth Amendment jurisprudence is a dichotomy between state action, which is subject to scrutiny under the Amendment's Due Process Clause, and private conduct, against which the Amendment affords no shield, no matter how unfair that conduct may be . . . . As a general matter, the protections of the Fourteenth Amendment do not extend to private conduct abridging individual rights.

> Careful adherence to the state action requirement preserves an area of individual freedom by limiting the reach of federal law and avoids the imposition of responsibility on a State for conduct it could not control . . . .

> In this case Tarkanian argues that the NCAA was a state actor because it misused power that it possessed by virtue of state law. He claims specifically that UNLV delegated its own functions to the NCAA, clothing the Association with authority both to adopt rules governing UNLV's athletic programs and to enforce those rules on behalf of UNLV.

> These contentions fundamentally misconstrue the facts of this case . . . the NCAA's several hundred other public and private member institutions each similarly affected those policies . . . .[They] did not act under color of Nevada law. It necessarily follows that the source of the legislation adopted by the NCAA is not Nevada but the collective membership.

UNLV retained the authority to withdraw from the NCAA and establish its own standards. The University alternatively could have stayed in the Association and worked through the Association's legislative process to amend rules or standards it deemed harsh, unfair, or unwieldy.

The Court then concluded that the NCAA actions were not state actions and, therefore, that Tarkanian could not sue the NCAA for violation of his Fourteenth Amendment rights. The Court, however, did concede that UNLV's decision to suspend the coach was such a state action.

Think Critically

1. Does the Fourteenth Amendment require that a private employer afford you due process—notice and a hearing of your side of the story—before firing you? What if your employer is a state government?

2. Was due process in such instances required of state governments before the passage of the Fourteenth Amendment?

3. Assume that your employer is a private guard company that hires you out to the state to do security work at a state installation. At the installation, you have the power to issue citations for violation of the state's laws. Can you claim a right to due process under the Fourteenth Amendment before being fired from this position?

CHAPTER 4

State and Local Legal Systems

GOALS

- ◆ Know the basic courts in a state and local court system
- ◆ Understand the functions of each type of court in the system
- ◆ Identify the cases the various courts have jurisdiction over

Powers of the State Courts with General Jurisdiction

The typical state legal system mirrors the federal system in most instances. The state legislature makes the laws. The state executive branch enforces them before the courts of the state judicial branch. There also are state administrative agencies with powers given them by the state legislature. These agencies, for example, the Missouri Department of Natural Resources, often complement their counterparts at the federal level (in this instance, the Environmental Protection Agency). Even though they vary from state to state, there are some common characteristics among the state court systems.

State Trial Courts with General Jurisdiction

In most states the courts with general original jurisdiction over both criminal and civil matters are known as circuit courts. In some states, however, they are named superior courts, district courts, or courts of common pleas. Regardless of their title, they are the courts of record of the state system. In a **court of record** an exact account of what went on at trial is kept so as to allow appeals. This account may include a transcript of what was said, the evidence that was submitted, statements and determinations of the court officials, and the judgment of the court.

Courts of record will at times review the decisions of or handle appeals from courts of inferior jurisdiction. These courts will be discussed later in the chapter. When this occurs, however, they actually retry the cases in full so as to make the proper record, again for the purpose of potential appeals. Because it has original jurisdiction over a case before it, a court of record will make determinations of the facts in the case by using a jury or, if a jury is not requested for the case, by having the presiding judge determine the facts. Then the court of record will select and apply the law to the facts to reach a verdict in the case.

State Courts of Appeal

In approximately half of the states, an appeal from the determination of a case in a court of record is reviewed by a panel of judges from a state court of appeal. In states where this intermediate level of **appellate court** does not exist, the appeal goes directly to the highest state court, usually referred to as the state supreme court, which will be discussed in the next section. The panel of judges from the state court of appeal, usually consisting of no more than three judges, evaluates the record of the case and then hears the attorneys' oral and written arguments. The facts remain unchanged because evidence can only be introduced at the lower trial court level. The judges instead check to be sure that the correct law was used to resolve the case.

The court of appeals panel of judges may conclude that the trial court used the wrong law. If so, the panel may enter the correct judgment or send the case back down for a new trial. On the other hand, the judges may conclude the lower court used the correct law in the proper way and, consequently, let the lower court's judgment stand.

State Supreme Courts

Generally, we are all entitled to a trial and, if it is filed in a timely manner and in the proper form, to one appeal. As mentioned above, an intermediate state court of appeal handles that appeal in about half of the states. Otherwise, it is handled by a state's supreme court.

In states with the intermediate level of courts of appeal, only cases that involve the most complex legal issues are taken to the justices of the state supreme court. **Justice** is the title given to judges who sit on state supreme courts and the federal Supreme Court. At the state supreme court level a panel of three or more justices reviews the legal issues and listens to the attorneys' oral arguments.

State supreme courts issue the final decision on matters of law appealed to them unless the U.S. Constitution or other federal issues are involved. In that case, a further appeal can go to the U.S. Supreme Court.

In addition to its appellate jurisdiction, in several states the state supreme court has original jurisdiction over most state impeachment cases. **Impeachment cases** involve the trial of governmental officials for misconduct in office. Finally, some states name their court of final authority something other than "supreme court." For example, New York State's highest court is called the Court of Appeals.

Functions of the Specialized State Courts

As indicated in Figure 4-1, a number of courts with specialized jurisdiction or jurisdiction inferior to that of the courts of record exist in every state. These courts include the associate circuit, municipal, small claims, juvenile, and probate courts.

Associate Circuit (County) Courts

Many states have a layer of courts below their courts of general original jurisdiction. These lower courts are referred to as associate circuit courts or county courts. Such courts hear minor criminal cases, state traffic offenses, and lawsuits in which relatively small amounts are in contention (usually no more than *$25,000*). Generally, these courts are not courts of record. However, they take a significant burden off the higher courts, even though appeals from their decisions can be taken to the circuit courts for a trial on the record.

Municipal Courts

Cities typically have courts that administer their ordinances. These municipal courts are usually divided into traffic and criminal divisions. As city ordinances often overlap or duplicate state laws, less serious violations occurring within city limits end up before such municipal courts for their first trial. The result can then be appealed to the circuit court level if necessary.

FIGURE 4-1   A Typical State Court System

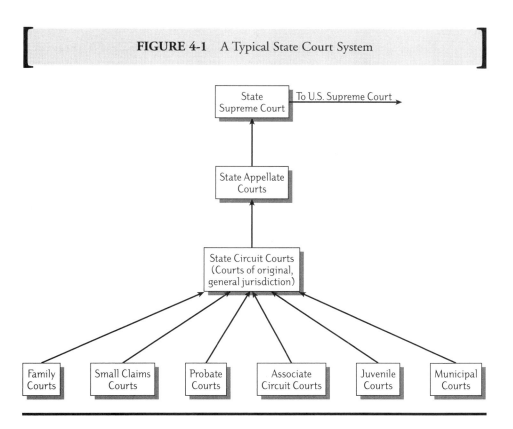

Small Claims Courts

Many relatively minor individual suits would not be heard if not for the small claims courts. These courts handle cases in which small amounts, generally $2,500 or less, are in contention. The cases are handled informally before a judge and without a jury. The costs of filing such cases are held to a minimum. Often attorneys are not allowed or are allowed only if they're acting for themselves or for a corporation of which they are salaried employees. The decisions of the small claims court can be appealed to the circuit court level.

Juvenile Courts

Individuals under the age of full responsibility for their criminal acts (generally set at 18 years) are known as **juveniles**. To protect such individuals from the full consequences of their criminal acts, special courts have been set up. These courts ensure that most of the criminal cases involving juveniles do not become public knowledge. The courtroom is closed while an informal hearing into the charges is conducted. Any records made are not open to the public. The juvenile is entitled to his or her full constitutional rights, including the right of representation by an attorney. Should the juvenile be found guilty of the charges brought, the court has wide powers in determining what should be done for rehabilitation. Possibilities open to the court include release into the supervision of parents, guardians, or governmental officials; placement in foster homes; and detention in correctional facilities.

Note that most states also provide that a juvenile, usually at least 16 years old, can be tried and punished as an adult. This occurs only in cases in which a very serious offense was allegedly committed by the juvenile. For example, murder and certain other crimes may bring about such treatment. Appeals from actions of the juvenile courts are directed to the circuit courts.

Probate Courts

The **probate court** is charged with administering wills and estates. When an individual dies, the interests that the deceased had in various assets must be allocated according to the deceased's wishes and the appropriate laws. The procedure to accomplish this is formal and complex. The probate court (referred to as the *surrogate court* in some states), is therefore staffed with experienced professionals so as to properly settle the deceased's affairs.

Other Courts

Other courts of inferior jurisdiction that are found in some states include domestic relations or family courts for divorce and child custody cases, justice of the peace courts for traffic violations and some ceremonial duties, and drug courts. The justice of the peace courts, which usually employ non-lawyers as judges, are being phased out.

Chapter Review

USE LEGAL TERMS

Fill in the blanks with the appropriate term.

appellate court   impeachment cases   juvenile
court of record   Justice   probate court

1. A court that needs an accurate transcript of trials is a(n) ___?___.
2. In a lower court, this person would be referred to as "just" a judge. ___?___
3. The legal title of an individual under the age of criminal responsibility. ___?___
4. In a(n) ___?___ an exact account of what went on at trial is kept so as to allow appeals.
5. ___?___ involve the trial of governmental officials for misconduct in office.
6. The ___?___ is charged with administering wills and estates.

TEST YOUR READING

7. Name the three levels of the typical state court system and explain their jurisdiction.
8. Compare the jurisdiction and rules in an associate circuit court with the jurisdiction and rules in a small claims court.

THINK CRITICALLY ABOUT EVIDENCE

Match the legal issue with the court that will decide it by putting the letter of the court most likely to decide the issue in the blank after each one.

The courts:

  a. state supreme court
  b. state court of appeals
  c. circuit court
  d. associate circuit court
  e. municipal court
  f. juvenile court

  g. small claims court
  h. probate court
  i. federal district court
  j. federal courts of appeal
  k. U.S. Supreme Court

The legal issues:

9. At 9:13 A.M. on Friday, March 13, Nelson Bates III, an Addamsville, California, resident, is ticketed by a policeman of that city for driving 39 mph in a 20-mph school zone. Mr. Bates protests that he was driving too fast to see the school zone sign. He must appear before the Addamsville ___?___.

10. Later in the morning of March 13, Mr. Bates is ticketed by a California patrol officer for driving 78 mph on an interstate highway. Mr. Bates must appear before the ___?___.

11. That afternoon, Hy Biscus, an avid gardener, files suit against Nelson Bates III for $275 in damages done when Nelson allegedly cut down Mr. Biscus's rare roses while employed to mow Mr. Biscus's yard. Neither party wants to hire an attorney. The ideal court to hear their case is the ___?___.

12. Just after school is out, Nelson Bates III's 13-year-old son is charged with attempting to steal a Seeing Eye dog. The attempted theft failed because the dog slowed young Bates's getaway by waiting for the streets to clear before crossing. The court that will try young Bates's case will be the ___?___.

13. As he is leaving the jail after visiting his son, Nelson Bates III unexpectedly meets his 17-year-old daughter, Lala. She informs him that she is about to turn herself in for stabbing her boyfriend to death. The court likely to hold her trial is the ___?___.

14. That evening Mr. Bates meets with the attorney handling the division of the property of his grandfather, who recently died. The attorney informs him that his sisters Rhea and Dee will receive almost everything. The court over-seeing the division of the deceased's property is the ___?___.

15. The same attorney informs Mr. Bates that it will cost almost $20,000 to further appeal his father's convictions on embezzlement and fraud charges. A noted televangelist, Nelson Bates II made himself famous by proclaiming that there was a pet heaven in which he could guarantee Fido or Fifi a place in return for an appropriate contribution. The California Supreme Court ruled against him last month, but the attorney is confident that victory is around the corner due to the federal constitutional issue in the case. The court to which the appeal will be directed is the ___?___.

REAL-WORLD CASE

Texas v. *Johnson*
109 S. Ct. 2533

Read this case to see if you, like Voltaire, would defend to the death Gregory Lee Johnson's right to "speak" by way of the burning of an American flag. It also shows the working relationship between federal and state court systems.

The protest march swirled through downtown Dallas during the Republican National Convention in 1984. One of the marchers pulled an American flag from a flagpole and handed it to Gregory Johnson. The march ended in a prolonged demonstration in front of Dallas City Hall. There Johnson unfurled Old Glory, drenched it in kerosene, and set it on fire.

As the American flag burned, the demonstrators chanted, "America the red, white, and blue, we spit on you." Although no one was threatened or injured physically by Johnson's actions, many witnesses later testified that seeing the flag in flames had offended them deeply.

Johnson was charged with violating a Texas Penal Code provision relating to "desecration of a venerated object," tried and sentenced to one year in prison, and fined $2,000. After this trial and conviction in the state court with original criminal jurisdiction, he appealed the conviction to a Texas intermediate appellate court. That court affirmed the conviction. Johnson then appealed to the Texas Court of Criminal Appeals, the highest state court with appellate jurisdiction over his case. That court reversed his conviction on First Amendment grounds, namely that Johnson should not be punished for symbolically exercising his freedom of speech.

The state of Texas then petitioned the U.S. Supreme Court to review the case. Justice Brennan wrote the deciding opinion:

> The act for which appellant [Johnson] was convicted was clearly "speech" contemplated by the First Amendment. To justify Johnson's conviction for engaging in symbolic speech, the State asserted two interests: preserving the flag as a symbol of national unity and preventing breaches of the peace.
>
> The Texas court [Texas Court of Criminal Appeals] concluded that furthering this interest by curtailing speech was impermissible. The Texas court also decided that the flag's special status was not endangered by Johnson's conduct. As to the State's goal of preventing breaches of the peace, the court concluded that the flag-desecration statute was not drawn narrowly enough to encompass only those flag-burnings that were likely to result in a serious disturbance of the peace. And, in fact, the court emphasized, the flag burning in this particular case did not threaten such a reaction . . . .

Johnson was convicted for engaging in expressive conduct. The State's interest in preventing breaches of the peace does not support his conviction because Johnson's conduct did not threaten to disturb the peace. Nor does the State's interest in preserving the flag as a symbol of nationhood and national unity justify his criminal conviction for engaging in political expression. The judgment of the Texas Court of Criminal Appeals is therefore affirmed.

Think Critically

1. Who won? Will Johnson have to serve his time and pay his fine?
2. Are the rights "guaranteed" by the Bill of Rights absolute? What part of the opinion supports your answer?
3. Assume that Johnson burned his draft registration card. Is there a state or federal interest that might overcome his right to freedom of speech so as to allow his punishment for that act?

CHAPTER 5

Criminal Law

GOALS

- Understand how crimes are defined and why
- Realize the significance of the various steps in criminal procedure
- Know the elements of the most common crimes affecting business

How Are Crimes Defined?

Crimes must be carefully defined in a free society. A crime too vaguely or too broadly defined may cause some citizens to stop doing legitimate productive work for fear of being prosecuted. In addition, such a statute may be used for purposes not intended by the legislature. For example, recently enacted statutes have created severe penalties for using lethal weapons in committing a crime. These statutes were intended to be employed against individuals using guns, knives, and the like in committing robberies or other serious crimes. Some prosecutors, arguing that a car is a lethal weapon, have employed the statutes against reckless or drunken drivers. Although the result may be commendable, the effect is to improperly place the legislative power in the hands of prosecutors and courts.

The Elements of a Crime

To stand the best chance of avoiding such unintended results, the definition of a crime should include at least two elements: the physical act—referred to at law as the *actus reus*, and the mental state—or the *mens rea*.

The Physical Act
Oh, you can't be put in jail for what you're thinking.
Matter of fact, neither can I.

This lyric from a classic song reflects some commonsense wisdom about our criminal laws. A properly worded criminal statute should prohibit the **actus reus**, defined as a movement directed by the actor's will. Thoughts *without* actions should not be prosecutable. Of course a few statutes wisely make it criminal to refuse to act when a person has a legal duty to do so. For example, a lifeguard who does not try to rescue a drowning person may be charged with manslaughter if the person drowns.

Note that involuntary acts, such as movements while asleep, while hypnotized, or during convulsions, do not bring on criminal liability.

The Mental State (Intent)   To be prosecutable as a crime, the act must be accompanied by the appropriate **mens rea** or the specific state of mind required in the statute defining the crime. For example, some statutes require that the alleged criminal act be performed "knowingly," that is, with the knowledge that a particular harm is likely to result from it. A person who, seeing a loved one suffering without hope of recovery, cuts off the power to the loved one's life-support system does so knowing that the loved one will probably die as a result. Other mental states often used to define criminal behavior include *recklessness*, which is acting without consideration of the high risk that harm will result from the action, and *negligence*, which is acting in a way that violates the due care a reasonable person owes to others. Driving the wrong way on a one-way street would be reckless conduct, whereas exceeding the posted speed limit by five miles or so per hour would be negligent conduct.

Too often the mental state used to define criminal behavior is referred to as "criminal" or "evil" intent. Such phrasing causes uninformed persons to incorrectly assume that there is a moral character to this part of a crime's definition. This, in turn, leads to focusing on the actor's motive or reason as an excuse for committing the crime. The law does not allow such analysis. In order to rest on the stabilizing pillars of fairness and justice, society must factor out individual moral judgments. It must conclude that those who steal food and money to help the starving, burn draft cards, or bribe legislators to vote one way or another on abortion issues are nonetheless common criminals and deserve to be prosecuted.

Strict Construction of Statutes

As previously indicated, a free society presumes that all forms of behavior not specifically prohibited by the law are permissible. The possession and use of cocaine, opium, and heroin were legal a century or more ago. For example, according to a 1920s U.S. Supreme Court case, until 1903 each small bottle of Coca-Cola contained the equivalent of one line of cocaine. Alcohol, as well, has been on and off the list of illegal drugs during the past century. However, regardless of how permissive society is toward an activity at a particular time, it is vital that if the activity is prohibited, it be defined as clearly and restrictively as possible. In legal terms, this means that it is vital that a crime be "strictly construed."

As an example, consider the crime of burglary. The definition we used earlier, "the breaking and entering of the dwelling house of another at night with the intent to commit a felony therein," actually originated centuries ago in the English common law. It seems pretty definite and specific, doesn't it? Even so, from the time of its origination to the present, the definition has required more and more clarification. Why? Because, practically each time the definition has been tested in court, it has had to be applied to a new set of facts. The question of when a garage is a part of a dwelling house was one such test. The answer, "when it is permanently attached to the main structure," sets the precedent for future cases in which a similar question might arise.

Other elements of burglary required clarification as well. For example, has a person broken into a house if he or she found the door unlocked and just turned the handle and walked in? The precedents say yes. Any time force is used, even to turn a handle to gain unauthorized entry, there has been a "breaking." If the door or window is open wide enough for the intruder to gain entry without moving it, then there is no "breaking." "Entering" has been held to require that a part of the intruder's body penetrate the plane of the house. So, a thief who is standing outside a dwelling pokes a stick through a window in order to snare a $10,000 pearl neck-lace lying on a dressing table has not "entered" the house. No part of the thief's body penetrated the plane of the house. Therefore, if a prosecutor mistakenly charged and tried the thief solely for burglary, the thief would be found not guilty and could not be retried for the same offense. This prohibition of retrial for the same offense after being found not guilty, referred to as **double jeopardy**, is a protection afforded by the Fifth Amendment to the U.S. Constitution. For the common law definitions of other crimes see Figure 5-1.

FIGURE 5-1   Common Law Definitions of Crimes

Burglary	Breaking and entering the dwelling house of another at night, with the intent to commit a felony therein.
Arson	The malicious burning of the house of another.
Forgery	The false making or the material altering of a document with the intent to defraud.
Fraud	An intentional perversion of truth for the purpose of inducing another to part with some valuable thing belonging to her or him or to surrender a legal right.
Murder	The unlawful killing of a human being by another with malice aforethought, either express or implied
Rape	Unlawful sexual intercourse with a person of the opposite sex without the latter's consent.

Note: Definitions of the specific terms used to define crimes can be obtained from the case law or from such publications as *Black's Law Dictionary*.

Is an apartment a "dwelling house"? When is it nighttime? (Defense attorneys have been quick to point out that it is still light for some time after the sun goes down, so "after sundown" can't be the answer.) Can a married person legally separated from his or her spouse burglarize the family home if both parties own it?

All of these questions and many, many more had to be answered by the courts to thoroughly define the crime of burglary, a crime that originally had been defined more clearly than most. In general, all of these questions could not have been anticipated by a lawmaking authority that drafted the crime's definition. The same is true for all of the hundreds of other crimes in the statute books. Crimes become fully defined by being applied to actual behavior. As a result, alleged criminals often do not know whether or not they have violated a law until a court reaches a decision like those mentioned above. This element of uncertainty rightfully causes the courts to strictly construe crimes so as to protect the citizenry from the misapplication of laws, if nothing else.

Classification of Crimes

The last element of the definition of burglary, "with the intent to commit a felony therein," brings us to the subject of the classification of crimes. Crimes are classified by their degree of severity and according to their origin. A **felony** is a crime severe enough to be punishable by death or by imprisonment for a year or longer. Examples of felonies include murder, arson, burglary, robbery, and rape. So, in accordance with the definition of burglary, breaking and entering the dwelling house of another at night with the intent to commit arson would be burglary.

A **misdemeanor** is a crime punishable by a relatively minor fine and/or imprisonment for less than a year. Shoplifting, disorderly conduct, and most traffic offenses are examples of misdemeanors.

Criminal statutes can be drafted by either a state or the federal government. However, whereas the definition or punishment of a crime may vary greatly from state to state, the federal government's criminal code remains the same throughout the country. Note that the federal government adds treason as a special category of crime. Treason is the levying of war against the United States or giving aid and comfort to the enemies of this country. Some states add minor offenses called *infractions*, such as littering and parking offenses, to the categories of crimes.

Finally, crimes are considered to be either *mala prohibita* or *mala in se*. **Mala in se** crimes are inherently and essentially evil in their nature and consequences. They include murder, arson, larceny, and acts that have been defined as crimes by the common law. A **mala prohibita** crime is not inherently evil. Such a crime is considered wrong only because it has been defined as such by the legislature or Congress. Speeding, jaywalking, and other minor offenses fall into this category.

Stages of Criminal Procedure

Criminal procedure begins with the violation of a criminal statute. At that time, according to our laws, an offense has been committed against the governmental body that drafted the statute. This is because almost all criminal offenses involve an actual or constructive *breach of the peace*. Such a breach is a violation or disturbance of the public tranquility and order. The offense is not considered to be against the victim of the crime. It therefore becomes the duty of the citizen to report such incidents to the proper authorities as the first step in criminal procedure. Those authorities, as representatives of the government that made the behavior criminal in the first place, have the power to decide whether to prosecute the person who allegedly committed the crime. It is not up to the victim, although whether the victim will aid in the investigation and prosecution is a significant factor in the decision to go forward with such efforts.

The Arrest

Upon the reporting of a crime by a private citizen or the observation or discovery of a crime by the police, an *investigation* is conducted. This investigation may result in an immediate **arrest**, which is taking into custody a suspect to answer a criminal charge. It may also result in the development of facts indicating that a certain person was responsible for the crime. At the state level, if the facts are conclusive enough, the responsible public officer—the state attorney general or the local prosecutor—will swear out an accusation based on his or her oath of office. This accusation is known as an **information**. At the federal level, where only a grand jury can issue an indictment, the decision to put the matter before such a jury belongs to such individuals as the U.S. attorney general and his or her assistants. In either system, however, the victim's willingness to testify if a prosecution is attempted often is crucial to the decision to go forward.

If the facts gathered by the investigating officers are not conclusive, either the state prosecutors or federal district attorneys may refer the case to a "jury of inquiry," which can compel witnesses to testify under oath and can demand the production of evidence. This jury, made up of 20 or more members, is referred to as a **grand jury** in most states because it is larger than the **petit jury**, which has 6 to 12 members. If the grand jury develops enough evidence to indicate that a certain individual should be tried for the crime, it will vote out an indictment based on its oath. The **indictment**, like the information, is an accusation of criminal conduct against an individual. The indictment or information is forwarded to a judge or similar public official with the power to issue an **arrest warrant**, an order that a person be arrested by competent authority.

Pretrial Procedure

Once arrested, a person must be informed of the charge or charges against her or him and be allowed to plead guilty or not guilty. This is done at a court proceeding called an **arraignment**. After hearing the accused's plea, the court will hold a hearing to set bail, if such is to be allowed the defendant. **Bail** is the posting of property or bond with the court to ensure the accused's later appearance. If the accused fails to appear, the amount posted is forfeited to the court. If the accused pleads guilty at the arraignment, the appropriate court will pass sentence at a later time. If the accused pleads not guilty, he or she is scheduled to be tried as soon as possible in accordance with the constitutional guarantee of a speedy trial.

If the defendant has been charged by an information, and should he or she request it, the court is required to hold a preliminary hearing before trial. (Persons charged by grand jury indictment do not have the right to such a hearing.) During this **preliminary hearing**, the evidence against the accused will be presented by the prosecution. The court will then determine whether there is reasonable basis or **probable cause** to proceed with the trial. If the court decides that there is not, the accused will be freed and the charge or charges dropped. This does happen at times. If, for example, a necessary witness will not testify or if the use of certain evidence is disallowed by the court, the case against the accused will be terminated. Usually, however, the court will find that there is probable cause to proceed with preparations for the trial.

At times, as a result of the presentation of the evidentiary case against the defendant at the preliminary hearing, the prosecution or the defense, or both, will seek a plea bargain. A **plea bargain** is an agreement in which the defendant agrees to plead guilty to a reduced charge in exchange for the prosecutor's recommendation of a lighter sentence. Plea bargains are also used to lighten the workload of the prosecutors and the overcrowding of the courts by eliminating the trying of relatively minor cases.

The Trial

If the court deems it proper and no plea bargain interrupts, the trial must take place without unreasonable delay. The trial jury, a group of persons selected according to law to impartially determine the factual questions of the case from the evidence allowed before them in court, is at the heart of the U.S. criminal system. Potential jurors are chosen from voter rolls in most jurisdictions. They are then carefully screened to eliminate any potentially biased persons. The right to a jury trial, if requested by the defendant, is guaranteed by the U.S. Constitution. Certain types of defendants do not request a jury, especially those charged with such crimes as child abuse or the performance of especially gruesome acts.

During the trial, the prosecutor will present evidence to prove the guilt of the accused "beyond a reasonable doubt," and the defense attorney will present evidence disputing that conclusion. Exactly what evidence it is proper to place before the trier of fact is determined by the judge. If the material or testimony that either the prosecution or the defense desires to put into evidence might improperly bias the jury, it will not be allowed.

At the conclusion of the presentation of evidence by both sides, the judge will instruct the jury as to what it is to determine. The jury will then retire and try to reach a verdict. A **verdict** is a statement of whatever conclusions the jury has reached on the questions of fact submitted to it. If, after extensive deliberations, the jury cannot reach agreement on a verdict, it is labeled a **hung jury** and the case is dismissed. After such a dismissal the case may be retried or perhaps even dropped by the prosecutor.

If the jury returns a guilty verdict, the court will generally delay sentencing for a time in order to examine the criminal's past history and other circumstances. Some crimes require a mandatory sentence as dictated by the legislature or Congress.

Hypothetical Case

Charles DuBois was on trial for the armed robbery of a liquor store. His defense attorney called Bernard Strong to testify. Strong had been in the store when the crime was committed. When the police arrived, Strong overheard one of the police officers say, "It couldn't have been DuBois. I saw him in the park when this robbery was being committed." If the prosecution objected to it, Strong's testimony would probably be thrown out by the court because it is *hearsay*, evidence stemming not from the personal knowledge of the witness but from what the witness heard another say. The jury would be ordered to disregard his testimony in reaching its conclusion.

Posttrial Procedure

A court may suspend the sentencing procedure and only place restrictions on the defendant's behavior for a certain period of time. If the defendant complies, there will be no official record of the conviction as sentence was never passed down. A court also may pass sentence but suspend its execution, allowing the convicted party to go free on **probation**. The sentence will not be carried out if the person on probation leads an orderly life and complies with the terms set by the court. Even if sentence is imposed and carried out by placing the convicted criminal in the county jail or the state penitentiary, the criminal may be given **parole**. This is a conditional release when there is still a great deal of time left to be served. If the terms of parole are violated, the criminal is returned to jail or the penitentiary to serve the rest of his or her term.

If the convicted party believes that errors of law were made in the trial or in the disallowing of certain defenses, an appeal may be taken to a higher court. Bail may be allowed pending the result of that appeal. If errors are found, the conviction may be thrown out. The prosecutor may then elect to retry the case or to let it drop, as shown in the following hypothetical example that parallels an actual case.

Hypothetical Case

Conner was arrested for committing a felony. Shortly thereafter, his lawyer appeared at the police station but was not allowed to see him. Meanwhile, Conner was told that if he would confess, he could consult with his attorney. Conner thereupon confessed, and his confession was used to convict him. Upon appeal, the U.S. Supreme Court ruled that before suspects in police custody are questioned, they must be informed of their rights, such as their rights to remain silent and to have counsel present if desired. Because these rights were denied Conner, both his confession and the conviction that resulted from its use were thrown out.

Constitutional Protections and Defenses for Suspects of Crimes

You have learned that the essential elements of a crime are the physical act and the mental state. Unless these are proven to the trier of fact beyond a reasonable doubt, the accused cannot be convicted. Therefore, most defenses go to proving by competent evidence that either or both of these elements do not exist. Constitutional protections, on the other hand, are most often used to exclude improperly obtained evidence that could be used to prove the crime if presented at trial. So, to keep things in the order of events, let's look at the constitutional protections first.

The Miranda Warning

As indicated in the situation involving Conner, any person taken into custody in a criminal case is protected by a number of rights. The *"Miranda warning,"* stemming from the 1966 Supreme Court case of *Miranda* v. *Arizona*, is commonly read to all suspects of federal and state crimes. This protection is not afforded to violators of municipal ordinances. The warning, based primarily on the guarantees contained in various amendments to the U.S. Constitution, details many of the protective rights. Any confession or other evidence developed by the authorities before a suspect has been properly informed of those rights cannot be used to convict the suspect. The warning has four parts:

1. That the person in custody has a right to remain silent (Fifth Amendment)
2. That any statement the person makes may be used as evidence against her or him
3. That the person in custody has a right to an attorney's presence (Sixth Amendment)
4. That if he or she cannot afford an attorney, one will be appointed for him or her prior to questioning if so desired

Other Significant Constitutional Protections

In addition, amendments to the U.S. Constitution afford several other protections. As mentioned earlier, the Fifth Amendment prohibits double jeopardy. It also states that no defendant in a criminal case can be compelled to be a witness against himself or herself. Also, according to the Fourth Amendment, searches must be a result of probable cause. If not, the courts will not allow the use of whatever evidence developed as a result of the search to convict the defendant. Among the other rights of defendants are the right to confront their accusers, the right to a speedy and public trial, and the right to be free from cruel and unusual punishment.

All of these constitutional protections, which often exclude evidence that would clearly show the guilt of the accused, are touted as safeguards against overzealous police efforts. Through these safeguards the legal system tries to live up to the idea that it should "free a thousand guilty lest one innocent be convicted." Critics of this approach say that present-day reality puts that ideal in question. Innocents are still convicted. In addition, the thousand guilty who are freed by the exclusion of evidence showing their guilt all too often prey on countless more innocents after their release. A California study showed that for every thousand or so released, approximately 580 committed other felonies within two years.

Moreover, the fruit of the truly successful criminal's labor often brings him or her substantial rewards that allow the hiring of the best defense attorneys. These attorneys ensure that their clients, who may be the most wicked and perverse persons in our society, receive the fullest protection of the law, whereas poorer defendants and certainly the victims do not. Rather than excluding improperly obtained but actual evidence of criminal behavior, an action that only hurts society, reformers today suggest that the defendant whose rights have been violated only be allowed some form of action, such as a lawsuit, against the law enforcement officer and organization. This would leave the prosecutor with all the evidence she or he needs to have the best chance for a successful prosecution.

Defenses to the Showing of the Criminal Act

Even if legitimate and conclusive evidence is admitted against the defendant who committed the act in question, certain defenses are still available. One of these defenses stems from the attempts of prosecutors to make a law already on the books cover conduct it cannot legitimately reach. Consider this example:

Hypothetical Case

A criminal statute that prohibits the making and distribution of certain addictive drugs lists each of them by chemical formula. Sam Powers, the defendant, found a way to combine two of the cheapest "street drugs" on the list to make a third that was even more addictive. The combination drug had a formula different from those prohibited under the statute. If Powers were caught and tried for a violation of the statute, he could defend himself by pointing out that the drug he manufactured was not specifically prohibited. If he were nonetheless convicted by the trial court, the conviction would probably be thrown out on appeal as a too broad or too far-reaching application of the statute.

Other defenses to a showing that the defendant committed the act in question include the defense that the statute was ambiguous in its definition of the act or that the statute makes a status, such as drug addiction, a crime. Note, however, that possession is not treated as a status and may therefore result in a conviction. The exercise of control over an item or even a vehicle, say one in which illegal drugs are found, is **possession** and enough of an act to satisfy the courts. Even refusing to act may be enough of an act to bring on criminal liability where the act is to fulfill a legally required duty. As mentioned, a lifeguard who refuses to attempt a rescue of a drowning person may be charged with manslaughter.

Defenses Relating to the Required Mental State

The second element of most crimes, the mental state, also provides grounds for many defenses. Note that in a trial the mental state of the defendant may be inferred by the trier of fact from the act itself. For example, a jury can conclude that the driver acted recklessly from a showing that she crossed and recrossed the interstate highway median at high speed prior to the collision. In such situations, the defense must present evidence that focuses directly on the defendant's actual mental state and not on what the act alone indicates it might have been.

The **insanity defense** is applied in this way. When this defense is used, it must be shown that the defendant was suffering from a mental disease or defect that prevented her or him from understanding the difference between right and wrong. Such an inability would prevent the defendant from formulating the evil intent that the criminal statute was meant to prohibit. A similar defense stems from the effect of an **irresistible impulse**. This defense is known as *temporary insanity* or *temporary mental defect*. This means that, because of a mental disease or defect, the defendant is temporarily unable to resist an impulse to commit a criminal act.

 # Hypothetical Case

Francis X. Tenguish, the fire chief of Flammable, Connecticut, returned home early from a stress clinic he had been attending for two weeks in rural Pennsylvania. The clinic had been prescribed as part of Chief Tenguish's treatment for job-related mental disorders. Unfortunately, the chief's unannounced return caused him to catch his wife in bed with another man. Chief Tenguish immediately grabbed a 37 Magnum "extinguisher" from a bedside cabinet and shot his wife's lover twice in the lower abdomen. When the chief was charged and tried for criminal assault, his defense was that he had acted out of an irresistible impulse. The fact that he had just been undergoing treatment for a mental defect showed that his ability to choose right from wrong was seriously weakened and that it was easily destroyed by the singular emotional impact of the event. Consequently the jury found the chief not guilty.

A defense that, like insanity, dispels the appearance of the criminal mental state is **entrapment**. If government agents have induced a person to commit a crime that she or he did not already contemplate, the accused has been entrapped and will be found not guilty. On the other hand, if the government agents provide only the opportunity for the crime to be committed, there is no defense. For example, individuals who sell goods they have stolen to an undercover cop acting as a fence have not been entrapped.

Mistake can be a defense when, because of honest error, the required criminal mental state is negated. Such a defense is provided if you take someone else's property because you honestly and reasonably believe it is your own.

🖼 Hypothetical Case

Nikki purchased a gift for her friend, and then took it to a gift-wrapping service. She asked for a box of a particular size and for a particular style of wrapping paper. She then paid for the service and was told to return in 15 minutes to pick up her package. When she returned, a package just like the one she ordered was on the counter. Not seeing anyone around the counter area, she picked it up and left with it, not knowing that it contained someone else's very expensive purchase. Mistake would serve as a defense to charges of theft that might stem from the incident.

Finally, accusations of criminal intent can be overcome if it can be shown that the defendant acted in **defense of self or others**. This defense is available if the defendant reasonably believed that there was danger of severe bodily harm or death from an unprovoked attack and used only enough force to repel that attack. Generally, retreat "to the wall," as it was once expressed, before defending oneself or others, is now required in only a few states and then only if faced with the use of deadly force and the retreat is not hazardous. When force is used in defense of others, some states require that those defended be members of the defender's family or household or someone else that the defender had a legal duty to protect. Other states allow the use of force in defense of others only if the party being defended actually, not just apparently, had a right to self-defense. In conclusion, note that only non-deadly force can be used in the defense of property alone.

Crimes That Affect Businesses

In order to take proper precautions, businesspeople must be able to recognize the criminal behavior that affects businesses. Criminal behavior can be classified as either violent or nonviolent.

Violent Crimes

You've probably seen the scenario on TV a dozen times—the armed bandit in front of the bank teller's cage or across the counter from the convenience store operator. But until the twin muzzles of a sawed off shotgun or similar weapon have been pointed at your own chest, it's all make-believe. Nevertheless, this scenario is an example of robbery, the most frequently practiced crime of violence against businesses. The modern definitions of robbery and of other crimes are given below.

Robbery   The taking of goods or money in the possession of another, from his person or in his immediate presence, by the use of force or fear is **robbery**. Notice that the items taken need only be in the possession of another and need not actually belong to that person. Also, in a number of jurisdictions the use of certain weapons, such as a handgun, in carrying out the crime of robbery, brings on a stiffer penalty. Generally, the additional penalty is a mandatory period of imprisonment beyond the usual term for robbery.

Burglary   The original common law definition of burglary, which was discussed earlier, has been altered in ways that make it applicable to business situations. "At night" or "nighttime" has been struck from the definition. "Dwelling house" has been replaced by "building" or "structure." So breaking into and entering a structure belonging to another to carry out a felony is now burglary in many states. The felony involved could also be grand larceny or even arson. These terms will be discussed shortly.

Arson   Like burglary, **arson** was made a crime by the common law to protect the home, where, while sleeping, citizens were most vulnerable either to a fire raging out of control or to theft or other felonies. Today, as with burglary, the definition of arson has been broadened, so that it now means more than intentionally setting fire to a dwelling house. Currently, arson is defined as the willful and malicious burning of a structure. *Malice* in such a case implies a wrong, evil, or corrupt motive.

Extortion   A potentially violent crime that also takes its toll on businesses is extortion. **Extortion** is defined as using threats of injury to the victim's person, family, property, or reputation to get consent to take property. Popularly referred to as *blackmail*, extortion must be dealt with firmly and immediately. Otherwise, the more resources the extortionist receives, the more likely she or he is to increase demands or carry out threats.

Nonviolent Crimes

Violent crimes catch the spotlight far more frequently than do nonviolent crimes. Yet, according to FBI figures, the total annual losses in all bank robberies around the country seldom, if ever, exceed $50 million. In contrast, the losses in one scandalous savings and loan failure—Lincoln S&L in California, bailed out by tax dollars—totaled more than $2.5 billion. Obviously, nonviolent crimes account for losses far greater than those caused by violent crimes and thus pose a far greater threat to the vast majority of businesses.

Larceny   Take away the threat or use of violence from robbery, and the result is **larceny**. Defined as the unlawful taking and carrying away of another's goods or money, larceny is usually divided into two categories: grand and petit. Taking and carrying away more than a certain amount of another's goods or money, say $250 or more, is considered **grand larceny** and a felony. Doing the same to goods or money of less than that amount is **petit larceny** and considered a misdemeanor. The dollar amount that is the dividing line between the two crimes is set by the various state legislatures. Note that what is commonly known as *shoplifting* actually is larceny.

Embezzlement and White-Collar Crime   A crime similar to larceny is embezzlement. The only difference between larceny and embezzlement is that in **embezzlement** the property taken is entrusted to the embezzler, who then wrongfully converts it to his or her personal use. Embezzlement poses a continual concern for businesses, as most of those who commit it have no criminal record. Up until the time they act criminally, usually to support a lifestyle that has gotten out of hand, they are model employees, agents, executives, and the like. As noted above, embezzlement and similar criminal activities by well-respected agents and executives, called white-collar crime, account for losses far greater than those caused by crimes of violence.

Computer Crime   The computer is an accomplice in many white-collar crimes. A computer program often consists of thousands of lines of complex directions and logic. As a consequence, white-collar criminals are attracted by the ample opportunities it provides to conduct embezzlement or larceny schemes. Also, computers and the data they contain are vulnerable to unauthorized use or destruction. Computer crime is a developing area of the law that deals with these problems.

As the following hypothetical situation illustrates, the law has a great deal of trouble with defining what is punishable as computer crime. Many of the computer crime statutes currently on the state lawbooks are vulnerable to constitutional challenge. Valid federal laws, however, do make it a crime to access certain governmental computers without authorization.

Hypothetical Case

As she neared the completion of her task, Bitsy Binari once again asked her boss, Sam Shadee, whether he would keep her on after she completed it. "Of course, of course," he replied. Nonetheless, as soon as she finished the program, Shadee fired her. Bitsy said nothing as she left. The next month, however, according to instructions she had programmed into the computer, it checked to see whether her Social Security number was still on the payroll. Seeing that it was not, the computer inverted the pay scale for the 12,000 employees of the business. Custodians received what Shadee normally did, and Shadee received the minimum wage. Then the computer completely erased the payroll program, the payroll database, and a variety of new project records before programmers discovered what was happening and pulled the plug. Shadee attempted to have Bitsy prosecuted for what she had done, but the evidence had been wiped out. In addition, the prosecutor pointed out that Bitsy's alleged "logic bomb" had only changed electronic impulses. There had been no taking of property. Without a taking of identifiable property, no crime had been committed under state law.

Bribery   Often crime flourishes because public officials find it more personally advantageous to look the other way. When something of value has been offered, given, received, or asked for in return for influence on how an official carries out a public or legal duty, the crime of **bribery** has occurred. Whether or not the offer is accepted, a crime takes place when it is made. If, however, the offer is accepted, both parties are equally guilty.

Public officials often face bribery charges. In a notorious case that started in early fall of 1973, Vice President Spiro Agnew denied accusations that he had accepted bribes from contractors for aid in getting contracts with the state of Maryland. It was charged that he had received these bribes while an executive of Baltimore County, governor of Maryland, and vice president of the United States. At University Hall in Charlottesville, Virginia, the Vice President elicited cheers from the assembled thousands when he said, "I will never resign," and then concluded his speech with characteristic attacks on the media and liberal politicians. On October 10, 1973, however, he proved himself a liar and resigned his position of trust a "heartbeat from the presidency." Subsequently, Agnew pleaded **nolo contendere** (no contest) to a single charge of failure to pay his full income tax for 1967. The judge in the case declared his plea a full statement of guilt, sentenced him to unsupervised probation for three years, and fined him $10,000. However, other bodies did more than just slap his wrist for his wrongdoing. In 1974 the Maryland Court of Appeals disbarred him, an action that prevented him from practicing law in the state. Finally, in 1981, another Maryland court ordered the ex-vice president of the United States to pay the state $248,735. This was the amount of the bribes that Agnew had taken in his positions of public trust plus interest.

Bribery goes beyond payoffs to public officials. In most states it is also a criminal act, usually referred to as *commercial bribery*, to pay business employees to influence their actions for their employer. For example, the Joseph Schlitz Brewing Company was convicted of commercial bribery because it had its salespeople grossly overtip for service they received at bars to induce the buyers for those establishments to buy Schlitz products. In an attempt to curtail such activity, many employment contracts have a "non acceptance of gift" clause. Overseas, American businesspeople are prohibited from bribing the officials of foreign nations in order to obtain or retain business. However, the federal statute involved, the Foreign Corrupt Practices Act, does allow what are called *grease payments*. Such payments are made as a matter of course to get public officials overseas to perform or expedite routine services, such as the issuance of a visa or a permit to do business.

Forgery and Bad Check Offenses   Whenever someone who has an intent to defraud falsely makes or alters a written document so as to create or change a legal effect of that document, a **forgery** has taken place. This crime takes in everything from altering the age on a driver's license to signing another's name on a deed or a check. Where checks are concerned, however, another crime encountered even more frequently than forgery is **issuing bad checks**. In committing this crime, a person writes a check on his or her account knowing that funds to cover the check are not available and that the check will probably not be paid by the financial institution on which it is written. If the financial institution does indeed fail to pay it, the person who wrote it is chargeable with issuing a bad check.

Racketeering   Most crimes against businesses are isolated events, planned and carried out by one person or a small group. For at least the last 35 years, however, Congress and many state legislatures have also worried about the effects of organized crime on businesses. As a consequence, Congress passed the Racketeer Influenced and Corrupt Organizations (RICO) Act in 1970. This act prohibits using a pattern of racketeering activities, such as murder, kidnapping, arson, and mail and wire fraud, in the conduct of business. It also prohibits using a pattern of such activities or the income from them to acquire or maintain an interest in a business. In addition to providing for the criminal prosecution of violators, RICO also allows lawsuits for damages by the victims.

Monopolizing Conduct   Although it is now popular to think of government with its regulations and paperwork as the main adversary of business, history shows that another adversary puts far more companies out of business than any other. That adversary is *competition*. Seldom is government more than a thorn in the side of businesses. Competition, however, eliminates inefficient companies and keeps the economy healthy by keeping it populated mainly with companies that sell quality products for the lowest cost. As a consequence, in the past some businesspeople sought to eliminate competition. The common law responded by making conduct that tended to consolidate control over the production of a good or the provision of a service into one person's or one firm's hands illegal. Such control was referred to as a **monopoly**. The initial victims of monopolizing conduct are those who seek to compete with the would-be monopoly. Ultimately, of course, the consumer has to bear the loss in the form of higher prices and diminished quality of the monopolized product.

As businesses grew in size, the ability of a single state's legal system to stop monopolies from forming decreased. Near the turn of the 20th century, the U.S. Congress passed the first of several statutes intended to stop the monopolizing conduct that it saw as threatening to dominate interstate commerce. This first statute is known today as the Sherman Antitrust Act. At the time of its passage, the primary way of consolidating control over businesses into a monopoly was though the use of a legal device called a *trust*. Thus, the word *antitrust* was applied to acts opposing such behavior. (See Chapter 27 for a full discussion of antitrust law.)

FIGURE 5-2 Comparative Sentencing Ranges for Crimes

Crime	Sentencing Ranges
Arson	From 5 to 15 years
Bad checks	Up to 1 year
Bribery of a public official	From 0 to 5 years
Burglary	From 5 to 15 years
Commercial bribery	Up to 1 year
Computer crime	
Damage under $1,000	From 0 to 5 years
Damage over $1,000	From 0 to 7 years
Forgery	From 0 to 7 years
Library theft	Up to 15 days
Murder (first degree)	Death or life without possibility of probation or parole (except by governor)
Rape (forcible)	From 10 to 30 years or life imprisonment
Robbery	From 10 to 30 years or life imprisonment
Unlawful receipt of a food stamp coupon	From 0 to 5 years

Chapter Review

USE LEGAL TERMS

Fill in the blanks with the appropriate term.

actus reus	grand jury	monopoly
arraignment	grand larceny	nolo contendere
arrest	hung jury	parole
arrest warrant	indictment	petit jury
arson	information	petit larceny
bail	insanity defense	plea bargain
bribery	irresistible impulse	possession
defense of self or others	issuing bad checks	preliminary hearing
double jeopardy	larceny	probable cause
embezzlement	mala in se	probation
entrapment	mala prohibita	robbery
extortion	mens rea	verdict
felony	misdemeanor	
forgery	mistake	

1. The judge enters the judgment. A jury reaches its ___?___ .
2. A(n) ___?___ crime is one that is not inherently evil.
3. Accusations of criminal intent can be overcome if it can be shown that the defendant acted in ___?___ .
4. The conditional release of a convict before her or his full time is served is ___?___ .
5. The conditional suspension of the carrying out of the sentence is ___?___ .
6. The source of indictments is a(n) ___?___ .
7. A potential defense to criminal charges because government agents induced the commission of the offense is ___?___ .
8. A(n) ___?___ is a crime punishable by death or imprisonment for a year or longer.
9. A(n) ___?___ is an honest error that negates the criminal intent usually required to convict someone of a crime.
10. At a preliminary hearing, the court will examine the evidence to see whether there is ___?___ to go to trial.

TEST YOUR READING

11.   List and explain the stages of criminal procedure.
12.   List and describe both the violent and nonviolent crimes that affect businesses.

THINK CRITICALLY ABOUT EVIDENCE

13.   Todd Chase Larue III, fresh out of the University of Virginia law school and destined to join the lucrative family law practice headed by Larues I and II, chuckled when he saw the motorcycle cop's lights flash in his mirrors. He didn't react at once. Instead he let his own motorcycle's big engine push him a quarter of a mile more down the shore road. Finally, he pulled onto the shoulder. As she dismounted, the cop took off her helmet. Five minutes later, a citation for riding without a helmet was in Todd's hands. Todd vowed that he would never pay it or any of the seven others like it he had received for the same offense. They had no right to tell him he had to wear a helmet!

   Does society have any interest to protect by requiring that we use helmets and other protective devices while traveling our roads, working in our factories, and so on? What has society invested in Larue III? What does society stand to lose beyond that investment if he is launched over the handlebars without a helmet on?

14.   Marcia Benton watched the rain falling outside her hospital window, then, amused at herself about how vulnerable she was to suggestion, reached slowly for the glass of water by her bedside. Her hand trembled from the exertion. But she kept it moving, forcing it toward the glass by an act of will. A light sweat appeared on her forehead. Her body had withered away these last few years. The disease had so sapped her energies that just raising a hand took enormous concentration. Her children didn't understand her weariness, however. They remembered their mother from the days when she had protected them against all harm, comforted them with love, given them direction in life. She had told them of her current desire to die, but they had not taken her seriously. "You're kidding, Mom. You'll miss so much, grand-children and all that," Bill had replied for all four of them. Even when the doctor had given them an estimate of the bill for keeping her on life support, they had remained resolute. She knew, though, that to keep her alive they would be paying the money they'd saved for their children's clothes, education, future . . . . So when the other doctor had slipped into her room the day before and introduced himself, she was glad, even joyful. She had prayed that he would come, prayed that the hospital orderly would contact him as promised. The doctor would return this evening with his machine, set it up, and then she would activate it with a push button. When she did, it would gently administer a lethal dose of a drug that the doctor had assured her would be painless. Her children would ultimately realize that she had ended

her life because she had to protect them . . . even from herself. Of course, the doctor would be in jeopardy. He was out on bail for rendering suicide assistance in another state. She grasped the water glass at last, but it fell from her hand and shattered on the floor. Marcia closed her eyes in dismay and sank back onto her pillows . . .

   a.   Should it be a criminal act to assist in suicides? If you believe that assisting suicides should be a crime, what should be the punishment for that crime? Compare your answer with sentencing ranges for various crimes listed in Figure 5-2.

   b.   Attempted suicide is a crime in some jurisdictions. What should be the punishment for it?

   c.   If an innocent bystander is accidentally injured in a suicide attempt (because in such an attempt a car crashes into the bystander), should the person who made the attempt be punished for that injury?

15. Assume that you are the head prosecutor of a major metropolitan area. Two alleged rape cases on your desk are awaiting a decision on whether or not to go forward with trial. The first case involves a female victim who becomes hysterical whenever she is questioned about the incident. There is a high likelihood that the stress of a trial would cause her to suffer a severe breakdown. However, there is a great deal of evidence against the defendant, much of which suggests the use of extreme force: torn clothing, and bruises and cuts on the alleged victim's body. The police also recovered a knife from the defendant similar to the one that the alleged victim described. The second case involves a defendant from a well-known and very wealthy entertainment family. The media coverage surrounding this case has been intense, and a decision not to prosecute would be regarded as favoritism. However, the only evidence in the case is the testimony of the alleged victim.

   a.   Which of the cases do you order to trial?

   b.   You have two assistant prosecutors who handle rape cases. One is an inexperienced woman. The other is a man with a superior conviction record over the six years he has been with your office. Which of these assistant prosecutors would you assign to the first case if it went to trial? Which would you assign to the second?

16. Assume that you are being arrested for a major felony. The police have hand-cuffed you and placed you in a patrol car for transport to headquarters. During the ride you have a few moments to think. As a person accused of a crime, what rights are you guaranteed under the federal Constitution? Given your present circumstances, what practical steps can you take to obtain the protection afforded by those rights?

REAL-WORLD CASE
United States v. *John W. Hinckley, Jr.*
525 Federal Supplement 1342

Consider the case of U.S. *v.* Hinckley, *in which able and expensive attorneys utilized available constitutional protections and the insanity plea in the defense of their client.*

On March 30, 1981, as President Ronald Reagan left the Washington Hilton Hotel after giving a speech, he was wounded by one of a series of bullets allegedly fired by John Hinckley. Three other men also were wounded, including James Brady, the president's press secretary, who received a severely debilitating wound in the head. President Reagan underwent surgery shortly thereafter at a nearby hospital. Before the surgery he commented to his wife, "Honey, I forgot to duck," then eyed the surgeons and said jokingly, "Please tell me you're Republicans." He recovered and served two full terms.

John Hinckley was arrested at the scene with "smoking gun" in hand. Soon after his arraignment, he underwent two psychiatric examinations by order of the magistrate and then the chief judge involved in the case. Both examinations found him to be competent. On August 28, after being indicted by a federal grand jury, Hinckley pled not guilty to a battery of charges, including attempted assassination of the president.

His lawyers, however, were hard at work. First, they moved to suppress evidence garnered from Hinckley's interrogation by law enforcement officials soon after the shooting and before he had legal counsel at hand. The court held that although Hinckley had been informed of his *Miranda* rights three times prior to making his statements, his expression of a desire not to answer certain questions until he had consulted with his attorney was enough to invoke that right. The court therefore held that interrogation should have been suspended until legal counsel was present and that Hinckley's answers to all questions relating to the investigation when he was without counsel would not be allowed as evidence. Second, Hinckley's lawyers moved to suppress evidence garnered from the diary and notes that he had maintained in his cell. In checking Hinckley's cell for contraband and indicators of a potential suicide attempt, his jailers had discovered allegedly incriminating material that he had written in the diary. Hinckley's lawyers argued that the substance of his writings had been improperly violated. The court held that the material garnered from those writings should be suppressed as the search and seizure rights of Hinckley's jailers went only to the two problem areas that they had been supposed to check. Finally, at trial, the defense was able to convince the jury, which debated almost 24 hours before returning a verdict, that John Hinckley was not guilty by reason of insanity. The defense introduced evidence of his psychiatric care immediately prior to the shootings and of his fixation on actress Jodie Foster. Hinckley apparently mused that Foster would have to notice him if he carried out an act such as the attempted assassination.

Hinckley was ordered confined at St. Elizabeth's Hospital, a mental institution in Washington, DC.

Think Critically

1. Hinckley was the son of very wealthy parents, and the law worked quite well in his defense. Do you think it would have worked as well in defense of an unemployed construction worker?
2. Should incriminating evidence be suppressed regardless of how it was obtained? Are there any alternatives to suppression?

CHAPTER 6

Civil Law

GOALS

- Understand the nature of tort law and its relationship with contract and criminal law
- Know the elements of the major torts
- Be able to identify the torts that affect business

What Is a Tort?

- A shopper backs his car into your new vehicle in the mall's lot
- A drunk punches you in the nose
- A newspaper improperly identifies you as the shoplifter picked up yesterday in a local store
- A truck overturns and spills gasoline that pollutes your land
- A competing business "bugs" your office with listening devices
- A doctor improperly diagnoses your problem as stomach flu when, in reality, you have appendicitis
- A lawyer improperly advises you, causing a $10,000 loss

Do any of the above situations sound familiar? A wrong has been committed in each of them. In all of them the victim can use the courts to seek compensation. These personal injuries or wrongs for which the law will provide remedies are known as **torts**, and the person who commits a tort is known as a **tortfeasor**. It is the right of the injured party to sue the tortfeasor. If the injured party wins the lawsuit, the court will order the tortfeasor to pay that party an appropriate amount of money for the harm done. This compensation is known as a damage award or just as **damages**.

History has shown us that if the opportunity to right personal injuries in a court of law is not available, wronged individuals often seek revenge with their own hands. The resulting violence endangers, and may even destroy, the peace and stability that mark civilization.

Tort Law's Relationship to Criminal and Contract Law

Note that tort law differs from other types of law in significant ways. For example, criminal law requires that the wrong be defined beforehand. Citizens then owe a duty to society not to commit criminal acts. When a crime is committed, it is society that has been injured because it is the peace of society that has been violated. Therefore, it is up to the prosecutor for the state or federal government to seek the fining and/or imprisonment of the violator on behalf of society. Tort law, on the other hand, is far more flexible than criminal law. It recognizes only a general duty of each citizen to refrain from harming another in negligent or intentional ways. The specific harmful act does not have to be identified beforehand and could occur in an ever-growing number of possible ways. If such harm occurs, it is then up to the injured person to seek damages and/or other suitable remedies in court. These available remedies are far less severe than the fine and/or imprisonment punishments meted out to violators of the criminal law. However, criminal acts often include conduct that constitutes a tort: Angered when a female fan at ringside repeatedly insulted his hairdo, famous wrestler Stan ("The Hummingbird") Solo hit her over the head with a folding chair. As a result, he was arrested and prosecuted for criminal assault. Afterward the fan sued him for the tort of battery and recovered $75,000 in damages.

FIGURE 6-1   The Overlapping Duties of Criminal, Tort, and Contract Law

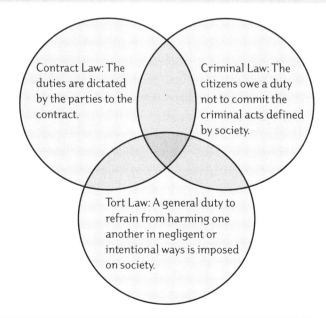

Tort law also differs from contract law. As with criminal law, under contract law the enforceable duties are defined beforehand. However, the definition of those duties is written by the parties to the contract and not by society. In addition, the contractual parties owe the duties primarily to each other. It is up to the party injured under the contract to sue to collect damages when such a duty has been unfulfilled or violated. Regardless of the differences between the parties, however, contracts also can produce grounds for tort actions.

Hypothetical Case

The Melbourne Marsupials, an Australian team of the World Outreach Experimental Football League (WOEFL), needed a coach. Desperate, the Marsupials contracted with Danny Uprights, successful head coach of Pennsboro State University (PSU) of Missouri, for his services. Coach Uprights, however, had just signed a five-year contract with PSU and would have to break it to be able to coach the Marsupials. Should he do so, PSU could sue the Marsupials for the tort of intentional interference with contract.

Remedies Available to Correct Tortious Conduct

A person who initiates a tort suit is attempting to correct the supposed wrong done by asking for damages or an injunction, or both. An **injunction** is a court order directing that some action be either taken or halted. For example, if your neighbor is dumping toxic waste into a stream that flows onto your land, you might sue for a court order directing that the neighbor stop the dumping and clean up the toxic waste.

Although the availability of an injunction as a remedy is significant, it is the promise or threat of a damage award that most often draws natural persons, associations, partnerships, corporations, and even the government, acting as a private individual, into court under the tort law. So, before discussing torts in detail, let's take a look at the various types and amounts of damages that may be available to **litigants**—those who engage in a lawsuit.

Actual damages, also referred to as compensatory damages, are the most important and most frequently sought damages. These damages are intended to compensate the victim for the real harm done. If property is damaged or destroyed, then the amount necessary to repair or replace it would be awarded. If a person is injured, damages would include payment for lost wages, medical bills, and the pain and suffering that the person endured.

In some cases the victim may be awarded even more than actual damages in order to punish or make an example of a defendant who acted maliciously or wantonly. These additional amounts, called **exemplary damages**, or "punitive" damages in some jurisdictions, are arbitrarily set by the jury and bear little, if any, direct relationship to the amount of actual injuries sustained by the victim. For example, imagine that, after waiting in line overnight, you are about to buy the last available tickets to a live concert of your favorite rock group. Suddenly, Anthony ("Little Mountain") Sanderson pushes you out of the way to get them for himself. You resist, and he punches you in the stomach. Then, while you are lying on the sidewalk, he buys the tickets, and leaves. Even if the punch did you no lasting harm, most courts would allow you to recover a small amount for it and thousands of dollars in exemplary damages from Sanderson to prevent the recurrence of such conduct. Unlike damages awarded for negligently caused harm, such exemplary damages are not dischargeable in bankruptcy.

In situations where there has been improper conduct but little in the way of actual loss, as in the preceding example, the law still awards a small amount of damages to the victim. Such awards are referred to as **nominal damages**. At times, these damages may be all that the victim receives as a result of her or his lawsuit. However, they do represent an acknowledgment by the law that the victim's rights have been violated.

Finally, do not forget that attorney's fees and expenses will not be awarded by the court in these cases. They are instead payable out of the pocket or recovery of the litigants. Many tort suits are brought on a percentage of recovery basis. Under such an arrangement, anywhere from 25 percent to 40 percent of the recovery may go to the attorney.

What Kinds of Conduct Bring on Tort Liability?

For a defendant in a tort case to be required to pay damages, it must be shown that he or she has harmed someone in one of three basic ways. These ways are

1. Intentionally, as reflected in the intentional torts recognized by the law
2. Accidentally, due to a failure to exercise reasonable care
3. By engaging in certain enterprises that bring on liability regardless of the degree of care taken, referred to as strict liability

Intentional Torts

Intentionally or purposefully bringing about harm to another's person or property is the basis for **intentional torts**. You've probably heard of some of the best known of these torts, such as assault, battery, and false imprisonment.

Placing an individual in reasonable fear of a harmful or offensive touching is an **assault**. Actually touching someone in a harmful or offensive way is a **battery**. Improper restraint or confinement of another without authority, justification, or consent is **false imprisonment**. Case examples of assault and battery will be discussed shortly in order to show how intentional tort law works. Other intentional torts and their specific impact on businesses will be discussed at the end of this chapter.

The victim of an intentional tort is able to recover not only actual damages but exemplary damages as well. So the stakes can be extremely high. To win an intentional tort case, several key elements must be proven to the jury. For the case of battery these elements include:

1. *An act*   This must be a result of the actor's will and not of a reflex or spasm. Thus, if a person hits me because he is in the throes of an epileptic seizure, I cannot recover for battery, as he did not hit me willfully.
2. *An intent*   The defendant must have intended to bring about a harmful or offensive touching. Note that intentionally hitting someone with either a baseball bat or an unwanted, and therefore offensive, kiss can be the basis for a battery suit.
3. *Actual contact*   There must be actual contact, not just a swing (or pucker) and a miss. Hitting a person's clothes while they are being worn or a person's purse while it is being carried is considered the same as hitting the person.
4. *Causation*   The defendant's action must be a substantial factor in the injuries suffered by the victim.
5. *Damages*   Evidence of the harm caused by the defendant must be shown.

These elements differ a little for the closely related intentional tort of assault. Assault requires that the defendant intended to place the victim in reasonable apprehension of a harmful or offensive touching. *No actual touching has to occur*, it simply has to be reasonable to presume that you're about to suffer such a touching. However, there has to be an overt act by the defendant to bring on that presumption. Words alone are not enough.

To understand assault and battery better, consider this example. You are in an English class in which the teacher frequently hurls pieces of chalk at sleeping or inattentive students. Kelsay, who sits in front of you, is whispering with a new female student while the teacher is lecturing. As the teacher's voice drones on, you stare at the back of Kelsay's head thinking about last weekend . . . . Suddenly, the teacher fires a piece of chalk at Kelsay. Seeing it coming, Kelsay ducks violently, pinches a nerve in his neck, and loses consciousness. Unseen by you, the chalk pops you in the mouth and breaks off part of your front tooth. Both you and Kelsay can bring suit for actual damages. His hospitalization caused him to lose $80 by missing two days' work. He paid $4,500 in medical fees. Also, he allegedly suffered $20,000 for pain and suffering and exemplary damages, which will be arbitrarily set by the jury and may total $50,000 or more due to the nature of the incident. His suit will be based on assault as the force set in motion (the chalk) by the teacher did not actually hit him. Your suit will be for battery only as you were the victim of a harmful touching but had no notice or apprehension of a forthcoming harmful touching. Your actual damages would include the $1,200 you paid for dental care. You could also sue for your lost wages and your pain and suffering. Finally, you too could pursue exemplary damages in an amount necessary to punish the teacher for this conduct.

Defenses to Intentional Tort Suits   As is obvious to any participant in or observer of a contact sport, not all injurious physical touching results in a successful lawsuit. That is because **consent**, a willing and knowledgeable assent to what would otherwise be tortious conduct, is a defense in intentional tort cases. The consent of the injured party may be implied or actual, and it must not be acquired by fraudulent means.

Self-defense and defense of property also provide limited protection against intentional tort suits. For information on these defenses, read the following scenario and consider the questions that follow.

Hypothetical Case

At 3 A.M., JJ awakened when she heard a car engine idling roughly on the street. Knowing something was wrong, she slid out of bed and peered out the window. A car was parked at the head of her driveway with its lights out and its trunk partly open. The side door of her new car, which was also parked in the driveway, was open, but its interior lights weren't on. A dark, shadow-like figure was sprawled on the seat of her car working at something under the dash. JJ called 911 and reported what was going on. As she hung up, she realized that the person was after her CD system, which was worth nearly $2,500 and uninsured. She grabbed her dad's old .45-caliber service pistol from the drawer in the night table and slipped out the side door. As she reached the driveway, the figure in the car got out, carrying her CD system. JJ was between him and his car. "Stop," she yelled, aiming the pistol at him. The man smiled at her and started walking to his car. As he walked past her, JJ chambered a round and yelled again: "Stop, I'll shoot, and you better believe it!"

If JJ shoots the man in the knee, do you think he should be able to successfully sue her for doing so? The answer is that JJ will certainly be liable if she shoots him merely to prevent him from taking her property. The law holds that reasonable force may be used in defense of property. This does not include force that might cause substantial bodily harm or death. Presume that JJ doesn't shoot at first but that after putting her CD system in the trunk of his car, the man walks toward her with a tire iron in his hand, saying, "Now get out of the way so I can get the speakers." Would his subsequent lawsuit against her be successful if she kneecaps him at that time? The law holds that in self-defense a person must use only reasonable force to prevent a threatened battery. Such force may include inflicting substantial bodily harm or death on the aggressor, but only so long as a convenient or reasonable means of escape is not available. As JJ could have gotten out of the thief's way and not had to use deadly force, she would probably be held liable for assault and battery.

Negligence

The second way in which a defendant may be held liable under tort law is to harm someone or something accidentally due to a failure to exercise reasonable care. This is termed **negligence**. If your property or person has been injured because of another's negligence, you may sue in court for the actual damages. Exemplary damages are not awarded to compensate for the harm caused by negligence.

Elements of Negligence   Filing suit alleging that another negligently caused us harm is one thing, but actually proving negligence is another. Proof of the tort of negligence typically requires producing evidence that shows each of the following elements:

1. *An act or omission*   Unlike intentional torts, which require an overt act, negligence may occur if the defendant simply fails to act when there is a special duty to do so. A bridgekeeper might be negligent if he or she fails to lower the traffic barriers before raising the bridge, for example.

2. *A duty of due care*   This is defined by asking how a reasonable person would have acted under the circumstances. We all have the obligation to recognize and take reasonable precautions against harming others. In some instances society may inform us on what it thinks is due care, for example, with highway speed limits, but even these indicators are not conclusive in all cases. It still comes back to an individual decision as to what is reasonable under the circumstances. It would not be a defense to negligence to claim that you were under the 65-mph speed limit when you were driving 63 mph on a road sheeted with ice and snow immediately before you crashed into the highway department's truck.

3. *A breach of the duty of due care*   The trier of fact (usually a jury, but a judge if a jury is not requested) will compare the defendant's behavior with the standard it created by defining how a reasonable person should have behaved under the circumstances. If the defendant's conduct, as shown by the evidence, falls below that standard, then there has been a breach of the duty of due care. In certain situations where there is not enough evidence to show the conduct of the defendant, such as airline crashes, the law will presume a breach of the duty of due care and will require the alleged tortfeasor, the airline, to show otherwise. The idea here is that the act, in this example, the crash, speaks for itself. Similarly, in assessing the potential liability of professionals, they are charged with knowledge of the facts they "reasonably should have known," not just the facts they were actually aware of.

4. *Causation*   The law tries to be just by requiring that the negligence of the defendant be both the actual and the proximate cause of the harm done. By **actual cause** the law means that the harm would not have occurred but for the defendant's negligence. If the harm would have occurred regardless of that negligence, the defendant is not held responsible. By **proximate cause** the law means that the harm caused must fall within the range of consequences of the negligent act for which the defendant is legally responsible. If the defendant's negligent act is not both the actual and proximate cause of the harm done, then the defendant is not liable.

5. *Damages*   Actual damages are awardable for negligence. So evidence of such damages, for example, lost wages, medical bills, and pain and suffering, is needed here.

▶ Hypothetical Case

"Spoke too Sooooon," a bicycle delivery service, was employed by several businesses in New York City for the speed of its bikers. Delivery of important packages and messages was guaranteed within 30 minutes from the point of pickup in a four-mile radius. After picking up a box marked "Danger, Explosive" from the Caustic Chemical Company on Fifth Avenue, Sue E. Side, Spoke's best delivery person, raced cross-town. Unfortunately, she was delayed by an accident on Broadway, so that she arrived at the destination with barely seconds to go. In her haste to beat the deadline, she negligently dropped the box, which exploded as it hit the ground. Sue was blown into some bushes and walked away with minor scratches. Glass shattered from nearby windows by the blast cut several individuals. Hiram Hackster, while driving his cab nearby, heard the noise and took his eyes off the road to see where the explosion came from and then crashed into the rear of a bakery truck, causing $8,500 in property damage. Spoke and Sue would be liable for the injuries to the individuals cut by the glass as their negligence was both the actual and proximate cause of the harm done. However, Hackster and the cab company would be liable for the harm done in the collision as Hackster's negligence in diverting his attention from his driving was the most proximate cause of that harm.

Defenses to Negligence   The defendant in a negligence case can offer a number of defenses. The most effective defense is **contributory negligence**, which disallows any recovery whatsoever for an injury if the injured party's own negligence contributed to that injury. In actual practice, contributory negligence has caused some very unfair results. Even so, it was enforced in most states for many years, and it is still the rule of law in several states. For an example, consider the case of Sammi Shovel, licensed private investigator:

▶ Hypothetical Case

Driving to a late night surveillance job, Sammi was tailed by undercover police detectives. One of the detectives had just clocked her driving 37 mph in a 35-mph zone when she was hit broadside in an intersection by a huge garbage truck negligently driven through a red light. Her car was totally destroyed, and she suffered internal injuries and broken bones. After a short foot chase, the police detectives apprehended the truck driver, Stan Langston, and arrested him for driving while intoxicated. Langston suffered no personal injuries from the crash, and his truck had only a small dent in the right fender. Langston, who persisted in calling himself a "refuse manager" throughout his interrogation, proved to be the owner of the local trash collection service and had a long record of traffic convictions. Nevertheless, when Sammi brought suit for the injuries to her property and person, which totaled more than $125,000, she could not recover. Under her state's contributory negligence rule, proof that she had been driving over the established speed limit immediately prior to the crash was enough to show negligence and to totally preclude her recovery.

Fortunately, most states have replaced contributory negligence with comparative negligence. **Comparative negligence** is a defense that does not deny all recovery when the injured party is somewhat negligent. Instead, it allows recovery according to the relative degree of fault of the parties to the accident. In Sammi Shovel's case, comparative negligence would require the trier of fact to assign each party a percentage of responsibility for the harm done. So if Langston were held to be 95 percent responsible, he would have to pay for 95 percent of the damages he had inflicted on Sammi and to bear 95 percent of his own damages. Sammi would be responsible for the remaining 5 percent of each.

A final defense worth mentioning is **assumption of risk**. If the injured party knew of the specific risk involved, yet voluntarily assumed it, recovery may be limited or even precluded. The operator of a portable TV camera on the sidelines of a football game would probably be held to have assumed the risk of the "Bubba factor," that is, the risk that a 245-pound linebacker would crash out of bounds into the operator.

Strict Liability

Ultrahazardous Activities   Under the doctrine of **strict liability**, regardless of how much care has been taken, if harm results from a defendant's abnormally dangerous conduct or activity, the defendant will be liable for it. This doctrine is applied when the defendant is involved in a hazardous activity, such as detonating explosives or damming streams. Also, keeping wild animals, other than in a zoo or for public exhibition, exposes the owner to strict liability. So if your pet cobra, mongoose, or lion escapes from you and wreaks havoc, no matter how much money you invested in a restraint system, you're going to be liable for the harm it does.

Product Liability   One constantly growing area of business law that embraces strict liability principles is *product liability*. Until the last few years, if you were injured by a defective product, your only way to collect was by producing enough evidence to prove the negligence of the manufacturer. Attempting this often proved to be difficult, expensive, and unsuccessful. This was due mainly to the complexity of the engineering involved in modern products and to the fact that the evidence was initially in the hands of the manufacturer.

Gradually the law has changed, so that today the injured party does not have to show how the product came to be defective due to the manufacturer's or seller's violation of the duty of due care. Instead, it is enough to show

1.   That the injury came from the use of the product in the manner intended
2.   That there was an unreasonably dangerous defect in the product
3.   That the defendant was engaged in the business of manufacturing or selling the product
4.   That the product had not been substantially altered by the time of the injury

Therefore, a person injured while using his lawn mower to trim his hedge could not recover. However, the family members who were injured in a car crash caused when the car's air bags deployed upon hitting a dropout pothole in a bridge could bring suit and recover.

Other Defenses to Torts—the Immunities

"The king can do no wrong" was the binding adage of the English legal system for the simple reason that the courts were set up by and belonged to the monarch. The judges only had power because the King or Queen granted it to them, and they certainly were not about to "bite the hand that fed them." After our Declaration of Independence on July 4, 1776, this freedom from responsibility changed only slightly. In the main it was retained as what we know today as "governmental immunity." This protection for the government from the consequences of tortious governmental acts has been weakened in recent years, but it still remains as a reasonably effective shield that most governmental bodies can hide behind. In particular, today the federal government can be sued for its negligent conduct or to hold it strictly liable. But it cannot be recovered from for its intentional torts. As an example, consider this true story.

> To study the spread of infectious diseases, a U.S. "intelligence" agency released a unique viral strain in the San Francisco Bay area. The agency then monitored how long the disease took to show up on the east and southern coasts. Lawsuits against the U.S. government for losses due to the medical bills and lost wages of those who fell ill would be thrown out of court due to governmental immunity, as the agency had acted intentionally.

At the state level, governmental immunity is still the rule. Charitable immunity, due to the availability of insurance and the size of many charitable organizations, is generally a thing of the past. So a negligence suit against a hospital run by the Order of Merciful Medical Missionaries, a charitable group, which would have been thrown out of court in decades past, would be tried today. Intrafamilial immunity, which once prevented all parent/child suits for tortious conduct, now applies only to negligence. A child can now sue his or her parents for intentional torts such as assault and battery. Interspousal tort immunity still holds in several states for personal injuries, due to the worry that a husband and wife might conspire in a fraudulent scheme to collect money under a liability insurance policy. However, suits for property damage inflicted by one spouse on holdings of the other spouse are now prosecutable, whereas a few decades ago they were not.

Torts That Affect Businesses

Without question, criminal behavior takes a severe toll on businesses. However, so does tortious conduct. Crimes are public wrongs for which the law provides a penalty. Torts are private injuries or wrongs for which the law provides a remedy. Several of the most serious and frequent torts that target business operations are discussed in the following paragraphs. Again, it is extremely important for businesspeople to be able to identify them so as to take appropriate action when they pose a threat to business operations.

Wrongful Interference with Business Contractual Relationships   Every business is encouraged by our systems of law and economics to compete fairly with other businesses. Advertising a product's strong points or the true weak points of another's product is at the heart of capitalism. Luring customers away from competitors with better prices and financing, if these are not set artificially low, drives the market mechanism. However, when a company breaches the level of fair competition by making false attacks on another company's reputation or products or by preying directly on another company's customers, an intentional tort has been committed.

Inducing Breach of Contract   Causing one party to an already existing contract to breach that agreement also may give rise to an intentional tort lawsuit. Certainly, a person adversely affected by another's failure to perform her or his contractual obligations can bring suit against the nonperforming party for breach of contract. But if it can be shown that an outside party intentionally caused the breach, that third person can be sued for the intentional tort of inducing breach of contract.

Hypothetical Case

Slippery Oil, Inc., of Dallas contracted to sell its outstanding shares of stock to a group of Japanese investors for $115 per share. Two weeks after the agreement was signed, the president of Slippery accidentally met the president of another American oil company, Continental Shelf Unlimited (CSU) at the Los Angeles airport. When Slippery's president told CSU's president of the impending deal, the CSU president offered $125 a share for the same stock. Slippery's president accepted the offer. When told that the deal with it was off, the Japanese investor group filed suit against CSU for inducing breach of contract and won. Because the suit was brought as an intentional tort rather than a contract action, the damages awarded included punitive damages and therefore ran into the billions of dollars.

Infringement of Patents, Trademarks, and Copyrights   In Section 8 of Article I, the Constitution gives Congress the power to "promote the Progress of Science and useful Arts, by securing for limited Times to Authors and Investors the exclusive Right to their respective Writings and Discoveries." Congress used this power to reward those who produce useful goods, often called *intellectual property*, with their minds instead of their backs. The **patent**, a nonrenewable legal monopoly over the right to make, use, or sell a device, was made available to the inventor of the device. The **copyright**, an exclusive right to the publishing, printing, copying, reprinting, and selling of the tangible expression of an author's or artist's creativity, was given to the copyright holder. A system for the registration and protection of the right to exclusive use of **trademarks**—the identifying symbols, words, or designs by which a business distinguishes its products to consumers—also was created by Congress in response to its constitutional charge.

When these rights of inventors, authors, artists, and businesses are violated, the tort of infringement of patent, copyright, or trademark has occurred.

Disparagement of Reputation   **Defamation** is the damaging of another's reputation by the making of false statements. It is divided into the intentional torts of slander and libel. **Slander** involves the communication of the false statements in a temporary form, such as orally. **Libel** involves the communication of the false statements in a more permanent form, such as in writing or in the visual medium of videotape. To base a lawsuit, the false statements must be made or conveyed to a third party. If the person defamed is the only one to hear the false statement, no tort has occurred.

U.S. laws give journalists and their publishers, the members of our society with the greatest ability to spread false statements to others, special protection against certain lawsuits for defamation. Specifically, this protection is against libel or slander actions brought by public officials or public figures. In the eyes of the law, public officials and figures seek to gain the attention of the people by means of news carriers of all kinds, from supermarket tabloids to the most serious daily papers, and must therefore take the good with the bad. So the law allows public officials and figures to recover for defamation only if they can show actual malice by the journalist in putting together the alleged falsehoods in a story. Actual **malice** means that the reporter or publisher had to know the story was false or had to recklessly disregard the possibility that it was false. These are hard standards to overcome. As a consequence, nearly all such suits fail. It is significant to note that other nations require a higher standard of truth from their media and yet maintain a free press.

A person other than a public figure or a public official need only prove that the published statements were false and show damages in order to recover in court. In a step beyond that, some categories of statements have been identified by the law as so harmful that the plaintiff does not even have to prove damages. These categories include falsely accusing someone of having a communicable sexual disease, of committing a criminal offense, or of lacking the ability to perform the duties of an office, employment, or profession. Such statements are said to be **defamatory per se**.

Businesses confront the effects of defamation in two main areas. One of these areas involves the making of false statements about the reputation of the business itself or about the quality of its products. This is called **disparagement of reputation**. The other area involves defamation suits by former employees. Such suits stem from statements made in letters of reference written by businesses to prospective employers of former employees. The legal systems of most states recognize a need for candor in these letters and therefore require that actual malice by the former employer be shown before the former employee can recover. Regardless, because of the large number of lawsuits and the high legal fees involved in defending against them, many businesses now refuse to provide useful references.

Injuries Stemming from RICO-Prohibited Activities   As mentioned in the subsection on racketeering in Chapter 5, in addition to allowing criminal prosecutions of violators, RICO also allows civil suits. In such suits the victims can recover three times the actual damages, court costs, and attorney's fees. RICO's provision for civil lawsuits, and especially for the recovery of attorney's fees, has led to some very creative applications of the statute by lawyers. This is especially true because the "pattern of racketeering activity" prohibited in the statute may be found in as few as two instances of related criminal activity within 10 years.

Hypothetical Case

The prestigious John W. Booth School of Graduate Studies in Acting at the State University let the parents of several marginally qualified applicants know that their children would be admitted only if the parents contributed $15,000 each to the Booth School Foundation. The foundation regularly gave Christmas and summer fellowships to the deserving faculty and administrators of the graduate school. Over the course of five years, some $300,000 was raised in this manner. The parents of a student who dropped out after the first semester brought suit for a violation of RICO. The court held that they had been damaged to the extent of their contribution to the foundation. They were awarded $45,000 in treble damages (3 x $15,000) plus their attorney's fees of $17,000 and court costs.

Court Procedure for Resolving Tort and Other Civil Cases

Parties to the Action

Court actions that are brought because of a private injury or wrong, such as those arising under tort or contract law, are called **civil cases**. Such an action usually is begun when an injured party files a document called a complaint with the clerk of a court with original jurisdiction over the matter. The **complaint** states the injured party's version of the facts of the case and shows why the court has jurisdiction over it. The complaint then makes a request or "prayer" for relief in the form of damages and/or a court order directing the defendant to do or to stop doing something. The person who initiates a lawsuit in this fashion is called the **plaintiff**. The person complained against is known as the **defendant**. Note that the law also allows lawsuits against entities that are not flesh and blood persons. For example, corporations are considered artificial persons and can sue and be sued.

Requiring the Defendant to Appear and Answer

Upon receiving the complaint, the clerk will see that a summons is issued and served upon the defendant along with a copy of the complaint. This informs the defendant of the nature of the claim involved and the court that has jurisdiction over it. The **summons** also demands that the defendant respond to the complaint within a given time.

Presenting the summons and complaint to the defendant, termed **service of process**, is vitally important. Otherwise, the defendant will not have proper notice of the lawsuit and cannot exercise the right to be heard. Once notice has been given, however, the defendant may react in a number of ways. First of all, the defendant may dispute whether the court is the proper one to judge the matter. For example, if the complaint is filed in a state circuit court, but the matter involves more than $75,000 and the parties to the dispute are from different states, the defendant may request removal of the case to a federal court. Second, the defendant may suggest that the service of process was improper and, therefore, that the summons was not effective. If the defendant is correct about improper service, no response to the complaint is required.

Defining the Issues to be Resolved

If both the court and the service are proper, however, the defendant must answer. The **answer** is the defendant's response to the complaint. In it the defendant either admits to or denies the claims of the plaintiff. The defendant may also make claims at this time. A claim that the defendant makes against the plaintiff based on the incident at hand is called a **counterclaim**. A claim that the defendant makes against another defendant in the same case is a **crossclaim**. Another procedural device, called a **third-party complaint**, reaches beyond the original parties and makes a party not previously involved a part of the suit.

The good thing about the use of the complaint, the answer, and claims is that they tend to clarify and narrow the issues to be resolved at trial. For example, if you file a complaint against me based on my alleged negligent driving that ended in a collision with you, my answer may dispute the issue of negligence but will probably admit that I was involved in an accident with you on the date and under many of the circumstances you stated. In court, then, you won't have to prove that I was present or driving the car or even that there was a collision. You may focus instead on proving the heart of your case, the allegation of negligence. This makes for a far more efficient use of the court system than would otherwise be possible. Formal written statements exchanged prior to trial, such as the complaint and the answer, are referred to as the **pleadings**.

It is very important to understand that at times a comparison of the various pleadings may reveal that there are no factual issues to be resolved in the case. When this occurs, a party may make a **motion for judgment on the pleadings**. This motion notes that since there is no factual issue, there is no reason to hold a full trial. Instead, the judge should just decide which laws to apply to the facts agreed to in the pleadings and enter judgment accordingly.

Pretrial Preparations

If a trial is to be held, the legal system wants all sides to have the best evidence available in their hands to present to the trier of fact. The system also is biased against surprises during trial, thinking it better that each side have the fullest possible ability to know the other side's case before it is presented. Such knowledge often leads the parties to settle out of court. Many jurisdictions enhance the possibility of such a settlement by requiring a **pretrial conference**. In such a conference, the judge and the attorneys for both sides try to get the parties to settle their problems without a formal trial.

If settlement efforts fail, either side is empowered to determine the evidence that the other side has to offer at trial. The process by which this is accomplished is appropriately termed **discovery**. Discovery involves a variety of ways in which one side can request information from the other side:

1. By **interrogatories**—a written list of questions that the other side must answer. Interrogatories are used to find out the names of the witnesses and their likely testimony or documents and physical evidence that are likely to be used as evidence.

2. By **depositions**—a procedure allowing witnesses or other parties to be placed under oath and made to respond to questions from opposing attorneys. A record of the answers given is made by court personnel and can be used against those testifying if their stories change.

3. By physical examinations conducted by qualified medical personnel. This allows the determination of injuries and conditions.

4. By requests for tangible evidence to allow the opposition to examine significant evidence such as documents, photographs, weapons, or products.

If a party does not comply with proper requests for discovery, the court will compel it to do so and will penalize it for refusing.

Trial Procedure

If the case goes to trial and a jury is requested, the selection of that panel becomes the first order of business. (If a jury is not requested, the judge will sit as the trier of fact.) The members of the jury must be impartial and competent. Prospective jurors are therefore interrogated to ensure that they do not have a relationship to anyone involved in the case that would affect their judgment.

After the jury panel has been selected, the trial formally begins with the opening statements of the attorneys. These statements tell the jurors what the case is about and what each side will endeavor to prove. After the opening statements, the plaintiff's case is presented through her or his attorney. Documents, physical evidence, and the testimony of witnesses are introduced to convince the jury that the plaintiff's statement of the facts is correct. The evidence is not allowed to be considered by the jury if, among other things, it might unduly bias the jurors. Evidence also is rejected if it is not the best evidence for the purpose, if it is hearsay, or if it is solely the product of leading questions by the attorney. Objections to the admission of various types of evidence dot the average trial. The judge must make the proper legal ruling on each objection or face the possibility that the trial result will be overturned on appeal.

The attorney who calls a witness conducts what is termed a **direct examination** of that witness. The opposition is then given an opportunity to challenge the testimony of the witness by **cross-examination** of that person. Note that the cross-examination is confined to topics introduced in the direct examination. If the opposition wishes to introduce a new subject area, it must call the witness as its own. The calling side may conduct a re-direct to clarify matters developed by the cross-examination, and, finally, the opposition is given the chance for a re-cross.

After the plaintiff completes the presentation of evidence, the defense takes over. When the defense rests, the attorneys give their closing statements, which stress what they consider significant evidence and what they expect the jurors to conclude therefrom.

The judge then instructs the jury on the rules of law that it must use to reach proper findings of fact as to whom, if anyone, is liable and as to damages. These findings of fact are referred to as a *verdict*. After the judge finishes instructing the jury, it retires. If the jury is able to agree on a verdict, it returns to the courtroom and announces it.

If a verdict is returned by the jury, the judge will review it to be sure it has been correctly and fairly arrived at. If so, the judge will accept the verdict and enter judgment accordingly. Typically, the losing side will be required to pay a fee for the use of the court and the public officers involved in the trial. Generally, each party must pay his or her own attorney, regardless of whether the party won or lost.

Appeal

After judgment has been entered, the losing side has a set period of time to file a notice of its intent to appeal. An **appeal** is a complaint made to a higher court of an error of law made during the conduct of a case. An appeal cannot be based on supposed errors in factual conclusions. For example, if a videotape made by a bank camera showed a defendant holding a submachine gun during a robbery, the defendant could appeal the judge's decision to allow the jury to see the tape. The appeal could be based on the claim that, as a matter of law, the tape would have such an impact on the jury that any and all other evidence could not overcome that impact. The appeal could not be based on the claim that the jury made an improper conclusion of fact once the tape was admitted into evidence.

If a judgment of liability and damages is allowed to stand by the appellate court or courts that review it, the loser has to pay the judgment. If payment is not made "voluntarily" within a set time, the court can order property of the loser seized and sold by the sheriff to satisfy the judgment. Such a court order is called a **writ of execution**. Any proceeds of the sale remaining after the judgment has been paid are returned to the loser. Some individuals to whom a judgment is owed will ask the court to order the loser's wages or bank account paid into the court. Termed a **garnishment**, such an order is quite effective as it is directed to an established third party, say an employer or a bank, that is much more likely than the loser to comply rather than risk being held in contempt of court.

Chapter Review

USE LEGAL TERMS

Fill in the blanks with the appropriate term.

actual cause	defamatory per se	negligence
actual damages	defendant	nominal damages
answer	deposition	patent
appeal	direct examination	plaintiff
assault	discovery	pleadings
assumption of risk	disparagement	pretrial conference
battery	of reputation	proximate cause
civil case	exemplary damages	service of process
comparative negligence	false imprisonment	slander
complaint	garnishment	strict liability
consent	injunction	summons
contributory negligence	intentional torts	third-party complaint
copyright	interrogatories	tortfeasor
counterclaim	libel	torts
crossclaim	litigants	trademark
cross-examination	malice	writ of execution
damages	motion for judgment	
defamation	on the pleadings	

1. When Brenda Hone did not repay the loan of $500 she had made to her, Jan Stokes sued her in small claims court. She received a judgment in her favor of $500 plus $52 in interest and costs. Brenda did not pay the judgment. So, 30 days later, Jan asked the court to order her employer to pay part of the money due her as wages to satisfy the judgment. Such a court order is called a(n) ___?___ .
2. Damages arbitrarily set to punish the defendant are termed ___?___ .
3. The ___?___ initiates a lawsuit by filing a complaint.
4. The ___?___ must answer the complaint and may then counterclaim or crossclaim.
5. The process by which one litigant is able to find out about the case the opposition will present is termed ___?___ .
6. A(n) person who commits an assault, a battery, or a negligent act would be known as a(n) ___?___ .
7. Token damages, which are generally awarded to acknowledge that a party was correct in suing but lacking in injury, are known as ___?___ .

8. To intentionally cause in someone a reasonable apprehension of a harmful or offensive touching is to commit a(n) __?__.

9. To intentionally touch someone in a harmful or offensive way is a(n) __?__.

10. A(n) __?__ served on a prospective litigant gives notice of suit, of the court's claim of jurisdiction over the matter, and of a required appearance.

11. Legally harmful false statements made in print are termed __?__.

12. Falsely calling someone a murderer orally or in print is __?__.

13. An exclusive right to an author's or artist's creative work is termed a(n) __?__.

TEST YOUR READING

14. What is the relationship of tort law to criminal and contract law?

15. Name and describe the remedies that are available to correct tortious conduct.

16. What are the three kinds of conduct that bring on tort liability?

17. What are the four things the injured party must show in bringing a product liability case?

18. Name and describe at least four torts that affect business.

19. Describe the court procedure for resolving tort and other civil cases.

THINK CRITICALLY ABOUT EVIDENCE

20. Woody Blankbrains' vacation was over. He had just lost his trip funds at the Hot Springs, Arkansas, racetrack on a 20-to-1 shot named Thunderchicken. The horse finished nearer the 20 than the 1. Angry, Woody went to a local bar to have a few drinks and "settle down." An hour later, he threw a beer bottle at a fellow gambler who called him a fool for betting on "the chicken," as Woody's steed was affectionately called around the track. The bottle mistakenly hit Darlene Dramshop in the face. Injured severely, Darlene called the police, but Woody was not prosecuted over the incident. Later, upon hearing that Darlene had filed a lawsuit against him for more than $40,000 in damages, Woody returned to his home in New Orleans. Because he was not served with process while in the state, the Arkansas courts could not hear the case. (Remember the federal courts require more than $75,000 in contest before they'll serve as a forum for a diversity of citizenship case). As a consequence, Woody swore never to return to that state. A year later, Woody boarded a commercial jet in St. Louis, Missouri, for a nonstop flight to New Orleans. About halfway through, Woody's seatmate, an attractive woman, pointed out the window. "Look," she said "isn't that Little Rock, Arkansas, down there?" Woody looked out and replied, "Sure enough, little

lady." As he did so the woman grabbed his hand and slapped a court summons and complaint from the Dramshop case in it.

    a.   In your opinion, has Woody been properly served with process within the boundaries of the state and therefore brought under the jurisdiction of the courts of Arkansas? How far above and below the ground does the state of Arkansas extend? Consider what would happen if someone had shot at a plane and hit someone high above the state or if someone had killed someone in a plane high above the state. Who would have jurisdiction then?

    b.   Presume that the Arkansas courts do have jurisdiction. When the case goes to trial what type of tort action will Darlene pursue? Negligence, assault, battery?

    c.   Would any of the defenses we have mentioned work in Blankbrains' favor? Consent, assumption of the risk, contributory negligence, immunity?

21.   Would you believe that Darlene recovered $38,000 from Woody in the lawsuit? Her attorney, who had been working under a contingency fee agreement, ended up with 40 percent or $15,200 for the trouble. In a surprise ending, a few months after the payoff, Woody bumped into Darlene in Hot Springs. They started dating and eventually married. Two years later, Darlene, in a fit of anger picked a large flower vase that she hated off the mantle and tossed it at her husband. It hit a dodging Woody square in the head inflicting an injury that caused more than $20,000 in lost wages and doctor's bills, as well as the loss of the $7.99 vase. Could Woody recover for any of these losses? If so, which?

22.   Presume you are a judge on an appellate court. An attorney is appearing before you claiming that new evidence has been discovered that would reverse the result of a recent trial in a lower court and produce instead a holding in his client's favor. Which of the following factors do you consider important in determining whether or not to grant the new trial?

    a.   The severity of the effect of the result on the loser.

    b.   Whether it was a criminal or civil trial.

    c.   How easy it was to find the new evidence.

    d.   The workload of the lower court.

    e.   The likelihood the new evidence would alter the original result.

23.   Suppose you invented a beacon-type device that allows physically distressed individuals to identify their residences to emergency personnel summoned to help them. To give you time to profit from your stroke of genius, you might seek a 17-year government-awarded monopoly called a(n) ___?___. If you give your product a unique name, such as Rescue Ray, you might protect the name by registering it as your ___?___. If you write ad copy to promote the sales of the Rescue Ray, you might secure a(n) ___?___ for the ad to prevent others from using it.

REAL-WORLD CASE
Nader v. General Motors
Court of Appeals of New York
255 N.E.2d 765

Like the law as a whole, the area of torts is constantly growing and being refined. The following opinion concerns the right of privacy and its development in the latter half of this century. The case involved a David in the form of Ralph Nader and a Goliath named General Motors.

The well-known consumer advocate Ralph Nader came to national prominence in the mid-60s as a consequence of a book he authored entitled *Unsafe at Any Speed*. The book alleged serious safety problems with the Chevrolet Corvair, a General Motors (GM) product. A few years later Nader brought suit against GM, alleging various invasions of his privacy. Specifically, Nader alleged that GM (1) had had him accosted by women for the purpose of entrapping him into illicit relationships; (2) had conducted interviews with his acquaintances about him and had cast aspersions on his political, social, racial, and religious views, his integrity, his sexual proclivities, and his personal habits; (3) had kept him under surveillance in public places for an unreasonable length of time; (4) had made threatening, harassing, and obnoxious telephone calls to him; (5) had tapped his telephone and eavesdropped, by means of mechanical and electronic equipment, on his private conversations; and (6) had conducted a continuing and harassing investigation of him. In a landmark decision, the highest court in the New York State system, the Court of Appeals, addressed each of these allegations to determine if any of them constituted a basis for an invasion of privacy suit. Part of that opinion reads as follows:

> The classic article by Warren and Brandeis ("The Right to Privacy," 4 *Harvard Law Review* 193) was premised to a large extent on principles originally developed in the field of copyright law. The authors thus based their thesis on a right granted by the common law to "each *individual* . . . of determining ordinarily to what extent his thoughts, sentiments, and emotions shall be communicated to others. Their principal concern appeared to be not with a broad "right to be let alone" but, rather, with the right to protect oneself from having one's private affairs known to others and to keep secret or intimate facts about oneself from the prying eyes or ears of others . . .

> It should be emphasized that the mere gathering of information about a particular individual does not give rise to a cause of action under this theory. Privacy is invaded only if the information sought is of a confidential nature and the defendant's conduct was unreasonably intrusive.

Just as a common law copyright is lost when material is published, so, too, there can be no invasion of privacy where the information sought is open to public view or has been voluntarily revealed to others . . . In order to sustain a cause of action for invasion of privacy, therefore, the plaintiff must show that the appellant's conduct was truly "intrusive" and that it was designed to elicit information which would not be available through normal inquiry or observation.

. . . We deem it desirable that we . . . indicate the extent to which the plaintiff is entitled to rely on the various allegations in support of his privacy claim.

. . . we cannot find any basis for a claim of invasion of privacy . . . in the allegations that the appellant (GM), through its agents or employees, interviewed many persons who knew the plaintiff, asking questions about him and casting aspersions on his character. Although these inquiries may have uncovered information of a personal nature, it is difficult to see how they may be said to have invaded the plaintiff's privacy. Information about the plaintiff which was already known to others could hardly be regarded as private to the plaintiff . . . If, as alleged, the questions tended to disparage the plaintiff's character, his remedy would seem to be by way of an action for defamation, not for breach of his right to privacy.

Nor can we find any actionable invasion of privacy in the allegations that the appellant caused the plaintiff to be accosted by girls with illicit proposals or that it was responsible for the making of a large number of threatening and harassing telephone calls to the plaintiff's home at odd hours . . . where severe mental pain or anguish is inflicted through a deliberate and malicious campaign of harassment or intimidation, a remedy is available in the form of an action for the intentional infliction of emotional distress.

The one [allegation] that most clearly meets the requirements [for an invasion of privacy cause of action] is the charge that the appellant and its codefendants engaged in unauthorized wiretapping and eavesdropping by mechanical and electronic means. [Finally,] it is manifest that the mere observation of the plaintiff in a public place does not amount to an invasion of his privacy. But, under certain circumstances, surveillance may be so "overzealous" as to render it actionable. Whether or not the surveillance in the present case falls into this latter category will depend on the nature of the proof. A person does not automatically make public everything he does merely by being in a public place, and the mere fact that Nader was in a bank did not give anyone the right to try to discover the amount of money he was withdrawing. On the other hand, if the plaintiff acted in such a way as to reveal that fact to any casual observer, then, it may not be said that the appellant intruded into his private sphere.

Think Critically

1. After this appellate decision Nader was able to go forward in the court with original jurisdiction with suit based on invasion of privacy on only two of the six grounds he originally alleged. Which two?
2. Would it be an invasion of my privacy for you to listen in to calls I make on an unscrambled cellular phone? Assume that it is a phone whose transmissions are easily intercepted on any and all of the frequency scanners sold at Radio Shack and other electronic stores.

UNIT 2

Survival Skills for Dealing with Contracts

CHAPTERS

CHAPTER 7

Legally Enforceable Contracts

GOALS

- Understand the purpose of protecting the freedom to contract
- Know the essential terms of contract law
- Be able to identify the six essential elements of a valid contract

What is a Contract?

A **contract** is an agreement between two or more parties that creates an obligation. The freedom to make such agreements is so important to our economic system that the framers of the Constitution guaranteed it. In Article I, Section 10, just before the clause forbidding the states to "grant any Title of Nobility," the states are ordered not to "pass any . . . Law impairing the Obligation of Contracts." This restriction on state power has been echoed by numerous legal decisions through the two-plus centuries since the Constitution was adopted. Even so, the freedom of contract is not without legal bounds. For example, note that it is the states that are prohibited from interfering with contracts, not the federal government.

In addition, realize that having the freedom to make contracts does not necessarily mean you can get the court system to enforce them. For example, the law will generally not waste its time enforcing social contracts.

There are many other situations in which courts will not enforce contracts. Certainly, if a person can't get such help from the legal system, the risk of loss in contracting goes way up. Thus, the ability to pick out which contracts can be enforced in court and which cannot is very important to us all.

Useful Terms for Working with Contracts

Express, Implied, and Quasi Contracts

Contracts can be categorized in many ways. First, they can be categorized as to how explicitly their terms are stated. An **express contract** has its terms set down in a clear-cut fashion either orally or in writing. On the other hand, the terms of an **implied contract** are not stated. Instead, they must be determined from the surrounding circumstances or a foregoing pattern of dealings.

Hypothetical Case

JJ bought his roast beef sandwich at Joe's Deli every lunch hour. Joe always had a joke or two that he would pass on while he rang up the transaction on the deli's cash register. Then JJ would buy a soda out of the machine, grab a section of the paper the store provided, and settle into one of the booths to read. JJ had only 20 minutes for lunch. So he made the most of them. One day he came in to find the store packed with Benton high school students. On their way to a semifinal game in the state basketball playoffs, their bus had stopped for them to buy lunch. Twelve of them were waiting in line at the register. Seeing his lunch time evaporating, JJ held up the sandwich where Joe could see it and laid the customary price on the back counter. Joe nodded, winked, and grabbed the money for the register. An implied contract between the two, based on their foregoing pattern of dealings, had just been made.

Unlike express and implied contracts, a **quasi contract**, also referred to as an *implied-at-law contract*, exists only by the direction of the court. It does not stem from the agreement of the parties to it. In reality, it is not even a contract, as *courts cannot impose contractual obligations on someone who has not assumed them.* (Remember that the freedom to contract is protected by the Constitution.) Instead, it is best viewed as a remedy that the courts utilize to return value to someone who has enriched another person in the absence of an express or implied contract between them. Generally, the price in such a contract will be set at a "reasonable amount" by a jury as trier of fact, or by a judge if a jury is not present. Consider the following example.

Hypothetical Case

Basil swerved and hit the brakes as soon as he saw the front tire of the kid's bike stick out from behind the parked car. The brakes locked. Basil's 18-wheeler skidded sideways across the opposite lane and into a guardrail. The impact snapped Basil's head into the door glass. He felt the blood streaming down over his ear. He opened the door of the cab and staggered out. A man in a postal uniform ran up to him. "Is the kid . . . all right?" Basil stammered. "Sure. Good job. The kid's fine but you're not," came the man's reply, which seemed to fade off at the end. Basil realized he was losing consciousness. "Please don't send me to a hospital . . . can't afford it." Basil slumped to the ground. An ambulance came and rushed him to St. John's, where quick treatment saved his life. When he awoke in a hospital bed, he tried to leave and refused to pay. Regardless of his refusal, a court would find that a quasi contract existed. As a consequence, it would force payment of a reasonable value for the hospital's services. Otherwise, Basil would be unjustly enriched.

So, whenever

1.   The plaintiff has conferred a benefit on the defendant,
2.   The plaintiff had a reasonable expectation of compensation in so doing, and
3.   The defendant will be unjustly enriched if he or she is not required to compensate the plaintiff,

the courts will utilize the quasi-contract theory to set things right.

Valid, Voidable, and Void Contracts

Another set of terms that is useful in describing contracts is *valid, voidable*, and *void*. A **valid contract** is one that is legally binding and enforceable. Most of the chapters on contracts coming up in this book will be about how to form or recognize such a contract. In the event of a problem, any party to a valid contract can take it to court for enforcement.

A **voidable contract** is a contract whose legal effect can be cancelled by one or more of the parties to it. This power to cancel or **avoid** a contract is given by law to individuals whose ability to enter into binding agreements is in question. Contracts made by minors, for example, are voidable until some time after they enter their legal adulthood, usually at age 18. When they do enter into contracts, they can legally fulfill their contractual obligations. However, when a minor uses his or her right to avoid, the contract is **rescinded**. This means not only that any current or future effect of the contract is cancelled but also that the minor is restored as much as possible to her or his previous position. Chapter 9 provides a full explanation of a minor's contractual rights.

Hypothetical Case

Lola ("Wheels") Rattler took a last look at the car. The Model A Ford Coupe was a classic. She had restored it during her junior year in high school. She drove it every day until she went away to college. Coming home on summer vacation after her freshman year, she knew it was time to sell it. She placed an ad in the hometown paper. To no one's surprise, the "A" car sold immediately. Moments later the buyer returned with the cash to pick it up. He was young, not more than 17, Shawn somebody, and he had been saving his funds since he was 12. He handed over the cash, took the keys and title, and jumped into the car. He let the engine idle for a moment, then shifted into reverse, and, with a wave to Lola, backed out of the driveway directly into the path of an oncoming garbage truck. In the collision, the Model A was destroyed. Shawn survived without a scratch. He then avoided his contract with Lola. She refused to return his money at first, but her father's attorney informed her that she had no choice. Lola was left with the pieces and with a lesson about the dangers of contracting with minors.

Finally, a **void contract** is one that has no legal effect whatsoever. Generally, the courts will not even recognize its existence. Gambling and bribery agreements are typical examples. A man recently sued in the Arkansas court system to recover a bribe he allegedly paid to one of the system's judges for a favorable verdict. The judge did not deliver, so he wanted his money back. The case was dismissed.

Executed and Executory Contracts

An **executed contract** is one that all parties have fully performed. On the other hand, a contract in which some performance, however slight, has yet to be rendered is termed an **executory contract**. When a dispute about a contract arises, the types of remedies available in a court of law depend on whether the contract is executed or executory. More about this in a later chapter.

 Hypothetical Case

> Ed Cell contracted to sell his car to Stew D. Baker for $4,000. On May 1, Cell delivered the car to Baker and received his $4,000. However, as Cell still had to procure the legal title from his credit union, which was holding it due to a loan the union had made using the car for security, the contract was still deemed executory. It was not considered executed until the title form had been properly obtained, made out, and transferred to Baker.

Unilateral and Bilateral Contracts

A **bilateral contract** is one that places a mutuality of obligations on its parties to fulfill their promises. A **unilateral contract** is a contract in which one party is obligated to fulfill a contractual promise only if another party performs.

To really understand what we're discussing here and how the terms are applied, we have to define some more basic contractual terms. To begin with, someone who proposes a bargain or exchange to another party or parties is making an **offer**. The person making the offer is termed the **offeror**. The person to whom it is made is termed the **offeree**. For example, if I proposed to sell you my laptop computer for $1,200, I would be the offeror and you the offeree in relation to that offer. I made the offer to you. Assume that we haggle for a while. Finally, you counteroffer $1,000, and I agree. We thereby form a contract that calls for you to buy the computer for that amount. That contract involves two promises or declarations to which we may be bound: I promise to transfer ownership of the computer to you. You promise to pay me $1,000—in cash, unless we agree otherwise—at the time I do so.

In relation to my promise to transfer ownership, I am the maker of that promise, or, at law, the **promisor**. You are the person to whom the promise is made, or the **promisee**. In relation to your promise to pay, you are the promisor and I am the promisee. Finally, our exchange of promises to each other creates obligations to fulfill those promises. I am the **obligor** who must fulfill my obligation to transfer ownership. Your are the person to whom I am obliged, or the **obligee**. In like manner, you are the obligor in relation to your promise to pay $1,000 in cash for the computer. I am the obligee of that obligation. In short, we are mutually obligated, one to another, to fulfill our contract. When a contract includes such a mutuality of obligations, the law terms it a *bilateral contract*.

Unilateral contracts are most often found in reward situations. I offer to pay $25 to anyone in my class who returns to me the notebook I left behind the last time the class met. Does the offer obligate any of my classmates to perform the act? Not at all. But if any of them does perform that act, I am obligated to pay that person the $25. Thus, the contract is unilateral. As such, it obliges me to perform only if another party performs according to my offer.

Elements of a Legally Enforceable Contract

Having defined some of the most important contractual terms and classifications, we will now take an introductory look at the key elements of a contract. There are six of these, and they are "essential" to successful contract formation. The six elements must be found to be present before a court will conclude that one or all of the parties to a contract are bound to carry out its terms. Specifically, the essential elements of a legally enforceable contract are

1. An agreement
2. Between competent parties
3. Based on genuine assent
4. Supported by consideration
5. In the proper form, and
6. For a legal purpose.

The Agreement

Composed of the offer and the acceptance, this cornerstone of contracts will be covered in Chapter 8.

Between Competent Parties

In most instances, minors, the intoxicated, and the insane lack the capacity to contract. Chapter 9 details how the law handles contractual situations in which such people are involved.

Based on Genuine Assent

At times, individuals may enter into contracts as a result of circumstances that deny them the ability to say no. Duress, the undue influence of others, mistake, misrepresentation, and fraud may all compel less-than-genuine assent to a contract. Chapter 9 also reveals when the lack of genuine assent will allow a party to back out of a contract.

Supported by Consideration

Generally, the law will not enforce against us a promise for which we receive nothing in return. What the promisor in a contract says he or she wants in return for giving a legally enforceable promise is referred to as consideration. Chapter 10 deals with this indispensable element of a legally binding contract.

In the Proper Form

Generally, oral contracts are legally valid, binding, and enforceable. In certain legal situations, however, a written statement of the contract terms signed by the person against whom enforcement is sought is necessary. Chapter 11 tells when to put your contract in writing.

For a Legal Purpose

As mentioned earlier in this chapter, the law will not enforce contracts for improper objectives such as bribery or gambling. Chapter 11 covers these eventualities.

After the in-depth discussion of the essential elements of contracts provided in Chapters 8 through 11, Chapter 12 discusses how contractual duties are ended. Then it discusses the remedies that are available in court if contractual duties are not properly accomplished. This unit on contracts should leave you with a clear idea of what contracts are enforceable. It will also inform you as to the results you can expect if you resort to a court for the enforcement of such contracts.

 # Technology Insights

Computer-Generated Simulations

A Cass County Missouri judge recently allowed the use of a computer simulation of a murder during the trial of its alleged perpetrator. The defendant claimed the shooting was accidental. He said he was going to perform a safety check on the handgun when it discharged in an upward direction as it was being drawn from its holster. The prosecution presented a computer-generated animation of the murder to demonstrate that the bullet that hit the deceased came from a leveled gun. The defendant was subsequently convicted.

Such computer simulations could have a significant place in contract law. They could enable either or both parties, for example, to demonstrate in detail how much work was or remains to be done under a particular construction agreement. They could make the description of the alleged contracting far more realistic so that the jury could better discern if a contract had been formed. Similar potential lies in the use of simulations of accidents in tort law.

Think Critically   Do you think that such simulations, especially as the capacity for realism increases, could unduly influence a jury? If you were creating such a presentation, can you think of ways in which you might prejudice the jury while still showing the contracting or murder scene, such as using the defendant's face, having the contracting party nod in assent, or having the accident's result be grave and graphic?

Chapter Review

USE LEGAL TERMS

Fill in the blanks with the appropriate term.

avoid	obligee	quasi contract
bilateral contract	obligor	rescinded
contract	offer	unilateral contract
executed contract	offeree	valid contract
executory contract	offeror	void contract
express contract	promisee	voidable contract
implied contract	promisor	

1. John and Bill agree to the sale of John's Fiat to Bill for $2,000. In relation to his promise to transfer ownership of the car to Bill, John is both a(n) ___?___ and a(n) ___?___. In relation to John's promise, Bill is both a(n) ___?___ and a(n) ___?___.
2. Once John has delivered the car and Bill has paid, the contract will be deemed a(n) ___?___.
3   Because the terms were explicitly stated, the contract between Bill and John is termed a(n) ___?___.
4. If Bill turns out to be a minor, the contract is deemed a(n) ___?___. If Bill chooses to cancel or ___?___ it, the courts will see that the contract is ___?___.

TEST YOUR READING

5. What difference does it make whether a contract is executed or executory?
6. What legal effect does a void contract have?
7. What is meant by a mutuality of obligations?
8. Name the six essential elements of a legally enforceable contract.

THINK CRITICALLY ABOUT EVIDENCE

9. Bart Sampson, a bachelor, lived at 353 East Nucleus Avenue in Reactor City, Florida. One day he drove home for lunch only to find a swarm of Acme Painters' workers painting his house. Bart noted they were using a nice shade of white. For a moment this puzzled Bart. Then he remembered that Bandy Simpson, his next-door neighbor, had mentioned that his (Bandy's) house was going to be painted. Bandy lived at 355 East Nucleus. Bart smiled and drove away. As he did, an Acme worker saw him. Later Acme discovered its mistake. It then sued Bart for payment for the work it had done. The worker is sure to testify that Bart drove by when his house was being painted. Should Acme win? Under what type of contract or contractual theory would Bart have to pay? Who would set the price?

10. Sandy walked to the window for the umpteenth time. Where was Ben? The prom started in 10 minutes, and her parents wanted to take pictures and be sociable for a while. She pushed back the curtain and started out into the street. Where was "Benjamin Bradley the Third," as he was fond of calling himself? The phone rang. Sandy started for it, but her dress and heels slowed her down. Her Mom picked up the phone, scowled, then handed it to Sandy. "SS . . . Sandy?" The voice was slurred.

    "Sandy??" "Yes, Ben," she answered. "SS . . . Sandy, sssome of my old buddies showed up and got me drunk. I'm afraid we're going to have to call it off. I'm sick." Sandy heard the phone clatter as Ben dropped it, heard him stumble away. Then a glass broke and a door slammed. Sandy laid the phone down and cried. The next day she filed a small claims action against Ben for breaking their contract. She sought $575 in damages—$450 for her prom dress, $75 for the shoes that were dyed to match the dress, $40 for her perm, $10 for her nails. Should she recover? Will she recover?

11. Clyde ("Da Bears") Longstreet of Springfield, Illinois, gave his friend Hank Billings $750 to place a bet on a certain Chicago team to beat the point spread in a playoff game. The Monday after that team did beat the point spread, Clyde asked Hank for his winnings. Hank replied that he had not placed the bet and was keeping the money. Clyde threatened to sue him for breach of contract. What kind of contract did the two men have? Will Clyde recover? If so, will he recover the $750 or the amount he would have won had the bet been placed?

12. The key to separating the contracts that the law will help you enforce from all other contracts is to examine these contracts for the required six essential elements. These six elements must be found before a court will bind the parties to a contract. Specifically, a legally enforceable contract has to have an ___?___ made between competent ___?___, based on genuine ___?___, supported by ___?___ in the proper ___?___, and for a ___?___.

REAL-WORLD CASE
Brooke Shields v. *Garry Gross*
451 N.Y.S.2d 419

Consider the case of the mother who consented to pictures being taken of her 10-year-old daughter in the nude.

When Brooke Shields was 10 years old, her mother and professional manager, Teri Shields, signed broad consent forms giving photographer Gross the unrestricted right to "use, reuse, and/or publish or republish" various photographs he took of Brooke. The photos were taken pursuant to arrangements made by Playboy Press. Some of the photos were nude shots of the 10-year-old in a bathtub. In others she was clothed. Several of the photos were later published in *Photo*, a French magazine. At that time negotiations were begun to buy back the rights to the photos. When these negotiations broke down, a lawsuit seeking damages and a permanent injunction to prevent further use of the photos was brought under sections 50 and 51 of the New York Civil Rights Law. At this time Brooke was 16. The lower court, sitting without a jury, dismissed the complaint and denied the injunction except to order that the photos not be published in pornographic publications or in publications of a predominantly prurient appeal. The Appellate Division of the Supreme Court of New York State then took the case and decided it. (Note that the courts with original jurisdiction in New York are the supreme courts. Above them are the courts of the Appellate Division, and above those courts is the highest court in New York State, the Court of Appeals.) The decision of the Appellate Division was as follows:

> In this state, as elsewhere, it has long been the general rule that an infant has the right to disaffirm a contract even when the contract has been entered into on behalf of the infant by a parent or guardian . . .

> We do not perceive in the wording of [our] Civil Rights Law, sections 50 and 51, any clear manifestation of a legislative intent to limit the long-established rights of infants to disaffirm contracts approved by a parent with regard to actions brought under those sections. Section 50 provides:

> "A person, firm, or corporation that uses for advertising purposes, or for the purposes of trade, the name, portrait, or picture of any living person without having first obtained the written consent of such person, or if a minor of his or her parent or guardian, is guilty of a misdemeanor."

> Section 51 makes a violation of section 50 actionable in a civil suit [such as this one].

. . . The manifest purpose of the requirement of parental consent in these sections was to protect someone who secured such consent from being prosecuted criminally, or subject to an action for damages or injunctive relief, with regard to activities embraced in the sections during the period the consent was effective. Nothing in the sections even purports to address the infant's right to disaffirm such consent, and we see nothing in the language of the sections nor the rights that they were designed to protect that would require an interpretation so inconsistent with the general common law principle and the clear meaning of the statutory pattern described above.

Accordingly, the judgment dismissing the complaint, and denying, except in one limited respect, plaintiff's right to a permanent injunction is modified and defendant is enjoined from using any pictures of plaintiff at issue here for purposes of advertising or trade.

Think Critically

1. Can the photos be used? Why or why not? What form of relief is used by the appellant court in this case?
2. Under the New York laws cited above, would a child have the right to disaffirm an agreement in which a parent contracts for the child to play a violent professional sport?
3. Is the result ethical?

CHAPTER 8

Valid Agreements

GOALS

- ◆ Know the tests to determine if an offer is valid
- ◆ Recognize the many ways an offer may be terminated before acceptance
- ◆ Understand why acceptance has to be absolute and unconditional

In the last chapter, we discussed the six essential elements that are required for a contract to be legally enforceable. The first of these, the agreement, is the most crucial. In this chapter, we'll break down the agreement into its two elements, the offer and the acceptance, and test them for their legal validity.

How Do You Determine Whether an Offer is Valid?

Over the years, the law has devised several tests to tell whether an offer, defined in the last chapter as a proposal of a bargain or exchange with another, is valid. These tests pose three main questions: Did the party making the offer intend a contract to result? Was the offer definite enough to be accepted? Finally, was the offer properly communicated to the offeree?

The Test of Contractual Intent

Often our lips blurt out things before we can think to stop them. We'd prefer that most such statements not be repeated and that even fewer be held against us in court. So when a pickpocket or a purse snatcher is running away with your valuables and you scream out, "Stop thief—I'll pay anyone who stops that person $5,000," the law regards the statement as having been made in the heat of excitement without enough thought to involve contractual intent. As a consequence, if someone chases and stops the thief and recovers your valuables, you will not be legally bound to pay the $5,000.

As discussed in the last chapter, the law does not find contractual intent in social invitations either. So, in the vast majority of states, individuals cannot sue or be sued over broken dates, missed birthday or dinner parties (RSVP or not), and so on.

An offer made as a joke also has been held to lack contractual intent. The only problem here is that in most cases the law uses an objective standard to determine whether contractual intent is present. This means that, if a reasonable person observing the occurrence impartially would conclude from the conduct of the parties that the offer embodied contractual intent, a contract can be formed. In the case of some alleged jokes, this can work a very harsh result, as in the following example based on an actual case.

Hypothetical Case

Buford Jones and his wife agreed that Yancy was a social climber. He had next to nothing, yet he was constantly badgering them about selling their family estate in Dorchester County to him. When they met him that night in the bar at the Elk's Head Inn, he started in on them again. Finally, they had had enough. While Yancy was in the restroom, Buford suggested to his wife that they play a cruel joke on the upstart. They would offer to sell him the estate for $250,000, just half of its market price. Not being able to pay would show Yancy up once and for all. So, when Yancy returned. Buford made the offer. Yancy thought for a moment, then thrust out his hand. "A deal for sure, Buf." They shook hands. Then Yancy suggested that they put the deal in writing. Buford did so by scrawling it on a cocktail napkin. Before Yancy signed, he proofread the agreement and suggested changes due to typos and misspellings. Buford redrafted the document with the changes and signed. Yancy then also signed. A few minutes later, Yancy said good bye and left with his copy. He was barely out the door when he turned around, came back to the bar, and had Mrs. Jones sign the contract as well. A few weeks later, in accordance with the contract, Yancy produced the $250,000. The Joneses then discovered that their "ne'er-do-well" had just married a very wealthy woman. They refused to sell, claiming that the offer was a joke, although a cruel one. Yancy sued for title to the estate. The court concluded that a reasonable person using the objective standard would have believed from the conduct of the parties in drafting and redrafting the document, then having Mrs. Jones sign, that no joke was being played. It then ordered Mr. and Mrs. Jones to sign over the estate.

Judging from the above example, sometimes the better the deception, the more likely it is that the objective standard will bind the parties to the joke's legal punch line—a contract.

Another area in which contractual intent is *not* found is in an **invitation to negotiate**. Such invitations may take many forms, but they are most commonly found in advertisements. Whenever most Americans see a product priced for sale in a store window, on a store's shelves, in a magazine or newspaper, or on television, they believe that the person who placed and priced it is legally obligated at law to sell it for that amount. In most cases this is not so. Generally speaking, an ad is construed by the law as merely a way of inviting someone to make an offer, or, in other words, to open negotiations. Haggling over the price of an item for sale, whether in the finest shop or with a street vendor, is a way of life in other countries.

Hypothetical Case

Andy Pottero of Plainview, Nebraska, visited Costa Rica on his first trip abroad. In a small native shop, Andy found a beautiful scarf for his wife. It was priced at only $0.50 in American money. He laid the purchase price down on the counter and was shocked by the shopkeeper's scornful look. Afterward, Andy asked a Costa Rican friend why the shopkeeper had reacted in this way. The friend informed him that by not haggling over the price, Andy had impliedly said to the shopkeeper that he was too wealthy to bother with such trivial matters, thus placing himself in a social status way above that of the shopkeeper. "Let it go," said the friend. "Most Americans display the very same insensitivity. That's why you are not as well liked as travelers of other nationalities."

Haggling over prices was the expected standard in this country as well until J. C. Penney supposedly made it a policy of his stores that they would sell at the same marked price to all comers. Penney's policy did not change the law, however, which was based on the premise that placing a price on a good is just an invitation to get the customer into the store to make an offer.

Hypothetical Case

Before she married Tom Terra of Bloomingville, Indiana, Annie lived to surf. After the nuptials and the move back to Indiana, however, Annie found that the closest experience to surfing offered by the Midwest was slashing across some boat's wake on a pair of water skis. So she placed a "want ad" in the Bloomingville paper to sell her surfboard. Thinking there would be little appreciation of the board's quality, she priced it at $750, about half of the price it would bring in California. The day the ad appeared, her phone rang for a solid hour with people asking for her address so that they could come by and see it. Annie, realizing that the price she put in the paper was far too low, waited until a crowd had assembled and then sold the board to the highest bidder for $1,150. One man objected, saying that she should have sold it to the first person to arrive with $750 in cash. Annie replied that the price in the ad was just an invitation to negotiate. She insisted that she had as much right to talk people into paying more as they had to get her to lower her price. A professor of law in the audience assured them that Annie was correct.

To prevent sellers from taking advantage of ads that they consider invitations to negotiate only, statutes outlawing fraudulent advertising and **bait-and-switch schemes** exist. In such a scheme a seller lures a buyer with an extremely low price on an understocked, underfeatured item, and then "switches" the buyer to a far more expensive product. However, even if convicted of these crimes, a seller does not have to go through with the deal set out in the "invitation." In this situation, as in those mentioned earlier, contractual intent is a necessity.

The Test of Definiteness

Many times, what appears to be an offer will prove unenforceable in court because its terms are vague, ambiguous, confusing, or just incomplete. For example, if I offered to pay you "a little over minimum wage to guide a few of our tours to the tulip festival in a nearby town," the offer would be unenforceable due to a lack of definiteness. At a minimum, the court must be reasonably certain of these four items in each enforceable contract:

1. The parties involved
2. The cost in money or value paid for the good or service, referred to as the price
3. The good or service involved in the contract, called the subject matter, and
4. The time for performance.

Be aware, however, that courts will overlook the absence of these terms in certain instances. For example, many contracts requiring a great deal of research and development are made on a cost-plus basis. Under a **cost-plus contract**, the purchaser must pay the developer the amount of money it cost to create the product plus a certain percentage of that cost for a profit. Weapons systems are often developed for our government under cost-plus contracts.

 # Hypothetical Case

"Yeeouch. Come 'ere you little . . . " Major General H. E. Airburst, U.S. Army, was under attack by his son's remote-controlled miniature dune buggy. Traveling faster than a man could run, the device had just slammed into his foot. "Next Christmas, you get the violin," the General screeched at his son as he tried to stomp the shiny black toy into a state from which no battery could resurrect it. Suddenly, an idea followed the pathway that the pain had opened into his brain. The "Wheeled Remote Controlled Land Mine Project" was born. The next fiscal year the Army contracted with Childproof, Inc., a leading toy company, to develop the weapon. Because new materials would have to be built into the device to withstand battlefield conditions, the contract was made on a cost-plus basis. Three years later Congressman Hynd Syte, noted for his crusades against government waste, found that Childproof had just billed the government for $77 million under the contract. Syte raised such a furor over the project that the government refused to pay the money, saying that the contract was indefinite and unenforceable because it did not have a price term. Childproof sued the government. In court, the company was able to show that the $70 million in development costs had been reasonably and fairly arrived at. Those costs plus the agreed-to 10 percent profit of $7 million totaled $77 million. The court responded to Childproof's evidence by holding that there was an enforceable contract. It then ordered the government to pay immediately.

Other types of enforceable contracts that seem too indefinite include requirements and output contracts and reference to standard form contracts. A **requirements contract** obligates one party to buy all it needs of a particular kind of good from the other party for a set period. An **output contract** is similar. Under it the maker of a product must sell all of its output of that product during a set period to the other party to the contract. The amount of the subject matter cannot be determined from the contract in either instance. However, the court produces an enforceable contract by simply requiring both parties to act in good faith in making or requiring the product during the set period.

The **"reference to standard form" contract** appears even more indefinite than all of the others, yet remains enforceable. Such a contract typically refers the parties to a page in a recognized publication. The page contains a contract form with blanks to fill in the names of the parties, the price, the subject matter, the time of performance, and other terms. One of the parties numbers the blanks, and then, on the contract beside the appropriate numbers, fills in the terms. The resulting contract looks like a sheet of paper with some unconnected but sequentially numbered facts on it. If, however, it is signed and otherwise valid, that sheet of paper and the terms it incorporates by reference are enforceable. With the widespread use of photocopying equipment, the rate of use of this type of contract has become very infrequent.

The Test of Communication to the Offeree

Hypothetical Case

Kim knew what Sharon would do, could only do, to return the deep forehand. A feeling of triumph swept through Kim's body. Years of training to get here, and now she had her arch-rival at match point for the championship. Sharon swung, aiming to lob the ball into Kim's backcourt. As the ball arced skyward, Kim smiled. It wasn't hit deep enough. It would allow Kim the perfect putaway, an overhead right at the net. The ball floated down. Kim heard the crowd draw in a collective breath. Sharon was running off the court to get out of the way. Now! Kim swung . . . and completely missed the shot she had hit dozens of times in a row in practice. The ball bounced off her head. Laughter skipped through the sun-drenched crowd. Overcome, Kim fell to her knees and pounded her fists into the clay. Finally, she rose and walked up to the judge. "I forfeit," she heard herself saying. Then she left. That evening she ran into Bobby, one of the touring pros in town for the pro-am tourney. "Bobby," Kim said, "I've thought about this since I left the court today. I'm quitting tennis. I'm going to sell my racket to Sharon for $75 and buy a bowling ball." Bobby laughed. "That racket is worth 10 times that. Come on now." Kim scowled at him. "Yep, I'm doing it," she insisted. "Maybe that racket will curse her the way it has me." Kim rose and left. A few hours later, Bobby saw Sharon and told her Kim's intentions. Sharon cashed a check for $75, then found Kim and pressed the money into her hand. "Bobby told me about your offer, and it's a deal," she said. "Go get me the racket." Kim refused, saying that she had changed her mind. Can Sharon enforce a contract of sale for the racket against Kim in court?

As you may have guessed, the answer to the above question is no. The courts have held that it takes communication of the offer to the offeree . . . by the offeror (or by some mechanism that the offeror sets in motion—for example, telling Bobby to tell Sharon if he saw her) to have a valid contract result. Such communication confirms the contractual intent of the offeror. Without it, there can be no resort to the courts for enforcement.

Events That Can Terminate an Offer Before It Can Be Accepted

Of course, a valid offer standing alone doesn't make an agreement. It takes timely, appropriate action of at least one other party to produce a legally enforceable contract. Before that action occurs, a number of events can take place that will kill the offer before it can be accepted. These include:

- Expiration of a reasonable time
- Revocation by the offeror
- Rejection
- Counteroffer
- Death or disability of a party
- Destruction of specific subject matter
- Subsequent illegality

Expiration of a Reasonable Time   One of the most common of these events is the expiration of a reasonable time during which acceptance should have taken place. All too often, offers are made without pinpointing a specific time at which the ability of the offeree to accept ends. As it would be unfair to require that such offers remain open indefinitely, the courts will hold that only a "reasonable time" is available within which a binding acceptance can be communicated to the offeror. The length of this period varies with the subject matter of the contract. For an offer to sell 1,000 shares of IBM stock at a set price, a reasonable time might be measured in minutes. For an offer to buy a house or farm, it might be measured in weeks. The court will rely on its trier of fact—a jury, if one is sitting in the case—to tell it how long the period was. If this period had expired, no contract was formed by the attempted acceptance.

Revocation by the Offeror   Whether or not the offeror set down a period within which the offeree could accept, he or she can still recall or take back the offer as long as this action, called a **revocation**, is taken prior to acceptance.

Hypothetical Case

Henry walked quickly down the sidewalk toward the storefront. He recognized it as soon as he turned the corner. It was the same shop they'd been in a few hours earlier, one of the dozens lining the streets near the corner of Orchard and Delancey in New York City. He could still remember the way Diane had looked at the bracelet. A copy of some top designer's work, it sparkled with precious stones. The owner of the shop had made a great offer to them—$500. It was worth several times that, but she had said no. It was all the "mad money" they had, and if they didn't spend it, they could use it to fix up their apartment after the honeymoon. Just as they left the shop, the owner had said the offer was good all day, then winked at Henry. He had taken her back to their hotel room and then had made an excuse to go back out . . . He pushed the shop door open. The owner looked up, recognized him, and shook his head sadly. "I'm sorry, sir. I thought you'd come back. Your wife is so beautiful, but I have to cancel my offer. Just after you left, another person came in and wanted it. I told her you might be back. She'll pay $750. You can have it for that, but no less." Henry was crestfallen, but he knew the law. The shopkeeper could revoke his offer before acceptance if he wanted to even if he'd offered Henry a month to take him up on it. Henry shrugged and left the shop.

Henry could have made sure the offer would still be open by making an **option contract** with the shopkeeper. Such a contract binds the offeror to his or her promise to keep an offer open for a set period of time. For example, Henry could have paid the shopkeeper $10 for an option to buy the bracelet for $500 anytime that day. He would then have had a legally enforceable position if the shopkeeper promised it to another.

Rejection and Counteroffer   The actions of the offeree can also terminate an offer. Suppose I offer to sell you my Fiat Spyder convertible for $2,000, and you reply that you'd never be caught dead in a foreign car. That expression of a lack of interest in my offer, called a **rejection**, terminates it. Afterward, if you suddenly remembered that an acquaintance of yours had told you she would pay $4,000 for a car exactly like mine, you could not come back and accept my offer. It was terminated at the time of your rejection. Any subsequent statement you made to me of being willing to buy it for $2,000 would be considered a new offer by the court. It would not be an acceptance of my offer. The same result would occur if, instead of rejecting my offer, you said, "I wouldn't pay $2,000 for it, but I will pay $1,000 just to help you out." Your response to my offer, which alters the terms of the original offer, is labeled a **counteroffer**. It terminates my offer, just as the rejection did.

Death or Disability of a Party   The death of an offeror, whether or not communicated to the offeree, automatically terminates the offer. The same result occurs if the courts find the offeror to be insane or a habitual drunkard.

Destruction of Specific Subject Matter   Belinski offered to sell Chance the 2-carat or better cuttings from a 122-carat diamond just discovered in the Carpathian mines. While Chance considered the offer, the diamond was safely flown to New York for cutting. Unfortunately, when the cutter's tool smashed into the stone, it hit a previously undetected flaw. The diamond shattered into tiny pieces, the largest of which was one-third of a carat. That destruction of the specific subject matter of the offer terminated it.

Subsequent Illegality   Some offers are terminated when a lawmaking body renders their subject matter or performance illegal. For example, assume that Sherlock Holmes had a standing offer to pay Dr. Watson 5 quid for every fresh pack of opium he brought in for the famous detective's use. If Parliament later declared possession and use of opium illegal, performance would be made legally impossible by the new law. Consequently, the offer would be unenforceable.

Why Is Complete and Unconditional Acceptance of an Offer Important?

The Mirror Image Concept   Technically, an acceptance under contract law is a sign by which the offeree indicates that she or he will be bound by the terms of the offeror's offer. As you can tell from the preceding section on rejection and counteroffer, an offer must be accepted without change. In other words, the acceptance must be a mirror image of the offer. If not, what seemed to be an acceptance will be treated as a counteroffer and will terminate the original offer.

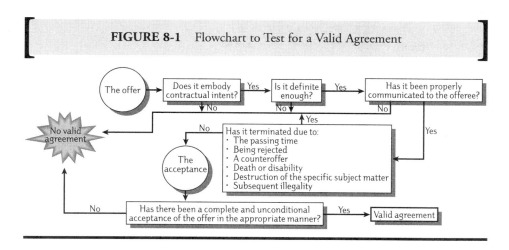

FIGURE 8-1   Flowchart to Test for a Valid Agreement

Communication of Acceptance   In unilateral contracts, problems with letting the offeror know the bargain is accepted generally do not occur. Action, not a return promise, is what is expected from the offeree. If I offer a reward for my missing dog, I expect someone to show up with the dog, not to call and promise to do so.

In bilateral contracts, however, a return promise is expected. This usually poses no problem if the contract negotiations are being conducted face-to-face or over the phone. If, instead, the parties are communicating by mail, telegram, e-mail, fax, or a like medium, the rules become complex.

First of all, the offeror may require that a certain medium be used. If such is the case, remember that the offeror is master of the offer. So, "acceptance by mail required" means just that, and a communication of the acceptance by fax, phone, or otherwise will not bind the bargain.

If the offeror doesn't stipulate the medium, then the best idea is to send an acceptance in the same medium that was used to send the offer. If this rule is followed, the acceptance is effective when it is placed in the control of a representative of that medium—for example, when it is delivered to the post office with the proper address and postage. If a different medium is used, say the offer came by mail and the acceptance is faxed to the offeror, the acceptance is effective only when it reaches the offeror's office, home, or other location, usually whatever is indicated as a return address on the offer. The offeror doesn't actually have to open or read the acceptance for it to be binding. Note that unlike the acceptance, a revocation is effective only when the communication bearing that revocation arrives at the offeree's location.

Before closing out your study of this chapter, realize that all of the rules concerning the agreement and the other essential elements of contracts are the result of centuries of common law experience. People in business today benefit greatly from that experience. In effect, the costly mistakes of our predecessors enable us to prevent our own. Ignorance of such law, therefore, is definitely not bliss.

CHAPTER REVIEW

USE LEGAL TERMS

Fill in the blanks with the appropriate term.

bait-and-switch scheme
cost-plus contract
counteroffer
invitation to negotiate
option contract

output contract
"reference to standard form" contract
rejection
requirements contract
revocation

1. If you say to me, "I'll pay you $50 to keep that offer open for a month," you are attempting to make a(n) ___?___ with me.
2. If you agree to buy all the computer chips you need for the next month from me, we have made a(n) ___?___.
3. If you agree to buy all the computer chips I can make for the next month, we have made a(n) ___?___.
4. If you agree to repay the reasonable amounts that I spend for developing a new chip and throw in an additional amount for a profit, typically a percentage of the reasonable amounts I spend, we have made a(n) ___?___.
5. Suppose you come into my store in response to my ads for a two-cycle push lawn mower at a truly incredible low price. Once through the doors you are told by my salesperson that the lawn mower has been sold out. She then proceeds to talk you into buying our new, air-conditioned, riding, garden plowing, and, oh yes, lawn cutting apparatus. Should this scenario occur you might suspect that you are being manipulated in a(n) ___?___.

TEST YOUR READING

6. What are the three tests of the offer?
7. What standards does a court use to enforce a requirements contract?
8. Why should the offer be communicated to the offeree at the direction of the offeror?
9. Why would someone purchase an option?
10. If a person made me a written offer that had 75 different terms, and I only changed one, signed the document and sent it back to the other party, would I have accepted the offer? Why or why not?
11. Why must an acceptance be in the form required by the offeror?
12. If no particular form is required by the offeror, what is the safest way to indicate acceptance?

THINK CRITICALLY ABOUT EVIDENCE

13. Luna Teek, a notorious sports fan, saw a television ad for the famed "Couch Potato" Recliner. The ad gave a sale price of $175 at Wild Bob's Furniture Outlet. To Teek's knowledge, the Recliner, famous for its size (a much greater "spud space" according to the ads), a universal remote built into one arm, and a small refrigerated space in the other (capable of holding six beverage cans), had never been advertised for less than $500. At Wild Bob's, however, when Luna thrust her $175 at the clerk, he refused to sell her a recliner. She was informed that the ad price was a mistake and that the actual price was $575. Luna claimed that there was a valid contract regardless. Is she correct?

14. Madilyn Sanderson purchased her seat on the stock exchange right after she sold her real estate business to a large corporation. Since that time she had bought and sold with the best of them. Two days ago, when she saw a chance to make financial history, she jumped at it. It happened when BMI anounced that it had received a major order for its new computer line. Madilyn had just finished researching the computer line and knew that BMI could not produce all the chips for the new order internally. The company would have to buy those from external sources, and there were only two. Madilyn immediately placed a "buy at market price" order for the stocks of the two companies with a Philadelphia broker who made a market in them. The broker responded that she would try to find some of the stock for sale and would get back to Madilyn. Now, 48 hours later, BMI had just announced that it was turning down this particular order because the purchaser was not able to pay enough up front. Madilyn tried to reach the broker to withdraw her offer but could not get her. Would Madilyn's buy offer still bind her? Why or why not?

15. Colossal Discounters advertised a compact 10-disc player/changer for $75. When Anton Snider made it to the store on the morning the ad first ran in the local newspaper, the player/changer stock was sold out. Anton slipped around and asked a friend of his on the sales staff how many of the item had been stocked. His friend replied, "One." Later that morning, Anton went to the courthouse and swore out a criminal complaint against Colossal for a ____?____.

16. If the prosecutor is successful in pursuing the charge and brings in a conviction, will Anton then be able to buy the player/changer for $75?

17. If my offer to you stipulated that you had to appear in person and verbally accept, would there be a contract if you sent me a videotape in which you stated that you accepted?

REAL-WORLD CASE
United Steel Workers of America v. *U.S. Steel Corporation*
492 Federal Supplement 1

The significance of the method of acceptance of a contractual offer can be dramatic. In the following case, it meant the difference between having a job and a home or not to the workers in a U.S. Steel plant.

When the losses at its Mahoning Valley plants became intolerable, U.S. Steel Corporation made plans to close them down. In response, the workers at the plants indicated a willingness to work hard at making them profitable and keeping them that way. U.S. Steel Corporation acknowledged these statements by the workers and communicated its willingness to keep the plants open if and so long as the workers made them profitable. When continuing losses eventually forced the shutdown of the plants, the workers brought suit for breach of contract and damages.

In its decision the court held that the offer to the workers was unilateral. It, therefore, required acceptance in the form of performance. The contract would not come into existence until the workers achieved and sustained profitability. Since the contract had not come into existence, it could not be breached.

Think Critically
1. Did U.S. Steel Corporation have to pay damages to the workers?
2. Would the decision have been different if the offer had been characterized as bilateral?

CHAPTER 9

Capacity to Contract

GOALS

- Understand the meaning of capacity to contract
- Know the times when a particular legal status will remove an individual's contractual capacity
- Be able to recognize the circumstances that will remove an individual's contractual capacity

Contractual Capacity

It is a fact of life that individuals often hire attorneys to get them out of unfavorable contracts. Many times these individuals, looking for a loophole to slip out of, are disappointed because "the law loves a bargain." In other words, the law works to keep in effect contracts that have been fairly negotiated and entered into by able parties who had their eyes open at the time. If such contracts are now working a hardship on such parties, the law leaves them with only the option of blaming the person they see in the mirror each morning.

In certain limited situations, however, the law will allow a party out of an otherwise binding contract. These situations generally involve individuals who do not have the ability or the freedom to properly evaluate and control the contracts they enter into. The crucial ability to appreciate the consequences of entering into a contract is termed **contractual capacity**. The following sections discuss the types of parties that can legally be excused from their contracts because they lacked the ability to enter into them.

Minors

According to the law, a child under the age of seven can commit neither a crime nor a tort. This is because the law recognizes that such youngsters usually lack the ability to appreciate the consequences of crimes or torts. Therefore it does not hold them legally responsible for those consequences. Under contract law there is a similar rule relating to minors. In particular, contractual capacity is only recognized in individuals who are in their **majority**, or in other words, in those who are at or beyond the legal age to contract. This age varies from state to state but is generally set at 18. A person under this age is deemed a **minor** and therefore to lack such capacity to contract. The insane or mentally incompetent and, and in some cases, intoxicated persons also are deemed to lack such capacity under our laws.

Power to Avoid Their Contracts . The primary way in which the law protects minors from those who would take advantage of their lack of capacity to contract is to allow minors to avoid or **disaffirm** their contracts. Note that this power to avoid is given only to minors and not to the adults involved in contracts with them. The power was discussed somewhat in Chapter 7. In most states, even minors who lie about their age to cause adults to contract with them can avoid the contracts that result. If avoidance is allowed, the contracts will be rescinded and the minors put back on their original footing. Minors enjoy this status under the law to prevent them from being taken advantage of by adults.

Note that, upon avoidance, minors are required to return any consideration still in their possession that they have received from the bargain. A businessperson who deliberately or inadvertently chooses to deal with a minor, even if the businessperson realizes the error, must continue to follow the terms of the contract. This holds true even if doing this increases the businessperson's potential losses should avoidance occur.

Ratification   Even after minors enter majority, they are given a reasonable amount of time to evaluate their contracts and to avoid them if they so desire. By the same token, minors may instead choose to ratify their contracts. **Ratification** is the display of a willingness to be bound by a contract's terms. Ratification can be inferred from certain actions. For example, either letting the reasonable period of time after turning 18 pass without avoiding the contract or making payments called for by the contract after turning 18 would be enough to prove ratification. Note, however, that a minor cannot effectively ratify a contract before entering majority.

Unavoidable Contracts and Necessaries   As you may have guessed, there are exceptions to the rule allowing minors to avoid their contracts. For example, some states bind minors to contracts in which they have misrepresented their age or to contracts that benefit their business interests. With this in mind, consider the following situation.

Hypothetical Case

Both Ronald's and Sharlene's parents had known the marriage wouldn't last, but they had caved in and allowed the two minors to marry. Now, five months later, the two 17-year-olds were having big problems. Ronald was despondent over the pay he was earning at the car wash. Without even mentioning the possibility to Sharlene, he had just enlisted for a five-year stint in the army. He would be in boot camp and advanced training for months. It was the last straw for Sharlene. She was packed and out of their tiny apartment just hours after he told her. Ronald was shocked when she left and even more shocked when she called and said that she would avoid their marriage contract if he went into the army. Realizing that he had made a tremendous mistake, he called the army recruiter to avoid his enlistment contract. Will either of these minors succeed in avoiding the contracts that bind them?

As you may have suspected, the answer is no in both instances. Minors cannot avoid valid enlistment or marriage contracts. In a somewhat similar vein, minors can be made to pay a reasonable value under executed contracts they make for items required to sustain life. Such items are termed **necessaries** by the law. In most states they include only food, clothing, and shelter. A few states added televisions and cars to the list. If the law allowed minors to completely avoid contracts for necessaries, sellers would fear that after eating the food, wearing the clothing, and using the shelter, the minor would demand his or her money back. Sellers would therefore refuse to provide necessaries to anyone under 18.

Parental Liability   Generally, parents are not liable for their minor child's contracts. They may, however, agree to assume such liability by serving as cosigners. However, the minor's right to avoid is not taken away by the parents' action.

Hypothetical Case

Billie Buchard, barely 17 years old, watched as her dad cosigned the purchase contract and loan papers for her new speedboat. She had paid $2,000 down from her savings, and she could make the $147.60 monthly payments from her paycheck at McDonald's. The boat was perfect for her water-skiing and for entertaining her friends. As soon as her dad laid down the pen, Billie grabbed the keys on the salesperson's desk and ran down to the dock. She warmed the 100-horsepower engine for a moment. By then her dad was at the dock shouting at her to wait. She laughed, waved at him, then gave the boat full throttle. Too late she thought of the stem line. As the boat shot forward, the thick rope played out for a fraction of a second, then stiffened and, with a tearing sound she would remember for years, ripped the back third of the boat off. Billie was thrown free and swam to shore as the boat, totally destroyed, sank to the bottom of the inlet. Her parents were so angry that they grounded her for six months. Out of spite, Billie then avoided her contract with the dealership. The dealership paid her back her $2,000 down payment and then billed her dad for it and the monthly payments. If her parents had not cosigned, the dealership would have had to bear the whole loss, as Billie, upon avoiding, would have received her $2,000 back regardless.

The Insane

In legal issues relating to capacity to contract, the insane are treated somewhat like minors. This holds especially true for individuals found by a court to be insane when they entered into a contract. If such individuals are found to be only temporarily insane, they are allowed to affirm or avoid their contracts whenever they become clearheaded (lucid) again. In the case of the permanently insane, as described below, their court-appointed representative may act to affirm or avoid. Regardless, the parties claiming this defense will be held liable to pay a reasonable value for necessaries. Note that mentally retarded individuals are presumed to have full capacity to contract unless the contrary is shown in court.

The treatment given the permanently insane under contract law is quite different. Realize that it takes a court proceeding to confer this status on a person. If the court does determine that a person is permanently insane, it will appoint a guardian for that person. The **guardian** is an individual who has been given the responsibility of taking care of the insane party. The guardian also is given the power to manage the **estate** of the insane party, meaning the real and personal property interests of that party, for the insane party's benefit.

Once a person has been held to be permanently insane, that person's subsequent contracts, checks, notes, deeds, wills, and other legal actions are considered void. The court will intervene to rescind the contracts and otherwise preserve the interests of the insane party. It is even a crime in many states to knowingly take advantage of such a person. However, obligations for a reasonable value for necessaries provided to the insane can be enforced against the estate of an insane person.

Hypothetical Case

Algernon L. Flowers, 84 years old and of substantial wealth, was declared permanently insane by the Greene County Court. Three months later, in response to her advances, he fell madly in love with Sally Benton, his nurse at the Last Daze Retirement Home. Nurse Benton, 41 years his junior, convinced Algernon that they should run away and be married. The following Saturday, Sally drove Algernon to a nearby state, where they were married. She then persuaded Algernon to sell his rings and expensive watch to finance their honeymoon. He did so. With the proceeds of the sales Algernon immediately rented the honeymoon suite in a nearby hotel and ordered champagne and caviar for their wedding feast. Algernon then gave Sally the remainder of the money he had with him, some $2,500. She was counting it when a deputy sheriff, alerted by a suspicious desk clerk at the hotel and by a missing person's report, knocked on the door of the suite. As a result of the deputy's investigation, Algernon was immediately returned to the retirement home. The legal effects of the "elopement" were longer lasting. Sally was charged under a state statute making it illegal for anyone to take advantage of an insane party. Sally's later claims to half ownership of all Algernon's property based on their marriage were rendered groundless when Algernon's guardian had the marriage contract canceled. The contracts for the sale of the rings and watch also were rescinded. Finally, the hotel was paid out of Algernon's estate for the reasonable value of the shelter and food it had provided at his request.

The Intoxicated or Drugged

The law handles intoxicated or drugged individuals in a manner similar to its handling of the insane. Those individuals whom a court holds to have been temporarily incompetent due to alcohol or other drugs during the time they were making a contract will be allowed to avoid the contract. However, to be considered temporarily without capacity due to alcohol or other drugs, the persons claiming such incapacity must show that at the time they did so they did not even know they were entering into a contract. This is much harder to prove than the normal standard for lack of capacity, which is just being unable to understand the consequences of a contract.

A person considered by the law to be permanently without capacity to contract due to alcohol or drug use is termed an **habitual drunkard**. An habitual drunkard is a person who exhibits an involuntary tendency to become intoxicated as often as the temptation to do so is presented. The person may be more often sober than drunk. However, once the court has been shown that the person lacks the willpower needed to control his or her appetite for alcohol or drugs, it will relieve the person of his or her capacity to contract permanently.

As with the permanently insane, a guardian will be appointed to handle the estate of the habitual drunkard. All contracts, checks, notes, wills, deeds, and other legal actions taken by the incompetent will thereafter be considered void. However, the doctrine of necessaries will apply to the habitual drunkard's contracts for food, clothing, or shelter.

Genuineness of Assent

Hypothetical Case

John Elza taught a high school business law class. One day, to explain a point about contract law, he offered to sell his 1982 convertible to anyone listening for $2,000. No one from the class spoke up, but another teacher, Sandra Pugh, who was walking past the classroom's open door, heard the offer. Sandra had ridden in the car and liked it. She poked her head in and said, "I'd pay $1,800." John replied, "$1,900." Sandra responded, "It's a deal." At that moment the bell rang. Most of the students left. Three hung around to ask questions. Before turning to the students, John asked Sandra whether she was serious. "Certainly," she responded. "I just can't pay you until the first of next month." John thought a minute, then said, "It'll cost you $1,925 if I have to wait that long." Sandra grimaced but agreed. John then turned to the students and answered their questions. After they left, John mentioned that the car's transmission was having problems that would take around $200 to fix. Sandra frowned. "Then I'll pay only $1,725." As if in agreement, John sat down and wrote out a contract. They photocopied it in the principal's office and signed both copies, each keeping one. That evening Sandra read the written contract for the first time and was angered to find that John had made the price $1,825. Would Sandra be bound by the written contract?

At times, competent individuals may be forced, tricked, or otherwise improperly induced to enter into contracts. The desire of these individuals to be bound by such contracts may seem genuine. However, once they discover that they have been duped or once they are no longer threatened by whatever forced them into the bargain, they turn to the courts for release from the contractual obligations. The law does not always allow such individuals a way out. The freedom to contract we so prize includes a freedom to enter into bad bargains as well as good. In the following paragraphs we'll take a look at the most common problems in this area to see how the courts handle them. We begin with mistake, the excuse most commonly used by individuals who want out of their contracts.

Mistake

Mistakes can be made by one or all parties to a contract. A mistake made by only one party is called a **unilateral mistake**. If both or all parties err, it is termed a **mutual mistake**.

Unilateral Mistake   Unilateral mistakes can be of law or of fact. Where the mistake is in not knowing a law or not knowing how a law is to be applied, the answer the courts give is simple. "Ignorance of the law is no excuse" expresses that answer best. The contract in question is then held to be valid and is enforced against the protesting party.

The most frequent unilateral mistake of fact is a failure to read the contract. In the Hypothetical Case on page 115, Sandra Pugh committed such an error, and it could be costly to her. The law is impatient with individuals who do not act to protect themselves, especially by not doing something so simple and effortless as reading. Also realize the complexity of the dispute involved if this written contract is placed in question before a court. Most of the business law class could be called on to testify that the real contract was for $1,900. Three students would indicate that the contract was for $1,925 with payment due on the first of the next month. Then the actual parties to the contract would offer two other versions, one for $1,725 and the other for $1,825.

Because of these and like problems, the law has devised several rules to simplify and lessen the burden of the court in such matters. The first rule is called the **doctrine of incorporation**. This doctrine disregards oral bargains struck before a contract has been reduced to writing. It utilizes the commonsense argument that the parties will much more carefully deliberate over and choose the terms of a contract that they put in writing. They will pick whatever terms they want from any preceding oral attempts at the same bargain and incorporate those terms into the final written deal. So the doctrine of incorporation properly focuses exclusively on that writing.

Reinforcing the effect of the doctrine of incorporation is a second rule of like importance. This is called the **parol evidence rule**. It supports the doctrine of incorporation by disallowing oral (parol) testimony that contradicts, adds to, or modifies a written contract. The only exceptions to this rule are for situations in which evidence of fraud, incompleteness, ambiguity, or a similar problem is inherent in the contract.

As you have probably guessed by now, these rules mean that bad news is in store for Sandra. Given the facts above, she will have to pay $1,825 for the car under what the law will hold to be a valid contract. Her unilateral mistake in failing to read the contract cost her $100. The only exceptions allowed by the courts in cases like Sandra's are for fine print appearing on what are essentially claim checks, such as those given out by parking garages, cleaning establishments, and so forth. The courts have consistently refused to enforce the fine print terms against the customers of such establishments. The courts feel that such customers only view the tickets as the means to reclaim their property, not even suspecting that they contain contract terms.

As a general rule, then, unilateral mistakes, whether of fact or law, do not release the mistaken parties from their contracts. The contracts remain valid, legally binding, and enforceable against those parties.

Mutual Mistake   Mutual mistakes can also be of either fact or law. As you can probably infer from the discussion on unilateral mistakes of law, mutual mistakes of law still result in a valid contract. Mutual mistakes of fact, however, are a different story.

Hypothetical Case

Angelica owned an art gallery located in a very exclusive section of New York City. Her collection included two landscapes by a French painter named Slopée. One of the landscapes, entitled "Parisian Fields," was valued at more than $50,000; the other, entitled, "Same Old Field," at less than half that. Late one afternoon Gaston Dubarr the third came into her office. He pounded his ivory-headed walking stick on the floor to get her attention, then announced, "I'll buy the Slopée landscape for $30,000." Angelica, presuming that he was bidding on the "Same Old Field," since a Dubarr would never make such an insultingly low bid on "Parisian Fields," immediately accepted. She asked an attendant to place the painting in a suitable container while she collected Mr. Dubarr's check. Just as the shop closed, Mr. Dubarr left with his painting. That evening Angelica purchased three new sculptures for the shop with the funds from the Slopée sale. The next morning Mr. Dubarr's cane was banging on the shop door a half hour before opening time. Angelica let him in. With him came his chauffeur, who unceremoniously thrust the "Same Old Field" at Angelica. Mr. Dubarr then insisted that he had bought "Parisian Fields" and demanded that painting. Angelica refused. Mr. Dubarr then demanded his money back. Angelica refused again. They next saw one another in court.

Angelica and Mr. Dubarr have made a mutual mistake of fact as to the identity of the subject matter of the contract. If their mutual mistake had been one relating to the appropriate value of a particular painting, such as "Parisian Fields," the court would rule the contract valid. However in this situation, in which the parties were negotiating for altogether different items, the court will hold the contract not voidable but void. The court will then rescind the contract. As a consequence, Angelica will have to return the $30,000 to Dubarr, and he will have to return the "Same Old Field" painting to her.

If the mutual mistake concerns a difference in the valuation of an item properly identified to both parties, that difference is a matter of opinion and the contract is valid. If the mistake concerns the identity of the subject matter, the contract is void but will be rescinded by the court.

Concealment

As a general rule, a person negotiating a contract is not under a duty to voluntarily reveal everything known about the subject matter. The resulting contract is valid regardless. If the other parties want to know something, they are free to ask. The answer, if given, cannot knowingly be false, however. In addition, if the other parties should be able to discover a material fact about the subject matter with a reasonable investigation, the contract will be enforceable even by a party with knowledge of it who says nothing. **Material fact** as used here means a fact crucial to making or not making a contract. The court's logic here is simple. It does not want to spend its time getting people out of situations that they themselves could have prevented with reasonable diligence. A contracting party who wants to find out should ask. The other party will be held legally accountable if he or she then gives a knowingly false answer.

There are exceptions to this rule, however. In particular, courts recognize that certain relationships are rightly founded on trust. These are called **confidential relationships**. They are also called *fiduciary relationships*. For those in such a relationship who are contracting with each other, the law recognizes a legally enforceable duty that all material facts be revealed. So when contracts are formed, for example, between parents and children, doctors and patients, and attorneys and their clients, concealment of material facts, or, as it is legally phrased, "silence when it is one's duty to speak," can render the contracts voidable by the party from whom material information is withheld.

Misrepresentation and Fraud

Rather than concealing material facts, parties to contracts often misstate them. If this is done innocently, the resulting contract can be avoided by the improperly informed party. For example, if I am selling you my big-screen TV and tell you the three-year "parts and labor" warranty that still has 22 months to run will transfer to you when it will not, you can cancel the contract due to that misstatement. In other words, if I innocently misrepresented a material fact such as that, the courts will rescind the contract. We'll each get back what we put into the bargain.

However, if I intentionally lied about it, you might be able to show fraud. The courts would then allow you to cancel the contract, get your money back, and recover damages. **Fraud** occurs when someone makes an untrue or reckless statement of a material fact to induce another party to enter into a contract. The other party must enter the contract as a consequence of relying on the misstatement and be damaged as a result. To prove fraud, some courts even add the requirement that the person who relies on the misstatement be unable to check on its accuracy by exercising due diligence. In short, fraud is rather difficult to prove. Making this even more difficult is the law's acceptance of the natural tendency of a seller to elaborate on the qualities of whatever is up for sale. As long as the salesperson's statements are of opinions and not of facts, they are not considered fraudulent. For example, someone trying to sell parents a set of encyclopedias might state that having them available would raise their children's grades. This would not provide a basis for a fraud suit if little Jenny's grades plummet instead.

Undue Influence and Duress

Mistake, concealment, innocent misrepresentation, and fraud all deal with not knowing the correct facts to be used in deciding whether to enter a contract. Now we turn to undue influence and duress, which deal with forces that destroy the capability of persons to make a reasonable decision about contracting, whether or not they know the facts of the matter.

Both undue influence and duress involve domination of one party by another. The means by which this domination is effected is what makes them different. **Undue influence** is found where the dominating party to a confidential relationship (attorney to client, physician to patient, parent to young child, child to aging parent) has exerted irresistible pressure on the dominated party to enter a contract that benefits the former. Whether or not the dominating party lost his or her free will to contract under such circumstances is usually a question for the jury. If the jury concludes that such is the case, the contract is voidable by the dominated party.

Legal **duress** is a wrongful threat that denies a person her or his free will to contract. The resulting contract is voidable by the party upon whom the duress was inflicted. Generally, a threat of bodily harm or death against the contracting party

---

FIGURE 9-1   Who Will the Law Excuse from the Requirement to Fulfill Contractual Obligations?

Parties Excused Due to a Lack of Capacity	Parties Who Contracted Without Giving Their Genuine Assent Due to
◆ Minors	◆ Mistake
◆ The insane	◆ Concealment
◆ The intoxicated	◆ Misrepresentation
	◆ Fraud
	◆ Undue Influence
	◆ Duress
	◆ Unconscionability

or his or her immediate family, a threat to burn down the contracting party's home, or a threat to bring a criminal action against the contracting party is considered legal duress. A threat of a civil suit or a threat that involves economic harm, such as "sign or you'll never do business in this town again," is not considered legal duress and thus does not render voidable the contract that results.

Unconscionability

All of the problems with genuineness of assent that we've discussed so far are individual ones. They focus on the contracting party's lack of ability to properly evaluate and freely enter a contract due to factors peculiar to that person or the contractual setting. However, the courts also have had to deal with cases in which fully informed, capable individuals out of necessity entered contracts that gave lopsided advantages to the other parties. Typically, such contracts met all of the traditional tests for a valid, legally enforceable, contract. To somehow grant relief from such oppressive bargains, the courts had to formulate a new doctrine. That doctrine was unconscionability.

An **unconscionable contract** is one entered into as a result of the greatly unequal bargaining power of one party, who makes a take it or leave it offer to the other party without any viable market alternative. If the resulting contract is grossly unfair to the weaker party, the offending section of the contract is void.

CHAPTER REVIEW

USE LEGAL TERMS

Fill in the blanks with the appropriate term.

confidential relationships   guardian   parol evidence rule
contractual capacity   habitual drunkard   ratification
disaffirm   majority   unconscionable contract
doctrine of Incorporation   material fact   undue influence
duress   minor   unilateral mistake
estate   mutual mistake
fraud   necessaries

1. "This car is the best bargain I've had on my car lot since I opened it." "Of course, I can do your surgery. I have the steadiest hand in the entire country when it comes to working on a person's brain." "I'm sure I can win this case. I always put the best interests of my clients ahead of my own, just like all other attorneys."
    These exaggerations would probably not be a basis for a ___?___ suit.
2. How many miles a car has been driven is usually a(n) ___?___ in the bargaining for the sale of a car.
3. "Sign the contract, or I'll report your tax dodge to the IRS for prosecution" is a good example of ___?___ .
4. A person under the age of capacity is termed a(n) ___?___ .
5. "Every party I go to with her she gets intoxicated. I'm afraid to let her drive home. She just can't turn down a drink." These words might describe a(n) ___?___ .
6. If a court declares the person described in item 5 incompetent, it will appoint a(n) ___?___ to manage the ___?___ of that person.
7. Making four monthly payments on a financing contract for a car after turning 18 is good evidence that a(n) ___?___ of the contract by the minor obligor has occurred.

TEST YOUR READING

8. What is the definition of contractual capacity?
9. What is the purpose of the doctrine of necessaries?
10. Why should it be a crime to take advantage of the insane?
11. Which type of mistake renders a contract void?
12. What does a guardian do?
13. Explain the doctrine of unconscionability.

THINK CRITICALLY ABOUT EVIDENCE

14. Brenda Sanders, 17 years old, bought the dune buggy from a dealership in Santa Monica, California. She drove it home, parked it in the driveway, got out and found her father waiting for her. "Take it back right now. The bank called and said you'd cleaned out our joint account of all your college money for a down payment. Go get your money and your future back." Brenda frowned, then shrugged her shoulders and without comment fired up the engine. She drove around the house's circular drive and came to a stop at the street. To the left was the beach, to the right was the dealership. Brenda turned right and smashed head-on into a new limousine. Luckily, no one was injured. The property damage totaled more than $7,000. When Brenda filed for coverage under the family car insurance policy, which covered new purchases without requiring notification up to 10 days, the insurance company refused to pay, saying that the car dealership's policy should cover the damages because Brenda had avoided the contract. Do you agree? Why or why not?

15. Can a minor ever avoid his or her contracts after attaining majority? Why or why not? Can a minor ever ratify her or his contracts before attaining majority? Why or why not? Should minors be able to use their minority status to take unfair advantage of parties that would sell to them? For example, should minors be able to buy tickets from airlines, use the tickets, and then avoid the contract to get their money back? Why or why not?

16. A court-determined habitual drunkard goes into a bar and runs up a $357 tab. He then buys two bottles from the liquor store affiliated with the bar. He writes a check to pay for the amount he owes and leaves. What is the status of the contracts the drunkard made in the bar and liquor store? Who can stop payment on the check? Is it ethical to treat such businesses as the bar and liquor store in this manner?

17. Now drop back over a century for a classic true case. Two ships, each bearing the name *Peerless*, were scheduled to leave Bombay, India, for England. One was to leave it in October, the other in December. A buyer accepted an offer to sell bales of cotton on the ship he believed was sailing in October. The seller was instead referring to bales of cotton on the ship sailing in December. How do you think the court resolved the breach of contract suit that the buyer filed when the cotton did not arrive on time?

18. Bill and his wife, now divorced, were separated when he signed an agreement dividing up the marital property. Today he greatly regrets entering into the agreement and claims that he did so only because of his wife's threat to bring criminal child abuse charges against him. Can he get out of the agreement if this is shown to be true? Could be get out of it if he maintained that he entered into it because of his wife's threat to sue him for damages for battering her?

REAL-WORLD CASE
United States v. Gorham and Wilkerson
532 F.2d 1088

Consider the "appeal of the miffed escapees" based on the idea that "if you can't trust the commissioner of corrections who can you trust?"

For some time prior to October 11, 1972, while appellants Gorham and Wilkerson, the latter a/k/a Robert Jones (hereinafter Jones), were confined as inmates at the District of Columbia jail, they conspired to escape from that facility. In furtherance of the plan, they obtained a loaded .38-caliber pistol. In the early morning hours of October 11, 1972, Jones pretended he was sick. When two correction officers entered his cell to assist him, Gorham assaulted them with the pistol and took them as hostages. Gorham and Jones proceeded to take control of the entire cell block and to release other prisoners to assist them in obtaining additional hostages. These hostages eventually included Kenneth L. Hardy, District of Columbia Corrections Director. In furtherance of their demand that they be released, appellants made numerous threats of violence against their hostages, used some of them as shields, and with the inmates who had joined them employed other strategies in pursuit of their freedom. All of their efforts were thwarted, and the jail authorities eventually reacquired control of the cell block and the entire jail complex.

In the aftermath of this episode Gorham and Jones were transferred to the maximum security "penthouse" area of the jail. While they were confined there, appellants obtained several hacksaw blades, sawed through two iron bars in a window, and on October 25, 1972, effected their escape by means of a "makeshift Jacob's ladder, fashioned from bed sheets in the classical manner" (quoted from trial brief).

In this appeal, appellants contend that the trial judge's failure to recognize as binding an agreement made during the riot was reversible error. This agreement, in which the government agreed not to punish the prisoners for their actions, made the subsequent confinement of Gorham and Jones in the maximum security cells improper. The agreement was extracted from DC Corrections Director Kenneth Hardy while he was a hostage.

In ultimately deciding this case, the Court of Appeals stated, "We find no merit to these contentions and no error in the trial and affirm all convictions on all (22) counts."

Think Critically

1. On what basis do you think the courts refused to regard as valid the agreement not to punish the prisoners?
2. Considering the possibility of future hostage situations, is disregarding the agreement a wise policy decision? Do you think "policy" entered into the judge's decision to ignore the agreement?

CHAPTER 10

Contractual Consideration

GOALS

- ◆ Know what constitutes contractual consideration
- ◆ Understand the use of consideration in identifying enforceable agreements
- ◆ Be able to recognize the exceptions to the doctrine of consideration

At the very heart of the freedom to contract is the ability to "name your price." In other words, you have a right to indicate what you must receive in return for being bound to your offer. For example, let us assume that we are bargaining over the sale of my grand piano to you. After considerable discussion, you finally state, "All right, I'll buy that piano for $2,500." Now you'd expect to be bound to your offer only if I promised to transfer ownership of that piano to you in return for that amount of money. That promise to you is, in effect, what you demanded in return for making your offer into a promise that is binding against you. In general, then, the supplying of what would-be promisors require in return for being bound to their offer is one of the main things the law looks for in a contract suit. This chapter focuses on how the law makes sure this essential element of an enforceable contract, labeled *consideration*, is present.

What Is the Legal Definition of Consideration?

To express it in more concise legal terms, **consideration** is what the offeror demands and, in most situations, must receive in return for making his or her offer into a promise that is legally binding against him or her.

Legal Effect of a Promise without Consideration

If someone offers to do something for you without naming the consideration that she or he wants in return, the offer can be no more than a stated intent to make a gift. A **gift** is a transfer of property by one party, acting voluntarily and without consideration, to another party. Under the U.S. legal system, a statement of intent to give, standing alone, is unenforceable in a court of law. "I'll give you my piano" is far different from "I'll give you my piano if you'll pay me $2,500 for it." The former is interpreted as a stated intent to make a gift and needs much more to be legally binding. The latter, of course, is a contractual offer.

In almost all gift situations, the stated intent to donate must be accompanied by a delivery and acceptance of the subject matter of the gift to be of any legal signif-icance. As a consequence, getting the promisor of a donation to complete the intended gift typically remains only a moral issue between the would-be **donor** (giver) and the **donee** (intended recipient of the gift). This is not the case in several other Western legal systems, particularly those of Western Europe, in which a promise to make a gift can be legally enforceable against its maker. The U.S. legal system, however, rather than making all such promises enforceable, lets the presence or absence of consideration be the guide in picking which promises the courts will enforce.

Adequacy of Consideration

As long as the would-be promisor is capable of making a genuine offer, the law gives each person the latitude to determine what amount of consideration is

Hypothetical Case

Madison Barnes was in his last year of law school when his mother was approached by Horace Highhorse. "He just walked right up and asked me to sign away my rights in that old warehouse your dad owned before he died," Mrs. Barnes told Madison over the phone. "He said he'd been in it more than 10 years now and that if I didn't sign, even though he can't find the deed to the property he claims your dad gave him, he'd take me to court for it. You're about to become a lawyer, son. Can you come out and defend me if he does?" Madison thought a moment, then replied. "Sorry, Mom, I can't do that till I'm licensed by passing the bar exam, and that'll be months yet. Otherwise, the only way I could argue the case would be if it were my own property. Then I could appear on my own behalf. Anyone can argue their own case under our system. It's called appearing "pro se." Of course, here in school they say that the lawyer who argues his own case has a fool for a client." Both Barneses laughed. Finally, Mrs. Barnes said, "All right, Madison, how about this? Would you like to buy my rights for $1? You may end up owning a warehouse." Madison replied quickly, "Good idea, Mom. I'll buy it for that. At least Horace won't get the property without a fight, and legal fees can be expensive. The only thing is, I've got to actually give you the $1. The courts won't care how much I bought your rights for, but the other attor-ney will check to be sure that we went through with the transaction." Madison then sent Mrs. Barnes a check for $1, which she cashed and spent. He used the canceled check and a written contract of sale he'd drawn and had Mrs. Barnes sign as evidence of his rights in the warehouse. Later that year, after gradu-ation from law school and while studying for the bar, Madison argued and won the lawsuit for himself. He later sold the warehouse for $45,000 and gave an undisclosed amount of the sale price to his mother.

adequate for the good or service they are offering. If I want to sell my Picasso painting to you for $10,000 cash, even though its market value is more than $100,000, the law leaves that decision to me. Perhaps I need the money right away, or perhaps my decision is based on tax considerations. The reason doesn't matter as long as I am a capable adult making a legally enforceable offer.

What Does the Law Hold to Be Legally Binding Consideration?

The law is full of surprises. Some of these surprises come in what the law does and does not hold to be legally binding consideration.

Legally Binding Consideration

Generally, a *promise* is held to be legally binding consideration. For example, when a person offers to sell you a big-screen television for $2,000, he or she doesn't expect that you'll have the cash with you. Instead, the offeror will want you to accept the offer by giving him or her a promise to pay that amount at some time in the future. That promise is consideration, and it will legally bind the offeror to a promise to transfer ownership of the television to you.

Exchange of Value   Another form of valid consideration is found in things of value that are immediately given to the promisor to bind her or him to his promise. The thing of value most frequently used in this way is **money**. It is a medium of exchange that a government has selected or created for just this purpose. Typically, what we refer to as "cash" has little, if any, functional use except to serve as a standard for determining relative value. Without money, we must barter good for good for the things we need or desire. Without money, statements like, "I'll give you two chickens and that stack of cherrywood over by the barn for that rocking chair you just made" would be the rule, not the exception. Of course, goods and services are legal consideration in their own right. When they are exchanged for other goods and services without the use of money, the exchange is called a **barter**.

Forbearance

Hypothetical Case

Marsha Hollander glared across her desktop at the soles of Will Stuart's size 10s. His desk fronted on hers. Now, head thrown back, staring at the ceiling of the newsroom, Will was smoking another of his cigars. The smoke rose two feet above his head, where it formed a spiraling cloud of toxic elements that reached out to engulf her. As in the past, Marsha felt her sinuses tightening. She knew that the first of a freight train of body-convulsing sneezes was on its way. He had ignored her past complaints, and so now it was time for plan B. Marsha grabbed her nose, then made Will Stuart an offer she prayed he couldn't refuse. "Look, Will, you know what those cigars do to me. I know you've got every right to smoke them" (smoking had not yet been banned by their employer), "but they're killing me. Would you take $500 not to smoke in here for a year?" With a smile, Will nodded and stuck out his hand.

If Will did not smoke for a year, would he be able to hold Marsha to her promise in a court of law? The answer is yes. Refraining from doing something you have a legitimate right to do is termed **forbearance**. Either a promise to forbear or the actual forbearance is sufficient consideration to bind those who demand that forbearance in return for their promise. A promise not to follow through on your intention to sue someone where you have a reasonable right to do so is also consideration. So if I promise to pay for the harm done to your car plus $250 if you won't sue me for my negligence in an accident, your forbearance would bind me to my promise.

Non-binding Consideration

Past Consideration   Sometimes, however, promises that appear to be valid consideration are not. Consider the following example.

 # Hypothetical Case

> Grateful to his friend, Helen, who had taken him in one bitterly cold evening years ago, John Stroll, formerly a homeless person, wrote out the following promissory note: "For goods provided and services rendered, I promise to pay to the order of Helen Santos $15,000." The note was dated and signed. When John presented it to her before leaving, she frowned and said, "No, John, I can't." He smiled. "Remember, Helen, how you said we all need our dignity. This will help preserve mine." She thought a moment, then took the note. "Goodbye John . . . You were the son I never had." John hugged her, grabbed his suitcase, and walked out the door.

A nice story, a gracious lady, and a gentlemanly exit, but Helen could not collect on the promise John put in writing. Why? Because all that Helen did for John is termed **past consideration**. Such consideration is not legally binding as it was given without expectation of or demand for a binding promise in return. Even when placed in the form of a promissory note, a promise without legally binding consideration is unenforceable in a court of law.

Promise to Perform a Preexisting Obligation   Another circumstance in which what appears to be consideration is not occurs when the return promise requires the performance of a task that the promisor is already obligated to do. Such a return promise is not taken as legal consideration. For example, suppose you promise to pay:

- A member of the city fire department $50 a month to check your building every night before she goes off duty.
- An on-duty cop $7.50 each time he shows up at your store at closing to protect you as you transfer your cash to the bank.
- Windblown, Inc., $950 for each sail it provides, instead of the $750 price it agreed to under its two-year contract with your sailboat manufacturing company.

Are these promises legally binding against you? The answer is no. This is because in each instance the consideration you received for your promise is merely a **promise to perform a preexisting duty**. In other words, it is a promise to do something that the promisor is already legally obligated to do, either by a previous contract with you or by a duty owed to the public. In the first two instances, the public servants involved are already obligated to perform the duties mentioned, so their promises cannot be valid consideration. The promises you made in return are therefore not legally binding on you. In the last instance, the result is the same, but it stems from the private contractual obligation to you that Windblown, Inc. had previously assumed.

Exceptions to the Rule Requiring Consideration for Binding Promises

In the following circumstances the law will abandon the general rule that consideration is required for a promise to be legally binding.

When a Debt Is Barred by the Statute of Limitations or a Bankruptcy Proceeding

If I borrowed money from you 12 years ago and have not yet repaid it, your right to enforce that debt against me today in a court of law would be barred by the **statute of limitations** in our state. Such statutes limit the time a person has to bring suit. The limits vary, depending on the nature of the possible action. For oral contracts, the limits range from a minimum of 2 years in a few states to a maximum of 10 years in one state. Most states set the limits between 3 and 5 years. For written contracts, the limits range between 3 and 15 years.

However, even after the statute limits have been passed, if I reaffirm the debt, no consideration is necessary to bind me to my new promise. The same rule applies to debts I owed you before I filed bankruptcy but which, because of the legal effect of that process, now cannot be collected through the courts. For example, if I meet you at our 15th high school reunion and promise that I will pay back the money you loaned me on graduation day, that promise will be effective against me without consideration. In most states the promise is enforceable even if made orally. If the promise is to reaffirm a debt barred by bankruptcy, however, the current federal Bankruptcy Act requires a formal statement at a hearing. (Read more about the fascinating, tricky, and sometimes even rewarding world of bankruptcy in Chapter 23.)

When the Court Uses Promissory Estoppel

At times a rigid adherence to the letter of the law can produce injustice. As a consequence, the law allows courts to counteract this effect by taking certain actions in the name of **equity**, or basic fairness. One such action that the courts can take is the use of the doctrine of promissory estoppel. When brought into use—or "invoked," to be more accurate—by the courts, **promissory estoppel** prevents promisors from stating that they did not receive consideration for their promises. Under the doctrine of consideration, if the courts stop people from stating that they didn't get what they demanded in return for being bound to their promises, then those promises can be enforced against them.

To get a court to invoke promissory estoppel, the person who requests it has to show first of all that a promise was made that could reasonably be expected to induce action on the promisee's part. Then, if the promisee acts in response to that promise and if an injustice can be avoided only by the court's enforcement of the promise, it will invoke promissory estoppel. All of these requirements filter out a lot of situations in which the doctrine cannot be used, mainly because centuries of experience have provided other remedies. Promissory estoppel therefore remains only as a last resort used by the legal system to correct injustices that have slipped through the cracks of established contract law.

Hypothetical Case

Diamond Gym, a regionally famous East Coast entertainer whose real name was James Barrett, had been offered a six-month run as a single act at the Lagoon Lounge in Atlantic City. The owner of the Lagoon, Arty Slaw, had said he would pay three times what Barrett was making. So Barrett had given notice that this evening would be the last show of his current engagement. He fished in his pocket for Slaw's card, found it, and called him. The phone rang for only a fraction of a second. "Yeah," Slaw's voice thundered. "Arty," Jim responded, "I just ended my current contract, and I'm ready to appear at the Lagoon. Didn't you mention that I could start next week." There was a pause at the other end. Then Slaw said, "Look, kid, I hired a new act just yesterday. Shoulda called you but didn't. Them's the breaks. Keep in touch." Without waiting for a reply, Slaw slammed down the receiver. Diamond Gym stared at his phone for a while. It was true that there wasn't a contract, but Slaw must have known that Barrett would end his current contract so that he could go to work at the Lagoon. The other clubs where Barrett normally performed were booked months ahead. Despondent, he picked up the phone to call his lawyer.

Should Diamond Gym elect to sue Arty Slaw, his attorney will probably request that the court use the doctrine of promissory estoppel. If the court agrees, it will not let Slaw raise lack of consideration as a defense. As a consequence, Slaw

FIGURE 10-1   Exceptions to the Requirement of Consideration for a Legally Binding Promise

♦ A promise to renew a debt barred by the statute of limitations or a bankruptcy proceeding.

♦ Instances in which a court estops a promisor from claiming a lack of consideration for his or her promise.

♦ Situations in which a promise is made for the support of a charitable institution or another nonprofit organizations.

will be bound to his promise of employment and will have to pay damages to Barrett for breaking it.

Promises Made for the Support of Charitable Institutions or Other Nonprofits

Universities, hospitals, public broadcasting, churches, charities ranging from the Red Cross to Save the Seals, and many other beneficial organizations depend on donors for their very existence. Their annual budgets and the special projects they undertake are based on reliable sources of funds. Therefore, as a matter of public policy enforced by the application of promissory estoppel, courts have held that pledges of contributions to such organizations are binding on the parties who make those promises.

CHAPTER REVIEW

USE LEGAL TERMS

Fill in the blanks with the appropriate term. Some terms may not be used.

barter	gift
consideration	money
donee	past consideration
donor	promise to perform a preexisting duty
equity	promissory estoppel
forbearance	statute of limitations

1. Bart said to Brett, "I'll trade you this fine stallion of mine for that quarter horse colt of yours." This is an example of a proposed ___?___ contract.

2. To bind Brett to his promise in item 1, Bart has named the ___?___ he must receive.

3. If Bart had instead said, "Because you took care of my ranch while I was in jail, even without my asking you to, this stallion is yours," the delivery of the stallion by Bart and its acceptance by Brett would have completed a(n) ___?___.

4. Brett's taking care of the ranch would be ___?___ ___?___ for Bart's promise to transfer ownership of the stallion to him.

5. Assume that Brett relied on Bart's promise to give him the stallion and spent a lot of resources in anticipation of owning it and that Bart then changed his mind and decided to keep the stallion. Out of a sense of basic fairness or ___?___, a court might listen to a request by Brett to force Bart to transfer ownership of the stallion to him.

6. The court might even use the doctrine of ___?___ ___?___ to disallow any attempted showing by Bart that he didn't get any consideration to bind him to his promise.

TEST YOUR LEARNING

7. Why is a stated intent to make a gift unenforceable in the courts?
8. How does consideration reinforce the idea of freedom of contract?
9. Name three types of consideration.
10. Explain why past consideration is not legally binding consideration.
11. Name the two situations in which debt reaffirmations do not have to have consideration.
12. Explain how promissory estoppel affects the requirement of consideration.

THINK CRITICALLY ABOUT EVIDENCE

13. Terry Firm owned a minerals and precious gems shop. He often sold his merchandise at weekend flea markets. At such a market Crystal Beam, a seven-year-old, bought a "pretty rock" from Terry for $5. Crystal paid for the stone with her own money. Later a licensed gemologist valued her purchase at more than $24,000. Hearing of this, Terry then sued to undo the sales contract because he had not received adequate consideration for the purchase and because Crystal was a minor. Will Terry succeed? (This account is based on an actual incident.)

14. The football coach of the LeBrea High School Reptiles, Brutus ("Who Needs a Helmet") Concussionus offered to pay the LeBrea math teacher $20 per hour to tutor the team each day during a free school period. The money was to be paid in December out of the Reptile's Nest Booster Fund. The teacher accepted the offer. By the end of the season, the teacher was owed some $1,700. However, the fund's board of directors refused to pay. The teacher brought suit, but the court upheld the board's refusal because of a problem with the consideration that the teacher gave to bind the Reptile's boosters to the contract. What was that problem?

15. Bono Chumpson loaned his son's baseball coach $750 to keep the bank from foreclosing on the coach's house. The coach never repaid the loan. When Bono finally brought suit in small claims court more than four years later, the judge threw out the case as the statute of limitations had run out. One day at the mall, Bono asked the coach in front of witnesses why he had not repaid the loan. The coach was embarrassed and promised to do so. Can Bono enforce this new promise? Why or why not?

16. Al Lumus of Brooklyn, New York, was contacted by a representative of Hosanna High during its "buy a piece of heaven" fund drive. Hosanna High was set up by the famous televangelist Helen Razor. It was supported by charitable contributions from around the United States and Latin America. Caught up in the spirit of the moment, Al, a 1978 Hosanna graduate, pledged more than $72,000 to help fund a new media center at the school. A few weeks later Al noticed an article in New York-based *SSSHHHH! Magazine* relating that Hosanna was making films opposing family planning of any and all types and sending the films to developing countries. As Al believed fervently that the overpopulated developing countries needed family planning, he thereafter refused to send in the amount of his pledge. Can Hosanna High legally compel him to pay it the money he promised? Why or why not?

REAL-WORLD CASE

United States v. John McBride, Michael Allen Worth, Theodore Duane McKinney, and Jill Renee Bird

571 Federal Supplement 596

On September 28, 1982, the president and the three vice-presidents of Gulf Oil Corporation received a letter announcing that the "Gulf Chemical Cedar Bayou Plant and one other Gulf facility have been sabotaged." The letter also stated that "in excess of 10 explosive charges have been placed within the Cedar Bayou Plant. These charges are both radio actuated and time actuated. The radio charges may be detonated from any point within a 20-mile radius of this facility. The time-actuated charges will self-detonate starting 120 hours after 10:00 A.M. on the morning you receive this letter; the time charges will continue to detonate up to seven days after this time . . . The purchase price to Gulf for the locations and deactivation sequences for the bombs at Cedar Bayou and one other plant to be discussed is $15 million, a fraction of Cedar Bayou's value and annual producing income."

Investigating FBI agents arrested Michael Worth and Theodore McKinney in Phoenix, Arizona, in the course of arranging by telephone to have them pick up the $15 million. Agents later traced the plot to John McBride and Jill Bird and arrested them in Durango, Colorado. Shortly after McBride's arrest, he stated to an FBI agent that he would give the government everything it needed in exchange for the government's agreement to certain terms, including the release and non-prosecution of Bird.

Assistant U.S. Attorney Patrick T. Murphy, under pressure to accept McBride's offer from a variety of sources, including the FBI, bargained with McBride concerning these terms. In considering his decision, Murphy contacted an assistant U.S. attorney in Houston, Texas, because both Colorado and Texas had jurisdiction over the matter. Murphy later testified that he accepted the deal after suitable consultation, during which he received approval to go ahead. McBride thereupon revealed that all of the bombs had already been found and dismantled.

Regardless, Bird was released by order of the Colorado U.S. Attorney's Office in accordance with the agreement but then indicted by the U.S. Attorney's Office in Texas. She made a motion to dismiss the indictment based on the government's agreement.

The testimony of Assistant U.S. Attorney Langoria, who was the party in the Texas office contacted by Murphy before he decided to make the agreement, is extremely significant in the court's decision. That testimony, as summarized by the court, is as follows:

> He [Langoria] said that he viewed McBride's offer as coercive, that it seemed to him they were being extorted, and he indicated to Murphy that he believed the agreement was voidable. On the other hand, he testified that he did not express dissatisfaction with approval of the

agreement but, on behalf of the United States Attorney in Houston [who later secured the indictment of Bird], agreed that the agreement was a good deal. He testified that the government was getting something in exchange for something: that the something they were getting was the peace of mind that they would have in knowing that there were no more bombing devices in the refinery, and that the government entered the agreement in good faith. He testified that the government's reputation is only as good as its word, but also that good faith meant that the government would keep its promise, all other things being equal . . . Langoria concluded his testimony by stating that the government should honor its agreement, assuming it was valid and the government was going to get what it bargained for.

Think Critically

1. Would you rule to uphold the agreement in this case? Why or why not?
2. How do you think the court ruled?
3. Can you trust the government?
4. If you reach an agreement with the federal government to avoid prosecution under a federal criminal statute for, let's say, kidnapping, do you think you could still be prosecuted by a state government for the same crime?

CHAPTER 11

Statutory Requirements for Contracts

GOALS

- ◆ Recognize the validity of oral contracts and enforcement difficulties
- ◆ Know when a written contract is needed and what to include
- ◆ Identify contracts as unenforceable because of improper objectives

Valid and Enforceable Oral Contracts

Whether an oral contract is enforceable involves the historical connections of our legal system to English law. We can trace the origin of our contract law back more than five centuries to a time when few people could read or write. As you may infer, the people of that day made mostly oral contracts. The law confirmed the existence of those contracts through the testimony of witnesses under oath. Although relying on oral testimony was sometimes problematic, the courts had no choice if they were to serve the needs of the people. The general rule of that time remains in force today: Oral contracts are legally valid, binding, and enforceable in a court of law.

Practical Matters of Enforcement

Of course, such a rule presents a number of practical problems. Chief among them is finding witnesses who heard and accurately remember all the terms the parties to the contract agreed to. Perjury runs a close second. However, the alternative of not enforcing oral contracts at all presents problems of far greater magnitude. At the extreme, it is possible for a contract case to be conducted without witnesses other than the parties to the contract. In such a case, only those parties could testify in court as to what was involved. It would then be up to the trier of fact to determine whom to believe. The court would then enforce the resulting contract.

The Statute of Frauds

Since the time contract law was first established, the number of literate people has obviously increased. Concurrently, courts have become more and more uncomfortable with the enforcement of oral contracts because of uncertainty in their terms and the possibility for injustice that they present. In the mid-17th century, allegations of widespread lying under oath concerning some very important contracts swept through England. In reaction, in 1677, Parliament passed the Act for the Prevention of Fraud and Perjuries. This act, which is today still in use in some form in each U. S. state, has become known as the *statute of frauds*.

Hypothetical Case

Liz Fisher shook her head and began to cry. They were going to take it all from her. Today three pushy real estate developers were going to testify against her in court. Their stories parroted one another. They would each lie by saying that she had promised to take their combined offer of *$1.5 million* for her 40-acre estate. Oh, they had talked with her about a $7.5 million deal. And it was true that they had even given her a check for $50,000. She had deposited the check and was spending it because she needed the money. But they had given it to her in return for her promise not to sell the estate to anyone else for three months. She hadn't agreed to sell it to them. Now one of the developers even said that right after their negotiations he had made a memo of the deal that he would show the court. It may be hopeless. Liz thought, "But if I have to fight, then fight I will." She went into her bedroom to change clothes for court.

Form and Interpretation

In its current form, the **statute of frauds** requires that in certain contract situations, a written contract must be produced in court. This "writing" must be signed by the party against whom enforcement of the contract is sought. For Liz in the above situation, this is good news, as agreements to sell land come under the statute of frauds. Therefore, if she denies that there was a contract for the sale of her estate, the developers will have to produce a writing. Such a writing must, at minimum, identify the subject matter of the contract (the estate), specify the consideration (the price), and be signed by the party against whom enforcement is sought (Liz). The signatures of the developers are not necessary as they are bringing suit for the contract's enforcement and must therefore submit to those terms. Note, however, that if Liz admits to the contract in court under oath, the contract will be enforceable without a writing.

We will discuss all the situations that require a writing in just a moment. However, now is a good time to emphasize that getting a contract in writing is a good idea anytime, not just when this is required by the statute of frauds. The old saying, "Strong fences good neighbors make," has its place in contract law. A writing is a strong guarantee that a court will enforce what the contract contains. Therefore, all parties are more likely to act in accordance with a written agreement than an oral agreement.

Rules of Evidence Reinforcing the Statute of Frauds

The Parol Evidence Rule   Also realize that the strength of a writing used as evidence in court is reinforced by court procedure in the form of parol evidence and best evidence rules. As discussed previously, the **parol evidence rule** does not allow oral (parol) testimony in court that would change or add to the terms of a written contract. This is because a written contract takes more time and deliberation to prepare and is therefore more likely to be in a final form agreeable to all before it is signed. Also, oral negotiations may appear to be contract formation to innocent witnesses, but they may actually only be a step toward a final agreement. To illustrate:

Hypothetical Case

Professor Lee Galese used his car, a Fiat convertible, as the subject matter for his examples of how contracts work. He would lecture, then make an offer to sell the car to a class member. "I'll sell you my 1982 Fiat convertible for $2,000" became a joke among many students. During one lecture however, a student named Johnson surprised Galese by making a serious counteroffer of $1,700. Just as the period ended, Galese agreed to the deal in front of the whole class. The classroom emptied quickly. As the last three students filtered out, they overheard Galese's and Johnson's oral contract fall apart when Johnson said he could not pay Galese until the first of the month. Galese then said that he would take $1,750, the additional $50 being his payment for waiting until the first. Johnson agreed. The three students then left. As the classroom door closed behind them, Galese remembered that his alternator light had been coming on as he drove in that morning. "I just remembered," Galese said, downcast. "The car probably needs a new alternator. It will cost $100." Johnson thought a moment, then replied, "Tell you what, I'll pay you $1,625 for it as is. That's the $1,750 less the $100 for the part and $25 for my labor in installing it." "Fine," said Galese. "Let's put it in writing." Galese wrote out the contract, then they photocopied it, and each signed the other's copy. The first of the month came around and Galese refused to take $1,625 for the car, saying he had a classroom with some witnesses who would say that the deal was for $1,700 and others who would say that the price was $1,750. Which contract would the courts enforce?

In this and similar situations in which a party denies the validity of a written contract, the law avoids a complex trial by enforcing the parol evidence rule. If it did not, the courts would face innocent, sincere witnesses (such as the various class members in the above situation testifying to the existence of contract terms totally different from those of the real bargain). So, in the case of *Johnson v. Galese*, Galese would have the written contract enforced against him for $1,625 as long as Johnson held on to his copy for evidence. Note that if the writing leaves important terms out or is ambiguous, then parol or other less reliable evidence is allowed to clarify the intent of the parties.

The Best Evidence Rule   As mentioned earlier, the **best evidence rule** also reinforces the strength of a writing as the ultimate evidence of a contract. It does so by allowing only primary evidence, for example the original of a contract, to be placed before the court. Secondary evidence, such as copies of the contract, are allowed only if the original contract has been lost or destroyed.

The combined effect of the parol and best evidence rules is to make the original of a written contract vastly superior to any other documentation of that agreement in the eyes of the court.

Contracts That Must Be in Writing

In most states in the U. S. the statute of frauds specifies several situations in which a writing is required. The most frequent conditions are discussed in more detail in the next paragraphs.

Contracts for the Sale of Real Estate

Land and things permanently attached to land are referred to as **real estate**. When a contract is made to transfer or sell an interest in such property, it must be in writing to be enforceable. More details about real estate and real property interests appear later in this book.

Note that there are a number of important exceptions to the general rule requiring a writing in this area. First, in most U. S. states, if you make a contract for the rental of real property for less than a year, the contract does not have to be in writing to be enforceable. Second, even if the contract for the sale of land is oral, should the seller convey the title, he or she can collect the purchase price. This is because the main purpose of the statute of frauds is to protect sellers against untruthful allegations that they made oral contracts for the sale of land. Buyers were not considered in the development of this statute.

Contracts That Cannot Be Completed within One Year

Hypothetical Case

Abe Backus stared at the mailbox. It was one minute before midnight, April 15. The carrier from the main post office took out his key and slid it into the box's lock. Abe waited till the last second, then slipped the tax return through the slot. The carrier grinned, unlocked the box, picked out the mail including Abe's return, then looked up, "Not letting them have your money till the last minute, eh?" Abe nodded. The federal mismanagement, the congressional perks and scandals—of course they weren't getting his money till the last moment, and not at all if he could work it. Unfortunately, the tax rules were becoming too complex and time-consuming to keep up with. So, just a few hours previously, Abe had made two contracts with a tax preparation service, Loopholers, Inc. One contract was to do his taxes for this calendar year; and the other covered the calendar year after this. Did either of these contracts have to be in writing?

The rule is reasonably simple. When the performance required under a contract cannot be accomplished within a year from the date on which the contract was made, the contract has to be in writing. This rule was put into the statute of frauds because over the course of a year, people often forget the detailed terms of an oral contract. The result, in the eyes of the law, is avoidable litigation and loss of resources. In applying the one-year rule however, problems arise in determining which contracts truly cannot be finished within a year. In Abe's example, the answers are relatively straightforward.

Loopholers, Inc., can do his taxes for the current calendar year within a year, although this company may actually take longer. Therefore, the contract for the current calendar year does not have to be in writing. However, the contract to do the taxes for the next calendar year obviously cannot be fulfilled until that year is over. That is a year and three quarters from now. Therefore, a writing is required.

Now assume you contract to buy 50,000 standard washing machines from my factory. Using our sole assembly line, we are currently able to produce only 24,000 per year by running three continuous shifts. Comparing those figures, you might think that a writing would be required. But, because we can purchase any shortfall on the open market, the contract can be done in a year. Therefore, no writing is required under the one-year rule. However, see the next section on contracts for the sale of goods valued at more than $500.

Employment contracts are often made with an indefinite term because such contracts may continue for the lifetime of the employer or the employee. However, because that lifetime may end before the year is up, no writing is required under the one-year rule. Similarly, unilateral contracts with demanded action that can be performed within a year, even though the promise that initiated the contract takes longer than a year to actually perform, do not have to be in writing. For example, if someone offers to pay $1,500 at the rate of $100 a month for 15 months for the return of a champion Irish setter that escaped, the promise would not have to be in writing to be enforceable by the party returning the dog.

Contracts for the Sale of Goods with a Purchase Price of $500 or More

In the washing machine purchase mentioned above, the contract may need to be in writing if the amount of the purchase equals or exceeds $500. There are a number of exceptions to this rule. One exception is for goods specially manufactured for the buyer, such as an expensive tailored suit, that cannot be resold for its value elsewhere. Another exception is made for that part of a goods shipment that has been paid for or the delivery of which has been accepted.

Promises to Stand Good for the Debt of Another

Hypothetical Case

Abraham Klaus stared at the door handle as the knocks began again. They were louder this time, more insistent. "Whoever it is must know I'm here," thought Abe. His hand shook as he opened the door. Two men in coveralls stood on his porch. One of the men spoke, "Mr. Klaus?" Abe nodded. The man went on. "Mr. Klaus, we're from Garton's Appliance Store. I'm sorry, sir, but we're here to repossess your refrigerator because of delinquent payments. If you make any move to stop us, we'll leave and return with a police officer who will ensure there's no breach of the peace while we do our jobs." Abe moved slowly aside, head down, and motioned the men in. "Stop right there," a voice boomed from behind the two. "Garton's men, right?" The voice continued, "You don't even put your name on the side of the truck." Abe looked up just as his neighbor, Bill, and two other men reached his porch. "Abe here's retired and spent every dime to help his wife fight her cancer. But he owes you, right?" Both of the men in coveralls nodded, but Abe noticed that they had begun backing off the porch. One of them fumbled in his pocket and produced a bill for $252.50, Abe's balance due. Bill looked at it, then shoved three 20s at the Garton's men. "That'll bring him up to date. If he has trouble paying in the future, have your office get ahold of me and I'll take care of it. Got it?" The men nodded, grabbed the $60, and trotted toward their truck. As they clambered into the cab, one yelled back at Bill, "We'll remember that. When the old coot doesn't pay, we'll send the law to come knocking on your door. You got that!" The truck roared off. Abe turned to Bill and said, "I'll pay you back somehow, Bill. It's just that the hospital and funeral bills are chewing me up right now. They'll probably be dogging you with a court suit next month." Abe shook his head. Bill smiled. "Forget it, Abe. I remember how good you and Ruth treated my kids. Besides, those boys don't know much about the law."

Bill is correct. By law, the promise he just made to Abe's creditors has to be in writing to be enforceable against him. The general rule under the statute of frauds is that whenever a person promises a creditor to pay a debtor's debt if the debtor cannot, the promise must be in writing to be enforceable. Note however, that if the promise is made to the debtor instead of the obligee creditor, it does not have to be in writing. So, if Bill had promised Abe instead of Garton's Appliance Store, the promise could have been enforced without a writing. Also, the statute of frauds requires a writing only if the promise is to pay if the debtor cannot. Therefore, if a person promises to be directly liable as a codebtor, regardless of whether the other person can pay, no writing is required.

Promises to Stand Good for the Debts of a Deceased's Estate.

When a person dies, someone is selected to manage and distribute that person's property according to the laws. Whenever this manager makes a promise to pay the debts of the deceased person out of the manager's personal funds, the promise must be in writing to be enforceable. In the eyes of the law, this situation closely parallels the one discussed earlier, in which someone promises a creditor to stand good for the debts of a certain debtor.

Promises Made in Consideration of Marriage

🔲 Hypothetical Case

Brenda Koch looked across the table at her brother Brent, who was four years her junior. "It doesn't matter, Brent," she whispered. "Besides, Mom knows enough to take care of herself." Brent shook his head and spoke out loud, "She's in love. He's some young stud that she has the hots for, but after they're married, when she dies he might sell the ranch, the business . . . everything . . . everything Dad built, then take half of the money and disappear." As he spoke the last few words, Brent glanced up from his coffee. Brenda was looking over his shoulder, eyes wide. Brent didn't turn around. He knew that his stepfather-to-be had come quietly down the stairs into the kitchen and overheard all he'd said. "But you'd never do that, would you, Stephen?" Brent continued. Stephen Kline slapped Brent a little too hard on the shoulder and replied quietly, "Of course not, Brent, all that belongs to you two. I just love your mother, nothing more. That's good enough for me. You've got my word on that. You two can keep all the property." After a confirming hearty slap on Brent's shoulder, Stephen left. Brent waited, then spoke, "I think we need to get that in writing, Brenda. Don't you?" Brenda shrugged and dialed her attorney.

As you might suspect, Stephen's verbal promise is not enough under the statute of frauds. However, it is true that the basic marriage contract, to meet and exchange vows, is fine in an oral form. To be enforceable, any additional promises given as consideration for marriage beyond those vows must be placed in a writing before the marriage. Such a writing is known as a **prenuptial** (also premarital or antenuptial) **agreement**.

A summary of the situations requiring a writing under a typical statute of frauds appears in Figure 11-1.

FIGURE 11-1 When Writing Is Required under the Statute of Frauds

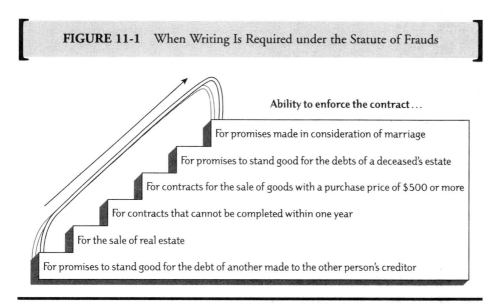

Ability to enforce the contract . . .

For promises made in consideration of marriage

For promises to stand good for the debts of a deceased's estate

For contracts for the sale of goods with a purchase price of $500 or more

For contracts that cannot be completed within one year

For the sale of real estate

For promises to stand good for the debt of another made to the other person's creditor

Contracts Unenforceable Because of Improper Objectives

Contracts otherwise enforceable may fail because they have improper objectives. Contracts with illegal objectives and those against public policy are two such situations.

Contracts with Illegal Objectives

Hypothetical Case

"The winner is number 3913. Who's got the winning ticket?" The voice reverberated throughout the gymnasium. Sanford Davis looked around. A man was running toward the stage from the other side of the floor. It was Brandon Johnson, the son of Michael Johnson, owner of Johnson's Exotic Car Shop. The '67 Mustang was his. Odd, thought Sanford, out of over 2,000 purchasers of the $25 tickets, the son of the man who had donated the car for the lottery had won it. Of course, buying new uniforms for the high school's Marching Terrapin band was a great cause. Still . . . Impulsively, Sanford pushed forward through the crowd. Near the stage he found the band director carrying a box with the receipts in it. "I want my money back," said Sanford, "or I'll prosecute you for holding an illegal lottery." The band director replied that it had been an honest drawing and that he wouldn't refund Sanford's $25. Sanford nodded and without another word turned and pushed his way out of the gym. The next morning, after a lengthy session with Sanford, the local prosecutor brought felony gambling charges against the organizers of the lottery.

Gambling Contracts   **Gambling** is paying something of value for the possibility of winning a prize, usually of greater value, in a game of pure chance. Most gambling contracts, including the ones in the preceding example, are illegal. A positive motive, e.g., charitable support, behind drawings such as the one in the hypothetical case does not give them a legal status. However, most prosecutors shy away from bringing charges against organizations holding such games unless a complaint is filed. If a complaint is filed however, the charge and the result are very serious. Most gambling contracts are considered void by the courts. Therefore, the individual who ends up with the prize keeps it, regardless of the bargain he or she struck to obtain it.

Many U. S. states have legalized state-run lotteries to generate revenue. The billions of dollars that these games of chance bring to the states each year are used for schools, roads, and general state needs. In some states, not-for-profit civic groups can also run games of chance, such as bingo. However, these exceptions do not make other lotteries legal or make the contracts underlying illegal games of chance enforceable in a court of law. Also note that many people associate investing in the stock market or on commodity exchanges with gambling. However, such investing is not gambling in the legal sense. Certainly, a lot of money is won and lost in such investing but, because investing incorporates the elements of skill, experience, and knowledge along with chance, it is not held to constitute "gambling" under the law.

Bribery Contracts   As mentioned previously, in a recent Arkansas case, a citizen of that state sued one of its judges for the return of bribery money he had paid the judge. Normally, as you know, contracts involving improperly buying the influence of a public official are void. In the Arkansas case however, the person who paid the bribe maintained that he was not **in pari delicto** (of equal guilt) with the judge. If this claim is proven to the satisfaction of the court, the court can step in to protect, usually by the return of consideration, the innocent or more nearly innocent party to an illegal contract. In the Arkansas case, of course, the courts refused to do so. Therefore, allegedly, the judge was left with the money from the bribe and certainly with a damaged reputation.

Usurious Contracts   Many U. S. states set a maximum on the interest rate chargeable for the loan of money. Charging an interest rate in excess of this legal limit is **usury**. In most states, usury limits are currently set at around 10 to 15 percent. (Note that we are talking about the lending of money, not the sale of goods on credit. For such sales, the interest rate can exceed 30 percent in some jurisdictions.) Some states hold that a contract charging more than the set limit is void. Therefore, the lender cannot collect the amount due through the courts, and the borrower cannot get back excess interest paid. Other states just enforce the contract for the maximum interest chargeable and refund any excess amount to the borrower.

Other Illegal Objectives   Contracts for prostitution, the sale of illegal drugs, or other objectives that involve the commission of a crime are treated as void by our legal system.

Contracts Against Public Policy

Hypothetical Case

Barth ("Rug") Baldwon stared at his image in the large mirror of the clinic. "Hair," he cried. He grabbed a small mirror off the sink and checked the back of his head. "More hair!" he shouted. The replacement surgery had been successful. Dr. Claudia Von Klippen, the noted ex-East German hair specialist, watched her patient for a moment, then walked out of the room. Dr. Klippen's administrative assistant met the specialist in the hallway. "He's ready for the bill," said Dr. Klippen with a smile. The assistant nodded and winked. Dr. Klippen's practice, opened when she arrived from Berlin barely three months ago, was doing well. There was some question about the validity of Dr. Klippen's license, which was not recognized by the New York State Licensing Board for Physicians, but it hadn't stopped the customers or the cash flow . . . at least not yet. The assistant made a mental note to find out what effect lack of a license would have on the contracts the good doctor made.

Where Unlicensed Parties Are Involved   Dr. Klippen and her assistant have quite a bit to worry about. If a license is required for the protection of the public, such as a license for a physician, contracts made without the license are treated as void. Therefore, if Barth Baldwon refused to pay, Dr. Klippen could not use the courts to recover the money due. However, if a license is required just to generate money for a community, such as a license for a typical business, the contracts are enforceable.

Contracts Made on Sunday   Despite the constitutional requirement of the separation of church and state, some courts continue to uphold the use of state statutes or local ordinances to give workers a "day of rest" on Sunday. In states that utilize this approach, the treatment of contracts made on this day of rest varies widely. For example, some states allow contracts made on Sunday to be ratified or confirmed on a weekday. Other states hold that such contracts are illegal and therefore, altogether void. Some states even delegate the choice of prohibiting or allowing such contracts to local governments. In the jurisdictions that retain them, laws that regulate the making or performing of contractual obligations on Sunday, called **blue laws**, are still a factor to be considered in determining the enforceability of contracts.

Contracts Curtailing the Freedom to Marry   Society places great emphasis on the family and home. A part of this emphasis concerns the preservation of the freedom to marry. Except for laws reinforcing **monogamy** (being allowed only one spouse), most limitations on that freedom are against public policy. This is especially true for contracts that restrict or prohibit marriage and contracts that foster divorce. For example, if Jane takes $5,000 in return for agreeing never to marry, or not to marry for the next three years, or not to marry a particular individual, she may do so anyway, because such contracts are void. Similarly, if Jane is paid $5,000 in return for promising to divorce her husband, she may keep the money and her husband if she so desires, as that contract is also void. However, property settlement agreements between divorcing spouses are not void.

Other Contracts against Public Policy   In addition to looking with disfavor on the contracts mentioned above, the law looks with similar disfavor on contracts that interfere with the administration of justice and public service, such as contracts that place restraints on trade and commerce and contracts that improperly limit liability for a party's actions.

CHAPTER REVIEW

USE LEGAL TERMS

Fill in the blanks with the appropriate term.

best evidence rule	monogamy	real estate
blue laws	parol evidence rule	statute of frauds
gambling	prenuptial agreement	usury
in pari delicto		

1. Yi-Ling put $1 into the jar, then walked out on the first tee. The $5,000 hole-in-one prize had last been awarded when the pro tour came through several years ago. One of the tour leaders had put in $121 before hitting the cup. The flag was only 220 yards away, but on a dogleg turn. Yi-Ling teed up her ball, made three or four practice swings, then smacked a drive that banked near the hole and rolled in. When she went into the office to claim her prize, the manager refused to pay, even with the witnesses. Yi-Ling brought suit, but the lawyer for the golf course said that the game involved a prize, chance, and consideration and therefore was ___?___ and illegal. Therefore, the court should declare the contract void and not force the golf course to pay. The judge listened for a moment, then said, "Sure there's a prize, $5,000, and sure there's consideration, the $1 Ms. Yi-Ling chipped in, but that hole in one wasn't chance, that was skill. Pay her, gentlemen."

2. Fisk looked down at the contract. He had signed it, sure, but these weren't the terms that they'd agreed to. Why did he ever let Henson put it in writing? Why didn't he read it as a precaution before signing? Now Fisk's attorney advised him that because of the ___?___, Fisk couldn't even testify to the real terms. Fisk put his head in his hands and sighed in resignation.

3. Hester held a garage sale. Thelma, her friend, advised her not to open on Sunday because the ___?___ made contracting on that day illegal.

4. When Saundra and her bookie, Angela, were caught by the police, Angela was holding a $1,000 bet of Saundra's. Angela refused to return the money, and Saundra sued for it, claiming that she was not ___?___ with a bookie. Therefore, Saundra argued, the court should not throw the case out but instead order her money returned.

TEST YOUR READING

5. Why are oral contracts still valid today?
6. What is the importance of the statute of frauds?

7. Why do the courts enforce the parol evidence and best evidence rules?

8. Name the times that a contract has to be in writing to be enforceable under the statute of frauds.

9. Name three instances where illegal objectives will prohibit the enforcement of contracts.

10. Name three instances where contracts are rendered unenforceable because they are against public policy.

THINK CRITICALLY ABOUT EVIDENCE

11. What other approaches could the law take today to preserve the enforceability of oral contracts rather than having them reduced to writing? Evaluate the strengths and weaknesses of each.

12. Laurel Davis put her house up for sale after her divorce from David became final. She offered it as "for sale by owner" by putting an ad in the local newspaper, placing a large sign in her front yard, and even sending out a notice over the computer network at the plant where she worked as a drafting engineer. After several months, Holly Seeler, a fellow worker at the plant, contacted her through the electronic mail. She asked to see the house. The day after Laurel took her through the house, Laurel found an offer from Holly to buy it on the computer bulletin board. Laurel counter-offered and Holly agreed. Afterward, Laurel and Holly left the contract for sale in the computer database. Therefore, when a dispute arose about the terms, the only contract they could produce was a printout from a source that either of them could have tampered with. The printout, of course, did not contain the signature of either Laurel or Holly. Would it satisfy the statute of frauds? Should it be considered best evidence?

13. Which of the following contracts have to be in writing?

    a. A contract giving the phone company permission to run underground lines across your real property.

    b. A contract for the purchase of $450 in model train equipment that usually takes more than a year to make by hand.

    c. A promise to your friend to pay his debts if he cannot.

14. Which of the following contracts would the courts enforce?

    a. A contract under which you owe $2,500 to a dentist who performed root canal surgery on you without the appropriate state license.

    b. A contract with a customer of your retail business that you made before you secured a city license to do business.

    c. A contract with a professional engineer to draw up the structural plans for your new office building. The engineer is licensed in several neighboring states but not in the state where the building is to be erected.

REAL-WORLD CASE

In the Matter of Baby M (a pseudonym for an actual person)
Supreme Court of New Jersey
537 A.2d 1227

When William Stern learned his wife was in considerable danger of blindness and paraplegia if she had children, he was deeply concerned. All the other members of his family had been destroyed by the Holocaust. As the only survivor, he very much wanted to continue his bloodline. Consequently, Mr. Stern, Mrs. Mary Beth Whitehead, and Mrs. Whitehead's husband at the time entered into a surrogacy contract. The contract provided that Mrs. Whitehead (since divorced and remarried) would be artificially inseminated with Mr. Stern's sperm. She would then carry the child to term, deliver it to the Sterns, and thereafter do whatever was necessary to terminate her maternal rights so that Mrs. Stern could adopt the child. For these services, Mr. Stern would pay Mrs. Whitehead $10,000 after the child was delivered to him.

Not wanting anyone at the hospital to be aware of the surrogacy situation, Mr. and Mrs. Whitehead posed as the parents of the newborn baby, which was named Sara Elizabeth Whitehead on the birth certificate, with Mr. Whitehead listed as the father. The Sterns visited the hospital unobtrusively to see the child.

Almost from the moment of birth, however, Mrs. Whitehead concluded that she could not part with the child. She broke into tears when the Sterns told her what they were going to rename the child. She also commented on how much the baby looked like her other daughter.

Ultimately, Mrs. Whitehead refused to turn over the baby to Mr. Stern. Mr. Stern filed suit for custody, but the Whiteheads fled to Florida with baby M. The Whiteheads, fearing the loss of the child, lived in roughly 20 different hotels over the next three months. Finally, the police located the baby and forcibly took her into custody. The trial court then heard the Sterns' complaint, which, in addition to seeking possession and custody of the child, sought enforcement of the surrogacy contract. The contract, among other things, required that Mrs. Whitehead's parental rights be terminated and that Mrs. Stern be allowed to adopt the child.

The Superior Court (trial court) upheld the validity of the surrogacy contract and granted the Sterns' request for its enforcement. The case was appealed to the New Jersey Supreme Court, which ruled as follows:

> We invalidate the surrogacy contract because it conflicts with the law and public policy of this State. While we recognize the depth of the yearning of infertile couples to have their own children, we find the payment of money to a "surrogate" mother illegal, perhaps criminal, and potentially degrading to women. Although in this case we grant custody to the natural father, the evidence having clearly proved such custody to be in the best interests of the infant, we void both the

termination of the surrogate mother's parental rights and the adoption of the child by the wife/stepparent. We thus restore the "surrogate" as the mother of the child. We remand the issue to the trial court . . . We find no offense to our present laws where a woman voluntarily and without payment agrees to act as a "surrogate" mother, provided that she is not subject to a binding agreement to surrender her child. Moreover, our holding today does not preclude the Legislature from altering the current statutory scheme within constitutional limits, so as to permit surrogacy contracts. Under current law (prohibiting the sale of babies), however, the surrogacy agreement before us is illegal and invalid. [Mrs. Whitehead was allowed visitation rights with the child.]

Think Critically

1. Do you feel that the court's decision reflected the "wisdom of Solomon" that we discussed earlier?
2. Should surrogacy contracts be allowed? What problems do you foresee if they are?
   a. Can you distinguish surrogacy contracts from contracts to aid in the suicide efforts of a terminally ill patient? What are the similarities between these two types of contracts?
   b. Should Mr. Stern have to pay child support?

CHAPTER 12

Discharge of Contractual Obligations

GOALS

- Be able to identify the party or parties who are to receive the contractual performance as well as the parties to whom it is to be rendered
- Understand the various levels of performance required
- Know the remedies available when contractual duties are not performed

Rendering Contractual Performance

Parties to a Contract

In most contractual situations, the rights and duties created by the agreement fall on the parties to it. In fact, the law requires that for every right there is a corresponding duty. Persons who are not parties to a contract however, do not have to perform its duties. By the same token, such persons generally cannot expect to receive benefits from the contract. Generally, contractual performance is rendered by and for the benefit of the parties who negotiated and concluded the agreement.

However, there are exceptions to this rule. At times, the parties to a contract may intend that benefits flow to persons besides themselves. Such persons are known as **third-party beneficiaries**. Life insurance contracts made between the insured and an insurance company are a good example. Such agreements call for a payment to a third party outside the contract in the event of the insured's death.

In addition to creating rights in others during contracting, parties to a contract may later transfer their rights and duties to others who were not original parties. Such a transfer of rights is termed an **assignment**. A transfer of contractual duties is termed a **delegation**.

Third-Party Beneficiaries   Before we discuss assignment, we need to take a closer look at third-party beneficiaries. This designation is important because true third-party beneficiaries can sue to enforce a contract that benefits them. Realize that contracts often benefit many parties. For example, a contract to buy a new car might benefit the dealership, the dealership's employees, its creditors and suppliers, and its owners. The same contract might benefit the purchaser; the purchaser's children, spouse, and other relatives; and the purchaser's lending institution, insurance company, and garage. Obviously, the courts could not open themselves up to suits by all these potential beneficiaries if the contract were not properly performed.

As a consequence, the courts allow only true third-party beneficiaries to sue. Others, labeled **incidental beneficiaries**, are considered to be only unintended recipients of a contract's direct or indirect benefits. Incidental beneficiaries therefore cannot bring suit to enforce the contract.

Among third-party beneficiaries are **creditor beneficiaries** and **donee beneficiaries**. A creditor beneficiary is a third party to a contract to whom payment of some obligation is expressly directed by a contractual party who has incurred that obligation. In the above example, the entertainer's creditors were creditor beneficiaries. As such, they could sue to enforce the contract between the entertainer and the promoters. By law, such a suit on behalf of a creditor beneficiary can be directed against either of the parties to the contract.

Hypothetical Case

The thunderous cheer cascaded down the aisles and crashed over him as he came on stage. His blood surged into his fingers. The first notes from his guitar slashed back at the audience. The roar increased momentarily, then died away as the crowd of more than 60,000 packed into the St. Louis Wonderdome settled in to enjoy the concert. Three hours and five encores later, he was back in his hotel room. Ben Jackson, his agent, had just told him that the box office gross was more than $1.5 million. This amount was more than enough to bail out the overdue bank loans on his estate and the new theater he'd opened in Branson, Missouri. Now that drugs were behind him, he hoped it would be a new world. Just to be sure however, his contract with the concert promoters stipulated that the money due him was to be paid directly to his creditors as third-party beneficiaries. Whatever was left after that, he would party on, without drugs, please, please without drugs.

A donee beneficiary is a third party who receives rights under a contract as a gift from a party or parties to that contract. Most life insurance contracts are made in favor of a donee beneficiary. By naming a person as the recipient of the face value of a life insurance policy, the insured is making a gift, not responding to the demands of an obligee. Unlike the situation with a creditor beneficiary, a donee beneficiary can sue only the promisor of the benefit, not the promisee. So as a third-party beneficiary under a life insurance policy, one can sue only the insurance company for failing to abide by the policy's provisions, not the person who took out the policy.

Assignees of Contractual Duties   After an agreement has been concluded, one of the contracting parties may want to transfer to someone else the right to receive a performance due under the agreement. If I construct an apartment building, for example, as part of the deal I might transfer to the bank making the construction loan the right to receive the rent from the tenants for a certain time. I might also contract to transfer to a private repair firm the duty of keeping the building in good shape. As noted earlier, the transfer of a person's rights under a contract to another party is known as an **assignment**. The party who assigns the contractual rights is known as the **assignor**. The party to whom they are assigned is known as the **assignee** (see Figure 12-1).

FIGURE 12-1   Assignment

Generally, a landlord has:

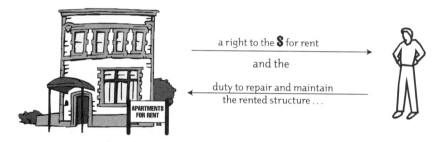

a right to the **$** for rent

and the

duty to repair and maintain the rented structure . . .

However, the landlord may assign the right to the rent money and delegate the repair and maintenance duty. For example:

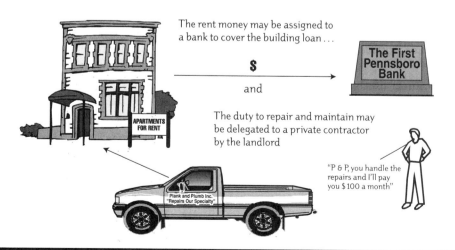

The rent money may be assigned to a bank to cover the building loan . . .

$

and

The First Pennsboro Bank

The duty to repair and maintain may be delegated to a private contractor by the landlord

"P & P, you handle the repairs and I'll pay you $100 a month"

Plank and Plumb Inc. "Repairs Our Specialty"

In general, contractual parties can assign their rights and delegate their duties as they see fit. In fact, the transfer of an entire contract to a third party by a contracting party carries with it a full assignment of rights and a full delegation of duties. Of course, contracting parties can secure a complete release from their contractual duties if the other parties allow it. When contracting parties secure such releases by substituting others to perform their contractual obligations, the maneuver is termed a **novation**.

Hypothetical Case

When Halfman Construction Company (Hafa) discovered it had run out of low-cost fill material for construction of the concrete foundation at the new stadium, its executives were able to secure a novation from the other contracting parties by finding another company, Gem Construction Company (Gem), to perform the same work for the agreed-upon price. Unfortunately, Gem's fill material was substandard and the concrete foundation was too weak. Gem was sued and recovered against as a consequence. When Gem later brought suit against Hafa for some of the money it paid out as damages, the court held that the release Hafa had obtained as part of the novation prevented any such recovery.

Note that if no release is obtained, even with a legally allowable assignment of rights and delegation of duties, the original party remains liable on the contract. In the preceding example, if Hafa had not secured the release, even if it were blameless for Gem's failure to perform the contract, it would have remained liable to the original obligee for damages for not fulfilling its obligations under the contract.

By law, some contract rights cannot be assigned. For example, an assignment of contractually required personal services that greatly increases the obligation of the person providing those services is not allowed. In other words, if you contract for the services of a certified public accountant to do your company taxes, you cannot assign that accountant's services to my much larger company instead of using them yourself. Also, restrictions on the assignment of contractual rights may be put in the contract itself.

Hypothetical Case

"Just sign at the bottom on the blank line, sir." The rental car clerk smiled at Eddie Bonet. The car keys dangled from her left hand. Eddie read the wording above the blank signature line. "This says I've read the terms on the back of the agreement and agree to the incorporation of those terms into our agreement." The clerk smiled and shrugged, "That's right, sir. Nobody reads them, though." Eddie thought a moment. "Well, let me take a few minutes anyway," he said as he flipped the contract over. The back contained a full page of small print. The first few terms were general statements that had little impact on the rental contract. "Whoa, what's this?" Eddie blurted. "I can't let anyone drive it who's under 21, and every time I leave the vehicle, the doors are to be locked and the windows up." The clerk nodded, "Standard terms, sir. Also, you can't assign your contract rights to the possession and use of this car to anyone else." Eddie thought a moment, then said, "So if I violate any of these terms, even for the best of reasons, and something goes wrong, I'm automatically liable for breach of contract." Again the clerk nodded, "That's right, sir. Take it or leave it." Eddie looked out the window at the car, shrugged his shoulders, and signed.

So, in this true-to-life example, Eddie could not assign his right to the car to anyone else because of the contract terms themselves. Note that an assignment, unlike a contract, does not require consideration to be enforceable. Also, assignments need be in writing only if the original contract was required by law to be in writing.

Finally, it is important to provide notice of the assignment to the person who must render the assigned performance. If notice is not given and the obligor performs for the assignor, the assignee cannot demand that a similar performance be rendered for her or him. For example, presume that I assigned to you the right to receive a $100,000 payment owed me by a debtor under a contract. If the debtor, acting without notice of the assignment, paid me and I disappeared, you would have to get the money from me, if you could find me. However, if you gave the debtor notice of the assignment and the debtor still paid me, you could legally take the debtor to court for the $100,000 payment, regardless of whether the debtor could find me to recover the mistaken payment.

Delegatees of Contractual Duties   Delegation of duties under contracts requiring personal services is also limited.

Hypothetical Case

Angie heard her husband, Dave, from across the yard. "Do we know? You bet. It's a boy. You ought to see the ultrasound!" Angie didn't hear the rest, but Dave and their neighbor, Bill Bradford, burst out laughing a moment later. A smile flashed across her face, then faded. Angie was worried about her doctor. During her first pregnancy and through most of this one, she'd been with Susan Medford, MD. Now, barely two months before her due date, they'd received a letter stating that Dr. Medford had gone into partnership with the two male doctors Angie had met during her last office visit. Angie liked Dr. Belton, who was short and rather pudgy. But Dr. Davis, who was tall and pale, gave her the creeps. As Dave walked toward her, she could hold back no longer. "Dave, I just don't want Dr. Davis to touch me. If he's on call the night I deliver, I won't let him handle it. But when I called the hospital to tell them this, they said that if I didn't use Dr. Davis, I'd just have to wait my turn for an emergency room doctor. It isn't fair. Can Dr. Medford do this? Our contract was with her."

The legal answer to Angie's question is a simple "no." Without Angie's permission, Dr. Medford cannot delegate such a personal contractual responsibility to either of the other two doctors. Only a standardized performance, such as one performed by unskilled labor, can be delegated.

Joint and/or Several Liability   Where two or more parties sign a contract as obligors, the very wording of the contract is crucial in determining which of them may be required to perform or who may be responsible if performance is not properly rendered. If all three doctors promised in the same contract to deliver Angie's baby as a cooperative effort, they would be **jointly liable** for whatever occurred. This means that if Angie had a problem with the birth procedure, she would have to sue all three doctors to recover. If the doctors instead each promised to do the same thing individually, they would be **severally liable**. To recover, Angie would have to sue only one of the doctors for the full amount due. Finally, for some obligations, such as the payment of income taxes by a husband and wife, the obligors are **jointly and severally liable**. This status allows the obligee of the performance to bring suit against any one, a few, or all of the obligors should the obligation not be properly fulfilled.

Discharge of Contractual Obligations

In a legal sense, **discharge** means to free from a legal obligation. When talking about effective discharge under contract law, it is crucial to realize that the vast majority of contractual obligations are discharged simply by performing them. Of course, where performance is complete and satisfactory, little law is made. The U.S. society could not survive without full compliance with most contracts. In this section, we'll discuss various levels of performance and other means of discharging contractual obligations.

Performance Level

Ideally, every contract is concluded by **complete performance**, that is, performance in which all parties fulfilled every promise as expected. Given the complexity of many contracts, it should come as no surprise that reality often falls short of this standard. As a consequence, in most cases, the law allows "substantial performance" to discharge the contractual obligations owed by the parties. **Substantial performance** results from a good faith effort that meets contractual expectations except for minor details. The difference between complete performance and substantial performance is that reimbursement for the minor shortcomings of substantial performance can be obtained at law.

Even so, at times individuals are not satisfied with any performance short of that which meets their full personal expectations. These individuals insert such words as "performance to my satisfaction" or "satisfactory to [a named individual]" into the contract requirements. The courts do not always enforce such **satisfactory performance** terms, however. If an objective standard exists that the courts can use to determine whether performance is satisfactory, they do so. If none exists, the courts hold the obligor to the requirement that the performance must satisfy the obligee' s personal tastes.

If the contract is silent as to certain terms relating to performance, the law places its own terms into effect. For example, if the time of performance is not mentioned, the law reads "in a reasonable time." If a lawsuit develops, the court asks the trier-of-fact to determine what that time should have been. When "time is of the essence" is used in a contract to bind a person to a set performance date, the courts look at the circumstances closely to find out whether time truly was of the essence before allowing any consequential recovery. For example, if I arranged for a $7,500 shipment of a variety of ice cream flavors to be delivered on the day before the grand opening of my ice cream shop, I would be able to justify a "time is of the essence" requirement in a contract I make with you for the installation of my freezer.

If the method of payment is not stipulated, U. S. coin or currency is required. A check may be used as a substitute only if this is approved by the obligee. Finally, performance may hinge on the satisfaction of a condition concurrent, a condition precedent, or a condition subsequent.

A **condition concurrent** requires both parties to perform their contractual obligations at the same time. Payment on delivery is the most common condition concurrent term. Even when this condition is not explicitly mentioned, it is often implied by the courts.

A **condition precedent** is a contractual term specifying an event that must occur before an obligation to perform is placed on one or all parties to a contract. An example is, "If you'll mow the yard before 5 P.M., I'll pay you $15."

A **condition subsequent** is a contractual term specifying an event that extinguishes an obligation to perform if it occurs. Let me paraphrase offers we've all heard for an example: "Keep the 10 compact disks of oldies remastered off Edison's original recordings for up to 30 days. If you're not satisfied, return them before that time expires and pay nothing." If you contract for the disks, fulfilling the condition subsequent by returning them within 30 days terminates your obligation.

Nonperformance Means of Discharging Contractual Obligations

A number of ways can lead to the discharge of contractual obligations without performance. The release involved in a novation and the action of a condition subsequent, both already mentioned, can accomplish this end. Other means include mutual rescission, tender of performance, and impossibility of performance.

Mutual Rescission   **Mutual rescission** can discharge contractual obligations without performance. Typically, it involves an agreement whereby the parties to a contract can obtain a discharge from the contractual obligations by returning whatever they've received under the contract (or equivalent value). If the original contract was required to be in writing, the agreement calling for mutual rescission must also be in writing.

Tender of Performance   Having a tender of performance turned down also discharges most contractual obligations. A **tender of performance** is a ready, willing, and able offer to perform in accordance with the terms of the contract.

Hypothetical Case

James Ford was in charge of booking a band for the 50th reunion of the Miller High School Class of 1945. Reviewing the listings of available bands, he came across the Bennie Goodman Band and mistakenly presumed it was the famous swing era band of nearly the same name. He called the number given and contracted for a two-hour show. When the band arrived on the fateful night, James realized he had mistakenly booked a rap group composed of female impersonators. He then refused the band's tender of performance and thus discharged its obligation to perform under the contract. However, Bennie and the band would still be able to claim their paycheck.

Note that a tender of payment of a debt is an exception to this rule. If such a tender is refused, the refusal does not discharge the duty to pay. Out of fairness however, any interest and charges for nonpayment stop running at the time such a tender is made.

Impossibility of Performance

Hypothetical Case

To Sandra Stuart, it felt like opening a time capsule. The old garage had stood behind her grandfather's house for years and years. He had never mentioned anything about it to her. Now, through his will, whatever was in there was hers. She turned the key that the attorney had given her in the old but well-oiled padlock. It clicked open. She removed it from the hasp, grabbed the door, and tugged. The light of day stabbed into the dark interior, disclosing something white . . . a car. Not just any car. Sandra remembered the movie *American Graffiti*. The car was a very rare '55 T-bird, portholes and all, and Sandra noticed that the odometer read 7,700 miles. All in all, the car looked just as it had when it was driven from the showroom so long ago. Three weeks later, Sandra sold it for $27,000 to a Ford dealer in Chicago. Then tragedy struck. A grass fire started by derelicts in a nearby vacant lot burned across her grandfather's yard, not mown since his death, and destroyed the garage and the car. The car dealer and Sandra were discharged from their contract because of the obvious and irreversible impossibility of delivering the car.

Destruction of specific subject matter   The destruction of the '55 T-bird is a good example of the first of several forms that impossibility of performance can take, that is, the destruction of subject matter specifically referred to in the contract. The destruction of such subject matter will terminate the contract. If the contract is not specific, the promisor must bear the extra expense of locating like subject matter and providing it to the obligee instead.

Incapacity of the performing party   Death, disability in relation to a necessary skill, or incompetence as a result of insanity or substance abuse terminate certain contractual obligations requiring special talents. For example, whether a star guitarist dies, breaks an arm, or is declared incompetent because of drug use, she or, upon her death, her estate, is no longer bound to meet the demands of a personal appearance tour. However, her estate is liable to pay a bill for a new guitar she had purchased just before her death, because making the payment is a simple effort that does not require special talent.

Commercial frustration   In exceptional cases, the law excuses a party from performing a contractual obligation when such performance requires an extraordinary and wasteful commitment of resources. For example, fulfilling a contract to supply gasoline during an oil embargo might require buying crude petroleum at triple its pre-embargo price. Enforcing such a contract would serve no practical public policy end. Therefore, the obligor might be discharged from this obligation. Before releasing the obligor, courts usually look for the occurrence of an unexpected event the risk of which was not allocated between the parties by either the contract or custom. If such an event makes performance commercially impracticable, the doctrine of commercial frustration is utilized; if not, the obligation remains. Several decades ago, the Suez Canal was closed because of international hostilities. Its closure greatly increased costs for ships leaving the U. S. for Iran, India, and other destinations in the Middle and Far East because now they had to detour around Africa's Cape of Good Hope. A U. S. federal court refused to use the doctrine of commercial frustration to allow shippers to recover additional costs under contracts for such journeys made before the canal's closing, saying that the increased costs were not great enough (approximately $45,000 added to a contracted price of $305,000).

Effect of law   A number of laws may also affect the legal necessity for an obligor to perform. For example, the law occasionally changes so as to ban the performance of certain contractual obligations. Such changes discharge the contractual obligations in question. So, if you have a contract to distribute a fine Scotch whiskey distilled in Great Britain throughout the U. S. just as another prohibition act goes into effect, you are no longer legally required to fulfill your promise. The same holds true for drugs that the Food and Drug Administration takes off the market and for other products subject to governmental regulation.

Statutes of limitation may also affect performance. Such statutes set time limits within which a lawsuit must be brought. Each state has such a statute. For action on a written contract, the case must generally be brought within 6 to 10 years, depending on the state. If it is not, the right to use the courts to resolve contract disputes over a lack of or improper performance is lost.

The federal bankruptcy statute produces the same effect for obligors under the control of its procedure. One result of a "successful" bankruptcy filing is that obligees are barred from using the courts to secure performance of the obligations due them. The bankruptcy statute is covered in Chapter 23.

Note that both the bankruptcy statute and the statute of limitations do not actually discharge performance obligations. They merely bar the obligee from using the courts for enforcement of those obligations. The means of discharging contracts are summarized in Figure 12-2 on page 158.

FIGURE 12-2   Means of Discharging Contracts

- Performance
- Mutual rescission
- Tender of performance

- Impossibility
- Effect of law

Breach of Contract

When **breach of contract** (an unexcused failure to perform according to the terms of the agreement) occurs, the injured party has a right to a legal remedy. As you might suspect, improper performance by one party also discharges the other party from having to perform further. It also enables the injured party to seek a legal remedy to the problem.

Potential remedies include damages, rescission, and specific performance. We'll get to those in a moment. Before we do, realize that there are times when obligors under a contract expressly state or clearly imply that they are not going to perform at all. When such a statement is made even before performance has begun, it is termed a **repudiation**. In response to a repudiation, obligees can either bring suit immediately or wait to see whether the person who has repudiated will change his or her mind before the date performance was to begin. The latter is the wisest course as it is usually a far more practical way to obtain the desired performance, rather than by relying on a court-imposed substitute. If suit is brought however, the repudiation is treated as an **anticipatory breach** because it precedes the beginning of performance.

Damages

You have already been introduced to compensatory damages, the type of damages most often sought in a contract lawsuit. As you may recall from Chapter 6, those damages are meant to provide the injured party with the amount of actual loss. They are therefore often called actual damages. Compensatory damages can be arrived at by calculating (1) how much a like performance would cost from a source other than the obligee, (2) the incremental cost of making a substandard performance whole, or (3) the lost profit on a sale. The trier-of-fact, usually the jury, fixes such damages to equal the financial loss borne by the injured party.

Consequential damages also are recoverable. These are damages reasonably foreseeable as caused by the breach. Do not forget however, that lawyer's fees, perhaps up to 40% or more of the damage award, almost always come out of that award. This is one reason that, in most circumstances, bringing a hasty lawsuit rather than waiting for proper performance is not a good idea.

Punitive or exemplary damages are not available in most contract suits. Some statutes do allow them in consumer contract cases where one party has behaved extremely improperly. Nominal damages are also awarded at times under contract law to acknowledge that someone who suffered only minimal harm had a cause of action. In addition, courts may award **incidental damages** to cover the costs incurred by an innocent party.

Finally, realize that, like most of us, courts do not like uncertainty. As a consequence, the law does not speculate as to the amount of a loss just to see a recovery of some sort by the injured party. If a monetary figure for harm done cannot be determined with reasonable certainty, the court does not allow damages to be awarded. So, if you're opening that brand new ice cream store we spoke of earlier, you cannot recover lost profits when the refrigeration company doesn't put in the freezer in time for the opening. In the eyes of the court, the amount of lost profits cannot be reasonably ascertained because you don't have any history of income for the store.

The way around this dilemma is to stipulate an amount for liquidated damages in the contract. **Liquidated damages** are a realistic approximation of the damages that a court should award in the event of a breach of the contract. Liquidated damages must be determined in good faith by the parties to the contract. If the liquidated damages are excessive given the nature of the breach, the court will not award them because they would be punitive.

Mitigation of Damages

Finally, a party injured by a breach of contract has a duty to act to minimize the harm done, in other words, to **mitigate** the damages. So, given time, the Bennie Goodman group must try to find another booking when its tender of performance is turned down. The ice cream store, without a working freezer as a result of the refrigeration company's contractual breach, must try to find another location to store the ice cream delivery rather than just stand by and see it melt. Even if the efforts fail, the injured parties must try to mitigate. If they fail to do so, they may lose part or all of their right to recover. Assume that if the effort were made, Bennie Goodman could still have secured a suitable booking for later that night. If this were shown in court, the amount that would have been paid or that was paid for that booking would be deducted from the damages due under the Miller High School reunion contract.

Rescission and Other Equitable Remedies

Another remedy for breach of contract is rescission. Injured parties who have performed may simply sue to recover what they have put into the contract. If the contract is for the sale of goods, damages may be sought in addition to the recovery of the items sold.

Of course, there are times when damages and rescission simply are not adequate remedies. For example, assume you have entered into a contract for the purchase of seven acres on the best corner in town. You have already lined up your financing and prospective tenants for a new shopping center when the seller breaches. Would you be satisfied with available damages, rescission, or even another seven acre tract? Of course not. Land is unique, as are certain other items, such as paintings, ancient relics, and collector's items. You may therefore request as a remedy that the court order the other party to fulfill the contract. This remedy is called **specific performance**. Note that the court will not order specific performance of contracts calling for non-standardized personal services because this would come too close to a violation of the Thirteenth Amendment's prohibition of involuntary servitude (slavery).

Hypothetical Case

"What do you mean he isn't coming," Burl Wilson screamed into the phone. "We've sold over 3,000 advance tickets at $25 plus a pop. The show's been scheduled for months." Burl's eyes bugged. "You squirrelly little . . ." Benton Ellis clapped his hand over Burl's mouth and grabbed the receiver. "Look, Mr. Charles, if Rod doesn't appear here, we'll go to court and sue for damages. We've got our time in this, it cost a bundle to print the tickets, and we'll have to refund every one of the advance sales." Benton stopped and listened. "You will. Well, that'll help some. We'll consider it. I know the courts wouldn't give us our lost profits yet because there are still 11,000 tickets to sell for the concert, so your covering our expenses will help. Still, he's supposed to appear here, not in the Twin Cities." Benton listened a moment longer, and then said, "I'll call you back on this," and hung up the phone. He turned and put his hands on Burl's shoulders. "Look, Burl, our little promotion just dies unless we can find some way to get Rod to change his mind. The courts can't order him to perform here, and Rod's management promised to pick up our expenses. Still, it's nowhere near what we could make if he showed up and sang. Tell you what, let's call our lawyer and see if we've got any other options."

Although it is true that, because of the Thirteenth Amendment, a court would not order Rod to appear, Burl and Benton's lawyer may advise them that other remedial court action is possible. The most effective remedy in this situation might be an **injunction**. An injunction is a court order prohibiting or requiring someone to do something. Rod could be prohibited from appearing at any other location on the date that he was to be onstage for Burl and Benton. If Rod disobeyed, he could be held in contempt of court and fined or imprisoned, or both. The fine would go to the court and thus, would not help the promoters financially. However, the threat of such a consequence might force Rod's management to reach a satisfactory compromise with Burl and Benton.

The contractual remedies we have discussed above are satisfactory as a last resort. But it is important to realize that they do not take the place, from either an individual or a societal perspective, of satisfactory performance under the contract. The reliance that can be placed on such performance in most contractual situations is what fuels our culture's growth and independence.

CHAPTER REVIEW

USE LEGAL TERMS

Fill in the blanks with the appropriate term. Some terms may not be used.

anticipatory breach	creditor beneficiary	mitigate
assignee	delegation	mutual rescission
assignment	discharge	novation
assignor	donee beneficiary	repudiation
breach of contract	incidental beneficiary	satisfactory performance
complete performance	incidental damages	severally liable
condition concurrent	injunction	specific performance
condition precedent	jointly and severally liable	substantial performance
condition subsequent	jointly liable	tender of performance
consequential damages	liquidated damages	third-party beneficiary

1. A(n) ___?___ involves the release of one party from contractual duties and the substitution of another party.

2. To be ___?___ is to be individually fully responsible for certain contractual obligations.

3. If a carpenter builds your gazebo to your contractual specifications with just a few minor deviations, the carpenter has rendered a(n) ___?___.

4. If a court responds to your complaint by ordering the electrician to complete his contract with you by installing wiring in the gazebo, the remedy used by the court is termed ___?___.

5. When you also try to get the court to order the painter to fulfill her contractual obligations, the court notes that the contract requires completion of the carpentry and the wiring before any latex goes on the structure. This requirement is termed a(n) ___?___ to the painter's obligation.

6. When the roofers hear about your court actions against the electrician and the painter, they ask to be let out of their contract. As you have spent a lot of money pursuing those lawsuits, you agree. Each party to the roofing contract will return the other party to that party's previous position. This is an example of a(n) ___?___.

7. A ready, willing, and able offer to perform contractual obligations is termed a(n) ___?___.

TEST YOUR READING

8. Is a third party beneficiary an actual party to the contract? Why or why not?
9. What is the effect of a novation?
10. What duties cannot be assigned?
11. Explain the difference between a condition precedent and a condition subsequent.
12. What is the most effective means of discharging contractual performance?
13. What is tender of performance?
14. Exactly what is a repudiation?
15. What is the wisest response to an anticipatory breach?
16. Why will a court not order specific performance of contracts calling for non-standardized personal services?

THINK CRITICALLY ABOUT EVIDENCE

17. When Bob Hayes' wife died, her insurance company refused to pay Bob, as beneficiary, the amount of her insurance policy because of the suspicious nature of her death. Bob was in debt to a number of creditors, including the local bank, at the time of his wife's death and had planned to use the insurance proceeds to pay them. When the insurance company refused to pay him, he decided to just let the matter drop and take bankruptcy to clear his debts. In relation to the insurance contract, what type of beneficiaries are Bob's creditors? Can they sue to enforce the policy?

18. In Problem 17, assume that Bob threatens the insurance company with a lawsuit. What type of beneficiary is he? Can he sue to enforce the contract with the insurance company?

19. Good news for Bob's creditors: The insurance company decides to pay off to avoid being sued. Bob then assigns the right to receive the policy amount to the creditors and in writing informs the insurance company of his assignment. The insurance company erroneously pays Bob, who then buys a ticket for Brazil and disappears with the payoff amount. The creditors then sue the insurance company for the money due them as a result of the assignment. The insurance company replies that the creditors must find Bob and get their money from him. Who is correct? Why?

20. Bernice contracts with XXXX-Terminate to rid her property of various insects. She owns some stock in the company and likes to think she will get a part of her money back as a dividend payout. Bernice is upset, however, when XXXX-Terminate, so as to fulfill its obligations under a big government contract, delegates its contractual duty to another established exterminator. She maintains that only XXXX-Terminate can perform the contract. XXXX-Terminate replies that any unskilled laborer can accomplish the job and that it can therefore delegate the job as it sees fit. Who is correct?

21. The Bombay or Bust Shipping Company contracted to transport several thousand tons of concrete yard ornaments to India by the beginning of the new year. Unfortunately, a major conflict in the Near East caused the Suez Canal to close and shipping costs to quadruple. Bombay or Bust wants to be released from its contract. You are the company's attorney. On what theory would you base your argument?

22. Our Grass Is Greener Company, a lawn care firm, contracts to mow the two acre yard of Mrs. Bailey's estate for $200 a month during the current year. Later Mrs. Bailey's grandson offers to do the same job for $50 a month. Mrs. Bailey tells Our Grass Is Greener that she is canceling the contract. The company responds by noting the $2,000 liquidated damage clause in the contract. What would be the effect of this clause in court?

23. Assume that in a lawsuit based on the scenario of Problem 22, it is shown that Our Grass Is Greener could have taken another job to replace Mrs. Bailey's that would have paid $150 per month at the estate next door to hers. How does this affect any potential recovery by the company?

REAL-WORLD CASE
Neal v. Republic Airlines, Inc.
605 Federal Supplement 1145

Consider the case of the missing deceased and how the court used contract law to solve it.

When Mrs. Neal died in Chicago on November 23, arrangements were immediately made between Inman Nationwide Shipping and Republic Airlines to ship her remains to her birthplace in Sulligent, Alabama.

Republic Airlines took charge of her remains on November 24 for its Flight 480 to Alabama. Through some error however, the remains were instead flown on other flights from Chicago to Memphis to Atlanta to Greenville, Mississippi, and then back to Memphis again. They did not arrive at the proper destination until the afternoon of the 25th, which significantly "interfered with the timely and proper burial of their mother by plaintiffs" (to quote the complaint).

The Neals thereupon brought suit against Republic Airlines for breach of contract and for other causes of action based on the breach.

Think Critically
1. What should the Neals attempt to recover as damages in this action?
2. Should the Neals be allowed to recover by the court? Why or why not?

UNIT 3

The Law of Sales

CHAPTERS

CHAPTER 13

The Uniform Commercial Code

GOALS

- Recognize the benefits of having uniform state laws governing commercial activity
- Understand how the law of contracts differs from the law of sales
- Know the specific terms associated with the law of sales

Origin and Significance of the Uniform Commercial Code (UCC)

If you're doing business with individuals in another state, it is important to know just how likely you are to receive what you bargained for. If the risk is great because of political or economic instability or underhanded dealings, you increase your bargaining demands to compensate for that risk. Doing so reduces your economic activity and, therefore, impairs the well-being of all concerned. To correct this situation, a drive to standardize commercial laws has been underway in these "united" states since the late 19th century.

Since its founding in 1892, the National Conference of Commissioners on Uniform State Laws (National Conference) has turned out nearly 200 uniform acts. These "acts" lack the force of law until they have been adopted by the states that decide to accept them. Each uniform act includes the best part(s) of existing state laws on a particular subject. The resulting act is then referred to state governments for consideration and possible adoption.

This approach reflects the application of a school of jurisprudence (remember from Chapter 1 that *jurisprudence* is synonymous with *legal philosophy*) called **legal realism**. This school holds that the law should reflect the most desirable real-life practices in a particular area. Judging from the economic success of our nation, brought about in part by the adoption of the National Conference's uniform and predictable laws in most states, this idea seems to have worked.

Origin of the Uniform Commercial Code

In the early 1940s, the National Conference took on its most ambitious assignment: the creation of a uniform code of laws covering most commercial areas. It enlisted the help of the American Law Institute, whose membership comprised hundreds of the country's leading judges, lawyers, and law professors. A decade later, the first edition of the **Uniform Commercial Code (UCC)** appeared. It has since been adopted in whole or in substantial part by nearly all the states, and significant portions were updated as the need arose.

Current Significance of the UCC

In the remaining chapters of this book, we lean heavily on the UCC as our source for the most likely form of the law in the legal areas it covers. As the UCC is statutory, it supersedes conflicting common law holdings in these areas. Figure 13-1 shows what areas the UCC covers and where in this book they are discussed.

Just reading the list of articles in Figure 13-1 gives you some idea of how much business law you can learn from the UCC. The UCC facilitates the operations of businesses. It was drafted to keep businesspeople out of court, not to lay roadblocks requiring detours that lead to litigation. As you can tell from Figure 13-1 on page 168, Article 2 of the UCC pertains to sales. This is probably the most important area covered by the UCC.

Relationship between the Law of Sales and the Law of Contracts

This relationship is relatively simple. The law of contracts applies to any and all contracts made within our society. The law of sales, on the other hand, is tailored to businesses.

Contract law may cover agreements relating to transfers of merchandise, land, buildings, services, and other things tangible and intangible. The law of sales deals only with transfers of rights in and to "goods"—a term referring to a relatively narrow class of items that we will define in a moment.

Also, the UCC's law of sales often requires knowledge beyond that required of the layperson by the law of contracts. You will quickly see that Article 2 both recognizes and demands the possession of more knowledge by a certain class of businessperson. (Note, however, that this article also provides standards for non-businesspersons involved in sales.) In return for its demands, it gives such businesspersons the ability to cut corners in ways not possible under contract law.

UCC Articles and Coverage	Topic Area	Covered in Chapter(s)
Article 1: General Provisions—Definitions and general guidelines on how to apply the act.		13–16
Article 2: Sales—Laws that cover transactions in goods as well as the laws on contracting, performance, and remedies.	Sales of Goods	13–16
Article 2A: Leases—Laws that cover the leasing of goods.	Property Law	30
Article 3: Commercial Paper—Laws that cover the use of checks, notes, drafts, and similar instruments.	Commercial Paper	17–20
Article 4 and 4A: Bank Deposits, Collections, and Transfers	Financial Institutions	17–20
Article 5: Letters of Credit—Laws that cover conditional commitments by banks to honor instruments drawn on them.	Commercial Paper	17–20
Article 6: Bulk Transfers—Laws that govern the sale of major parts of the transferor's materials, supplies, and merchandise.	Sales of Goods	14
Article 7: Documents of Title—Laws that control the use of instruments that signify ownership of goods.	Sales of Goods	15
Article 8: Investment Securities—Laws that help govern the issuance of stocks and other securities.	Security Regulation	24–27
Article 9: Secured Transactions—Laws that govern the interests lenders and sellers may have in the property of others.	Debtor/Creditor Relationships	21–23

FIGURE 13-1   Summary of the Uniform Commercial Code (UCC)

So, really, after having provided a great deal of background in this book, we are just now embarking on the study of true business law. We begin, as noted, with Article 2 of the UCC. The knowledge it imparts is specialized, challenging, and, like all knowledge, either gives you an advantage in your dealings or comes back to haunt you if you fail to acquire it.

Crucial Terms in Applying the Law of Sales

Goods

As mentioned above, Article 2 of the UCC, the law of sales, governs the transfer of rights in and to goods. **Goods** are defined as things that are movable at the time they are identified as the subject matter of the sales agreement. This definition is given in section 105 of Article 2, which is expressed as "2-105" in the common notation used to identify UCC sections. Note that section 2-105 specifically excludes money and investment securities, which are covered in Article 8 of the UCC. Excluded by implication from the definition are things not traditionally considered "movable" in the eyes of the law, particularly real property.

Real property is defined as land, buildings, and items permanently attached to land and buildings. Note that the transfer of ownership rights in real property is covered by areas of the law that have been established for longer than the UCC. (Real property will be discussed in detail in Chapter 30.) Put another way, Article 2 generally focuses on things other than real property.

This brings us to the subject of personal property. **Personal property** is best defined as all things that are not real property, such as clothes, cars, books, and so on. The law of sales found in Article 2 thus applies to the transfer of ownership of most tangible, movable personal property. (Some personal property is intangible—contract rights, for example. Again see Chapter 30 for a fuller explanation.)

Of course, none of these terms from property law mesh exactly with the UCC. This is because the UCC is based on current business experience, which is constantly changing. The time-tested but relatively inflexible rules of property law, on the other hand, reflect centuries of development. They embody the conflict between the historical school and the legal realism school of jurisprudence.

Sale and Contract to Sell

Another vital term is sale. In UCC 2-106(1), a **sale** is defined as the passing of title to goods from a seller to a buyer for a price. Two terms in this definition—price and title—require explanation. The **price**, as you might suspect from contract law, is defined as the consideration required to be transferred in exchange for the goods. This price can be in money, other goods, or services.

The other term, **title**, requires an explanation grounded in the area of property law. Simply put, property as we know it comprises many rights. For example, you may have the property rights of possession and use of this textbook, but some other party may really "own" it. In other words, that party may have the formal ultimate legal right to the textbook's ownership. This is the property right that the law refers to as title.

 # Hypothetical Case

> Horton rented his specially constructed buses to rock groups on tour. Such a group would have possession and unrestricted use of a bus during the tour and then would have to return it. One group, Wild Irish Rose, liked its bus so much that, a month after its tour ended, it made an offer to purchase the wheeled home. Horton finally accepted a price of $250,000 and transferred title to the group. However, Wild Irish Rose would have to wait until the bus was returned by the group currently using it before they could take possession and use it.

The point of all this is that the seller may not have possession and use of goods at the time their sale takes place. In addition, the law of sales in Article 2 is applicable even if the goods are not in existence or identified in the contract at the time of the contracting. The law refers to such goods as **future goods**. An agreement involving future goods is known as a **contract to sell**. Note that even though Article 2 governs the transaction, according to UCC 2-105(2), no interest in goods can pass until they are both in existence and identified in the contract. As a consequence, the distinctions between goods and future goods and sale and contract to sell become important when questions of performance or risk of loss are raised by the parties to the contract. More about that later.

Finally, it is important to realize what a "sale" under Article 2 is not. It is not a gift, providing services (e.g., automobile repair or restaurant tablewaiting), a transfer of only possession for money (e.g., a rental or lease; see Chapter 30), or a process in which a creditor is given rights in goods to secure payment of the obligation (e.g., a security interest—a very important tool for sellers and creditors; see Chapter 21).

Merchant

The more you understand the definitions of goods and sale, the clearer the pervasive coverage of Article 2 is. Given the fact that most of you studying this material either have a career in business or are planning one, another term of considerable importance is "merchant." Under the law of sales, a person classified as a merchant is held to a higher standard than the layperson. The definition is more detailed than most, so read it carefully.

A **merchant** regularly deals in the goods involved in the transaction at hand. The term also covers someone who, by occupation, has knowledge or skills peculiar to the practices or goods involved in the transaction or to whom such knowledge or skill may be attributed by his employment of an agent or broker or other intermediary. The agent or intermediary, of course, also has such knowledge or skills.

This definition may be complicated, but it also is very important. (Sometimes it seems that the same person who writes assembly instructions for children's toys was hired by the Uniform Law Conference to formulate the UCC definitions.) So let me paraphrase and clarify it. People who regularly buy and sell the goods in question are considered merchants by the UCC. Also considered merchants are two other types of people: (1) those who make a living by selling their expertise in the goods involved in the transaction and (2) those who hire individuals with that expertise.

Good Faith

We've just noted that under the UCC merchants are held to higher requirements than laypeople. Now let's see what that means in terms of good faith, the one unalterable standard that affects the interpretation of every UCC contract. **Good faith** is defined as honesty in fact by UCC 1-201(19). For merchants however, it carries a further meaning (or requirement) added by UCC 2-103(1)(b). That UCC section demands of merchants not only honest behavior, but also the observance of reasonable commercial standards of fair dealing in the trade.

⚖️ Hypothetical Case

Barney Stallings stood in the kitchen and stared out the screen door at the dark clouds on the southwest horizon. Just after he had cut and baled the hay on his north 40 acres, Barney had contracted with a regional stockyard. The stockyard people agreed to buy the hay at $2.40 a bale and had promised to pick it up from the field within seven days of the contracting. Of course, every farmer knew that the contract was void if it rained on the hay before they could get to it. This was because of the possibility of spontaneous combustion and spoilage when wet hay was put in storage. The stockyard people knew that too, and Barney suspected that they'd been watching the weather forecasts just as he had. The price of hay had fallen by a quarter a bale right after the contract was made, so maybe they had decided to play it cute by letting it rain on his bales and then buying cheaper from someone else. They still had two days to pick up the hay before the week was up, so they could wait if they wanted to, couldn't they? Suddenly the rain began. Barney groaned. Then he turned away from the screen door and placed a call to an attorney he knew in town.

Barney's attorney should have some good news for him. Even though the stockyard people may have been within the bounds of good faith in waiting to pick up the bales until near the end of the seven days, as merchants they are held to a higher standard. If they indeed postponed picking up the hay so as to get a better deal elsewhere, they are in violation of the UCC's requirement of reasonable fair dealing in the trade. In short, they should have picked up the hay because of the possibility of rain. Under these circumstances, Barney should be able to recover damages from the stockyard.

CHAPTER REVIEW

USE LEGAL TERMS

Fill in the blanks with the appropriate term.

contract to sell	personal property
future goods	price
good faith	real property
goods	sale
legal realism	title
merchant	Uniform Commercial Code (UCC)

1. The formal legal designation of ownership of goods is ___?___.
2. An apartment building is classified as ___?___.
3. A wristwatch is classified as ___?___. If the same wristwatch were the subject matter of a sales contract, it would be classified as ___?___.
4. Jonathan wanted to buy a horse for his wife. He knew little about evaluating horses, so he hired Jack P. Allance, a horse trader and ex-cattle drive boss, to pick one out. In relation to this transaction, Jonathan is considered a(n) ___?___.
5. The consideration paid for goods in a transaction is termed the ___?___.
6. If I contract to buy the first 500 television sets you manufacture next month, the sets are ___?___. The contract is a(n) ___?___.

TEST YOUR READING

7. Why have uniform state laws governing commercial activity?
8. When the National Conference issues them, do the uniform acts have the force of law? Why or why not?
9. What organization assisted the National Conference in drawing up the UCC? Why is this organization so significant?
10. What is the difference between the law of contracts and the law of sales?
11. What article of the UCC is devoted to sales?
12. Are items of real property generally considered goods?
13. What are future goods?
14. What is required, other than good faith, from a merchant in a sales transaction?

THINK CRITICALLY ABOUT EVIDENCE

15. Which article of the UCC covers each of the following transactions?
    a. You sign a contract to purchase your new car, a Fordolet Thunderchicken.
    b. You sign a note to finance the purchase of the car.
    c. You write a check for the down payment on the car.
    d. The car dealership deposits your check in its bank, which then collects the funds to pay the check from your bank.
    e. The dealership makes so much money on your purchase that it decides to sell more stock to finance its expansion.
    f. The dealership contracts with Fordolet to buy 100 Thunderchickens.
    g. The bank receives rights from the dealership to take control over the Thunderchickens in the dealership's stock if the dealership's debts are not paid off properly.

16. Consider each of the following disputes, and determine whether it could be resolved by contract law or by the law of sales in Article 2 of the UCC.
    a. John Holland will not turn over the title to seven acres as required by a contract for sale of the land.
    b. Jean Holland, John's wife, sues her employer for overtime that she says her employment contract allows.
    c. Joe Holland, John's brother, sues John concerning the delivery terms in a contract by which Joe bought 100 bags of concrete from John.
    d. Jerri Holland, John's aunt, sues the department store from which she bought a $250 bottle of Confusion perfume, on the grounds that it did not throw her intended mate into a state of ecstasy, as advertised.
    e. Jim Tunnel, the Holland family lawyer (known to them as the Holland Tunnel), brings suit against each member of the Holland family mentioned above for nonpayment of attorney's fees.
    f. The Fordolet Corporation sends the Thunderchickens mentioned in problem 15 to the dealership by rail and sends the dealership separately a document showing that it has title to the cars in the shipment.
    g. A few months later, the dealership, unable to find enough customers to buy its remaining Thunderchickens, has to sell off its assets, equipment, and inventory.

17. Amy Irvine holds a garage sale each weekend. Would she be considered a merchant under the UCC?

REAL-WORLD CASE

Liberty Financial Management Corp. v.
Beneficial Data Processing Corp.

670 S.W.2D 40

Finally, consider how the characterization of a contract as a sale of goods (or not) made a million dollar difference to two feuding companies.

Liberty Financial Management Corporation (Liberty) contracted with Beneficial Data Processing Corporation (Beneficial) for online computer data services for Liberty's many accounts. Dial, a company with which Liberty had grown disenchanted, had previously provided it with similar services. To provide these services to Liberty, Beneficial had to transfer to its own system thousands of accounts and records from data tapes it obtained from Dial. In the transfer, Beneficial allegedly negligently lost some 5,000 account records and duplicated 20,000 others. The loss to Liberty was enormous, and it brought suit.

In the contract between Liberty and Beneficial was a clause limiting the liability of Beneficial for negligence to out-of-pocket expenses but not lost business. Citing public policy considerations embedded in the UCC, the trial court threw out the limited liability clause and awarded Liberty nearly $2 million, mainly for lost business.

Beneficial appealed on the grounds that because it was providing a service, not selling goods, the law of contracts applied, not the UCC, and the limitation on liability should be enforced.

Think Critically

1. What good or service is being transferred?
2. Does the transaction fall under the UCC or not?
3. Who ultimately wins as a consequence of your decision in question 2? Why or why not?

CHAPTER 14

Requirements of a Valid Sales Contract

GOALS

- ◆ Understand the wisdom of the general approach of the UCC to sales
- ◆ Know how the UCC changed contract law to apply it to the area of sales
- ◆ Be aware of the special UCC rules that apply to bulk transfers and auctions

Proper Form for Sales Contracts

Approach of the UCC

Frankly, UCC standards for determining whether a contract exists are quite relaxed. Any conduct showing that the parties have reached an agreement binds them unless the statute of frauds requires a written contract. In other words, the basic thrust of the UCC is to support as legally binding any oral contract, any written contract, and any contract implied from the actions of the parties. Thus, under the UCC, many elements of a contract can be omitted without dooming it.

To keep the basic contractual intent intact, at various times the UCC rules will fill in price, subject matter, date of execution, and other items, the omission of which would easily render a contract unenforceable under the common law of contracts. Preserving bargains is the watchword of the sales portion of the UCC. It goes to seemingly extraordinary limits to do this. Compared with the more ordinary contracts we discussed in Unit 2, it is much easier to get into and much harder to get out of sales contracts. Do not forget that.

Impact of the Statute of Frauds

As far as the statute of frauds is concerned, UCC 2-201(1) states formally what we have already discussed in Chapter 11:

> (1) Except as otherwise provided in this section, a contract for the sale of goods for the price of $500 or more is not enforceable by way of action or defense unless there is some writing sufficient to indicate that a contract for sale has been made between the parties and signed by the party against whom enforcement is sought or by his authorized agent or broker. A writing is not insufficient because it omits or incorrectly states a term agreed upon but the contract is not enforceable under this paragraph beyond the quantity of goods shown in such writing.

Hypothetical Case

Jennifer Robinson owned the Fender-Bender Repair Shop, which specialized in fixing and selling top-of-the-line guitars. When one of her best-selling manufacturers came out with a new line, Jennifer immediately ordered by phone 20 of each of the manufacturer's four new models from her wholesaler. During the phone conversation, the wholesaler's salesclerk advised her that the bill would be over $52,000. Seven weeks passed, and Jennifer's customers asked time and again when she would be getting the new line. Finally, a competing store obtained the guitars and Jennifer began losing sales. She contacted the manufacturer and was told that she could buy such a large order direct from it at a considerable savings. She then placed an order with the manufacturer. The very next day the guitar shipment arrived from her wholesaler. She refused it. When the wholesaler sued, Jennifer claimed that there was no writing to clarify what was agreed on and to prevent fraud. Because the wholesaler could not satisfy the requirements of the statute of frauds, the court dismissed the case.

As noted earlier, $500 is the limit for oral contracts. Section 2-201 makes that plain. The last part of the section also states clearly that mistakes or omissions of terms do not signify the death of a contract. We'll discuss shortly what the UCC does in that event. However, we must now take a look at the exceptions to the UCC requirement for a writing. Section 2-201(1) alludes to them at the start. See Figure 14-1 for a listing of these exceptions.

FIGURE 14-1   Exceptions to the Statute of Frauds Requirement for a Writing

- Admissions to the contract have been made in court.
- The goods have been specially manufactured.
- The goods have been accepted.
- Written confirmation of an oral agreement between merchants meets with no objection from its recipient.

Exceptions to the Statute of Frauds

Three of these exceptions are applicable to everyone. The last exception applies only to merchants and is part of the specialized knowledge that merchants need to come out ahead in the game of buying low and selling high.

However, the first three exceptions get top billing. They deal with (1) court admissions, (2) specially manufactured goods, and (3) the effects of payment, receipt, and acceptance.

Court Admissions   If the person against whom enforcement is sought admits in court pleadings, testimony, or otherwise that a contract for sale was made, the statute of frauds barrier is lifted. Note however, that the contract is good only for quantities up to the amount admitted to by the party making the pleading, giving the testimony, and so on. In the case of the Fender-Bender Repair Shop, for example, if, in answering the wholesaler's complaint, Jennifer's side admitted that the contract existed, the UCC's requirements would have been satisfied.

Specially Manufactured Goods

 # Hypothetical Case

Yi-Ling stared at the black cookie, broke it in her hands, and pulled out the slip of paper concealed inside. "You will not leave the restaurant alive," it read. She shook her head and tore it into tiny pieces. It would have been far better if she had never heard of "misfortune cookies." Kuo Ming, who had come up with this idea, had intended to use such cookies as a joke for his new restaurant. He had ordered thousands, over $4,200 worth, from Yi-Ling's Chinese Bakery. Then the bank had cut off his financing. Yi-Ling opened another cookie. Its slip said, "You will meet three tall, dark, and handsome IRS agents." Then another: "You don't look a day over 70." Now Kuo was refusing to pay for the cookies. Yi-Ling had not made him sign a written contract, although a number of people could testify to their oral discussions. No one in his or her right mind would buy the cookies. Without a written contract, Yi-Ling felt, there was no way she could win a lawsuit. Is she correct?

As you might suspect, the answer to the above question is "no." Yi-Ling could win a lawsuit even without a writing signed by Kuo Ming, the party against whom enforcement is sought. The UCC makes an exception to its requirement of a writing in the case of specially manufactured goods. As long as those goods are not suitable for resale to others in the ordinary course of business and the seller has made a "substantial beginning of their manufacture or commitments for their procurement," the contract is enforceable without a writing.

Accepted Goods   A third exception to the requirement for a writing is made for goods that have been either paid for and accepted or received and accepted. **Acceptance** occurs when the buyer, after a reasonable opportunity to inspect the goods, signifies to the seller that the goods are fine, performs an act inconsistent with the seller's continued ownership, or simply fails to reject the goods.

Transactions between Merchants   As mentioned earlier, the three previous exceptions apply to all parties. A special exception however, deals specifically with transactions between merchants. Remember the definition: merchants deal regularly in the goods involved, hold out their expertise in the goods for hire, or hire someone with such expertise.

Assume that, as often happens, two merchants come to an oral agreement that is then confirmed in writing by one or the other of them. Unless the recipient of the written confirmation objects to the terms stated in it within 10 days, the written confirmation allows enforcement of the oral contract. In the hypothetical situations described above, Jennifer Robinson's wholesaler and Yi-Ling would have saved a great deal if they had sent such a confirmation and it was not objected to within 10 days after receipt.

Requirements of the Writing under the UCC

As mentioned, the UCC's bottom line requirements for a writing to satisfy the statute of frauds are minimal. A writing does the job if it contains some reference to a contract for the sale of goods, specifies the quantity, and is signed by the person against whom enforcement will be sought. Realize however, that the ability of a party to get past the hurdle of the statute does not necessarily mean that the party will win the case. However, without a writing or the use of one of the exceptions, the case will not be heard.

The UCC, the Law of Contracts, and Sales Situations

As mentioned earlier, the purpose of the UCC is to streamline the process of making binding contracts. The UCC simplifies the law of contracts, especially in the areas of offers, acceptances, and performance. For some, this benefits all concerned because it encourages more contracting, more exchanges of goods, and more business activity. To these UCC supporters, more business activity means progress and a better standard of living for all concerned. To others, of course, the UCC means more resources converted or destroyed, more pollution, and more uncontrolled growth. Regardless, one thing is for certain; the UCC rules have curtailed the diversion of a great deal of funds into litigation. Here's how:

Offers Under the UCC

A lot of things can go wrong when an offer is made. Terms crucial to the bargain may be omitted. Other terms may still be under discussion when the bargain is made or, if agreed to, may conflict with pre-existing terms. In addition, these potential problems may be affected by the fact that the parties are merchants or parties who deal with one another regularly. As such, they may have ongoing understandings from previous dealings, or they may be subject to rules that others in the trade adhere to. The UCC is equipped to handle all these situations.

Absent Terms   One of the most important terms that can be omitted from a contract is the *price*. Under the law of contracts, no contract results if the price is not specified. Under the UCC however, an **open price term** does not eliminate the reality of a contract (UCC 2-305). The court holds that a contract exists whenever it is the intent of the parties, regardless of whether they've agreed on a price. The parties are then given time to agree to that term. If they cannot agree, the court sets the price at a reasonable amount determined as of the time of delivery.

 ## Hypothetical Case

Wayne C. Barnum knew a good thing. The 74 merry-go-round horses were extravagantly designed and painted. They were exactly what he needed to get his new amusement park off the ground. Smiling, Wayne approached Jim Bailey, the craftsman who made them, with an offer. Bailey counter-offered. Barnum said, "Look, we've got a deal here. I need to get my employees on the job setting up the Merry-Go-Round. So let me get busy on that. We'll agree to the price later." Bailey agreed. A court enforcing the UCC would give them time to work out a price. If they could not, the court would have the trier-of-fact determine what a reasonable price for the horses was at the time Barnum's employees took delivery of them.

Where the exact *quantity of the subject matter* purchased is omitted in favor of such statements as "all of the item we need" or "all of the item we can produce," the UCC enforces the contract. We have already discussed such requirements and output contracts. The law of contracts did not support them until the UCC's standards of good faith and performing to reasonable expectations proved workable in these areas. The courts, through these standards, may also infer terms of payment and place of delivery.

The UCC's course of dealings and trade usage rules are additional sources of aid to courts trying to keep alive a sales contract with missing terms. **Course of dealings** refers to the understandings that the parties to the contract have developed in their previous transactions. **Trade usage** is a pattern of dealing established in the area of commerce in question that the parties to the contract can be expected to adhere to. Finally, the course of dealings of the parties to the contract at hand and what they did and did not do this particular time may also be referred to for guidance. All these sources can be drawn on to fill in terms absent from the contract. However, when the actual terms of the contract conflict with or rule out the use of either course of dealings or trade usage, the contract's terms prevail.

Hypothetical Case

The Baldknobber's Noose, a tourist-oriented store in Branson, Missouri, sold concrete lawn furnishings. Normally, the Noose placed an order for 25 concrete miniature outhouses from its supplier in midseason and the supplier accepted the order and delivered the outhouses to the Noose's front door. This time, however, because he was being extremely busy transporting a large order to a national park in the Southwest, the supplier did not deliver them. Orville Waxworm, owner of the Noose, called the supplier when the outhouses were not delivered. When told that he would have to bear the cost of having a truck line transport them, Orville did so under protest and then sued the supplier for the extra expense. Will Orville recover?

As you might suspect from our discussion, the court handling the "Noose" suit held that the course of dealings between the two merchants indicates that the supplier was to deliver the outhouses and was responsible for the costs of so doing.

Firm Offers   For offers, as for other areas, merchants must adhere to a higher standard than that required of non-merchants. In particular, no consideration is required to hold a merchant to a promise to keep an offer for the sale of goods open for a certain time. This is true as long as the offer is made in writing, is signed by the merchant, and is not to be effective for more than three months. Such an offer is referred to as a firm offer under the law of sales (UCC 2-205). Under the law of contracts, we knew it as an option. Other than under the law of sales, such an option has to be supported by consideration to be legally enforceable. Put differently, any offeror other than a merchant under the law of sales has to be paid something of value to keep an offer open. Otherwise, the offeror can withdraw the offer at any time even before the promised period has run.

Hypothetical Case

Jeremy Bean placed a newspaper ad to sell his old bike for $50. His first call came from Mike Terratola, who offered Jeremy $40. Jeremy counter-offered with $45. Mike said he'd have to come over and take a look at the bike before he'd go any higher. Jeremy replied that he'd keep the $45 offer open for 24 hours. By the time Mike showed up two hours later, Jeremy had sold the bike for $55.

Even though a sale of goods was in question, Jeremy was able to do this because he was not a merchant and had not made a firm offer. Had Jeremy been a merchant and had he put the offer to sell at $45 anytime before the next morning in writing and signed it, the offer would be binding against him.

Acceptances under the UCC

The UCC has made three important changes with regard to acceptances. The first change involves the mode of acceptance; the second involves additional terms in the acceptance; and the third involves the more specialized case of prompt shipment.

Mode of Acceptance   Under the law of contracts, if the offeror as a part of the offer requires a particular mode of acceptance, such as phone, letter, telegram, or fax, that mode must be followed to produce a contract. Also under the law of contracts, if no particular mode is required, the acceptance is effective if it is sent in the same mode as that used by the offeror to make the offer. For example, contracts result at the moment that, in response to a mailed offer, offerees drop their acceptance in the mail. If a different mode is used, if a fax is sent in response to a mailed offer, for example, the acceptance is effective only when the offeror receives it. Got all those rules? There are more, but . . .

The UCC simplifies all that. UCC 2-206 states that "unless unambiguously indicated by the language or circumstances," the offeree is allowed to accept in any reasonable manner or by any reasonable medium. Such an acceptance is effective when sent. End of discussion.

Additional Terms in the Acceptance   In the same vein as its rules relating to mode of acceptance, the law of contracts dooms any would-be acceptance that contains additional terms. Successful acceptances are required to be absolute and unconditional. Again, this is not so under the UCC.

According to UCC 2-207, which deals with additional terms in the acceptance, a sales contract is formed even if the "definite and seasonal expression of acceptance . . . sent within a reasonable time" includes some different terms. These additional or altered terms are treated as proposals that are added to the contract if and when non-merchant parties agree to them. Merchant parties however, have to be more alert. Why? Because for merchants, if the new terms are not **material** (essential), they become part of the contract unless the recipient gives some notification of objection to them within a reasonable time. However, if the offeror expressly limited acceptance to the terms of the offer, no additional or altered terms are enforced. If the terms are material, they cannot become a part of the contract without the actual assent of the offeror.

Hypothetical Case

Murphy Anderson ran Chips 'n' Dips, an electronic goods store. Late one fall, she mailed the following order to her wholesaler: "Send me 250 computer chips set to run at 1,000 megahertz at the price shown in your fall catalog. If you don't have that chip at that price, just forget it." The wholesaler faxed back an acceptance of her offer that read as follows, "Will ship 250 chips at Fall Catalog price but set at a slower megahertz unless we hear from you within 10 days. We will ship by UPS second-day air COD with insurance." Murphy did not communicate further with the wholesaler, who then sent the order some 15 days later. When Murphy refused to pay upon delivery, the wholesaler sued for enforcement of the contract and the shipment costs. The wholesaler argued that the additional terms it had proposed in its acceptance had not been rejected within a reasonable time and that Murphy was a merchant, so those terms therefore became part of the contract. The court held for Murphy, stating that she had restricted acceptance to the goods requested in her original offer and that the subject matter in question, namely the type of chip, was a material term. Therefore, UCC 2-207 prevented a contract from coming into existence. Without a contract, the additional terms of the acceptance relating to shipment had no bearing.

Prompt Shipment   The latitude that the UCC rules allow sellers when buyers demand prompt shipment also has a significant impact on acceptances. If Murphy

Anderson had said, "I need these chips yesterday" or had used other words to indicate the necessity of prompt shipment, the wholesaler could have accepted by simply shipping immediately. Doing so brings problems, however. If all is proper, the shipped goods are **conforming goods**, that is, goods specifically fulfilling the seller's obligations under the contract with the buyer. If, however, the goods deviate from the buyer's specifications or are defective in some way, they are labeled **nonconforming goods**. The shipment of nonconforming goods may act both as an acceptance binding the seller to the contract and as a breach of that contract. This is true unless the seller notifies the buyer that such goods are being offered merely as an accommodation.

An **accommodation** is an arrangement or favor to the buyer, done perhaps because the seller who could not fill the order as given wants to stay on the buyer's good side. It is not treated as consideration that binds the buyer to the contract. If the buyer accepts the accommodation of substitute goods, then a contract results only for the purchase of those goods. So, if the wholesaler promptly shipped Murphy Anderson the nonconforming goods without giving notice that the goods were merely an accommodation, the wholesaler would be bound to the contract. If, however, the wholesaler sent notice that the substitute goods were an accommodation, then the wholesaler could not be sued for breach because no contract would be held to exist for the goods originally ordered. If Murphy refused the substitute goods, then no contract would have resulted for either set of goods.

Performance under the UCC

Once the contract has been solidified, the UCC is very plain as to what it expects of the parties. UCC 2-601 states that "if the goods or the tender of delivery fail in any respect to conform to the contract, the buyer may (a) reject the whole; or (b) accept the whole; or (c) accept any commercial unit or units and reject the rest." In short, a **perfect tender** is expected. Should it not be forthcoming, the buyer may use any of the remedies listed above.

Perfect Tender Requirement   We'll discuss these remedies in more detail in Chapter 16. The important point here however, is the absolute nature of the requirement on the seller of the goods. Note that when a contract requires performance to the satisfaction of the buyer, that performance is judged from the perspective of what the buyer's reasonable expectations should be, not what they actually are.

Hypothetical Case

Grandma Jones was a "whittler" in the language of the Ozark Mountains of Missouri. Well known regionally, she turned out statuettes of hillbilly figures. After viewing some of her work, representatives of a large New York City department store contracted with her for several carvings "suitable for our customers." When the whittled figures were delivered, the department store sued because they were not of sufficient detail to meet the standards of its customers. The carvings closely resembled those that Grandma Jones made for her regional trade. The court held that they were acceptable goods under the sales contract, as they should have matched the reasonable expectations of the buyer.

Tender of Delivery   Another hedge on the perfect tender requirement is the seller's opportunity to cure. **Cure** under the UCC means the ability to replace a defective tender with one that is proper under the contract.

UCC 2-508 allows the seller to cure in only two circumstances. If there is still time to perform properly under the contract or if the seller had reasonable grounds to believe that the tender of nonconforming goods (with or without a money allowance for the shortcomings of the tender) would be accepted, the seller can give notice and try again. In the latter situation, even if the time to perform has expired, the UCC allows the seller "a further reasonable time to substitute a conforming tender."

Tender of Payment   Unless otherwise agreed, the tender of conforming goods is contingent on the concurrent requirement for a proper tender of payment. Such payment can be made by any means normally used in business unless the seller demands payment in legal tender (money). If the seller makes this demand, she or he must give the buyer a reasonable time to obtain it. If the seller accepts payment by check, it is conditional on the payment of that instrument by the bank (UCC 2-511).

That about does it for the UCC changes in the standard way of handling things under the law of contracts. However, before concluding our discussion, we need to look at the auction and the bulk transfer, two sales situations given special treatment by the UCC.

Special Rules for Bulk Transfers and Auction Sales

Both bulk transfers and auction sales involve the sale of goods. However, because of their unique problems, special rules apply to them.

Bulk Transfers

Under the UCC, a **bulk transfer** is a trading away of a major part of a commercial enterprise's inventory, supplies, and/or equipment in a transaction that does not occur during the ordinary course of business.

Problems occur when a business tries to undercut the rightful claim of its creditors by such a transfer. The creditors expect the debts owed them by the business to be satisfied at least in part by the value of its inventory, supplies, and equipment. In the past, merchants who saw the end of their businesses nearing all too often sold such assets. They then used the proceeds from the sale in ways (such as payments to investors in the business) that left unpaid creditors with nothing to execute their claims against. Bulk transfers were therefore made the subject of UCC Article 6.

This article puts a special burden on the transferee of the goods involved in a bulk transfer. Certain very specific requirements must be met. If not, creditors of the transferor can demand the return of all the goods involved without compensating the transferee. The requirements are as follows:

1.   The transferee must get a list from the transferor of the latter's creditors, their addresses, and the amounts due each of them.
2.   The transferee and transferor must make out a schedule of the property subject to the transfer so the items can be identified.
3.   The transferee must have the list and the schedule available for inspection for up to six months after the transfer.
4.   The transferee must give the creditors notice of the transfer at least 10 days before paying for the goods or taking possession of them, depending on which occurs first.

Creditors who fail to stop the transfer after the transferee has observed these requirements lose all rights to do so in the future.

Auction Sales

An **auction** is defined as a public sale of property to the highest bidder by someone authorized to conduct the sale (the auctioneer). UCC 2-328 covers this type of sale. It mentions two types of auctions. In the first, an **auction sale with reserve**, the auctioneer is able to withdraw an item at any time before completion of its sale. In the second, an **auction sale without reserve**, the auctioneer cannot withdraw an item after asking for bids.

Note that the description of the items up for sale and the request for bids all fall under the heading of an invitation to negotiate from contract law. The bids are considered offers. As such, they may be withdrawn by the bidder at any time before a contract has been concluded by the auctioneer. The auctioneer usually indicates this conclusion or acceptance by banging down the gavel and saying "sold." The bidder (offeror) can withdraw the offer at any time before this indication has been given. Such a retraction however, does not revive any previous bid.

If the gavel is falling just as a new bid is made, the auctioneer may go ahead with the auction using the new bid or just sell the item under the bid on which the gavel is falling.

Some auctions are rigged by the sellers. They may plant individuals (often called *shills*) in the crowd who bid against innocent, unsuspecting bidders to produce higher prices for the goods on sale. This practice is forbidden by the UCC except in a forced sale, such as a sale of foreclosed property by the sheriff. In a normal sale however, if a shill is utilized, the buyer can avoid the sale or buy the good at the last good faith offer made prior to the completion of the sale. This penalty often produces a significantly lower price for the buyer at the seller's expense.

CHAPTER REVIEW

USE LEGAL TERMS

Fill in the blanks with the appropriate term.

acceptance
accommodation
auction
auction sale with reserve
auction sale without reserve
bulk transfer
conforming goods

course of dealings
cure
material
nonconforming goods
open price term
perfect tender
trade usage

1. Hanson's business was on the ropes. Before his creditors knew what was going on, he sold his inventory and delivery fleet to a competing store for a fraction of its value. He then took the proceeds of the sale and paid himself a high salary. The sale of the goods was a(n) ___?___ .
2. An offer to produce goods that conform exactly to the sales contract is a(n) ___?___ .
3. Omitting the amount of consideration payable for the goods sold is to leave a(n) ___?___ .
4. The pattern of doing business that the parties to the sales contract have established in their previous transactions is termed a(n) ___?___ .
5. A(n) ___?___ term to the contract is essential to its enforceability.
6. A shipment of obviously nonconforming goods to the buyer as an apology for not filling the buyer's order is labeled a(n) ___?___ .
7. The ability to replace a defective tender with one that is proper is referred to as the right to ___?___ .

TEST YOUR READING

8. Why is the approach of the UCC so lenient when it comes to satisfying the statute of frauds?
9. List the four exceptions to the UCC requirement for a writing?
10. What must be in the writing required under the UCC?
11. What will be done by a court under the UCC if a sales contract is missing a price or subject matter term?
12. What is an accommodation?
13. Under the law of sales, must a payment be in money unless otherwise agreed to? Does this differ from the common law of contracts' position on the matter?

14. What is a bulk transfer?

15. What rules must be followed in a bulk transfer?

16. What is the difference between an auction with reserve and an auction without reserve?

THINK CRITICALLY ABOUT EVIDENCE

17. Assume Sports Wholesalers sent a written confirmation that Putting Green received on May 15. Putting Green, a golf pro shop, rejected the confirmation's terms on May 30. Would Putting Green be bound to the confirmation's terms? Why or why not?

18. On May 12, Putting Green orally ordered $1,500 worth of golf gloves from Sports Wholesalers. The gloves came on May 18. Six weeks of the season passed before Putting Green tried to negate the contract by refusing to pay. Putting Green claimed that because there was no writing, it was not obligated. Do you agree? Why or why not?

19. Colling's Hardware Store ordered 500 pounds of 12 and 16 penny nails from its usual supplier. When Colling's checked on the price by phone more than a week before it placed the order, the nails were wholesaling for 18 cents a pound. However, no price was mentioned when the order was placed. When the nails were delivered, a bill for $100 (20 cents a pound) came with them. Colling's refused to pay, saying no contract existed because a price term had not been agreed to. When the case was litigated before the small claims court, the nails were selling at 15 cents a pound. The court found in favor of the supplier, holding that under the UCC, a contract did exist between the two merchants. What price will the court require Colling's to pay for the nails? Why?

20. When Phil's Floral Shoppe ran out of poinsettias for the holidays, it placed an order for prompt shipment of five dozen more with its wholesaler. The wholesaler shipped five dozen Irishsettias, a similar potted plant, with notice that they were an accommodation. Phil's kept the Irishsettias and sold several. After the season however, Phil's sued the wholesaler for a breach of contract for the poinsettias. Will it succeed?

21. Glory Daze, a religious broadcasting station with its own satellite transponder, bought the equipment and tape library of a competing station. The deal, a tremendous bargain, was closed quickly. Two months later Glory Daze received notice that creditors of the competing station were demanding the return of its assets. Under what law could they take this action? Would Glory Daze have to return the assets even if it could not get back the money it paid for them?

REAL-WORLD CASE
Sedmak v. Charlie's Chevrolet, Inc.
622 S.W.2d 694

In July 1977, Dr. Sedmak read in *Vette Vues*, a Corvette fancier's magazine, that the Pace Car, a special edition of the Corvette, would soon be manufactured. He was a collector of Corvettes and wanted one of the 6,000 that were to be placed on sale. In January 1978, Mrs. Sedmak gave Charlie's Chevrolet a $500 check as a deposit on a Pace Car and specified the options that the Sedmaks desired. She was then informed that the purchase price of the car would be around $15,000. In April 1978, the Sedmaks were notified that the Pace Car, equipped as specified, had arrived but because of the increased demand for the car, it would be put up for bids. The Sedmaks did not submit a bid; instead, they filed a suit for specific performance.

The trial court found that the parties had entered into an oral contract. If that contract could be excepted from the application of the statute of frauds, the court would order specific performance as requested. Charlie's would then have to sell the car to the Sedmaks at a reasonable price, which, given the options added, would be around $15,000.

Think Critically

1. Should the oral contract be excepted from the application of the statute of frauds?
2. Assuming that the contract should be so excepted, which one or more of the acceptable grounds would you use to justify the exception?

CHAPTER 15

Ownership of Goods

GOALS

- Understand what is meant by ownership under the UCC
- Know the rules of title transfer, risk of loss, and insurability in sales transactions
- Be able to recognize the special situations affecting application of these rules

Ownership of Goods

When we began our study of sales in Chapter 13, we defined title as the ultimate legal right to ownership of property. The concept of ownership however, encompasses a great many other rights as well. Possession, use, the right to sell or mortgage, and a number of other rights are all bundled together to form our concept of ownership of goods.

It is possible for each of these different rights to be in the hands of a different person simultaneously. For example, I may have possession of my son's car, but allow my wife to drive it while I ride as a passenger. My son is the legal titleholder, true, but he has allowed the bank the right to take the car away from him if he fails to make payments on his car loan. In a sense, all three of us and the bank have property rights in the car, but the predominant right is title.

Valid and Void Title

Whenever goods are purchased, the presumption is that the seller has **valid** (legally enforceable) **title** to them. This is not always the case, however. The seller may be offering stolen goods for sale; in this case, the title that passes to the buyer is termed a **void** (nonexistent) **title**. In short, the buyer receives nothing but possession and use. The true owner retains valid title to the goods and may claim them at any time. This is true no matter how innocent the purchase may have been or how many innocent purchasers and sellers may have transferred the goods previously. The innocent purchaser of stolen goods is left with only the alternative of suing the seller, who, all too often, has disappeared with the money.

Voidable Title

Instead of receiving void title by purchasing stolen goods, a buyer may buy problems by purchasing voidable title. **Voidable title**, like a voidable contract, may be terminated at the option of one of the parties. Until that occurs however, the title is considered valid. Such a faulty title can occur if goods are obtained from minors or others without capacity to contract. In addition title is considered voidable if it is obtained through duress, undue influence, or fraud. The difference in effect between void and voidable title is that the innocent purchaser of a good whose seller has voidable title receives valid title.

 # Hypothetical Case

Stanley Spoke decided to have a garage sale to raise money for his motorcycle group's annual road ride to a biker's get-together in the Midwest. Herb Ignatius, a Boy Scout leader who happened by during the sale, bought a color television set for the Flaming Bison troop's den room and four handheld scanner radios for the upcoming all-troop hike to the headwaters of the Santa Ana River in lower California. Later, the police visited Herb. They informed him that the radios had been stolen from an electronics store in downtown LA and that the color TV set had been purchased by Spoke from a widow for $5 after members of the club threatened to beat her cat. Because Herb was an innocent purchaser, he would have to return the stolen merchandise, as his title to it was void. However, he and the scouts did have valid title to the color TV. Nevertheless, Herb and the troop voted to return it to the widow.

Title to Entrusted Goods

 # Hypothetical Case

Helene Heartburn, noted star of the long-running TV soap opera *Destiny's Fate*, took her new watch in for repairs. The watch was nearly pure gold with diamond-studded settings. Unknown to Helene, the jeweler, Mitch Wastrel, had run up some very serious gambling debts. To cover these debts, Mitch put her watch up for sale, then returned to her a cheap replica. Winna Winsome, an innocent purchaser, bought the real watch for $27,500. A few months later, Helene was showing the replica to another jeweler, who exclaimed that it was a fake. Helene then realized what had happened. In the meantime however, Mitch Wastrel had gone out of business and disappeared. Helene then determined from his business records that Winna had purchased her watch. Can she recover her valuable timepiece from Winna?

Especially since the Great Depression, when confidence in the market system was greatly shaken, giving consumers assurances about what they buy has been a major emphasis of the law. The UCC follows suit in section 2-403(2), which states:

> Any entrusting of possession of goods to a merchant who deals in goods of that kind gives him power to transfer all rights of the entruster to a buyer in the ordinary course of business.

A later subsection states that this holds true regardless of "any condition expressed between the parties" to the entrusting. In short, whenever you turn over your possessions to a merchant, you give that merchant the power to transfer good title to any innocent purchaser of those possessions in the ordinary course of business. Therefore, you should consider the merchant's reputation and many other factors in deciding who to entrust with your valuables. The more important the possession, the more care you should take. As you may suspect, Helene's only recourse is against Mitch. Under the UCC, Winna has acquired good title by virtue of her good faith purchase in the ordinary course of business. The watch cannot be retaken from her by legal action.

Title, Risk of Loss, and Insurable Interest in Sales Transactions

All too often, even when you have complied with all the requirements for forming a valid contract for a sale, something goes wrong. Goods are lost, stolen, damaged, or destroyed before, during, or after transit. Whenever something of that nature occurs, it becomes necessary to determine whether the buyer or the seller must suffer the loss. This risk of loss is often determined by simply finding out who has title because generally, the loss then falls on that title holder. However, there are exceptions to this rule. We discuss these exceptions in the last section of this chapter.

Insurable Interest

Knowing the hazards involved, a wise party to a sales contract may take out insurance to cover a potential loss of the goods. As a consequence, it becomes important to determine who has an insurable interest in them. An **insurable interest** is a property right in goods whose potential loss can be indemnified (protected against).

The seller has such an interest until title passes to the buyer. The buyer obtains an insurable interest as soon as the contact has been made and the goods have been identified to it. **Identified to the contract** means that specific goods are selected as the subject matter of the deal. They may be tagged, marked with the name of the buyer, placed in a certain part of the warehouse or shipping area, wrapped together, gathered from shelves into the buyer's cart, and so on. How the goods are identified is generally immaterial.

Fungible goods are the only exception to this rule. Salt, grain, sugar, oil, and gas are examples of such goods. In essence, a unit of a fungible good is acknowledged by trade usage to be identical with any other unit of the same good. Therefore, identification of a certain amount of fungible goods occurs whenever the bulk from which it will come is indicated. The exact amount of salt or other fungible good for sale does not need to be segregated for that fungible good to be identified to the contract.

The point however is that both the buyer and the seller may have an insurable interest in the goods at the same time during the sales transaction. Typically, this overlap occurs between the time the goods are identified to the contract and the time they are received and accepted by the buyer. During this time, both parties would recover if the goods were to be damaged or lost.

Title and Risk of Loss

Aside from this overlap, title remains the most important determinant of which party (or which party's insurance company) must bear a loss when it occurs. Unless the parties specifically agree otherwise, as soon as the goods are identified, title typically passes to the buyer when the seller delivers those goods in accordance with the contract terms.

There are two categories of delivery terms in sales contracts. The first is the **shipment term**. This category calls for the seller to turn goods over to a carrier for delivery to the buyer. Once this has been done, the seller has no further responsibility for seeing that the goods reach their destination. In a sales contract with a shipment term, title and risk of loss pass to the buyer upon the seller's delivery of the goods to the carrier.

The second category is referred to as a **destination term**. Such a term requires the seller to be responsible for the delivery of the goods to their destination. Title and risk of loss then pass to the buyer when the seller makes a **tender of delivery** (an offer to turn over the goods to the buyer) at that location.

The business world uses shorthand to specify the type of term controlling a particular sales contract. If you read "Free On Board (FOB) place of shipment" in the contract, this indicates that the costs of shipment to the destination are being paid by the buyer. "FOB place of destination" indicates that the costs of shipment to the destination are being borne by the seller. Risk of loss and title then pass as described above. A term with similar effect relating to sea transportation is Free Alongside Ship (FAS), either at the seller's or buyer's dock or port, again with title and risk of loss passing accordingly. If no terms of shipment are specified, the contract is assumed to be a shipment contract.

Other terms that affect delivery include Cash on Delivery (COD) and Cost, Insurance, and Freight (CIF). COD requires the shipper to collect the cost of the goods (and often shipping costs as well) before turning them over to the buyer. CIF (or sometimes just CF if insurance is not included) requires the carrier to collect the cost of the goods, the insurance, and the shipping in one lump sum.

Hypothetical Case

While Missouri Valley tennis champion in the 60 and older category, Jonas Crowson purchased 12 cases of tennis balls from Double Fault, a mail order discount house for tennis supplies in San Andreas, California. As the contract did not cover shipping, Double Fault arranged for the pickup and delivery of the cases by a local trucking firm. When the balls were destroyed in a wreck of the trucking firm's only vehicle, Jonas had to bear the loss because Double Fault's risk ended with the satisfaction of the contract, which was implied to be a shipment contract according to the UCC. However, should it still be solvent, Jonas might recover from the trucking firm.

Exceptional Situations

"Buyer Pick Up" Sales Contracts   When the buyer agrees to pick up the goods rather than have them delivered, special rules apply. The title passes at the time of contracting. If the seller is a merchant however, the risk of loss passes when the buyer actually receives the goods. If the seller is not a merchant, the risk of loss passes to the buyer when the seller makes the goods available for pickup by the buyer.

Hypothetical Case

Stacy Portman had just moved into her first apartment since graduating school, and it was bare. But it wouldn't be long. Smiling, Stacy made a left turn into McClernon's Furniture. It was having its big annual red-tag sale. Half an hour later, she drove out of the McClernon's lot, the proud owner of a new living room set. Rather than pay the shipping charges, Stacy had told McClernon's that before the day was out, she would return with her pickup truck to get the furniture. McClernon's had promised that it would be on the loading dock waiting for her. On her way to get the pickup, Stacy bought a bedroom suite at a yard sale. Regrettably, a sudden rain-, wind-, and hailstorm hit without any warning and destroyed both sets of furniture. Because McClernon's is considered a merchant under the UCC, even though Stacy owned the set as of the time of contracting, the risk of loss stayed with the store because she had not received the goods. Therefore, it must bear the loss. In the case of the bedroom suite however, the seller is not a merchant. Therefore, both title and the risk of loss passed to Stacy; the title passed to her at contracting; the risk of loss passed to her when the goods were tendered by the seller, who said, "Take them with you" (in other words, when the seller made an offer to turn them over to Stacy). Stacy must therefore bear the loss of the bedroom suite.

Documents of Title   Another exception to the general rules for passage of title involves the use of ship's bills, bills of lading, warehouse receipts, and other **documents of title**. These instruments are evidence of the power of the person who possesses them to control the instruments themselves and the goods they cover. In certain sales situations, the purchaser is given a document of title instead of immediate possession. When presented to the appropriate warehouse or carrier, the document of title allows the purchaser to receive the goods. Unless the parties agree otherwise, when a document of title is used in a sales transaction, both the title and the risk of loss are transferred to the buyer upon the delivery of that document.

Hypothetical Case

José purchased 100 video cameras from their manufacturer in Yokohama, Japan. As José wanted the goods delivered to the United States, the manufacturer placed them aboard a merchant ship headed for San Diego, California. The ship's master inventoried them as they came on board. When the ship left port, the manufacturer was issued a ship's bill, a document of title to the video cameras. When the manufacturer received payment for the goods, it signed the ship's bill over to José and sent it to him by Express Mail. When the goods arrived in San Diego, José was able to pick them up by presenting that document of title. He had become the titleholder and was responsible for any loss of the video cameras at the time the document arrived.

Agreements   As has been mentioned, if the parties to the contract specifically agree on the time when title and risk of loss are to be passed, that agreed-to time takes precedence over the UCC rules concerning the matter. This is not the case only when the parties agree that the seller is to retain title even after shipment or delivery to the buyer. In section 2-401, the UCC identifies this arrangement as the retention of a security interest by the seller. A **security interest** is a property right that allows its holder legal recourse against specific property (in this case the goods) if a debt or obligation is not paid off. (Chapter 21 covers security interests in depth.) When such a situation occurs, title passes as if there were no agreement of the parties.

When the Buyer Says No   UCC 2-401(4) covers a ticklish area:

A rejection or other refusal by the buyer to receive or retain the goods, whether or not justified, or a justified revocation of acceptance, revests title to the goods in the seller. Such revesting occurs by operation of law and is not a "sale."

"Justification" in the meaning of 2-401(4) is usually found in defective or nonconforming goods. Of course, revesting title in the seller still leaves the risk of loss undetermined. UCC 2-510 controls that issue. If the rejection occurs because the goods are nonconforming, the risk of loss remains with the seller until cure or acceptance. If a defect is discovered after acceptance and the acceptance is consequently revoked by the buyer, the risk of loss depends on the insurance coverage of the buyer. According to 2-510, the buyer must cover the loss up to the amount of her or his insurance, if any, and the remainder of the loss falls on the seller.

That covers the buyer's justifiable actions. Now presume instead that the buyer breaches the sales contract after the goods are identified to the contract for an unjustifiable reason. In that case, the risk of loss beyond the seller's insurance coverage may be shifted to the buyer for a commercially reasonable time. Let that sink in a moment. That's right. The risk of loss shifts after identification, not after shipment, delivery, or acceptance. Also, if the seller has no insurance coverage, the buyer has the full risk of loss during the period. This makes breaching a sales contract potentially even more damaging should a loss of the goods occur.

"Sale on Approval" and "Sale or Return" Deals

The desire to capture customers often causes suppliers of goods to offer special deals. These deals often pose particular problems for the application of the rules we have just discussed. The two most often encountered deals are sale on approval and sale with the right of return.

Sale on Approval

Hypothetical Case

Angela Coy listened enraptured as the announcer spelled out the terms of the transaction: ". . . and if you do not want to keep the Wonder Carpet Coater, simply return it before the 3-day trial period is up for a full refund . . . just call 1-800-289-7226—that's 1-800-BUY-SCAM—and never have to vacuum your carpet again." Angela punched the 1-800 number into her portable phone without hesitation. A few days later the device came complete with supplies. Angela immediately ran the Carpet Coater over her rugs. Afterward, the pile of the carpet glistened with the newly-applied stain- and dirt-repellent coating. Sure enough, as guaranteed, the carpet did not have to be vacuumed. In fact, the carpet pile had turned as hard and slippery as sheet ice. Consequently, Angela decided to return the device. She informed 1-800-BUY-SCAM of her decision. Unfortunately, as she was driving downtown to ship her purchase back, her car was sideswiped by a large truck and overturned. The Carpet Coater was destroyed. Who had the risk of loss of the Carpet Coater at the time of the accident?

Under **sale on approval** terms, the buyer is allowed to return the goods within a reasonable period even if they conform to the contract. A sale on approval is distinguished from a sale or return, which is discussed next, by the fact that the goods involved are intended primarily for the buyer's use instead of for resale.

In a sale on approval, the title and risk of loss stay with the seller until the buyer accepts the goods. This acceptance may be found in the oral or written statements of the buyer. It may also be indicated by showing extreme carelessness in handling the goods or by keeping them beyond a reasonable time. Acceptance is not found in the trial use of the goods in an expected way. So in Angela's case, her working on her carpet would not show acceptance. Therefore, the risk of loss was still on the seller when the Carpet Coater was destroyed. Also note that as title had not passed to Angela, none of her creditors (should any exist) could satisfy the amounts due them from the value of the Carpet Coater.

Sale or Return

In a **sale or return**, goods sold primarily for resale may be returned even though they conform to the contract. Title and risk of loss pass to the buyer upon acceptance. Therefore, the buyer's creditors can reach the goods after that time. Also, if the goods are destroyed after acceptance, the buyer must still pay for them. The buyer must take reasonable care of the goods in case they are to be returned. Finally, the return is at the buyer's expense and risk.

 ## Technology Insights

High Tech Gadgets and the Law of Sales

After buying a computer-enhanced dump bed for his wife's new truck, an over-the-road driver went back onto the highway. His wife's business required the ability to use such a device if he were not present. The truck was also used for family transportation. Unfortunately the dump bed malfunctioned. the purchasers entered into a dispute with the seller and refused to make further payments on the purchase price. Finally, in apparent violation of a term in the sales contract (making the seller in the sale of consumer goods and any successor in interest subject to any defenses that might be raised against the collection of the sales price), the finance company repossessed the truck. The repossession occurred about 5 A.M. one morning while the husband was on the road. The wife saw the truck being driven from her driveway and, thinking it was being stolen, contacted the sheriff. the repossession was in violation of a contract term that required permission from the buyers before a repossession occurred on their premises. The buyers brought suit against the finance company and recovered $67,000 in actual damages and $250,000 in punitive damages.

Think Critically What argument could be made against the buyers winning this case? What harm did the $67,000 award likely compensate? Why were punitive damages awarded? Do you think $250,000 is enough when the finance company is making tens of millions of dollars a year?

CHAPTER REVIEW

USE LEGAL TERMS

Fill in the blanks with the appropriate term.

destination term   sale on approval   tender of delivery
documents of title   sale or return   valid title
fungible goods   security interest   void title
identified to the contract   shipment term   voidable title
insurable interest

1. Bills of lading, airbills, and warehouse receipts are examples of ___?___ .
2. A legally enforceable claim of ownership to goods is referred to as ___?___ .
3. A(n) ___?___ involves the contractual right to return conforming goods that were purchased for resale.
4. Waldo bought a new car by borrowing money from his credit union. In return for the loan he agreed to make payments of principal and interest to the credit union. He also created in the credit union the right to repossess and sell the car if he failed to keep up with the payments of principal and interest. This right is referred to as a(n) ___?___ .
5. A contract provision calling for the seller to transfer the goods to a shipper for delivery to the buyer is known as a(n) ___?___ .
6. Salt, grain, sugar, and other items with identical units when taken as subject matter to a sales contract are termed ___?___ .

TEST YOUR READING

7. Name the rights that are in the bundle of rights we refer to as ownership.
8. What is the legal effect of voidable title?
9. Why should a merchant be able to transfer valid title to an innocent purchaser of entrusted goods when the purchaser buys them in the ordinary course of business?
10. Generally, when does title pass in a sales transaction?
11. Generally, when does risk of loss generally pass in a sales transaction?
12. When does the buyer acquire the ability to insure the goods in a sales transaction?
13. What do FAS and FOB mean?
14. When does the buyer assume the risk of loss in a sale on approval?
15. Who pays the expenses of returning the goods in a sale or return transaction?

THINK CRITICALLY ABOUT EVIDENCE

16. Marshall Mishappe innocently bought a wristwatch from Deals in Digitals, a watch repair and sales shop. The watch he bought had been mistakenly placed on sale after Annie Analog brought it in for repair. What kind of title did Marshall have to the watch? What claim does Annie Analog have, and against whom?

17. Marshall Mishappe innocently bought a stolen bicycle for $375 from Deals on Two Wheels, a cycle repair and sales shop. What type of title did he acquire to the bike? What legal action was open to him after the original owner reclaimed her property? In what court would he be likely to file his action?

18. Marshall Mishappe and his wife, Missy, ran a religious bookstore called HyMMMs. A church in the Mishappe's community ordered 100 hymnals from them. The hymnals were taken out of the Mishappe's warehouse and stamped with the name of the church. Before they could be shipped however, the church replaced its old pastor. The new pastor called the Mishappes, informed them that the ordered hymnals were blasphemous, and tried to cancel the order. The hymnals were destroyed that very evening, when the Mishappes' store was hit by a bolt of lightening and burned to the ground. The Mishappes did not have insurance. Who bears the cost of the loss of the hymnals?

19. Before the fire, the Mishappes had on display several racks of greeting cards for sale. These cards were transferred to them under a contract with a sale or return feature. When their store burned, the cards were destroyed. Who bore the risk of their loss?

REAL-WORLD CASE

Prewitt v. Numismatic Funding Corp.
745 F.2d 1175

On February 10, 1982, Numismatic Funding Corporation mailed Frederick Prewitt, a commodities broker in St. Louis, Missouri, gold and silver coins valued at more than $60,000. The corporation sold rare and collector coins by mail throughout the United States. It had dealt with Prewitt on two previous occasions. The terms were stated in literature enclosed with the coins: "Everything is available to you on a 14-day approval basis." The invoice stated that title did not pass until the buyer paid the account in full and the buyer had 14 days from the date of receipt in which to settle the account. The literature gave no directions on how to return unwanted coins.

In the words of the court, "Upon receiving the coins, Prewitt instructed his wife to return them via certified mail for the maximum amount of insurance available—$400 for each package (2 packages). She mailed the coins on February 23,

1982, but Numismatic never received them. Thereafter, Prewitt brought this action seeking a declaration of his nonliability for the loss in mailing."

Think Critically

1. Who must bear the $60,000-plus loss for the coins, Prewitt or Numismatic? Why?
2. Numismatic's sales technique was to ask each buyer by phone to agree to consider a number of coins for purchase. Upon the prospective buyer's agreement, Numismatic would then send the coins out on the terms cited above. Prewitt informed the court that he had complained to Numismatic that it often sent out more coins than had been agreed to (unsolicited merchandise). Given your answer to Question 1, would you recommend that Numismatic change its tactics? If so, how? If not, why not?

CHAPTER 16

Breaches of Sales Contracts

GOALS

- ◆ Be able to identify express warranties in a sales transaction
- ◆ Understand implied warranties and when they are in effect
- ◆ Know what action to take when a warranty or a contract has been breached

In the three preceding chapters we have dealt with the law covering sales. Without question, it comprises an area of the law vital to how we live in the U.S. We have seen how a relatively new body of law, the UCC's Article 2, was established to enhance sales transactions. The intent of the UCC is to provide clear, uniform, and current standards by which sales contracts and performances are judged. According to most legal professionals, the effort was successful. However, beyond the sales contract are other legal concerns of extreme importance to successful buying and selling. Among these are warranties, product liabilities, and the remedies for breach of warranties or underlying sales contracts. This chapter is dedicated to these topics.

Warranties in Sales Transactions

A warranty is a guarantee. It is used to describe the product and its quality and performance. Within the context of a sale of goods, a **warranty** is an assurance expressly made by the seller (orally or in writing) or implied against the seller by a court of law.

Express Warranties

To be legally exact, an **express warranty** is an oral or written term or its equivalent in the sales agreement in which the seller makes some statement of assurance about the good being sold. According to UCC section 2-313, an express warranty can be created by a sample, a model, a description, or an "affirmation of fact or promise made by the seller to the buyer," any of which then becomes part of the "basis for the bargain."

Hypothetical Case

Jo Lee demonstrated a working model of his Life-light to a large department store chain. The customer would use enclosed Velcro strips to affix the Life-light to a visible outside portion of a house or apartment. Then, when the customer dialed 911 in an emergency situation, the light would come on and be a beacon to emergency vehicles. The department store chain bought 5,000 Life-lights. When these arrived, it was found that they lacked the computer chip necessary to turn on the light when 911 was dialed. Based on the model, which did contain such a chip, the department store chain brought a successful suit for breach of an express warranty.

The UCC distinguishes between an express warranty and "puffing." **Puffing** is an exaggerated statement of opinion by a salesperson. Such statements as "This is the finest, most reliable car I've ever tried to sell off my lot," are easily recognizable as puffing by most people. Statements of this kind do not become the basis for the bargain and thus, cannot be considered a warranty.

Magnuson-Moss Warranty Act

Important to the area of express warranties is the Magnuson-Moss Warranty Act. Passed by the U.S. Congress in 1975, its purpose was to ensure that consumers were better informed about product warranties. However, this act is strictly limited in its application. In effect, it applies only to voluntarily issued written warranties on consumer products costing more than $15. These **consumer products** are defined as items of tangible personal property used for personal, family, or household purposes.

Whenever a written warranty is given on goods that fall under this act, three requirements must be met. First, the warranty has to be available before the consumer's "buy" decision. Second, the warranty has to be expressed in easily understood language—no "legalese." Finally, the warranty must state whether it is a **full warranty** (the seller's promise to cover the costs of the labor and materials necessary to fix the product) or a **limited warranty** (a written promise extending some of the coverage of a full warranty).

Methods of limiting a full warranty are numerous. The warranty may cover parts and not labor, or *vice versa*. Other limits include covering only the first purchaser within a fixed period; refunding damaged goods only partially, depending on how much of the warranty period has expired; and requiring the owner to transport heavy goods back to the seller or to a repair facility. Regardless, the point is that any written warranty on consumer goods costing over $15 that does not contain all the attributes of a full warranty is treated as a limited warranty.

Hypothetical Case

Tiny's Ice Cream Parlor ordered a new freezer. The freezer came with what the manufacturer labeled a full warranty. However, the warranty limited the warrantor's responsibility to replacing the defective parts. Labor and other costs of repair were the responsibility of the owner. When, barely a month after its delivery, the freezer broke down and $17,000 worth of ice cream melted, Tiny's owner, Tim, sued the warrantor for the costs of both the labor and parts necessary to repair it. Tim insisted that those costs should be covered under the "full warranty" required by the Magnuson-Moss Act. Is he correct?

The answer to the question in the hypothetical case is "no." Magnuson-Moss applies only to consumer products. Warranties on business equipment cover only what is stated by the issuer.

Implied Warranties

Implied warranties, the second basic type of warranties, are guarantees imposed by law that do not have to be expressly stated to be effective. They contrast sharply with the express warranties contained in the statements, samples, or product descriptions given during negotiations between buyers and sellers. Implied warranties are intended to bring about higher standards of conduct in business transactions. There are three such warranties: implied warranties of merchantability, fitness for a particular purpose, and title.

Merchantability   From the standpoint of the purchaser, the most important implied warranty is that of merchantability. This warranty is read by the law into every sale by a merchant (manufacturer, wholesaler, or retailer) of goods of the type sold in the transaction. Nonmerchant sellers are not bound by it. At its heart, the **warranty of merchantability** guarantees that the goods sold are fit for their ordinary intended use. UCC section 2-314 sets the following standards for merchantable goods:

> They must at least be (a) able to pass without objection as goods of the contract description in the trade area involved, (b) fit for the ordinary purpose for which such goods are used, (c) uniform in quality and quantity within each unit, (d) adequately "contained, packaged, and labeled as the agreement may require," (e) in conformance with facts or promises made on the container or labels, and (f) in the case of fungible goods, of reasonable average quality within the description of the goods given.

Given the detail of these requirements, you can easily see why the warranty of merchantability is a favorite of buyers. As is implied, this warranty applies to food and drink as well as other goods.

Hypothetical Case

John sat in his car in the Barnyard Burger parking lot holding his newly purchased triple cheese-burger with reverence. After a moment, he turned to his friend Lissa and said, "I look forward to this moment every day. This burger is made exactly the way I want it. It just doesn't get any better." He took a bite. Soon after he began chewing, a shriek erupted from his lips. A large piece of bone had come between his good teeth and a new partial filling his dentist had put in place earlier that day. Most of the filled tooth was crushed. John found the bone, showed it to Lissa, and headed into the Barnyard Burger. The bone was large enough to violate the warranty of merchantability pertaining to adulterated food. As a consequence, when the dentist told John the next day that the remnant of the tooth would have to be capped, Barnyard Burger had to pay for the procedure plus the pain and suffering and other damages that John incurred.

A stumbling block to many suits based on the implied warranty of merchantability is showing that the goods were nonmerchantable when they were sold. Often the defect does not surface until the product has been in use for an extended period. It therefore can be difficult to prove the problem was not caused by ordinary wear and tear. This is especially true in suits alleging defects in motor vehicle tires, shock absorbers, and muffler and steering systems.

Fitness for a Particular Purpose

Hypothetical Case

When Claude first came up with the idea of glassing-in their porch to produce the hot, humid environment necessary for growing night crawlers, Gladice tried to stop him. Finally, she gave up and called an air-conditioning firm. She told the firm's representative that the system had to keep the house at around 70 degrees on the hottest days, even with the extra heat from the "worm room." Consequently, the firm installed the system it thought best. However, since it started operating three weeks ago, the system could not decrease the temperature of the house below 80 degrees during the heat of the day. Gladice asked the firm to check the system; it was running perfectly. Gladice then thought of the public broadcasting show on consumer law she had watched last night. Several warranties had been mentioned. One of them was an express warranty. Unfortunately, the air-conditioning firm had made no express representations as to how cool the house would be after the system was installed. The warranty of merchantability didn't apply either, because there was no defect in the equipment. Gladice had to admit it was running fine—continually, but fine. So what was left? Gladice shook her head in dismay. Maybe an answer would come to her.

One answer to Gladice's dilemma is found in UCC 2-315, which describes the **warranty of fitness for a particular purpose**. It implicitly guarantees that the goods will fulfill the buyer's expectations as to intended use. This warranty applies to all sellers, not only merchants, who know or should know their buyers' intended uses for the goods. Buyers rely on the sellers' skills and judgment to obtain suitable goods. Note that it is the seller's duty to ask the buyer questions that define the buyer's intended use. The warranty of fitness for a particular purpose fills a void, as Gladice's case has illustrated, where no express warranties are extended and no defects occur in the goods that could otherwise involve the warranty of merchantability.

Title   A **warranty of good title** is another implied warranty effective against any seller, not just merchants. Sellers impliedly give this warranty, expressed in UCC 2-312. It guarantees that the title transferred to the buyer is good and the transfer is rightful. It also provides that the goods will be delivered free from any claims of other parties about whom the seller has knowledge.

Hypothetical Case

Bertram sold Angela a freezer he had recently purchased on credit from Sears. Sears had a claim for the unpaid credit balance that it could bring against the freezer no matter who owned it. When Bertram stopped making payments on the freezer, Sears did exactly that. Angela could and would have to sue Bertram for breach of the implied warranty of good title to cover her loss.

Elimination of the Implied Warranties

A prospective seller might ask, "Is it possible to eliminate all such warranties?" The answer to this question is, as you might suspect, "Yes." The UCC sanctions three main ways to remove warranties:

1. By using the words "as is," "with all faults," or similar language in the contract. Such phrasing cancels all implied warranties except title.

2. By allowing the buyer to examine the goods. Whether the buyer does so or not, any implied warranty that would have covered a defect discoverable through a reasonable inspection is thereby terminated.

3. By using specific disclaimers for the implied warranties of merchantability and fitness for a particular purpose. If such disclaimers are in writing, they must be conspicuous, typically in large and very bold type. In addition, a disclaimer of the implied warranty of merchantability must mention it by name. For example, **"THE SELLER OF THIS TEXTBOOK HEREBY EXCLUDES THE WARRANTIES OF MERCHANTABILITY AND FITNESS FOR A PARTICULAR PURPOSE."**

FIGURE 16-1   The Implied Warranties

- Title
- Fitness for Particular Purpose
- Merchantability

In the area of consumer goods however, the Magnuson-Moss Warranty Act curtails the seller's ability to eliminate warranties by the above means. In other words, if either a full or limited express written warranty is given or if a service contract for the goods is sold within 90 days of their sale, the implied warranties of merchantability and fitness for a particular purpose cannot be disclaimed during the effective period of the warranty. Finally, any clause attempting to eliminate or limit **consequential damages** (indirect but foreseeable at the time of contracting) must be conspicuously noted on the warranty.

Recovering for Breach of Warranty and Product Liability Law

Lawsuit for Breach of the Warranty

The primary remedy available when a warranty is breached is the threat or actual initiation of a lawsuit against the violating party. However, to be eligible to recover for a breach of warranty under the UCC, the injured party must satisfy two requirements, notice and privity.

Requirements for Recovery

Notice   UCC 2-607 provides that a buyer must give the seller **notice** of any breach within a reasonable time after the breach has been or should have been discovered. If this is not done, the buyer is barred from any remedy.

As you may suspect, this failure to give notice within a reasonable time also adversely affects the buyer's chances of recovering for breach of the sales contract itself, not just for breach of warranty. Remedies for breach of the sales contract are discussed in the next section.

Privity   If you reflect a moment, you may realize how much the availability of warranties depends on the interaction between the parties to the sales contract. This mutual relationship between buyer and seller based on the establishment of a bargain between them was known as **privity**. Prior to the UCC, warranties were regarded as extended only to the actual buyer by the seller because only those two were "privy" to the deal. Typically, the seller did not look beyond the original buyer to other potential users of the product, nor did the buyer bargain for warranties for such later users. However, it ultimately became obvious that confining warranties to those in strict privity to the contract left others who might be injured by a defective product without any remedy. Therefore, the UCC abolished the requirement of privity and provided three replacement options that U.S. states could choose from when they enacted the code. In addition, a state could draft its own option, and a few did. The UCC options are summarized as follows:

> *Option A:* Extends express or implied warranties to any natural person who is a member of the buyer's family or household or a guest of the

buyer if it is reasonable to expect that such person will consume, use, or be affected by the goods. Limits recovery to personal injuries.

Option B: Is the same as A but drops the requirement that the natural person be a member of the buyer's family or household or a guest of the buyer.

Option C: Drops the requirement of a natural person and the restriction of recovery to personal injuries.

Most states have adopted Option A, the most restrictive option. Fewer than 10 states have adopted Option B. Only a handful have adopted Option C, the most liberal option. If you live in the U.S., check your state's commercial code, section 2-318, to see which option covers breach of warranty. Note that fewer than five states have retained the original privity requirements.

Once a person is authorized to sue under the UCC for breach of warranty, the question of who can be sued arises. All too often, the retailer who sold the defective product does not have sufficient assets against which to recover. Fortunately, the trend has been to allow suits against the manufacturer of the defective product. This is because usually the manufacturer's massive advertising campaigns engendered demand for the product in the first place.

Product Liability

It is important to remember that, although this chapter emphasizes remedies based on warranty or the sales contract itself, an important alternative exists. That alternative is a product liability action under tort law rather than contract law. This alternative was covered in detail in Chapter 6. Product liability law focuses on the safety of the product rather than on the conduct of the parties involved in its sale. Potential plaintiffs for product liability actions are not limited to the parties described in the UCC options. Individuals without any relationship to the original sales transaction may seek damages for injuries brought about by a defect in a product. Despite this broad applicability of product liability tort law however, warranty law retains great significance within the area of sales.

Remedies for Breach of the Sales Contract

Adequate Assurance of Performance

One of the most important remedies can actually forestall a possible breach of the contract. It is termed an "adequate assurance of performance." Often during the contractual period, the actions of one party can be interpreted as an intent to breach the contract. UCC 2-609 provides a means of clarifying this intent short of having the other party stop performance and go into a breach mode. Under this section, the worried party may suspend performance and demand an **adequate assurance of performance** (action satisfactorily indicating intent to fulfill the contract) from the other party. The demand must be in writing, and the party making it must wait for the assurance for a reasonable time (but not more than 30 days). If this assurance is not provided, the party demanding it may safely treat the contract as repudiated. Under the UCC, a repudiation allows the injured party to suspend his or her own performance and either wait for performance by the repudiating party or choose from the remedies for breach of contract discussed in Figure 16-2.

When there is a breach of contract, which we defined in Chapter 12 as an unexcused failure to perform according to the terms of the agreement, the injured party has the right to a legal remedy. This same right extends to those injured by a repudiation leading to an anticipatory breach of the contract. As Figure 16-2 shows, under the UCC, the potential remedies from which such a party may choose are rather extensive for both the buyer and the seller.

These remedies, broad and thorough as they may seem, are worth nothing without the resolve to right the wrong done within a reasonable time. The UCC recognizes this fact by providing a statute of limitations of four years on breach of contract actions under Article II. Beyond that time, there appears little reason to allow the threat of a potential lawsuit to hang over the heads of the litigants.

FIGURE 16-2   The Legal Remedies Available for Breach of the Sales Contract

Remedies Available to the Seller

- To *cancel the contract.* Upon breach by the buyer, the seller stops all efforts to comply with the terms of the agreement. The seller may also select any of the following remedies if appropriate. (UCC 2-106)

- To *withhold or stop delivery of the goods,* if appropriate (UCC 2-703 and 705).

- To *resell undelivered goods and sue for damages.* This remedy applies whether the goods are in finished or partially finished condition. The seller is not required to invest additional resources to bring the goods into compliance with the order. The unfinished material may be sold as scrap and suit brought for the difference between the price of the scrap and the contract price. Note that good commercial judgment to minimize loss must be used in this procedure. Any good faith purchaser of the goods at such a sale takes them free and clear of the buyer's rights (UCC 2-706).

- To *retain the goods and sue for damages.* The seller may then sue for either the lost profit, which includes incidental damages of stopping delivery of, transporting, caring for, and attempting to resell the goods, etc.; or the shortfall between the contract price and the market price when the breach occurred [UCC 2-703(e)].

- To *sue for the price.* If the goods have been accepted, the seller may initiate an action to recover the sales price (UCC 2-709).

Remedies Available to the Buyer

- To *cancel the contract and sue for money paid.* In addition, the buyer may select from any of the following remedies that are appropriate.

- To *sue for damages.* When the seller fails to deliver the goods, the buyer may bring suit for the difference between the contract price and the market price at the time of the breach. Incidental and consequential damages may also be recovered in such an action (UCC 2-710 and 2-711)

- To *cover.* The buyer exercises the right to **cover** the sale by purchasing similar goods in the marketplace within a reasonable time. Suit for damages for any increase in cost may then be brought as described above [UCC 2-711(a)].

- To *retain improper goods already delivered and seek an adjustment.* If no adjustment is forthcoming, suit may be brought for damages measured as the difference between the value of the goods delivered and the value of the goods contracted for (UCC 2-714).

- To *sue for specific performance.* This remedy is allowed under UCC 2-716 where the goods are unique and money damages will not suffice.

CHAPTER REVIEW

USE LEGAL TERMS

Fill in the blanks with the appropriate term.

adequate assurance of performance	full warranty	warranty
	implied warranty	warranty of fitness for
consequential damages	limited warranty	a particular purpose
consumer products	notice	warranty of good title
cover	privity	warranty of merchantability
express warranty	puffing	

1. Flashy Dan, "The Used Car Man," looked at you straight in the eye and said, "You don't want these drag slicks on this car if you buy it? No problem. I'll put some recaps on. They'll be better than new tires. Frankly, I don't see why they bother making new tires with such bargains as recaps on the market." When Flashy Dan said that, he was probably ___?___ in relation to the capabilities of the recapped tires.
2. The implied warranty that covers adulterated foods is the ___?___.
3. A written warranty that covers the cost of the labor and parts necessary to repair a defective product is a(n) ___?___.
4. You ask a hardware store employee for a nontoxic paint to cover and seal the interior walls of your concrete swimming pool. When she sells the paint to you, you receive an implied warranty with the paint. It is the ___?___.
5. The right to purchase similar goods in the commercial marketplace within a reasonable time of a breach is referred to as the right to ___?___.
6. The mutual relationship between the buyer and seller in a sales contract is referred to as ___?___.

TEST YOUR READING

7. How is puffing different from a warranty?
8. What kind of products does the Magnuson-Moss Act cover?
9. Name the implied warranties.
10. What are the two requirements for bringing a lawsuit for a breach of warranty?
11. What is meant by privity?
12. How does product liability law extend the potential for lawsuits beyond breaches of warranties?
13. What is an assurance of performance?

14. Name three remedies available to the buyer for breach.
15. Name three remedies available to the seller for breach.

THINK CRITICALLY ABOUT EVIDENCE

16. Hiram Stone knew he needed to have his car painted. So, when a car repair shop in town advertised its "Watch Out for the Early Bird" special, he drove to the shop immediately. Under this special, the shop would paint any car for $250 in any of the five paint colors it had overstocked. After looking at five cars in the shop's parking lot, each painted in one of the colors, Hiram selected the "sunburn red." When the shop finished painting his car however, the color looked more like "blush pink" than the red he had picked. After considerable argument, the shop admitted it had thinned the red with some white to make it go further. Hiram felt that the shop had breached its warranty to him and refused to pay. What type of warranty is Hiram referring to?

17. Is the following a full or limited warranty under the Magnuson-Moss Act? Why?

    "This warranty covers any defect or malfunction of the RB-71 unit. Repairs will be made free of charge for labor or materials within a reasonable time after notice of the problem is given, if such notice is provided within ONE YEAR AFTER DATE OF PURCHASE. This warranty applies to anyone who is a member of the purchaser's household. If repairs cannot return the unit to a serviceable condition within one month after notice, a new unit will be provided free of charge."

18. If they are to be eliminated, what implied warranties must be mentioned by name in a written disclaimer?

19. L. A. Botomy prided himself on the condition of his yard and shrubbery. One summer day, just hours before the city's annual "best lawn" contest was to begin, L. A.'s hedge trimmers fell apart. Knowing that he had to act decisively or lose the contest he had won each of the past five years, L. A. picked up his lawn mower and proceeded to trim his shrubs with it. (Believe it or not, this problem is based on an actual case!) As he was about to finish, a stout part of the bush he was working on snapped and was flung back, hitting L. A. in the face. L. A. brought suit for a breach of the warranty of merchantability and on product liability grounds. Review both areas and make the best case for Mr. Botomy that you can. Do you think he recovered?

20. Henpecked Farms, Inc., sold three tons of chicken parts to the Mystery Meat Hot Dog Packers Company. The chicken parts were to be delivered in three one-ton shipments. What pre-breach remedy would you recommend to Henpecked Farms if Mystery Meat's check for the first shipment bounced?

21. If Mystery Meat was thereafter deemed to be in breach of contract, what remedy or remedies would you recommend to Henpecked?

REAL-WORLD CASE
Blevins v. Cushman Motors
551 S.W.2d 602

Maxwell and Blevins teed off on hole 13, then hopped into their golf cart and motored out to Maxwell's ball. Maxwell fired his second shot, then drove the cart toward Blevins' ball. As the cart approached the ball at approximately 5 mph, it entered a shady area of the course, on which a light dew lay. At that point, the cart went into a skid for 10 to 15 feet—"it was like being on ice"—and then tipped over. Maxwell was thrown free. However, Blevins, who failed in his attempt to jump from the cart, was pinned under it when it came to rest.

Blevins brought this suit on product liability grounds based on strict liability in tort, not negligence. He sued for personal injuries. In addition, his wife brought suit for loss of consortium (the fellowship of husband and wife in companionship and sexual relations). Both of them received very substantial awards in the trial court and these awards were upheld before the Missouri Court of Appeals. The case was then appealed to the Missouri Supreme Court.

Among other unsuccessful contentions, Cushman Motors argued that although Missouri courts had used strict liability in tort to decide cases involving a defect in manufacturing, the courts of the state should not use this theory to decide cases involving a defect in design. Instead, the negligence theory should be used in such cases to determine whether the maker of the product was liable. The Missouri Supreme Court replied:

> In Kenner (a precedential case in Missouri on this issue), this court established that an action in strict liability in tort may lie to recover for injuries caused by a product which is unreasonably dangerous as manufactured. It is only logical that in this case we permit an action in strict tort liability to obtain for the recovery of injuries caused by a product which is unreasonably dangerous as designed because, "There is no rational distinction between design and manufacture in this context, since a product may be equally defective and dangerous if its design subjects protected persons to unreasonable risks as if its manufacture does so."

Think Critically

1. According to what the court said, was strict liability in tort to be used to determine this case?

2. Consider the following:

The Elements of Negligence

Act or omission
Duty of due care
Breach of the duty of due care
Actual cause
Proximate cause
Damages

The Elements of a "Strict Tort" Product Liability Action

Injury from intended use
Unreasonably dangerous defect
Manufacturer is the defendant
No alteration before injury

a. Which would you rather try to recover under, negligence or a "strict tort" product liability action?

b. What actual proof requirements would be added in this case if the court chose negligence as the standard instead of strict liability in tort? Would this represent a significant difference to the plaintiff?

UNIT 4

Checks, Notes, Drafts, and Other Negotiable Instruments

CHAPTERS

CHAPTER 17

Nature and Use of Negotiable Instruments

GOALS

◆ Understand the need for negotiable instruments

◆ Know the types of negotiable instruments

◆ Identify risks of dealing with negotiable instruments

What Are Negotiable Instruments?

For our purposes, a **negotiable instrument** is defined simply as an unconditional written promise or order to pay a sum of money. The definition is generic because it needs to encompass checks, promissory notes, and a number of other financial instruments. Article 3 of the UCC provides the laws that govern the use of such instruments.

First, we need to understand why we have "negotiable instruments." The best way to do that is to go back to the 1930s and the Great Depression in the U.S.

Hypothetical Case

Hutton L. ("Nub") Adamson stood in the cold of an early winter day and watched the crowd file in and out of the building. The word that the Farmers and Merchants Bank was about to go bankrupt had spread like wildfire among those who still had money. Fearful they would lose all they had, anxious depositors had lined up before 6 A.M. to withdraw their cash. Nub had no such worries. Instead, he had come on the scene at about 11 A.M., when the line was at its peak. As time went on, about 25 other out-of-work men and women had joined him. Nub checked the City Hall clock. It was past 11:30 A.M. on this Tuesday, the 28th of November, 1932. Most of the people watching with Nub were surely as hungry as he was. Many had families who were also hungry. They stood silently, immobilized by what was happening and by the steady gaze of two mounted police officers. In desperation, they eyed those who were walking out of the bank with cash stuffed in their pockets. For the ex-depositors, the story was always the same. Relief at having retrieved their money was written on each ex-depositor's face as he or she came out through the bank's doors. Then they paused. The expression on their faces changed. They sensed the destitute mass of raggedly clothed people watching them. At the same time, they knew that the cash they were carrying meant food, warmth, and shelter to the watchers. They each then turned and walked resolutely to the bank across the square from the Farmers and Merchants. They deposited their funds in that bank, and left it carrying a new checkbook. They preferred to trust their funds to the machinations of yet another banker rather than risk the desperation of the people on the street.

This "hypothethical case" is based on a true story. It illustrates the classic purpose of negotiable instruments, such as checks, drafts, and notes, over the last several centuries. That purpose is to relieve individuals of the need to carry large sums of gold, silver, or cash by providing them with a safe means of payment in commercial and other exchanges. In fact, the forerunner of the check was called a **bill of exchange**. It was simply a piece of paper on which the owner of precious metals wrote an order requiring that a certain amount of those metals be transferred to the person named in the order. The order was addressed to an individual or a company who made it their business to hold such metals in safekeeping. The individual or company holding the precious metals carried out the order after validating the signature of their owner.

Even though the current system is more sophisticated, a check still fulfills the same function. By this instrument, we order a certain financial institution in which we have deposited our money to "pay to the order of" a particular individual or company to whom we want to transfer cash. The point here is that, although today there's a lot of law and electronic encoding surrounding the use of such instruments as checks, those instruments are still understandable from a commonsense viewpoint. Why? Because their basic use or purpose hasn't changed. So don't be overcome by the terminology we're going to study. It has to be precise because of the great importance of such commercial exchange. Recognize it as necessary for your professional knowledge. Once mastered, this terminology helps you understand what's going on.

Negotiable Instruments and Their Uses

The two basic types of negotiable instruments are drafts and notes. We start our discussion with a very familiar negotiable instrument: a type of draft called the check.

Checks

A check is the most important type of draft. A **check** is defined as an unconditional written directive to a bank to pay deposited funds on demand to the order of an individual named on the instrument or to the **bearer** (a person in possession of a valid instrument that does not specifically identify its owner). Here are some important points to note about this definition:

1.   A check must be drawn on an institution that falls under the definition of a bank in UCC section 4-105. That section defines a *bank* as a person engaged in the business of banking and includes institutions chartered as banks by the U.S. federal and state governments. It also includes savings banks, savings and loan associations, credit unions, and trust companies. Any instrument drawn on other "persons," both natural and artificial, fall into the broader classification of drafts, which are discussed later in this chapter.

2.   "On demand" means the check is to be paid whenever it is physically presented to the bank for payment by the person authorized to do so. Other terms, such as "at sight" or "on presentment," imply the same thing.

3.   The instrument must be unconditional. Such conditions as "Pay to the order of Ajax Construction as soon as it finishes the construction of my home" make instruments that bear those conditions ineligible to be a check.

4.   The instrument must be in writing. The following subsection, "Form of the Check," explains how this requirement applies.

The legal terminology associated with a check is relatively simple. The person who issues the order to pay found in a check (or in any other draft) is termed the

FIGURE 17-1   Check drawn (issued) by Lois Kent ordering a payment to be made out of the funds she has deposited with the First National Bank in a checking account

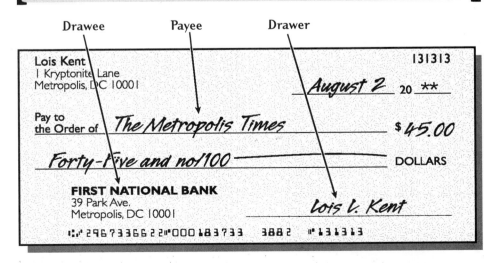

drawer. The drawer in the check shown in Figure 17-1 is Lois L. Kent. The bank that is directed in the check or draft to pay to the order of someone is termed the **drawee**. The drawee ordered by Lois to pay the $45 is the First National Bank of Metropolis. For that order to be effective, Lois must have sufficient funds in the drawee bank. The person named to receive the funds or the power to order them paid to someone else is labeled the **payee**. Again referring to the above example, the *Metropolis Times*, one of the two newspapers serving the city of Metropolis, is named as the payee.

More than one individual may be named as payee on the same instrument. The UCC specifically allows **joint payees**. In this arrangement, the payees' names are separated by the word *and*. "Pay to the Order of Joan and Ted Stanley" is an example of joint payees. Both parties so named must consent before the instrument can be exchanged for value. In other words, both Joan and Ted have to **endorse** (sign the reverse of the instrument) before the instrument can be cashed.

The UCC also allows **alternative payees**, in which case the payees' names are separated by the word *or*. "Pay to the Order of Joan or Ted Stanley" is an example. In the case of alternative payees, the instrument can be cashed if only one of the two payees consents. Typically, consent is shown by the payee's endorsement.

Now here's an important question: Assuming you have a checking account in a bank, are you the debtor or the creditor of the bank in relation to that account?

"Creditor" is the correct answer. You have given the bank your money for safekeeping. They are your debtor. Think about how your creditors treat you when you are dealing with your bank concerning your checking account.

Form of the Check   Today most bank depositors are accustomed to writing checks on uniform, neatly printed, electronically encoded forms provided by banks at their depositors' expense. The uniformity and encoding facilitate the speedy processing of these instruments by financial institutions. However, such uniform checks were not used when checking systems originated and they are not required today. By law, any written instrument that fulfills the definitional requirements of a check is acceptable as such.

Hypothetical Case

Chad Keck turned to Bill Glass, his buddy, for a favor. "Bill, I wrote my last printed check for the groceries back at that convenience store, but I still need some cash. Could you lend me $50?" Bill thought a minute, then replied, "Sure thing. But instead of an IOU, just write me out a check for that amount on this sheet of paper. I'll cash it when I get back to town." Chad frowned. "You can't do that. It's not a check unless it's on the form." Bill smiled. "Tell you what, Chad, make it out for $100. If I can't cash it, you don't owe me a thing. If I can, the $100 is mine." Chad agreed. Figure 17-2 shows how the instrument read. Bill presented the instrument at the People's Bank of Pennsboro the next day. The teller called a supervisor, who, in turn, called the bank's lawyer. After studying the instrument for a short time and comparing Chad Keck's signature on it with the signature the bank had on file, the lawyer told the teller to pay the check.

FIGURE 17-2   Legally Effective Check Written Without a Printed Form

August 8th, 20**

To the People's Bank of Pennsboro,
Pennsboro, Missouri. Please pay to the order of Bill Glass
on demand $100.00 from my checking account.

Chad Keck

Several special types of checks, such as cashier's and certified checks, are discussed in Chapter 20. In this chapter we concentrate on basic types of negotiable instruments.

Drafts

A **draft** is similar to a check in many ways. It is defined as an unconditional written order to a person to pay money, usually to a third party. Notice that the order is given to "a person." This means either a natural person or an "artificial person" such as a corporation (in the case of a check, for example, this could be a banking corporation or a similar institution). Also, the payment is not necessarily due on demand. It may be due after a certain period, such as a number of days or months, in which case it is a **time draft**. On the other hand, it may indeed be payable on demand, which would make it a **sight draft**. It is also possible to combine the two. A draft that reads in part "due and payable 90 days after sight" is an example of such a combination. Finally, note that a **postdated check** (a check issued bearing a future date as its effective date) is treated as a time draft. It will become a demand instrument on the date entered on its face. An **antedated check** (a check issued bearing a past date as its effective date) is treated as a check in all respects. UCC 3-113 requires that the date on any dated instrument be presumed as correct.

Figure 17-3 shows a time draft. It was written because Joey Kleeman, the drawer, had completed a construction job for Collyer Hardware, the drawee, as a part of Collyer's expansion plan. Collyer owed Joey $6,500 as a consequence. When B. A. Hill asked Joey for the $5,000 Joey owed him for backhoe work in Joey's new subdivision, Joey convinced him to take the draft instead. B. A. then presented the instrument to Jim Collyer for **acceptance** (an assurance that he would be liable on the draft and would pay it according to its terms). If you look at Figure 17-3, you can see that Collyer has correctly indicated this by writing "accepted" and his signature across the instrument. If Collyer refused to pay the draft, it would be considered **dishonored**. Banks make the same type of decision daily on millions of checks.

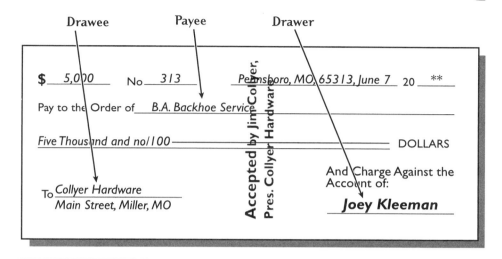

FIGURE 17-3   Time draft drawn by Joey Kleeman to pay B. A. Hill from money owed him by Collyer Hardware, an instrument on which Jim Collyer has accepted primary liability and which he must pay when it is due.

Trade Acceptances

Like the check, the **trade acceptance** is a type of draft. It can be extremely helpful in certain business situations. It is written by sellers of goods on the money owed to them by the buyers of those goods. If the buyers accept the liability on the instruments, the sellers have valuable negotiable instruments that can, in turn, be sold. Here's an example of how it works in real life:

Hypothetical Case

Susan Bently's clothing store, Unmatronly, was in trouble. Antoinette ("Toni") Zelos, salesperson for Femuline, the store's main supplier of women's business suits, knew it. The new freeway was being constructed nearby. During the construction, Unmatronly's business had dropped off by 40 percent. Still, Toni thought, the freeway will be done in two months and then Unmatronly will be doing twice its original level of sales. The only question was how to provide a stock for Unmatronly in the meantime. Toni had been selling to Susan's store on "open account." In other words, Toni's company would provide whatever stock Susan ordered on terms requiring that it be paid for in 30 days. Unfortunately, the winter shipment, with an invoice price of $7,000, hadn't been paid yet. In fact, it had been over 90 days since that batch of suits had been shipped to Unmatronly. As a consequence, Toni's company had just informed her that it would not meet Susan's new order for $4,000 of additional merchandise on the same terms. Suddenly, Toni recalled her old business law teacher talking about how a trade acceptance was used. It might work. She called the company's legal adviser and her boss, received permission, and drew one up. It is shown in Figure 17-4.

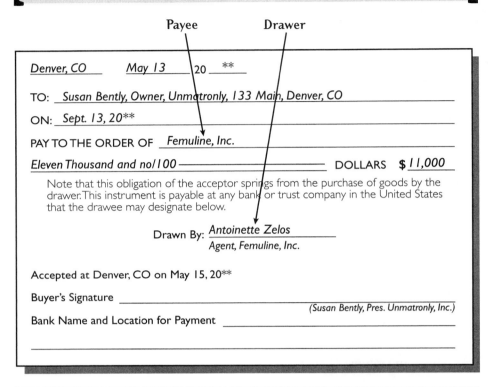

FIGURE 17-4   Trade acceptance drawn by the seller, Antoinette Zelos, acting as an agent of Femuline, in favor of that company as payee. This trade acceptance is drawn on Unmatronly but will have to be accepted by an appropriate representative of that shop (Susan Bently by her signature on the line for the drawee, Unmatronly, Inc.) before it is payable according to its terms.

Payee   Drawer

Denver, CO   May 13   20 __**__

TO: _Susan Bently, Owner, Unmatronly, 133 Main, Denver, CO_

ON: _Sept. 13, 20**_

PAY TO THE ORDER OF _Femuline, Inc._

Eleven Thousand and no/100 ———————————— DOLLARS $ _11,000_

> Note that this obligation of the acceptor springs from the purchase of goods by the drawer. This instrument is payable at any bank or trust company in the United States that the drawee may designate below.

Drawn By: _Antoinette Zelos_
                  Agent, Femuline, Inc.

Accepted at Denver, CO on May 15, 20**

Buyer's Signature _____
                                                    (Susan Bently, Pres. Unmatronly, Inc.)
Bank Name and Location for Payment _____

_____

When the new shipment of goods arrived, Susan would inspect them, then sign the trade acceptance. The advantage is that this instrument (for the $11,000 balance that would then be due on the account) could be **discounted** (sold at less than its face amount) to a financial institution. Even if it brought only $10,000 from the financial institution, that money would at least be available for Femuline to use. When the instrument came due, the financial institution would make money because it would collect the full $11,000 from Susan. Susan would stay in business, and Toni would keep a customer and get a commission on the sale.

From this example, you can see how handy the trade acceptance can be. Of course, the same is true for checks and basic drafts. These negotiable instruments were developed out of the necessity to solve various problems. They continue to be used because they continue to solve those problems. The second basic type of negotiable instrument, the promissory note, has a similar role.

Promissory Notes

Hypothetical Case

Gomeranna Pyle and her mother, Anna Pyle, walked into the dealership. Her car to be, a brand-new Ford Patriot, was waiting on the showroom floor. Their salesperson, Manbart Sampson, motioned for them to come into the "settlement room." There they were given various documents to sign, including the contract of sale. Finally, Manbart said, "Now we just need a check for the $3,000 down, and then you both must sign this note. Ford Credit will send you," he nodded to Gomeranna, "a payment book in about a week." Gomeranna wrote out the check. She and her mother then read the promissory note, shown in Figure 17-5, and signed it. Manbart smiled, dug in his pockets for a moment for the keys, then stood up and ceremoniously presented them to Gomeranna. "The temporary tags are on her. Happy driving."

A **promissory note** is a written promise by one party to pay money to the order of another party. It is often used, as in the above example, as evidence of a debt. Unlike an IOU, which merely acknowledges the existence of a debt, a promissory note is legally enforceable because it contains a promise to pay.

The promisor on a promissory note is termed the **maker** (two or more promisors are referred to as **comakers**); the person named to receive the money is again termed the payee. In the above example, Ford Credit was the payee of the promissory note and Gomeranna and her mother, Anna Pyle, were its comakers.

FIGURE 17-5   Promissory note evidencing obligation undertaken by the Pyles to repay $12,000 in installments over five years

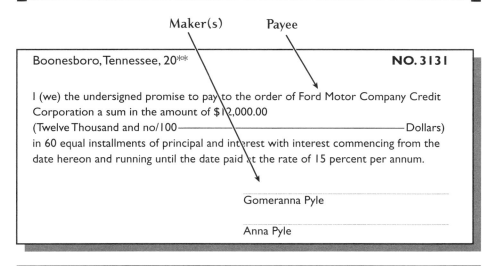

Maker(s)   Payee

Boonesboro, Tennessee, 20**   **NO. 3131**

I (we) the undersigned promise to pay to the order of Ford Motor Company Credit Corporation a sum in the amount of $12,000.00
(Twelve Thousand and no/100——————————————————————Dollars)
in 60 equal installments of principal and interest with interest commencing from the date hereon and running until the date paid at the rate of 15 percent per annum.

Gomeranna Pyle

Anna Pyle

There are various types of promissory notes. A **demand note**, an example of which is shown in Figure 17-6, becomes due and payable whenever the payee or a subsequent owner presents it for payment. Both the face amount of the note (called the **principal**) and any interest are payable at that time A **time note**, unlike a demand note, is payable at a set future date noted on the face of the instrument. The note is said to "mature" or become due on that date. An **installment note** (refer to the instrument that Ford Credit used in the example involving Gomeranna) requires a series of payments of principal and interest until the debt is paid off.

Certificates of Deposit

A **certificate of deposit**, or CD, as it is often called, is a written acknowledgment by a bank of the receipt of money coupled with a promise to pay it back, usually with interest, on the due date. Such certificates are issued rather frequently because they give the bank some security as to how long it gets to keep (and make money with) the depositors' money. Also, depositors are pleased because they receive a higher interest rate on a CD than, for example, a savings account.

Letters of Credit

A **letter of credit** is a promise by a person (typically a financial institution such as a bank) that it will honor and pay drafts drawn in compliance with the terms set forth in the letter of credit. This instrument is often used to assure payment for foreign purchases when the buyer and the buyer's credit standing are unknown to the seller. Say you have just taken a job with Harvey's Stereo Warehouse, a small electronics retailer in the Midwest. Harvey's makes most of its profits on the sale

FIGURE 17-6   Promissory note payable on demand of Lincoln Savings and Loan or anyone to whom Lincoln properly transfers the right to collect. Bernard Bilgewater III is the maker of the note and obligated to pay it plus interest when it is presented.

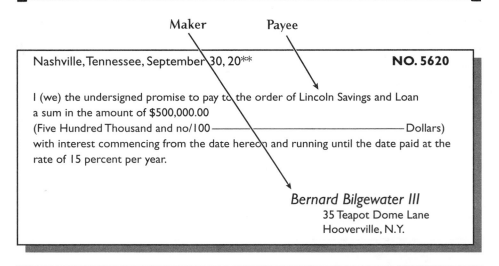

Maker   Payee

Nashville, Tennessee, September 30, 20**   **NO. 5620**

I (we) the undersigned promise to pay to the order of Lincoln Savings and Loan
a sum in the amount of $500,000.00
(Five Hundred Thousand and no/100 ————————————————— Dollars)
with interest commencing from the date hereon and running until the date paid at the
rate of 15 percent per year.

Bernard Bilgewater III
35 Teapot Dome Lane
Hooverville, N.Y.

of the Sony MX-11 compact disc player and its installation in automobiles. You have been at Harvey's less than three weeks when Greatest Buy Electronics, a national chain with a store less than a mile from Harvey's, starts offering the MX-11 and its installation at a price less than your cost. After a day or so of panic, you tell your boss that the only hope is to buy direct from Sony. Eliminating the reseller will bring your costs down to where you have a chance at competing with Greatest Buy. Your boss says that Sony will never sell to Harvey's because Sony doesn't know Harvey's from the Grand Old Opry. You tell him that you're sure Pennsboro National Bank, with which Harvey's keeps its accounts, will write a letter of credit to the bank of Yokohama that will give Sony the reassurance it needs to sell 250 MX-11s to Harvey's. Your boss asks you to give it a try. A few days later, after some negotiations, the President of Pennsboro National Bank writes the letter of credit shown in Figure 17-7.

You then notify Sony of your order and the letter of credit being held at the Bank of Yokohama. Sony's places the goods you ordered on a ship bound for the U.S. The shipmaster inventories the goods and issues a ship's bill of lading for them. The Sony representative takes the ship's bill to the Bank of Yokohama, where it is compared with the letter of credit requirements. If satisfied that these requirements have been met, the Bank of Yokohama issues a draft for the amount of the purchase. The draft is drawn on Pennsboro National Bank and payable through the Bank of Yokohama. Sony's representative may then cash the draft or deposit it

FIGURE 17-7   Letter of credit allowing Bank of Yokohama to issue draft on Pennsboro National Bank payable to Sony Corporation, if Sony ships ordered goods to Pennsboro client

Letter of Credit
PENNSBORO NATIONAL BANK
PENNSBORO, MO 65713
July 27, 20**

TO: BANK OF YOKOHAMA, Yokohama, Japan

Good Day

Upon receipt of suitable bill of lading showing the transshipment of 250 Sony Model MX-11 Compact Disc Players to Harvey's Stereo Warehouse, Springfield, MO, you are authorized to draw on the Pennsboro National Bank a sum of up to $50,000 in favor of Sony, Inc. in payment for said goods. This letter will expire 90 days from above date. No partial shipments are to be allowed or compensated.

Hutton L. (Nub) Turnback II
President

in Sony's accounts, from which it will make its way back to the bank of Yokohama. That bank will pay the draft, then demand the amount paid plus a service fee from Pennsboro. When payment is received, typically electronically, from Pennsboro, the ship's bill is sent to that bank. Pennsboro then requires that Harvey's pay it the amount it has expended plus a service fee. When Harvey's pays, it receives the ship's bill showing ownership of the goods. As Harvey's representative, you can then go down to the local warehouse to which the goods were shipped, present the ship's bill, and receive the goods. The point here is that in a global economy, the use of such instruments as letters of credit is crucial to businesspeople who hope to compete today and in the future.

Risks in Using Negotiable Instruments

Properly used, checks, drafts, and other negotiable instruments greatly reduce the possibility of such dangers as theft of cash. As already discussed, the idea of reducing such dangers probably brought on the use of what we now know as negotiable instruments. But every solution gives rise to new problems. Crimes involving lost and stolen instruments, forgery, embezzlement, insufficient funds checks, and so on have marked society's increasing use of substitutes for hard cash. In response, laws governing the use of negotiable instruments have been altered to reduce the risk of such problems to a manageable level. Much of the next few chapters covers the laws aimed at protecting people from the most common problems related to negotiable instruments.

CHAPTER REVIEW

USE LEGAL TERMS

Fill in the blanks with the appropriate term.

acceptance	dishonored	negotiable instruments
alternative payees	draft	payee
antedated check	drawee	postdated check
bearer	drawer	principal
bill of exchange	endorse	promissory note
certificate of deposit	installment note	sight draft
check	joint payees	time draft
comakers	letter of credit	time note
demand note	maker	trade acceptance
discounted		

1. ____?____ occurs when an individual agrees to pay a draft according to its terms by writing a word or words to this effect across the instrument and signing below that.
2. A check that the bank refuses to pay has been ____?____.
3. The person in possession of an instrument made out to "cash" can be labeled a(n) ____?____ of that instrument.
4. A check, issued today but bearing an earlier date, is labeled a(n) ____?____ check.
5. The face amount of a note, not including interest, is called the ____?____.
6. A note containing a promise to pay the amount due in a series of payments over a number of periods is a(n) ____?____.
7. To sign the reverse of a negotiable instrument is to ____?____.
8. The person to whom a note is payable is labeled the ____?____.
9. The issuer of a check is termed a(n) ____?____.
10. The bank upon which a check is drawn is labeled the ____?____.

TEST YOUR READING

11. Why was a bill of exchange so useful?
12. What other phrases mean the same as "on demand?"
13. In reference to your checking account, are you the bank's debtor or creditor? Why?
14. Why should a postdated check be treated as a time draft?
15. How does a certificate of deposit differ from a note on which the bank is a maker?

16. Who is the drawee on a trade acceptance? Why?

17. If you were a business owner closing down your shop at night, would you rather be leaving with $10,000 in checks made out to you or $10,000 in cash? Why?

THINK CRITICALLY ABOUT EVIDENCE

18. Will negotiable instruments become obsolete? Consider the alternative forms of rendering payment and transferring resources in your answer.

19. Flora and Deplora Adams, twin sisters, were arguing over the best place to establish a checking account. Flora wanted to place the account with her credit union, which paid interest on such accounts. Deplora wanted to place the account in Pennsboro Bank because she received a lot of out-of-state checks and these would clear (be paid by the issuer's financial institution and thereby produce usable funds) almost a week sooner at the bank than at the credit union. After several days of dispute, Deplora pointed out that there was no such thing as a checking account in a credit union because checks had to be drawn on banks. Was she correct? Why or why not? Where would you prefer to "bank?"

20. Tim Schulyer sold the Going-Going-Gone Company a load of ash timber for use in making baseball bats. As a result, the company owed him $7,500 on the purchase price. Before receiving the payment due, Tim found a used tractor he wished to purchase. Its price was $5,000. Tim needed it immediately and did not want to borrow from the local bank for its purchase. What type of negotiable instrument could he use to order Going-Going-Gone to pay the seller of the tractor the $5,000 due? Is the negotiable instrument likely to be a demand instrument or a time instrument?

21. Sure-Fire Wood Stove Company delivered five of its airtight models to Taylor's Stove and Hardware Store more than six months ago. The store has still not paid on its account. Several Sure-Fire executives have recommended suing Taylor's for the $3,500 balance due. The salesperson in charge of the Taylor's account has pointed out that the store was a good customer in the past and that the winter just concluded was mild and the costs of fuels competing with wood were therefore low. What type of negotiable instrument would you recommend that Sure-Fire require Taylor's to sign in lieu of bringing a lawsuit against it? What could then be done with that instrument to provide working funds for Sure-Fire?

22. Abraham Manufacturing Company sells Omar's, a chain of clothing stores, 100 suits. In the trade acceptance based on this transaction, which firm was the drawer? Which firm was the drawee? Which firm was the acceptor? Which firm was the payee?

23. What risks are associated with using means other than negotiable instruments for transferring resources? How could these risks best be avoided? Consider credit cards, voiceprint money ordering, electronic fund management, and so on.

REAL-WORLD CASE
Means v. Clardy
735 S.W.2d 6

Gary Means and his coappellant, Fred Barry, brought this case before the Western District of the Missouri Court of Appeals. They were seeking to collect on a promissory note in the amount of $31,000 purportedly signed by Nancy Clardy as partial payment for a cabinet-making business she allegedly purchased. Two weeks after the note was made, it was to be paid by $5,000 in cash. Then, the remainder of the principal and interest was "to be paid in cabinets figured at the prevailing builder's price for Jefferson City," and in a final lump-sum payment. When the note was not paid, Means and Barry brought suit for the nearly $22,000 still due. During the trial, Nancy Clardy testified that she did not sign either the note or a bill of sale buying the business. She alleged that her son, Bruce, had done so and had drawn $5,000 from a "remodeling" fund to make the initial payment on the note. Bruce took the Fifth Amendment (protection against self-incrimination) when asked about this at the trial. However, a witness to the signing of the promissory note and the bill of sale testified that Bruce Clardy placed the signatures of Bruce and Nancy Clardy on the note.

Think Critically

1. Is the jury most likely to hold that Bruce Clardy forged his mother's signature?
2. If the note is payable in money, the Uniform Commercial Code will apply. The UCC requires that a forger be liable on the signature she or he forged. If the note is not payable in money, Gary Means and Fred Barry will be treated only as assignees of the contract rights to collect on it. In addition, although Bruce Clardy may face criminal charges for forgery, neither Bruce Clardy nor Nancy Clardy will be personally liable on the note. Is the note payable in money?
3. Why do the courts give a decided advantage to takers of an instrument that falls under the coverage of the UCC?

CHAPTER 18

UCC Protection for Negotiable Instruments

GOALS

- Understand the benefits of being a holder in due course
- Know how to qualify as a holder in due course
- Be able to identify negotiable instruments

Reducing the Risks of Using Negotiable Instruments

At the end of the last chapter, we discussed briefly some of the problems associated with the use of negotiable instruments. These problems, which include worthless instruments, embezzlement, forgery, and many others, can never be eliminated, but they can be brought under control by a variety of means. Good management is at the top of the list of those means. Among the wise courses of action that indicate good management in this regard are selecting personnel only after suitable background checks and incorporating internal audit procedures in day-to-day business operations. Of course, carefully screening customers from whom checks, drafts, promissory notes, and other instruments are taken is also crucial. Finally, the application of foresight and good negotiating skills to agreements from which negotiable instruments may issue can also help a great deal. (In this regard, note that the UCC does not define the word *default*. That definition is left to the contracting parties. For example, late payments, the obligor's bankruptcy, or the obligor's insolvency are among the definitions that could be included in the agreement on which the issuance of negotiable instruments is based.)

This chapter and the next few chapters, however, are meant to make another means of protection very clear. In particular, the material in these chapters is meant to show you how to utilize the holder in due course status made available by the UCC's Article 3 as a shield from the risk of taking negotiable instruments.

Advantages of the Holder in Due Course Status

The holder in due course status allows a qualified **holder** (a person possessing an instrument issued or endorsed to her or him or made payable to bearer) to overcome legal defenses that often prevent someone from collecting on a negotiable instrument.

What are these defenses? The ones most commonly used are breach of contract and failure of consideration, both of which should be familiar to you from our discussion of contract law.

 # Hypothetical Case

Commerce Bank bought two promissory notes from their payees at a discount. One note was issued by Babbling Brook, Inc. (the maker), to Fearless Chemical Company (the payee) in part payment for a shipment of cleaning chemicals. The face amount of this note was $2,000; Commerce bought it for $1,750. The other note was issued by Aggressive Agriculture, Inc. (the maker), to Kikkstart of Japan (the payee) for two garden tractors. Its face amount was $5,250; Commerce acquired it for $4,500. When the notes became due, Babbling Brook refused to pay because the chemicals did not do the job warranted (this is a failure of consideration defense). Aggressive Agriculture also refused to pay, stating that it had never received the tractors as promised by Kikkstart (a breach of contract defense). Commerce Bank could legally overcome both of these defenses and collect on the notes if it has the status of holder in due course. If Commerce is an assignee or a mere holder of the notes, the defenses, if valid, will be upheld by the court. Therefore, collection will not be possible against the makers.

Definition of a Holder in Due Course

A holder qualifies as a **holder in due course** (HDC) by giving value for a negotiable instrument in good faith without any notice of defect or dishonor. Let's take a close look at what is meant by the various elements in this definition.

Value   Under Article 3 of the UCC, **value** is defined as akin to consideration in contract law. However, there are some significant differences. For example, value must actually have been given to qualify under Article 3 rather than merely promised as under contract law (remember that under contract law a promise is taken as consideration to support another promise). Also under Article 3, value is considered given if an instrument is issued as payment of a foregoing debt (this would be considered past consideration under contract law and, therefore, would not bind a promisor to a promise).

Hypothetical Case

Xuan Li's restaurant, Little Saigon, was behind by 180 days in paying on the balance in the open account provided to it by its major supplier, Oriental Foods, Inc. Finally, before Oriental Foods would fill another order for Li, it required him to sign a promissory note in the amount of the overdue balance. By law, this substitution of the note for the antecedent (preexisting) debt, would be taken as value given by the payee, Oriental Foods, Inc.

Note that the adequacy of the value given, as in the analysis of the adequacy of consideration, is immaterial. Whether $1 or $50,000 is given for an instrument with a $50,000 face value does not matter in determining whether value has been given. However, if the instrument is transferred as a gift, the donee is not credited with giving value.

Finally, realize that, by law, value is not given when an instrument is acquired in a sale brought about through legal process or as part of a bulk transfer.

Good Faith   To qualify as a holder in due course in relation to an instrument, a person must take the instrument in good faith. **Good faith** is most closely defined as honesty in fact or subjective honesty. Although the adequacy of the consideration given for an instrument is immaterial in determining whether value has been given, adequacy is very relevant to the question of whether the acquirer of an instrument has acted in good faith. Giving $1 for a $50,000 instrument may be taken as a clear indication that in the buyer's opinion something is wrong with the transaction. Therefore, it may be concluded that the buyer did not act in good faith.

Without Notice of Defect or Dishonor   Notification of a defect in an instrument or the past dishonor of an instrument that would prevent a holder becoming a holder in due course may be acquired in a number of ways. Such notification may be by actual knowledge given by someone or something directly to the would-be holder in due course. Being told by a credible witness that a promissory note was issued because of an illegal gambling debt, for example, would disqualify the recipient of the information from being a holder in due course of that instrument.

Notification may also be found in knowledge that is imputed to the would-be holder in due course. Imputed knowledge may be inferred when such a person is aware of a circumstance from which he or she should have concluded that there

FIGURE 18-1   Requirements of the Holder in Due Course Status

- Give value
- In good faith
- Without notice of defect or dishonor

was a defect or dishonor. Acquiring an instrument already past its due date is one example of this. Consequently, you need to know that a time instrument becomes overdue the day after the maturity date specified on its face. Also, by law (UCC 3-304), a check is overdue 90 days after it has been issued. This does not mean that it cannot be cashed even years after the 90-day period. It does mean, however, that anyone who takes the check after those 90 days have elapsed cannot be a holder in due course. Other demand instruments become overdue after an "unreasonably long (period) under the circumstances of the particular case in light of the nature of the instrument and usage of the trade."

There are other signs from which notice of potential defect or dishonor can be inferred. Discovery of these signs requires more than a cursory glance at the face of the instrument. For instance, a person should inspect an instrument to see whether there has been an obvious alteration, such as crossing out one figure and entering another for it. Individuals sometimes even initial such changes as though that would reduce their effect. It does not. Other important inquiries that should be made include the following: Does the amount deliberately written out in long-hand agree with the amount shown in numbers? Is the instrument incomplete? Does the instrument have missing or incomplete endorsements? Is there evidence on the face or reverse that the instrument has been presented for payment and dishonored? Any one of these defects will prevent a would-be holder in due course from acquiring that less risky status in relation to the instrument.

Finally, there is always the danger of some type of public notice, say a bankruptcy filing by the issuer of the instrument, that would eliminate the possibility of this status.

Powers of Mere Holders or Assignees in Relation to an Instrument

Mere Holders   The failure of a person to qualify for the status of holder in due course does not mean that the amount due on the instrument involved cannot be collected. A mere holder of the instrument has the power to transfer ownership of that paper, to demand payment on it, and to exercise any and all rights that the person who transferred the instrument to the holder could have exercised.

This last power of a holder, to have and exercise the rights of her or his transferor, led to the creation of the status of a holder through a holder in due course in the UCC's Article 3. A **holder through a holder in due course (HHDC)** is a holder who cannot become a holder in due course (HDC) on his or her own but who acquires an HDC's rights by acquiring the instrument after an HDC has held it.

Hypothetical Case

Due to lack of attention, Bill Blast bought a promissory note that had already matured. When he presented it for payment to the maker (a local business, Trailrides, Inc.), he was told that the maker would not pay it because of a defect in each of the 10 saddles that had been supplied by the original payee, Hi!-in-the-Saddle, Ltd. The note had been issued in payment for those goods. Since Bill had taken the instrument too late, he could not be a holder in due course and thereby able to overcome Trailrides' defense and collect. He contacted his lawyer, who asked Bill to find out whether the person who had transferred the instrument to him, an equestrienne named Stacy Shipman, had been an HDC. Bill learned that she had been. He therefore acquired her rights, and as a holder through a holder in due course he could recover the amount due on the instrument despite the maker's defense of failure of consideration.

Note, however, that a previous mere holder of an instrument cannot improve her or his status by reacquiring it. For example, if Hi!-in-the-Saddle knew or should have known of the saddles' defects, it could not be a holder in due course of the instrument but only a mere holder. The UCC would not allow it to improve its position by reacquiring the instrument from Stacy Shipman, an HDC. Hi!-in-the-Saddle would still be restricted to the powers of a mere holder. Therefore, it could not improperly use the law associated with the HDC status to overcome the defense of failure of consideration stemming from defects in the saddles it supplied.

Assignees   Thus far we have focused our attention solely on the requirements of persons who try to acquire the powers of holders and, more important, the powers of HDCs. If such persons, no matter how qualified, take a defective instrument, they are treated as only assignees of that instrument. They retain this status until the defects have been corrected, if this is possible, at which time they can become a holder, an HDC, or an HHDC. Unfortunately, some defects cannot be corrected. It therefore becomes important for businesspersons to examine an instrument to determine which are defective and which are not. In the terms of the UCC, before acquiring an instrument, a potential investor or buyer should determine that it is negotiable and that it has been properly negotiated. Otherwise, the investor or buyer will end up being treated as only an assignee of the instrument and will thereby lose out on the protection that the UCC can afford the wise acquirer.

Determining Which Instruments Are Negotiable

In the remainder of this chapter, we will devote our attention to determining in detail what a negotiable instrument is. Chapter 19 will then cover how an instrument should be transferred so as to have been properly negotiated. A **negotiable instrument** is

1.   A writing
2.   Signed by its maker or drawer
3.   That is unconditionally payable
4.   In a sum certain in money
5.   On demand or at a specific time
6.   To order or to bearer.

Most of the elements of the definition have been discussed in a superficial way in the preceding sections and chapter. Now, however, we need to focus in depth on the case law and the UCC sections pertinent to each of these elements.

A Writing

This requirement is very flexible. The writing may be done in pen, pencil (although this invites alteration), or even blood as long as it is legible. The surface on which the writing is executed must be capable of being circulated (so writing an instrument on a 10-ton rock is out), but that's about the only constraint. Of course, the use of anything out of the ordinary invites detailed examination and delay, so the most practical choice is to execute your instruments in the same way as others do.

The fact that an instrument is in writing means that the parol evidence rule governs the admissibility of oral evidence to contradict the terms of the instrument. Therefore, evidence of fraud, incompleteness, inconsistency, and the like is required before testimony on the terms of the instrument will be allowed in court. There are also rules for interpreting problems that tend to recur frequently in the making out of such an instrument. When there is a conflict of terms, for example, the written term takes precedence over the typewritten term or over any printed form term. In other words, flexibility is emphasized. On the other hand, if there is a conflict between the written amount and the amount expressed in numbers, the written amount wins out due to the deliberation required to write it.

Signed by the Maker or Drawer

This second requirement is relatively straightforward. The actual or authorized signature of the issuer is required for the instrument to be negotiable. Unlike situations that require the interpretation of the writing, in which the parol evidence rule may potentially block testimony, oral evidence is admissible to identify the signer of an instrument. In any region of the country, after all, there are typically several people bearing the most common names. So we allow the appropriate person to testify as to which of the ten John Smiths possible actually was the maker of the note or draft.

Further, if another person signs for the issuer (for example, all corporations must employ this method to utilize negotiable instruments), the person signing must be authorized to do so or be bound personally to pay the instrument. A failure to indicate that a person is signing in such a capacity, even if so authorized, obligates the signer personally as well as the issuer.

Hypothetical Case

The Reverend Billie Samuel was president of the Bible College of the Ozarks, a small accredited four-year school located in Pennsboro, Missouri. Each Friday, she signed the payroll checks and other pieces of negotiable instruments for the school. She was authorized to do so by the school's governing body. She signed only her own name and did not indicate that she was signing in her capacity as president of the institution. Recently, due to the publicized infidelities of several TV evangelists, the level of donations to the school dropped overnight. As a result, the payroll checks and several other outstanding instruments were dishonored. If the college cannot pay these instruments, their employees and other obligees may take Reverend Samuel's home, car, bank account balances, and so on, by bringing suit against her for the money due.

Two final points: First of all, any form of signature is permissible as long as it indicates an intent to issue the instrument. So any instrument signed with the proverbial X is sufficient (witnesses to such a signing are usually a good idea but not required technically). Second, the signature may appear anywhere on the face of the instrument, not necessarily at the end. Obliquely across the face and embedded in the body are both acceptable options. For example, the instrument in Figure 18-2, written by the obligor, Thomas Hart Benton, was considered complete with signature.

Unconditionally Payable

This requirement maintains that the promise or order to pay contained in a negotiable instrument must not be conditional on any outside event. The requirement is based on the role of negotiable instruments in our economic system. To enhance the transferability of such instruments as checks and notes, we want to avoid a situation in which every potential purchaser of an instrument must somehow take time to determine whether a condition has been fulfilled. Allowing instruments bearing such statements as "Pay to the order of Wilmouth Builders, Inc., if it has completed construction on our house" to be negotiable would so inhibit the transfer of negotiable instruments that their use would practically disappear. Requiring that something be done or that a specific event occur before an instrument can be collected on reduces the instrument to the status of a simple contract whose rights, at best, can merely be assigned. Note that requiring payment strictly from a particular account (which might or might not have the funds in it to pay the instrument) still leaves the instrument negotiable according to UCC 3-106(b)(ii).

> **FIGURE 18-2**   Handwritten Promissory Note Containing Valid Signature of Thomas Hart Benton

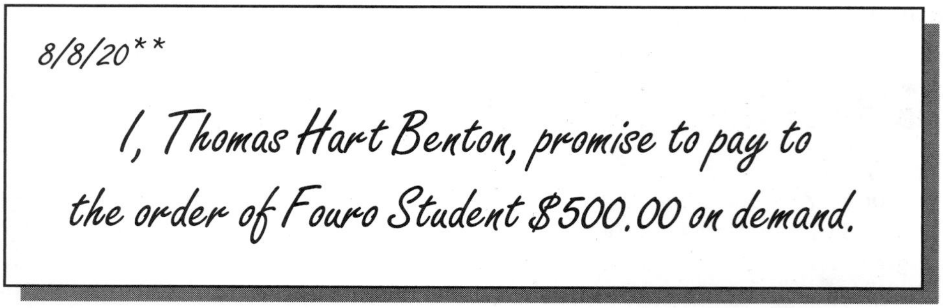

8/8/20**

I, Thomas Hart Benton, promise to pay to the order of Fouro Student $500.00 on demand.

A Sum Certain in Money

The requirement of a **sum certain** means that the amount must be clearly ascertainable from the face of the instrument. To qualify the instrument in question as negotiable, this must be capable of being done at two distinct times. First of all, when the would-be holder considers buying the instrument, he or she should be able to calculate from the information on its face the exact minimum amount payable on it. Second, at maturity, the holder must be able to calculate from the face the exact amount due.

It does not disqualify an instrument if it is payable in installments or with a particular interest added on because even if this is the case, the amounts mentioned above can still be calculated. Even if an instrument promises the recovery of reasonable attorney's fees and court costs in case of default, the courts have held that it is still negotiable.

A second requirement is hidden in the requirement of a sum certain, namely the requirement that the instrument be payable in money. **Money** is defined as the medium of exchange that any government (including international organizations) has officially adopted as currency. So if an otherwise negotiable instrument states that it is "payable in 10,000 German marks," we have no problem with it.

In addition, if an otherwise negotiable instrument bears such wording as "payable in 10,000 German marks or my 1986 Ford Pickup at the holder's option," it too would still be negotiable as long as the holder (obligee/owner) of the instrument can choose to be paid in *money*. Whether or not she or he does so is immaterial; the instrument is negotiable.

On Demand or at a Specific Time

To satisfy this requirement, the time the instrument is payable must be determined in one of two ways. We are more familiar with "on demand" because this is the only way legally allowable for checks. At law, *on demand* is synonymous with at *presentment* or *at sight*. All of these terms reflect the acceptable condition that the holder has the option of choosing the time when she or he is to receive payment. Equally acceptable is specifying the time when the instrument matures. Such expressions as "due and payable on or before March 3, 20**," "due and payable 60 days from sight," or "due and payable 60 days from March 3, 20**" (that is, a particular date, such as the date of issue), are all acceptable. The point is that the holder must be able to determine from the face of the instrument the latest possible time it can be paid without default.

Even if the instrument is subject to an **acceleration clause** (a clause allowing the obligee to declare the full amount due and payable upon the occurrence of a particular event, such as the failure to make a payment), as long as a specific date is otherwise named, the instrument is still negotiable.

Note that making an instrument due and payable upon the death of a person, although such is sure to occur, is not acceptable because the date is not specific enough. Finally, even though an instrument's due date may be extended, at the holder's option, it is negotiable. However, this would not be the case if, instead, the obligor could extend the time of payment indefinitely.

Payable to Order or to Bearer

This last requirement is the most straightforward. An order instrument must be "payable to the order of the named payee(s)," "payable to the named payee's order," or some equivalent wording. A bearer instrument must be written "pay to bearer," "pay to cash," "pay to the order of the bearer," "pay to the order of the named payee(s) or bearer," or something very similar. Finally, if an instrument is made out to an obviously fictitious person, such as Superman, it is treated as a bearer instrument.

A negotiable instrument, then, is one that satisfies all of the above requirements. The negotiability of an instrument is something that is basically determined or determinable when the instrument is first issued. Just because an instrument is negotiable, however, does not necessarily mean that a holder who acquires it in good faith and gives value without notice of defect or dishonor can be a holder in due course. The instrument must also have been properly negotiated as it made its way to that holder for him or her to attain the valuable status of an HDC. As mentioned above, we will discuss negotiation itself in the next chapter.

CHAPTER REVIEW

USE LEGAL TERMS

Fill in the blanks with the appropriate term.

acceleration clause

good faith

holder

holder in due course

holder through a holder in due course

money

negotiable instrument

sum certain

value

1. An individual who cannot of himself or herself be a holder in due course but acquires the same rights as those of a holder in due course by taking an instrument from a holder in due course is labeled a(n) __?__ .

2. Subjective honesty is known at law as __?__ .

3. A person possessing an instrument issued or endorsed to her or him or made payable to bearer is known as a(n) __?__ .

4. A(n) __?__ allows the obligee of an instrument to declare it fully due and payable if certain conditions occur.

5. The euro, a unit of currency created by the European Union, would be considered __?__ .

TEST YOUR READING

6. Why isn't "default" defined in the UCC?

7. How does being a holder in due course reduce the risks of taking negotiable instruments?

8. Name three ways in which a person could receive notice of defect or dishonor of a negotiable instrument.

9. Could a donee of an instrument be a holder in due course? How could such an individual receive the rights of a holder in due course?

10. When is an "X" a valid signature?

11. Why is it important that we eliminate conditions from negotiable instruments?

12. Why should a note made out to an obviously fictitious person be considered a bearer instrument?

THINK CRITICALLY ABOUT EVIDENCE

13. On Christmas Eve, Christina Cringle was racing to catch her plane for home. As she reached the boarding area, she realized that she needed to phone a friend and ask him to pick her up on arrival. Desperate to place the call, she had to trade for $1.25 in coin a $50 check her parents had given her during her Labor Day vacation. Why would Ebeneezer Grennich, the person who paid $1.25 for the check, not be a holder in due course?

14. Would Grennich be able to collect on the instrument anyway? Why or why not?

15. Horatio Bornlower, principal of the East London Home for Wayward Boys, signed so many documents that he had his signature duplicated onto a rubber stamp and used it instead. One day, when about to write out the home's payroll checks, he hit upon the idea of using the signature stamp to sign these checks as well. Can he do so and still produce a negotiable instrument?

16. Assuming that all other requirements for negotiability have been satisfied, would an instrument bearing the following wordings be negotiable?
    a. "Payable upon completion of the construction contract for our home."
    b. "Payable to Ajax Construction Company as required in the construction contract for our home."
    c. "This debt is secured by a mortgage."
    d. "Payable out of account number 313 only."

17. A promissory note issued by Chet Brinkley to payee David Huntley included this statement: "The obligor of this instrument reserves the right to extend the due date indefinitely." All the other requirements of negotiability were satisfied. Was the instrument negotiable? Would your answer be the same if the statement read, "The obligor reserves the right to extend the due date by one six-month period"?

18. Is the instrument in Figure 18-3 negotiable?

> **FIGURE 18-3**   IOU given by Carlton Marlboro in exchange for $500 payment to Him from Benjamin Longstreet III

To Benjamin Longstreet III
August 9, 20**

I.O.U. $500.00

Carlton Marlboro

REAL-WORLD CASE
Centerre Bank Of Branson v. Campbell
744 S.W.2d 490

Decide whether or not the instrument in the following case is negotiable.

The Campbells signed a note obligating them to pay $11,250 that contained the following term: "Interest will be payable semiannually. Interest may vary with bank rates charged to Strand Investment Company." The note was sold to Centerre Bank. Upon default Centerre sued to collect. The Campbells refused to pay, claiming that there had been a failure of consideration when Strand Investment Company failed to establish the limited partnership promised in return for issuance of the note. The trial court entered judgment in favor of the bank, saying that it was a "holder in due course of the note sued upon." As such, it could overcome the Campbells' defense of failure of consideration and recover.

Think Critically

1. Assume that you are the judge and that you are about to write the deciding opinion for the appellate court. Would you consider the bank a holder, an HDC, an HHDC, or what? What is the basis for your classification?

2. Should Centerre Bank be allowed to recover from the Campbells as a consequence of that classification?

CHAPTER 19

Acquiring and Transferring Negotiable Instruments

GOALS

- ◆   Know how to properly negotiate a negotiable instrument
- ◆   Identify the defenses that can be overcome by an HDC
- ◆   Understand the effects of warranties

How Are Negotiable Instruments Negotiated?

Negotiable instruments must be both negotiable and properly negotiated to enable a transferee to become a holder in due course (HDC). **Negotiation** is defined as transfer of possession, either voluntarily or involuntarily, from someone other than the issuer to another person. If either of these elements (negotiability or negotiation) is missing or improper, transferring the negotiable instruments is regarded as merely an assignment. The potential for becoming an HDC is lost. As has been alluded to earlier, HDC status can be extremely important. In fact, it can mean the difference between collecting and not collecting on an instrument.

The final section of the preceding chapter focused on determining whether an instrument is negotiable. In this chapter, we deal with properly negotiating negotiable paper. Under UCC 3-203, the required purpose of a transfer under the definition of negotiation is giving the person receiving delivery the right of the transferor to enforce the instrument. It is crucial therefore to provide evidence of this purpose in such transfers. How this is done hinges on whether you have bearer or order paper; bearer paper is negotiated one way and order paper another. Let's consider bearer paper first.

Bearer Paper

Bearer paper is a negotiable instrument that is: (1) issued payable to cash, bearer, or the equivalent and without any endorsements; or (2) issued payable to cash or to the order of someone, but the last endorsement is a blank endorsement. A **blank endorsement** does not designate a person to receive the payoff on the instrument. It is merely a signature.

Proper negotiation of bearer paper is accomplished by a mere transfer of possession. No endorsement is necessary.

Order Paper

Order paper is a negotiable instrument that: (1) has been issued to a specific party and has not yet been endorsed; or (2) whether issued to cash or to a specific person, it has a special endorsement at the end of its endorsement chain. A **special endorsement** names the endorsee and directs that the instrument be paid to the endorsee. In such an endorsement, the expression "pay to the order of" or "pay to" is followed by the name of the recipient. Note that, for brevity's sake, on the reverse of an instrument, "pay to" is legally treated as the equivalent of "pay to the order of."

Proper negotiation of order paper must occur by endorsement of the holder accompanied by a transfer of possession to another party. A transfer without the proper endorsement is classified as an assignment.

Consider the accompanying examples closely.

◆ An instrument created as negotiable order paper

Carryl Taylor bought a shipment of vitamins for his business from his supplier, Wayne Washam. He made out a check to Wayne, naming him as payee, and handed it to him. At that point, the check was considered order paper and required Wayne's signature and transfer of possession for a proper negotiation.

Carryl Taylor	1313
Rt. 2	
Pennsboro, MO 65707	December 10 20 **
Pay to the Order of **Wayne Washam**	$ 237.50
Two Hundred and Thirty-Seven and 50/100	DOLLARS
People's Bank of Pennsboro	*Carryl Taylor*
⑆366222967⑈000373318 8238 ⑈1313	

◆ Endorsed in blank, thereby becoming bearer paper

Wayne used the check to pay off a debt to Buff Chassie. To do so, Wayne endorsed the instrument in blank and transferred possession to Buff.

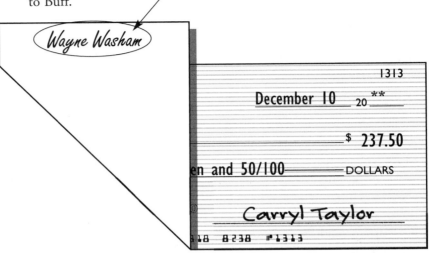

◆ Left unchanged as negotiable bearer paper

Chassie bought some fuel for his furnace. The bill came to $250. Chassie negotiated Taylor's check over to Shore Oil, Inc., simply by handing it to their cashier (transferring possession, as it was bearer paper) and paid the additional $12.50 in cash.

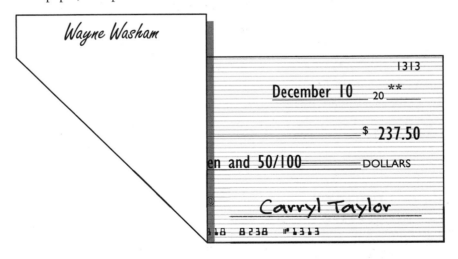

- Given a special endorsement to become negotiable order paper

  Shore Oil Company's President, Paula Sweetcrude, then signed the check over to Shore's supplier, Cielnoir, Inc. with a special endorsement and a transfer or possession. *Note that the transfer of possession was all that was required for a proper negotiation in this instance* but Sweetcrude wisely created order paper by her special endorsement. She did this so that Cielnoir's endorsement would serve as some evidence of the transaction.

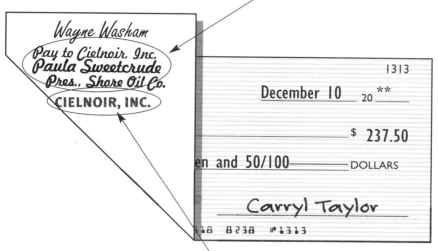

- Deposited in bank for collection

  When Cielnoir deposited the check in its bank, it endorsed the instrument (this time with a stamp) in blank. When the bank tried to collect, Carryl Taylor refused to pay the instrument because the vitamins he had bought with it proved to be spoiled once the containers were opened. Because the instrument was negotiable and properly negotiated to it and because it gave value in good faith without notice of defect or dishonor, Cielnoir was an HDC and could recover the amount of the check from Taylor regardless of his defense of failure of consideration. Carryl would have to sue Wayne Washam to recover for his (Carryl's) loss.

Other Kinds of Endorsements

As shown above, the proper method of negotiating a negotiable instrument in the future may be determined by using either a blank or special endorsement. However, two additional endorsements, the qualified endorsement and the restrictive endorsement, may also affect the use of negotiable instruments. The qualified endorsement helps determine the degree of the transferor's exposure to liability based on his or her use of the instrument. The restrictive endorsement curtails the rights of the endorsee, but it does no more than that.

Sources of an Endorser's Potential Liability   Whenever a check, note, or other form of negotiable instruments is circulated, two types of potential liability may attach to parties through whose hands the instrument passes. The first type of liability stems from warranties the courts may imply against parties to any transfer of such an instrument. These warranties are discussed later in this chapter.

The second type of potential liability comes from signatures. As a general rule, only a person whose signature appears on the instrument is exposed to this type of potential liability, although there are a few exceptions to this rule. One exception makes a forger or someone who signs another's signature without authorization liable on that signature as if it were his or her own. A second exception makes the person whose signature is forged or given without authority liable if she or he **ratifies** (approves or confirms) the act. Typically, other than in these cases, a person must sign the instrument in his or her own name to be liable on that signature.

Signature-based liability on negotiable instruments is either primary or secondary. **Primary liability** is defined as the unconditional responsibility to pay an instrument whenever it is due. The maker of a promissory note or a certificate of deposit is primarily liable thereon. Although no one is primarily liable on a draft when it is issued, the drawee becomes so on acceptance.

Secondary liability is the legal responsibility to pay an instrument whenever the party primarily liable does not. It is owed to the current holder and all subsequent endorsers. Secondary liability attaches only when the instrument has been properly presented for payment to the party primarily liable, when that party has refused payment, and when notice of the refusal or dishonor has been given to the parties who are potentially secondarily liable. The drawers of drafts are secondarily liable thereon. Endorsers of all forms of negotiable instruments can be secondarily liable unless they use a qualified endorsement.

Effect of Qualified Endorsements on Liability   A **qualified endorsement** uses "without recourse" or a similar phrase in conjunction with an endorsement. Qualifying an endorsement in this manner eliminates signature-based liability, but not liability based on the warrantee. Figure 19-2 is an example of using the words, "without recourse" as Wayne Washam did to cancel his potential signature-based liability on the instrument.

FIGURE 19-1	Parties Who Are Primarily and Secondarily Liable Based on Signature	
	Notes	Drafts
Primary	Maker	No one until acceptance of primary liability by drawee
Secondary	Endorsers unless qualified (see the section on "Effect of the Qualified Endorsement")	Drawer and endorsers (unless endorsers are qualified)

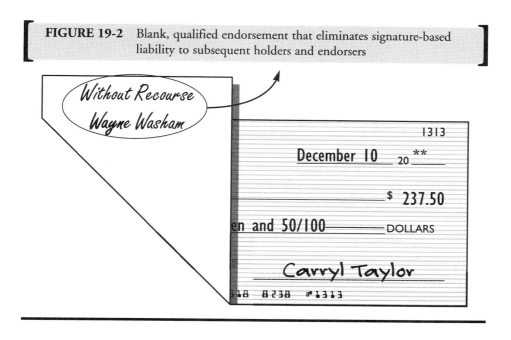

Restrictive Endorsements and the Rights of the Endorsee A **restrictive endorsement** curtails or restricts the rights of the transferee. Examples include expressions such as "for deposit only," "for collection only," "pay to [endorsee's name] only," and the wording in Figure 19-3, which would be considered a special, restrictive endorsement.

There are two important things to remember about restrictive endorsements. One, already mentioned, is that the endorsement restricts only the rights of the immediate transferor and does not prevent further negotiation. So, a check endorsed "for collection only, Bill Blaase" could be treated as though it had only a blank endorsement by future holders except for the party who took it from Bill Blaase and, for some reason, did not collect on it. An immediate transferee who does not follow the restriction imposed by the endorsement may be liable for the tort of conversion.

Second, putting restrictive endorsements on a conditional basis may not affect the negotiability of the instrument. Recall that a condition imposed at the time of issuance (e.g., "pay to the order of Cielnoir, Inc., only upon delivery of T–32 pump as per order" on the face of the instrument) defeats the instrument's negotiability. But such conditions can be imposed on the reverse of the instrument to accompany endorsements without any effect on negotiability.

A Few Miscellaneous Points about Endorsements If wording on the reverse of an instrument reads like an assignment, the UCC insists that it is to be treated as an endorsement. Thus, if the reverse reads "I hereby assign all my rights under this instrument to Timothy Leery" and is signed by the holder, Bill Blaase, then the effect of the transfer is that of a negotiation.

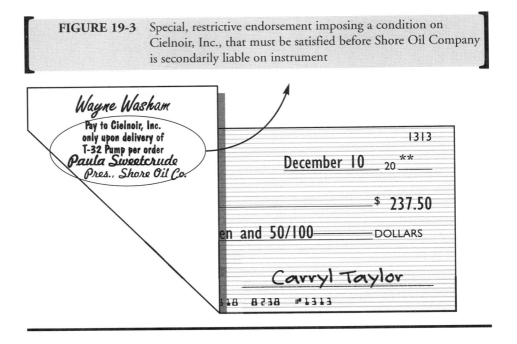

FIGURE 19-3   Special, restrictive endorsement imposing a condition on Cielnoir, Inc., that must be satisfied before Shore Oil Company is secondarily liable on instrument

Another quirk in the law comes from the pressure of necessity. In particular, the law allows a **depository bank** (the first bank to which an instrument is transferred for collection) to act as an agent of its customer (the depositor) by supplying his or her endorsement if it is missing from the instrument. This facilitates collection by eliminating the delay of holding the instrument until the proper signature is obtained.

Finally, if the endorsee's name is misspelled, the UCC allows that party to endorse it with the correct spelling or the previous incorrect spelling, or both. However, a transferee giving value for the instrument may, again by the dictates of UCC, require the transferor to sign both ways.

How a Holder in Due Course Overcomes the Defenses of the Obligor

Basically, the crucial point of negotiable instruments law is that a holder in due course who takes a negotiable instrument that has been properly negotiated is more likely to collect on the negotiable instruments involved. This lowered risk of being unable to collect stems from an HDC's rights, which can overcome many of the defenses traditionally raised against collection on a check, draft, note, or other instrument. To build on this key point, let's look at the range of possible defenses and see which are good against all holders. Then, we'll examine defenses that can be overcome by the rights of an HDC.

In other words, a valid defense from the first category prevents holders, HDCs, HHDCs, and, of course, mere assignees, from collecting on a check, draft, or other negotiable instrument for which they may have paid good money. These are called **real** (or universal) **defenses**.

The second category of defenses works only against mere holders and assignees, but can be overcome by HDCs and HHDCs. These defenses are called **personal** (or limited) **defenses**.

Real Defenses

The key to most real defenses is that a void transaction is or was involved in the issuance of the instrument.

Illegality   An example of illegality as a defense occurs when an instrument has been issued in conjunction with an illegal gambling debt. Because the transaction underlying the issuance is void, the real defense of illegality can be raised in court and prevent collection by any and all holders of the check or promissory note that resulted. Instruments resulting from bribery or extortion also fall into this subcategory.

Forgery or Unauthorized Signature   Again, the underlying transaction is void. Consequently, the defense of forged or unauthorized signature of the maker or drawer is valid against all holders. The only exceptions to this rule are situations where the negligence of the drawer or issuer have contributed to the forgery or unauthorized signature.

Hypothetical Case

Bruce negligently left his checkbook in the child's seat of his shopping cart at the supermarket. It disappeared but was returned shortly by store personnel. They reported finding it near the magazine rack where Bruce had been standing. Bruce, thinking that he had merely dropped the checkbook, did not examine the numbered checks and thus, did not notice that the last five had been ripped out. Consequently, when checks in the amount of several hundreds of dollars were passed over his forged signature, the court had to choose between placing the loss on Bruce and placing it on the innocent holders of the instruments. Because Bruce's negligence was evident, he had to sustain the loss.

Discharge as a Result of Bankruptcy Proceedings   Chapter 23 discusses bankruptcy. Here, we just point out that the determinations of a bankruptcy proceeding can result in a real defense against the collection of any of the bankrupt's outstanding instruments.

Material Alteration   Among the many examples of material alteration are adding figures to the amount or deleting figures from it, no matter how small their significance; unauthorized completion; and changing the date or dates involved. If made with a fraudulent intent, such changes produce a real defense against collection of the instrument. The extent of the defense differs. It is a defense to the full amount due when a mere holder seeks to collect. A person with the rights of an HDC however, can enforce the instrument for its original amount (or even for an amount fraudulently inserted on an incomplete instrument resulting from the issuer's negligence in leaving part of the instrument blank).

Fraud in the Execution

Hypothetical Case

Billy Boots, a sudden smash country-and-western star, walked down the stairs after an evening performance at the *Star on Stage* review in Branson, Missouri. Several fans pushed toward him. Billy signed their playbills without glancing at them. One, a blank piece of stiff, white 67-pound paper, was immediately pulled back by the person who had offered it, a tall raven-haired woman of about 30. Billy caught her eye for a brief moment, and she self-consciously smiled at him, then disappeared into the darkness. Two months later Billy received a call from his business manager. Commercial Bank of Branson had just called for payment of a $100,000 promissory note it was holding. Commercial had bought the note from a "Suzanne Williams," one of its depositors. It had paid $95,000 for the note and wanted the $100,000, as the note had just become due. When Billy examined the instrument, he remembered the raven-haired woman, who had evidently printed the note around his signature on the blank piece of paper. In the meantime Suzanne Williams had disappeared. Will the bank as a holder in due course be able to overcome Billy's defense of fraud?

The answer is no (1) if Billy did not act negligently or carelessly in succumbing to the fraud, and (2) if Billy did not know he was creating an instrument or was totally deceived as to the instrument's essential terms. **Fraud in the execution**, in which the party does not even "realize that she or he is issuing a negotiable instrument," is a real defense. If that defense were successfully established in court, the bank could not collect from Billy. Given the above circumstances, such would probably be the case. The bank would then have to recover against Suzanne Williams, the secondarily liable party, or just bear the loss. In another section of this chapter fraud in the inducement is discussed, which should be compared with fraud in the execution.

Infancy   As you may suspect, minority as it relates to the capacity to contract produces a real defense to negotiable instruments issued in the contractual context. Otherwise, if, for example, a minor issued a check to pay for an expensive car, she could avoid the contract but would be required to pay the check.

Insanity and Habitual Drunkenness   As you probably recall, whenever the law recognizes either insanity or habitual drunkenness in an individual, it appoints a guardian for that individual. This process renders void all contracts made by the protected party. Thus, on behalf of the protected party's estate, the guardian can enter a real defense against any negotiable instruments the protected party issues.

Extreme Duress   If negotiable instruments have been issued by a person under extreme duress, the issuer can raise a successful real defense to their collection. In most states, **extreme duress** is defined as a threat against the issuer or his or her immediate family. The threat must be of death, severe bodily harm, or the destruction of the issuer's home, and it must cause the issuer to act in a way that she or he would not have acted otherwise. However, there is a difference between extreme duress and ordinary duress. Ordinary duress is discussed later in this chapter.

Statute of Limitations   Many states impose a statute of limitations on the collection of negotiable instruments. If this period has expired, it will produce a real defense.

Personal Defenses

The defenses in this category are good only against mere holders and assignees. HDCs and HHDCs are able to collect regardless of the personal defenses raised against them.

Breach of Contract or Failure of Consideration   In situations where negotiable instruments have been issued to bind a transaction, a personal or limited defense is available when the contract is not properly executed or the consideration is faulty or lacking.

Hypothetical Case

Stan Crucial owned a restaurant in St. Louis. Deciding to go into catering, he bought a new delivery van from Sally's Service Vehicles. He issued a check for $3,000 as a down payment for the van and signed a promissory note for the $27,000 balance. Unfortunately, the delivery of the van was delayed several weeks past the promised date. Consequently, Stan lost considerable business for which he had already signed contracts. When the van was finally delivered, its faulty heating and cooling systems caused food spoilage. Stan tried to use the breach of contract (late delivery) and failure of consideration (faulty good) as offsets to the amounts due on the negotiable instruments he had issued in the transaction. Unfortunately, Stan had to pay the check as Sally's had transferred it to an HDC, which could overcome the defenses. When Sally's tried to collect on the note however, Stan offset his damages from the amount due to Sally's Service Vehicles. He could do this because Sally's Service Vehicles had knowledge of the van's defects. Sally's therefore, could not be a holder in due course on the instrument. As a mere holder, it could not overcome Stan's personal defenses of breach of contract and failure of consideration.

Fraud in the Inducement and Similar Defenses   When a person is deceived or defrauded into issuing negotiable instruments, a personal defense of **fraud in the inducement** results. In fraud in the inducement, unlike fraud in the execution, the issuer knows she or he is making out an instrument.

Other circumstances leading to a voidable contract also produce personal defenses to negotiable instruments issued in the voidable transaction. Misrepresentation, undue influence, temporary insanity, and temporary intoxication all produce this effect in most jurisdictions. **Ordinary duress**, which is typically found in economic threats or legitimate threats of criminal prosecution, also results in a voidable contract and a personal defense.

Consumer Transaction Defenses

Finally, nearly 20 years ago, in response to many consumer complaints, the Federal Trade Commission (FTC) issued a rule that greatly affected the collection of negotiable instruments issued in consumer transactions. In effect, the FTC decreed that in a transaction in which a negotiable instrument is issued in payment, all claims and defenses available to a consumer are effective even against a person with the rights of a holder in due course in relation to that paper. In other words, where consumer credit instruments (drafts and notes) are concerned, HDCs and HHDCs are treated exactly the same as mere holders are treated and are subject to whatever defenses mere holders are subject. See *Blue Cross Health Services* v. *Sauer*, the case at the end of this chapter, for a real-life example of the difference this makes.

Warranties Flowing from Negotiable Instruments

Earlier in this chapter, we noted there were two bases for liability on negotiable instruments. Liability based on signature was the first basis we discussed. Now, we examine the second: warrantee-based liability.

Just as it does in sales situations, the law implies certain warranties against the transferor of negotiable instruments. If the transfer is made by endorsement and delivery, the warranties flow to the immediate transferee and all later holders who take the instrument in good faith. If the transfer is made by delivery alone, the signature of the transferor does not appear on the paper, and the warranties therefore flow only to the immediate transferee.

The warranties are as follows:

1. *Good title.* In effect, the transferor is held to warrant that she or he has good title or is authorized to act on behalf of the person who has good title to the instrument.

2. *Genuine or authorized signatures.* By this warranty, the transferor implicitly acknowledges that all foregoing signatures on the instrument are genuine. In the event of a forgery or an unauthorized signature on the instrument, no matter how distant from the transferor in the endorsement chain, the transferor is liable and may have to take the loss unless a transferor further up the chain can be saddled with accountability.

3. *No material alteration.* Given this warranty, you can understand the reluctance of a potential holder to take an instrument made out in pencil. With such an instrument, the possibility of undetectable alterations poses too great a risk.

4. *No defense against the transferor by any party to the instrument.* This warranty is softened somewhat for qualified endorsers. They are held only to a warranty that they have no actual knowledge of any such defenses.

5. *No knowledge of any insolvency proceedings against the issuer or acceptor of the instrument.*

Obviously, warranty coverages are quite broad. Taken together with signature-based liability, they reduce significantly the potential for loss on negotiable instruments. That diminished potential for loss combined with the convenience of negotiable instruments has led to the flood of checks, drafts, notes, and other instruments used in our capitalist economy.

Technology Insights

Counterfeiting in the Digital Era

The availability of scanners, appropriate software, and cutting-edge technology printers continues to make the Secret Service's job of preventing counterfeiting a nightmare. Current estimates indicate that approximately half of all counterfeiting is now done digitally using expertise widely available. Southern California leads all other jurisdictions with the introduction of more than $100,000 a day in counterfeit notes. Foreign nations such as Iran and Libya also are alleged to be falsifying U.S. currency. Consequently, at a cost of almost five cents a bill, the U.S. Treasury has introduced a variety of preventative devices, many of which are not generally known. They include

◆   A presidential portrait watermark that you can see from both sides when the note is held up to the light.

◆   The relatively obvious polymer security thread embedded vertically in the paper next to the portrait along with the denomination of the note. Unknown to most, however, is the fact that a flag also is embedded next to the portrait. The flag and the denomination are visible under bright light, and the security thread glows a different color under an ultraviolet light.

◆   All but the $5 denomination has a special embedded ink that turns different shades of green and black when the bill is held at different angles.

Think Critically   How important is the fight against counterfeiting? What would be the result if we let such activities go on unchecked? Can you suggest any preventative measures the government might consider? What is the key to effective anti-counterfeiting activities?

CHAPTER REVIEW

USE LEGAL TERMS

Fill in the blanks with the appropriate term.

bearer paper	negotiation	ratifies
blank endorsement	order paper	real defenses
depository bank	ordinary duress	restrictive endorsement
extreme duress	personal defenses	secondary liability
fraud in the execution	primary liability	special endorsement
fraud in the inducement	qualified endorsement	

1. The first bank into which a check is deposited for collection is referred to as the ___?___.
2. While he's on vacation, Randy Reelestate's secretary issues a check for a down payment on a piece of property he's been trying to buy for five years. When he returns, she informs him of what she has done. He will be liable on the instrument if he agrees to pay the check or, in other words, if he ___?___ it.
3. If a negotiable instrument has been properly transferred so as to make the transferee a holder of some kind, the paper has been ___?___.
4. "For Deposit Only" is an example of a(n) ___?___.
5. After Angelica threatened to vandalize his car, Bill gave her a check for $500. Bill's defense against collection of this instrument is ___?___.
6. The maker of a note and the acceptor of a draft have ___?___ on the respective instruments.
7. The drawer of a check has ___?___ on the instrument.

TEST YOUR READING

8. How is bearer paper properly negotiated?
9. How is order paper properly negotiated?
10. What type of endorsement limits an endorser's signature-based liability on an instrument?
11. Name four real defenses.
12. What is the difference between fraud in the inducement and fraud in the execution?
13. Under what circumstances do warranties not extend beyond the immediate transferee?
14. Do holders in due course have any advantage over mere holders in collecting on consumer paper?

THINK CRITICALLY ABOUT EVIDENCE

15. For the following examples (figures a through e), name the type of endorse-
     ment and then state the requirements for further negotiation of the instrument.

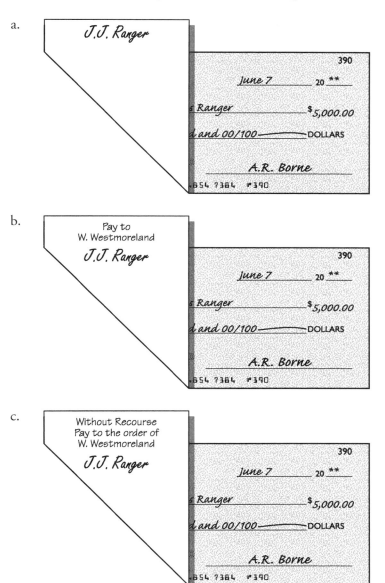

a.
b.
c.

d.

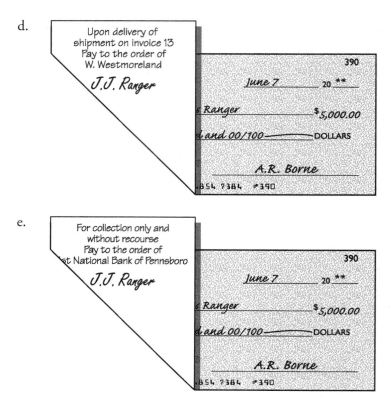

e.

16. For each of the following situations, determine whether the specified person with the rights of a holder in due course can recover on the instrument in question. In each instance, be sure to specify the type of defense the obligor would raise.

    a. Patsi Johnson wrote a $350 check in payment for a sophisticated electric-powered Jeep she bought for her granddaughter. The Jeep's battery exploded, ruining the vehicle. Could a bank that qualifies as an HDC recover on the check?

    b. M. T. Pockets went through bankruptcy. After the process, the 1st National Bank of Pennsboro (an HDC) requested payment from him on a note he had signed prior to his bankruptcy filing. Could the bank recover on the note?

    c. Charles Smith stopped payment on a check on which his name had been forged as a drawer. Could a bank that qualifies as an HDC recover on the check?

    d. Lee Infant, while 16 years of age, wrote a check to pay for some records he purchased with money he had been saving for college. His parents had him void the transaction. Could a bank that qualifies as an HDC recover on the check?

e.   Dee Seived wrote a $15,000 check to buy stock in a fraudulent scheme to purchase the Brooklyn Bridge and move it to England for use as a tourist attraction. Could a bank that qualifies as an HDC recover on the check?

17.   What is the advantage to the transferee of having bearer paper endorsed by the transferor?

REAL-WORLD CASE
Blue Cross Health Services v. Sauer
800 S.W.2d 72

Decide what to do about the more than $22,000 in checks that Blue Cross sent to the wrong person.

Because of a clerical error, 33 checks totaling more than $22,000 were sent to William Sauer of Chesterfield, Missouri, instead of William Sauer of Milwaukee, Wisconsin. The Missouri man had been in the hospital at about the same time as the Wisconsin man's son. Both Sauers had been insured by Blue Cross, and the 33 checks had been sent sporadically over a seven-month span. When Blue Cross brought suit to reclaim the money paid erroneously to Sauer of Missouri, he claimed he was a holder in due course of the instruments. Therefore, he maintained he could collect on them regardless of any defense of failure of consideration or breach of contract that Blue Cross might raise. In examining this claim, the court determined that each check sent to Sauer of Missouri had been accompanied by an "explanation of benefits" form and that his father, who had been paying his Blue Cross premiums, had stopped paying them before Sauer of Missouri's most recent hospitalization.

Think Critically

1.   Applying the definition of an HDC to Sauer of Missouri's circumstances, determine whether he must repay the money. What are your conclusions?

2.   Ethically, should Sauer of Missouri be forced to repay the more than $22,000 in checks sent to him by mistake if it is shown that in cashing and spending the checks he acted in good faith and without knowledge that mistakes had been made?

CHAPTER 20

Discharge of Negotiable Instruments

GOALS

- ◆ Understand how negotiable instruments are discharged
- ◆ Understand how financial institutions support the use of negotiable instruments
- ◆ Determine when special rules apply to negotiable instruments

Discharging Negotiable Instruments

In sections 3-601 through 3-605, the UCC lists methods of **discharging** (terminating a party's legal obligation to pay) liability on an instrument. Realize that even after an individual's obligation on a check, draft, or other negotiable instrument has ended, the paper can remain due and payable. When this occurs, the discharge is effective only if notice of it is given to subsequent HDCs. A qualified endorsement is an example of this. The expression "without recourse" gives notice to all later owners of the instrument that the qualified party is not liable on her or his signature. With that in mind, let's review the most significant items on the UCC's list of potential ways to be discharged from responsibility on negotiable instruments.

By Payment or Satisfaction

Obviously, for most negotiable instruments, discharge comes from full, complete payment. It is a tribute to the adequacy of the laws governing the use and flow of such instruments that relatively few cases need to be adjudicated.

In dealing with discharge by payment, some cases involve an accord and satisfaction. Basically, an **accord and satisfaction** involves the discharge of a party from a previous contractual obligation (satisfaction) by his or her fulfillment of the terms of a new contract (the accord). An example is given in the hypothetical case below.

Hypothetical Case

Jason Tarleton, a contractor, lost $6,000 in penalties because he was late in completing the Barstone Causeway Project. Jason blamed his tardiness on the tardiness of one of his suppliers, Reliable Rebar, Inc. When he threatened suit, Reliable Rebar sent him the following check:

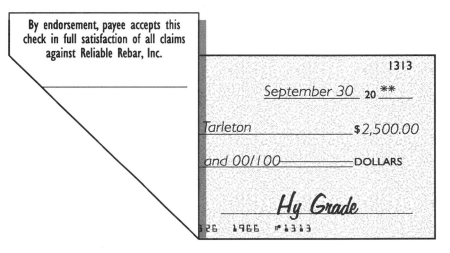

Jason took the check, then lined out the wording on the reverse and substituted his own, which read:

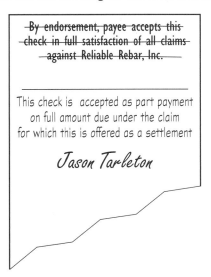

A court eventually held that regardless of Jason's reasons for cashing the check as expressed in his endorsement, the drawer had offered an accord by sending the check to him. In cashing the check therefore, Jason had brought about a satisfaction of the foregoing contractual dispute over Reliable Rebar's tardiness.

Note that some parties try to imply an accord and satisfaction by writing such comments as "payment in full" on the face of a check that is only one of many installment payments. Unless foregoing negotiations support an accord in which one payment cancels the whole obligation, the notation on the check has no effect.

Unlike the tender of a ready, willing, and able offer to perform under a contract, a **tender of payment** does not discharge the obligor's responsibility on a due instrument. However, it will discharge the tendering party from liability for subsequent interest, attorney's fees, and other costs associated with collection. It will also discharge any endorser and accommodation party to the extent of the amount tendered. If the instrument is not mature, a tender of payment has none of these effects unless the terms include the acceptability of payment "on or before" the due date.

By Cancellation or Renunciation

Any holder of an instrument may, with or without consideration, cancel any party's obligation. This is done on the face or reverse of the instrument by striking out the party's signature or by any other means that informs a prospective holder that the party is no longer obligated on the instrument. Cancellation can also be accomplished by simply destroying or mutilating the instrument.

Renunciation, the abandonment of a right without transferring it to another, can be accomplished by delivering a signed writing to that effect to the party so discharged. Surrendering the instrument to the party to be discharged has the same result (UCC 3-604).

By Impairment of Recourse or Collateral

This rule is a bit complicated, but once understood, it makes a great deal of common sense. Assume that Dannee Frail needed an education loan of $7,000 to pursue his studies. He borrowed the money from his friend, William Winton. Dannee then issued in Winton's favor a promissory note in that amount plus interest. To give further assurance that the loan would be repaid, Dannee also promised William Winton and anyone who took the note from him, the right, upon default, to sell Dannee's car and use the proceeds to satisfy whatever amount that might still remain to be paid. Winton then sold the note to Theodore K. Runamukus, who sold it to Georgio Bushini. Bushini, as holder, bipartisanly released Dannee from his promise to let Winton sell his car to pay for any default on the note. He also canceled Winton's signature and secondary liability by lining through Winton's endorsement. A copy of the face (top) and the reverse of Dannee Frail's promissory note issued to William Winton as they appeared when Bushini tried to collect the balance due appears in Figure 20-1.

However, when Bushini tried to collect on the note, he found that Frail could not pay. Bushini then gave proper notice of default to Runamukus so as to make him secondarily liable. Runamukus was quick to point out that Bushini had impaired Runamukus's chances of recourse against Winton by canceling Winton's

FIGURE 20-1   Face and reverse of Dannee Frail's promissory note issued to William Winton as they appeared when Bushini tried to collect the balance due

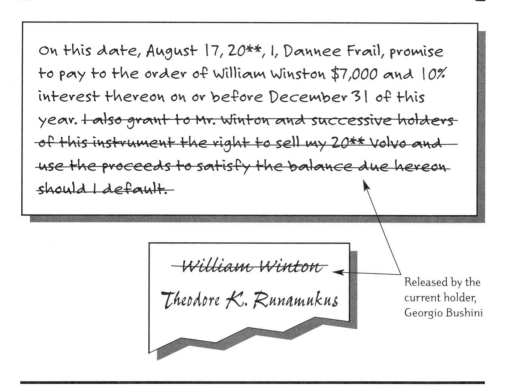

On this date, August 17, 20**, I, Dannee Frail, promise to pay to the order of William Winston $7,000 and 10% interest thereon on or before December 31 of this year. ~~I also grant to Mr. Winton and successive holders of this instrument the right to sell my 20** Volvo and use the proceeds to satisfy the balance due hereon should I default.~~

~~William Winton~~
Theodore K. Runamukus

Released by the current holder, Georgio Bushini

obligation and Runamukus's chances of recourse against the collateral (the Volvo) by releasing Frail from his promise to allow its sale to cover any amount due on default. As a consequence, according to UCC 3-605, Runamukus had been discharged. Bushini immediately called his lawyer, who reluctantly agreed with Runamukus.

The point is that it would be unfair to allow a current holder to cancel the rights of a previous holder of an instrument and then expect that holder to pay off the instrument without them. The UCC rule prevents this inequity.

By Reacquisition of an Instrument by a Prior Party

Remember the rule that no one can improve his or her status by reacquisition? We ran into that rule in discussing holders who could not be holders in due course on their own but tried to get the rights of an HDC by selling to one and then buying the instrument back. This rule follows the same principle. For example, forget about the release of parties and collateral by Bushini. Instead, presume that Winton reacquired the unaltered instrument from Bushini. This is shown in Figure 20-2.

FIGURE 20-2

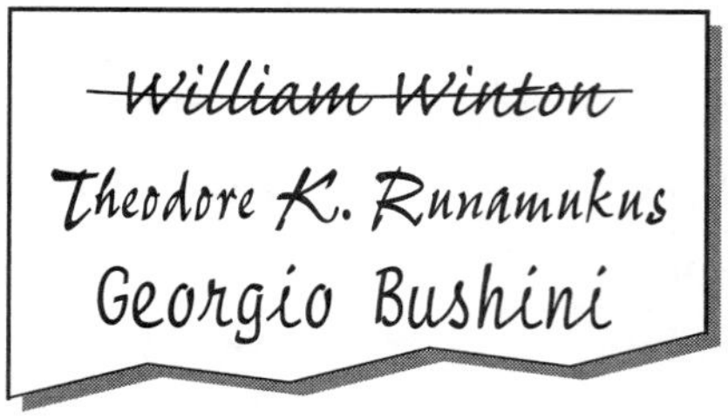

~~William Winton~~
Theodore K. Runamukus
Georgio Bushini

To be consistent with the HDC application, we cannot allow Winton, upon default by Frail, to pursue Runamukus and Bushini on their signature-based secondary liabilities. If Winton were able to do so, he would have improved his status by reacquisition. Therefore, Runamukus and Bushini are discharged.

Other Means of Discharge Listed in the UCC

* Certification of a check (discussed in the next section)
* Fraudulent and material alteration (discussed under Defenses in Chapter 19)
* Unexcused delay in presentment or notice of dishonor
* Acceptance varying a draft. When the potential acceptor negotiates with the holder to vary the terms of the draft itself as a condition of acceptance, the drawer and endorsers are discharged unless they agree to remain accountable under the new terms.

The obligation of the paper itself or that of any of the parties to the paper can be discharged in whole or in part by any of these means. However, it is important to remember that almost all negotiable instruments are discharged simply by being paid according to their terms. Considering the volume the negotiable instruments system must handle, its reliability has been proven many times over. It is an essential, smooth-functioning facilitator of commercial and personal endeavors.

Financial Institutions and Negotiable Instruments

Banks, savings and loans, credit unions, and other financial institutions are all crucial in making the negotiable instruments system work. In addition, the federal government administers a very efficient transmittal and clearance procedure for the instruments at the heart of the system.

Creating New Methods of Resource Transfer

A major innovation in the negotiable instruments system is **electronic fund transfers** (EFTs). In place of checks, drafts, and other paper instruments, EFTs employ a powerful combination of electronics and computer technology. Without any action by the depositor, paychecks are automatically deposited in employee accounts and drafted on to pay recurrent bills automatically; automatic bank tellers "work" around the clock, allowing customers to do their banking without contacting any human employee of the institution; retail purchases are charged directly against account balances; and on and on. The only paper trail is found in a computer-printed form notifying the party at interest of the various transactions.

Of course, this system invites unchecked error, fraudulent schemes, and theft. Because the system has great advantages for financial institutions as well as conveniences for its users, the financial institutions carry greater risks of loss in exceptional circumstances. For example, when an EFT card is lost or stolen and used without authority, the card's owner is reimbursed for losses of more than $50 if the issuing financial institution is notified of the loss of the card within two business days. After two days, regardless of when notice is given, the limit for such consumer losses is $500. When the consumer's card is not lost or stolen but just used without authority, the consumer has up to 60 days after the "transmittal of the statement" to provide notice to the issuer so as to receive reimbursement.

These rules are vital and require due diligence on the part of the consumer. All too often, the consumer tends to rely on the electronic transfer system to prevent errors. Nonetheless, although computers have an aura of infallibility, such errors occur all too frequently. For example, consider the case of an 85-year-old woman, Jewell M. Miller, who was recently indirectly declared dead by her bank. The bank's computer refused to deposit in her account her EFTs from the Veterans and Social Security administrations. Those agencies, "thinking" she was indeed dead, immediately stopped sending her the monthly checks on which she depended for her livelihood. Mrs. Miller checked her pulse and then reported the error to her financial institution. Nevertheless, it was a full three months before her income was reinstated. According to the Electronic Fund Transfer Act of 1978, the law that governs EFT transactions (and provides the rules for lost and stolen EFT cards), a consumer has 60 days to report such an error (discovered through a careful review of bank statements and receipts) to the responsible institution. Upon notification, the institution has 10 business days to investigate. If it takes longer to complete the investigation (up to 45 days are allowed), it must at least recredit the customer's account with the amount in dispute after the 10 days. In Mrs. Miller's case, this recrediting had to be done as the dispute took far longer than 10 days to resolve.

Providing Specialty Instruments

Financial institutions satisfy their customers' needs by offering several special negotiable instruments. Traveler's checks, cashier's checks, and certified checks are the most common.

Traveler's Checks   These checks are purchased for both security and the ease with which they are cashed even when their owner is far from home. These factors stem from how traveler's checks are circulated. According to UCC 3-104(i), a **traveler's check** is a demand instrument drawn on or payable at or through a bank and which, in order to be cashed, requires a countersignature by the person whose specimen signature appears on it. The UCC also requires that such an instrument bear the term "traveler's check" or similar term, in order to be effective. In other words, when traveler's checks are purchased, the buyer or potential user signs each of them in the presence of the issuer. Thereafter, each traveler's check can be cashed only if its possessor is identified to the payee and countersigns in the payee's presence. Thus, the risk for the person who takes the traveler's check in payment for merchandise or cash is greatly reduced by simply requiring a picture ID and comparing signatures. The risk for people carrying the checks is also greatly reduced because their signatures, given in the payee's presence, are required to negotiate them. Moreover, many issuers of traveler's checks pride themselves on their promptness in replacing lost or stolen checks.

Cashier's Checks   With a **cashier's check**, as with a traveler's check, a bank is both the drawer and the drawee. A cashier's check can be issued payable to its purchaser or to any party its purchaser specifies. Because the bank has drawn the check on itself, the check is as good as the creditworthiness of the bank itself. This greatly enhances the likelihood that the instrument will be taken by a third party in lieu of cash. Also, the payee or holder knows that, by law, payment cannot be stopped on such a check, because by issuing it, the bank has already accepted primary liability.

Hypothetical Case

Murkey Hubbell agreed to buy a new telescope for $1,300 from a discounter in New York State. The discounter required payment by credit card or cashier's check. Murkey went to a local bank and purchased a cashier's check for $1,305 (the bank charged nondepositors a $5 service fee). She mailed the check by Priority Mail. The discounter shipped her telescope on receipt of the cashier's check, so Murkey received her new purchase barely a week after her original phone call. When she opened the package however, she discovered the telescope's mirror was scarred. She immediately contacted the discounter, who referred her to the manufacturer. The manufacturer stated that the discounter was not an authorized retailer for its products and refused to talk to her. Murkey then tried to get the bank to stop payment on the cashier's check. The bank refused to do so, stating that, by law, it had already accepted the primary liability to pay the instrument. Note that some discount retailers will accept a personal check but will not ship the goods until the check clears.

Certified Checks   The bank on which a **certified check** is drawn has accepted primary liability for it. This acceptance is best noted by writing "accepted" or "certified" on the check, along with the date and the signature of a bank official. However, acceptance can be indicated by the drawee's signature alone. Certification can be obtained at any time after issue. By so indicating acceptance, the drawee guarantees that sufficient funds are available for payment. According to the UCC, this certification is the equivalent of actual acceptance. Note that, according to the UCC, a refusal to certify a check is not a dishonor. When most banks certify such an instrument, they immediately subtract from the depositor's account the funds for payment.

By certification, the bank acquires primary liability to pay the instrument. However, the determination of the secondarily liable parties on such an instrument depends on who requested the certification. If the drawer of the check requested the certification, then that drawer and all endorsers are secondarily liable. However, if a holder has the instrument certified, the drawer and the intervening endorsers are discharged. The hypothetical case below is an example.

Hypothetical Case

Boyer paid Javier by check for $7,500 of sports equipment. Javier used the check to pay a debt to White. White then signed it over to Euchre as a down payment on a business. While Euchre was discussing the matter with White, he received a call from his employer informing him that he was being transferred to the West Coast immediately. To obtain access to funds at this new location, Euchre took the check to Boyer's bank to have the bank certify it. When the bank did so, Boyer, Javier, and White were all discharged from secondary liability on the instrument. This is only fair, as their secondary liability was only contingent on the bank's refusal to accept the check. It was accepted, so their potential liability ended at that point.

Managing the Negotiable Instruments System

At the heart of the negotiable instruments system are the financial institutions that, through customer relationships, keep the system intact and efficient. These relations are most frequently defined in contract form, particularly depository contracts.

Depository contracts are solely between the financial institution and its depositors/customers. Rights under these contracts are not assigned by depositors or payees by the issuance of instruments. So, for example, if a bank refuses to pay a check even if there are funds available, the payee/holder cannot bring suit to force it to do so. Any suit for payment of the amount due must instead be directed to the parties secondarily liable on the instrument or against the issuer based on the underlying contract, if there is one. The depositor can sue the bank for its failure to pay as a breach of the depository contract, but, once again, the holders of the instrument cannot.

Because the depository contract is pivotal to the functioning of the negotiable instruments system, we need to take a closer look at the relationship it creates. Primarily, this contract establishes the financial institution as the caretaker of the depositor's funds. The financial institution is to preserve them, keep them safe, and place them at the disposal of the depositor on that person's demand. The financial institution also serves as the **agent** (a person authorized by another to act in her or his stead) of the depositor in collecting negotiable instruments payable to the depositor. Any use of the money that the depository bank (the bank into which the instrument is deposited for collection) gives the depositor before the instrument has actually been paid by the bank on which it is drawn is only temporary, however. As a consequence, the depository bank can, under the depository contract, revoke the use of the money if the instrument is dishonored.

Turning the situation around, the depositor's bank is under a contractual duty to honor all checks drawn on the depositor's account when there are sufficient funds in it. If sufficient funds are not in the account to cover a check, the bank may pay it nonetheless. It may then bill the depositor for an administrative charge in addition to the amount of the **overdraft** (the amount of the check in excess of the deposited funds). If a bank decides not to pay the overdraft, it still may charge the depositor an administrative fee for reviewing the situation. Many institutions negotiate a line of credit that can be automatically drawn against in the case of a depositor's overdraft. Whether by using a line of credit or by simply paying an overdraft, the bank converts its position from that of the depositor's debtor to that of the depositor's creditor.

Should a **payor bank** (the bank that is the drawee of the draft) wrongfully dishonor a check, for example, when there are adequate funds in the depositor's account to pay it, the bank is liable for the proximate (direct) damages to the depositor that follow. These may include (to quote UCC 4-402) "damages for an arrest or prosecution of the customer or other consequential damages. Whether any consequential damages are proximately caused by the wrongful dishonor is a question of fact to be determined in each case."

Hypothetical Case

Bart Black and J. Silverheels had a long-standing dispute over the ownership of a horse named Scout. Finally, Black agreed to pay Silverheels $500 to settle things. To do so, he drew a check in that amount on his account at the National Bank of Pennsboro. Unfortunately, even though there were sufficient funds in the account, the bank refused to honor the check. As a consequence, Silverheels brought bad check and grand theft charges (for taking Scout) against Black. Black later sued the bank and received payment for the harm caused him by the dishonor. His recovery included actual damages (the expenses of finding another horse to replace Scout) and consequential damages (his lawyer's fees and other costs).

Such mistakes, given the number of instruments presented for payment each day, are infrequent. An unavoidable factor complicating this process is the requirement that the decision to pay each instrument must be reached by the payor institution's **midnight deadline**. This refers to midnight of the banking day following the day on which the instrument in question has been received.

Although the potential risks to banks are increased by some rules, such as those relating to the midnight deadline and the availability of proximate damages for wrongful dishonor, other rules protect these institutions, such as the following:

Stale Check Rule   A **stale check** is a check presented for payment more than six months after the date of issue indicated on its face. A bank is not liable for failing to pay such a check. In addition, a bank is not liable if it in good faith honors such an instrument. These rules are especially important because of the time limits imposed on stop-payment orders.

Stop-Payment Orders   A **stop-payment order** directs the drawee institution not to transfer funds in accordance with the terms of a previously issued draft. The drawee institution is given a reasonable time to execute the order. Thereafter, however, if it pays the instrument, it is liable to the depositor. UCC 4-403 states that an oral stop-payment order is effective for 14 calendar days only unless it is confirmed in writing during that period. A written stop-payment order is effective for 6 months unless it is renewed in writing for further terms. Each successive renewal must be requested during the previous term. Should the stop payment order not be renewed and the bank pay the check, the bank could be exposed to potential liability were it not for the stale check rule.

Death or Incompetence of a Customer   Similarly, a drawee financial institution is not liable (UCC 4-405) if it pays a check before it has received notice of the death or incompetence of a depositor. Even with this knowledge, the bank may continue to certify or pay checks for 10 days after it has received notice unless a stop-payment order is given.

Forgeries and Unauthorized Signatures   Although the law holds that any loss on a negotiable instrument falls on the person that took the instrument from a forger, UCC 4-406 places squarely on the shoulders of depositors the duty to examine promptly and with reasonable care their account statements. The statements and accompanying items must be made available to depositors in a reasonable manner. Depositors must then report unauthorized signatures and other problems promptly to the bank. Depositors who fail to do so cannot hold their banks liable for any loss sustained because the banks paid on a forgery, an unauthorized signature, or a material alteration. However, should a depositor be able to show that the bank paid over a forgery, the depositor's account should be recredited unless she or he has been negligent.

The Impostor and Fictitious Payee Rules   In addition, financial institutions can avoid liability if it can be shown that the depositor's negligence contributed to a loss resulting from an unauthorized signature or a material alteration. For example, negligently leaving your checkbook on a golf cart from which it was stolen precludes you from forcing the bank to recredit your account for any forged check from the checkbook. Therefore, you would most likely take the loss for what occurred unless you could find and recover from the forger. This rule not only protects financial institutions but rightfully places responsibility for such problems on the party most able to prevent them, that is, the party whose negligence gave rise to the problems.

The idea of placing responsibility on the party most able to prevent the problem is also reflected in the **impostor rule**. If one party is duped into issuing an instrument to a person whom the issuer has misidentified, the loss from the resulting forgery falls on the careless issuer.

Hypothetical Case

Vaughn Richthoften's barnstorming air show business had just gone bankrupt, and he desperately needed money to start over. Finally, he hit on a plan. Knowing that Charles Shooltz, one of the 12 wealthiest persons in the world, supported almost all children's charities, Richthoften called Shooltz and posed as the local campaign chairperson for the Jerry Lewis Telethon. As such, he obtained Shooltz's promise to donate $100,000 to the latest effort. Richthoften later drove up to the Shooltz estate and collected the check personally. He then forged the telethon's endorsement and cashed the instrument. Shooltz's accountant discovered the deception a few days after the bank statement came. Richthoften could not be located. Shooltz sued to get the bank to recredit his account as it had paid on a forgery and the rule is that the loss falls on the person who takes from the forger. Unfortunately for Shooltz, his negligence in failing to unmask the impostor by requiring proper identification caused the court to shift responsibility from the bank to him. As a consequence, Shooltz had to bear the loss and the bank did not have to recredit the account.

The **fictitious payee rule**, a rule similar to the impostor rule, works similarly under slightly different circumstances. The rule is used when an employee tricks her or his employer by providing the name of a payee to whom the employer is to issue an instrument in payment of a supposed obligation that is, in reality, nonexistent. The employee then takes the instrument, endorses it with the payee's signature, and cashes it for his or her own benefit. In such an event, the rule is invoked to force the employer to bear the loss because the loss is held to result from the employer's negligence in placing the employee in the position of trust that allowed execution of the scheme.

The protection that the above rules afford is generally well deserved by our financial institutions, especially if they are to fulfill all that our negotiable instruments system demands and those who benefit from it expect.

CHAPTER REVIEW

USE LEGAL TERMS

Fill in the blanks with the appropriate term.

accord and satisfaction   fictitious payee rule   stale check
agent   impostor rule   stop-payment order
cashier's check   midnight deadline   tender of payment
certified check   overdraft   traveler's check
discharge   payor bank
electronic fund transfers   renunciation

1. Electronic tellers and direct deposits are examples of ___?___.
2. A(n) ___?___ must be signed by the user in front of the issuer and the payee.
3. A(n) ___?___, which is an instrument more than six months old, does not have to be paid by its drawee bank.
4. A(n) ___?___ has a bank for its drawer and drawee, and a stop-payment order is ineffective against it.
5. A bank accepts primary liability on a(n) ___?___ issued by its depositor, and then allows the instrument to be returned to circulation.
6. An agreement to discharge a party from a preexisting debt upon payment of a late charge of 10 percent on the debt plus principal and interest is an example of a(n) ___?___.
7. The amount of a check in excess of the checking account balance is known as a(n) ___?___.
8. An oral ___?___ is good for two weeks, but if placed in writing, it is good for six months.

TEST YOUR READING

9. List five different ways that liability under a negotiable instrument can be discharged.

10. Explain the effect of a tender of payment on a negotiable instrument's principal amount due. What is the effect on the interest?

11. Why do we not allow prior holders to improve their status by reacquisiton?

12. What is the difference between a cashier's check and a certified check?

13. What makes a traveler's check safer than an ordinary check?

14. What is a bank's potential liability if it wrongfully dishonors one of your checks?

15. Does a written stop payment order remain in effect indefinitely? Why or why not?

16. How is the depositor's negligence involved in the impostor and fictitious payee rules?

THINK CRITICALLY ABOUT EVIDENCE

17. Ben Cartwrong thought he could get out of making the remaining 34 monthly installments (totaling more than $14,000) on his new car by writing "accepted as payment in full" on the top of the reverse side of the current check he was sending in as payment. He had not communicated with the creditor at all.

    a. If the payee/creditor signs under the endorsement, does Ben still owe the remainder of the payments?

    b. Under what circumstances would such an endorsement be binding against the creditor?

    c. What legal terminology could be used to describe such an arrangement if it were effective?

18. Having unexpectedly received a large estate settlement, Anton went to his creditors to pay them off. He owed one of them, Silas, $5,000 on a promissory note that was to mature in a week. When he talked to Silas however, she refused to take the payoff at that moment. Anton set the money aside to pay her in a week, but instead spent it on a new car for his daughter. As a consequence, he did not have the cash to pay Silas when the note came due. When he finally went to pay Silas several months later, Anton refused to pay more than the principal plus the interest due up to the time he tendered payment. Is Anton correct in maintaining that he has to pay only this reduced amount?

19. Ajax made out a check to Bold, but before delivering it to that payee, Ajax took the check to the bank and had it certified. Once Bold had the check, she negotiated it by special endorsement to Chear. Chear then negotiated it, again by special endorsement, to Duzz. If the check is not paid upon presentment, which parties are secondarily liable on it? If, instead of being obtained by Ajax, certification had been obtained by Duzz, who would be secondarily liable?

REAL-WORLD CASE
Rotert v. Faulkner
464 S.W.2d 463

In reviewing this case, you may realize that you now know more about certain aspects of commercial paper law than do some judges and attorneys.

Charles and Alice Faulkner signed a $25,000 note as makers. The note was made out to Elmer Miller and Ronald Rotert as co-owners of the instrument. It was payable in monthly installments of principal and interest. However, the interest and principal came due only on the death of Elmer Miller. The note was delivered to Miller on issue. Nine months later, Miller wrote the following on the note:

> July 12, 1978
> Paid in Full
> for Services Rendered
> Elmer E. Miller

In fact, the Faulkners paid nothing to Miller during his lifetime, and they did nothing for Rotert before or after Miller's death. Because of the Faulkners' failure to pay upon Miller's death, Rotert brought suit. The lower court treated the instrument as negotiable and consequently applied a UCC section to it that read:

> An instrument payable to the order of two or more persons . . . if not in the alternative is payable to all of them and may be negotiated, discharged, or enforced only by all of them.

As the instrument was not payable in the alternative (i.e., "pay to the order of Elmer Miller or Ronald Rotert"), it has not been discharged under the UCC. Therefore, the lower court awarded Rotert a judgment against the Faulkners for the full $25,000 with interest from the date of Miller's death as well as attorney's fees, costs, and expenses of more than $3,500.

The Faulkners appealed to the Missouri Appellate Court. In their appellate brief, they admitted liability for the half of the amount of the note not discharged and for the attorney's fees, costs, and expenses.

Think Critically

1. Why was the lower court incorrect in treating the note as a negotiable instrument?
2. If the note was not negotiated to Miller, how was it transferred legally?
3. What body of law should be applied to resolve the situation, if the negotiable instrument law embodied in Article 3 of the UCC is not to be used? How much should the Faulkners pay ultimately?

Protecting Yourself in Debtor-Creditor Relationships

CHAPTERS

CHAPTER 21

Taking Security for a Debt Under the UCC

GOALS

- ◆ Understand the difficulties of collecting on debts and how a security interest helps
- ◆ Utilize the protection of a security interest
- ◆ Know the full extent of the protection afforded by a security interest

Collecting on Debts

In *Hamlet*, Polonius warns us, "Neither a borrower nor a lender be." In a society that, arguably, has flourished because of the credit device, we may be inclined to dispute the validity of that warning. However, it is highly "on point," as the legally inclined might say, whenever a default on a loan made against the general credit of the debtor occurs. For the person failing to pay, that defaulting on a loan brings on the potential of lawsuits, personal embarrassment and expense, and the loss of a positive credit standing.

For the creditor, matters are even worse, if possible. Upon default, the creditor's interest must be pursued in an environment of increasing animosity. Gentle reminders of an overdue payment give way to threats, veiled and otherwise, as to the debtor's loss of credit standing. The use of collection agencies and the filing of lawsuits against the debtor may soon follow. If the default has been anything but an oversight on the debtor's part, the creditor will ultimately have to utilize some, if not all, these alternatives.

Usually, the creditor finds other lenders in the same position relative to the defaulted debtor. So the game comes to involve not only unearthing any resources the debtor may have that can satisfy the outstanding balance, but also beating others to get to those resources first. If the creditor is a natural individual (usually individuals—friends and relatives—are turned to lastly by debtors on the verge of default), she or he is usually up against institutions that know far more about winning the collection game. If the creditor is an institution, a bank, a credit union, or some other financial entity, it is usually up against other institutions with the same expertise. In addition, such institutions are very closely monitored by their governmental auditors. Such careful monitoring occurs today because the "deregulation" trend a couple of decades ago led to a lack of governmental over-sight. This lack ultimately cost taxpayers almost as much as the entire conflict in Vietnam. Uncollectable loans hurt financial institutions and inhibit their ability to make money by future lending.

The strictly legal alternatives—lawsuits and bankruptcy—are very costly. Bankruptcy kills almost every chance that debtors will work their way out of the situation. In addition, as we will discuss, bankruptcy procedures take the better part of a year and usually return less than 15 cents on each dollar owed. On the other hand, a lawsuit also takes a long time. After other collection methods have failed, a lawsuit might be filed. Given scheduling problems, postponements, and other delays, the case might be heard four to six months after default. Even after a judgment has been entered against the debtor, most jurisdictions allow the debtor four additional weeks to pay what is due under that court directive. Only if the debtor fails to do this can court procedures, which still take time and money, be initiated to collect the amount due against the debtor's liquid (cash or readily convertible to cash) and static assets. The creditor may then find that those assets are already **encumbered** (subject to a legal claim other than that of the debtor). If such is the case, the creditor gets only what is left after the encumbrance has been satisfied, and please don't forget the legal fees and costs that must be paid as well.

In short, 99.9 times out of 100, it is a no-win situation if a creditor has no option other than to try to collect against just the debtor's assets in general.

Holding a Security Interest

Of course, there are remedies for this problem. However, they require varying amounts of knowledge, expertise, time, and expense. One remedy is the pledge. A **pledge** involves the transfer of possession of personal property to the creditor, who has the right to sell it upon default to pay off the debt. Such an arrangement is the basis for pawnshop operations everywhere. The problem with the pledge is that the debtor does not have possession of the **collateral** (the property subject to the creditor's claims) during the term of the obligation. This inhibits the use of the pledge, as the use of the collateral often figures significantly in the debtor's ability to pay off the debt.

As a consequence, another procedure has evolved that allows a creditor suffi-cient assurance that a loan will be repaid even if the debtor retains the collateral. This assurance, legally referred to as **security**, is obtained by having the debtor give the creditor a property right in the debtor's collateral. That property right, given to the creditor by the debtor in return for the loan, allows the creditor to sell the collateral on default and to satisfy (pay off) the loan as a result. The property right is known as a **security interest**. Be sure you understand this right is created in the creditor by the debtor. It is not automatically granted to the creditor just because he or she lends the debtor money. A **secured loan**, therefore, is one in which the creditor has a security interest in specific property that can be utilized in the event of default. An **unsecured loan**, the situation described in the first section of this chapter, provides the creditor no such option. To satisfy a defaulted unsecured loan, the creditor must instead proceed against the general asset position of the debtor.

Because of the importance of security interests to lenders, state governments in the U.S. have set up UCC procedures that streamline and coordinate the use of security interests taken in personal property. Similar procedures for recording encumbrances to land and other real property are followed in county recorders' offices throughout the U.S. These procedures offer creditors some protection regarding one very important drawback to using security interests: the fact that a debtor could use the same property as collateral for more than one loan. When this occurs, the first properly established loan has top priority. All the proceeds from the sale of the collateral are used to satisfy that debt. Whatever is left after that loan has been paid off trickles down to those who established their security interests later.

Hypothetical Case

When Wayne Myers needed $1,500 to start his own cable TV show, he borrowed the money from his uncle. In return, Wayne gave his uncle a security interest in his car, a slightly road-weary Pacer. Later Wayne needed more money, in this case $5,000, to fund a movie production. He borrowed it from his friend Dana Garth and gave her a security interest in the same Pacer. When the movie grossed only $500, Wayne defaulted on the loans. His uncle ultimately took possession of the Pacer and had it sold. The car brought $1,600, of which $1,435 was taken by Wayne's uncle to satisfy his remaining security interest and $165 went to Dana Garth. To recover the $4,865 still owed her, Dana would have to go wherever in the world the remainder of Wayne's property was located and start a court proceeding as a general creditor.

As a consequence of such difficulties, the UCC sets up an orderly procedure to be followed in establishing a security interest in personal property. It also provides for the maintenance of a registry of such security interests at a location designated by each state in the U.S. Typically, states require that security interests be filed with the secretary of state or with the county clerk of the debtor's county, or with both. So, when a lender is considering giving money to a person in exchange for a promise to repay that is secured by particular collateral, the lender need only check the registry to see whether this is a wise thing to do. If someone else has already taken out a security interest in the collateral, this fact should be on record. As a result, the would-be lender will probably say no.

Obtaining the Protection of a Security Interest

Security interests in land and buildings (real property) are covered in Chapter 30 of this book. Here, we concentrate on items other than land and buildings. Such items actually are more frequently used as security interests.

Article 9 of the UCC was created specifically to bring understandable uniformity to the wide and confusing variety of pre-UCC methods of obtaining security interests in items other than land and buildings. The statutory format and procedure required by Article 9 are the subjects of this section.

Attachment

The most important requirement for the creation of a legally effective superior security interest under Article 9 is that the agreement be in writing. The agreement is termed a **security agreement** by the UCC. It must clearly identify the collateral, and it must be signed by the debtor.

With few exceptions, the security agreement is indispensable to the procedure for creating the desired security interest. The procedure consists of two stages; the first stage is referred to as **attachment**. It begins when the creditor (who may be a lender of money or a seller of the collateral) acquires a legally enforceable right to take the collateral and sell it to satisfy the debt.

There are three requirements for attachment. First, the debtor must have property rights in the collateral. Typically, these rights stem from ownership of the collateral, although the right to possess the collateral may be sufficient in certain instances. Second, the creditor must transfer to the debtor something of **value**; typically, this refers to money from a lender, but it may also refer to the buying power in the form of credit to purchase the collateral that the seller extends. Value is technically defined in UCC Article 1-201(44) as contractual consideration, taking the security interest for a past indebtedness, or a credit extension. Third, the creditor must receive a security interest in the collateral from the debtor (as evidenced by a security agreement) or the creditor must take possession of the collateral (as in the pledge).

Once these requirements have been satisfied, the secured party acquires the right to **attach** (seize) and sell the collateral. The proceeds from the sale are then applied to the satisfaction of the debt involved. A problem here is that there can be more than one party whose debt has attached or may attach to the collateral in question. Therefore, the proceeds from the sale may have to be shared with others. There is, however, a way for a secured party to obtain the full use of the proceeds to satisfy his or her debt. That way is through the "perfection" of the secured party's interest in the collateral.

Perfection

After attachment, the next stage in the UCC Article 9 procedure allows a secured party to obtain a set priority in the collateral. This stage is called **perfection**. If a secured creditor is the first in priority, that creditor can satisfy her or his entire debt from the collateral or from the proceeds of its sale before anyone of lesser priority can claim a penny. (Of course, this holds true only if the collateral is valuable enough.) The priority thus established cannot be disturbed by subsequent attempts by others to satisfy judgments by attaching and selling the collateral.

Perfecting a security interest in collateral can be done in several ways. The method used usually depends on the circumstances of the underlying transaction.

Retention of Possession of Collateral   The first and simplest way is by possession. Remember that the last requirement for attachment is the security agreement or the pledgee's retaining possession of the collateral. Possession also provides the same result for perfection. If the creditor holds the collateral, perfection has been achieved as of the moment of possession. It's that simple.

Purchase Money Security Interests   The second way to perfect applies only to consumer goods. **Goods** are tangible and movable items at the time the security interest attaches. **Consumer goods** are goods used or purchased primarily for personal, family, or household purposes. A lender or seller who provides the value to purchase specific consumer goods acquires a perfected security interest in those goods at the time of attachment. This is called a **purchase money security interest**. Consider the example in the hypothetical case below.

Hypothetical Case

Sonny Salvatore bought a new home. After a week, he decided it was time to cut his 4-acre lawn for the first time. After mowing with his old push mower for a little over two hours, he decided it would be wise to mechanize. He and his new wife, Cherilyn, drove to a nearby mall and, after several hours of shopping, picked out the Blade Babe, a riding lawn mower. Unfortunately, the mower carried a price tag of more than $2,000. Just as the couple was about to break into "I Ain't Got You, Babe," a new song that they had written on the spot, a salesperson informed them that Sark's, the store that sold the mower, would be glad to finance their purchase with only 25 percent down. Salvatore slapped down the $500. Sark's produced a security agreement that described the mower in detail and gave the store the right to repossess and sell it upon default to help pay for any outstanding debt. Sonny and Cherilyn signed the agreement and took the mower home. Later a court judgment was entered against the couple. To satisfy the judgment, the sheriff tried to attach the mower and sell it. However, Sark's was quick to notify the court that its security interest had a superior priority because that interest had not only attached but been perfected (when the security agreement was signed). As a consequence, the court could not utilize the lawn mower or proceeds from its sale to satisfy the judgment. The court then used some of the couple's other property instead.

Allowing perfection through attachment greatly curtails the time, expense, and inconvenience associated with obtaining perfection in other ways. Perfection through attachment enhances the flow of consumer goods at a lower cost and protects the creditor against the claims of most others. Some additional risk over the other ways of perfection is involved, however. This risk is discussed later in this chapter.

Filing of a Financing Statement   The third way of achieving perfection is by filing a brief documentation of the security interest's existence with the appropriate governmental office. This documentation is referred to as a **financing statement**. It must contain three items:

1.   The debtor and secured party's names and addresses
2.   A description of the collateral
3.   The signature of the debtor. The financing statement's place of filing varies within the states in the U.S. and according to the type of collateral, as described below.

Collateral in this case can be tangible or intangible. As mentioned earlier, items that are tangible and movable when the security interest attaches are referred to as goods. This general category of collateral is broken down into four classes:

1.   **Equipment**   Goods used primarily in an ongoing business. A forklift in a warehouse or a dentist's chair fall into this class.
2.   **Inventory**   Goods bought for sale or lease.
3.   **Farm products**   Livestock, crops, and supplies used or produced in farming operations that are in the possession of the debtor-farmer.
4.   **Consumer goods**   As defined earlier, this class includes items bought or used primarily for personal, family, or household purposes.

Intangible collateral includes amounts owed on account to the debtor, negotiable instruments, and documents of title. All these are frequently used as collateral for a secured loan. It is interesting to note that under the UCC, money itself, as a medium of exchange, is not considered a good and therefore cannot be used as collateral.

In the U.S., such financing statements are usually filed at the local county courthouse for farm products and, if desired, for consumer goods. A financing statement identifying inventory or equipment as collateral is usually filed with the state's secretary of state. However, regardless of where the documentation is filed under law, if it is done properly, it will provide constructive notice to whomever else considers taking the same items as collateral. A prudent lender always checks for such filings before completing a loan.

A prudent secured party almost always files a financing statement for perfection, also. There are filing charges, of course, and in high-volume sales of consumer items, a significant amount of additional work is involved. As a consequence, some retailers just rely on the purchase money security interest rule that attachment is perfection.

When we discussed this option earlier, however, we mentioned that it entails additional risk. That risk stems from the fact that although a filing is constructive notice to all comers that a security interest has been perfected in the collateral, using attachment as perfection does not provide such wide notice. In fact, what is called the "neighborhood exception" haunts retailers in this area. Let's go back to Sonny and the Blade Babe to explain it.

Hypothetical Case

Sonny Salvatore was awakened at around 7 A.M. by someone knocking at the door. He staggered downstairs, still half-asleep, and opened his front door. A large woman with a huge pair of sunglasses pushed up into her hair stood with her hands on her hips in front of him. "The garage sale here, buddy?" she asked. Sonny shook his head, "Not until 8:30, lady." He started to shut the door, but she took a step forward. "Look, mister, I want to buy that Blade Babe in the worst way." Sonny paused. He needed the money for some hospital bills, but he hadn't planned on selling the mower. He still owed Sark's $1,200 on it. He'd parked it by the garage after mowing yesterday. Still . . . Sonny shrugged, "I'd sell it for $1,500," he said. "$1,200," the woman replied as she pulled her sunglasses down onto her nose. "$1,350," Sonny counter-offered, "but I've got to warn you that Sark's has a security interest in it and I still owe them $1,200." The woman scowled. "That's not good. Not a penny over $1,200." Finally, Sonny agreed to the $1,200. A few months later Sonny and Cherilyn hit on hard times and couldn't make any more payments on the lawn mower. When Sark's came to repossess it, Sonny admitted selling it. He was able to provide Sark's with the name and address of the purchaser. A few days later Sonny received a call from Sark's lawyer. The lawyer asked him whether he had told the purchaser about the loan on the lawn mower. Sonny said that he had. The lawyer then told Sonny that when someone sells a consumer good on which documentation of the security interest has not been filed, an innocent purchaser usually gets the title free and clear. If that were the case, Sark's could not take the lawn mower back and sell it. Because Sonny had given notice of the security interest to the purchaser, Sark's would be able to take the lawn mower back and sell it to satisfy the amount due from Sonny. However, the lawyer cautioned, the purchaser would be able to sue Sonny for the amount she paid him.

In other words, if retailers opt for the purchase money security interest exception to the rules, they run the risk of losing their security interest to an innocent, good faith purchaser. Filing as perfection would eliminate this risk, but it's more expensive and time-consuming.

Strength of Security Interest Protection

To begin, realize that upon default, Article 9 affords creditors substantial protection by providing for self-help repossession of the collateral and priority in the proceeds of its sale. In addition, under the Article 9 procedure, the **lien** (claim on property for payment of a debt) itself is both flexible and tenacious in addressing problems short of default.

Period of Effectiveness

The term of the lien, for example, can be as long as five years, and it can be renewed for another five if a continuation statement is filed in the last six months of the first five-year term. This is proving more and more important as the increasing price of items, such as automobiles and recreational vehicles, coupled with high interest rates, forces creditors to allow buyers longer to repay. When I purchased my first automobile, the maximum time allowed for repayment of such loans was 24 months and most car loans were made for 12 to 18 months. Today the typical financing period is 60 months (coincidentally, the Article 9 limit on unrefiled liens) and 72 months are available in certain situations.

After-Acquired Coverage

UCC 9-204 allows the security agreement to cover future advances made to the debtor. In addition, property acquired after the agreement to replace collateral identified in the agreement may be made subject to the lien set up by the agreement. Such an **after-acquired property clause** is found in many security agreements. It is especially useful when the collateral is inventory that may be sold and replaced frequently. Note that buyers who in the ordinary course of business purchase inventory subject to a security interest take their purchase free and clear of that interest unless they have actual knowledge that the sale violates the terms of an inventory loan.

Automatic Perfection in the Proceeds of the Sale of Collateral

Unless reinvested in replacement goods in accordance with an after-acquired clause, the proceeds from a debtor's sale of the collateral may disappear. With the proceeds go any hedge based on Article 9 that the lien holder may have against the risk of default. As a consequence, the UCC provides for the secured creditor to have automatic perfection in the proceeds from the sale of such collateral for 10 days. After that time, unless there is reinvestment under an after-acquired property clause, the creditor loses the priority position in relation to the debtor's assets. In the example with Sonny Salvatore, if Sark's had known of the sale of the lawn mower in time, it could have executed its security interest against the $1,200 in proceeds to pay off the remainder of the debt. Note that the 10-day period of perfection in the proceeds can be extended if the debtor agrees to the extension.

Out-of-State Coverage

An obvious ploy of a desperate debtor is to remove the collateral from the state in which the security interest is effective. Then, in a new state, she or he could use the property as collateral for a new loan. To deal with such situations, the UCC provides for the first creditor's perfection in the collateral in the new state by filing in that state within four months. If the previously secured creditor has not filed for protection in the new state by that time, that creditor's priority in the collateral is lost.

Hypothetical Case

Charles Berry pulled the last strap tight over the U-Haul trailer load of his goods, then jumped behind the wheel of his station wagon. Maybe Alabama would bring better things for him. It couldn't be worse there than here in Michigan. The plant where he had worked had shut down 18 months ago. His unemployment had run out several weeks ago. He was exhausted from job hunting and avoiding creditors. It was time to head back home. Fourteen hours later he was in Birmingham safe and sound. Four weeks later he'd found a minimum wage job and was looking for something better. In the meantime, he needed money for enrollment in a technical college. Desperate, he went to Templars, a local loan office that promised almost universal acceptance but charged extremely high rates. When it requested collateral for the loan, Charles offered the refrigerator and freezer he had brought down from Michigan. He knew that the appliances were still subject to the purchase money security interests he had given Sears back in Detroit. However, it was school and a future or nothing. So, with barely any hesitation, he signed the necessary papers and took the money. Templars filed a financing statement as required to perfect its security interest. A few weeks later Sears filed against Charles's appliances in Alabama and thereby perfected its Michigan security interest in the southern state. Because Berry missed several payments, Sears then repossessed the appliances and kept them in satisfaction of the amount due on them. Templars was left without collateral for its loan as a consequence.

Uniform Default Procedure

Another advantage of Article 9's reworking of the old laws on secured transactions is uniformity among U.S. jurisdictions regarding claim priorities and default procedure.

Priorities   When two or more parties claim an interest in the same collateral, the UCC provides a means of listing them in the order of their priority. Perfected claims are at the top of the list. They have priority over attached and unsecured claims. If two parties have perfected claims in the same collateral, the first to have perfected wins out. Remember that a "winner" here is permitted to satisfy the entire amount due from the proceeds before others further down the priority list get anything. If there are not enough proceeds to satisfy the entire debt of any party with a secured interest, that party becomes an unsecured creditor with a claim against the general credit of the debtor for the balance due. Finally, among those whose security interests have merely attached, the first in time wins out.

Procedure Upon Default   A self-help repossession (in the event that the security interest is not evidenced by a pledge) is the first step usually considered upon default. As long as this can be accomplished without a disturbance of the peace, it is the creditor's best hope of getting back the value it has invested. If a disturbance of the peace may result from an attempt at repossession, the person making the attempt must seek an alternative method.

If the collateral is repossessed, the creditor may either keep it in full satisfaction of the claim or sell it. If the creditor decides to keep it, the debtor and any other secured creditor must be notified. If any of these parties object within 21 days, the collateral must be sold and the proceeds used to satisfy the secured party's claims. Any money left over must be given to the other secured party or parties or to the debtor. If the sale doesn't produce enough money to pay off the debt(s), the debtor is liable for the remainder.

As you might expect, the law requires that any sale be conducted in a commercially reasonable manner. This typically calls for advertising and conducting the sale so as to bring top dollar from appropriate prospective buyers. Finally, if the collateral consists of consumer goods, this procedure is altered somewhat. In that case, if more than 60 percent of the cash price has been paid, the secured party is not allowed the option of keeping the goods. They must be resold, and the debtor must be told of the sale and have the right to buy the goods at the sale.

Once the debt has been satisfied, in the U.S., the secured interest holder who perfected by filing a financing statement must file a **termination statement** with the same governmental office at which the financing statement was filed. This termination statement gives notice that the property used as collateral is no longer encumbered. The debtor can then apply for other loans and offer the property as security.

FIGURE 21-1   Creditor Protection Under Article 9 of the UCC

- Extended time protection
- After-acquired property can be made subject to lien
- Automatic perfection in proceeds if sold
- Out-of-state protection
- Uniform default procedure

CHAPTER REVIEW

USE LEGAL TERMS

Fill in the blanks with the appropriate term.

after-acquired property clause

attach

attachment

collateral

consumer goods

encumbered

equipment

farm products

financing statement

goods

inventory

lien

perfection

pledge

purchase money security interest

secured loan

security

security agreement

security interest

termination statement

unsecured loan

value

1. The transfer of possession of collateral to a creditor by a debtor is called a(n) ___?___. It is the basis for pawnshop operations.
2. ___?___ can be found in consideration that would bind a simple contract or a preexisting obligation.
3. Goods used in the operation of a business are known as ___?___.
4. Goods for lease or purchase are labeled ___?___.
5. Both the tangible, movable items referred to in questions 3 and 4 above can be taken as ___?___ for the security interest of a creditor.
6. A(n) ___?___ is a document that is filed in a governmental office to give notice of the existence of a security interest.
7. At the direction of a court, a sheriff or a similar official may ___?___ or seize items.
8. Property subject to a legal claim of someone other than its owner is said to be ___?___.
9. ___?___ are purchased for personal, family, or household use.

TEST YOUR READING

10. At one time our culture had debtor's prisons. How would you justify such institutions?
11. Why is it so difficult to collect on defaulted loans?
12. What measures can you take to curtail the risk of default on a loan?

13. What information would you want to gather from a prospective borrower in case of default?
14. How does holding a security interest in the debtor's collateral decrease the risks of loaning money?
15. What are the various ways to perfect a security interest?
16. Why should a pawnshop be protected by special rules and allowed to charge high interest rates?
17. List four different ways a perfected security interest enhances the chance of recovery on a defaulted loan.
18. What is the purpose of a termination statement?

THINK CRITICALLY ABOUT EVIDENCE

19. Why does Article 9 of the UCC exist? Is there an obligation to assist creditors in lowering the risks of lending? Does the average person profit from such efforts?
20. Who "owns" a property right such as a security interest before it has been transferred to a creditor? Why does the law require that a security agreement be in writing and signed by the debtor?
21. Burney loaned Sampson $4,000 to buy a car. Sampson issued a promissory note in favor of Burney for that amount. Also, when he registered the new car, Sampson had Burney's name entered on the title as lienholder. Later Sampson took out a loan from the First National Bank of Pennsboro. After a few months, he defaulted on both the bank loan and the promissory note. The bank filed suit and obtained a judgment against Sampson that it sought to execute against the car. Burney maintained that he had a security interest in the car that took precedence over the bank's claim. Who do you think won?
22. Matt Lawnder bought a washing machine and a dryer from the Pennsboro Department Store. The store financed the transaction and perfected its security interest by filing shortly after the sale was closed. Two years later, still owing a substantial amount on the appliances, Lawnder sold his house and moved to another state, taking the washing machine and dryer with him. Three months after his move, Lawnder lost the job he had acquired in the new location. He then sold the appliances to a local dealer for $400 and deposited the money in his bank account. Two weeks later the Pennsboro Department Store discovered what had happened. The proceeds from the sale are still in Lawnder's account. Can the store recover the $358.75 still owed on the appliances from the account?

REAL-WORLD CASE

In re Midas Coin Co.

264 Federal Supplement 193

Finally, consider the following case and then use it to remind yourself that at times the statutory law goes a bit berserk and needs a judge to straighten it out.

In order to take out a loan, the Midas Coin Company offered some of its rare U.S. coins to St. John's Community Bank as security. The bank took possession of the coins and thought that it therefore had a perfected security interest in them. When problems arose concerning Midas's ability to meet its obligations, it was contended that as the UCC does not allow money to be taken as collateral, Midas did not have the priority of a perfected secured party in them. Therefore, other creditors could share in the proceeds from the sale of the coins.

Think Critically

1. Should St. John's Community Bank be allowed a secured position in the coins? What argument would you make to support the position that it does not? That it does?

2. Who will win if it does not? Will the bank lose out entirely if it does not have the highest priority security interest?

CHAPTER  22

Debtor and Creditor Protections Outside the UCC

GOALS

- Understand the differences between voluntary and involuntary encumbrances
- Identify types of involuntary liens
- Know the protections afforded debtors in our society

Protections for Lienholders

Chapter 21 covered liens established through the cooperation of the debtor. The law refers to such liens as "voluntary" encumbrances. Usually, debtors "volunteer" to subject their property to liens in return for value of some sort or for money. As you probably suspect or know from experience, there are also "involuntary" liens, to which we now turn our attention. These liens do not require the property owner's assent. Instead, they arise by operation of the law.

Involuntary Liens in Real Property

Tax Lien   The primary example of these involuntary encumbrances is the **tax lien**. If certain property taxes remain unpaid for an extended time, they become a lien against the property taxed. Ultimately, in the U.S., the government entity owed the taxes can cause the property to be sold to satisfy the amount due. Liens for nonpayment of governmental services can also be placed against the property.

Hypothetical Case

When the grass on his lot in downtown Pennsboro grew too high, the city asked disc jockey Robert ("Howling Bob") Logan to mow it. Insulted, even though the vegetation stood over 3 feet above the 1-foot limit set by city ordinance, Howling Bob took to the airwaves to protest. His loyal listeners picketed Pennsboro City Hall carrying signs that read, "Hell, no, we won't mow." After repeated warnings, the city sent its own personnel to mow Howling Bob's lot. Afterward, as called for by city ordinance, the city attorney filed a lien against the property for the cost of the mowing, some $14. Howling Bob again refused to cooperate. Finally, the city asked the court to sell the lot to pay for the mowing. The court complied. The lot sold for $1,725, from which the $14 plus the city's legal costs and the court costs were deducted. Ultimately, a little over $1,400 was returned to Howling Bob, who, because of the publicity the case attracted, had just been offered—and had accepted—a new job with a major station in Chicago.

Mechanic's Lien   Workers and suppliers of material used in building or improving real property have at their disposal a similar involuntary lien. This encumbrance, called a **mechanic's lien**, ensures the proper payment of those who add value to buildings or land through their labor or other resources. Plumbers, carpenters, electricians, landscapers, lumberyards, hardware stores, and so on, are all empowered by law to file a lien against property improved by their efforts or materials. The lien must be filed within a certain time after the work has been completed. Usually, the limit is no longer than 60 or 90 days. Once filed however, the lien typically takes priority over all other encumbrances.

Hypothetical Case

Martina and Nat met in graduate school and married soon after. After graduation, they dreamed of and designed their own house. A few years of saving later, they bought some land and found J. Elza Fudgling, a contractor they believed could build their dream house. Fudgling had been building custom homes in the area for years and liked their plans. His bid came in at $350,000. Martina and Nat quickly secured a line of credit for the project through the Pennsboro National Bank by giving the bank a security interest in the house. Eight weeks later, J. Elza presented them with the keys to the house. Nat checked the line of credit, found that only $335,000 had been used, and then gave J. Elza a bonus check of $5,000. A troubled look flickered over J. Elza's face as he took the check, but he quickly recovered, smiled, and thanked Martina and Nat for their business. A week later, as Nat went out to get the paper, he was shocked to see a parade of pickups in his driveway. Representatives of every firm that had put labor or materials into construction of the house, including the lumber company, the plumbers, the carpenters, the electricians, and even the installer of the automatic sprinkling system, came at him. None of the firms had been paid. J. Elza had guaranteed all of them their money by 5 P.M. the previous day and hadn't come through. "What do you mean?" said Nat. "I asked for and got releases from all of you." A lanky man wearing a carpenter's apron spoke for the assemblage, "Not from us you didn't. We've been checking, and ol' J. Elza may have outfoxed us all. He probably worked up his own copies of our release forms that he's handled over the years and made out the ones he gave you himself. There are three other high-dollar homes around town he's pulled the same thing on. Over one-and-a-half million dollars. Rumor is his wife was suing him for divorce, so he cashed it all in and headed south. Reckon you'll be owing us and your mortgage company now." Nat shook his head in dismay, turned, and reentered his house. As he slammed the door behind him, one of the men yelled, "See you in court." Nat watched through the window as the pickups pulled out of the drive, and, sure enough, headed toward the courthouse. A few days later Nat and Martina worked up a total of the full amount due. The mechanic's liens that had been filed against the house totaled over $250,000. Although those claims took priority over the $340,000 that Nat and Martina had drawn against the line of credit, the latter amount would still have to be paid back after the "mechanics" were paid. Nat looked up from the list, "Martina," he asked, "didn't your dad say he could recommend a good bankruptcy attorney for us?"

Involuntary Liens in Personal Property

Artisan's Lien   In case you hadn't noticed, a car mechanic in modern terms would not be able to avail herself or himself of a mechanic's lien. This contradiction becomes understandable if you realize that Webster's primary definition of the word mechanic reads "of or involving skill or manual labor." So painters, carpenters, and those in similar trades can take advantage of the protection of mechanic's liens because of the application of their skill and labor to real property. Car mechanics have to use the **artisan's lien**. This possessory lien is given to someone who has improved or added value to the personal property of another. Two points must be made here. First, a **possessory lien** is effective only while the lien holder maintains possession of the property that received the benefit of the artisan's efforts (legally, an **artisan** is a person skilled in a trade or craft requiring manual dexterity). Second, because the lien is intended to ensure the payment due for the services performed, it places the lienholding artisan in a very powerful position that is not under a court's immediate supervision. That position can lead to abuse.

Hypothetical Case

Herman Petite decided to have his convertible painted at The Reubens Auto Salon, an upscale car detailing shop near Beverly Hills, California. The "colour" he selected was "flaming fall," a muted reddish orange. The color was based, according to the "artistes" at The Reubens, on "the glorious daunting colours of a sugar maple in the autumnal pause." Regretfully, when Herman returned to pick up the car, he found that the color resembled a coat of rust inhibitor. Herman refused to pay the bill, and the Auto Salon, in turn, refused to relinquish possession of the car. The Salon's salesperson noted that if the bill remained unpaid for more than a month, the Salon would enforce its artisan's lien by having the car sold and taking the bill amount plus storage charges of $40 per day out of the proceeds. Unfortunately, Herman needed the car to drive to work. So, after a few phone calls, Herman found a friend who could come down to the Auto Salon. When the friend arrived, he told her what was going on and had her witness his payment of the bill under protest. (After hearing his complaints, the Auto Salon would take only cash.) The president of the Salon took the money, then relinquished possession of the car and, thereby, the Salon's artisan's lien. Herman realized then that to get his money back he would have to bring suit in court under contract law.

From the above account, it can be seen that physical labor and skill invested in the property of another may bring on an artisan's lien. It should be noted however, that in most states in the U.S., this does not mean that accountants or lawyers or doctors have such a lien on the materials of their clients or patients.

Hotelkeeper's Lien   Another possessory lien established without the property owner's consent is the **hotelkeeper's lien** (also referred to as the *innkeeper's lien*). This lien allows the provider of lodging to take the property a guest brought into the establishment, except for the property in the guest's immediate possession, as security for payment of that guest's bill.

Warehouseman's Lien   A similar possessory lien allows a warehouse to hold stored property as security for payment of the storage charges. This is termed a **warehouseman's lien**. The warehouse must be careful to list all property stored by a customer on a receipt provided to that person. Otherwise, its security interest in the unlisted, yet stored, property may not be recognized.

Hypothetical Case

The Attic, a storage warehouse in Boca Raton, Florida, repeatedly stored unused store fixtures (tables, racks, display counters, etc.) for Idling Shoppers, a chain of drive-through convenience stores. Because of the frequency of the chain's storage and retrieval trips to the warehouse, the Attic stopped issuing warehouse receipts to it. Late last year, Idling Shoppers went into bankruptcy and owed more than $7,000 in storage bills to the Attic. When the Attic tried to claim Idling Shoppers' nearly $20,000 worth of stored property as security for the storage bills, the bankruptcy court would not allow it because of the lack of receipts. The Attic therefore became an unsecured creditor, and when the bankruptcy proceeding was concluded, it received only $948.52 instead of the full $7,000 it would probably have received if its debt had been property secured.

Carrier's Lien   A **carrier's lien** is, as you may suspect, also involuntary and possessory. It is given to a person engaged in transporting cargo for hire. The specific cargo transported is the lien's collateral. Like the warehouse owner, the carrier must be careful to properly list all property received in the **bill of lading** (the receipt provided to the person contracting for the shipment).

Guarantors and Sureties

Although the law offers a great deal of protection through various provisions of the UCC and the liens we have just discussed, that protection comes with complexities, delays, costs, and uncertainties that may inhibit lenders. Consequently, the most practical protection for a creditor is often found by adding another person to the list of those responsible for paying off a loan. Both for the debtor who has yet to establish a credit standing worthy of the sought-after loan and for the prospective lender, this arrangement often provides the final measure of assurance necessary. The individuals who assume the responsibility for payment do so under varying conditions.

A person who agrees to be primarily liable for the payment of a debt (or the performance of an obligation) of another is known as a **surety**. A person who agrees to be secondarily liable for the payment of a debt (or the performance of an obligation) is known as a **guarantor**.

The difference between the positions of surety and guarantor is often quite significant. A surety makes the same promise as the principal debtor and is usually a party to the original instrument creating the debt or other obligation. An example, shown in Figure 22-1, is a promissory note signed by a father as surety for a loan made to enable his son to start a small business. The point here is vital. From the way the obligation is assumed, the surety is liable for the loan from the beginning. Such is not the case with a guarantor, who becomes liable only on the default of the principal debtor.

In particular, the guarantor does not make the same promise as that made by the principal debtor whom the guarantor is sponsoring. Instead, the guarantor promises to cover the debt only if the principal debtor defaults and on the provision of suitable notice. It is a separate undertaking altogether, and typically it must be supported by separate consideration. Also recall that under the statute of frauds, a promise to a creditor to stand good for the debts of another must be in writing to be effective.

Whether the additional party is a guarantor or a surety however, the increased assurance provided by that party's credit standing is often all that a sensible lender requires.

FIGURE 22-1   A note signed by Tyrone Lancaster II as surety for the loan of $50,000 to his son, Tyrone Lancaster III

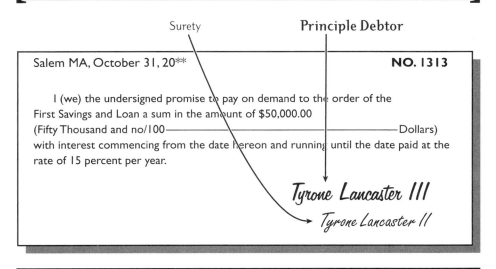

Protections for Debtors

To balance the various forms of assistance given to creditors, the U.S. legal system offers debtors—especially consumer debtors—certain protections. In addition, it offers all debtors the shelter and potential rehabilitation of the Bankruptcy Act.

Consumer Debtor Protection

Defenses Preserved Against HDCs   A primary means of protecting consumer debtors is the preservation of defenses against the enforcement of commercial paper by all types of holders (See Chapter 19 for more about this important area.). With the exception of bankruptcy provisions, the most significant other U.S. federal laws protecting debtors are found in the Consumer Credit Protection Act (CCPA). The act covers most aspects of the consumer-lender relationship (See Title 15 of the U.S. Code for the full text of this act.).

    Requiring Information Allowing Loan Comparison   A portion of the CCPA commonly known as the Truth-in-Lending Act (TILA) requires that prospective borrowers for personal, family, household, or agricultural purposes (and prospective purchasers of goods and services on credit) be provided with a written disclosure of comparative information about the loan. The most important items in that disclosure are

- The **finance charge**   The actual cost of the loan expressed in dollars and cents. This cost is computed by summing the interest plus add-on charges such as loan initiation fees.

- The **annual percentage rate**   The interest rate of the loan expressed as a yearly figure. An interest rate of $1\frac{2}{3}$ percent per month, for example, would be expressed as a 20 percent APR.

    Note that TILA only provides that the consumer be informed of the interest rates. It does not set limits on those rates. In the U.S., the states set interest limits in what are termed usury laws. These limits vary considerably from state to state. Also, many loans made with real estate as security are not covered by TILA.

    Finally, TILA requires a certain format in advertising credit terms. If an interest rate is mentioned, it must be in APR terms. If one credit term is stated (e.g., "no money down"), other credit terms must also be stated (See Figure 22-2 for our example.).

    Ensuring Equal Opportunity for Credit   The U.S. Equal Credit Opportunity Act, another act of significance to debtors, attempts to provide consumers with fair access to loans and other extensions of credit. All lenders who regularly extend credit must comply with the act. Such lenders include banks, finance companies, credit unions, retailers, and credit card companies. Individuals who apply for credit may not be asked to disclose the following information about themselves:

FIGURE 22-2 Example of Retailer's Advertisement Mentioning a Credit Term

THUNDERCHICKEN SALE

LIST — $20,000

YOUR COST only
$17,233

* With $2,500 cash down or equivalent trade. Payments calculated on a 4.9% 48 month basis with 47 payments. Final payment $6,030.90.

- Religion, sex, race, or national origin
- Marital status (unless applying for a joint account or in the states of California, Arizona, Nevada, New Mexico, Washington, Idaho, Texas, Louisiana, and Wisconsin, all of which have laws giving one spouse certain rights in property held in common with the other spouse) or whether widowed or divorced
- Plans for raising children
- Receipt of alimony, separate maintenance, or child support if that income is not a significant proportion of overall income
- Age (unless applicant is a minor or of advanced age and the information will result in favorable consideration)
- Receipt of public assistance, except in the same manner as other income

Applicants for credit have a right to know the results of their applications within 30 days. If rejected, they have a right to be advised of the reasons for that rejection within 30 days of the adverse action. Violators of the Equal Credit Opportunity Act can be sued by the applicant(s) harmed for their losses, attorney's fees, and court costs. Punitive damages are also possible.

Correcting Billing Errors Billing disputes that concern consumers are covered under the Fair Credit Billing Act. Under this act, a creditor must mail bills at least 14 days before they are due. A consumer who discovers an error has 60 days from the mailing date to notify the creditor. That notification must contain the identity of the consumer, the account number, and a description and explanation of the error. An acknowledgment of the consumer's notification is required within 30 days. The creditor then has up to 90 days to investigate. If an error is discovered, it must be corrected. If the account is believed to be correct, an explanation must be sent to the consumer.

Protecting Against Improper Bill Collection Practices   To prevent abusive tactics from being used to collect debts, the U.S. Congress passed the Fair Debt Collection Practices Act. The act regulates the activities of those who are in the business of collecting debts for others. In particular, a debt collector

- Must not attempt to locate a debtor by informing others that the debtor owes money. The use of postcards to collect debts is also forbidden due to the public nature of the message they carry.
- Must communicate solely with the debtor's attorney if one is known to be representing the debtor.
- Must not communicate with the debtor at the debtor's place of employment (if the employer prohibits such communication) or at unreasonable hours. The typical proper hours are 8 A.M. to 9 P.M. unless information to the contrary is provided to the collector.
- Must not communicate, in connection with collection of a debt (not locating a debtor), with anyone other than the debtor, the debtor's attorney, the creditor, the creditor's attorney, or a credit reporting agency.
- Must, upon the debtor's written notification of the debtor's refusal to pay the debt or the debtor's desire that the collector cease communication, cease contacting the debtor except to notify the debtor of a specific action.
- Must not use harassing or abusive means to collect the debt. For example, threats of violent action, profanity, criminal activity, and frequent telephone contacts are ruled out.
- Must not use a form of communication that would cause the debtor to mistake it for legal process.

Violators of the Fair Debt Collection Practices Act can be sued for actual and punitive damages, court costs, and attorney's fees.

Assisting in the Reporting of Accurate Credit Ratings   In a society such as the U.S., in which credit is often regarded as the vehicle to prosperity, the ability to utilize that vehicle often depends on the evaluation of our ability to repay made by certain credit bureaus. This evaluation is termed a **credit rating**. To enable U.S. citizens to be as certain as possible that such ratings are fair and accurate, the U.S. Congress passed the Fair Credit Reporting Act. If consumers are disallowed credit, insurance, or employment because of a bad credit report, the act requires that they be informed and provided with the name and address of the credit bureau from which the credit report was obtained. If consumers contact the credit bureau within 60 days of the issuance of the bad credit report, the act allows them to see without charge the files the credit bureau maintains on them. Such files contain reports from many sources and are reviewed by credit bureaus to determine the credit ratings of their subjects.

Upon reading the contents of such a file (including the sources of the information but excluding any medical information contained therein), a consumer can point out alleged errors to the credit bureau. The bureau must then investigate. If the investigation proves the consumer is correct, the improper information must be deleted or changed. If the investigation supports the accuracy of the contested information, consumers can still file their versions of the story with the bureau. The consumers' versions must be maintained in the files with the original versions.

Bankruptcy The bankruptcy provisions of U.S. federal laws assist greatly in maintaining fairness in the use of credit by consumers. Without these laws, the balance of power in such dealings would easily tip toward lenders. However, consumers are not the only debtors who at times need protection from the consequences of an overwhelming debt load. The availability of the protection afforded by the federal bankruptcy laws has been and will be of prime importance to businesses, charities, financial institutions, and all other classes of debtors. Bankruptcy protection and its attendant procedures are discussed in Chapter 23.

 ## Technology Insights

Facial Mapping, Thermography, and You

You've just received a large inheritance and want to spend some of it in an exclusive shop on Rodeo Drive. As you walk toward the shop's door, you notice a small camera swing toward you. Then, as you reach for the shop's door handle, you hear a soft click as the door is locked automatically in your face. You rattle the door handle, and then, bewildered, you stand aside as the door unlocks and allows other people to enter the shop. You slip into the shop behind them but are immediately confronted by a sales clerk with the build of a night club bouncer. He asks you to leave. When you inquire as to why, he responds that, according to the store's accessible databases, you do not have the economic resources to shop in the store. Plus, judging from where you normally shop, you are not suitably educated to the products in the store to appreciate them and buy. You are shocked.

"But how did you know who I was?" you stammer. The "bouncer" smiles as he grabs your elbow to escort you out of the store and says, "Your face told the story."

Well, maybe not all of the story. But the science of *facial mapping* (matching the distances between the tip of your nose to the corners of your mouth, eyes, or ear cavity, for example, to the same distances taken from your driver's license photo) together with the ability to access various private and public databases allows a business either to exclude you or to send a sales clerk your way to help.

Also useful in the quest to identify and obtain demographics on potential customers, terrorists, and even common criminals, is the process of *thermography*. This is based on comparing the heat patterns of a person's face with patterns on file.

Think Critically Is it morally proper for stores to discriminate in this fashion? Is it legally proper to do so? What are the advantages and/or disadvantages to retailers who allow the curious or the comparative shoppers into their store.

CHAPTER REVIEW

USE LEGAL TERMS

Fill in the blanks with the appropriate term.

annual percentage rate (APR)	credit rating	possessory liens
artisan	finance charge	surety
artisan's lien	guarantor	tax lien
bill of lading	hotelkeeper's lien	warehouseman's lien
carrier's lien	mechanic's lien	

1. A credit bureau evaluates your ability to repay debts and gives you a(n) ___?___.
2. A mother who agrees to pay off a car loan if her son cannot is a(n) ___?___ in relation to the loan.
3. The involuntary security interest afforded by the law to the unpaid plumber who installed the bathrooms at the Bates Motel is termed a(n) ___?___.
4. The involuntary possessory security interest afforded by the law to the person who repaired Mr. Bond's Lotus sports car is termed a(n) ___?___.
5. A mother who agrees to be primarily liable on a car loan made to her son is a(n) ___?___ in relation to the loan.

TEST YOUR READING

6. List two types of involuntary liens in real property.
7. Why should a mechanic's lien have priority over all other types of liens?
8. How does the statute of frauds affect the enforceability of a suretyship? A guarantorship?
9. Does TILA prescribe or proscribe any credit terms? Why or why not?
10. Name four pieces of information the would-be creditor cannot request under the Equal Credit Opportunity Act.
11. List five things a debt collector must not do under the Fair Debt Collection Practices Act.

THINK CRITICALLY ABOUT EVIDENCE

12. Which of the following involuntary liens are not possessory?
    a. mechanic's
    b. hotelkeeper's
    c. warehouseman's
    d. tax
    e. artisan's
    f. carrier's

13. Which type of lien in Problem 12 would each of the following businesses be able to levy if it were not paid for providing its goods or services?
    a. Bro' Lex's Watch Repair Shoppe
    b. Lawrence County Assessor's office
    c. Minnie Pixel's Television Repair Shop
    d. Hardis Nailz Carpenter Company
    e. Kent Nuke Ohm, Electrician
    f. Bill Lading's Commercial Storage Company

14. Flashy Dan, the Amusing Appliance Man, placed the ad shown below. What law is Dan overlooking? What must he do to comply with that law?

15. The Pennsboro National Bank of Pennsboro, Missouri, used the following application form for its individual line of credit:

PNB LOAN FORM 27-93: Individual Line of Credit

Please supply the following information:

Name: _____   Sex: M F   Date of Application: _____

Address: _____   Years at this Address: _____

Employer: _____   Years at this Job: _____

Salary: _____   Spouse's Name: _____

Spouse's Employer: _____   Spouse's Salary: _____

If single, have you been divorced? _____   Widowed? _____

Number of Children: _____   Planning for More? _____

Are currently involved in a lawsuit that may result in a judgement against you? (If yes, please explain): _____

_____

If you are currently receiving income other than your salary and want us to consider it, please list the amount and

its source: _____

Amount of Line of Credit Requested: _____   *Thank You. We will inform you of*
our decision in 45 days.

What is improper about the form? What recourse does an applicant have for dealing with the violations of law inherent in the form?

REAL-WORLD CASE
Carroll v. Exxon Co.
434 Federal Supplement 557

Now consider the real life effectiveness of the consumer credit protection laws.

When Exxon denied Kathleen Carroll a credit card, she requested that it furnish her with the specific reasons for its action. In its subsequent correspondence with Carroll, a single employed woman, Exxon failed to state the name and address of the credit bureau on which it had relied in denying the credit application. Carroll brought suit. In the court proceeding, it was shown that her credit bureau files contained little, if any, information. As a consequence, it was held that Exxon did not have sufficient information to determine her worthiness as a credit risk.

Think Critically

1. What consumer credit protection laws did Exxon violate? How?
2. What could Exxon have done to fulfill the requirements of these laws?

CHAPTER 23

Bankruptcy Laws

GOALS

- Understand protections provided by the U.S. bankruptcy laws
- Understand the wisdom of providing protection for individuals overcome with debts
- Know the procedures in Chapter 7 bankruptcy

Bankruptcy as an Alternative to Remaining in Debt

Similar to Great Britain, the 13 colonies that eventually formed the U.S. treated debtors harshly in their early history, and maintained prisons for people unable to pay their obligations. With the American Revolution in 1776 and the framing of the U.S. Constitution, an enlightened alternative was established. This alternative relieved individuals from bearing the burden of overwhelming debt loads for years. Specifically, in Article I, Section 8 of the Constitution, the U.S. Congress is given the power to "establish . . . uniform Laws on the subject of Bankruptcies throughout the United States." In other words, Congress was authorized to provide a procedure whereby citizens overburdened with debt could be **discharged** or released from their obligations.

However, Congress has not utilized this power frequently. The first federal bankruptcy act was not passed until 1800. The current U.S. bankruptcy statute, the Bankruptcy Reform Act of 1978, was the first substantial modification of the bankruptcy laws since 1898. The changes it brought about were controversial at best. In fact, this latest bankruptcy act was perhaps too generous in its terms. As a result, the rate of bankruptcies doubled almost overnight. The act also opened so many obvious loopholes and created so many administrative problems that most observers were amazed at Congress' seeming lack of competence in drafting it. Ultimately, the 1978 act was successfully challenged on constitutional grounds and substantially amended, first in 1984 and again in 1986. Most attorneys refer to its current form as the Bankruptcy Code.

The word "bankrupt" is not actually used in the Bankruptcy Code. Instead, the word "debtor" is used. This omission was intentional, perhaps to avoid applying the stigma of the term "bankrupt" to those seeking the protection of the code.

The word **bankruptcy**, however, also has a legal meaning. It refers to the procedure by which debtors' eligible assets are utilized to discharge them from some, if not all, their obligations. Note that the discharge of debts through bankruptcy is available to a debtor only once every six years, and that the debtor's credit record typically reflects the discharge for 10 years. However, neither U.S. government bodies nor private employers can discriminate against someone who has gone through bankruptcy (e.g., by firing an employee). Nevertheless, seeking protection under the Bankruptcy Code provisions should be considered only as a last resort.

Protections Provided by the Bankruptcy Code

The statutes of the U.S. contain the provisions of the Bankruptcy Code in Title 11. This title is subdivided into several Chapters containing eligibility requirements, procedures, and protections authorized by Congress. Note that each Chapter, with the exception of Chapter 12, has been given an odd number. So, if you look up the statute for more details, note that Chapters 2, 4, 6, 8, 10, and 14 simply do not exist.

Eligibility and Administration

The Chapters that you find fall into two general groupings. Chapters 1, 3, 5, and 15 contain procedures and information relevant to people who may become subject to the Bankruptcy Code. Chapter 1 gives eligibility guidelines; Chapter 3 creates and empowers official positions associated with the bankruptcy process; Chapter 5 contains the principles for determining which of the debtor's properties are legally accessible to satisfy creditors' claims; and Chapter 15 sets up the position of bankruptcy trustee and specifies the trustee's duties and powers. The **bankruptcy trustee** administers the debtor's estate in bankruptcy. An **estate** is a person's rights and interests in property of all types. The trustee's job is to maximize the estate's assets so creditors receive as much as possible on the **liquidation** (sale for cash) of those assets.

Types of Protection Available

Each of the remaining Chapters in the Bankruptcy Code—7, 9, 11, 12, and 13—describes different types of bankruptcy protection, as follows:

♦ *Chapter 7* "Discharge of Debts by Liquidation and Payout" is the form of bankruptcy most people are familiar with. It calls for the discharge of the debtor's eligible obligations after a payout to creditors. This payout comes from the proceeds of the liquidation of the debtor's statutorily unprotected assets. This form of bankruptcy is discussed in detail later in this chapter.

♦ *Chapter 9* "Adjustment of Debts for Cities" gives municipalities facing a funding crisis the latitude to restructure their obligations.

♦ *Chapter 11* "Reorganization to Avoid Liquidation for Active Businesses" provides ongoing businesses with a last alternative before full bankruptcy under Chapter 7. Compliance with the Chapter 11 procedure may allow a business that would otherwise be terminated to restructure its debts and other obligations, remain in possession of its most important assets, and continue doing business in some form. Participation in a Chapter 11 proceeding may be initiated voluntarily by the business or it may be forced to do so by its creditors.

The special considerations under Chapter 11 are based on the fact that keeping a business in operation, employing individuals, and filling a social need, is typically more beneficial to society than selling off its assets piece-meal. Often however, these results cannot be achieved without some losses to the business' creditors. For most creditors, these losses are generally far smaller than those they would sustain if the business were liquidated. As mentioned previously, a rule of thumb in a full Chapter 7 "straight bankruptcy" is that

FIGURE 23-1 Forms of Bankruptcy Protection Available for Debtors under the Federal Bankruptcy Statutes

Chapter 7 All of the debtor's assets, with certain exemptions, are sold. The cash proceeds are distributed to the creditors according to a statutory priority order. Then, except for certain non-dischargeable items, all debts, paid and unpaid, are discharged and thereafter cannot be collected by the debtor's creditors.

Chapter 9 Provides a means for reorganizing the debts of financially stressed municipalities.

Chapter 11 Emphasizes the preservation of the debtor as an ongoing entity. Therefore, the court reorganizes the debt and equity structure of the entity, often discharging some of its obligations in order to preserve it.

Chapter 12 Reorganizes family farms under court supervision with the objective of preserving each farm as an ongoing entity.

Chapter 13 Enables natural persons as debtors to discharge their debts without liquidating their assets, usually following a three-year plan of regular payments to creditors.

each unsecured creditor receives only about 15 cents on the dollar. Chapter 11 reorganization usually promises to pay back far more than that.

Under Chapter 11 procedure, a reorganization plan is filed with the court by the debtor or, if a trustee has been appointed for the debtor's estate, by any interested party. The plan must designate classes of claims, for example, secured debts, unsecured debts, business accounts payable, workers' claims, and pension plan claims, and it must indicate which classes will have their claims impaired (reduced). The plan is forwarded to the various classes of creditors to approve or reject.

Even if some classes of creditors do not approve the plan, if the court feels the plan is fair and equitable, it may put the plan into operation. These circumstances are called the "cramdown" provision of Chapter 11. The plan is imposed on some creditors even over their objections. Chapter 11 plans can even result in the modification or avoidance of collective bargaining agreements between workers and the debtor firm. However, such action by a bankruptcy court is the exception today.

- *Chapter 12* "Discharge of Debts without Liquidation for Family Farm Owners," added to the Bankruptcy Code in 1986, is modeled on the procedure for relief provided in Chapter 13. Chapter 12 provides assistance for farmers who find the debt limits of Chapter 13 too low and the expense of Chapter 11 filings too high. Chapter 12 requires that the farmer's debts not exceed $1,500,000. Note that Chapter 12 is not a permanent addition to the bankruptcy code as of this writing. Its status as a temporary addition must be renewed every few months by the U.S. Congress.

- *Chapter 13* "Discharge of Debts without Liquidation for Individual Debtors" (natural persons only) is commonly called the "wage earner's plan." It is available only to people with regular incomes. In addition, the person who voluntarily files a Chapter 13 action must have less than $250,000 in unsecured debt and less than $750,000 in secured debt. The Chapter 13 procedure requires the debtor to propose a plan that includes signing over future income to a trustee who pays creditors. Under a Chapter 13 plan, both unsecured and secured debts can be reduced in amount, or the time allowed for making payments can be extended. In most instances however, the plan cannot run for more than three years, although in some situations, it can be extended to five years. The plan is reviewed by the court to make sure it provides the creditors with advantages over what they might expect in a Chapter 7 liquidation.

If the plan is approved by the court, at the end of the three- or five-year period of payments, practically all debts have been discharged, and debtors retain title to and possession of all their property. Note however, that alimony and child support cannot be discharged by this method.

Regrettably, Chapter 13 provisions were poorly drafted originally. Before the U.S. Congress closed loopholes by amending this part of the code, many debtors used their prefiling credit standing to abuse the bankruptcy act. These debtors amassed luxury goods just before filing Chapter 13 bankruptcy. In other words, debtors acquired fur coats, jewelry, expensive cars, and so on, along with large cash advances. Timing was important so the credit load for one item would not show up on a credit report requested by the seller of another item. The debtor would then file for Chapter 13 protection, make modest payments for three years and end up with the property. In this way, individuals were collecting tens and even hundreds of thousands of dollars simply because they could read, understand, and follow the Chapter 13 procedures. After an almost inexcusable delay of six to eight years, the U.S. Congress finally stopped this practice. The corrective amendments made debts nondischargeable if they were acquired from the purchase of $500 or more of luxury items within 40 days of a bankruptcy filing or from cash advances totaling more than $1,000 taken out within 20 days of a filing.

Hypothetical Case

As a result of financial problems incurred during a retailing downturn, Herb's Department Store was in serious trouble. Although it owned its main building in downtown Springton, Herb's had entered into very expensive leaseholds in two upscale malls in the suburbs. The lease payments and a lack of turnover in its inventory left the store teetering on the brink of bankruptcy. In desperation, Herb's board of directors located a prospective buyer out of state. The buyer, Slashed Enterprises, had considerable resources and ran a chain of discount department stores in the Chicago area. Unfortunately, when the news of the impending sale was announced, the malls threatened to sue Herb's to block the transaction. The malls pointed to a provision in their agreement with Herb's prohibiting the marketing of low-quality and/or discounted merchandise on their premises. When Herb's attorneys admitted that the malls' suit would probably be successful, Herb's filed for a Chapter 11 reorganization. Ultimately, the bankruptcy court accepted a plan put together by Herb's attorneys that postponed some payments for Herb's inventory and eliminated other payments. The court also voided the provisions in Herb's leases with the malls that allowed the malls to sue to block the sale of Herb's but required that the buyers maintain Herb's reputation as an upscale store. As a consequence, the sale went through and Herb's is again flourishing.

Procedure for Chapter 7 Liquidation

The most common form of bankruptcy protection is also the harshest. Under the Chapter 7 procedure, the discharge of debts follows a liquidation of the debtor's property. This *quid pro quo* produces a more dramatic change in the debtor's financial environment than any other bankruptcy alternative.

Of course, there are exceptions. Not all of the filer's debts are eligible for discharge. Not all of the filer's property must be liquidated. To determine which debts and property belong in which category, a strict procedure is followed. See Figure 23-2 for an overview of this procedure.

Filing the Petition

Chapter 7 bankruptcy procedure begins with the filing of a bankruptcy petition. If the petition is filed by the **bankruptcy debtor** (any natural individual or business except those considered special cases, such as banks, savings and loans, building and loans, railroads, and insurance companies), the result is called a **voluntary bankruptcy**. A petition filed by a debtor's creditors results in an **involuntary bankruptcy**.

Although subject to the same basic liquidation procedure, these two Chapter 7 bankruptcies are fundamentally different. In a voluntary filing, petitioners may still be able to meet their debts when they come due, yet be eligible to file for voluntary bankruptcy. In a contested involuntary bankruptcy, on the other hand, creditors must show that the debtor is insolvent to be successful. **Insolvency** under the Bankruptcy Code is not a test based on a balance sheet assessment that a debtor has more liabilities than assets. It is a status afforded people who cannot meet their debts when they become due. If the bankruptcy court dismisses the involuntary petition for lack of evidence of insolvency, the debtor can be awarded costs, lawyer's fees, and damages (even punitive damages in certain cases).

FIGURE 23-2   Steps in Chapter 7 Bankruptcy

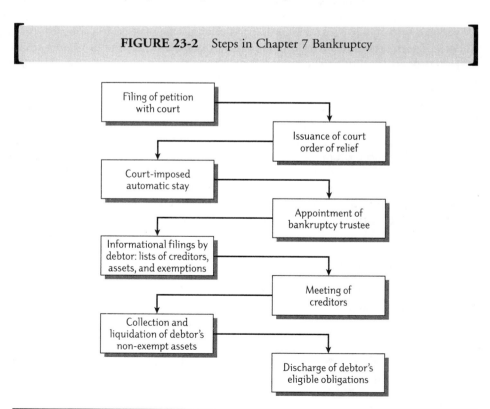

A husband and wife can join in a voluntary proceeding, whereas an involuntary proceeding is individualized. Also, neither a charity nor a farmer can be forced into involuntary bankruptcy (nor can the types of businesses listed above as special cases). The farmer or the charity can, of course, take voluntary bankruptcy without objection.

To force an eligible party into involuntary bankruptcy, only one signer of the petition is required if the debtor has fewer than 12 creditors and the signer is owed $10,000 or more. If a debtor has more than 12 creditors with unsecured claims totaling at least $10,000, at least 3 of them must sign the petition.

Hypothetical Case

As a result of medical problems, Victoria Baker fell behind in payments to her creditors. After several months, two creditors ignored her assurances that she would pay them back when she returned to work. The two creditors, Ava Rice and G. Reed, filed an involuntary proceeding against Baker showing that the total amount owed them exceeded $10,000. Baker contested the filing by saying that she had more than 12 creditors (the petition showed only 8), so that at least three of them had to sign the petition. Baker insisted that her attorney argue that her phone bill of $37.50, the $50 she owed her mother, her Sears credit card balance ($5.75), and the $12.50 she owed the paper boy brought the number of her creditors up to 12. The attorney reluctantly did so. The court examined the statute, found that no minimum amount was necessary to be listed as a creditor, and therefore dismissed the petition and awarded Baker enough in damages to pay off all her debts.

The Order of Relief

Once an involuntary petition has been filed, the court enters an **order of relief** (a declaration that the debtor is in a state of bankruptcy liquidation) if it determines the petition will not be contested. If the debtor contests the petition, the court must hold a trial. The purpose of the trial is to determine whether the debtor is insolvent or whether the debtor's property is in the custodial care of another. Only if the court determines that one of these circumstances is true will it issue the order of relief. Note that the very filing of a voluntary petition acts as an order of relief.

The Automatic Stay and Appointment of the Bankruptcy Trustee

The order of relief has two important effects. First, by law it triggers an automatic **stay** (suspension or halt) to judicial and administrative proceedings against the debtor. It also stops the enforcement of any judgment or the creation or enforcement (by self-help or otherwise) of liens against the debtor. Any violation of the stay can result in the violator being fined or imprisoned for contempt of court. Note that the stay does not freeze the collection of alimony and child support or criminal prosecution. Finally, the stay, enforced by the watchful eye of the court, also prevents creditors from taking unfair advantage of one another.

The second effect of the order of relief results in the appointment of a bankruptcy trustee by the court. As mentioned, the bankruptcy trustee administers the debtor's estate. This involves discovering, assembling, and protecting the rights and interests of the filer, then liquidating the assets, and using the proceeds to pay claims against the estate.

Informational Filings by the Debtor

Whether the debtor voluntarily files for bankruptcy or is involuntarily petitioned into bankruptcy, that party must provide certain information under oath, including:

- A list of creditors and the amount owed to each (an unlisted debt generally will not be discharged).
- A list of all the debtor's property, even if it may be exempt from the claims of the creditors. For the federal list of property exempted from liquidation procedures, see Figure 23-3. (Note that the Bankruptcy Code gives U.S. states the power to disallow their citizens' use of this federal list. Instead, states can compose their own lists and either require that debtors use it or give debtors the choice between the federal list and the state list.)
- A list of the debtor's current income and expenditures.
- A statement disclosing and explaining the debtor's financial affairs.

The Creditors' Meeting

Once the creditors have been identified, a meeting is scheduled for them. At that meeting, the debtor is required to answer their questions in person and under oath. If the creditors so desire, they can elect a trustee to replace the court-appointed

---

FIGURE 23-3   Exemptions Allowed under the Current Bankruptcy Act and Its Amendments

The federal list of exempt property includes:

1. A value of $15,000 in the debtor's residence (called the *homestead exemption* under state laws) and, in a macabre touch, the debtor's burial plot. For comparison, note that the state of Texas sets aside its homestead exemption by acreage—1 acre of urban or 200 acres of rural property, regardless of value, as long as the residence is there.

2. Household and personal items valued at less than $400 up to a total of $8,000. For several years there was no cap—the $8,000 total restriction—on this category. So, debtors were breaking down all manner of items, even cars, into small parts, each worth less than the exempted amount and thereby escaping their creditors' claims.

3. Up to $1,000 in jewelry, $1,500 in professional books and tools of the debtor's trade, and $2,400 of value in a motor vehicle.

4. Alimony, child support, Social Security, public assistance, pension, and veterans and disability payments.

5. Damages due in a personal injury suit up to $15,000.

Only state exemptions are allowed in more than half the states in the U.S. However, some states, especially California and Texas, have more generous exemptions than the federal exemptions shown here.

trustee already in place. They can also elect a creditors' committee to consult and advise the trustee.

The Collection and Liquidation of the Debtor's Assets

In a Chapter 7 proceeding, an estate in bankruptcy is formed from the debtor's property. This estate includes the property rights and interests of the debtor at the time of filing plus those to which the debtor becomes entitled during the next 180 days. In other words, insurance policy proceeds, gifts, inheritances, property awards and settlements from lawsuits (including divorces), and other property in which the debtor acquires rights and interests during this extra 180-day period are also used to satisfy creditors' claims. Thus, the end of this period acts as a cutoff point for the bankruptcy process. After the 180 days, the estate can typically be settled because no other property will become available that the trustee can liquidate for the creditors' benefit. Property acquired after the 180-day limit remains the debtor's.

During these 180 days a number of other events can occur, including:

- Creditors, especially those not listed by the debtor in the informational filings or those who allege a different amount owed, can file a **proof of claim**, which is a document showing the debtor's obligation to them. The court automatically allows such proofs of claim unless someone affected by the bankruptcy (trustee, debtor, or creditor) objects, in which case the court reviews the matter to be certain that the alleged debt is enforceable against the debtor. Obviously, a creditor that does not correctly establish itself during the 180-day period is not eligible for a portion of the payout when the estate is settled.

- Secured creditors in general may petition the court to be allowed to execute their security interest before the 180-day period is over. Such a petition is usually granted if the property is perishable or will decline greatly in value during that period. If the sale does not satisfy the full amount of the claim, the secured party is treated as an unsecured creditor for the balance due. If there is an excess of proceeds, the excess amount must be used to help the creditor pay off reasonable fees and costs brought on by the debtor's default. Anything still remaining is to be paid out to the unsecured creditors. Note that a consumer debtor must file a statement of intent regarding the secured collateral in her or his estate. This statement of intent, which must be filed before the creditors' meeting, details whether the debtor wants to surrender the collateral or keep it in the estate. The trustee is obligated to comply with the debtor's wishes within 45 days. If the collateral is to be turned over to the consumer debtor's creditors, they must determine whether to keep it in full satisfaction of the debt or to sell it for the proceeds, which are then utilized as in a non-consumer debt situation.

- The trustee in bankruptcy can accept or reject any of the debtor's executory contracts. In addition, the trustee collects the debtor's property and reduces it to money. This collection process may involve undoing some questionable transfers of property made by the debtor prior to filing for bankruptcy. In particular, the trustee is allowed to recover money or other property transferred by the debtor to a favored creditor on one of two grounds. The first condition involves a transfer made by an insolvent debtor within 90 days of the filing of the petition. This **preferential transfer** must give the payee creditor more than that person would have received in a Chapter 7 proceeding. If the transfer is to a **bankruptcy insider** (a person with a close relationship to the debtor, such as a relative or partner), the 90-day period is extended to a full year before filing. The second type of transaction that the trustee can void consists of transactions made with the intent to defraud, hinder, or delay creditors. These are called **fraudulent transfers**. The trustee can undo fraudulent transfers occurring up to one year prior to the filing.

Payout of Bankruptcy Proceeds

The Bankruptcy Code establishes a prioritized order in which the unsecured creditors are to be paid from the proceeds of the estate. Remember that secured creditors have priority over all other creditors in the proceeds from the sale of their collateral.

This payout of proceeds to the unsecured creditors is done in order of classes. All members of the class with the top priority must be fully paid before one cent is paid to anyone in the class with second priority. This procedure is followed through the eight classes until the money runs out. If a class cannot be fully paid, its members receive a pro rata share of the funds available. The priorities are as follows:

Class 1   Court costs and attorneys' and trustee's fees (typically labeled administrative costs).

Class 2   Claims against the debtor involuntarily petitioned into bankruptcy for expenses incurred between the filing of the petition and either the appointment of a trustee or the issuance of an order of relief

Class 3   Claims against the debtor for wages, commissions, and salaries earned within 90 days of filing. There is a $4,000 cap per claimant on this. The amount over $4,000 may be pursued as an unsecured claim (the last priority of claim).

Class 4   Claims stemming from unpaid amounts to employee benefit plans for the last 180 days prior to filing. Again, there is a $4,000 cap per employee.

Class 5   Claims against debtors operating fish and grain storage facilities brought by fishers and grain producers—$4,000 cap per claimant.

Class 6   Claims by consumers who have deposited funds to purchase or rent consumer goods or services that were not provided—$1,800 cap, with amount in excess of $1,800 eligible for treatment as an unsecured debt.

Class 7   Paternity, alimony, maintenance, and support debts.

Class 8   Unpaid income and property tax claims due various governmental bodies.

Class 9   Claims of general creditors and residual unsatisfied claims from the above categories.

Any money left after these claims have been satisfied is turned over to the debtor.

Discharge of the Debtor's Obligations

After the procedures detailed above have been properly followed, the bankruptcy court orders a discharge of most of the debtor's obligations. Some debts are not dischargeable by the court, however. These include

- Alimony and child support.
- Back taxes accruing over the three-year period prior to the filing for bankruptcy.
- Student loans owed to the government acquired over the last five years. However, a debtor can rid himself of this burden by proving that paying the loans would impose an undue hardship.
- Judgments or consent orders resulting from driving while intoxicated.
- Judgments against the debtor resulting from willful or malicious conduct injurious to the person or property of another, such as assault, battery, defamation, or other intentional tortuous conduct. Negligence awards however, can be discharged through bankruptcy.
- Claims against the debtor resulting from larceny, fraud, or embezzlement.
- Note that in certain instances the court does not order a discharge of even eligible debts. These instances include situations in which the debtor has fraudulently made a false oath, presented a false claim, used various means to withhold information on financial condition or business transactions, or attempted during the year before filing to keep property out of the creditors' grasp by fraudulent means. In addition, a debtor who fails to obey a lawful court order or who has received a bankruptcy discharge within the last six years will not receive a discharge.

Revocation of Discharge and Debt Reaffirmation

If the bankruptcy court should find at any time within one year of the discharge that the debtor acted fraudulently or in a dishonest fashion during the bankruptcy proceeding, the court may revoke the discharge. This leaves the creditors free to exact their claims against the debtor.

Also, it is often the debtor's wish to pay off a discharged debt owed to a family member, a friend, or a vital supplier of the business. This can be done legally through a **reaffirmation agreement**. However, the agreement must be made before the discharge and notice of it must be filed with the court. It may be rescinded by the debtor at any time up to 60 days after it has been filed or before discharge, whichever comes later.

Through the extended, formalized procedure of bankruptcy just detailed, thousands of Americans yearly seek the relief from debt necessary to allow them to become fully productive citizens once again.

As this text goes to press, the U.S. Congress is debating and will likely pass a new Bankruptcy Reform Act that seems necessary because of a number of factors. For example, approximately 1.3 million people filed for bankruptcy in the year

2000, a 75 percent increase over 1990. The resulting losses increased the cost of borrowing substantially to others; the banking industry cited figures of between $400 and $500 per person per year. Some of the very significant provisions under consideration for this new act include:

- *Restriction on individuals who can utilize Chapter 7*   Instead of being able to liquidate their debts totally and start over, bankruptcy debtors who can pay at least 25% of their debts over five years will have to file under Chapter 13. However, Chapter 13 allows debtors to keep their homes.

- *Curtailment of the Homestead Exemption*   "Wealthy" debtors preparing for bankruptcy had shifted millions of dollars' worth of assets into their homes, which could be shielded from creditors under some states' homestead exemptions (as mentioned, Texas has an unlimited homestead exemption). The U.S. Congress proposes either capping the exemption at $125,000 or denying it for a home bought within two years of filing for bankruptcy.

- *Ability of a Business Creditor to Block a Chapter 11 Reorganization*   Under the proposed changes, a single creditor could forestall a company's reorganization under Chapter 11, thereby forcing it into liquidation.

CHAPTER REVIEW

USE LEGAL TERMS

Fill in the blanks with the appropriate term.

bankruptcy	fraudulent transfer	proof of claim
bankruptcy debtor	insolvent	reaffirmation agreement
bankruptcy insider	involuntary bankruptcy	stay
bankruptcy trustee	liquidation	voluntary bankruptcy
discharged	order of relief	
estate	preferential transfer	

1. Paying off one favored creditor fully when the other bankruptcy creditors receive only 15 cents on the dollar owed is labeled a(n) ___?___.
2. Upon the filing of a voluntary petition, a(n) ___?___ is issued that would ___?___ other proceedings against the debtor.
3. A person unable to pay her or his debts when due is ___?___.
4. The sale for cash of the assets in the bankruptcy estate is called ___?___.
5. A transaction by the debtor made within one-year prior to filing that was intended to hide assets from the bankruptcy creditors is labeled a(n) ___?___.
6. A bankruptcy court will automatically allow a(n) ___?___ unless someone affected by the bankruptcy (trustee, debtor, or creditor) objects, in which case the court will review the matter to be certain that the alleged debt is enforceable against the debtor.

TEST YOUR READING

7. When a bank or other financial institution makes a bad loan that is then liquidated by a bankruptcy filing, who ultimately pays the price?
8. How often can a person take bankruptcy?
9. How long can a bankruptcy filing remain on a debtor's credit record?
10. What are the duties of a trustee in bankruptcy?
11. What type of protection is offered by Chapter 7? Chapter 9? Chapter 11? Chapter 12? Chapter 13?
12. What are the consequences of the Order of Relief?
13. List the informational filings of the debtor.
14. List five federal exemptions.
15. List the order of disbursement of the bankrupt person's estate.
16. List six debts that cannot be discharged in bankruptcy.

THINK CRITICALLY ABOUT EVIDENCE

17.   Considering the effects of taking bankruptcy on a debtor's credit standing, do you feel that the bankruptcy law is achieving its objectives? Why or why not?

18.   Under what ethical systems is the cramdown provision of Chapter 11 supportable? Do you agree with such actions?

Two Texas brothers, oil barons R. E. and I. N. Quest, were recently forced into involuntary bankruptcy. Problems 19, 20, 21, and 22 were taken from their filings of exempt property. Look through the problems, and inform them of just what the court will allow.

19.   Both brothers live in a penthouse on top of structures they own. R. E.'s penthouse is on the top floor of a $62 million office building. I. N.'s penthouse is on the top floor of a $71 million shopping complex. Each claims the 1 acre of urban property due him under Texas law. That acre encompasses both structures. Will both be allowed their multimillion-dollar exemptions?

20.   R. E. separated his rare china collection into 1,217 individual pieces, each worth less than $400, and claimed them under the personal property exemption. Will this method enable him to save the collection from liquidation? Could it have enabled him to do so in the past?

21.   One month before being forced into bankruptcy, I. N. retired from his position as president of the brothers' company. He then began drawing an amount equal to his old salary ($4 million per year) as his pension. He claimed that the pension was exempt from his creditors' claims.

22.   I. N. divorced his wife a month before the filing. As part of the property settlement, he signed over all his properties to his ex-wife. In turn, his ex-wife agreed to pay him alimony in the amount of $4 million per year. I. N. now claims that the $4 million is exempt from his creditors' claims.

The Quests were insolvent for a year before they were forced into bankruptcy. During that period, they made the following transfers, which are now the subject of the trustee's attention as possible fraudulent or preferential transfers. Which property will the bankruptcy court order returned to the estate? Explain, if appropriate, which type of transfer each is.

23.   R. E., a widower, gave his $13 million yacht to his son Charles a month before the filing.

24.   I. N. paid off in full a note held by his friend and business partner, Charles Smith, 92 days before the filing. I. N.'s creditors can expect to receive only 11 cents on the dollar as a result of the current bankruptcy proceeding.

The Quests want the court to order the following debts discharged. Will they be?

25.   An award of $2.5 million to Rodney Henry, a driver paralyzed in an automobile accident due to R. E.'s negligence.

26. A consent decree in which R. E. agreed to pay $1.2 million to the family of Bernard Tower, a driver killed in an automobile accident due to R. E.'s negligence. R. E. was issued a citation for driving while intoxicated.

27. Taxes amounting to $127 million owed to the federal and state governments since 1987.

28. Child support of $125,000 a year that R. E. agreed to pay as a result of a paternity suit brought against him four years ago.

REAL-WORLD CASE

Pennsylvania Dept. of Public Welfare v. Davenport
110 S. Ct. 2126

Now consider just how forgiving of debts society should be.

Ed and Deb Davenport pleaded guilty to welfare fraud and were sentenced to a year on probation. One condition of their probation was that they make payments of restitution for the welfare funds they had fraudulently kept from others. A few months after being sentenced, the Davenports filed for bankruptcy under Chapter 13. They listed the restitution payments as a debt from which they sought relief.

Think Critically

1. From an ethical perspective, should the relief be granted? What ethical system would support your answer?

2. The case was ultimately appealed to the U.S. Supreme Court, which ruled on it in 1990. What do you think the Court held? The citation below the case name refers to the Supreme Court case. Feel free to look up the answer in your local library or on the Internet.

3. What is your overall opinion of Chapter 13 plans?

UNIT 6

Selecting an Organizational Form for Your Business

CHAPTERS

CHAPTER 24

Forms of Business Organization

GOALS

- ◆ Identify various business forms
- ◆ Understand how a business is organized depending on the form
- ◆ Know the relative strengths and weaknesses of each form

Forms of Business Organization

Almost every businessperson dreams of one day becoming her or his own boss by establishing a business. The four chapters of this unit are dedicated to helping you make that choice either now or in the future. We'll begin by going over the most commonly used alternatives very concisely. Then we'll look in detail at the sole proprietorship, partnership, corporation, and specialty forms such as limited partnerships, S corporations, limited liability corporations, and limited liability partnerships. A good rule of thumb is that the more complex the procedure you use to organize your business—and therefore the more professional legal help you require, the greater the benefits you can derive from it.

That said, we start our discussion with the sole proprietorship, the form of business most easy to organize and most frequently used in the U.S.

Sole Proprietorship

A **sole proprietorship** is a business owned by one person. That owner alone is personally liable for the obligations of the business. Partnerships have two or more persons as owners. Corporations provide a shield that protects their owners from personal liability. But the sole proprietor stands alone. Typically, the business rises and falls on his or her contacts, contracts, expertise, business savvy, energy, or other resources. If it fails, the obligations it has incurred are enforceable not only against the assets of the business, but also against the home, car, furniture, and other possessions of its sole proprietor.

Why be a sole proprietor then? Why expose so much to the control of the marketplace, especially when the corporate form is available usually for less than $500 in legal and filing fees? Mainly, the reason is that the sole proprietorship is such an easy form to assume. Make your lemonade, set up a table on the street, and you are a sole proprietor. Aside from having a product, a price, and a prospective customer, the preparation involved is practically nil. The government may come along later and enforce such minor requirements as a tax number or a business license. However, you will not be shot or typically even fined for starting without these. "Just do it," seems the best way to express both the philosophy and the foresight required to get started in this form.

The sole proprietorship is also far more flexible and responsive to change than the other business forms—if the owner is properly involved in it. If not, the business is at peril. That's the major weakness of the sole proprietorship as well as its potential strength. Its very existence is the responsibility of one individual, the owner. If the owner loses interest, desire, financial or physical health, the business typically perishes. For this reason, it is difficult to hire long-term professional business people into a sole proprietorship. In addition, both the initial capitalization of the sole proprietorship and its financial ability to respond to change and opportunity are limited to the resources that the owner provides from personal savings or indebtedness.

General Partnership

If a businessperson needs more capital and greater skills than he or she alone can provide to make a business successful, the partnership form may be advisable. The basic partnership is known as the **general partnership**. It is statutorily defined as "an association of two or more persons to carry on as co-owners a business for profit." The use of the term *co-owners* here implies that, like the sole proprietor, each of the partners is individually liable for the obligations of the firm. As you may suspect, a partnership involves more legal considerations than does a sole proprietorship. These legal considerations are usually addressed in the partnership agreement. Issues not covered or resolved in the partnership agreement are governed in the U.S. by the Uniform Partnership Act (UPA). The UPA is a product of the Conference of Commissioners on Uniform State Laws. First offered to the states for adoption as law back in 1914, it has been enacted by every state in the U.S. except Louisiana

Note that should one of the partners die or withdraw from the business, the partnership's legal existence comes to an end. However, the business may continue if this is allowed by a wisely drafted partnership agreement. This is explained in more detail in Chapter 25.

Limited Partnership

The general partnership form involves the co-owners' unlimited personal liability for the obligations of the business. This can produce very unsatisfactory results.

Hypothetical Case

Dick Lobe and Lea Pold met in college, where they were both journalism majors. After graduation they kept in touch. Lobe became a successful TV news anchor. Pold became the editor of a biweekly regional literary magazine. When Lobe inherited $750,000 from an uncle, he mentioned the inheritance to Pold. She then suggested that they enter into a partnership and open a small publishing firm. Lobe agreed and put the $750,000 into the business. Pold agreed to do most of the managing in return for 50 percent of the profits. Lobe assisted by reading some manuscripts but mostly involved himself in his work and in writing his own novel, which he expected to have the partnership publish. When he finished the book, he presented it to Pold, expecting her to put it in print. She refused to do so, saying that she had just paid a large advance to a well-known defense attorney for his autobiography and that there wasn't any money left to do anything else. Several months passed. One day Pold called a meeting with Lobe. At the meeting, she quickly announced that because of personal problems, the attorney had not submitted a publishable manuscript. She went on to say that the partnership was out of funds and that she was dissolving it. After she left, Lobe checked the partnership books. Only then did he realize that as a result of contracts Pold had made, there were outstanding obligations of more than $1,300,000. Lobe could find no record of any scheduled income. When the creditors sued for their money, Pold was discovered to be judgment-proof (no recoverable assets). Lobe however, was forced into bankruptcy and stripped not only of what few assets remained in the partnership but of most of his personal possessions, including his home, his summer house, his cars and much more.

Because of experiences paralleling Lobe's, a statutory alternative to the general partnership form has been created, called the **limited partnership**. Such a partnership is composed of one or more general partners with full personal liability and one or more limited partners whose liability for partnership obligations extends only to the amount of their investment in the business. This is termed **limited liability**. To retain their limited liability, limited partners must not participate in the general management of the business. If Lobe had been a limited partner, he would have been liable only for the $750,000 that he put into the business. The creditors would not have been able to reach his personal wealth.

The limited partnership was created by the Revised Uniform Limited Partnership Act (RULPA). Potential partners must comply strictly with the formation procedure described in RULPA for the limited partnership status to be conferred. Because of the advantages of the limited partnership, many businesses employ this form.

Corporations

The ultimate in limited liability protection of investors is offered by the corporation, the form of business that almost all large firms choose. The **corporation** is a legal entity created as an artificial person through statutory authority. It can be owned by one or more persons (natural or artificial). Therefore, a corporation can sue or be sued without its investors acquiring personal liability. Also, it continues in existence beyond the withdrawal or death of its owners because ownership rights and equity are freely transferable in the form of certificates or shares of ownership called **stock**.

The protection of limited liability coupled with the possibility of perpetual existence made the corporation the foremost device ever created for attracting capital investment. Of course, the sheer size of some corporations renders them unresponsive to the best interests of their owners and to the immediate challenges of the marketplace. Also, the enormous earnings accumulated by corporations have made them the target of public criticism and, perhaps more important, of almost every public entity with taxing authority. Today, unlike the owner of a sole proprietorship or a partnership interest, the owner of a corporation is subject to double taxation. Because the corporation is considered a separate artificial person, its earnings are taxed. Then, when some or all of its after-tax earnings are paid out to the owners of the corporation, that is, the **shareholders**, these earnings are taxed a second time. This occurs because the stockholders are required to declare the earnings payouts as income on their personal tax returns.

Even so, if dollars were votes, the corporate form would be elected the world's most popular mode of business ownership for investors.

S Corporation

A significant stepping-stone between the partnership and the full corporate form is provided in the Internal Revenue Code. Called the S corporation, it is organized like a normal corporation, but differs in the fact that profits and losses are taxed directly to the stockholders. In that way, double taxation is avoided. To become an **S corporation**, a corporation merely has to file for the status with the Internal Revenue Service and meet the following criteria:

1. Has to be a corporation chartered in the U.S. with no more than 75 shareholders (partnerships and corporations are not allowed as shareholders).
2. Has the agreement of all stockholders to become an S corporation.
3. Has only one class or kind of stock shares.
4. Divides its profits and losses among its shareholders according to their proportionate holdings of stock.
5. Elects to become an S corporation by March 15 of the tax year in which the election is to be effective.

As with a normal corporation, limited liability, survivability, and free transferability of shares are features of the S corporation (as long as the 75-shareholder limit is not exceeded). Also, S corporation losses can be passed through to investors—as income is passed through. These losses can be used by stockholders to offset income from other sources. This reduces the investors' overall tax burden. In contrast, such losses cannot be passed through to the owners of a regular corporation.

If the corporation later needs to increase the number of investors for growth purposes, the S corporation status can be dropped with another filing. Since its creation as an alternative form of business, the S corporate form has been very popular with owners of closely-held businesses.

Other Business Forms

Limited Liability Corporation   This form of corporation has swept across the country since a favorable Internal Revenue Service ruling in 1988. Currently, almost all states have passed a prototype statute making the **limited liability corporation** (LLC) form available. The LLC combines the advantages of the limited partnership and the S corporation forms while eliminating the restrictions normally placed on each. In particular, the LLC, unlike the S corporation, is neither limited in its number of shareholders nor restricted to only one class of stock. At the same time, every member of an LLC is free to participate in management without losing the limited liability protection so important to a limited partner or a corporate shareholder. In addition, a general partner—the member who is fully personally liable in a limited partnership—is required under the LLC statutes of the various states that have adopted this form. Besides all these advantages, plus several others not covered here, an LLC can also pass losses as well as profits through to the member-owners. In short, the LLC seems almost too good to be true. Consequently, because of tax revenues lost by the growth of LLCs, the threat of its elimination by Congress arises periodically.

Business Trust   The **business trust**, which is still in use, was once a popular business form in some northeastern states that barred corporations from dealing in real property. It involves having selected trustees manage property (signed over to the trust by the business owners) so as to provide income or other forms of return to certain individuals (labeled **beneficiaries** at law). It is formed by an instrument that generally must be crafted by attorneys to properly describe the trust property, the trustees' powers, and the rights and interests of the beneficiaries and the trust's creditors.

At one time, the business trust was not subject to either double taxation or other forms of governmental regulation. In addition, its participants were free from personal liability. Now however, the business trust is taxed as a corporation and the trustees and any beneficiaries of the trust who have managerial power have personal liability for trust obligations. Accordingly, the popularity of the business trust has declined markedly.

Franchise   Another form of business that has recently become somewhat inhibited by regulation is the **franchise**. It is defined as a business arrangement surrounding the licensing of a trademark, trade name, or copyright for use in selling goods or services. A detailed and well-tested system of doing business often comes with the licensing. The capital for the business comes from the recipient of the franchise, called the **franchisee**. The franchisee can be a sole proprietor, a partnership, a corporation, or some other form of business, whatever is acceptable to the seller of the franchise (the **franchisor**). In return for her or his investment, the franchisee typically receives, in addition to the license and the business system, the benefit of national or regional goodwill from collective advertising and the cost-cutting power of collective purchasing. The franchisor receives the franchise fee, a percentage of the sales, and other reimbursements.

Successful franchises are practically legendary. They range from Ray Kroc's McDonald's to a multitude of other names that crowd the highly trafficked thoroughfares of America and the world. Unsuccessful franchises however, are equally numerous, if not more so. This has caused state and federal regulators to focus on how franchises are distributed. In 1979, the Federal Trade Commission required that prospective franchisors disclose material facts about their enterprises. Failure to properly reveal all information pertinent to a prospective franchisee's choice or a misstatement in the information disclosed may leave a franchisor wide open to suit. These informational requirements have been augmented by various state laws aimed at preventing franchisors from terminating franchises without good cause. Taken as a whole, the legal attention given to franchising has made it a field for the cautious and those with the resources to ensure compliance.

All the forms of business discussed above have advantages and drawbacks (see Figure 24-1 for a summary of these). In the next section, we will take a closer look at the establishment of a sole proprietorship. Then, in the chapters that follow, we discuss partnerships and corporations in more detail.

Sole Proprietorships

As indicated earlier, you can start a sole proprietorship almost by simply "opening the doors" for business. In most municipalities, a business license is required. Even so, unless the business comes under some regulation because of its product or service, for example, liquor, food, or toxic chemicals, obtaining a business license involves nothing more than the formality of paying a fee.

Hypothetical Case

Michael Mansfield opened his gaming store and playroom in April. Some six months later, a city inspector walked in and checked to see if the business was licensed. Finding no license displayed, he ordered Michael to procure one at his earliest opportunity. Michael did so at once. No fine or late charge was imposed. The license cost $10. The inspector returned the next week, saw the license, and thanked Michael for taking care of it so promptly.

Of course, if Michael had refused to obtain a license (a source of revenue for the city), he would have ultimately been closed down.

Another requirement for businesses is a tax number. This number is provided free of charge by the federal government upon request. It or a similar number

[**FIGURE 24-1**   General Attributes of Most-Used Forms of Business]

	Sole Proprietorship	Partnership	Corporations
Capitalization potential	Typically limited to proprietor's resources	Typically limited to partners' resources	Relatively unlimited
Owner's liability limited to investment?	No; proprietor's personal resources may be used to satisfy liabilities of business	No; partners' personal assets may be used to satisfy liabilities of business	Yes
Formal entry requirements	Negligible	Need partners' agreement; lawyer's services recommended	Relatively complex; lawyer's services usually necessary
Potential lifetime of business	Limited by duration of proprietor's involvement	Ends upon death, disability, or withdrawal of any partner	Can be perpetual
Potential for attracting and retaining professional management	Poor due to limited lifetime and growth potential	Poor due to inherent instability of partnership	Excellent due to extent of life of business and possibilities for growth
Ability to respond to changing business environment	Excellent in short term due to lack of institutionalization; poor strategically due to lack of capitalization potential	Moderately able both tactically and strategically	Relatively slower to respond to tactical changes; excellent for long-term structural changes due to capitalization potential
Is business taxed as a separate entity?	No; earnings taken as personal income by sole proprietor	No; profits taken as personal income by partners	Yes; corporation taxed on earnings; owners taxed on dividends paid to them out of those earnings

issued by an individual state is often used as identification to see that eligible businesses do not have to pay sales tax on their purchases of inventory. It also serves to identify businesses to the Internal Revenue Service to assure tax payments and other levies.

Beyond these minor requirements, the average sole proprietor need worry only about having the product, the price, and the prospective customer.

CHAPTER REVIEW

USE LEGAL TERMS

Fill in the blanks with the appropriate term.

beneficiaries	franchisor	S corporation
business trust	general partnership	shareholders
corporation	limited liability	sole proprietorship
franchise	limited liability corporation	stock
franchisee	limited partnership	

1. Shares of ownership in a corporation are evidenced by ___?___ certificates.
2. The seller of a franchise is known as the ___?___.
3. Individuals receiving the benefit of a business trust are labeled ___?___.
4. The form of business with one owner who has full personal liability for the business is known as a(n) ___?___.
5. The form of business with more than one owner, each of whom has full personal liability for the business, is known as a(n) ___?___.
6. The form of business with multiple owners, at least one of whom has full personal liability for the business, is known as a(n) ___?___.

TEST YOUR READING

7. What are the advantages of the sole proprietorship form?
8. Why would a professional manager not want to work for a sole proprietorship?
9. What is the greatest disadvantage of the partnership form?
10. When does a partnership end?
11. Who has unlimited personal liability in a limited partnership?
12. Under what circumstance(s) does a limited partner acquire unlimited personal liability?
13. What are the advantages of the corporate form?
14. Why are the S corporations and LLCs so popular?

THINK CRITICALLY ABOUT EVIDENCE

15. You are a business consultant. A young engineering graduate walks into your office one day. He has a patent on a new type of automobile braking system. He informs you that he knows a wealthy doctor who wants to invest in the development of the product. However, the doctor does not want to risk the possibility of liability from lawsuits if the product fails to perform and injures someone. The engineer does not want to use the corporate form because he feels that it might cause him to lose control of the business. What form of business do you recommend to him? Why?

16. Barney Phifendrum has worked for a large auto muffler shop for six years. Now he wants to go into the business of selling and installing mufflers at discount prices for himself. He has saved barely enough money to buy an initial stock of different sizes of mufflers and to lease a suitable garage for six months. What form of business is Mr. Phifendrum most likely to establish? Why?

17. A year has passed. Mr. Phifendrum's shop is a huge success. He has developed his own methods for advertising, pricing, and installing mufflers. The ads feature "Sy Lentz," the fictional spokesperson and owner of the shop that bears his name (Sy Lentz's Discount Mufflers). Mr. Phifendrum plans to establish a second shop on the other side of the city. However, he is worried about being able to attract a good manager for that shop and about the potential liability from improper installations. He does not like the corporate form because of the double taxation. What business form should he choose? Why?

18. Mr. Phifendrum's second shop is also successful. He has recently been approached by a number of people for help in setting up shops like his in nearby cities. What form of business would you recommend that Mr. Phifendrum consider at this stage of development of his business? Why?

19. Most of us have business ideas that we have promised ourselves to market-test someday. Think about yours, or reflect until you have such an idea. Then ask yourself, "Given my current situation in life, would I want to use the sole proprietorship form to develop a business around my idea?" What are the pros and cons of a sole proprietorship for you? Are you likely to use that business form?

REAL-WORLD CASE
Pilsbury v. Honeywell, Inc.
191 N.W.2d 406

Consider a case that points out the limits on the powers of ownership.

During the Vietnam conflict, Honeywell, Inc., made fragmentation bombs for use against enemy personnel. The bombs, nicknamed "shredders" by some veterans, were highly effective. Pilsbury, an antiwar protester, bought one share of Honeywell stock in order to communicate with other Honeywell shareholders. He wanted to persuade them to use their power of ownership to cause the company to cease production of the shredders and other munitions. As an "owner" of the company, he therefore requested a list of shareholders and records of its dealings with the Pentagon from its management. When his request was refused, he petitioned the court to order the documents released to him.

Think Critically

1. If Honeywell were a sole proprietorship and Pilsbury were its owner, would there be any question as to his ability to obtain the information he wanted? If it were a partnership and Pilsbury were a general partner, would there be any question?
2. The court refused Pilsbury's request. What reasons for its refusal can you think of?
3. Would the court be justified in refusing a similar request from a member of a competing corporation's management who bought a share to obtain inside information about Honeywell? Would the court be justified in refusing a stockholder who believed that corporate management was defrauding the shareholders by not reporting all of the income from its munitions sales to the Pentagon and needed the records to confirm that belief?
4. Is Pilsbury a true "owner" of a business? Why or why not?

CHAPTER  25

Partnerships

GOALS

- ◆   Understand the advantages and disadvantages of general partnerships
- ◆   Identify significant issues to be covered in a partnership agreement
- ◆   Know how to form and end a general partnership

Advantages and Disadvantages of General Partnerships

In comparing the different business forms in the last chapter, we mentioned most of the advantages and disadvantages of the general partnership. To quickly restate them, the advantages include ease of entry; flexibility; greater capital formation potential and managerial resource availability than are obtainable under a sole proprietorship; lack of direct governmental oversight; and no double taxation. The most notable disadvantages are full personal liability for the partners; termination of the partnership upon the withdrawal or death of any partner; and the practical problem of keeping partners acting as partners.

All too often, the greatest enemy of a partnership is that the effort or sacrifice required of each partner is not balanced. Usually one or a few partners "give" more than the others. As a result, resentment may build up. Before long, it occurs to some of the partners that they are rewarding "partners" whom they feel are not carrying their share of the burden. The ultimate result is that the "partnership" perishes. Consequently, a word to the wise is to never—repeat, never—go into a general partnership with anyone with whom you want to keep a long-lasting personal relationship.

Lawyers are typically aware of the perils of the partnership form of business. Therefore, when clients ask a lawyer to write a partnership agreement for them, the lawyer tries to include terms that anticipate and resolve possible conflicts. Unfortunately, to do this requires asking the potential partners how they would want to resolve these conflicts. The clients, who have come into the attorney's office caught up in the euphoria of what they think the partnership could achieve, thereby have the ice-cold water of experience poured on them. The lawyer's well-motivated questions remind them of all that might go wrong with the partnership. Before long, the euphoria changes to dread, and often, no partnership is formed. The lawyer again earns a reputation as a "deal killer." This situation can be avoided by addressing these issues in advance. The next sections of this chapter deal with the legalities of creating, running, and terminating a general partnership.

Creating a General Partnership

One of the advantages of the partnership form is ease of entry. Of the two principal ways of forming partnerships, the first way is by express agreement of the persons involved. Note that the "persons" referred to here may include various types of business organizations, especially corporations. This way of forming a partnership is discussed further at the end of this section.

By Court Acknowledgement

The second way a partnership is formed results from a court determination that a partnership exists because of how certain parties do business with one another.

If a person maintains in court that a partnership exists, the court examines the business dealings of the alleged partners to find some **prima facie evidence** (proof good and sufficient on its face on which a factual presumption can be based) of the partnership. The most common prima facie evidence is the sharing of profits. If the court discovers that practice, it holds that a partnership exists unless satisfactory evidence to the contrary is presented. For example, profits may be paid out to a creditor or other obligee without making the recipient a partner.

Hypothetical Case

McCord, Hunt, and Liddy formed a partnership to do household plumbing repairs. They leased office space in a well-known city landmark. To pay their rent, they agreed to share 25 percent of their profits with their landlord, Creep, Inc. When the partnership failed to meet its obligations, several of its creditors hired the law firm of Cox, Sirica, and Jaworski to try to recover the amounts due. The law firm produced evidence showing that the plumbers did indeed share their profits with Creep. One of the plumbers, John McCord, even alleged that Creep was a partner. This was enough prima facie evidence to cause the court to presume that a partnership existed and therefore, Creep could be held liable for the partnership's obligations. Creep then came forward with documents and tapes of the lease negotiations showing that the payout of profits was strictly for rent. This was enough evidence to cause the court to overturn its presumption that Creep was a member of the partnership. It then held that Creep was not liable for the partnership's debts.

Other profit payouts, such as to employees for wages, to creditors for debt repayment, to retirees as part of a pension plan, or to sellers as the price of goods sold, are not enough to make the payees partners, either. Remember however, that if prima facie evidence of partnership is found, then the party denying that a partnership exists must disprove the court's contrary presumption. The court does not look for evidence on its own. Once the prima facie evidence causes the court to erect its presumption, the court must be shown that there was no partnership.

By Statute

Typically, statutes do not interfere to any great extent with the formation of a general partnership. The statute of frauds does require however, that the express contract on which the partnership is based be in writing if it cannot be carried out in less than a year. However, the Uniform Partnership Act, discussed briefly in the last chapter, does provide terms that the courts use in handling partnership issues. These terms are used only if the partners do not reach agreement on their own terms. For example, section 18 of the UPA reads, in part:

> The rights and duties of the partners in relation to the partnership shall be determined, *subject to any agreement between them,* by the following rules:
> (a) Each partner shall . . . contribute towards the losses, whether of capital or otherwise, sustained by the partnership according to his share in the profits. . . .
> (e) All partners have equal rights in the management and conduct of the partnership business. . . .
> (h) Any difference arising as to ordinary matters connected with the partnership business may be decided by a majority of the partners; but no act in contravention of any agreement between the partners may be done rightfully without the consent of all the partners.

These are only a few of the UPA rules that apply unless the parties to the partnership agreement (referred to as the **articles of partnership**) stipulate otherwise. So, in a U.S. state that has adopted the UPA, if you don't want every partner to "have equal rights in the management . . . of the partnership business" [18(e) above] or if you don't want to have "ordinary business matters . . . decided by a majority of the partners" [18(h) above], then you need to stipulate the desired procedures in the articles of partnership.

In contrast to this approach, the UPA, in section 16, enables certain individuals to bear the full responsibility for partnership obligations. In this section, the UPA mandates the enforcement of partnership responsibilities against someone who improperly indicates by words or conduct that a partnership exists or who holds herself or himself as a member of an existing partnership. If an outside party is deceived enough to believe these misrepresentations, the person who made them is held responsible for any subsequent liability just as if he or she is a partner. This is termed a **partnership by estoppel**. However, no real partnership is created under these circumstances. Partners by estoppel do not share in the profits or assets of a partnership, if one exists. They simply lose the right to deny at law their involvement in the partnership so as to avoid paying its liabilities.

Hypothetical Case

A group of investors wanted to open a country music theater in Branson, Missouri. They pooled their money and formed a partnership. To attract customers, they paid famous country singer Ronny Money for the use of his name. A few months before the season was to begin however, it became obvious that Ronny Money Country Music Jubilee would not be able to open its doors without a sizable loan. Knowing that Ronny was well regarded in the community and had an excellent credit rating, the partners asked him to accompany them to the bank from which they wanted to borrow the needed money. Ronny, who would receive a substantial percentage of the jubilee's take when he appeared there in person, agreed to do so. He even pretended to be a partner and represented himself as such to the bank. Because the bank knew Ronny's credit rating, it lent money to the partnership.

As a result of other difficulties however, the country music theater never opened. When the bank sought funds to cover its unpaid loan, it was able to proceed against Ronny as a fully liable partner even though he really was not a partner in the enterprise. The court held that he was a partner by estoppel. He was therefore estopped or prohibited from denying that he was a partner for the purpose of avoiding responsibility for repaying the loan.

By Agreement

Although court acknowledgment focuses partnership responsibility on some, a partnership is most often created by express agreement of the parties. As mentioned, that agreement can be oral. However, if the agreement cannot be performed within a year, then it must be in writing to meet the requirements of the statute of frauds. Also, if the partnership is to deal with buying and selling real estate, the agreement must be in writing.

The flexibility of a partnership is underscored by the various types of partners involved in such businesses. For example, **general partners** participate in the management of the partnership and are personally fully liable for the partnership's obligations. **Silent partners** are properly and publicly acknowledged, but do not participate actively in the management of the partnership. **Secret partners**, on the other hand, are not publicly acknowledged. **Nominal partners** are not actually partners but present themselves as such or allow themselves to be presented as such. (As you have probably deduced, Ronny Money in the last hypothetical case was a nominal partner.) Finally, **dormant partners** are neither acknowledged publicly as partners nor do they actively participate in the management of the partnership.

Regardless of the partners' intentions (as mentioned, they may be corporations, individuals, or, in many states, other partnerships), the partnership form has proven to be flexible enough to serve just about any would-be partner's needs and imagination. The articles of partnership shown in Figure 25-1 present most of the items normally considered important in forming a partnership.

FIGURE 25-1   The General Partnership Agreement of Leaks Anonymous

Date, identity of partners, and purpose of partnership →

Name, location, and records availability →

Duration and termination procedure →

Capitalization →

Funding of reserve →

Division of profits and losses, payout schedule →

Account location, withdrawal procedure →

Duties and limitations →

Nonroutine decision-making procedure →

Signatures →

By agreement made this 30th day of September, 20**, we, John McCord, Glenda Liddy, and Eduardo Hunt, the undersigned all of Leavenworth, Kansas, hereby join in general partnership to conduct a plumbing installation and repair business and mutually agree to the following terms:

1.   That the partnership shall be called "Leaks Anonymous" and have its principal place of business at 715 South Oaklawn, Leavenworth, Kansas, at which address books containing the full and accurate records of partnership transactions shall be kept and be accessible to any partner at any reasonable time.

2.   That the partnership shall continue in operation for an indefinite time until terminated by 90 days' notice provided by one or more of the partners and indicating his, her, or their desire to withdraw. upon such notice an accounting shall be conducted and a division of the partnership assets made unless a partner wishes to acquire the whole business by paying a price determined by an arbitrator whose selection shall be agreed to by all three partners. Said price shall include goodwill, and the paying of same shall entitle the payor to continue the partnership business under the same name.

3.   That each partner shall contribute to the partnership: $5,000 for initial working capital and the inventory and equipment (including trucks—which shall be marked with the partnership name, address, and logo) of their current individual plumbing businesses.

4.   That in return for the capital contribution in article 3, each partner shall receive an undivided one-third interest in the partnership and its properties.

5.   That a fund of $25,000 be set up and retained from the profits of the partnership business as a reserve fund. It being agreed that this fund shall be constituted of not less than 15 percent of the monthly profits until said amount has been accumulated.

6.   That the profits of the business shall be divided equally between the partners, that the losses shall be attributed according to the subsequent agreement, and that a determination of said profits and losses shall be made and profit shares paid to each partner on a monthly basis.

7.   That the partnership account shall be kept in the First National Bank of Pennsboro and that all withdrawals from same shall be by check bearing the signature of at least one of the partners.

8.   That each partner shall devote his or her full efforts to the partnership business and shall not engage in another business without the other partners' permission.

9.   That no partner shall cause to issue any commercial paper or shall enter into any agreements representing the partnership outside the normal conduct of the plumbing business without notice to the remaining partners and the consent of at least one other partner and further that all managerial and personnel decisions not covered by another section of this agreement shall be made with the assent of at least two of the partners.

IN AGREEMENT HERETO, WE ARE

John McCord   Glenda Liddy   Eduardo Hunt
(signatures)

Operating a Partnership

The rules determining how a partnership operates may be spelled out in the partnership agreement, if one exists. However, if a partnership is not based on an express agreement or if it is based on an incomplete agreement, then some or all of the rules of its operation have to be found in the UPA. So, the UPA rules are covered in the following discussion. Remember that the partners are free to select their own rules for the partnership agreement, which typically then supersede the UPA rules.

Management

Under the UPA, day-to-day operations of a partnership can be conducted by any of the partners. Each partner has equal rights in the management of the ordinary course of business, no matter how small that partner's percentage of ownership may be. Any differences among the partners over routine matters is to be resolved by a majority vote of the partners. Should that method fail, then any previous pattern of conducting business is retained, if appropriate. If no previous pattern exists or the failure to resolve the issue impairs the business routine and its profitability, the partnership must be dissolved.

Hypothetical Case

Lance and G. Daland Webb formed a partnership and took over their father's prosperous real estate brokerage when he retired. Unfortunately, conflicts soon developed between the two partners over employee tasks and office locations. One partner employed a programmer to integrate computers into the office routine. The other partner saw this hiring as a budget problem and fired the programmer. Lance developed an advertising campaign. Daland canceled it. Before long, the well-meaning decisions of the two partners started to affect profits. Finally, because of their inability to agree on such ordinary business matters, the partnership had to be dissolved.

Extraordinary managerial decisions typically require the assent of all the partners. For example, using partnership property as collateral, bringing in a new partner, and selling the partnership's real property require unanimous consent of the partners. (Compare how the partners in Leaks Anonymous handled these decisions by reviewing Article 9 of Figure 25-1.)

Note that under the UPA, partners can assign their partnership interests, such as profits, to non-partners. However, the assignees who receive such interests are not thereby given the right to take part in the management of the partnership.

Profits, Losses, and Property Rights

Each partner is entitled to an equal share in the profits and losses of the partnership unless agreement to the contrary has been reached. As mentioned, however, partners who have extensive outside income may find it advantageous tax-wise to take a larger share of the partnership's losses than those that do not have such income. Such an allocation can easily be arranged in the partnership agreement. In addition, under the UPA, partners may call for an accounting of the partnership business to determine profits, losses, and other matters whenever this "is just and reasonable" [UPA section 22(d)].

In addition to a share of profits and losses, the UPA gives each partner a co-ownership in partnership property. This **tenancy in partnership**, set up in UPA section 24, provides each partner with an equal right to possess specific partnership property for partnership purposes. This right, unlike the partners' interests in the profits of the partnership, cannot be assigned. Likewise, specific partnership property cannot be used for personal purposes by any partner without the consent of the other partners. Consequently, a partner's creditors cannot attach or execute their rights against specific partnership property, whether or not the property is in that partner's possession. In addition, should a partner die, the deceased partner's rights in specific partnership property pass to the surviving partners. The surviving spouse, heirs, or other next of kin have no claims on specific partnership property.

Liability for Business Operations

All these provisions of the tenancy in partnership provide the best opportunities for preserving the partnership's business in the face of individual misfortune. However, the partnership is liable for torts that a partner or an employee commits while engaged in the partnership's business. The liability is both joint and several for the partners for everything chargeable to the partnership as a result. This means that each partner can be sued (or perhaps released from liability) separately without affecting the case against the other partners. It also means that several or all of the partners can be sued at once. If sued separately and recovered against in full, a partner is entitled to receive a proportionate share from each of the other partners (or, if necessary, the partner who has paid in full can secure such contributions by court action). If a partner commits a crime to further the partnership's interests, that partner is separately liable for the offense, however. A contract action, unlike those based on tortious or criminal conduct, must be brought against the partners jointly. The judgment received or the release given applies to all of the partners.

Fiduciary Duty Above All

Finally, in conducting the partnership's business, each partner owes a **fiduciary duty** to the partnership, and must put the partnership's interest above her or his own. The partner must act in good faith in all business dealings. Using partnership funds or other property for personal gain violates the partner's fiduciary duty. Competing against the partnership also violates the duty. Consequently, the courts hold the partner accountable to the partnership for any individual gain that he or she receives while on partnership business.

Ending a Partnership

In general, a partnership's legal existence may have to be terminated (brought to a legal end) because of intentional actions of the partners, automatic operation of the law, or a court decree. Any one of these may result in a **dissolution of partnership**. The UPA defines such a dissolution as a change in which any partner ceases to be associated with carrying on the partnership's business. However, the dissolution of a partnership does not necessarily mean the partnership's business must end. Often the partnership agreement provides a means by which the remaining partners can buy out the interest of the departing partner. Article 2 of the partnership agreement shown in Figure 25-1 allows the partnership business to continue under its established name after the departure of one or more partners.

However, if no such mechanism was established in the partnership agreement, or if no one uses an available mechanism, the partnership business itself needs to be terminated. Such a partnership can be "wound up" either by following procedures in the partnership agreement or, lacking that, according to UPA rules. The **winding up** of a partnership requires that all business be concluded (remaining partners cannot enter into new contracts except as necessary to fulfill existing obligations) and partnership property sold. After the cash accumulated this way satisfies the partnership's debts, any remaining funds are distributed to the partners. The partnership then ceases to function, and the partnership agreement is terminated.

Dissolution

Now that you have the general picture, let's examine various ways dissolution can be initiated.

By the Intentional Acts of a Partner   Many partnership agreements set down the term for the partnership. Once that period has run or a specified event has occurred (such as gross earnings falling below a certain amount, the expulsion of a partner, or a unanimous partners' vote for dissolution), the partnership is dissolved. Some partnership agreements hinge dissolution on the accomplishment of a partnership's purpose (construct a bridge, provide food service at home football games for the coming season, etc.) If nothing is set down in the partnership agreement about the term of the partnership, then the partnership is considered to be "at will." Any partner can dissolve a **partnership at will** at any time without incurring any liability.

By Action of Law   Certain events described in various laws dissolve partnerships automatically. For example, the law prescribes that the death of a partner ends the partnership. The bankruptcy of a partner or the bankruptcy of the partnership also end a partnership. The loss of a professional status or license also could bring on the dissolution of a partnership by making it inoperable.

Hypothetical Case

Fresh out of dental school, Tormentia, Gore, Lurem, and Skewerem formed a partnership to practice dentistry. For several years they were quite successful. Then Lurem was charged with using too
little anesthesia in her procedures. Eventually she lost her license to practice in the state. Because she
could no longer take part in the partnership's activities, the partnership was automatically dissolved
as a matter of law.

By Court Decree   Although not automatic, other legal grounds can be used
to dissolve a partnership by court **decree** (judgment). When circumstances render
the partnership inoperable, yet do not bring on its automatic dissolution under the
law or the partnership agreement, a court can be petitioned with the facts of the
matter. The court is asked to judge whether the partnership can or should be
continued. If the court decides in the negative, the court orders the partnership
dissolved. Typical reasons for such petitions include:

- Disputes among the partners that cannot be reconciled
- A significant willful breach of the partnership agreement
- The inability to carry on the partnership's business except at a loss
- The incapacity of a partner to carry out the partnership agreement

Regardless of how it happens, partnership dissolution affects not only the
partners but those who deal with the partnership. In the dentistry partnership, Dr.
Lurem's loss of her license may have significant effects on many of the partnership's
patients. The resulting reduction in partnership income also may affect the partnership's creditors.

Notice of Dissolution

Because dissolution of a partnership affects the third parties that deal with it, the
law has special provisions about the notice of dissolution due such parties.
Creditors must receive direct personal notice of the dissolution. Others, until they
receive implied or express notice of the dissolution, are protected if they continue
to deal with the partnership in the same manner they have dealt with it previously.

Winding Up

As mentioned, the dissolution of a partnership does not necessarily mark the
termination of its business. However, should that become necessary, an orderly
procedure must be followed. The procedure begins with the sale of the partnership's assets. The funds raised are then used to pay off the partnership's liabilities.
Whatever remains is distributed to the partners in accordance with the percentage
of the profits each normally receives. It is important to remember three things
about this procedure. First, until the partnership has been fully wound up, the
partners still owe a fiduciary duty to one another. Second, once the procedure has
begun, the partners are authorized to act only in ways that contribute to the

winding-up process. Third, in paying off the partnership's creditors, non-partner creditors receive their due before partner-creditors receive theirs.

Obviously, destroying an ongoing profitable business seldom does anyone any good in the long term. The employees lose their livelihood. The economy loses a viable participant. Even the partners who receive a payout from the process probably would receive a better return on their money if the business continued to function. Nonetheless, if the business has to be wound up, following a fair and orderly procedure is the best insurance against expensive subsequent lawsuits.

 ## Technology Insights

Medical Technology and the Law of Business Forms

After chronic back pain had almost disabled his patient, a neurologist referred the ill man to the clinic of a radiology service corporation for an MRI. The first MRI was taken on February 14, read by a clinic doctor and found to be negative. Nonetheless, the pain continued. On July 31 and November 3 of the same year, two other MRIs were taken. Each of these times, a doctor from the radiology service who interpreted the results found them to be negative. Ultimately, the patient was given an MRI by another radiology lab and a cancerous tumor was found on his spine. When the patient brought suit for what he claimed were the negligent readings of the first three MRIs, the court found that, although he could recover damages from the corporation, he could not recover anything from the individual doctors.

Think Critically   What rule(s) do you think protected the doctors from being sued individually? Do you think that the court's disallowing suit against the doctors will affect the performance of similarly situated doctors in the future? Was "justice" done?

CHAPTER REVIEW

USE LEGAL TERMS

Fill in the blanks with the appropriate term.

articles of partnership   partnership at will
decree   partnership by estoppel
dissolution of partnership   prima facie evidence
dormant partner   secret partner
fiduciary duty   silent partner
general partner   tenancy in partnership
nominal partner   winding up

1. The court formed its factual presumption from ___?___.
2. An individual member of a partnership who has full personal liability and participates in managerial decisions in the partnership is known as a(n) ___?___.
3. An individual member of a partnership who has full personal liability but is unknown to the public and does not participate in managerial decision making is known as a(n) ___?___.
4. An individual member of a partnership who has full personal liability and is publicly known but does not participate in the management of the partnership is known as a(n) ___?___.
5. An individual who is not a member of a partnership but holds himself as such or allows another to do so is known as a(n) ___?___.
6. An individual member of a partnership who has full personal liability and participates in managerial decisions but remains unknown to the public is known as a(n) ___?___.

TEST YOUR READING

7. Explain the reasoning behind the following textual statement: "Never—repeat, never—go into a general partnership with anyone with whom you want to keep a long-lasting personal relationship."
8. List three major advantages to the general partnership form of business.
9. What is the most likely way for a partnership to be formed? List two other ways.
10. If a partner assigns her or his profits to a non-partner, does the non-partner get to take part in managing the partnership? Why or why not?
11. Under the tenancy in partnership, what right does each partner have to possess the partnership property for a partnership purpose?

12. When does a partner get the right to use partnership property for personal use under a tenancy in partnership?

13. What is the difference between dissolving and winding up a partnership?

14. What type of notice must creditors receive of the dissolution of a partnership? Why?

THINK CRITICALLY ABOUT EVIDENCE

15. Explain the rationale behind each of the following observations
    a. "Do not go into partnership with your in-laws."
    b. "Lawyers are deal killers."

16. Houk wanted to involve everyone in her message delivery business. She therefore set up a compensation system under which her employees received a percentage share of the profits as their pay. Later, she extended this system to retirees from her business. Unfortunately, the business acquired an overload of debts during a recession. Its creditors then maintained that the employees, retirees, and Houk were partners so as to hold them all personally liable. Will the court find prima facie evidence of partnership here? Are the employees, retirees, and Houk partners? Why or why not?

17. In an effort to save her business, Houk applied to an investment capital syndicate for a debt consolidation loan. As an adviser during her interview with the syndicate, she took along Marisa Mantie, a wealthy, well-known friend, whom she introduced jokingly as "my partner in crime." The syndicate members made the loan because they assumed that Marisa was a partner. Marisa did not receive any profits (or losses) from the business. When Houk's business collapsed after the loan was spent, the syndicate sued Houk and Mantie as partners. What theory might be used to cause Mantie to be liable as a partner for the debts of the business? Will that theory work? Why or why not?

18. Again desperate to save her business, Houk took in a partner, Hubert Spoke. Spoke, an ex-employee of a competing firm, had inherited his Aunt Chaney's fortune. Spoke's money bailed the business out. Later he and Houk had a number of disputes over how the business should be run. One of the disputes concerned Spoke's authority to make contracts for the business. Another involved Spoke's suggestion that a third partner be brought into the business. Houk and Spoke have no express partnership agreement, but the UPA is in force in their state. How would their disputes be resolved in court?

19. Which of the following occurrences would force a legal end to the partnership?
    a. The state medical malpractice board removes the license of one of the two physicians in Trauma Treaters, a professional partnership.
    b. One of three partners dies.
    c. The partnership declares bankruptcy.
    d. All of the above would end the partnership.

REAL-WORLD CASE
Gridley v. *Johnson*
476 S.W.2d 475

Test your ability to judge whether a partnership exists in the following medical malpractice case.

Mr. and Mrs. Larry E. Gridley sued three doctors and a hospital for damages caused Mrs. Gridley by the alleged failure of the defendants to give her a pregnancy test before having her undergo a gall bladder operation and a dilation and curettage ("D & C"). Dr. Doane was one of the three doctors named as defendants. The plaintiffs were attempting to hold him liable for the alleged wrongful acts of Dr. Johnson by alleging that the two were partners in the operation of the Grandview Clinic, where Mrs. Gridley was seen. A letterhead sheet and billing statements submitted as evidence showed the name and address of the clinic at the center top and the doctors' names at the sides. Dr. Doane testified (Dr. Johnson was ill at the time of the trial) that the two doctors saw and charged their own patients. However, if one of the doctors were absent, the other would see the absent doctor's patient and receive the amount charged. The two doctors did not share each other's fees, but they did share the expenses of the clinic and its equipment.

Think Critically

1. Is Dr. Doane a partner of Dr. Johnson? Why or why not?
2. Should a partnership by estoppel be held to exist here? Why or why not?
3. What do you think the court decided in this case?

CHAPTER  26

Corporations

GOALS

- ◆ Identify the advantages and disadvantages of the corporate form of business
- ◆ Understand when it is optimal to organize a business as a corporation
- ◆ Know how to incorporate a business

When Is the Corporate Form Optimal?

Finally, our discussion turns to the corporation, the business form that large concerns choose almost exclusively. As mentioned in Chapter 24, although sole proprietorships and partnerships are far more numerous, based on the size of their capitalization, corporations win the popularity contest hands down.

The reason for this is the combination of attributes associated with the corporate form. It offers limited liability along with a practically unlimited ability to attract capital and professional management. It not only protects investors against full personal liability but also gives them an ownership interest that, typically, is freely transferable. It offers professional managers access to the resources necessary to carry out their plans. In addition, its survival—unlike that of a sole proprietorship or a partnership—is unaffected by the death or withdrawal of its owners.

For those who began a business as a sole proprietorship or a partnership, shifting to the full corporate form may eventually mean a loss of control. If the change breeds success, however, the higher profits may provide suitable consolation.

Steps in Forming a Corporation

Let's first define some terms related to specific types of corporations. The corporate form most familiar to people is the general or "G" corporation. Other, more limited forms developed specifically for small businesses, such as the S corporation and the limited liability corporation, are covered in Chapter 27. Also, because of the free transferability of most corporate stock among public or private investors, people often refer to corporate stock as "publicly held" and to the business form we are discussing as a "public corporation." However, most corporations are not "public." A real **public corporation** is an organization set up in the U.S. by a local, state, or the federal government to accomplish a governmental purpose. Corporations established to do business are legally referred to as **private corporations**. They are entities set up, funded, and run by private individuals to achieve private ends.

A private corporation may be organized as for-profit or not-for-profit. A **for-profit corporation** is set up to yield its owners a return on their investment. A **not-for-profit corporation** is created to achieve educational, charitable, or other ends without any return to its investors. As you may suspect, this chapter focuses on the for-profit form. By the time you're setting up not-for-profit corporations, you'll have enough expertise to do so (or, more likely, adequate funds to buy that expertise—and then some).

A few additional terms need to be clarified. Private corporations are often labeled "domestic" or "foreign," depending on their U.S. state (not country) of origin. Because the states write the laws controlling the creation and empowerment of corporations, a corporation doing business in the state under whose laws it was organized as a legal entity is known as a **domestic corporation**. In all the other states where it does business, the same corporation is properly labeled a **foreign corporation**. A corporation from outside the U.S. is referred to as an **alien corporation**.

Private corporations also may be called *closely held* or **close corporations**. These labels indicate that the stock-based control of the corporation is held by a single individual or a tight-knit group of individuals. The stock is not traded publicly. Some states even allow the imposition of restrictions on the transferability of the owners' shares.

Promoting a Corporation

The first step in the journey of forming a corporation is promotion. **Promotion** is the advocacy of the business idea and the corporate form for it to potential investors. The people who do this sales job are, as you might expect, labeled **promoters**. Some promoters are individuals bent on organizing the corporation and then participating in its day-to-day existence as officers, managers, and/or employees. Other promoters merely may be interested in selling the to-be-issued stock for a commission.

Even at this early stage, however, all promoters have a fiduciary duty to the corporation they intend to form and to its future stockholders. The promoters must put the interests of the corporation-to-be ahead of their own. They must act as its loyal servants. They must honestly and fully account for any contractual obligations they incur on behalf of the future corporation. If the corporation is not formed, or if, once formed, it fails to fulfill these contracts, the promoters may be held personally liable.

Hypothetical Case

Because of the repeated success of the Johnson Family Racing Team in regional "street" stock car races, the Johnsons finally decide to move into a higher level of competition. Because this new level, i.e., "modified" stock car races, requires much more funding, the Johnsons also decide to finance the move by forming a corporation tentatively named The Checkered Flag Company. They plan to sell shares in the corporation to fans and other investors. While promoting the unformed corporation, the two oldest Johnson brothers, Brad and Charley, enter into contracts for equipment, space in a garage, and endorsements on its behalf. In each instance, they work hard to secure the best deals for the corporation-to-be. To do so however, they have to cosign the contracts personally as well as on behalf of the corporation. As Brad, the older of the two promoters, said to Charley, his younger sibling, "If we don't get enough investors to put this corporation together, you and I are going to be in a real financial bind because of all these contracts we've signed." Is Brad correct in being concerned?

Brad is right to worry. Moreover, as mentioned, even when The Checkered Flag Company is formed, it will not be bound by any of the contracts that the two promoters made on its behalf until it performs some act indicating its acceptance of those contracts. For example, moving the corporation's tools and equipment into the garage or making a lease payment on it would show such acceptance and render the corporation liable. However, just having the corporation assume liability does not release the promoters from responsibility under the same contracts.

Stock Subscriptions

Despite the potential liability from contracts, the focus of the promoter must be on getting potential investors to commit themselves to buying the stock of the corporation-to-be. That stock becomes available only after the formation of the corporation. The formation of the corporation in turn occurs only if enough investment capital has been committed. Do you see the problem here? Which is to come first?

The resulting impasse usually is solved by large measures of trust and, especially in the case of large stock offerings, by **subscription agreements**. Such agreements are written contracts by which a potential investor agrees to buy a certain amount of stock if and when stock is issued. The resulting commitments, if sufficient in number, give those organizing the corporation a foundation on which to proceed with the next step, incorporation.

Articles of Incorporation

The process of incorporation begins with the filing of a written application for corporate status in a state the corporation's organizers have chosen. It does not have to be the same state in which the corporation is located. This application is called the **articles of incorporation** because a state requires various items (or "articles") of information pertinent to the corporation-to-be. The individuals signing the articles of incorporation are known as **incorporators**. The Model Business Corporation Act, offered as a prototype incorporation act to the states by the American Bar Association, requires that each application contain the articles of information shown in Figure 26-1.

The laws of the state of incorporation control how a corporation is run. These laws vary significantly from state to state. Some states allow a great deal of latitude to corporate management; others require shareholder approval for nearly all major decisions. Most large corporations in the U.S. have been formed under the laws of the state of Delaware, which provide management with a great deal of latitude. Businesses wanting to incorporate in Delaware need only follow that state's relatively simple regulations and employ a **registered agent** (a person to represent the corporation in receiving binding service of process) in the state. So a business with headquarters in New York City, for example, can still be "a Delaware corporation" if it so chooses.

Also note from the articles of incorporation displayed in Figure 26-1 that the name of the business must include the word or the abbreviation of *company (Co.),* *corporation (Corp.)*, or *incorporated (Inc.)*. Finally, the duration of the corporation can be set at any term up to and including the "perpetual" indicated for The Checkered Flag Company in article 7, as shown in Figure 26-1.

Issuance of the Charter

Once the articles of incorporation have been submitted, the appropriate state office will review them. This is usually the office of the secretary of state for whatever state the incorporators have chosen (the state of Missouri was chosen by the incorporators of The Checkered Flag Company). If all the legal requirements are met and all the fees are paid, the state issues a certificate of incorporation, called a **charter**, to the applicants. Through the powers vested in the state, the charter officially creates a separate legal entity, (i.e., an artificial person according to the law) called a corporation.

Sale of Stock

Once the corporation has been officially chartered, it can commence doing business. Its obvious first step is to acquire the necessary capital by selling stock to those who have subscribed to the initial offering and to others as necessary.

FIGURE 26-1   Articles of Information Required in an
Application for Corporate Status

The State of Missouri
Office of the Secretary of State
Articles of Incorporation
(As Required By Revised Statutes of Missouri Section 351.055)

1. **The Name of the Corporation shall be:** The Checkered Flag Company
2. **The Address, including street and number, if any, of its initial registered office in this state, and the name of its initial registered agent at such address:** Omar Bradley Johnson, Agent, at 213 First Street North, Miller, MO 65707.
3. **The number, class, and right of the holders of authorized shares:** 100,000 common shares of Class A each with full ownership rights and voting authority.
4. **A current shareholder's right to purchase shares in a new stock issue:** Each current shareholder shall have the right to purchase a pro rata share equal to her or his ownership percentage of each subsequent issue at the public offering price of that issue.
5. **The name and place of residence of each incorporator:**
   Omar Bradley Johnson   Miller, MO 65707
   Charles Edgar Johnson   Miller, MO 65707
6. **The number of corporate directors and the names and addresses of those chosen to fill those positions until the stockholders can elect their replacements:**
   Three (3) directors shall constitute the initial Board of Directors of The Checkered Flag Company. They are
   Omar Bradley Johnson, 213 First Street North, Miller, MO 65707
   Charles Edgar Johnson, 1717 East Delmar, Miller, MO 65707
   Jacqueline Alexis Johnson, 213 First Street North, Miller, MO 65707
7. **The number of years the business is to continue:** The business is to enjoy perpetual existence.
8. **The purpose(s) for which the business is formed:** The Checkered Flag Company is to involve itself in racing competitions with the hope of profiting thereby.

Organizational Meeting

The stockholders are then summoned to an organizational meeting run by the initial directors named in the articles of incorporation. Note that some states have adopted the Revised Model Business Corporation Act, which dictates that the incorporators run the initial meeting.

The first order of business at this meeting is typically the election of permanent **directors**. These stockholder representatives are charged with the overall responsibility for management of the corporation. Although most directors are shareholders, this is not required. Many large corporations have both **inside directors** (employees, officers, or major stockholders) and **outside directors** (individuals without a significant financial interest in the corporation). Collectively, the directors are referred to as the **board of directors**.

After their election, the directors formulate and adopt the corporate **bylaws**. These are the rules by which the internal organization and management of the corporation proceeds. Bylaws typically include provisions that

- Set the time and place for future meetings of the stockholders and the board of directors
- Determine the number required for a quorum for such meetings
- Stipulate how vacancies on the board of directors shall be filled
- Identify the corporate officer positions and the qualifications required of those who fill them
- Prescribe the duties of the corporate officers

Like the promoters and the incorporators, the members of the board of directors owe a fiduciary duty to the corporation and its investors. The formulation of the bylaws and consideration of the contracts made by the promoters for ratification should reflect the proper execution of this duty, as should the selection of officers by the board.

Commencement of Business

Once the company president, the company treasurer, and other necessary corporate officers and employees have been selected, the company can commence doing business. As long as the proper legal steps have been taken in its formation, the company is now a separate legal corporate entity called a **de jure corporation**. Neither private citizens nor the state can challenge its status.

If an error has been made in the process of incorporation, yet the effort to incorporate was made in good faith, the corporation is said to be a **de facto corporation**. Such a corporation is afforded the same status as a de jure corporation as far as a challenge by private citizens is concerned. Only the state can challenge its position so as to correct the errors of incorporation.

Why would a private citizen or the state want to challenge the corporate status of a company? The primary reason is to impose personal liability on the owners (i.e., the shareholders) of the company. This is referred to as **piercing the corporate veil**. Although frequently sought, piercing the corporate veil has been achieved only in aggravated cases. However, if a corporation has been organized as a shield behind which its owners carry out improper or illegal acts, the courts disregard the corporate status to make the wrongdoers pay.

By going through all the steps mentioned in this section and diagrammed in Figure 26-2, a corporation can be formed and readied to do business. However, as the next section details, legal considerations do not end when the business finally begins.

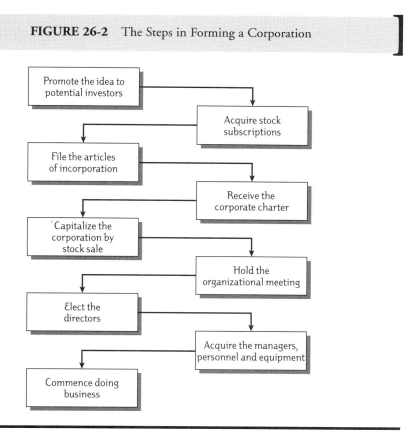

FIGURE 26-2 The Steps in Forming a Corporation

Legal Considerations in Corporate Management

In a typical corporation, the directors are not the day-to-day managers. However, they are charged by law with ultimate managerial responsibility. The directors fulfill this responsibility by appointing (hiring) what they feel is the necessary number of corporate officers. These officers may include a president, numerous vice presidents, a treasurer (with responsibility for financial plans and budgets), a secretary of the board, a comptroller (an official in charge of day-to-day expenditures), and a general counsel (attorney). In large corporations all these positions need to be filled. Typically, a different person holds each position. In some close corporations however, if allowed by state law, all these positions may be filled by only one person. In other words, the same person may be the sole director, the sole corporate officer, and the sole shareholder.

The Business Judgment Rule

The U.S. court system typically adopts a hands-off approach regarding daily business decisions made by corporate managers and other officers. The courts recognize the general overall competence of such people in making the resource allocation decisions for which they were hired. The courts adhere to this approach even when these decisions may place the good of the corporation ahead of the good of the community in which it is located.

Hypothetical Case

In response to the passage of federal legislation creating a free trade zone between the U.S., Mexico, and Canada, the management of the Zeno Corporation elected to move its Springfield, Missouri, manufacturing facility to Mexico. The move meant an end to the last domestic manufacture of certain electronic goods and the loss of more than a thousand jobs. Such a loss had a depressing effect on the economy of the Springfield region. Nonetheless, the decision could not be successfully challenged in a court of law.

Hypothetical Case

Rather than install costly preventive devices on its smokestacks, Dentox, Inc., chose to vent thousands of pounds of toxic wastes into the air breathed in by its neighbors in the Pennsboro, Missouri, community. The venting was allowable under the environmental control regulations of both the federal government and the state government.

In reviewing decisions such as the ones made by Zeno's or Dentox's officers, the courts use the **business judgment rule**. The rule's effect is to immunize management from liability resulting from business decisions made within the power and authority granted corporate officers in the corporate charter and state statutes. The decisions must be made in good faith and with due care for corporate interests. Moreover, in situations in which managers personally benefit from their decisions made on behalf of the corporation, the law requires that at a minimum they fully disclose all crucial information, including their own involvement. Similarly, if a business opportunity develops, officers who know of it and may take advantage of it themselves must disclose it to the corporation. If the corporation then rejects it, the officer may then and only then, take the opportunity. All this stems from the duty of loyalty to the corporation. If corporate officers violate the tenets of that duty, they are exposed to the full scrutiny of the court without the benefit of the business judgment rule.

Powers of the Corporation and Its Officers

The business judgment rule protects only the officers whose decisions are within the legitimate powers of the corporation concerned. The primary rule defining corporate power comes from the law's recognition of the corporation's status as a separate legal entity. This entity is considered at law to be an artificial person. Therefore, unless the articles of incorporation or the state laws under which the corporation is formed set limits, the corporation has the same powers as a natural individual. Consequently, it may do anything necessary to carry out its business and related matters. These actions typically include the power to

◆ Acquire, hold, and dispose of property
◆ Act in the corporate name to bring suit against (and be sued by) others
◆ Enter into contracts
◆ Borrow and offer corporate property as security for loans
◆ Participate in other business organizations
◆ Acquire, hold, and dispose of rights in those organizations
◆ Employ agents with appropriate compensation and pension plans so as to fulfill the purposes of the corporation
◆ Contribute to the public good
◆ Conduct inter- and intrastate business by means of the powers explicitly noted above and any other legitimate implied powers that further the business interests of the corporation

Any action taken by the corporation that goes beyond the powers granted by the express and implied delegations specified above or by statute is labeled **ultra vires**. In most states in the U.S., a corporation may use the fact that a corporate officer's act was ultra vires to protect itself from the enforcement of an executory contract against it. In fact, at one time all ultra vires corporate transactions were void. However, modern law does not hold a party contracting with a corporation to the responsibility of inquiring into what the corporation she or he is dealing with can or cannot do. If you are unaware of limitations placed on the actions of a corporation, then you are not bound by those limitations nor can you use them against the corporation. Similarly, the fact that a corporate act is ultra vires does not mean that it is illegal and void.

 # Hypothetical Case

As part of the "full service" facility at its downtown branch, the Greater Pennsboro Savings and Loan operated a small convenience store, a laundry, and a liquor store in its mall-like lobby. Chase LaRue, one of the town's leading citizens, ran up a large bill in the liquor store, and then refused to pay it. When Greater Pennsboro Savings and Loan brought suit for the balance due, Chase defended by contending that running a liquor store was an ultra vires act for a savings and loan. Therefore, the contract was void or, in the alternative, illegal and thereby void. The court disagreed, stating that as Chase had enjoyed the benefit of the contract without complaint, he could not now raise the ultra vires defense. The court also noted that even if the selling of liquor was ultra vires, this did not mean that the sales contract was illegal and thereby void. Many ultra vires acts are legal. Chase was ordered to pay Greater Pennsboro the full amount due.

Corporate Growth and Financing

As a corporation widens its business operations, encounters new obstacles, and overcomes them, its potential profit and exposure to liability expand accordingly. Although growth should not be considered synonymous with success, it parallels success in many cases. New markets beckon the company with the currently superior product or service. Often the expansion necessary to take advantage of such markets cannot be financed through the internal generation of capital from profits. Therefore, the corporation may decide to seek more funds by turning once again to potential investors. Generally, it can do this in two ways:

1. It can attract more capital by selling stock of various kinds to individuals who want to become part owners of the business or to increase the amount of their existing ownership. This is termed **equity financing** because it increases the investment of the owners in the business.

2. It can attract more capital by borrowing money from individuals and issuing them **bonds** (a certificate or some other evidence of debt requiring that the issuer/borrower repay the amount borrowed, the **principal**, plus interest according to a fixed schedule) in return. This is termed **debt financing** for obvious reasons.

Whatever method is chosen to generate capital—issuing stock or bonds—the transaction comes under the scrutiny of the federal and state governments in the U.S. There are advantages and disadvantages to either method. For example, bonds have a number of tax advantages, but if they are not paid as required, the corporation might face bankruptcy. Stock has no such demanding payout schedule. However, the issuance of more stock dilutes the ownership of the corporation, that is, it creates more owners to split the payout of earnings whenever these occur. Also, selling too much stock to newcomers may jeopardize the control of the original owners.

Because of these and other considerations, different types of stocks and bonds have been used in the past to capitalize a corporation. The basic type of stock, and the type generally issued at the start of corporate existence, is called **common stock**. This type of stock gives its owner the right to vote (according to the number of shares held) in corporate elections. The owner of common stock also gets a proportionate share in the distribution of corporate profits, called **dividends**, whenever these are authorized for issue by the board of directors. Should the corporation be terminated, the owner of common stock also receives a proportionate share of the payout, if any. Other rights that accrue to common shareholders (and generally to shareholders of all types) include the right to transfer their shares, the right to receive information (financial and other reports) about the company, and the right to inspect corporate books and records.

Contrast common stock with **preferred stock**, a type of stock whose dividend amount is usually set ($1 per share, for example) and whose owners get paid in full before common shareholders are paid any dividends. Unlike owners of common stock, preferred shareholders do not have voting rights in corporate matters. This causes some investors to shy away from this type of stock. However, if the corporation desires, the basic position of a preferred shareholder can be enhanced by making preferred stock cumulative and/or participating. **Cumulative preferred stock** requires that all unpaid preferred stock dividends be paid, even from previous fiscal years, before the common shareholders receive anything. **Participating preferred stock** means that preferred stockholders are entitled to receive a pro rata share of the money for common stock dividends left over after the preferred dividends have been paid.

Like stock, corporate bonds come in a variety of types. A **debenture bond**, or just *debenture*, as it is commonly known, is a bond issued without any security. It is to be paid back through the general credit of the issuing corporation without recourse against any specific corporate property. A **convertible bond** is exchangeable for a set amount of stock at the option of the bond's creditor.

Shareholder Rights and Responsibilities

In most U.S. states, the choice between these various forms of financing and several others not mentioned is left up to the voting stockholders of the corporation. In a widely held corporation, many of these owners cannot be present to cast their votes on significant corporate decisions. Such decisions might include the timing and amount of dividends, the type of financing, or even the directors who will oversee the corporation. Consequently, the law allows voting by proxy. A **proxy** is an authorization by which a shareholder allows someone else to cast his or her vote. Significant disputes over corporate control or similar issues often manifest themselves as "proxy fights" to see which side can get the most votes of those shareholders who cannot be present at shareholder meetings.

To enhance the possibility of treating corporate issues democratically, state incorporation statutes allow cumulative voting in the all-important election of directors. Under the rules of **cumulative voting**, each share is given a number of votes equal to the number of directors to be elected. So if a person owns 1,000 shares and five directors are to be elected, the person can cast 5,000 votes among a general field of candidates for the positions. The five candidates with the most votes are elected. This method improves the chance that a minority view is represented on the board. It contrasts sharply with the usual method, i.e., voting for each director's position individually, strictly between two or a few candidates for that specific position. Under this method, someone controlling only 51 percent of the common stock could elect all five directors.

In addition to cumulative voting, shareholders are given the power to bring what are called *derivative court actions* to safeguard their own and corporate interests. This is typically done if the officers and directors have either acted improperly or have failed to pursue a claim of the corporation against a third party. Such an action is allowed only if a demand for it is first made to the officers and directors.

Investors in corporations are protected by these shareholder rights, other devices and mechanisms, and by government oversight. Of course, none of these means or measures can replace individual vigilance. However, despite scandals of the greatest magnitude, colossal failures, and the unforgettable specter of the Great Depression, the corporate form today remains the foremost legal building block of the United States' economic well being.

CHAPTER REVIEW

USE LEGAL TERMS

Fill in the blanks with the appropriate term.

alien corporation	equity financing
articles of incorporation	foreign corporation
board of directors	for-profit corporation
bonds	incorporators
business judgment rule	inside directors
bylaws	not-for-profit corporation
charter	outside directors
close corporation	participating preferred stock
common stock	piercing the corporate veil
convertible bond	preferred stock
cumulative preferred stock	principal
cumulative voting	private corporation
debenture	promoters
debt financing	promotion
de facto corporation	proxy
de jure corporation	public corporation
directors	registered agent
dividends	subscription agreements
domestic corporation	ultra vires

1. A legal entity organized by the government to fulfill a governmental function is termed a(n) ___?___ .

2. A separate legal entity organized for charitable purposes without the promise of a return to its investors is a(n) ___?___ .

3. A corporation doing business in the state in which it was chartered is a(n) ___?___ .

4. A corporation improperly organized due to a good faith error is a(n) ___?___ .

5. A corporation owned by one or very few individuals is known as a(n) ___?___ .

6. Capitalization of a company through the issuance of bonds and similar instruments is called ___?___ .

7. Capitalization of a company through the issuance of stocks and other means of increasing the ownership investment is called ___?___ .

8. A type of stock with a priority claim on dividends yet without voting rights is referred to as ___?___ .

9. A type of stock like that defined in Question 8, but with the additional attribute that all of its missed dividends must be paid before any dividends are paid on common stock is termed ___?___ .

10. A debt instrument issued by a corporation that can be exchanged for a certain number of shares of the corporation's stock is termed a(n) ___?___ .

TEST YOUR READING

11. Give three advantages of the corporate form of business organization.
12. Give two disadvantages of the corporate form of business organization.
13. Can you have a close, domestic, for-profit corporation? Why or why not?
14. List the steps in corporate formation. Explain each.
15. Why are subscription agreements so important?
16. What is the difference between an inside and an outside director? Why would you want to have an outside director?
17. Why would professional managers prefer to work for corporations rather than sole proprietorships or partnerships?
18. Who elects the directors of a corporation?
19. Who picks the top level managers of a corporation?
20. When would an existing shareholder prefer a corporation to use equity financing?
21. When would an existing shareholder prefer a corporation to use debt financing?
22. Why is the business judgment rule so important to a corporate executive?
23. Could the availability of insurance make the business judgment rule obsolete? Why or why not?

THINK CRITICALLY ABOUT EVIDENCE

24. Consider a business idea you may have had in the past or create one. Then ask yourself, "Given my current situation in life, would I want to use the corporate form to develop a business around my idea?" What are the pros and cons of this form for you? Are you likely to use this form? If so, then explain how you would promote, incorporate, and start doing a profitable business with it. Be demanding on yourself. The more clearly you define the steps now, the more likely you are to accomplish them later.

25. Following up on Problem 24, consider these questions:
    Do you have to incorporate in the state where your corporate headquarters are located?
    Do you have to incorporate in every state in which you do business?
    If you choose to incorporate in a state other than one in which you have a corporate office, how do you legally establish a presence in that state so you can be chartered there?

26. Presume your corporation has been properly formed and has been in operation for more than a year. Your reputation is spreading. Business opportunities in your line of operation are popping up every day. However, your considerable profits are still not enough to finance what you regard as a need to expand. What type of financing for the expansion would you use if you did not want to dilute your control (you currently own 51 percent of the common stock). Would your answer be any different if you didn't want to be forced to make payments back to your new investors unless you had the profits from which to make them?

27. As your company grows and becomes more successful, some criticism develops about the projects you are funding. As a result, a block of dissident shareholders set out to secure a position on the corporation's five-member board of directors. You have retained your 51 percent block of common stock. Without cumulative voting, how many directors can the dissidents hope to elect at the next shareholders' meeting? With cumulative voting, how many of the 20,000 outstanding shares of the corporation's common stock must they control before they are assured of electing at least one director?

REAL-WORLD CASE

K.C. Roofing Center v. On Top Roofing

807 S.W.2d 545

Examine how the limited liability aspect of the corporation may be manipulated.

Creditors brought suit to pierce the corporate veil of On Top Roofing, Inc., and affix full personal liability on its owners. The evidence submitted at trial included the following information:

- That On Top Roofing, Inc. was actually incorporated in 1977 as Russell Nugent Roofing, Inc., but changed its name to On Top Roofing, Inc., in 1985.
- That Russell and Carol Nugent were the sole shareholders, officers, and directors of the corporation.
- That On Top ceased doing business in 1987 when RNR, Inc., was incorporated with Russell and Carol Nugent as the sole shareholders, officers, and directors.
- That RNR went out of business in 1988 and RLN Construction, Inc., was incorporated in its stead with Russell and Carol Nugent again the sole shareholders, officers, and directors.
- That RLN Construction went out of business in 1989 and Mr. Nugent then formed Russell Nugent, Inc.

♦ That all of the companies were located at the same address, 614 Main in Grandview, Missouri, which was owned by the Nugents, and used the same business telephone number.

♦ That although three directors were required, only Carol and Russell Nugent had been directors for several years.

♦ That Mr. Nugent's corporations did not produce records of any annual meetings in 1988 or 1989.

♦ That in 1987, K.C. Roofing Center (the plaintiff) advanced about $45,000 in roofing supplies to On Top, which went unpaid, and fostered this suit.

♦ That according to Mr. Nugent's testimony, he stopped buying materials from suppliers when they refused to advance any more material on credit.

♦ That Carol and Russell Nugent received rent for 614 Main in amounts varying with the success of the corporations they owned and in 1986, included a $99,290 payment in addition to their $100,000 in salaries for that term.

Think Critically

1. Why should the court pierce the corporate veil and hold the Nugents personally liable to the creditors of their various corporations?

2. What reasons could be used to argue against piercing the corporate veil even in this case?

CHAPTER 27

Specialized Small Business Forms plus Securities and Antitrust Laws

---

GOALS

- ◆ Know the advantages and disadvantages of various small business organizational forms
- ◆ Understand the importance of antitrust and security regulations
- ◆ Recognize potential problems from antitrust and security regulations

Small Business Organization

In Chapter 24, we briefly discussed two forms of business organization particularly useful for small businesses, the limited partnership and the S corporation. These two forms are decades old, and in the last few years, several additional forms, even more useful, have been made available. Two that warrant further discussion are the limited liability corporation and the limited liability partnership. To make an informed choice, a businessperson needs to understand the advantages and disadvantages of all four of these business forms.

Limited Partnership

As mentioned in Chapter 24, in a limited partnership, there must be at least one general partner with unlimited liability. However, one or more other partners may be limited partners with liability limited to only the extent of their investment in the business. The general partners in a limited partnership have a great deal of freedom in setting up their business as they desire. They are the ultimate decision makers about sharing profits and losses and responsibilities in making the business a success. Like a general partnership, if the terms of the partnership agreement are not established by the partners themselves, the law imposes its own terms. Moreover, in the U.S., the government intrudes further into the domain of the partners in a limited partnership than it does in a general partnership. This additional intrusive behavior is considered warranted because of the limited liability provisions given to the limited partners.

Forming a Limited Partnership   Unlike a general partnership in the U.S., a limited partnership can be created only by following the procedures in the relevant state statute. Some states have adopted the Uniform Limited Partnership Act (ULPA), and others have adopted the Revised Uniform Limited Partnership Act (RULPA). Under ULPA, and unlike the general partnership, a limited partnership can be created only by the proper execution, recording, and publication of a certificate that identifies the partners and lists basic facts about their agreement.

As indicated in the sample limited partnership certificate shown in Figure 27-1, the limited partnership is legally formed at the time of the filing provided it complies "substantially" with statutory filing requirements. If the filing requirements are not met, all business participants are treated as general partners, which means they all have unlimited liability.

[**FIGURE 27-1**   Certificate of Limited Partnership]

1. **Name** (must contain without abbreviation the words "Limited Partnership"):
     K & K Pictures and Paintings, A LIMITED PARTNERSHIP

2. **Address of Office** (need not be a place of business but must be location in this state where records required by RULPA are kept):
     5415 So. Kimbrough, Springfield, NM 87110

3. **Agent for Service of Process** (must be either a natural resident, domestic corporation, or foreign corporation authorized to do business in New Mexico):
     Kirsten Alexis, 1339 Picturesque St., Springfield, NM 87110

4. **Name and Address of Each General Partner**:
     Kimberly Adamson, 1313 Picturesque St., Springfield, NM 87110

5. **Latest Date Upon Which the Limited Partnership is to Dissolve**:
     MARCH 13, 2013

6. **Any Other Matters the General Partners Determine to Include Therein**:
     N/A

FILED WITH THE SECRETARY OF STATE, MARCH 13, 2000, AND EFFECTIVE AS OF THAT DATE.

Record Keeping for a Limited Partnership   In addition to the information contained in the Certificate of Limited Partnership filed with the appropriate government office (usually the Secretary of State), RULPA requires that certain records be kept at the office specified in paragraph 2 of the certificate. These records include

1.   The last known addresses of the general and limited partners with each properly identified as a general or limited partner
2.   Copies of the certificate of limited partnership and all its amendments
3.   Copies of the limited partnership's local, state, and federal income tax returns for the past three years
4.   Copies of any currently effective partnership agreement and any financial statements issued for the past three years
5.   Unless contained in the partnership agreement, the amount of cash and property contributed or pledged by any partner, times of any future contributions by any partner, and events that might lead to the limited partnership's dissolution and winding up

All these records can be obtained by subpoena and are subject to inspection and copying by the reasonable request of any partner during ordinary business hours.

Under ULPA, limited partners who participate in any managerial decisions lose their status and become liable without limit as general partners. This rule has been relaxed and redefined by RULPA, which has been adopted by most states in the U.S. Under RULPA, a limited partner is not viewed as having participated in the managerial control of the business when he or she consults with the general partner(s), acts as an agent or employee for the partnership, attends meetings of the general partners, or participates in the restructuring of the partnership.

Finally, with few exceptions, if a limited partner knowingly allows her or his name to be used in connection with the limited partnership, that limited partner is liable to creditors who extend credit without realizing that she or he is a limited partner, not a general partner.

S Corporation

Almost 20 years ago, the U.S. Congress authorized a new corporate form intended to give small business owners an alternative to the traditional corporation governed by subchapter C of the Internal Revenue Code. Subchapter C corporations are subject to double taxation. The corporation is taxed on corporate income, and corporate shareholders are taxed on dividends.

Advantages of an S Corporation   Under subchapter S of the Internal Revenue Code, an eligible corporation can elect to be taxed as an S corporation. When it does so, its earnings are treated the same as a gain (or loss) from a partnership and taxed only at the individual owner's level. This elimination of double taxation has resulted in many businesses adopting this form. Even though other alternatives are now available (see the next sections), the subchapter S form remains very popular.

Hypothetical Case

Chris Adamson and Ross Chaffin worked during the day as private investigators for a law firm. During the evenings and on weekends, they founded and owned Relics, Inc. The company was chartered by local museums to search for Native American arrowheads, spear points, and other items in the area surrounding the Osage River of Missouri. Knowing that the money they spent on specialized equipment to help them in their searches would lead to a loss in the first year they ran this business, the two wondered whether forming an S corporation would be advantageous.

In the hypothetical case, if Relics were an S corporation, Chris and Ross could take their business losses against their work income next year and avoid double taxation of income from Relics, Inc., in profitable years. In addition, the best elements of the corporate form, such as limited liability, perpetual life, and free transferability of ownership interests are all available under the S corporation form.

Eligibility Requirements for an S Corporation   Recall that to qualify as an S corporation under the IRS code, the business must satisfy several requirements, specifically:

1. *Timely filing*   A corporation wanting to be taxed as an S corporation must file the appropriate form indicating such an election with the IRS before March 15 of the tax year in which the election is to be effective. The election must reflect the unanimous choice of the stockholders. If an S-qualified company wishes to resume being taxed as a C corporation, the shareholders must agree to this unanimously as well.

2. *Domestic corporation*   The S corporation status is reserved for businesses incorporated in the U.S.

3. *Identity of shareholders*   Only natural persons, estates, or certain types of trusts can be shareholders in an S corporation. Other corporations, partnerships, and non-qualifying trusts cannot. In addition, nonresident aliens cannot be shareholders.

4. *Number of shareholders*   The corporation must have 75 or fewer stockholders.

5. *Classes of stock*   The corporation can have only one class of stock. However, all shareholders in that class do not necessarily have to have the same voting rights. *Note that the S corporation is not so much a corporate form as a tax status. To form such an entity, one needs to form a corporation in the normal fashion and then make a qualified filing with the IRS.*

Limited Liability Corporation

As mentioned previously, for years the best forms of business organization for small businesses were the limited partnership and the subchapter S corporation. These forms however, were flawed and limited. Improvements began to appear in the U.S. in 1977 when the state of Wyoming passed a statute creating a business form based on European and South American models. Florida followed in 1982.

However, it took a favorable IRS ruling in 1988 for other states to adopt similar statutes. By 1997, the limited liability corporation (LLC) had been legalized throughout the U.S.

Formation of an LLC Similar to a corporation or limited partnership, an LLC must be formed and operated in accordance with the law of the state in which it was organized. In most states, an LLC is formed by filing **articles of organization** in an appropriate state office (usually the Secretary of State's office). Typical articles of organization are shown in Figure 27-2.

The owners of an LLC are known as **members.** Their liability is limited to the amount they have invested in the business, and the earnings of the LLC are taxed as a partnership. However, some states allow certain members to declare themselves as fully personally liable at the time of organization, which may improve the LLC's creditworthiness.

Advantages of LLCs The significant advantages that make LLCs more attractive than traditional forms are

1. No limitation on the number of members (the S corporation currently limits the number of stockholders to 75).
2. No limitations as to whom or what can be a stockholder in an LLC. Therefore, foreign nationals, corporations, and other business entities can all be shareholders.
3. Members are allowed to participate completely in managing the business. There are no concerns about losing limited liability status for those who manage the corporation. In an S corporation, losing limited liability status is always a potential problem, even under RULPA.

FIGURE 27-2   Articles of Organization for an LLC

---

1. **Name:***
     The Moot Point LLC

2. **Nature of Business:**
     Retailer of the finest in accessories for the successful attorney

3. **Office Address:**
     1339 W. Synchronicity Blvd., Coincidence, Colorado

4. **Agent for Service of Process:**
     Ben Acausal, 1339 W. Synchronicity Blvd., Coincidence, Colorado

5. **Name and address of organizer(s):**
     Ben Acausal, 1339 W. Synchronicity Blvd., Coincidence, Colorado

6. **Names of initial LLC members:**
     Ben and Susan Acausal, 1339 W. Synchronicity Blvd., Coincidence, Colorado

*Note that the business's name must include the LLC designation or the full Limited Liability Company title.

Disadvantages of the LLC Prior to 1997, LLCs were subject to an IRS test. This test determined if the LLC could avoid being taxed at up to the federal maximum corporate rate of 34 percent on earnings and then again at the personal rate of the owners (up to 39.6 percent). It required that an LLC not possess more than two of the following four characteristics:

1. Centralized management. This situation would be different from the partnership form in which each general partner manages the corporation and all earnings pass through to the partners without taxation at the corporate level.
2. Perpetuity of life. If the LLC continues indefinitely, it appears more like a corporation and very unlike a partnership.
3. Limited liability. Again, this is indicative of a corporation, and corporate status usually carries double taxation.
4. Free transferability of ownership. This characteristic also is indicative of a corporation and not of the partnership form the LLC must imitate to remove the double taxation burden.

Just as the IRS arbitrarily set the rule that prevented LLCs from enjoying all the advantages of the form (i.e., they could demonstrate only two of the four characteristics above or lose LLC status), the IRS later just as arbitrarily revoked the rule. With this, the main disadvantages of being an LLC form were eliminated. The only significant problem in an LLC today is the tax ramifications associated with transferring assets from a partnership or corporation to an LLC.

Today, unless the business entity is a corporation formed under a state incorporation statute (not an LLC statute), a publicly traded corporation, or particular types of foreign-owned corporations, the IRS presumes the entity prefers to be taxed as a partnership. If the business entity wants to be taxed as a corporation, it can simply check the appropriate box on the IRS form.

Limited Liability Partnerships

Despite the obvious advantages of an LLC, already-existing business entities may find it difficult to convert to an LLC form. In particular, partnerships constructed for professionals find it difficult to deal with the complexity of ending the partnership, valuing the interests, and then reestablishing the concern as an LLC in a fair manner.

As a consequence, in 1991, Texas created the **limited liability partnership (LLP)**. An existing partnership could convert to an LLP easily, double taxation could be avoided, and partial limited liability protection established. By 1997, almost all the states in the U.S. had enacted LLP statutes, mostly by simply amending already-existing partnership statutes.

Under most LLP statutes, limited liability protection shields only against the consequences of tortious acts of others involved in the partnership. The Texas statute, for example, protects innocent partners from the consequences of errors, omissions, negligence, incompetence, or malfeasance stemming from partnership operations. Therefore, if a partner commits professional malpractice and the recovery from it exceeds the amount of liability insurance coverage the partnership or that individual carries, the other partners' personal assets are not endangered.

Laws Controlling Business Financing

On October 29, 1929, the death knell of the post-World War I prosperity in the U.S. tolled on Wall Street. On that "black Tuesday," the stock market fell disastrously. The New York Stock Exchange, the financial heart of the country, had been in questionable condition for some time. Its prices were artificially inflated by easy credit. Many investors paid only 10 percent of the purchase price of their shares with their own money and the rest with money typically borrowed from brokerage houses. The market also was debased by an ethic that tolerated fraud and unfair advantage. Even so, the stock market carried the faith and hopes of investors throughout the country, from churches to colleges to widows to banks. So, on that day, the very foundation of an entire nation was shattered.

Very few escaped the tragedy. One man who did managed to do so by observing that stock speculation had gotten out of hand. He then acted quickly on that observation. That man was Joseph P. Kennedy, one of the wealthiest and most active investors of the time. Legend has it that during a taxi ride only a few weeks before the Great Crash, Kennedy unexpectedly received stock tips from the driver. Thinking about it afterward, he realized that the market had become much like a horse race. He therefore determined it was time to get out. He did so and saved the fortune that, years later, would help make his son president of the United States.

On the vast majority of people however, the effects of the Crash were devastating. By 1932, when the economy was at its worst, the stock of US Steel and General Motors was selling at less than one-tenth of their pre-Crash prices. The Dow Jones Industrial Average plummeted from around 500 before the Crash to bottom out at 42. The steel industry as a whole was operating at less than 20 percent of capacity. Its customers did not need much steel, as demand for steel products had fallen drastically. The American Locomotive Company, which produced more than 600 train engines per year before the Crash, sold one in 1932. The gross national product of the U.S. fell from more than $100 billion to around $40 billion. More than 5,000 banks failed, obliterating the life savings of their depositors (at that time no federal deposit insurance was available). Nonfarm unemployment soared to more than 25 percent, leaving more than 30 million men, women, and children without any supporting income whatsoever. Hundreds of thousands of evictions from homes followed hard on the heels of the unemployment wave.

The pervasive effects of this unprecedented fall in the prices of an unregulated market in securities fostered a widespread demand for protective controls by the federal government. Soon after taking office, President Franklin Delano Roosevelt responded to that demand by proposing the Securities Act of 1933 and the Securities Exchange Act of 1934. These two acts established the Securities and Exchange Commission (SEC) and gave it the power to regulate the issuance, marketing, and reselling of investment securities. Roosevelt appointed Joseph P. Kennedy as the first SEC chairman. When asked about this appointment, Roosevelt responded that Kennedy knew all the loopholes in the current laws and therefore, could close them. A prosperous post-World War II economy free of severe problems attributable to stock market machinations supported Roosevelt's assessment.

The Coverage of Our Securities Laws

State Laws   Although the most comprehensive regulation of securities now originates at the federal level in the U.S., the states also regulate the area. Federal securities laws regulate interstate transactions; state securities laws are intended to control intrastate transactions. The state laws are referred to as **blue-sky laws**. Some say this label originated in the stock sellers' practice of praising each offering to the blue sky. Others say the purpose of the laws was to prevent stock purchases that were the equivalent of investing in a few square feet of the blue sky. As you might suspect, these laws vary greatly in the controls they place on the transfer of securities and the powers they grant holders of securities. Midwestern states, because of the frequent perpetration of fraudulent schemes on farmers, have some of the strictest laws of this kind. Generally, these laws set down registration requirements. They also detail the latitude of action that company management is allowed without seeking the approval of the stockholder owners. However, because a firm can choose the state in which it incorporates—even though it may do business and be headquartered in another state—these state laws do not control securities activities as much as federal statutes and regulations.

Federal Regulation   The scope of federal securities requirements, primarily SEC regulations, extends to all securities transactions—from issuance to every resale—in interstate commerce.

Definition of Security   Although the Securities Act of 1933 provides a detailed definition of the term *security*, our courts have developed a much more condensed and workable one. In particular, the Supreme Court considers a **security** to be an investment contract whereby investors provide the capital and share in the earnings generated through the management and control of the promoters.

Hypothetical Case

Blately built a 33-unit condominium development on the beach in Nag's Head, North Carolina. He then sold the units to prospective investors. A part of each sales contract involved Blately's employment to manage the upkeep of the development and the marketing of the condominiums as seasonal rentals for vacationers. The proceeds of the rentals were to be used to pay for Blately's management and to provide a return to the owners. A federal court held that the ownership interests in the condominiums were in fact securities and therefore, subject to SEC requirements.

Once an investment instrument has been determined to be a security, it becomes subject to the requirements of U.S. federal statutes. These statutes and SEC rules and regulations that implement them depend on the disclosure of all relevant information about the corporation and the security issue to protect the average investor. Broadly speaking, the Securities Act of 1933 covers the initial offering of a security on the public market, and the Securities Exchange Act of 1934 covers the public trading of a security after issuance.

In relation to issuing securities, note, first and foremost, that the SEC does not evaluate a prospective offering. The SEC merely requires that information about the offering be truthfully rendered and properly distributed to would-be investors. It is up to the investors to evaluate the offering. Therefore, the main enforcement emphasis under the 1933 Act is on the veracity and completeness of the information given to prospective investors.

As a mechanism for collecting this crucial information, all securities (unless exempted by statute) must be registered with the SEC prior to being issued. Such registration does not eliminate the requirements of any pertinent state statute, however. In particular, a **registration statement** must be filed with the SEC before a single share can be sold. This statement consists of detailed information on the company's financial status, its history, its management's experience, and the reason for and risks of a particular offering, among other data. A significant portion of the information contained in the registration statement must be made available to a prospective buyer of any portion of the issue. This information is published in what is called a **prospectus**, which also contains an invitation to buy. The prospectus must be approved by the SEC. Should false information be contained in the prospectus or other documents filed with the SEC, the company, its officers and directors, and the lawyers and accountants who compiled those documents may be personally liable in a civil suit for the losses suffered by investors. If the information is willfully falsified, criminal charges may be brought, with conviction resulting in a fine, imprisonment, or both.

Complying with the SEC procedure for issuing a security is both complex and expensive. As a consequence, many companies attempt to qualify their issues under one or another of the exemptions from the requirements of the 1933 Act.

Securities Exempt from SEC Registration

A businessperson looking for an exemption so as to avoid paying the hundreds of thousands of dollars needed to register a security issue properly must recognize two things. First, it is true that many stock issues do go unregistered as a result of the exemptions we are going to discuss. Second, improperly or unwisely bypassing registration often comes back to destroy those involved. With these points in mind, consider the following exemption categories.

Securities Issued by Government Entities and Not-for-Profit Organizations

Foreign countries, states, counties, cities, and their authorized agencies can offer securities issues without registering them. Corporations organized for educational, health, recreational, or charitable purposes are also exempt from registering their securities.

 # Hypothetical Case

The Pennsboro Turnpike and Intercounty Airport Authority issued and sold $30 million in bonds to finance the construction of a new airport terminal and runway system. In conjunction with that project, the Pennsboro Hospital, a nonprofit organization, issued $5 million in bonds to finance the acquisition of three Medevac helicopters and the construction of hangar and maintenance facilities at the new airport. Neither issue had to be registered with the SEC.

Short-Term Commercial Paper

As long as it is not advertised for sale to the public, a business may issue any form of commercial paper for financing. The only requirements are that the note, draft, or whatever must be due within nine months and arise out of a current business transaction.

 # Hypothetical Case

To purchase two new cabs for its fleet to be stationed at the new airport, the Pennsboro Independent Cab Company issued a 180-day promissory note in favor of the Pennsboro Bank. No registration was required.

Private Placements

In 1982, in what was labeled Regulation D, the Reagan administration carved out a number of new exemptions to the SEC registration requirements. These exemptions were intended to legitimize the general category of private offerings of securities.

There are three main exemptions under Regulation D. The first and broadest allows an issuer to sell up to $1,000,000 worth of securities in a year to an unlimited number of investors without providing those investors with any information whatsoever. Realize however, that, as mentioned, this does not exempt the issuer from the requirements of the states involved. In addition, as with the other exemptions under Regulation D, the issuer must refrain from publicly advertising the offering, must provide notice of a Regulation D offering to the SEC, and must mark the stock certificates as a **restricted security**. This means that the shares cannot be resold without registration unless the resale is another exempt transaction.

The other two exemptions allow a much greater number of securities to be issued. The key to having a security issue fall under one of these exemptions is directing the offering only to appropriate investors.

Who are these appropriate investors? Regulation D divides them into two categories: accredited investors and investors capable of evaluating the risks of the issue on their own (nonaccredited investors). If a nonaccredited investor is involved, it is up to the issuer who is claiming the exemption to prove that the investor is indeed capable of understanding the risks involved. This becomes a rather formidable task if the investor is claiming just the opposite and has losses to back up that claim.

Therefore, the first category, the accredited investor, represents most of the intended, truly safe havens for private placements. According to Regulation D, an **accredited investor** is one of the following:

- Any bank, investment company, insurance company, or employee benefit plan
- Any business development company
- Any charitable or educational institution with assets greater than $5 million
- Any director, executive officer, or general partner of the issuer
- Any person with a net worth of more than $1 million
- Any person with an annual income greater than $200,000

So, if all goes well, after finding interested and accredited investors as defined above, the issuer can take advantage of either of the remaining two exemptions under Regulation D.

The first of these two exemptions allows up to $5 million of securities in a 12-month period to be sold to an unlimited number of accredited investors and not more than 35 other purchasers. The latter purchasers however, must receive a registration statement.

The second exemption is more important. It allows an issuer to sell an unlimited number of securities to any number of accredited investors and no more than 35 nonaccredited purchasers. Again, it is extremely important that the nonaccredited purchasers to whom securities are sold are capable of evaluating the risks involved. This exemption covers the vast majority of the billions and billions of dollars of private placements made each year.

Small Public Offerings

Available to companies that wish to offer $1.5 million or less of securities to the general public within a 12-month period, the small public offering exemption provided by Regulation A is frequently used. An offering statement must be filed in the closest SEC regional office at least 10 days before the planned offering. An **offering statement** includes financial statements and other information contained in a typical prospectus. Unlike the financial statements provided for a full registration however, this information does not have to be professionally audited. Once the SEC is satisfied with the offering statement, the securities can be sold. However, a copy of the offering statement must be provided to purchasers and the issuer is exposed to liability based on the information contained in (or omitted from) that document.

Intrastate Offerings

As we have discussed in relation to other federal agencies, under the Interstate Commerce Clause of the U.S. Constitution, an action that affects only intrastate commerce cannot be regulated by the federal government. However, given past U.S. Supreme Court interpretations of that clause, it is possible that no stock issue can be considered truly intrastate. To clarify matters for those who would nonetheless try for such an exemption, the SEC passed a rule detailing its definition of an intrastate offering.

In particular, the rule says that, to be eligible to make an intrastate securities offering, the issuer must be incorporated in the state and at least 80 percent of the issuer's gross revenues must originate in that state. Once the issue has been sold, it continues to be considered intrastate only if no resales are made to nonstate residents within nine months. It is this last requirement that causes so many corporations to stay away from this exemption. Even if buyers sign agreements that they will not resell any shares for nine months, it is extremely difficult to prevent sales to residents of other states. Consequently, the risk of ultimately losing the intrastate exemption, as well as the fines and other liabilities that may result, cause most issuers to choose another exemption if they are eligible.

Although a registration exemption is tempting to young companies that need capital and, thus would like to save registration costs, it is important to remember that at some point most unregistered securities will be made available to the general public. At that time, whomever wishes to sell those securities will have to bear the expense of registration. Also, if a company is to tap the immense source of capital that the national stock markets offer, at some point it will have to "go public" and register its stock.

FIGURE 27-3   Exemptions from SEC Registration

- Securities issued by government entities and not-for-profit organizations
- Short-term commercial paper
- Private placements
- Small public offerings
- Intrastate offerings

Laws Governing Securities Trading

Unless exempted, all securities traded on a national exchange or over-the-counter must be registered with the SEC in accordance with the Securities Exchange Act. In addition, any company with more than 500 shareholders and over $1 million in assets must provide detailed information about the company and its financial position to its shareholders and the SEC. This information must be updated frequently (usually quarterly). Because of experience with past manipulative schemes, the SEC has also implemented several rules to alert traders—and thereby, it is hoped, to protect them—to significant changes in a reporting company's financial circumstances.

Rules Governing Insider Trading

Many observers of the market situation that precipitated the 1929 Crash identified lack of regulation of the actions of **insiders** (officers, directors, major stockholders, and others privy to confidential information pertaining to corporate activities) as a major cause of the financial disaster. As a consequence, the U.S. Congress included two sections in the Securities Exchange Act of 1934 to correct the situation. The first, section 16(a), requires a monthly disclosure of any change in the ownership position of an officer or director of a corporation or any stockholder with more than 10 percent of any class of the corporation's stock. The second, section 16(b), makes these same parties automatically liable to the corporation for any so-called "short swing" profits. These profits are realized by buying corporate stock and then selling that stock within six months of its purchase.

Hypothetical Case

Kendra Brian held an outside director's position on the board of Pennsboro Motors Corporation (PMC). Although she had not attended the last two quarterly board meetings because of illness, Kendra believed strongly in PMC and the employment opportunities it offered to members of the Pennsboro community. As a consequence, she purchased 1,000 shares of PMC stock at $14 per share in late August. Two months later, after PMC announced a merger with Giant Motors Corporation, the price of PMC stock shot up to $32 per share. Kendra immediately sold her 1,000 shares at a profit of $18,000. Under section 16(b), whether she knew about the merger beforehand or not, her profit is recoverable by the corporation or by a stockholder suit on its behalf brought in federal court.

Another federal statute that affects insider trading is the Insider Trading Sanctions Act of 1984. Under its provisions, a person profiting or avoiding loss by trading on the basis of material nonpublic information about a security can be made to pay as damages to the corporation involved three times the amount of that profit or the amount of the loss avoided. In addition, criminal liability in the form of fines into the hundreds of thousands of dollars can be imposed. Individuals who provide inside information that others use for trading purposes, even if they do not trade themselves, may also be held liable.

Hypothetical Case

> Although she did not trade in the security herself, Heather LaSulle, a stockbroker with a large, nationally known firm, was held liable for the profits made by several of her customers who acted on inside information that she provided.

Various publications provide information on legitimate insider trading they obtain from SEC reports to the general investment community. In addition, remember the old saw about the value of such activity as an investment indicator. Insiders may sell for a variety of reasons (they need money for the children's education; they need money for medical expenses; the corporation has fallen on hard times, etc.), but they buy for one reason only, because they have confidence in the potential of the stock price to go higher.

Rules Against Fraud and Manipulation

Section 10(b) of the 1934 Act makes it illegal for any person to use a manipulative or deceptive device in a manner prohibited by SEC rules. This regulation mirrors a basic common law prohibition with the same effect, but it leaves the door wide open for the SEC to carry the matter further by outlawing any specific manipulative or fraudulent conduct it considers especially improper. The SEC ultimately responded by producing Rule 10(b)-5. The applicability of the rule is extremely broad as is obvious from its text:

> It shall be unlawful for any person directly or indirectly by use of any means or instrumentality of interstate commerce, or of the mails, or of any facility of any national exchange:
>
> ◆ to employ any device, scheme or artifice to defraud
>
> ◆ to make any untrue statement of a material fact or to omit to state a material fact necessary in order to make the statements made, in the light of the circumstances under which they were made, not misleading
>
> ◆ to engage in any act, practice or course of business which operates or would operate as a fraud or deceit upon any person in connection with the purchase or sale of any security.

Notice especially that application of the rule is not limited to securities registered with the SEC or to companies of a certain size. It simply requires the involvement of "any means or instrumentality of interstate commerce, the mails, or . . . any national exchange . . . with the purchase or sale of any security." In addition to enforcement actions brought by the SEC, the courts allow private parties to bring civil damage suits for 10(b)-5 violations. As a result, the rule has been used by and against a wide spectrum of parties. The most pertinent outcomes of all this use include the following:

- Individuals who received tips from insiders have been held liable for their trading profits.
- Consultants, lawyers, accountants, and other professionals who legitimately acquired insider information as a result of a confidential relationship with the corporation have been held liable for the use of that information and for improperly revealing it or failing to disclose it as appropriate under the circumstances.
- Traditional insiders have been held liable for trading in securities of their corporation before fully disclosing significant information to the public.
- Rule 10(b)-5 and other, more specialized rules provide a working shield against improper acts that may rob investors of the confidence necessary to make our capital markets work. Without those markets, your ability to attract major financing for your own business is non-existent.

Antitrust Laws and Their Effects on Business

A good introduction to the topic of antitrust law comes from the text of a recent interview with a widely read legal scholar and professor

What is the greatest enemy of business in this country? Right off the top, I must tell you that this is a trick question. You might answer "the government" or "governmental regulation." As you may suspect, that answer is anticipated but wrong. If you keep trying you might eventually come up with the correct answer: *Competition!* Competition is the greatest enemy of business in this country. Government regulation may be a harassment and otherwise a bother, but only in the rarest of cases does it put someone out of business. Competition, on the other hand, does that to many businesses every day. The statutes and regulations to which we give the relatively obscure label "antitrust law" in this country are really our attempt to preserve competition and thereby keep businesses subservient to consumers through the market mechanism. Recent federal administrations have de-emphasized such laws along with other governmental regulation while encouraging bigness as a remedy for foreign competition and declining productivity. It hasn't worked, and now our even bigger companies are getting their socks blown off by companies one thousandth their size because those smaller outfits are far more competitive. It's sad, but we're about to relearn the lesson our forebears learned a century ago, a lesson about economic concentrations and bigness and how they threaten our way of life. Concisely put, the lesson is that without competition, our way of life is doomed. This simple truth is dearly bought each and every time it is learned.

Left alone, businesses act to eliminate competition. Thus, some governmental supervision is necessary to preserve free markets. Adam Smith recognized the need for such supervision and warned against what would happen without it. As is all too often the case, Smith's statements and the historical experiences confirming his position were ignored. Within a century of its founding, the U.S. confronted a challenge in which vast portions of its most important markets were being consolidated under the control of an elite group of businessmen. Railroads, banks, petroleum, and many other industries were being monopolized.

Nowhere was this trend more evident than in the petroleum industry. There, John D. Rockefeller accomplished a near miracle by bringing under one umbrella of control some of the most independent capitalists in the country, men who had truly earned their "wildcatter" nickname. Rockefeller did this through a legal holding device called a trust. A **trust** is a separate entity created by law to which ownership of property can be transferred, after which the property is managed by designated individuals in accordance with the wishes of the transferor. In essence, a controlling interest in the stock of companies once in competition with one another was transferred to the trust. The few parties in charge of the trust, called the **trustees**, then used their power to eliminate competition by fixing prices, territories, and so on. In essence, the bigger the trust, the greater the corner on the market obtained by its members and thus, the greater their profits.

By the late 1880s, the abuses of the market system caused by the trusts jeopardized the welfare of the country. The U.S. Congress, reacting to the concerns of the electorate, passed the Sherman Antitrust Act in 1890. What was initiated was a century of governmental defense of competition at the federal level. Unfortunately for those called on to enforce it, this initial antitrust act was written in such broad and absolute terms, it seemed to throw out the good with the bad. Eventually, problems inherent in the Sherman Act were corrected by the U.S. Supreme Court when it invoked the **rule of reason** test. This test called for each arrangement to be examined from the standpoint of reasonability to see whether it acted to eliminate competition or to promote it. The Sherman Act was then followed by other acts including the Clayton Act, Federal Trade Commission Act, and several amendments. What has evolved is a web of regulations and laws that govern competition in the U.S.

Common Potential Antitrust Violations

For self-protection, a businessperson today must be sensitive to conduct that can be construed as violations of the antitrust laws. Either as a victim of the violations of others or as an unwitting perpetrator, your ability to identify potential antitrust problems can be crucial to the success and longevity of your business. Note however, that certain businesses are exempt from antitrust regulations (see Figure 27-4).

These potential violations can be divided into two categories. The first category covers violations that interfere with **interbrand competition**. This type of competition involves individuals who should be working against each other to sell competing products from different producers (see Figure 27-5). Such violations are labeled **horizontal constraints** because they typically involve sellers at the same level of commerce (for example, a salesperson selling Gotcha Pagers conspiring to fix prices with a salesperson selling Nokayama Pagers). The second category comprises violations that interfere with **intrabrand competition**, which involves individuals who should be competing to sell the same product (see Figure 27-6). Such violations are labeled **vertical constraints** because they involve relations between parties that are at different levels in the chain of distribution of the product in question (for example, a salesperson from the local store selling Gotcha Pagers conspiring to fix prices with a Gotcha factory representative selling Gotcha Pagers).

FIGURE 27-4   Current Exemptions from the Provisions of the Antitrust Laws

Exempt Area	Regulator, if Any
Baseball	None as yet. The national pastime remains immune.
Trucking, airlines, railroads, and ships at sea	Although the trucking and airline industries were formerly regulated by the Interstate Commerce Commission (ICC) and the Federal Aviation Administration (FAA), respectively, their deregulation left their long-standing exemption in doubt. Railroads are still regulated by the ICC, and the Maritime Administration regulates oceangoing American vessels.
Farming and fishing cooperatives and similar enterprises	Department of Agriculture and Department of the Interior
Insurance companies	Insurance commissioners of the various states
Radio and television broadcasting	Federal Communications Commission, which grants monopoly rights to broadcast over certain frequencies
Banks and similar financial institutions	Can be chartered at the state or federal level. At the state level, they are regulated by various state agencies; at the federal level, the Federal Reserve Board exercises primary control over them.
Stock exchanges	Securities and Exchange Commission
Labor unions	Department of Labor and National Labor Relations Board

FIGURE 27-5   Interbrand Competitors for the Breakfast Cereal Market

FIGURE 27-6   Intrabrand Competitors for the Breakfast Cereal Market

Violations Among Competitors Selling Competing Products

Monopolizing   This is the cornerstone of antitrust prohibitions set down in the Sherman Act's section 2 ("Every person who shall monopolize . . . shall be deemed guilty.") To be held guilty, a firm must be shown to have **monopoly power** (in essence, the ability to control prices) and to have exhibited **monopolizing conduct** (behavior indicating that it achieved or abused its position of market dominance by improper methods).

Market power   As mentioned, when a business or some other entity no longer finds the prices it can charge dictated by a competitive market but is instead able to set its prices almost at will, it has market power. Until the mid-1970s, the various state bar associations sent out suggested fee schedules to their members. If a member violated such a schedule, the bar association could prosecute the member for a breach of the code of ethics and have the member disbarred. Finally, in a 1975 case, the U.S. Supreme Court held that these practices were a violation of the antitrust law (*Goldfarb* v. *Virginia State Bar Association* 421 U.S. 773).

Currently, courts focus on the answers to two questions to determine whether a business has monopoly power, allowing it to exercise a significant control over prices. First, what is the relevant market in which to consider questions of monopolization. Second, what is the market share of the business/defendant within the relevant market? In the antitrust case law, the phrase **relevant market** means the total demand for the product or service allegedly being monopolized and those interchangeable with it as determined within the geographic area in question. So, if charges are directed against a power lawn mower manufacturer for trying to monopolize, the court first determines the relevant market. To do so, the court begins with the sales of the defendant's mowers within the geographic area in question. Next, the court adds the sales of reasonably interchangeable products—other power lawn mowers, push lawn mowers, garden tractors with mower attachments, and the like—within the same area. Then, it would divide the defendant's sales by the total sales in the relevant market to determine the defendant's **market share** (the percentage of the relevant market under the defendant's control). Once this percentage has been calculated, it is matched to a "market power" scale provided by Judges Learned Hand and Augustus Hand in deciding the mid-1940s antitrust case against the Aluminum Company of America (Alcoa). To quote their opinion in that case, "That percentage we have already mentioned—over 90— . . . is enough to constitute a monopoly; it is doubtful whether 60 or 64 percent would be enough and certainly 33 percent is not" (*United States* v. *Aluminum Company of America* 148 F 2d 416).

With these percentage guidelines in mind, courts and businesses alike can determine whether monopolizing power (indicated by a market share of more than 90 percent according to the above) exists with reasonable certainty. As the market share slides toward the 33 percent level, so too does the possibility that such power does not exist. In addition, as mentioned, a business cannot be held guilty of a violation of the antitrust acts merely for holding such power. The business must also exhibit monopolizing conduct.

Monopolizing conduct   Common sense tells us we do not want to punish someone who obtains a monopoly position by working hard and offering the best product at the lowest price. Most people feel that businesses with a large market share should be punished only if they achieve or maintain that position by using underhanded methods to eliminate or forestall competition. The monopolies granted inventors under our patent laws testify to the wisdom of this view. The Sherman Act however, did not recognize any such exception. "Every person who shall monopolize . . . shall be guilty." Judicial interpretation eventually read "reason" into the application of the act, and business people were therefore no longer threatened with prosecution for superior work, efficiency, skill, and risk taking.

Instead the regulatory focus shifted to whether the possessor of monopoly power had acquired it by monopolizing conduct. In deciding the *Standard Oil of New Jersey Trust* case, the U.S. Supreme Court gave us a good description of such conduct by reciting some activities of that trust's founders:

> It suffices to say that such [monopolizing conduct] may be grouped under the following heads: Rebates, preferences, and other discriminatory practices in favor of the combination by railroad companies; restraint and monopolization by control of pipe lines, and unfair practices against competing pipe lines; contracts with competitors in restraint of trade; unfair methods of competition such as local price cutting at the points where necessary to suppress competition; espionage of the business of competitors, the operation of bogus independent companies, and the payment of rebates on oil, with the like intent; the division of the United States into districts, and the limiting of the operations of the various subsidiary corporations as to such districts so that competition in the sale of petroleum products between such corporations had been entirely eliminated and destroyed; and finally reference was made to what was alleged to be the "enormous and unreasonable profits" earned by the Standard Oil Trust and the Standard Oil Company as a result of the alleged monopoly. (*Standard Oil Co.* v. *United States*, 221 U.S. 1)

So, through the decisions cited above, the courts gradually evolved a position that evidence of monopoly power and a history of monopolizing conduct are required to place a defendant in jeopardy of conviction for monopolization.

Attempting to Monopolize   As far as attempts to monopolize are concerned, the prosecution must show that the defendant utilized established market power improperly in an "attempt" to consolidate market control. Without market power behind it, such an attempt is not considered a violation of the Sherman Act.

Proposed consolidations of competing companies that might substantially lessen competition "in any line of commerce in any section of the country" (section 7 of the Clayton Act) are fought by the Justice Department. Such resistance to mergers and similar business activities that might create a company with too much market power stems from the Sherman Act prohibition of "attempts to monopolize."

Conspiracy   Unlike monopolization or attempts to monopolize, which present prosecutors with significant problems of proof because of the relative ambiguity of the rule of reason approach, conspiracies between competitors either to restrain trade (section 1 of the Sherman Act) or to monopolize (section 2) are *per se* violations. A *per se* **violation** is conduct considered illegal under the antitrust laws regardless of its justification or reasonableness. The primary example of such conspiracies is price-fixing.

Price-Fixing   Price-fixing is the most clearly acknowledged antitrust offense. Price-fixing was made a *per se* violation by the 1927 Supreme Court decision in *United States* v. *Trenton Potteries*. Significantly, the *Trenton Potteries* case acknowledged that **price-fixing**, or joining with your competitors to set prices, is illegal *even if prices fall as a result.*

In fact, a number of America's largest corporations have faced the near disastrous consequences of a conviction for this offense. In the 1960s, for example, high executives of General Electric and Westinghouse got together to fix prices on the turbines used by electric utilities to generate power. Before the prosecutions were over, nearly 50 of these executives were found guilty. Although fewer than one-fifth of those found guilty served prison sentences, the careers of almost all of them were greatly harmed. In addition, the two companies involved were fined and were forced to pay treble damage awards to parties injured by the price gouging. The fines totaled only approximately $2 million but the treble-damage awards totaled over $400 million in 1960s dollars. This amount is equivalent to almost $2.0 billion today.

Conscious Parallelism   A common practice today in areas of our economy in which only a few companies control most of the market (a condition referred to as **oligopoly**) is for all of them to follow the pricing policies of the largest of these companies. This practice is labeled **conscious parallelism**. If the members of the oligopoly set prices independently of one another, the behavior is legal. However, if there is evidence of collusion other than the obvious patterning of prices, the behavior can be prosecuted as a *per se* violation of the antitrust laws. Even circumstantial evidence is allowed to indicate wrongdoing. As one court said:

> [We are not] so naive as to believe that a formal signed-and-sealed contract or written resolution would conceivably be adopted at a meeting of price-fixing conspirators in this day and age. In fact, the typical price-fixing agreement is usually accomplished in a contrary manner . . . A knowing wink can mean more than words . . . It is not

necessary to find an express agreement, either oral or written, in order to find a conspiracy, but it is sufficient that a concert of action be contemplated and that defendants conform to the arrangement . . . Thus, not only action but even a lack of action may be enough from which to infer a combination or conspiracy. (*United States* v. *Esco Corporation* 340 F 2d 1000)

In short, if a business is a member of an oligopoly, it must be extremely careful about the factors it considers in setting its prices and about its contacts with the other members about prices. Any evidence of collusion other than parallel prices can be persuasive in a resulting criminal case.

Boycotts   When competitors refuse to deal with (**boycott**) suppliers or customers unless transactions are concluded on terms that the competitors have mutually agreed to observe, a violation of the antitrust acts has occurred. Generally, such violations are considered illegal *per se*.

Territorial and Customer Allocations   *Per se* violations are almost always produced by conspiracies of competitors to divide territories or customers among themselves. The exclusive dealing zones so created represent a restraint of trade.

Violations Among Competitors Selling the Same Product (Vertical Constraints)

Resale Price Maintenance   Among firms competing to sell the same product, resale price maintenance is a violation as serious as price-fixing between sellers of competing products. The phrase **resale price maintenance** refers to the efforts of a manufacturer or distributor to control the price at which a product is marketed at a commercial level other than its own. For example, when a manufacturer tries to force retailers of its product to maintain a set price on that product, the manufacturer's efforts are referred to as resale price maintenance. Whether their purpose is to keep the price artificially low to preclude or injure competition or artificially high to ensure maximum profits, contracts to maintain prices of goods in such circumstances are illegal *per se*. The obvious loophole in this rule is the situation in which no contract is involved. Indeed, the Colgate Company tested that point in the early part of the twentieth century when it informed its resellers that if they failed to follow a suggested price list for Colgate products, they would no longer be able to buy them. Because no contract was involved, the U.S. Supreme Court held that the Colgate plan was legal.

However, should there be more to such an action than a mere refusal to deal, a contract may be found and a conviction result. Such a case occurred when, subsequent to the Supreme Court decision upholding the Colgate plan, a company instituted a plan in which it refused to deal with any resellers of its products that would not follow its suggested price list. However, this company did promise to reinstate such disenfranchised resellers if they changed their minds. This was too much for the Supreme Court. It found the condition of reinstatement to be similar to a contract and held that the company had committed a *per se* violation (resale price maintenance) of the antitrust laws.

This single Court-approved position—"If you sell my goods below my suggested price, I'll not sell any more of them to you"—has come to be known as the Colgate line. Businesses risk antitrust violations by stepping over it.

As you might suspect, rather than do that, some businesses have tried to side-step the Colgate line. One attempt was through the use of **consignments**. Under such an arrangement, the possession of goods belonging to one party (the consignor) is transferred to another party (the consignee) who will sell the goods. The ownership remains with the consignor, who, to avoid taking a loss, can rightfully set the lowest allowable sales price for the goods. The consignee usually gets a percentage commission on the actual sales price.

Consignment law was in place long before the antitrust laws, and its terms seemed a ready-made haven for those who wanted to circumvent the loss of control over price brought on by those laws. Nonetheless, the Supreme Court would have none of it. It held that if the substance of the transaction was an attempt at resale price maintenance, the transaction was illegal *per se* even if its form was similar to that of a consignment. It is important to note that, not wishing to destroy the consignment device, the Court held that such transactions were illegal only when conducted on a "large scale." However, it did not provide firm guidance as to the meaning of that term.

Price Discrimination   As mentioned, the amended Clayton Act outlawed certain forms of price discrimination, including selling below cost or discriminating in price between geographic areas in order to destroy competition; receiving the benefits of price discrimination; and hiding price discrimination behind discount or commission schedules, service contracts, or preferential payment plans.

Legislation also endorsed certain defenses to charges of price discrimination, including:

- Differences in costs of manufacture. Larger orders usually have a smaller unit cost than smaller orders because, while the setup costs are similar for orders of various sizes, they are allocated to more units in larger orders than in smaller orders.
- Differences in costs of delivery. Shipping costs are usually greater for smaller orders than for larger orders because of the greater handling requirements of smaller orders.
- Necessity for meeting competition. A good faith response (not below cost) to meet a price established by the competition is defensible.

Allocation of Territories and Customers   Antitrust violations stemming from assignments of the territory or customers of a particular product were once treated as *per se* violations of the antitrust laws. However, the U.S. Supreme Court decreed in 1977 that they would thereafter be evaluated by the rule of reason. To quote the court in that decision, "The market impact of vertical restrictions is complex because of their potential for a simultaneous reduction of intrabrand competition and stimulation of interbrand competition." (*Continental T.V.* v. *GTE Sylvania*, 433 U.S. 36).

It was this complexity that caused the Court to opt for a rule of reason evaluation. Among the many factors that can be cited is distance between retailers, flexibility of consumer travel, capitalization of the various entities involved, and shipping costs.

Exclusive Dealing Section 3 of the Clayton Act makes it illegal to condition a sale on the agreement of the buyer not to sell a competitor's products if such an agreement substantially lessens competition. The courts have interpreted this prohibition to be effective against any party with considerable market power that demands such an arrangement of a buyer. The degree of market power necessary to reduce competition substantially is generally determined by a product-by-product analysis similar to the use of the rule of reason.

Tie-In Sales As defined previously, a tie-in sale occurs when a seller agrees to sell one product only if the buyer agrees to buy another product. Such sales are treated as illegal *per se* whenever the seller has considerable market power. Otherwise, the tie-in sale can still be evaluated under the rule of reason test. Note that franchisers are afforded some protection by the Lanham (trademark) Act. As such businesses are often built around a particular mark, franchisers may utilize tie-in sales. For example, sales requiring that franchises purchase particular ingredients and a particular monitoring device to ensure the production of uniform Bunnyburgers throughout the world would be permissible.

Vertical Mergers Finally, a business owner needs to be especially wary of the vertical merger. All too often, manufacturers buy members of their distribution chain at the wholesale or retail level, or both. Section 7 of the Clayton Act makes such combinations illegal primarily if they tend to lead to situations where a great deal of the market is under one control, i.e., that of the merged companies. Obviously, if a manufacturer of, say, skimobiles merged with a company that owned 80 percent of a region's retail outlets for such vehicles, the resulting combination could reduce dramatically a competitor's chances of success in that region. On the other hand, if the same manufacturer instead merged with a company that owned only 10 percent or fewer of the retail outlets, the merger would be allowed without any thought of prosecuting its participants.

CHAPTER REVIEW

USE LEGAL TERMS

Fill in the blanks with the appropriate term.

accredited investor	offering statement
articles of organization	oligopoly
blue sky laws	*per se* violation
boycott	price fixing
conscious parallelism	prospectus
consignment	registration statement
horizontal restraints	relevant market
insider	resale price maintenance
interbrand competition	restricted security
intrabrand competition	rule of reason
limited liability partnership	security
market share	trust
members	trustees
monopolizing conduct	vertical restraints
monopoly power	

1. To form an LLC, an application known as the ___?___ must be filed with the appropriate state office. The owners of an LLC are known as ___?___.
2. A refusal to deal is also termed a(n) ___?___.
3. A(n) ___?___ is a legal entity capable of holding ownership of property that is to be managed according to the dictates of the entity's creator.
4. The ___?___ requires that the effect of certain restraints on trade be evaluated before they are considered illegal.
5. Competition between individuals selling the same product is termed ___?___.
6. ___?___ is a practice in which the members of an oligopoly follow the price leadership of one of their members.
7. Generally, prior to purchasing shares of a new issue, each potential stock investor is provided with pertinent financial information and an invitation to buy in the form of a(n) ___?___.
8. An exempted security that must be registered or exempted again before it can be resold is termed a(n) ___?___.
9. A(n) ___?___ is an investment whose profit is a function of the management of others.

TEST YOUR READING

10. How is a limited partnership formed?

11. What activities might cause a limited partner to lose that status?

12. What are the limitations imposed by the use of the S corporation form?

13. Where did the idea for the LLC originate?

14. Compare the current disadvantages of the LLC with the limitations of the S corporation. Would you rather use the LLC or the S corporate form? Why?

15. Why were LLPs created?

16. Why are Blue Sky Laws important?

17. What problems caused the federal government to start regulating security issuance and trading?

18. List three exemptions from security issue registration requirements.

19. What abuses caused the federal government to pass the Sherman Antitrust Act?

20. What is a security?

21. Does being a registered security indicate that a stock is a good investment? Why or why not?

22. Why was insider trading regulated?

THINK CRITICALLY ABOUT EVIDENCE

23. Missouri Water Providers, Inc. bought and sold used water towers. One of its 75 stockholders was a Canadian living in Chicago; the remainder were U.S. citizens. When the company filed its corporate tax return on April 15 of 2001, they elected to be taxed as an S corporation for the tax year their return covered (2000). Will the IRS allow their election? Why or why not?

24. Della Octaves, a well-known opera singer, was a limited partner in "Octaves and Clark, a limited partnership." The partnership's only project was the construction and management of Octaves Area, a residential retirement complex for senior citizens. When the partnership approached a group of local banks for an expansion loan, it did not mention that Octaves was just a limited partner. The loan was for $1.5 million and is now in default. Can the banks collect what is due from Octaves' personal fortune?

25. Three doctors were in a limited liability partnership with Dr. S. Kay Bell. The practice's offices were in Dallas, Texas. During a minor plastic surgery, one of Dr. Bell's partners severed a patient's artery and the patient died. The family brought suit and recovered more than $4 million dollars. The negligent surgeon is financially exhausted after paying nearly $1.5 million dollars of the recovery. The partnership's liability policy has covered all but $1 million of the rest. Now the other doctors want to take out a loan in the partnership's name to cover the remaining million. Dr. Bell has come to you for advice as to whether she should go along with the idea. How would you advise her? Why?

26. Could access to national TV advertising be viewed as a restraint on trade because of its cost and thereby its obvious slant in favor of large companies? Why or why not?

27. Of the various possible antitrust violations, which one has affected you as a consumer the most? Which one has affected you as an actual or potential competitor the most? Can you identify possible violations that exist in the marketplace around you right now that have gone unprosecuted?

28. George Armstrong purchased a franchise in a new fast-food restaurant chain famous for its grilled buffalo burgers. The franchise cost over $2.5 million. Later, Armstrong found that financial data and information on supply problems had been withheld from him. When his restaurant lost money for four consecutive years, he brought suit against the franchise. Armstrong based his suit on the claim that a franchise was a security. Was Armstrong correct in his assessment?

29. You are considering making an investment, but you need more information about the various securities that your broker has recommended to you. A friend has suggested that you check the local library for data furnished the SEC by the issuer of each. On which of the following would such information be available?

    a. A city of Pennsboro bond issue of $1 million.

    b. A $1 million note due in a year and issued by the Pennsboro Hospital.

    c. A $1 million stock issue available for sale only within the state of Missouri from the Hindleg Corporation, which is headquartered in its state of incorporation, Delaware.

REAL-WORLD CASE

Securities and Exchange Commission v. W. J. Howey Co.

66 S. Ct. 1100

Now, see how flexible the definition of security is.

When the Howey Company of Florida needed money, it simply sold off parts of the citrus grove it owned. As a part of the sale however, every purchaser was also required to enter into a service contract with Howey-in-the-Hills, Inc., which was owned by the owners of the Howey Company.

The land purchase contract did not allow the purchasers to work the land or sell crops grown there. Everything of that nature was reserved to Howey-in-the-Hills by the service contract. The purchasers did receive a share of the profits from those crops. Because of complaints, the SEC brought suit, claiming that the sales of land and service were actually securities and, as such, should have been registered.

Think Critically

1. What is the definition of a *security* under the securities acts?
2. Can you distinguish the Howey-in-the-Hills situation from that of a typical franchise arrangement?
3. Should the contracts of sale and service have been registered as securities?

UNIT 7

Earning and Keeping Your Money and Other Property

CHAPTERS

CHAPTER 28

Creating, Running, and Ending Agencies

GOALS

- ♦ Distinguish an agent from an employee or an independent contractor
- ♦ Know how agencies may be formed
- ♦ Understand how agencies are terminated

What Is an Agency?

Often in your life, you need to be in more than one place at the same time. You need to be out making a sale while clearing up the paperwork from the last sale back in the office. You need to be on vacation while keeping up with bills and business. If you are in the armed forces, you need to be on a combat mission while also managing your personal affairs. As is the case for many other kinds of practical problems, dilemmas of this kind have bred a legal solution, namely, the relationship called agency.

When two parties establish a relationship whereby one may legally bind the other by words or actions, an **agency** has been created. The person authorizing another to act in her or his stead is labeled the **principal**. The person so authorized is termed the **agent**. As long as the agent acts within the power granted her or him by the principal (called the agent's **scope of authority**), the principal is bound by any deals the agent negotiates with third parties.

Hypothetical Case

The Rasslin Reptiles, Cobrette and Vipera, could not find suitable matches for women with their talents. Wrestling promoters across the country would not return their calls. Finally, they hired a professional manager, Angela Drone, and gave her full authority to contract on their behalf as their agent. Drone then booked the Reptiles into a sequence of matches up and down the West Coast. In addition, she handled their finances, travel arrangements, and public relations through contracts she made on their behalf. The Reptiles were bound to those contracts, as Drone was their agent.

Agency Distinguished from Similar Relationships

To better grasp the meaning and practical functioning of agency, we must compare it to similar relationships, such as those existing between an employer and an employee or between an individual and an independent contractor hired for a project.

The principal-agent relationship is distinguished from a typical employer-employee relationship on the basis of the extent and type of control exercised. In the first place, while an agent can enter into contracts on behalf of her or his principal, the typical employee cannot. Second, although an employer (also labeled a "master" at law) can direct the on-the-job, physical actions of the employee (also labeled a "servant" at law), the principal does not have the equivalent power over her or his agent. Should the principal contract for this power as well, the agent becomes an employee in the eyes of the law. If this occurs, the principal, like any other employer, is held liable for the harm caused by the agent in the physical conduct of the agency duties. In the alternative, should an employee be granted the power to contract on the employer's behalf, that employee becomes an agent of the employer and can render the employer liable for the agreements that he or she makes on the employer's behalf.

An independent contractor, on the other hand, contracts only to provide a result. The independent contractor therefore, neither acts to bind another to legal agreements nor acts under the control of another. See Chapter 29 for full discussion of the employer-employee relationship and the legal status of the independent contractor.

An Agent's Authority

An agent may be empowered by a principal's express grants of authority or by implication from the nature of the agency. In addition, circumstances may indicate that individuals have agents' authority and thus, may cause those they represent to be bound to contractual obligations that result.

Express Authority   Express grants can either be made orally or in writing. Most important is that the terms are spelled out for both parties. A written agency authorization is called a **power of attorney**. That power may be either general or limited. A **general power of attorney** allows the agent to do anything legally necessary to conduct the principal's affairs. A **limited power of attorney** allows the agent to carry out only specific transactions or to act as agent for only a set period of time.

Hypothetical Case

When their agent booked the Rasslin Reptiles into a six-month string of matches in Europe, Cobrette gave her brother, Herb, a general power of attorney to handle her interests while she was gone. Vipera, on the other hand, did not want to trust anyone with so much power. Consequently, she gave her lawyer only a limited power of attorney that restricted him to paying all of her monthly bills and to contracting for the necessary maintenance work on her properties while she was gone.

Implied Authority   Whether placed in writing or merely stated orally, an express grant of authority to an agent carries with it implied authority to do whatever is reasonably necessary to carry it out. For example, if while Vipera is away on the European tour, her car needs to be driven occasionally to keep it in proper condition, her lawyer has the implied authority to buy gas for it.

Apparent Authority

Hypothetical Case

Snyder was a volunteer firefighter. She also ran a used car lot near the fire station in Pennsboro, Missouri. When a fire call came in early one afternoon, Snyder asked Angie Clark, a 16-year-old high school student who had stopped by to chat, to sit in the office of the used car lot and manage things until the emergency was over. Angie agreed. When Snyder returned from the fire, she found that Angie had accepted delivery on two used cars from a wholesaler. The wholesaler regularly toured the new car dealerships, bought trade-ins, and took the trade-ins to remote used car dealers. Snyder usually bought a couple each trip, but as sales had been slow, she had not planned to this time. Is she bound to the contract?

If one person "clothes" another person with the appearance of an agent, the courts often hold that the person so clothed had **apparent authority** to enter into contracts on the clothier's behalf. This was the case for Angie, whom Snyder placed in a position of responsibility in the used car lot. Because Snyder's actions created the appearance of agency in Angie, Snyder would be bound to the contract for the two cars. Those actions would cause a court to prohibit Snyder from denying the existence of the agency. In other words, apparent authority creates an **agency by estoppel**. The fact that Angie is a minor makes no difference if the principal is an adult. It should be noted here that the representations or conduct of an alleged agent cannot be the sole basis for the creation of such an agency. There must also be the reasonable appearance of authority originating from the alleged principal.

Generally, then, if a person acts without the express, implied, or even apparent authority of another, the alleged principal is not and cannot be bound. However, should the unauthorized act be **ratified** (expressly approved or impliedly approved by accepting the benefits of the unauthorized act), the ratifying party can be bound as a principal.

Note that if a minor becomes a principal in an agency relationship, that minor retains the power to avoid any contracts entered into in his or her behalf. In addition, the minor can avoid the agency contract itself. However, a person without contractual capacity, such as a minor, can be an agent. Therefore, the adult who makes a contract through an agent who is a minor cannot avoid the contract on that ground.

Duties of Agents and Principals

Once an agency has been established, the parties to the agency (depicted in Figure 28-1) owe distinct duties to each other.

Duties of the Principal to the Agent

To Compensate the Agent (if so agreed)   This duty can be the most important of all. In particular, the principal must pay for the agent's services if this is required under the agency contract. If such payment is not required, the arrangement is called a **gratuitous agency**.

To Reimburse the Agent   Again, if the agency contract requires, either expressly or impliedly, that the agent expend her or his own funds to carry it out, the principal is obligated to reimburse the agent for those expenses.

To Pay for the Agent's Liabilities to Third Parties   If, in properly carrying out agency duties, the agent incurs contractual or tort liability through no fault of his or her own, the principal has an implied duty to make good the agent's loss.

To Adhere in Good Faith to the Agency Contract   The principal must comply with the agency's terms openly and honestly. Also, the principal must not block or inhibit the agent's ability to carry out her or his duties.

All of these duties except the requirement of good faith are subject to revision or elimination by the agency contract.

FIGURE 28-1   The Legal Duties of the Principal-Agent Relationship

To the principal, the agent owes:	To the agent, the principal owes:
◆ Obedience	◆ Compensation as agreed
◆ Loyalty	◆ Reimbursement as agreed
◆ The exercise of reasonable care and skill	◆ Indemnification of contract and tort liability incurred by the agent without fault
◆ The segregation of funds belonging to the agency	
◆ A proper accounting upon reasonable demand	

🐾 Hypothetical Case

> The Nosmadas owned a shoe store. Wanting to retire, they listed the property with a realtor, Tex Porter. The agency contract with Porter stipulated that he would bear the expenses of advertising and showing the building as well as the responsibility for maintaining insurance to cover any liability he might incur in performing the agency. The contract also required that the Nosmadas pay him a 10 percent commission on the sales price of $50,000 if he produced a ready, willing, and able buyer. Two months after the Nosmadas made the listing contract with Porter, he produced such a buyer. Before the deal could be closed however, the Nosmadas learned that the pension fund of Mrs. Nosmada's employer had been looted. The previous management had used the money to fight a takeover bid. As a result, they could not retire and they therefore refused to go forward with the sale. Nonetheless, they owed Tex a $5,000 commission for fulfilling his part of the agency contract.

The Agent's Duties to the Principal

Obedience   Agents are responsible for obeying the lawful directions of principals. Any damages that result from their failure to do so are recoverable from the agents.

🐾 Hypothetical Case

> Kaila Moore managed the weekend early morning shift at the Rat Race Convenience Store in Pennsboro, Missouri. Because the Rat Race was open 24 hours a day and did a large cash volume, the owners required that all managers do a cash drop into a floor safe every time the cash on hand exceeded $200. Because Kaila found the procedure annoying, she ignored it. She deposited her excess cash just before her replacement showed up. At 7:30 A.M. on the Saturday on which deer season began, while Kaila was on duty, the Rat Race was held up. Receipts showed that the robbers made off with over $1,700 that Kaila had left in the cash drawer in defiance of her principal/employer's instructions. She was therefore held personally liable for $1,500 of the loss.

Loyalty   Just as the principal owes the duty of good faith to the agent, the agent is held to act loyally toward the principal. If the agent's personal interests are affected by a transaction for the principal, the agent must inform the principal. The agency's business must not be conducted with intimates or businesses of the agent without the principal's prior approval. Such approval is also required before the agent can represent other parties in an agency transaction. Without the required approval, the transaction is voidable by the principal.

Reasonable Care and Skill   When carrying out the principal's directions, the agent must exercise reasonable care and skill. Failure to do so renders the agent liable.

Hypothetical Case

Bronowski owned a car brokerage on a corner of an intersection of two busy streets. He convinced Jonathan Brown that Brown's van would sell in just a few days if it were left at that location. Brown turned the van over to Bronowski on a Tuesday. By Thursday Bronowski had sold the vehicle. When Brown came to get his money, Bronowski informed him that the buyer's check had bounced and that the buyer had disappeared with the van. Brown asked Bronowski whether he had run a credit check or obtained any information from the buyer other than what was printed on the buyer's check. Bronowski replied that he had not, as the buyer had shown up at closing. Brown sued and recovered the value of the van from Bronowski because of Bronowski's failure to exercise the degree of care that a prudent person would have exercised under the circumstances.

Segregation of Funds and Accounting   Agents are charged with keeping agency funds and other property separate from their personal resources. In addition, agents must be prepared to account for all agency funds and other property under their control. If for some reason, the agent commingles personal and agency property so it is impossible to distinguish personal property from agency property or to separate personal property from agency property, the principal can claim all of the property.

Hypothetical Case

Farmer Joan Jones made the Pennsboro Seed Company her agent to sell the barley crop of her north 40 acres. The company had barley of its own stored in a silo at company headquarters. When Jones appeared with her truckloads, the company mistakenly had her put her barley in the silo in which theirs was stored. Since neither Jones nor the company had any way of determining their respective shares of the barley in the silo, all of the barley in the silo was later awarded to Jones.

Principals' and Agents' Liability to Third Parties

The potential for liability between principals and their agents stems from the duties listed above. However, both parties can also become liable to third parties.

Principals

Certainly, principals are bound by any contracts with third parties as long as those contracts were negotiated by agents acting within the authority granted to them. As mentioned, principals can also be held liable to third parties whenever they have clothed agents in apparent authority or ratified the actions of their agents, even if those actions were not initially within the scope of the agency. In addition, any tortious conduct committed by agents when acting within the guidelines set for the agency renders principals (and agents) liable. Finally, principals are usually held to be without liability for criminal acts committed in carrying out an agency unless the specific criminal acts were approved by the principals or were later ratified by them.

Agents

Generally, agents are not liable on contracts they negotiate for principals under the terms of the agency. However, there are exceptions to this rule. For example, should the agent exceed the boundaries of the authority granted by the agency, the agent is liable under the contract that results. The principal, as indicated, is not liable in such a situation unless he or she has clothed the agent in apparent authority or has ratified the contract.

Agents can also incur liability when they act for **undisclosed principals**, that is, under an agency contract that forbids the agents to reveal they are acting for principals, much less those principals' identities. In such cases, the third party may hold either, but not both, the agent or the principal liable for losses. If the principal's existence, but not identity, can be revealed, that party is referred to as a **partially disclosed principal**. Finally, should the principal be shown not to exist or not to have capacity to contract, the agent is held liable.

Hypothetical Case

The law firm of Williams and Manchester contracted to act as agents for a large amusement park chain that wanted to buy land near Branson, Missouri. Afraid that knowledge of its plans would drive land prices sky-high, the chain required that Williams and Manchester not disclose their principals. After thousands of dollars of land purchase contracts had been negotiated in the name of Williams and Manchester, the amusement park chain went bankrupt. The third-party sellers of the land could hold the firm liable under the purchase contracts.

Agency Termination

By Actions of the Parties to the Agencies   Agencies are so dependent on the relationship between the parties that the law generally gives both agents and principals the power to terminate agencies at any time, even before the terms of the contract may cause it to expire. Except for cases in which the agency is terminable at will however, the power of the parties to terminate their relationship does not mean that either has the legal right to so do. If an agent or principal exercises the power to terminate even though legitimate contractual requirements remain in the agency, the courts hold those who exercise that power responsible for any resulting harm. In other words, even though the courts cannot force us to remain in agency contracts we do not wish to be in, they can make us pay damages for the liability that results from our refusal.

Note that in one situation, even the power to terminate the agency relationship is denied. If the agent is given an interest in the property in which she or he is dealing, that interest must be above and beyond the payment for the agent's services. The parties thereby create an **agency coupled with an interest**, which is irrevocable by the principal.

The agency can also be terminated by success, in other words, by the achievement of the purpose for which it was created. Finally, the agency can be terminated by mutual agreement of the parties.

By the Law   As you might expect, the death or permanent incapacity (for example, through insanity) of either the principal or the agent usually leads to an automatic termination of the agency. If an agent makes a contract with a third party on behalf of a principal who has, without the agent's knowledge, become incapacitated or deceased, the agent may be liable to the third party. This is because an agent is held to an implied warranty of having the principal's authorization to act. However, the third party cannot recover against the principal's estate.

Bankruptcy terminates many agencies. If the principal is the subject of the bankruptcy proceeding, the agency is canceled. If the agent is the subject, the agency may continue at the wish of the parties involved unless the agent cannot perform because of the need to commit personal funds to the endeavor. For example, a real estate agent who is the subject of a bankruptcy proceeding might lack access to the resources necessary to advertise and sell the principal's property.

Finally, if carrying out the agency becomes impossible, the agency relationship is terminated. The destruction of the subject matter or a change of law rendering essential agency actions illegal discharges the agency, for example.

Notice of Termination Is Required   Except where the agency is discharged as a matter of law, the principal has the duty to give notice of its termination. This notice must be given to parties with whom the agent has had prior dealings for the principal. If the principal fails to give adequate notice, he or she is liable on contracts negotiated by the former agent with such parties.

CHAPTER REVIEW

USE LEGAL TERMS

Fill in the blanks with the appropriate term.

agency   limited power of attorney
agency by estoppel   partially disclosed principal
agency coupled with an interest   power of attorney
agent   principal
apparent authority   ratified
general power of attorney   scope of authority
gratuitous agency   undisclosed principal

1. An agency that neither party has the power to terminate is the ___?___ .
2. When the court stops a person from denying that an agency exists, a(n) ___?___ is in effect.
3. A written agency agreement is referred to as a(n) ___?___ .
4. The range of power given an agent is called her or his ___?___ .
5. An agency in which the agent does not receive any compensation is labeled a(n) ___?___ .
6. If a principal's existence, but not her or his identity, can be revealed, that party is referred to as a(n) ___?___ .

TEST YOUR READING

7. What is the definition of agency?
8. How do you distinguish between an agent and an employee?
9. How do you distinguish between an agent and an independent contractor?
10. List and explain the difference(s) between the two types of powers of attorney.
11. List the duties an agent owes a principal.
12. List the duties a principal owes an agent.
13. Give four ways an agency may be terminated.

THINK CRITICALLY ABOUT EVIDENCE

14. Which of the following statements (is) are true?

    a. A minor can be an agent.

    b. A minor can be a principal.

    c. An employee can be made an agent of her or his employer.

    d. A power of attorney must be in writing.

15. Wyn Drow sold used farm equipment as an agent for Agri-Vate Corporation. The terms of his agency agreement allowed him to keep half of whatever amount over cost he was able to obtain from the sale of the equipment. Wyn kept his money receipts from the agency in his personal bank account along with the money receipts from his other businesses. When a fire burned his records, he could not determine how much of the money in the account he owed Agri-Vate. Agri-Vate brought suit. How much of that money could the court award Agri-Vate to satisfy its claim?

16. Chung ("Stretch") Minh delivered custom-made limousines to various points around the country for the Elegant Transportation Company of Pennsboro, Missouri. He also served as the company's agent in selling such vehicles to those who inquired about them during his trips. Unbeknownst to Elegant, Chung took several friends along on these trips. His friends would enjoy use of the limos' built-in TVs, VCRs, sound systems, liquor cabinets, and other luxury appointments. They would also pose as famous personalities. During Chung's last trip, his friends got out of hand and caused him to negligently run off the road, through a fence, and into the African game preserve of the famous Animal Land of Ohio. The downed fence permitted several exotic animals to escape, some of which were never recovered. In addition, in an argument that followed the accident, Chung assaulted the preserve's owner. Is Elegant liable for the damages to the preserve or to the person of its owner?

17. The limo was barely damaged. When Chung reported the accident, he was ordered to return to Pennsboro and told that not only was he no longer an agent of Elegant but that he would be terminated as an employee as soon as he got back. Acting out of spite, Chung then drove the limo to the home of an individual who had asked him about buying one several weeks earlier. There, he negotiated the sale of the limo to that individual for about one-third of its regular price. Is Elegant bound by the sales contract? Does Elegant have any recourse against Chung?

REAL-WORLD CASE
Missouri Farmers Association, Inc. v. *Willie May Busse*
767 S.W.2d 109

Consider whether one spouse has the authority to bind the other spouse to contracts without the knowledge of that other spouse.

Tom and Willie May were farmers. Raising cattle was part of their business. On March 18, 1978, Tom executed a credit agreement with the Missouri Farmers Association, Inc. (MFA). That agreement obligated Tom to pay the balance due, court costs, attorney's fees, and finance charges if the account became delinquent. When Tom died, an outstanding balance of $17,000 was owed to the account. Although Willie May did not dispute that supplies were received from MFA and that $17,000 was due on the account, she asserted that she was not liable personally for the amount due. She stated that although her part in the cattle business included ordering and picking up cattle feed and grain from the MFA, she did not know of the credit agreement and did not remember being present when Tom signed it.

Think Critically

1. Do you think that one spouse should be an implied agent able to bind the other spouse to contracts? Why or why not?
2. Do you think the law holds that, without any other proof, the marital relationship alone creates such an agency?
3. What argument other than the existence of an implied agency could you make for binding Willie May to the credit agreement?

CHAPTER 29

Employer/Employee Do's and Don'ts

GOALS

- Understand the basis of the employer-employee relationship
- Know the rights and duties of employees and employers
- Identify when the government becomes involved in the employer-employee relationship

Employment Differs from Similar Relationships

Why distinguish employment from similar relationships? Simply put, without that relationship, most productive work in our society would not get done. The alternatives to that relationship, such as slavery, the feudal system, and the communist production credo ("From each according to his ability, to each according to his need") have been cast aside. Basically, if we want to properly feed, clothe, and house ourselves, employment is essential. However, a second reason is probably more relevant to the subject matter of this book, namely that the employment relationship is blanketed with more statutory and administrative regulations than any other. For now, it is sufficient to say that a manager or business owner who fails to distinguish employees from agents or independent contractors and who fails to treat employees differently from agents and contractors quickly becomes ensnared in violations, regulators, and legal fees.

Actually, **employment** is simply defined as a relationship in which one party (the **employer**) pays another party (the **employee**) to do work under the control and direction of the first party. The detailed terms of this relationship are found in the employment contract that binds the parties, which can be oral or written. The terms of the contract can be either expressly set down or implied by the court from the course of dealings. Like any other contract, it must contain all the essential elements of a contract to be enforceable.

The employment relationship is different from an agency in that an agent is authorized to contract on behalf of a principal, but the employee under the basic employment contract is not. An **independent contractor**, like an employee, is someone who agrees to do a job for another. However, unlike employees, independent contractors perform jobs as they see fit; they are not subject to the direction and control of the person with whom they contracted to do the job. Generally, only the final result needs to be satisfactory to that person for whom the independent contractor is working. Of course, that is not the case with the employer-employee relationship, in which the employer controls the details of the employee's performance.

Hypothetical Case

The Large Area of Pennsboro Stock Exchange (LAPSE) needed a new manager. Consequently, it decided to pay an independent contractor, ExecuTrak, $5,000 to locate five candidates with the special skills necessary to do the job. When ExecuTrak submitted its list, the LAPSE made its former manager its agent to interview the candidates and ultimately negotiate an employment contract with the one he considered best qualified. The former manager did so, and thereby provided the LAPSE with a new manager who was also a new employee.

The degree of employers' responsibility for what happens to employees, products, and consumers is the rationale for the close regulatory scrutiny that employers come under. Before we examine the regulations that envelop the employment relationship, we need to review the basic duties that common law says employers and employees owe to each other.

Basic Duties of Employers and Employees

Before detailed regulation of the work environment began several decades ago, the common law had created legal standards enforced against participants in an employment relationship. Those standards are still valid today. They are usually stated in terms of the duties owed by participants to each other and are in addition to the duties expressed in an oral or written employment contract. Most of them parallel the duties pertinent to agency law.

Duties of Employers

Compensation   As you may suspect, the employers' primary duty to employees is to compensate them, primarily by wages or salaries, for their work. Such compensation can include **fringe benefits**, or forms of payment not directly related to work performance, such as pensions, vacation time, and insurance.

Many employment contracts are **terminable at will** unless they specify a fixed term. Such "at will" relationships can be ended without notice by either party at any time without producing a litigable cause of action. However, if the employer has contracted for a fixed period of employment, and compensation has not been provided according to the terms of the contract, the employee is justified in quitting. In fact, as long as employees show themselves ready, willing, and able to perform during the fixed period, compensation is due whether any work was performed or not.

Hypothetical Case

The Miracle Motor Company of Lockewood, Colorado, hired three full-time employees for a period of one year. The three were to do the dealer prep work on the new car models the company sales staff sold during this period. Unfortunately, as a result of a strike at the manufacturing plant, no new models were available for sale during most of the year. Nevertheless, the three showed up for work each day, ready, willing, and able to perform. Miracle Motor Company therefore had to pay them for the entire period.

Reasonable Range of Duties and Treatment A second duty owed by employers to employees is to properly set out a reasonable range of tasks for employees and to treat them properly in the performance of those tasks.

Employers cannot demand that employees perform work outside the scope of the job defined in the employment contract. Such demands give employees adequate legal grounds to justify termination of the employment relationship. However, quitting a job merely because the treatment is harsher than expected or the tasks are more difficult than expected is not legally defensible.

In addition, employers are not permitted to subject employees to unreasonably harsh treatment, such as assaults or batteries. For example, should an employer beat an employee, the employee can quit without any fear of liability for breach of contract.

Hypothetical Case

To make money for school, O'Neil agreed to work through the summer as a detail person at a local car wash. She would dry each car with a chamois, then clean the ashtrays and floors of the vehicle. Late one afternoon, she inadvertently spilled a half-full container of milk that had been left open on the dash of a brand-new luxury car. Her boss saw her do so and yelled at her, calling her a "clumsy fool." He then helped her clean up the mess. Unfortunately, they could not get out all the milk. When the milk that had soaked deep into the pile curdled and started to smell, the owner brought the car back and demanded new carpeting. The cost to the car wash came to over $1,100. When O'Neil's boss got the bill, he walked up to her, pulled her by the hair, and threatened her. O'Neil then quit and sued him for assault and battery.

Note that insulting O'Neil by calling her a "clumsy fool" did not give her a legal basis for quitting. Only the later assault and battery provided her with a legal basis for quitting without being sued for breach of the employment contract.

Proper Work Environment   Because employees lack control over how work is done, the law maintains that, as a minimum, they are entitled to a safe work environment. Unsafe working conditions provide employees with another justification for ending the employment relationship without liability for breach of contract. Employees' recourses against employers for injuries sustained in an unsafe work environment are covered later in this chapter.

Duties of Employees

As are the duties of employers, many employees' duties, such as obedience, loyalty, and reasonable care and skill, are based in agency law. However, the first duty of employees discussed below, providing production in return for compensation, is the center of the exchange inherent in all employment relationships. Note that this duty is not found in all agencies.

Production   The primary duty of employees is to produce a satisfactory work product. Work that is below standard in either quality or quantity can result in an employee's justifiable discharge.

Obedience   Implicit in the employment relationship is the employee's agreement to submit to the detailed control and direction of the employer. As noted earlier, it is this detailed oversight that distinguishes the employment relationship from those of independent contractors and agents. Unlike them, employees must obey the lawful orders and rules of their employers that fall within the scope of employment. Failing to do so provides grounds for dismissal.

Hypothetical Case

A government safety inspector ordered Dark-Oak Enterprises, a woodworking firm, to provide all its employees with safety glasses. The firm did so and issued a rule that all employees were to wear the glasses while within 5 feet of a woodworking machine. Johnson found the glasses annoying, especially in the heat of summer. She therefore refused to wear them. After several warnings, Dark-Oak properly terminated her employment.

Loyalty   In return for the compensation paid, the employer buys not only obedience but also an expectation of loyalty. Loyalty does not extend beyond the job, however. Employers cannot demand that employees use company products in their private lives, for example. Of course, it is certainly justifiable for employers to expect that their employees not reveal confidential information or otherwise harm the business at any time.

Reasonable Care and Skill   Unless hired to take part in a training program, employees implicitly warrant that they have the skills needed to perform the job properly and with the appropriate care. If experience shows that this is not the case, employers are justified in discharging these employees.

One of the main reasons that employers discharge improperly qualified employees is the potential liability if such employees injure someone or something while acting within the scope of employment. In such a situation, employers can be held vicariously liable for the harm done. **Vicarious liability** is a legal doctrine that imposes responsibility on one party for the actionable conduct of another party based on an existing relationship between the two parties. In employer-employee or principal-agent relationships, the rule of law placing vicarious liability on the employer or principal is known as **respondeat superior** ("let the master answer"). This rule allows an injured party to hold the servant and the master jointly liable for the harm done by the former. As you probably suspect, the justification for the rule lies in the high degree of control that an employer exercises over an employee. As long as an employee acts within the scope of employment, the detailed training and directives given by the employer make the employer accountable for the employee's harmful actions. However, holding a "deep pocket," such as the employer, liable does not release the employee from responsibility.

In contrast to the willingness of the courts to affix civil liability on the employer for an employee's tortious acts, criminal acts generally remain the sole responsibility of the employee. Unless an employer has specifically authorized the crime, the criminal intent of the master simply cannot be inferred from the servant's acts. However, there are exceptions to this rule. For example, criminal responsibility is placed on the employers of those who, even against their employers' directions, sell impure foods or alcoholic beverages to minors or to persons too inebriated to drive.

Terminating Employment Contracts

Generally, unless termination is inhibited by an employment contract or a collective bargaining agreement, the employment relationship can be ended at any time by any party to it for practically any reason. This is the "at will" termination

---

FIGURE 29-1   Duties of the Employee and the Employer

Employee's Duties:

- To produce a satisfactory work product
- To obey lawful orders and rules of the employer that are within the scope of the employment
- To be loyal to the employer's best interests
- To perform with reasonable care and skill

Employer's Duties:

- To compensate the employee
- To be reasonable in defining jobs
- To treat employees properly
- To provide a proper work environment

mentioned earlier. Such terminations do not ordinarily lead to any litigable causes of action unless there is a contract or an agreement setting standards for dismissal.

There are exceptions to this rule. Some states in the U.S. require that firings be made as a result of good faith evaluations of the various factors involved in employment. Other states protect employees who are fired for refusing to violate the law or for failing to waive their rights under certain laws, such as workers' compensation. Most states however, still cling to the "at will" perspective. Finally, the federal government has legislated exceptions in favor of **whistle-blowers**, persons who alert authorities to improprieties in the conduct of their employers, even when the federal government is the employer.

Note that employers who must impart secret information on product formulas or vital processes often have **agreements not to compete** in their employment contracts. Such agreements prevent workers from competing with their former employers for a reasonable period after termination of the employment relationship. If written too broadly, agreements of this kind conflict with federal laws intended to spur competition. The courts either void such agreements or "blue-pencil" (reduce) them to reasonable proportions.

Hypothetical Case

Angela Pilet worked for Crowson's Fried Chicken in Columbia, Missouri, for three years. Shortly after she left its employment, she started her own fried chicken restaurant, using the recipes and the cooking and serving processes that she had learned at Crowson's. Crowson's promptly filed suit asking the court to enforce the agreement not to compete in Angela's employment contract. The contract term read, "I will not compete with Crowson's for a period of three years after leaving its employ or within a 10-mile radius of any of its stores." The court agreed to uphold the agreement, but only after blue-penciling it down to one year and one mile from the Crowson's outlet in which Angela had worked.

Government Regulation of Employment   In the U.S., the government often intervenes in the employment relationship, typically to balance the degree of control vested in the employer. Such intervention comes mainly from the federal government in the form of statutorily authorized regulations.

The National Labor Relations Act

Prior to the passage of the National Labor Relations Act (NLRA) in 1935, government measures legitimized **collective bargaining**, or negotiations over conditions and terms of employment between representatives of a work force and its employer. Nonetheless, the NLRA, also referred to as the Wagner Act, went further by creating a system of governmental oversight that assured fairness and order in the process. It set up procedures for selecting a bargaining representative as well as for conducting collective bargaining. In addition, the NLRA made certain union and management activities illegal. The prohibited activities were referred to as

unfair labor practices. They included refusing to participate in collective bargaining, the firing of employees or other discriminatory actions in retaliation for union activity, inhibiting employees' right of organization, and improperly interfering with or controlling the creation or running of a union.

Finally, the NLRA created an administrative body to oversee its application. This body, the National Labor Relations Board (NLRB), investigates and makes determinations on complaints of NLRA violations, especially unfair labor practices.

After World War II, in a much more positive economic environment than that of the depression-burdened 1930s, the U.S. Congress passed amendments to the NLRA in the Taft-Hartley Act of 1947, which was passed over then-President Truman's veto. The Taft-Hartley Act attempted to better balance the provisions of the NLRA by stipulating a number of unfair labor practices that restricted unions as well as employers. It prohibited union coercion of individual employees, made it illegal for unions to refuse to bargain collectively with an employer, required unions to give notice of their intent to **strike** (refuse to work for an employer in order to win contract demands), allowed employers more freedom of speech to comment on unionization, and prohibited secondary boycotts. A **boycott** is a refusal to do business with a particular person or firm in order to obtain concessions. A **secondary boycott** involves causing third parties to agree to cease doing business with a firm with which a union is involved in a dispute.

Hypothetical Case

> The Retail Clerks and Busboys Union of Pennsboro, Missouri, had organized the workers in that community's largest chain of grocery stores. Other stores remained without unions but paid union scale wages. In response, the Retail Clerks placed billboard ads at a number of locations near the non-unionized stores urging the general public to boycott those stores. One of the non-unionized stores, Smithson's, filled a complaint with the NLRB against what it termed the secondary boycott urged by the ads. The complaint, however, was disallowed as no provision in the agreement with the unionized store required the advertising.

The Taft-Hartley Act also contained provisions allowing the President of the U.S. to request through the U.S. attorney general that a federal district court order an 80-day "cooling-off" period to possibly ward off a strike. This cooling off period could be invoked only if the potential strike severely endangered the nation's well-being. During the 80 days, strikers must return to work and may be required to vote on the latest contract offer between the 61st and 75th days. Finally, the Taft-Hartley Act allowed individual states to pass laws prohibiting collective bargaining agreements from requiring union membership as a condition of employment. Such laws, called **right-to-work laws**, are in place in 20 states currently.

In 1959, more significant amendments were made to the federal labor laws. These provisions were intended to help clean up corruption within the unions. Titled the Labor-Management Reporting and Disclosure Act, and also referred to as the Landrum-Griffin Act, the law contains a statement of rights for union members, including the right to vote in union elections, the right of access to union financial statements, and the right to voice concerns at union meetings.

The Fair Labor Standards Act

Another law that directly affects the employment relationship also originated in the 1930s. The Fair Labor Standards Act (FLSA), passed in 1938, sets the basic parameters of hours and wages for any person who works in or produces goods for interstate commerce. Many state laws echo the FLSA standards and make them applicable to persons not covered under the FLSA. Under the provisions of the FLSA, no covered worker can be employed for more than 40 hours a week without being paid time and a half for overtime. In addition, the law sets a floor under hourly wages, called the **minimum wage**, and prohibits the employment of individuals who are 13 or younger.

Exemptions from the FLSA standards are numerous. Among those who lack the protection of the act's provisions are managers; scientists; local, state, and federal employees; employees of retail and service businesses with gross annual sales of less than $250,000; outside salespeople; and other exemptions based on special permissions from the U.S. Department of Labor. In the same vein, exemptions are granted to certain occupations for minors. For example, minors 13 and under can be employed to deliver newspapers; perform as actors; and work on farms as long as the work is not hazardous. Between the ages of 14 and 16, minors can also be employed as office workers and gas station attendants, but not in factories or around machines or in hazardous work areas.

The Occupational Safety and Health Act

In 1970, Congress created the Occupational Safety and Health Administration (OSHA). OSHA's purpose is to establish and enforce federal health and safety standards in the workplace. Employees have the right to request an OSHA inspection if they suspect a violation of an OSHA rule or regulation. If the inspection reveals such a violation, the employer is cited and required to appear at a hearing to defend against penalties. OSHA inspectors conducting an investigation are required to have search warrants if they do not receive the employer's voluntary assent to enter the workplace.

Hypothetical Case

Willy Hastings worked in the paint shop of a small manufacturer in Tabletop, Kansas. His co-worker, Tom Allen, had been painting the manufacturer's products for years. After work Willy and Tom would occasionally meet for a few beers at a local pub. Willy would watch as Tom hacked up clots of the orange rust inhibitor they used in most of their jobs. The "paint shack," as their boss called it, was not ventilated, and even though Willy and Tom wore masks, the hovering vapors penetrated into their air passages and lungs. One day, Tom did not show up for work. When Willy inquired, he was told that

Tom had collapsed at the bowling alley the previous evening and was in the hospital. Two months later Tom died of a rare lung disease. Willy then called OSHA and, requesting anonymity, reported the lack of ventilation in the paint shack. OSHA investigated and cited the employer. Eventually, a ventilator was installed. However, the employer came to suspect Willy as the reporting party. Although the employer never questioned him about the matter or discussed it with him directly, the employer served Willy with implicit notice that his future with the company might be limited. Willy quit the next year to return to school. [This is based on an actual incident.]

Discrimination and the Equal Employment Opportunity Commission

Every time factors other than the ability to perform the task at hand affect the decision as to who to hire, promote, or discharge, we all pay a higher price for our goods and services. This is because those goods and services have not been produced by the most efficient employees. In addition, when the best workers are turned away because of discrimination based on such factors as sex, race, and color, we are lowered in an ethical sense. The apathetic acceptance of such activities by a citizenry and its leaders debases a nation.

In recognition of these facts, the U.S. Congress passed the Civil Rights Act of 1964. That act established the Equal Employment Opportunity Commission (EEOC) and authorized it to utilize litigation and conciliation to fight against **discrimination in employment**. Title VII of the Civil Rights Act makes such discrimination illegal and defines it as hiring, promoting, or discharging on the basis of race, color, sex, religion, or national origin. Amendments to the Civil Rights Act gave the EEOC power to compel employers (with more than 15 employees and whose business has an impact on interstate commerce), unions, employment agencies, and other entities to eliminate direct discrimination on these bases. In addition, the EEOC can act against the more subtle discrimination inherent in supposedly neutral rules that have an improper impact. For example, by requiring security guards to be at least 6 feet tall and to weigh at least 200 pounds, the resulting force is very likely to be all male.

The EEOC also enforces the Equal Pay Act of 1963, which precludes the use of sex as a basis for paying one worker less than another who is performing similar work. The opportunity for all aspects of compensation, from overtime to pensions, must be equal for men and women doing jobs that are performed under similar working conditions and require the same levels of effort, skill, and responsibility.

Another act enforced by the EEOC is the Age Discrimination in Employment Act. This federal law, passed in 1967, makes it illegal for private employers to discriminate against persons because they are 40 or older. In addition to prohibiting age discrimination in hiring, firing, promotion, or pay, the act prohibits advertising for job applicants in terms that suggest a preference for youth or for persons in a particular age bracket. Even advertising a desire for a "recent graduate" is improper.

Other statutes in the area of discrimination include:

♦ *The Rehabilitation Act*   Requires the hiring and promotion of handicapped individuals by employers who do a significant amount of government business in a year.

♦ *The Pregnancy Discrimination Act*   Requires that an employer treat pregnancy, giving birth, and the recovery from delivery in the same manner as other physical problems producing an inability to work are treated.

♦ *Federal Regulation 29*   Requires the elimination of harassing sexual advances, requests for sexual favors, and other verbal or physical abuse of a sexual nature. When such sexual harassment comes from a supervisor, the employer is strictly liable for the improper conduct. When it comes from co-workers, the employer is liable only if the supervisor knows or should have known of the conduct and has not taken effective action to eliminate it.

Bona Fide Occupational Qualifications   It is important to note that exceptions are made in some of the discrimination categories mentioned above. These exceptions typically fall under **bona fide occupational qualifications** (BFOQs), which are occupational qualifications that allow types of discrimination that are reasonably necessary to the conduct of a specific business. Here, what is "reasonable" is the issue. Is it reasonable to have only Baptists as faculty members at a Baptist college? Is it reasonable to have only men as guards in an all-male maximum security prison? Is it reasonable to have only men as front line combatants in war? The answers vary dramatically from person to person, interest group to interest group, government entity to government entity, political party to political party, time to time, and at law.

Affirmative Action Plans   One of the most controversial current areas in discrimination law involves **affirmative action plans**. Such plans are "voluntarily" created by employers according to EEOC guidelines. They set down methods and time frames for actions to eliminate the adverse impact of an employer's past discriminatory practices on certain subgroups such as women and racial minorities. Percentages are used as general guidelines to determine whether an adverse impact exists. Individuals in the adversely impacted subgroups may then be hired or promoted ahead of similarly or better-qualified employees to achieve a satisfactory balance. Such actions lead to charges of **reverse discrimination** (government-endorsed favorable hiring, promoting, or discharging based on the prohibited categories of sex, race, etc.) and the use of **quotas** (the setting aside of a certain number of positions to be filled exclusively by the adversely impacted subgroup.)

Workers' Compensation Laws

Long before OSHA, the common law offered workers some hope of protection from unsafe working conditions. If injured because of such a condition, an employee could bring a negligence suit against the employer. If victorious, the employee not only secured compensation for his own injury but also served notice on the employer that failure to correct the condition responsible for the injury could result in additional successful suits. Regretfully, the state of the law at the time was such that even if the employer's negligent violation of the duty to provide reasonably safe working conditions could be shown, recovery by the employee was often prevented by certain defenses. These defenses included contributory negligence, assumption of the risk, and the acts of fellow workers.

The contributory negligence of the injured employee, for example, in not observing safety rules set down by the employer, precluded any recovery even in situations where the negligence of the employer far outweighed that of the employee. Recovery was also precluded by assumption of the risk, as evidenced by the employee remaining on the job even after he or she had been shown the dangerous condition that later caused the injury—for example, the open pit or the unsheathed saw blade. Finally, the fellow servant defense meant that if the employer could show that another employee caused the harm, the injured employee could recover only from that employee, not from the employer.

In the 19th century, these defenses were commonly available in part because our society wanted to protect its growing businesses. Therefore, the legal system enforced rules that caused individual employees and their families to bear the consequences of disabling on-the-job injuries. Around the turn of the century, as the capitalization of our industrial base became more secure, these defenses slowly eroded. Negligence suits brought by employees became more frequent, and the dollar awards of such suits increased. As an alternative to possibly ruinous recoveries, employers then supported the passage of workers' compensation statutes at the state level. These statutes required employers to buy insurance that would pay injured employees appropriate benefits regardless of fault. Such assurance of benefits was given to employees as a substitute for bringing a negligence suit against the employer. The benefits awardable by the statutes generally encompassed only medical expenses and a certain percentage of the injured employee's lost wages. This eliminated recovery for the pain and suffering derived from the injury, however. It also proved a good bargain for employers because usually recovery for pain and suffering in a court of law is 5 to 10 times the medical expenses.

If employees cannot continue in their former occupations because of injuries, the system provides for **vocational rehabilitation** (training to assume another type of job). This takes the place of a recovery for lost future earnings under negligence law.

Hypothetical Case

Sherman Henry, the sole breadwinner for his family of six, worked as a master carpenter for an Arkansas construction company. While constructing the roof on a new house, one of Sherman's fellow employees, newly hired and without proper training, placed a thin sheet of plywood over a chimney hole. Sherman stepped on the sheet, fell through, and plummeted three stories. In the fall, he broke his pelvis and several bones in his arm. The workers' compensation system paid for his medical treatment, reimbursed him for several months of lost wages, and assisted in his vocational rehabilitation at a nearby university.

Eligibility   Most of the injuries that fall under the workers' compensation systems occur while the employee is on the job and are related to the work. In the phrasing of the typical state workers' compensation statute, the injury must "arise out of and in the course of the covered employment."

Potential for Lawsuit Regardless of Workers' Compensation System   In certain exceptional instances, the employee is not bound by the workers' compensation laws and can pursue suit against the employer. For example, if the employer does not subscribe to the workers' compensation insurance program although required to do so, the employee may bring suit. In that event, the employer is forbidden to use the defenses mentioned above (fellow servant, assumption of risk, contributory negligence).

The employee may also bring suit if the employer has intentionally acted to harm the employee or has permitted conditions it knows will bring injury to the employee.

Hypothetical Case

Karen Silkwood's father, as administrator of her estate, brought suit against Kerr McGee because his daughter had been contaminated by plutonium at that company's Cimarron nuclear fuel plant, where she worked. The jury found for Karen's estate and awarded $10 million in punitive damages for the company's tortious conduct.

Finally, suit is still allowed where the employee or the injury is not required to be covered by workers' compensation. In such cases however, the employer may use the previously mentioned defenses.

Social Security Programs for Workers

The Social Security Act provides programs that supplement some of the others mentioned above. These programs provide relief for qualified individuals who lose their jobs, become disabled, or retire. See the discussion in Chapter 32 for more details of these programs.

Americans with Disabilities Act and Family and Medical Leave Act

The statutory requirements imposed by the Americans with Disabilities Act (ADA) also affect what an employer must do for disabled employees. Under the ADA, an employer must provide "reasonable accommodations" for a qualified worker who happens to have a substantial physical or mental impairment. What accommodations are reasonable varies with the nature and cost of the impairment and the work requirements. The impairments can be the result of diseases or accidents. The accommodations can include visual aids, hearing aids, alterations in ventilation, lighting (in one case a teacher was allergic to fluorescent light and a classroom therefore had to be rewired for incandescent bulbs), and other elements of the work environment.

The Family and Medical Leave Act (FAMLA) also imposes new requirements on employers. Specifically, employees in covered businesses (those with 50 or more employees) must be allowed to take up to 12 weeks of leave without pay if a child is born or adopted or if the employee or member of the employee's immediate family develops a serious medical condition. In addition, the employer must maintain health insurance on the employee during the leave and reinstate the employee in the same job or an equivalent job upon return.

CHAPTER REVIEW

USE LEGAL TERMS

Fill in the blanks with the appropriate term.

affirmative action plans
agreements not to compete
bona fide occupational qualifications
boycott
collective bargaining
discrimination in employment
employee
employer
employment
fringe benefits
independent contractor
minimum wage

quotas
respondeat superior
reverse discrimination
right-to-work laws
secondary boycott
strike
terminable at will
unfair labor practice
vicarious liability
vocational rehabilitation
whistle-blowers

1. The ___?___ is the lowest legal hourly wage.
2. A(n) ___?___ is a work stoppage intended to coerce employers into yielding on disputed issues.
3. The doctrine of ___?___ allows an employer to be held as the respondeat superior of her or his employees.
4. ___?___ provides training in new occupations for the disabled.
5. Pension plans, vacation time, and profit sharing are all ___?___ of certain jobs.
6. ___?___ laws make it illegal to require that an employee be a union member.
7. A(n) ___?___ involves a refusal to do business with someone.

TEST YOUR READING

8. In terms of control over his or her work, distinguish an employee from an agent and an independent contractor.
9. List the duties of an employer relative to his or her employee.
10. List the duties of an employee relative to his or her employer.
11. What is the general rule governing when employment can be terminated?
12. What is a whistle-blower?
13. What are the options a court has when reviewing an agreement not to compete?
14. Name the various types of discrimination the EEOC works to protect against.
15. What is the main legal issue associated with the BFOQs?
16. Why is the use of quotas to fulfill affirmative action plans in dispute?

THINK CRITICALLY ABOUT EVIDENCE

17. The Pennsboro Baptist Church employed Hiram Goodrest, a retired carpenter, to drive a bus for the church school. One evening, while driving the school's basketball team to an away game, Hiram negligently rammed the rear of a car, thus injuring several elderly women. If the women bring suit, whom do you think they will probably name as defendants? What legal doctrine allows this? Would they be able to sue the same parties if Hiram Goodrest were an independent contractor hired to drive for this one trip only?

18. Mike Mass owned and operated a nationwide job hunt service for nuclear engineers. To help him in his work, he hired Sharon Newtron. Mike taught her the entire business. He introduced her to many of his clients and to the entities with which he found them jobs. After five years, Sharon quit to found her own job search business for all employees in the nuclear industry, including the engineers. Mike brought suit to enforce the agreement not to compete in Sharon's employment contract with him. The agreement specified that for three years after leaving his employ Sharon could not open a competing business or contact any of the clientele or employers she had become acquainted with while in his employ. Sharon responded that, because the nationwide nuclear industry consisted of only a small number of employing entities, enforcing the agreement would exclude her from the market. What do you think the court should do?

19. Every day at the morning coffee break, the office secretaries gather in the lounge. Steve, the only male secretary, is often chided by female secretaries and occasionally propositioned by them. He has reported the problem to his boss, Victoria Adams, but nothing has been done to correct matters. Can he sue and recover against his employer for sexual harassment?

20. Caprice Whimsey worked as a chemist in a secure area leased by a defense contractor from Grand Bluffs Air Force Base in Kentucky. While working late one evening, she was raped, badly beaten, and left for dead by Jeremiah Stanton, a custodial employee who had a record of sexual assaults. Her employer had neglected to check its staff for criminal records. Will she be covered by workers' compensation or instead be allowed to sue her employer for negligence? Why?

REAL-WORLD CASE
John Doe v. *William H. Webster,*
Director, Central Intelligence Agency
769 F. Supp. 1

Consider the case of a covert CIA operative who was fired when he told the agency about his homosexuality.

"John Doe" was hired by the Central Intelligence Agency (CIA) in 1973. By 1977, thanks to consistent evaluations of his performance as excellent or outstanding, he was promoted to a position as a covert electronics technician. In early 1982, Doe voluntarily informed a CIA security officer that he was a homosexual. The CIA then placed him on administrative leave and conducted an investigation of the ramifications of his homosexuality. During a polygraph examination, he admitted that he had engaged in homosexual conduct but denied ever having had homosexual relations with any foreign national or ever having discussed classified information with a sex partner. After the evaluations were concluded, Doe was asked to resign. He refused and was then, in May 1982, dismissed by order of the director of the CIA. At that time, he was informed that the agency would give him a positive job recommendation during his job search but that if he applied for a job requiring a security clearance, it would inform the prospective employer of its conclusion, namely that his homosexuality posed a threat to national security.

Doe maintained that he was denied due process because his dismissal resulted from a blanket CIA policy banning homosexuals who engaged in homosexual activity from CIA employment. Doe maintains that without the individualized appraisal guaranteed by due process through notice and a hearing, he cannot present evidence showing his trustworthiness and employability.

Think Critically

1. Do homosexuals pose a greater risk to the intelligence services than heterosexuals? (If you have access to a law library, read *High Tech Gays* v. *Defense Industrial Security Clearance Office*, 895 F.2d 563 at p. 568 for a detailed consideration of this issue.)
2. If homosexuals do pose a greater risk, should that justify a blanket policy against their employment by the intelligence services?
3. Should Doe receive the due process he requests?

CHAPTER 30

Holding On to Your Property

GOALS

- ◆ Identify what property is
- ◆ Understand the concept of bailments
- ◆ Know the types and attributes of leaseholds

What Is Property?

> Behold, my brothers, the spring has come . . . Every seed is awakened, and so has all animal life. It is through this mysterious power that we too have our being, and we therefore yield to our neighbors, even our animal neighbors, the same right as ourselves, to inhabit this land. Yet, hear me, people, we have now to deal with another race . . . They claim this mother of ours, the earth, for their own and fence their neighbors away; they deface her with their buildings and their refuse.
>
> *Sitting Bull, Sioux warrior and chief in 1877, reacting to a U.S. government order that the Sioux leave their treaty-guaranteed hunting grounds, where gold had been discovered*

The Definition of Property

The seemingly simple question of what is property has a complex answer. Many of us think of property as things—things we can own or **rent** (pay consideration for the right to use or occupy) or otherwise obtain some right or interest in. In the law however, a more proper and accurate definition is emphasized. There, **property** is best defined as the rights and interests we recognize that each of us can have in things. *Property is not the things themselves.* In fact, under our capitalist system, many people can have rights and interests ("property") in the same thing at the same time. For example, you may have the right of ownership of this book by virtue of having purchased it from its previous owner, a campus bookstore. However, you might rent the book to a friend for a semester so that she doesn't have to buy her own. She may, in turn, let another student temporarily take possession of it to check his notes. All of these individuals have distinct property claims (ownership, possession, and use) of the book. To put it directly, all have property in the same thing. So, it is crucial that you recognize at the outset that, "technically" at least, a particular thing is not property. Property is only the rights and interests in things that a particular society allows its citizens. Societies other than ours did not and do not always place the same value on property as we do.

> As long as the sun shines and the waters flow, this land will be here to give life to men and animals. We cannot sell the lives of men and animals; therefore we cannot sell this land. It was put here for us by the Great Spirit, and we cannot sell it because it does not belong to us.
>
> *A Blackfoot chief rejecting an offer of money by U.S. delegates in return for the tribal lands of the Blackfoot*

The Rights and Interests We Recognize as Property

The most important of the rights and interests that the law labels property is title. **Title** in property law means a legally endorsed claim to the ultimate ownership of something. **Ownership**, in turn, refers to a variety of rights allowing the use and enjoyment of things. These rights, as indicated by the discussion in the preceding section, may be split among many individuals, but the claim of title is their origin and the point to which they return.

Possession is another property right. Most of us have heard that it is nine-tenths of the law. Although this greatly overstates the case, **possession** does mean immediate control or power to the exclusion of all others over something. Given what can be done to something in a person's possession, other rights and interests may prove irrelevant.

Use is a third right of importance. In the case law of property, **use** is defined as the enjoyment of things by their employment. Don't be misled by the word enjoyment in the definition. At law, *enjoyment* means the exercise of a right, not the taking of pleasure, which is what the word commonly means.

Finally, there are the rights that allow the owner of property to destroy, consume, and **alienate** (transfer title by sale, gift, will, etc.) some or all of it.

Hypothetical Case

Eileen bought the old *Pennsboro Press* building from the last editor of the newspaper. Her purchase included all of the property located in the building. Back issues of the *Press* were part of that property. Although Pennsboro's mayor and other Pennsboro citizens asked her to have the issues microfilmed at their expense to help preserve the city's history, she declined to do so and burned the issues.

Types of Property

Property is divided into two classifications, real and personal. **Real property** is defined as rights and interests in land, buildings, and fixtures. Note that land is viewed as extending downward to the very center of the earth and upward into the atmosphere above it.

Fixtures are tangible, movable things that become permanently attached to land or buildings, such as an oven built into an apartment wall or a trailer permanently moored to a foundation on a piece of land. Generally, once a tangible, movable thing has become permanently attached to real property, its ownership vests in the owner of that property. This is true regardless of who owned the thing before it was attached.

Trade fixtures are an exception to this rule. Such items are attached to another's realty by a renter to facilitate a business the renter is carrying on in the property. Pizza ovens bolted to a storefront wall or walk-in freezers in a grocery store or an ice-cream parlor are examples. The ownership of trade fixtures remains with the party renting the **premises** (real property subject to the legal action at hand) and may be taken with her or him after the rental period is complete.

Personal property is basically everything that is not real property. It can be tangible (e.g., shoes or a pen) or intangible. Intangible property is generally some evidence of value, such as a stock certificate, a promissory note, a patent, a copyright, or a trademark. These last three items are the main evidences of intellectual property as defined in Chapter 7.

FIGURE 30-1 Rights and Interests People May Have in Things

- Title
- Possession
- Use
- Destruction
- Consumption
- Alienation

Acquiring Personal Property

By Creating Intellectual Property

Acquiring a Patent   Article I, Section 8, of the U.S. Constitution empowers our government to grant qualified applicants the exclusive rights to use, make, and sell their inventions for a set period. Such a grant is called a **patent**. It is the equivalent of a legal monopoly. However, it requires that the inventor make public the substance of the invention so that others may use the ideas it contains as a basis for further developments. The two most important types of patents are the design patent and the utility patent.

A **design patent**, good for 14 years, protects the unique configuration or appearance of an object's surface or components. Note that some items that qualify for a design patent can also be copyrighted (see below).

The most common type of patent however, is the utility patent. Its 17-year run of exclusive rights is granted for a novel and useful invention that is not obvious. By novel, the law implicitly means a previously unknown idea that represents a "burst of genius." An idea is "obvious," and therefore not patentable, if it is plainly evident to a person with average skill in the field involved. "Useful" implies that the invention has a utility of some kind that will reward society in return for the patent rights granted to the applicant.

The invention can be a machine (such as an intermittent windshield wiper), a process (such as xerography), a composition of matter (various prescription drugs), or other articles of manufacture.

If a person infringes another's patent (exercises any of the rights granted without authority to do so), the holder of those rights may sue for an injunction to stop the **infringement**. The holder may also sue for damages, which are usually set in the amount of a reasonable **royalty** (compensation for the use of property) for the patent rights in question.

Hypothetical Case

Arnold Cruise invented a device that "scrubbed" or cleaned more than 99.9 percent of the pollutants in the smoke from coal fires for a fraction of the cost of the scrubbers currently in use. On the advice of people he approached to invest in the development of his device, Arnold contacted a patent attorney. The attorney immediately had a computer search conducted through the U.S. Patent and Trademark Office's database to see whether similar devices had already been patented. Two "hits" came back. The attorney then ordered descriptions of the patented devices. She and Arnold studied the descriptions and determined that they were not that close to Arnold's idea. Next, the attorney had a draftsman draw up detailed plans of Arnold's invention. Then the attorney and Arnold wrote up the "claims" they would make for his invention. These claims or distinguishing points had to be sufficient to cause the patent office to agree that Arnold's invention differed significantly from those previously registered. The patent application was then submitted to the patent office. In the meantime, Arnold made a prototype of the invention and marked it "patent pending." Many investors promised their financial support if the patent was indeed issued. Unfortunately, the patent office turned down the application. Arnold, nonetheless, collected a small amount of capital and began making the devices. Soon, the holder of one of the other patents brought suit against him and received an injunction requiring Arnold to cease production. The patent holder was also awarded some $97,000 in damages for lost royalties.

Acquiring a Copyright   Article I, Section 8, also empowered the federal government (the U.S. Congress in particular) to "promote the Progress of . . . useful Arts, by securing for limited Times to Authors . . . the exclusive Right to Their . . . writings." The original copyright statute, passed in 1790, granted exclusive protection for such writings for 14 years with a provision for renewal for another 14. Under the current statute, which was revised in 1998, authors of books, composers of music, and originators of similar artistic productions have their works protected for the life of the creator plus 70 years. The copyright thus awarded places the exclusive rights to copy, publish, and sell published or unpublished works in the hands of their creators. The works that can now be copyrighted include everything from traditional books to sound recordings, motion pictures, and videos. Should a copyright be infringed, the holder may sue for injunctive relief, damages, and lost profits. Also, the injured holder may ask that the unauthorized copies be destroyed.

Creating and Protecting a Trademark   The maker or seller of particular goods often identifies them with a distinctive name or symbol known as a trademark. From Coca-Cola to the MGM lion, such marks identify to consumers the level of quality, reliability, and many other attributes of products. For many, the Campbell soup label represents protection against the possibility of botulism that haunts users of generic brands. However, the holder of the trademark can license its use to others. Also, under a relatively new federal statute, businesses can even preregister a mark for up to three years before using it if they file the proper application, certify they intend to use the mark, and pay a fee every six months.

Other Means of Acquiring Personal Property

Asked how to acquire personal property, one person jokingly suggested, "You steal it." Surprisingly, in a sense she was correct. You can acquire possession in that way. However, possession is all you will have. Title remains forever with the true owner, to whom you, and all future possessors, innocent or not, have a legal duty to return the stolen item. Of course, what we are looking for here is how you legitimately acquire full ownership of personal property.

By Reducing It to Your Possession   The best place to start is where most law school courses on property start—with wild animals. Back when our forebears were hunter-gatherers, a lot depended on whose property the deer or other felled game happened to be on. Once a society was stable enough for such questions to be answered by courts, the answer came through loud and clear:

 ## Hypothetical Case

Barney of Oxfordshire and Fred of Bree, shooting from opposite sides of the deer, each lodged an arrow in it at the same time. The deer bolted. Both men gave chase. The deer collapsed and died after running about 100 yards. Barney was first to it and claimed it. When Fred arrived, he noted that both arrows had produced a mortal wound. To whom should the deer be awarded?

The answer, said the courts, is that the deer belongs to Barney, the first person to reduce it to his possession. Barney's family eats well. Fred's ends up hunting lots of edible roots in the forest.

By Finding Lost, Mislaid, and Abandoned Property   A similar rule applies to **abandoned property** (property in which the owner has given up all intention of maintaining rights or interests). In such cases, the first party to establish dominion and control over whatever has been abandoned owns it. **Lost property** is a different story. The owner has parted with the property involuntarily. When lost property is found, the finder is allowed to retain it until the true owner is located.

Lost property must be distinguished from mislaid property. **Mislaid property** is consciously laid aside by the owner, who intends to retrieve it later, but now cannot find it. When mislaid property is found, the finder must surrender it to the person most likely to contact the true owner during the true owner's search for the property. Whether property is considered lost or mislaid depends on what can be inferred from where it was discovered. For example, a $50 bill found on the floor of a barbershop would probably be treated as lost property and retained by the finder until the true owner appeared. The same bill found on a counter near the coat rack of the barbershop would be considered mislaid and legally should be given to the barber to improve the chance of its being returned to the true owner.

Both the finder and the ultimate holder of mislaid property have a duty to try to return the property to its rightful owner. Many states have statutes that allow individuals with lost or mislaid property to acquire ownership by making a sincere effort to locate the true owner over a period of time (usually by advertising the situation in a publication of general circulation for a certain number of times over a period of one year). In many jurisdictions, converting lost property to the finder's own use without attempting to find its true owner is considered larceny. In addition, failure to take reasonable care of found property can result in liability for the finder or holder.

Hypothetical Case

Professor Abraham folded up his notes and then watched the students file out of his 9 A.M. Law I class. The last one, Bill Turner from nearby Springfield, turned to him. "Here, Dr. Abraham, this was left in the row down from mine. It's not from our class." Turner handed Abraham a large backpack. Abraham thanked him, then put the backpack on a chair near the door and left a message on the board about it. The backpack disappeared. Because of his failure to take reasonable care (for example, by storing it in his office rather than leaving it where anyone could make off with it), Professor Abraham could be liable if the backpack were taken by someone other than its true owner.

Lost or abandoned property without any rightful claimants eventually, usually after several years, becomes the property of the state. The right of the state to property without existing claimants is referred to as **escheat** by the common law. Today, many states have put into law the Uniform Disposition of Unclaimed Property Act to cover this and similar issues. It was rumored that W. C. Fields, a famous comedian of the 1930s, opened accounts under fictitious names in banks throughout the country, and then never returned to collect the money he deposited. In most states, after 20 years, the unclaimed funds would have escheated to the states where the banks were located.

By Receiving Gifts   Although it may not happen as often as you'd like, personal property may also be acquired by having it given to you. What could be more simple, right? Well, as you may by now suspect, simplicity in the law is like fairness in the Tax Code—it hasn't happened yet. First of all, the law has determined that you need three elements to have a transfer of ownership. Those three are the intent to give, the delivery of the gift, and the acceptance.

The intent of the **donor** (the person or other entity giving the gift) is controlling. If the intent is to make a gift at the present time, then for the gift to be complete, all that needs to be shown is that the item was delivered to and accepted by the **donee** (the recipient of the gift). Such an absolute, unconditional gift is labeled **inter vivos** (between the living).

A gift given in anticipation of death, on the other hand, is labeled **causa mortis**. In other words, if a living person, in contemplation of her or his death from a known cause, gives someone a gift, the gift is regarded as conditional. Therefore, should the donor not die as anticipated, either within the projected time frame or of the supposed cause, the gift is legally ineffective. Ownership of the intended gift is then returned to the would-be donor or the donor's estate. The same result (that is, the return of the gift to the donor) is reached if the donee dies before the donor or if the donor takes the gift back before dying of any cause.

Hypothetical Case

Sensing his death from cancer to be near, Jim Jones gave Antoine Carver, his longtime friend, a check for the $210,000 in his checking account. Jones then took an overdose of sleeping pills and died. Since Jones did not die of the anticipated cause, the court ordered that the $210,000 be returned, as the gift was *causa mortis*, that is, conditional on Jones' near immediate death from cancer. As Jones died without a will, the court would split up the money along with the rest of Jones' assets among Jones' surviving relatives.

Legal questions regarding gifts also arise as to delivery. Because people often publicly state their intent to make a gift but do not follow through, the courts must see evidence of delivery to have a completed gift. Transfer of dominion and control over the subject matter of the gift is typically good enough. Even if the physical delivery of the property is not made, for example, transferring the means of access or control to the donee (e.g., the key to the safe deposit box containing the jewelry) is enough. Such a symbolic act is known as **constructive delivery**.

Finally, to be complete, a gift requires the donee's acceptance. Such acceptance is generally presumed or, if questioned, can be inferred from an act of the donee indicating that he or she intends to treat the subject matter as his or her own.

Hypothetical Case

When she found out that her friend Taipei had voted a split ticket in a recent election, Hillary bought her a mule and a young elephant. She then had them delivered to Taipei's house along with a card indicating the nature of the gift. Taipei, although amused and flattered by Hillary's attention, wanted to refuse the gift. Indecisively, she waited so long to act that the reasonable time during which she could have repudiated it passed. As a result, the animals became hers by law.

The area of gifts poses a few other problems for the law. For example, common law held that gifts given to minors really belonged to the parents. As a consequence, many states have passed Uniform Gifts to Minors acts that prescribe procedures for making sure that such gifts are used in the minor's best interest or kept for the minor until she or he reaches adulthood. Another problem is the gift of an engagement ring. In many states, the courts hold that if the engagement is broken, the ring is to be returned to the donor. The courts of some states hold just the opposite however, if the donor broke the engagement. In several states, the position of the courts on this problem seems to change every few years, leaving it a question to which the law cannot give a conclusive answer.

By Purchase   Purchase is the most frequently utilized means of acquiring personal property. **Purchase** is defined as the transmittal of property from one person to another by voluntary agreement based on valuable consideration.

By Descent or Will   Personal property is also acquired through the distribution of the assets of a deceased. Such a distribution is done either according to the wishes of the deceased as expressed in a will or according to the provisions of state statutes should no will be involved, or both. A **will** is a person's expression of how his or her property is to be distributed upon death. A person who dies leaving a valid will dies **testate**; a person who dies without leaving a valid will dies **intestate**. As a will can be altered almost anytime during the lifetime of its maker (who is labeled the **testator** if male, the **testatrix** if female), the law has imposed strict requirements to prevent forgeries of wills and to resolve conflicts that develop between different versions of wills. In particular, to be valid, a will must reflect the true intent of the deceased unaffected by duress, fraud, or undue influence. It must be in writing, although a few states allow oral wills, termed **noncupative wills**, for the distribution of personal property up to a modest monetary limit under $10,000.

The makers of wills must have legal capacity, know what they are doing and sign in front of at least two witnesses (more witnesses are required in certain states). These witnesses must be disinterested adults who have been told they are observing such a signing. Finally, the will must not be revoked by a later will's explicit statement to that effect or by the action of statutes that terminate its effectiveness because of marriage, birth of offspring, or divorce. Nonetheless, wills may be amended by a formally witnessed and executed document called a **codicil**. About half the states in the U.S. allow **holographic wills** (written and signed in the decedent's hand but not witnessed). If no will can be proved to the satisfaction of the probate court, the property of the deceased is divided according to formulas in appropriate state statutes. Finally, should the deceased be survived by a spouse, he or she may have the right to take one third to one half of all the property in the estate regardless of what is in the will.

All this may sound complex, and it is. To handle it all, once proof of death has been established, the court selects or endorses an individual to handle the estate. This appointee is labeled an **executor** (male) or **executrix** (female) if there is a will. If the deceased died intestate, the appointee is labeled an **administrator** or **administratrix**. This person can be held liable if the estates they handle are improperly executed.

By Accession and Confusion   Both of these means of acquiring personal property are rather specialized. **Accession** involves the acquisition of property by the natural increase of property already owned (for example, when a cow produces a calf, the calf belongs to the cow's owner). It can also occur by affixing things to property already owned (for example, a carburetor placed on a car's engine during repairs becomes the property of the car's owner). **Confusion** is blending together the indistinguishable goods of two or more owners so the share of each owner cannot be identified. When such a situation arises, the most innocent party usually receives the ownership of the intermixed whole.

By Bailment   A **bailment** is the legal relationship created by the acquisition of possession of the personal property of another, subject to an agreement to return it or to deliver it to a third party. Although short of full ownership, this transfer of a personal property right is also worthy of mention. Bailments actually occur frequently in our society. We just use less accurate terminology to describe them in real life. For example, if you need to use my textbook, you do not ask me if I'll bail it to you. Instead, you want me to "lend" or "give" it to you for a few days so you can study for the exam. If you need a trailer to move your furniture and other belongings to a new apartment, you do not look under **bailors** (individuals who bail goods) in the Yellow Pages. Instead, you look under "rental centers" or "trailer rentals." Similarly, if you need someone to transport a package for you to a friend in a faraway city, you do not look under **bailees** (individuals to whom goods are bailed). Instead you look under "delivery services" or, perhaps, "common carriers." If you need money and pawn your compact disc player to get a quick loan or if you find someone else's lost money—all of these situations and many more involve bailments but just aren't called that. There are actually three types of bailments: bailments requiring ordinary care by the bailee, bailments requiring extraordinary care by the bailee, and bailments imposed by law.

Bailments requiring ordinary care can be broken down into gratuitous bailments (bailments for the sole benefit of one or the other of the parties) and mutual benefit bailments. The intent of mutual benefit bailments is that both the bailor and the bailee receive payment of some kind. A common example of a mutual benefit bailment is a pawn (also referred to as a *pledge*). In a pawn arrangement, the bailor transfers his or her personal property to the bailee as security for a loan.

Gratuitous bailments involve a flow of use or value in one direction only. For example, if I let you borrow my riding lawn mower to finish a part of your yard where the grass has grown exceptionally high, that is a bailment for the sole benefit of the bailee—you. I do not expect payment for my neighborly favor. The next time we go on vacation however, look for me to show up on your porch with all of my wife's ferns and a note with the following directions: "They need watering every day, and I was hoping you wouldn't mind if I left them with you. Don't forget to talk to them—Marge keeps them up on all the neighborhood gossip. Thanks, Flanders." This arrangement is a gratuitous bailment for the sole benefit of the bailor. Under modern bailment law, ordinary care is required in all situations involving mutual benefit and gratuitous bailments.

In certain bailment arrangements, bailees must take extraordinary care of the property entrusted to them. Extraordinary care implies a standard of responsibility that holds the bailee liable for any loss or damage unless it is solely attributable to unforeseeable circumstances, war time, or the acts of God. In short, the bailee becomes a near insurer of the goods. Such strict liability arises in business settings only. The foremost examples of bailees who must take extraordinary care are hotelkeepers and common carriers. A hotelkeeper (also occasionally labeled innkeeper by the law) operates an establishment that provides overnight accommodations to the public. The common law imposed on hotelkeepers a duty to accept all guests. Furthermore, hotelkeepers become insurers of property that their guests turn over to them for safekeeping.

This unenviable level of responsibility for bailed goods is also placed on businesses that transport goods for a fee. Such businesses are referred to as common carriers. They, like hotelkeepers, must take extraordinary care of items bailed to them. Common carriers must be distinguished from private carriers, such as Sears, i.e., companies that transport in their own vehicles their own goods or goods they have sold or leased; and contract carriers, companies that transport goods only for those with whom they care to do business. Of the three types of carriers, only private carriers are not regulated by the U.S. Interstate Commerce Commission, and only common carriers must exercise extraordinary care.

A bailment of goods to a common carrier for shipment is known as a **consignment**. When the common carrier receives goods for shipment, it issues a document called a **bill of lading**. The bill of lading states the terms of the shipping contract for the consigned goods. It also contains a description of those goods and details who has the right to demand the goods by presenting the bill of lading when the goods arrive at their destination. Some bills of lading are negotiable. Like commercial paper, they (and thereby the right to receive the shipped goods) can be made to the order of a named person or to a bearer. Other bills of lading are nonnegotiable, which means that the consignee of the goods involved must deliver them to the person named on the bill of lading.

A situation in which personal property inadvertently ends up in the hands of a stranger is referred to by the law as an involuntary bailment. The misdelivery of a package and a finder taking lost property into his or her possession are both examples of involuntary bailments. The person who thereby holds the property must then exercise a level of care similar to that required of a bailee in a bailment for the sole benefit of the bailor (ordinary care in most states).

Finally, note that when personal property wrongfully comes into another's hands, a tortious bailment is created by law. Tortious bailees are the equivalents of insurers for any damage that occurs to property in their possession. All of the following represent situations in which the court would impose a tortious bailment:

- James buys a stolen compact disc player.
- Harry keeps the $175 in a wallet he found even though the owner of the wallet is clearly identified by documents contained in it.
- Sandra borrows Angela's car to drive back and forth to work but on occasion uses it to go shopping in a nearby city.
- John refuses to return Carlos' jack after changing a tire.

Acquiring Real Property

By Gift or Purchase   Like personal property, the ownership of real property can be acquired by gift or by purchase. Should either of these methods be involved, the result is evidenced by a **deed**, a formal written instrument that transfers title to real property. The most frequently used type of deed is a **warranty deed**. This deed not only conveys title from the **grantor** (transferor of property) but also contains several warranties for the benefit of the **grantee** (person who receives the property). These warranties include legally enforceable assurances that the grantor has title and the right to transfer it, that the grantee will not be disturbed in her or his ownership by someone with a superior claim, and that the property is free from all encumbrances (liens) at the time of transfer. Such assurances are usually very important to a new owner of real property.

Another type of deed, in contrast to the warranty deed, has none of these protective assurances. Instead, a **quitclaim deed** merely passes whatever claim or interest the grantor may have or might receive in the real property. So, if the grantor has only a disputed or partial claim, that's all the grantee gets. No warranties are made in the deed.

By Descent or Will   Like personal property, real property may also be acquired through the distribution of the assets of a deceased person. Such distribution is done either according to the wishes of the deceased as expressed in a will or according to the provisions of state statutes, should there be no will, or both. For more details, refer to the parallel personal property discussion earlier in this chapter.

By Adverse Possession   In all 50 states in the U.S., ownership of real property can be acquired by occupying it for an extended period. Such occupancy must be open, continuous, exclusive of others, notorious (generally known), and under some rightful claim. The period required varies from 5 to 30 years, depending on the state. Note that land belonging to the government cannot be adversely possessed. Also, the possession has to be without the owner's permission. In some states the adverse claimant's payment of taxes on the land shortens the period necessary for adverse possession. Finally, adverse possession can apply to small portions of land. For example, presume that after a neighbor builds his fence one foot onto your land, you protest but take no further action. After the statutory period has run, the neighbor owns the land enclosed by the fence.

Hypothetical Case

After her husband, Hutton Larue, died and left her several pieces of real property, Jewell Larue, then 75 years old, became something of a recluse. As a consequence, she neither realized nor cared when Benton Hill moved onto one of her pieces of property. Benton claimed that Jewell's husband had sold the property to him before he died. A little over 10 years afterward, Benton Hill sued in court for an acknowledgment that he had adversely possessed the land and thus obtained a title to it. The court agreed and awarded the land to him.

By Eminent Domain   At times, ideally for the good of the whole, private land has to be taken for public use. The right of governments and other public bodies at the federal, state, and local level to do so is referred to as **eminent domain**. Hospitals, schools, parks, and highways for public use are all made possible through the use of this right. The original owners of the land must receive "just compensation" according to the Fifth Amendment to the U.S. Constitution. The amount of this compensation can be determined by a court, if necessary. However, as has often been pointed out, no amount of money can make up the loss to the elderly widow who is forced out of the home she shared with her husband and family for a lifetime.

Hypothetical Case

Mrs. McWilliams, an 85-year-old widow living near campus, refused the University of Springfield's final "fair value" offer for her home. The university's population was expanding, and the land was said to be needed for a parking lot. Upon her refusal, the university went to court for a final determination of the amount that Mrs. McWilliams would have to accept for her property.

By Leasehold   Rights and interests short of full ownership are also acquirable in real property. For example, a **leasehold** gives the recipient the right to the exclusive possession of the premises involved for a certain term. It is important to distinguish leaseholds from "leases." A lease has a somewhat broader and more ambiguous meaning. It is best defined as "an agreement under which temporary exclusive possession of real property or possession, use, and enjoyment of personal property are transferred." A person who rents the real or personal property of another is termed a **lessee**. A person from whom real or personal property is being rented is termed a **lessor**. However, when the subject matter of a lease is solely real property, more specific terms are used (although lessor and lessee are accurate still). In particular, a party who rents real property to others is often called a **landlord**. A renter of real property is referred to as a **tenant**. A **lodger**, on the other hand, occupies the premises, but has only the use of them, not their exclusive possession.

A tenant is also distinguishable from business invitees, licensees, and, certainly, trespassers. **Business invitees** are implicitly invited onto the premises of another to conduct commercial transactions (a Christmas shopper at a toy store, for example). **Licensees** are afforded the privilege of entering another's real property through the possessor's explicit or implied promise. A UPS delivery person is a good example of a licensee. Finally, **trespassers**, persons who willfully enter the property of another without consent, are easily distinguishable from leasehold tenants.

Note that the property holder's duty (and, therefore, potential liability) varies according to these types. For example, the property holder is only required to refrain from doing intentional harm to a trespasser (such as setting traps), but must warn a licensee of known dangers (such as hidden pits). Business invitees must be provided with safe premises on which to conduct business with the property holder. So, business people are charged with conducting reasonable inspections of their stores to ensure that no harm comes to their customers while they are there.

Generally, leaseholds can be categorized by the time allocated for the tenancy. The four principal types are the periodic tenancy, the tenancy for years, the tenancy at will, and the tenancy at sufferance. Of the four, the periodic tenancy is the most common. When you rent an apartment from someone on a month-to-month or week-to-week basis, you are a tenant in a periodic tenancy. At law, the definition of **periodic tenancy**, although relatively imprecise, generally requires that a tenancy be a leasehold that continues for successive, similar intervals subject only to termination by proper notice from one of the parties.

At common law, subject to change by the terms of the lease, the rent is due at the end of each such period, be it monthly, weekly, daily, or whatever. The timing of the termination notice is important in a periodic tenancy. Unless the lease provides differently (for example, by requiring "30 days' notice"), a full period must elapse between the time of notice and the effective date of termination for any period less than year to year. This means that if you want to terminate your monthly periodic leasehold on January 1, you need to give notice before the preceding December 1. If you give notice on December 1 or afterward, you cannot terminate the leasehold before February 1. For periodic tenancies of a year or longer, three months to a full year's notice is required, depending on the law in the jurisdiction. Again, all this can be changed in the lease agreement.

The second type of tenancy's name is misleading. A **tenancy for years** should instead be called a "tenancy of fixed duration," as that is all it is. The duration can be any length of time as long as it is definite. The tenancy for years automatically terminates when the set length of time has run. No notice is required. According to the statute of frauds, the lease for the tenancy for years must be in writing if the duration is for a year or more. An oral lease is enforceable for durations of less than a year. However, oral leases are best avoided. In most U.S. states, ownership to the intended tenant, not just exclusive possession, is conveyed by a tenancy for years that runs for 100 years or more.

Hypothetical Case

The McKlernon family owned a large acreage in Pennsboro, Missouri. When the McKlernons were approached by the Mount Etna Development Corporation with plans to build a regional mall on the site, they agreed to lease their land for 99 years. Under the laws of the state, if they had agreed to a longer lease, they would have passed ownership of the acreage to the corporation.

Note that some U.S. states hold that a periodic tenancy is created if a landlord permits a tenant for years to remain in possession after the lease has ended. Other states hold that this action creates a **tenancy at will**. This third type of tenancy is a leasehold that permits the exclusive possession of real property for an indefinite period. Two characteristics distinguish this type of tenancy from the other types. First, its termination is subject to the current will of its parties instead of determined by a fixed length or a repeating term specified in a lease. Proper notice of the impending termination of the tenancy at will may have to be provided to the other party, however. State statutes or common law usually set the notice requirement anywhere from no advance notice to 30 days' notice in writing. Because of the undetermined length of the tenancy at will, there is no requirement that the lease be in writing, however. The second distinguishing characteristic of a tenancy at will is that the tenant remains on the property with the owner's permission. The tenancy therefore ends with a change in ownership. This is important in many situations, because a periodic tenancy and a tenancy for years continue to bind new owners.

Hypothetical Case

Avalone wanted to sell her apartment house to a firm involved in redeveloping the neighborhood in which the house was situated. To make the house more marketable. she did not renew the tenancies for years as they expired. If the tenants wanted to stay, they could, but only under a tenancy at will, which would not burden any new ownership. Therefore, should the redevelopers purchase the building, they could move all such tenants out simply by giving proper written notice and then waiting for the two-week notice period required by state statute to run.

The fourth and last tenancy, a **tenancy at sufferance** is a leasehold created by law whenever a periodic tenant or a tenant for years wrongfully retains possession of the premises after the lease has expired. A tenant at sufferance is liable for rent for the time involved and is not entitled to any form of notice before **eviction** (the act of removing a tenant from possession of the premises). However, should the landlord accept rent from a tenant at sufferance who remains in possession, either a tenancy at will or a periodic tenancy is created, depending on state law.

Before leaving this subject, it is a good idea to consider the relationship between the landlord and the tenant in a little more detail. Typically it is based on an essential exchange: possession of the premises in return for rent. However, unless agreement to the contrary is reached, the responsibilities of the parties go deeper than just this simple bargain.

For example, where the premises are to be used for human housing, they should be in a condition fit for living. Ensuring this was at one time left up to the tenant and the market. If a tenant did not find the premises in proper condition, he or she could look elsewhere before finalizing the lease. Such is not the case today in most jurisdictions. Today, even small cities have housing codes that set minimum standards for rental properties offered for human habitation. Such codes generally require certification by a qualified governmental inspector before occupancy can begin. The inspector ensures that rental properties are free from structural problems, leaky roofs, improper wiring, improperly vented fixtures and gas appliances, and security and health problems. In addition, although at one time landlords were not liable for injuries sustained on leased premises, today courts often hold them accountable. This is especially likely if the injuries are sustained in the common areas, such as stairwells or elevators, or result from negligently made repairs or hidden defects that the landlord should have been aware of but did not disclose to the tenant.

The landlord also has the duty to pay the property taxes on leased property, be it apartments or rental homes. However, the terms of a long-term commercial lease often obligate the tenant to pay these taxes. An apartment dweller, on the other hand, pays them indirectly by way of rental payments.

To balance out these duties, the landlord has two fundamental rights. The first is simply the right to be paid rent. The second is the right to regain the possession of the real property upon the termination of the lease or upon its violation by the tenant. If the tenant has improved the premises with fixtures, except for trade fixtures, they belong to the landlord. Given a violation of a lease condition, such as a failure to pay the rent, the landlord can evict the tenant. Realize however, that landlords may not take matters into their own hands and personally throw tenants out. Sheriffs or other suitable officials carry out evictions upon petition to and order of the proper courts.

The tenant's duties, as compared to the landlord's, are simpler. The primary duty is, of course, to pay rent. The payment must be tendered in a timely fashion and in the medium agreed to, be it money from the tenant's income, a part of the harvest from the land, or a percentage of the gross receipts from a concert. Beyond paying rent, the tenant is responsible for taking reasonable care of the premises. The tenant must make minor repairs, such as fixing a leaky faucet or replacing light bulbs or fuses. For a major problem, such as a hole in the roof or a worn-out combustion chamber in the furnace, the tenant's duty is to notify the landlord of the problem. After having given notification, the tenant must take reasonable steps to prevent avoidable damage, such as placing buckets under a leak and taping a cardboard shield over a broken window. The idea is to return the premises in basically the same shape they were in when they were received from the landlord. However, the tenant is not liable for the toll taken by reasonable wear and tear.

The fundamental right of the tenant is exclusive possession of the premises. "Exclusive possession" means just that. Even the landlord cannot enter the leasehold without the tenant's permission. However, this right has to be balanced by the landlord's need to enter the premises to make repairs. Should the landlord fail to make proper repairs or provide necessary services (such as heating during the winter), so that the premises are rendered uninhabitable, the tenant may abandon the leasehold and refuse to pay rent. The law terms this a **constructive eviction**. Note that to justify nonpayment of rent, the tenant must truly leave the premises. Otherwise, the leasehold is held to still be habitable.

Hypothetical Case

On one of the hottest days of summer school, the students living in the university's high-rise apartment building woke up to discover the air-conditioning system was no longer working. The breakdown of the system was caused by a defective part that took three weeks to replace. During this period, the students sweltered in temperatures that remained near 90 degrees even in the "cool" of the night. The only ventilation for the fifteen-story building was provided by small sliding windows in the apartment bathrooms. Near the end of the third week, the topic of constructive eviction came up in a business law class attended by one of the sweltering students. When she suggested that the university had constructively evicted her by not providing air-conditioning, the professor noted that inasmuch as she had remained in residence, a court would hold that the premises were still habitable. Had she left and rented elsewhere, a court would probably have excused her from her lease with the university. She would have also been able to seek damages covering moving expenses and any additional rent she was forced to pay for a leasehold comparable to the university apartment.

Note that this fundamental right of possession is accompanied by a right to use the premises, but only for customary purposes. So, unless some lease provision allows it, a structure normally used as a residence cannot, for example, be turned into a warehouse for pets.

Finally, unless a lease term prohibits it, the tenant has the right to transfer her or his rights and interests in the leasehold to someone else. Transferring all of these rights and interests to another is termed **assignment of the lease**. Retaining some of these rights and interests while transferring others is termed **subletting**. A lease assignee becomes directly liable to the landlord for the rent and fulfilling other duties. Even so, the assignor still remains liable under the lease if the assignee fails to fulfill the duties. In a sublet, the sublessor continues to be immediately liable to the landlord under the terms of the lease.

By Easements and Profits   An **easement** gives someone the right to use the land of another for a variety of purposes. Utility companies often need to obtain easements from property owners to run their lines. Also, owners of an adjacent parcel of land may have an easement across another's property to allow them access to theirs. A **profit** is the right to take from the soil of the land of another, for example, to mine for minerals, extract timber, or drill for oil.

Hypothetical Case

Wildcatters, Inc., bought the right to drill for oil on Tricia Horton's land. However, to reach the spot where they intended to place their oil rig, Wildcatters purchased an easement from Grant, who owned the adjacent property. Wildcatters did not have to purchase a similar right from Horton because the profit they had already obtained from her implied the right of access across her land. When Grant subsequently leased his land to Buford, Buford still had to allow Wildcatters its access.

Other Interests in Real Property

Creditors often acquire interests in the property of their debtors. A **mortgage**, for example, is a device that transfers the right to have the subject real property sold to satisfy an unpaid debt. Such a right or lien is given by the debtor (**mortgagor**), who thereby transfers one of the ownership rights that he or she has in the property to the creditor (**mortgagee**), who lends value to the debtor in return for such secured repayment. Mechanic's and tax liens, discussed in Chapter 23, allow roughly the same rights as the mortgage, but generally without the debtor's direct assent. Finally, individuals can have certain privileges in using the real property of others. For example, a delivery person or a business customer may be allowed access to real property, depending on the circumstances.

Legal Forms of Property Ownership

Individual Ownership

Persons who own property may do so individually or with others. In the former situation, where there is only one owner, that owner is said to hold the property in **severalty**. This is the simplest and most common form of ownership. When there are two or more owners, property can be held in a variety of ways. Tenancy in common, joint tenancy, and tenancy by the entirety are discussed below.

Joint Ownership

All three of the above-mentioned tenancies involve different rights that various co-owners enjoy in the subject property. A **tenant in common**, for example, is a co-owner of the undivided property in question who can transfer her or his ownership interest without the permission of the other co-owners. Like the other cotenants, a tenant in common is entitled to possess the entire premises. The creditors of a tenant in common can use her or his interest to satisfy their legal claims. Also, a tenant in common can call for **partition** (division of the property or of the value received for it) if desired. Finally, the shares of tenants in common do not have to be equal.

Like a tenant in common, a **joint tenant** is defined by and enjoys a different set of rights in relation to the subject property. Specifically, a joint tenant is legally considered to own all of the subject property. As all joint tenants are considered to have equal rights in the subject property, this means that each of the two, three, or more owners is considered by the law to own all of a single thing. Life in general teaches us that such an obvious divergence from reality is indicative of a need for either therapy or a good lawyer. In this case the divergence is what is known as a *legal fiction* and as such, is accepted as an irrefutable tenet of belief by the entire legal profession, and so you must accept it as well. In addition to owning all of the subject property, each of the joint tenants also has the right of survivorship. This means that when a joint tenant dies, the entire ownership remains with the surviving tenants and is not subject to the claims of the deceased's family or estate. If a joint tenant transfers his or her ownership rights, the transferee becomes a tenant in common with the other joint tenants. Finally, partition is allowed and the creditors of one joint tenant may reach the property held by all of the other joint tenants to satisfy outstanding debts.

The final form of joint ownership is more specialized. In particular, **tenants by the entireties** must be husband and wife. Old common law treated spouses as one person, so such tenants each own all the property in the same manner as joint tenants. Thus, each spouse has the right of survivorship in relation to the subject property. However, the separate action of one spouse, such as falling into debt, cannot work a detriment on what is owned by both as tenants by the entirety. In other words, neither creditors solely of the husband nor creditors solely of the wife can reach property that both hold as tenants by the entirety. Both husband and wife must have signed any debt instrument to allow the creditor to take the collateral held in tenancy by the entireties upon default. Should the couple divorce however, they are no longer considered tenants by the entirety, but instead become tenants in common and the creditors can descend on them and their holdings. Note that, unlike the situation in U.S. states accepting the common law approach that each spouse owns whatever he or she earns unless both spouses agree to share, in nine U.S. states, each spouse is automatically considered to have an undivided one-half interest in whatever the other spouse earns. These are referred to as *community property states*. In those states, the creditors of one spouse can reach the property of the other spouse, at least partially, without the other spouse's signature.

 Technology Insights

Stem Cell Research and Property Law

The most promising biotechnical advances of all time could be forthcoming due to stem cell research. These base cells, extracted from embryos, can generate other specialized cells to perhaps replace destroyed nerves or organs. The idea to grow colonies of these cells originated with a Sri Lankan Veterinarian who was observing the mating habits of water buffalo. The actual patent on the establishment of the cell colonies was awarded to the University of Wisconsin. Under the patent laws, the University has the right to the process for over a decade. Anyone utilizing this technology must pay them for the stem cells they provide or for utilizing the patented process. The University also is demanding a cut of any profits made from products developed from the research. As a consequence, the amount of research that could be accomplished has been reduced substantially.

Think Critically   Do you think the purpose of the patent laws has been fulfilled in this case? Can you think of any amendments to the laws that might enable vital developments to be more freely utilized?

CHAPTER REVIEW

USE LEGAL TERMS

Fill in the blanks with the appropriate term.

abandoned property	executrix	possession
accession	fixtures	premises
administrator	grantee	profit
administratrix	grantor	property
alienate	holographic will	purchase
assignment of the lease	infringement	quitclaim deed
bailee	inter vivos	real property
bailment	intestate	rent
bailor	joint tenant	royalty
bill of lading	landlord	severalty
business invitees	leasehold	subletting
causa mortis	lessee	tenancy at sufferance
codicil	lessor	tenancy at will
confusion	licensee	tenancy for years
consignment	lodger	tenant
constructive delivery	lost property	tenants by the entireties
constructive eviction	mislaid property	tenants in common
deed	mortgage	testate
design patent	mortgagee	testator
donee	mortgagor	testatrix
donor	noncupative will	title
easement	ownership	trade fixtures
eminent domain	partition	trespasser
escheat	patent	use
eviction	periodic tenancy	warranty deed
executor	personal property	will

1. A creditor who receives the right to have property taken as security sold to satisfy a debt is known as a(n) ___?___ .
2. A co-holder of a transferable ownership right to a share of the subject property is a(n) ___?___ .
3. The division of the property of an ownership tenancy or the division of the value received for it is termed ___?___ .
4. Rights and interests in things are known at law as ___?___ .
5. The right of governments to take land for public use is called ___?___ .

6. Rights and interests in land, buildings, and fixtures are known collectively as ____?____.

7. Compensation paid for the use of intellectual property is known as a(n) ____?____.

8. A(n) ____?____ gift is one given in anticipation of death.

9. ____?____ is a term applied to someone who rents either personal or real property to another.

10. ____?____ is a term applied to someone who rents real property to another.

11. A tenancy involving a holdover tenant who has the permission to remain is known as a(n) ____?____.

12. The landlord's failure to provide heat in the winter can be a reason for a tenant to ____?____ the leasehold.

TEST YOUR READING

13. Define property.
14. Name five rights and interests we have in things.
15. Name six ways a person can acquire personal property.
16. Name five ways a person can acquire real property.
17. State the difference between lost and mislaid property.
18. Name four requirements of a valid will.
19. What are the types of bailments? What level of care is required in each?
20. What are the elements of a completed gift?
21. Name and explain the four types of tenancies in real property.

THINK CRITICALLY ABOUT EVIDENCE

22. Given the quickly diminishing resources of our planet and the skyrocketing population, is it wise of us to adhere to a concept of property that says everything can be exclusively owned and controlled by one person or a few persons?

23. Are people really nothing more than property? Ask yourself what rights and interests other people have in you. Who has the equivalent of title, possession, use, and alienation in you and under what circumstances? When does your body itself become property? (*Hint*: Consider blood and tissue donations, parental rights over children, life-support systems, professional athletes, etc.)

24. Bartholomew Wentworth III of Sandcranial, California, buys two high-quality cooking stove and oven combinations. One he builds into the wall of the townhouse he is renting; the other he bolts to the floor and wall of his restaurant, which is located in space rented from the Sandcranial Mall. Who now owns each stove and oven combination? What legal terms and doctrines are applicable to this question?

25. Which of the following is not a bailment?
    a. Your neighbor lends you a cup of sugar.
    b. Your mother has you hold her purse while she tries on some clothing.
    c. You lease a yacht for a round-the-world cruise.
    d. You find $20 on a football field after the game.

26. Paula borrows John Henry's gasoline-powered chain saw to cut firewood for the fireplace of her lake cabin. John Henry lets her use the chain saw for free. However, he has just finished cutting with it and the chain is loose. When Paula fires it up, the chain slips off and slashes her arm. Three stitches and a tetanus shot are needed. The total expense is over $250. Who is ultimately responsible for the bill?

27. Because of John Henry's generosity in letting her borrow the chain saw, Paula decides not to pursue the issue. Instead, she waits a day, then borrows a pickup from her neighbor, Beau Lombard. She drives into the nearby national forest, where she has a permit to cut pine trees. While she is cutting, two things happen. First, she forgets to replace the oil cooling the blade and engine of the chain saw. As a result, the chain saw overheats, ruining its motor. Second, a strong wind blows a tree trunk over the cab of Beau's pickup, doing severe damage. Who is liable for the harm in each situation?

28. Paula still needs to bring in the firewood she has cut. To do so, she borrows an all-terrain vehicle (ATV) from another friend, explicitly for that job. This time her mission is a success. After unloading the firewood, however, she uses the ATV on a night fishing trip near the waterfall on the other side of the lake. Regretfully, during the night, the ATV is stolen even though Paula has hidden it and removed its key. The ATV is never recovered. Who is responsible for the loss?

29. Which of the following are business invitees, licensees, and trespassers? What duty do you owe to each of these persons?
    a. A young boy cutting across your vacant lot without your knowledge on his way home from school.
    b. A pizza deliverer bringing your anchovy and peanut butter deluxe pizza to the door of your house.
    c. A hunter on your land without permission.
    d. A utility company employee checking the electric meter on the side of your house.
    e. A customer of your restaurant parking in your parking lot.
    f. A person invited to your spouse's Tupperware party in your house.

30. Flaire Cambell majored in engineering at Central State University. During her last year of school, she leased an apartment from Lagree. Her lease was a month-to-month periodic tenancy. Flaire moved out of her apartment on May 31, the day before her graduation. She mailed notice of her termination to Lagree immediately after the graduation ceremonies. Her rent was $325 per month. Under common law rules, how much money does she owe Lagree for unpaid rent?

31. You invite your apartment mate's parents to visit for a surprise birthday party for their child. Unfortunately, the father is injured when he falls after his foot catches in the ragged rug that covers the outside stairwell. Who is liable? Who would have been liable if he had slipped on a throw rug you had on the apartment's hardwood floor?

32. It is the middle of a cold January in Yukon City, Montana. The average daytime high since the beginning of the new year has been just a little over freezing. You return home from work to find that you can see your breath inside your apartment. You check to see whether you've left a window open, then realize that the heat is off. You call the landlord and find that the old fuel oil furnace has broken down. She intends to replace it with a natural gas furnace, but you will be without heat for several weeks. She therefore advises you to buy several electric floor heaters, but will not reimburse you for them or for the increased electric bill they will generate. Your budget is extremely tight. What should you do?

REAL-WORLD CASE

Draper and Kramer, Inc. v. Baskin-Robbins, Inc.

690 Federal Supplement 728

Test your knowledge of leaseholds on a "hard pact."

Baskin-Robbins, Inc. (BR), entered into a lease of commercial property in a mall in Decatur, Illinois. The lease contained the following term:

> Lessor hereby agrees and covenants that no other premises of the building or group of the buildings, owned or controlled by Lessor, of which the leased premises are a part, shall be leased or used for the business of selling hand packed ice cream, ice cream cones, or soda fountain items . . . [excepting] co-tenants that have executed leases prior to February 28, 1968 unviolated.

Several years after Baskin-Robbins entered into this lease, the mall entered into a lease with TCBY Yogurt for the operation of a TCBY franchise at the mall. When BR learned of the new lease, it contacted the lessor. BR maintained that as TCBY would sell soda fountain items, TCBY would represent a violation of the exclusive use clause of BR's lease. Although the lessor conceded TCBY would sell soda fountain items, it contended that as these items would not be made with ice cream, BR's lease would remain unviolated. BR countered by stating that, whether made with ice cream or yogurt, sodas, sundaes, and cones are still soda fountain items. Eventually, the parties sought the forum of a federal court to resolve the dispute.

Think Critically

1. Do you feel that our society is well served by allowing such issues to be resolved in our federal court system? Can you think of a better forum?
2. Should "exclusive use" clauses be enforced? What do consumers gain if such clauses are broadly enforced (in this case, if TCBY is precluded from serving soda fountain items)? What do consumers gain if exclusive use clauses are narrowly construed (in this case, if the exclusive use clause merely means that no other store can sell ice cream-based soda fountain items)?
3. How would you decide the issue? How do you think the court resolved it?

UNIT 8

Decreasing the Risks of Life

CHAPTERS

CHAPTER 31

What Can Be Insured?

GOALS

- ◆ Identify the risks that can be covered by insurance
- ◆ Understand the necessity for insurable interests
- ◆ Know the requirements of a valid insurance contract

What Is Insurance, and Why Is It Necessary?

Consider the risks of life. Falling down stairs, inhaling the air near a broken gas line, looking away from the windshield while driving, a match in a small child's hands—all these scenarios can lead to calamitous, life-altering consequences. Such disastrous events can happen to anyone. You can prepare for them by saving large amounts of cash, but usually this requires severe self-deprivation. Thus, it is very difficult to prepare for disastrous events individually.

Collective action however, can make preparing for possible disasters manageable. Many people, each contributing small amounts, can form a resource pool big enough to **indemnify** (compensate for loss or damage) those individuals who suffer from harm that occurs randomly. Whether the government, a corporation, or private individuals form the resource pool, the result can be the same.

The primary device used to transfer the risk of loss from specific perils from one person to another is called **insurance**. Insurance comes in many forms and types. Typically however, it involves a contract by which an **insurer** (the party who agrees to accept the risk of loss) commits to covering an **insured** (the party who transfers the risk of loss to the insurer) against a certain peril or risk for an amount of consideration called a **premium**. The written insurance contract is called a **policy**. Such a policy usually states a maximum amount that can be paid if the harm insured against actually occurs. This maximum is referred to as the **face value** of the policy. Note that depending on the type of risk covered by the policy, the compensation for the loss may be paid to a third party, called the **beneficiary**, rather than the insured. This is the case when the loss covered is the life of the insured.

Once an insurance contract has been made, the courts treat it as a personal bargain between the insurer and the insured. As a consequence, the insured cannot assign her or his rights under the policy to a third party without the insurer's permission.

Hypothetical Case

Joe ("Crash") Dumi bought a used Corvette from his cousin. Because Crash had a poor rating with the insurance industry as a result of past problems, he offered his cousin $750 for the six months of automobile insurance coverage left on his cousin's policy on the car. The cousin took the money and wrote out a statement assigning the policy rights to Crash. When Crash lived up to his name and totaled the Corvette a little over two weeks later, he tried to get the insurance company to cover the loss under his cousin's policy. The insurance company refused to do so. Crash's attorney then pointed out to him that insurance policies are not assignable by the insureds. Crash sued his cousin for his $750 payment for the policy and recovered it, but he lost the $17,000 he had in the Corvette.

Insurable Interests

In a similar vein, to prevent insurance from being viewed as another form of wagering, insurers determine who is eligible to acquire insurance on property or persons by requiring that the insured have an insurable interest in the subject matter of the policy. Having an **insurable interest** means that the insured would suffer some pecuniary (monetary) loss if the insured property were damaged or destroyed or the insured individual died. As mentioned, if such an interest were not required, I could, for example, take out fire insurance on your home. Why would I do that? Well, perhaps because I know that the wiring is bad and will probably start a fire soon. Perhaps because my brother-in-law installed the wiring, and judging from the job he did in my home, I am sure that a fire is imminent in yours. Or, perhaps because I intend to torch your home one of these nights. Whatever the motive, such "wagering" through insurance contracts would be highly detrimental to our society.

Insurable Interests in Property   To collect on a policy covering property, the insured must not only have an insurable interest in the property at the time the policy is taken out, but must also have such an interest at the time of loss. Also, note that it is possible for many persons to have an insurable interest in the same property.

Hypothetical Case

Walston Baskit bought a brand-new thresher. Its air-conditioned cab had tinted windows and a built-in CD player and AM/FM stereo. The Pennsboro National Savings Bank held a security interest in the thresher because it had lent Baskit $87,500 to purchase the machine. Kleen Kut Harvesters, Inc., leased the thresher from Baskit for the month of August so it could harvest its Kansas crop. Baskit, Pennsboro National, and Kleen Kut all have insurable interests in the thresher, and all of them could purchase insurance on it. If it were destroyed, all three could collect for their individual losses.

Insurable Interests in Life   Unlike property insurance, an insurable interest in life need be shown only when the insurance is taken out—not at the time of loss. As with property insurance however, many persons can have an insurable interest in one individual's life. Generally, each of us has such an interest in our own life. If we are married, our spouses have an interest in our lives. If we have creditors, each of them has an interest in our lives. Our business partners or employers have such interests as well, if they can show they will suffer financial loss upon our deaths. However, the law typically disallows children's claims that they have an insurable interest in an elderly parent or sibling.

Basic Types of Insurance

Four basic types of insurance stand out from all the rest. These include social insurance, life insurance, property and casualty insurance, and automobile insurance.

Social Insurance

Many of the industrialized nations around the world, including the U.S., rely on governmentally funded insurance plans to protect citizens against the risks of advanced age, unemployment, disability, poverty, and catastrophic medical expenses. Chapter 32 discusses eligibility for and coverage of U.S. social insurance programs.

Life Insurance

Chapter 32 also deals with available life insurance coverages, ways to increase coverage for accidental death, and how much can be collected on life insurance policies, by whom and when.

Property and Casualty Insurance

This category encompasses a broad range of coverages. From fire insurance policies that can be augmented to include storm and earthquake damage, to theft and liability policies that provide protection against the frailties of people, property and casualty insurance fills tremendous needs. It is covered in detail in Chapter 33.

Automobile Insurance

A complex form of property and casualty insurance crucial to our mobile society, automobile insurance requires a detailed discussion. Comprehensive, collision, uninsured motorist, and underinsured motorist coverages and many more are explained in Chapter 33.

Other Forms of Insurance

A less common form of insurance, **fidelity insurance** provides protection against forms of dishonesty and laxness in fulfilling obligations owed to the insured.

Hypothetical Case

Although the Mutual Farmer's Association of Pennsboro trusted its employees completely, Bea Kanton, the manager, kept a $100,000 fidelity insurance policy in force. One day in late summer, a farmer came into her office to question some erasures on his grain storage ticket. Because Emma Beason, the secretary-treasurer of the company, was on vacation, Bea had to straighten out the matter herself. When she found the copy of the ticket in the company's files, it became obvious that Emma had altered the amounts on the ticket. Bea spent the next weekend going through the files and discovered that Emma had embezzled over $40,000 from the company in the last two years alone. Although the fidelity insurance would cover the losses, when Emma returned from vacation, she found herself confronting criminal charges.

Another form of insurance of some importance is **marine insurance**. Its coverage indemnifies for losses resulting from the perils of water transport. Both ships and cargoes are covered by marine insurance.

In addition to the types of insurance already mentioned, as many types of insurance are available as insurers see fit to write. The famous insurer of last resort, Lloyd's of London, specializes in **underwriting** (insuring) against all manner of risks, from loss of dexterity in a pianist's fingers to the effects of war. Even so, one type of insurance is not available, namely insurance on the profitability of a business. Insurance companies will not directly insure a person against his or her failure to conduct a commercial operation properly. To do so would rob the business-person of the fear of failure that promotes success. However, for a list of insurance types tailored to other business risks, see Figure 31-1.

FIGURE 31-1   Insurable Business Risks

Risk	Insurance
Disruption of daily business events resulting from fire or other peril	Business interruption insurance
Professional negligence	Malpractice insurance
Defective products	Product liability insurance
Employee injury liability	Workers' compensation insurance
Employee dishonesty	Fidelity insurance

Insurance Contracts

The principles of contract law apply to the agreements embodied in an insurance policy. Some special rules also apply as well, but before we discuss them, we need to take a closer look at the parties offering indemnification, i.e., the insurers.

Insurance has always been a lucrative and stable industry. It is well regulated in the U.S. by state insurance commissions. Insurance companies and associations are given publicly available letter rankings after intensive audits of their cash, management, and the policies they have written. The insurance industry thrives on the large-scale predictability of individually random events ranging from deaths to car crashes. Because of the reliability of statistical projections (referred to as the *law of large numbers*), profitability is reduced to a question of mathematics and marketing. Consequently, insurance companies have become some of the largest of our financial reservoirs.

Types of Insurers

Several types of organizations can sell insurance in today's marketplace. The government, at times in cooperation with the insurance industry, offers types of insurance that would probably be unavailable commercially. These include workers' compensation insurance and retirement insurance. Traditional insurance products, such as life and fire insurance are typically offered by stock and mutual insurance companies. Some fraternal organizations also offer such coverages to their members.

A **stock insurance company** has been capitalized by investors who expect a return on their money from its profits. A **mutual insurance company** is capitalized through the premiums of the insureds. These premiums are used to meet the administrative expenses of the firm and to form a pool of money from which the resources for indemnifying the policyholders are to be taken. If a mutual insurance company shows a profit, it can be paid back to the policyholders in the form of a nontaxable refund of their premiums.

Applicability of Contract Law

With the exception of insurance contracts involving the government, which can legislate its own rules, the law of contracts governs the formation, issuance, and application of insurance contracts. All the essential elements that we studied earlier must be present for an insurance contract to be valid and enforceable. However, there are some rules and terminology that apply specifically to insurance law.

Agreement and Genuine Assent   The agreement between the parties that calls on one party to indemnify the other is typically formed as a result of a detailed examination of both the policy terms and the applicant's level of exposure to risk. The insurance companies, through their agents and their advertising of coverages against various perils, widely extend an *invitation to negotiate* to potential insureds. The wise person considering the purchase of insurance does a great deal of informed comparison shopping of the various policies. Comparison shopping is a near necessity because an insurance agent seldom, if ever, has the authority to alter the terms of a policy to tailor it to an individual situation. Instead, the terms are placed before would-be insureds on a take-it-or-leave-it basis. Taking time to understand the extent of the coverages and the premium structure may save the insured tens of thousands of dollars. Once the would-be insured finds a suitable policy, she or he must apply for coverage. In other words, the would-be insured becomes the offeror with her or his submission of the application for coverage. The insurer can either accept or reject the offer based on the facts presented by the applicant and, at times, on its own investigation.

Hypothetical Case

Joanna Sturgeon married Bill Prentiss. She was 35 and an executive making in the high five figures with a leading stock brokerage firm. He was 23, just out of graduate school, and an unpublished writer. He stayed home, took care of Joanna's three children by her first marriage, and wrote. Worried about her family's livelihood if she should die, Joanna took out a $5 million life insurance policy. When she applied for the coverage, she answered a detailed set of questions about her health and her ancestral family's medical problems. Before the insurance company would issue the policy, it required Joanna to undergo a series of medical tests, including one for AIDS. Once its investigation was successfully concluded, it accepted Joanna's offer, cashed her premium check, and covered her for the $5 million.

Statements that the applicant makes in her or his offer, such as information regarding the incidence of cancer in Joanna's family or the presence of safety devices in an automobile or home, may prove extremely significant to the validity of the policy. If such statements are not included in the policy, they are termed **representations**. Statements in the application that are made a part of the issued policy are known as **warranties**. Even if not a part of the policy, an applicant's false representation of a **material fact** (one that, if known, would have caused the insurer not to issue the policy) renders the policy voidable by the insurer. Should it be shown that a warranty is false, whether it is material to the issuance and/or believed to be the truth by the applicant or not, the policy is voidable by the insurer. The same result holds should a material fact not be disclosed when the insurer requests it (this is referred to as **concealment**).

Although the insurance industry normally follows a deliberate and careful approach to risk assumption, it responds quickly to certain insurance needs. In the property and casualty area, for example, agents can enter into temporary oral agreements to extend coverage to those with immediate insurance needs. Let us say that you have just purchased your second Rolls-Royce and that you do not want to drive it until it's insured. You can call your agent from the dealership and secure temporary insurance merely through the agent's say-so over the phone. The policy goes into effect at once, but the agent confirms the transaction by issuing a written voucher of insurance called a **binder**. This satisfies the legal requirement for a writing. As you might expect, the insurance company reserves the right to cancel any such agreement upon review. However, you are covered for any loss insured against until the cancellation occurs.

Consideration   Mutual consideration in the forms of a premium and the indemnification it buys binds both parties to the insurance contract. Although certain large insurance premiums can be paid in installments, payment is usually due in advance of the coverage period. This is especially true for automobile insurance. Also, certain eventualities can compel the return of premiums or the reduction of the coverage bargained for. For example, when it is discovered that a person lied about his or her age in purchasing life insurance coverage, the policy's payoff is typically reduced to the amount of insurance that the premium would have purchased had the true age of the insured been known.

Form of the Contract   Insurance policies must be in writing. Insurance laws uniformly require this. State insurance statutes also typically require that significant terms not be hidden in lengthy paragraphs of verbiage or at least that they be highlighted by color or large print. Failure to follow such statutory requirements usually results in the voiding of the hidden terms by the courts. Another rule working in favor of the insured is that any ambiguity in the policy is construed against the drafting party.

Hypothetical Case

Edith Walker's life came to a tragic ending one summer night as she staggered on her way home and fell into the path of an oncoming car. She was highly inebriated according to a test of her blood alcohol content. The Pennsboro Life Insurance Company refused to pay on its $100,000 policy on Ms. Walker because the policy specifically excluded payment when "death occurs as a result of alcoholism." The local chapter of Alcoholics Anonymous (AA), ironically named as the beneficiary of Ms. Walker's policy, brought suit. The AA claimed that one incident involving drunkenness did not constitute the disease of alcoholism. The court agreed and construed the ambiguous term against its maker. As a consequence, Pennsboro Life had to pay AA the $100,000 face value.

Capacity of the Parties   As discussed in principle in Chapter 9, the insane, habitual drunkards, and minors are held to be without capacity to enter into insurance contracts. Minors in particular are able to avoid most such contracts with the notable exception of life insurance.

Termination of the Insurance Contract

In general, insurance policies end either through expiration of the coverage period or by action of a party or parties to the contract. For example, in the case of property or casualty insurance, even a substantial payout for damage does not end the policy. Homeowner's or automobile insurance policies cover the subject properties until they are canceled or the coverage period expires.

Hypothetical Case

Travis Lear's recreational vehicle was vandalized during a stopover in a desert campground. The insurance company paid $7,230 to have it put back into shape. Leaving the repair garage, Travis ran over a high curb and bent the frame. The insurance policy was still in force, so the insurance company paid another $4,800 to correct the problem. Lear's insurance remained in effect even after the second incident as neither party sought to cancel it and the coverage period had not expired.

Cancellation, unlike expiration, usually requires notice. The length of time required depends on the type of insurance and varies widely. Should the coverage period paid for extend beyond the effective date of cancellation, the insured generally has the right to a refund.

Technology Insights

Surveillance Cameras and Workers' Compensation Insurance

Feeds from surveillance cameras sometimes pay off with information on employees rather than shoplifters. A recent case involved an employee of a large retailer who had fallen down steps after purchasing some items from the employer. The videotape revealed the employee's purpose for being on the stairs. It was extremely suasive in causing the Workers' Compensation Commission to rule that the employee was not providing employment services at the time of the accident.

Think Critically Do workers have to give permission for such taping? Compare this with the necessity of workers agreeing to lie detector or drug testing as a condition of employment. Are there privacy issues involved in such surveillance? What would be your answer if the surveillance cameras were in the employee break or wash room? What limits on the use of the resulting tapes would you as an employee bargain for?

CHAPTER REVIEW

USE LEGAL TERMS

Fill in the blanks with the appropriate term.

beneficiary	insurance	premium
binder	insured	representations
concealment	insurer	stock insurance company
face value	marine insurance	underwriting
fidelity insurance	material fact	warranties
indemnify	mutual insurance company	
insurable interest	policy	

1. ___?___ would cover losses incurred when a trusted employee embezzled money from my business.
2. The consideration you pay for insurance is called the ___?___.
3. The party to whom the insurer will pay upon the covered loss is termed the ___?___.
4. ___?___ is another term for the act of insuring.
5. ___?___ are statements of facts, that you make in applying for insurance that become part of the written insurance contract.
6. The failure to disclose a material fact to a potential insurer is termed ___?___.
7. The written insurance contract is termed a(n) ___?___.

TEST YOUR READING

8. What "law" allows insurance companies to remain profitable?
9. Explain the concept of insurable interest and why it is necessary to insurance contracts.
10. When is an insurable interest required for property insurance? For life insurance?
11. Name five different types of insurance and their areas of coverage.
12. What is the difference between a stock insurance company and a mutual insurance company?
13. What is the difference between a misrepresentation and a warranty in insurance law?
14. In what ways can an insurance policy be terminated?

THINK CRITICALLY ABOUT EVIDENCE

15. While Angela and John were married, Angela took out a $500,000 life insurance policy on John. Even after their bitterly contested divorce, she kept the policy in effect with regular premium payments. Six months after their divorce, John died a violent death under suspicious circumstances. However, nothing could be proven against Angela. Will she collect on the policy? Why or why not?

16. During their marriage, Angela and John owned a large yacht on which Angela had also taken out insurance. As a part of the divorce settlement, John received the full ownership of the yacht. As with the life insurance, Angela kept up the payments on the yacht insurance even after the divorce. In fact, John died in an explosion that destroyed the yacht. Will Angela collect on the yacht's insurance policy? Why or why not?

17. Which of the following are generally not insurable risks?
    a. Atie Ate, the renowned concert pianist, wants to insure her fingers for $1 million against any accident or disease that would prevent her from performing during the next five years.
    b. Jim Hofta wants to take out life insurance on himself that would pay the face amount of the policy to him if he lives to the age of 65.
    c. Sandy Andreas wants to take out earthquake insurance on the parking lot of her business.
    d. Sandy Andreas wants to take out life insurance on Kay Junn, the chef she has just employed to cook in her new restaurant.
    e. Sandy Andreas wants to take out insurance to cover the risk that she will not make enough money in the restaurant to cover the mortgage payments on the property.

18. In the final estimate, which policy should cost less to cover identical risks— the policy of a mutual insurance company or the policy of a stock insurance company? Why?

19. Cindy Swanson, the famous child star, was beset by financial problems as she neared 18 years of age. Realizing that she had paid thousands of dollars to her insurance companies over the last decade, she decided, as a minor, to avoid the policies and demand the return of the premiums. When she totaled it up, she found that she had paid in $32,000 for homeowner's insurance on her Beverly Hills townhouse and $45,000 for her life insurance coverage. How much is she likely to get back? Why?

REAL-WORLD CASE

Lakin v. Postal Life and Casualty Insurance Company
316 S.W.2d 542

Test your skill in discerning when it is insurance and when it is just gambling.

Lakin took out a life insurance policy on Hankinson, who Lakin claimed was his business partner, and was listed as the beneficiary of the policy. Lakin faithfully paid the policy premiums. When Hankinson died and the insurance company refused to pay, Lakin brought suit for the amount due under the policy's terms. The evidence revealed that Hankinson had not paid in any capital or contributed any expertise to the alleged partnership. In addition, Hankinson was not permitted to issue partnership checks or to hire or fire employees. Finally, upon Hankinson's death, no settlement of his alleged partnership share had been made.

Think Critically

1. Upon what basis should the court make its decision?
2. What, if anything, might Lakin receive from the insurance company?

CHAPTER 32

Life and Social Insurance

GOALS

- ◆ Identify the life insurance policy best for you
- ◆ Understand the terms in a life insurance contract
- ◆ Understand the need for social insurance

Life and Social Insurance Protections

We begin our in-depth look at insurance with the types that protect against the gravest risks. These risks are those associated with the loss of life, limb, and vitality. Although society gives lip service to the idea that every life is priceless, in actuality, we each have a dollar value. This value is significant to the people who depend on us in some way. To these people, be they family, employers, or members of a public we serve, the loss of our productivity and our accumulation of assets would be significant. Without us, our spouses and children might not be well supported. Without us, our employers might not be able to produce or sell as good a product. Without us, the services offered by our group might be less adequate. Insurance, through its pooling of monetary resources and its payout of these resources as needed to insured people, helps alleviate losses of these kinds.

Life insurance, for example, provides a contractual means for transferring to an insurer the potential losses resulting from the death of an individual. The insurer will pay a prearranged amount of money to a named beneficiary that will help offset the practical result of the loss.

Social insurance provides similar protection against forced retirement, disability, severe illness, unemployment, and other risks. Without such protection, members of our society would be far less likely to take the financial and personal risks that are the lifeblood of progress. However, because of the enormity of the potential losses, only the government has been able to bring together the pool of resources necessary to offer social insurance protection to the general public.

Terms in a Typical Life Insurance Policy

A large number of insurance companies offer policies to cover the most serious of all risks, the loss of life. The life insurance contract is based on the representations and warranties made by the insured person and on the tests and investigations performed by the insurance company. The insurance company evaluates this information to determine the premium it demands for the face value of the life insurance policy.

Exclusions

That evaluation is also reflected in the **exclusions**, or terms eliminating coverage in certain situations, found in life insurance policies. "War clauses," for example, exclude coverage when the insured person is involved in armed hostilities. Other possible exclusions include:

- Death of the insured resulting from piloting or being a passenger on an airplane
- The execution by act of law of the person whose life is insured
- Suicide of the insured
- Murder of the insured by the beneficiary (but if the beneficiary is involved criminally in the insured person's death in some other way, the insurance company must pay)

Most policies set a time limit on the suicide exclusion. Usually, the insurer must pay if the suicide occurs more than two years after the policy is issued. If the suicide occurs before this time, the insurer has to return the premiums paid only.

Hypothetical Case

Benjamin Fishery was doing 75 miles per hour when his car left the road, burst through a hedge, and slammed into a tree in the yard of Peter and Mary Martin. When the Martins ran out to help, Ben was climbing out of the car with hardly a scratch on him (the air bag on the driver's side having saved his life). Unfortunately, Ben's wife was dead on arrival at a local hospital. The state highway patrol arrived at the scene of the accident almost immediately and arrested Ben for driving while intoxicated. His blood alcohol content was almost double the legal limit. He was later convicted of both the DUI charge and manslaughter, for which he received a total of six months in jail. Nonetheless, Ben recovered $250,000 under his wife's life insurance policy. He was involved in a criminal way in her death, but he did not murder her.

Various other exclusions exist. These are generally tailored to hazardous occupations that insured people reveal in preissuance questionnaires. However, fraud or misrepresentation in supplying answers to these questionnaires may result in the mistaken issuance of policies. As mentioned in Chapter 31, the insurance company has the right to void a policy based on erroneous material representations or warranties by the applicant. Even so, most policies contain an **incontestable clause** that puts a time limit on the exercise of this right, usually one or two years from the policy issue date. Afterward, if the insurance company has not voided coverage, the policy is in full force. This occurs regardless of any misrepresentation, fraud, or concealment by the applicant unless it is discovered that the applicant has lied about her or his age. In that case, the face amount of the policy is adjusted to the face amount that the premium would have bought had the correct age been known.

 # Hypothetical Case

> When Connie Stinson took out a life insurance policy from a Pennsboro insurance company, she concealed from the company that she had had cancer, was a heavy smoker, had been treated several times for alcoholism, and was a licensed pilot. Two years and one day after the policy was issued, Connie committed suicide by crashing her twin-engine plane into a mountainside. Because of the incontestable clause, the insurance company could not void the policy on the ground of suicide and had to pay the face value of the policy, $1 million, to her estate.

Days of Grace

Another term of considerable importance to an insured person relates to the **days of grace**. This is the period, usually a month, during which an overdue life insurance premium can be paid to keep the policy in force. The payment can be rendered even if the insured has died in the interim. If the payment is not rendered, the policy **lapses** (terminates).

Double Indemnity and Disability Coverages

In today's information-rich world, life expectancy tables, often developed and maintained by insurance companies, affect our expectations of personal longevity. Such expectations are often a major factor in determining the amount of insurance coverage we buy on our lives. Obviously, if we live a long life, our employment income is likely to be sufficient to put our children through college and send them out on their own; to put away savings for retirement; and so on. After all that has been achieved, the need for payouts to our survivors upon our deaths is minimal.

Many people therefore insure themselves with that final, minimal need—usually to cover burial costs—in mind. But what if an accident prevents us from living out our natural span of days? How can our families replace the income lost for this reason? A partial solution to this problem is coverage that can be placed in a life insurance policy for a relatively small increase in the premium. This coverage is referred to as **double indemnity**. It causes the insurer to pay twice (or three or four times for triple or quadruple indemnity, respectively) the face amount if the insured person dies accidentally.

Disability coverage protects against a devastating consequence of accident and disease, namely a permanent inability to work. Innovative life insurance policies provide for the payment of a regular income supplement if a physician certifies that the insured person is unable to work. Earlier policies provided for the cancellation of further premium payments if the insured person could no longer work because of an accident or disease.

Insurance of Insurability

A common term in a life insurance policy obtained by paying slightly higher premiums is **insurance of insurability**. Such coverage allows the insured person to purchase new amounts of life insurance coverage or to continue current amounts without being required to pass a physical examination or other test.

New Forms of Coverage

Innovative coverages are constantly being developed and offered to potential insureds. Life insurance that pays if the insured person is diagnosed with a terminal illness, not when he or she dies from that illness, is one of these newer coverages. Also, as discussed in the next section, various new policies are frequently developed to respond to changes in parallel markets for investment funds. One way or another, the insurance industry tries to remain competitive and to fill the needs of a changing population.

Types of Life Insurance Policies

Whatever the changes in its name or its packaging, there is still one basic type of life insurance. Simply put, it is based on a contract whereby a premium is paid for a period of coverage at a certain dollar level of indemnification. At the end of the period of coverage contracted for or on the payout of the face value because of the death of the insured person, the contract comes to an end. Such pure life insurance, without any frills involving savings plans or other marketing gimmicks, is called **term insurance**.

Hypothetical Case

Bixier bought a $50,000 term life insurance policy on herself through the university where she taught. She paid $35 per month during the academic year for the coverage. At the end of the year the coverage ended. As the $35 per month had gone strictly for the purchase of insurance, she had not built up any savings during the year. She noted that her premium would rise to $37 per month if she took out the same amount of insurance next year because she was older, and the statistical probability of her death had increased accordingly.

Term Insurance

Term insurance policies can be set up with one or two basic forms of payment. In return for a constant face value, **level term** life insurance policies require the payment of a set premium throughout the period that the insurance is in force. In return for a steadily decreasing face value, **decreasing term** policies' premium is smaller than the level term premium for the initial face amount. However, like the level term, the premium is constant throughout the time that the insurance is in force. This cheaper form of insurance often comes closer than level term insurance to satisfying the requirements of insured people whose need for a large face value declines as they grow older, as their mortgages are paid off, and as their children grow up and become independent.

Term insurance's simple function means it is common in our everyday lives. For example, the **travel insurance** policy bought to indemnify for the loss of the insured's life during a trip is term insurance. So too is the **group insurance** policy offered to each member of a group with some common characteristic, such as all the employees of a state university or all dentists, all veterans, or all senior citizens. Finally, the **credit insurance** policies that pay off lenders if the debtors die are also term insurance.

Fund Accumulation Policies

Many types of policies other than term insurance flood the life insurance market, as well. Almost all of these policies have a built-in savings function made possible by the regularity with which the insured person pays premiums to keep the insurance coverage in force. These payments (inaccurately called premiums) are split by the insured company into two amounts. One (the true premium) pays for the insurance, and the other goes into an accumulation fund.

A major type of policy with accumulation funds is the whole life policy. **Whole life** insurance policies pay a moderate interest rate on the accumulated funds. The interest and principal in the fund account are referred to as the **cash value** of the policy. Insured people may borrow against this cash value, but absurd as it may seem, they must pay interest, usually at a lower than market rate, on this lent amount of their own money. When the insured person dies, the insurance company must pay the beneficiary the policy's face amount plus the cash value less any loan amount outstanding.

FIGURE 32-1 Common Types of Life Insurance Policies

Term	Fund Accumulation
Level term	Whole life
Decreasing term	Endowment
Travel insurance	
Group insurance	
Credit insurance	

Endowment life insurance is another type of fund accumulation policy. Under its terms, the insured person typically pays a very high premium for insurance coverage and the right to receive the face value, if still alive, at retirement or the end of a certain period. This type of policy makes sense to individuals who may need a large lump sum of money at a particular time in their lives, to buy a retirement home in the Sun Belt, for example.

The interest paid by insurance companies on the funds accumulated in these types of policies is typically significantly lower than that available through other investment means. Consequently, financial advisers regularly cite the advantages of buying term insurance and investing the difference. Nonetheless, the forced regularity of the savings causes many to avail themselves of these types of insurance.

Newer types of fund accumulation policies have recently been developed. Some allow the insured person to control how the accumulated funds are invested; others guarantee minimum returns on the funds. Regardless, fund accumulation policies remain popular among insured people and lucrative for insurers.

Beneficiaries under the Various Policy Types

As discussed in Chapter 31, the beneficiary is the individual named to receive the payout from an insurance policy. With the possible exception of the insured person with an endowment policy who lives long enough to receive its benefits, all life insurance policies pay off to someone other than the person whose life is insured. The beneficiary may be a family member, a business associate, or an estate. As long as the required insurable interest can be shown by the person taking out the insurance, that person can name any potential recipient for the funds. Two or more beneficiaries can be named to receive equal shares. On the other hand, primary and contingent beneficiaries may be preferred. A **primary beneficiary** (the person named first in priority to receive the whole policy payout) must still be alive when the person whose life is insured dies. The **contingent beneficiary** is the person named to receive the policy payout should the primary beneficiary die first.

One way or another, it is the prerogative of the person who has taken out the policy to name the beneficiary and to change the beneficiary by notifying the insurance company in writing.

Social Insurance

The federal Social Security Act of 1935 as amended provides most of the social insurance we are familiar with in the U.S. Retirement, Survivors, Disability, and Health Insurance (labeled RSDHI by the Social Security Administration) coverages are available to those eligible. (See Figure 32-2 for an acronym that helps in remembering the social insurance coverages available.) Also provided is unemployment coverage, which the states in the U.S. administer in compliance with the Federal Unemployment Tax Act (FUTA).

FIGURE 32-2 Types of Social Insurance

S urvivors

O ld age

D isability

U nemployment

H ealth

Eligibility for Social Insurance Benefits

To be fully insured and therefore, eligible to receive RSDHI benefits, people must have recorded proof with the Social Security Administration that they worked at least a set number of **quarters** (three-month periods in which the person earned at least approximately $830). Up to four quarters can be awarded in each year. Retirement benefit eligibility requires 40 quarters of credit.

Disability and Survivors benefit eligibility is determined on a sliding scale requiring from as few as 6 quarters at age 24 to as many as 40 quarters at age 62. To be eligible to receive its benefits, **Medicare** (a program that helps eligible individuals pay for hospital, physician, and other health care expenses) only requires that the recipient be 65 or older or be eligible for disability payments for 24 months under RSDHI. Finally, although unemployment program eligibility varies somewhat from state to state, almost all states require that the recipient be totally out of work for a set period, be registered with the state, and be actively looking for employment, and ready, willing, and able to work if suitable work is found. For work to be "suitable," it must be within a reasonable distance from the worker's residence and, even though for lower pay, in a field in which the worker has experience or training.

Securing Benefits

Retirement Benefits   The steps that must be taken to secure benefits vary from program to program. Any eligible party 62 years of age or older may receive retirement benefits by simply applying for them. The full benefit amount however, is payable when the retirement benefits are requested at full retirement age (which may vary from 65 to 67 depending on the recipient's date of birth) and not before. The closer the person is to age 62 when the benefits are requested, the lower the amount of the monthly check. Note that until retirees are age 65, their retirement benefits are reduced if they make more than a set amount of outside income.

Survivors' Benefits   Survivors' benefits can be obtained by persons related to a deceased worker (who, to render the possible recipient eligible, must have had more than six quarters of coverage in the three years prior to her or his death) in the following ways:

- By being the worker's parent over 62 years of age and dependent on the worker for support
- By being the worker's surviving spouse and at least 60 years old (or at least 50 if disabled) or being of any age if also caring for a disabled child or any child under 16
- By being the worker's dependent child under age 18

Disability Benefits   Disability benefits are payable to fully insured individuals with an appropriate disability who are under 65 years of age and have worked 20 quarters within the 10 years preceding the disability.

Health Insurance Benefits   Under the Medicare program, health insurance benefits to cover hospital, physician, and other health care expenses are available to persons over 65. Such benefits are provided under the Medicaid program to persons under 65 who lack the financial ability to pay health care costs. If a person does not apply for Medicare within the three-month period before or after the insured's 65th birthday, a considerable delay in receiving benefits occurs. Medicaid requires only proof that the person is currently indigent. Medicaid currently pays health care expenses for more than 30 million individuals.

Unemployment Benefits   Finally, unemployment benefits are available to eligible parties upon filing. However, depending on the applicable state rules, these benefits may be reduced or denied if workers:

- Quit their jobs without just cause (unsafe working conditions, for example, is a just cause)
- Turn down or don't even try to find suitable work
- Are full-time students
- Lie about job skills
- Were fired because of criminal or other improper conduct
- Lost their jobs because of participation in a strike or other labor dispute
- Are receiving a pension or Social Security retirement benefits

The various forms of social insurance discussed in this chapter reflect the fact that we are all part of the same society and therefore, responsible to one another for one another. From the homeless to the residents of grand mansions, our differences from one another are not great enough to justify denying the needs of the former for the purpose of indulging the wants of the latter.

CHAPTER REVIEW

USE LEGAL TERMS

Fill in the blanks with the appropriate term.

cash value	exclusions	primary beneficiary
contingent beneficiary	group insurance	quarters
credit insurance	incontestable clause	social insurance
days of grace	insurance of insurability	term insurance
decreasing term	lapses	travel insurance
disability coverage	level term	whole life insurance
double indemnity	life insurance	
endowment	Medicare	

1. ____?____ is offered to a certain class of similarly situated individuals.
2. ____?____ eliminates coverage in certain situations, for example, the coverage of a life insurance policy if the policyholder dies during air travel.
3. Providing insurance that covers hospital, physician, and other health care costs, ____?____ is a program that has been set up under the Social Security Act.
4. A(n) ____?____ is a period in which a worker earned at least a certain amount of money. The accumulated number of these periods is used in determining eligibility for certain social insurance programs.
5. The ____?____ is the person named to receive the payout from a life insurance policy as long as she or he is alive at the time of the insured's death.
6. A(n) ____?____ insurance policy requires higher than usual premiums but pays out the face value if the person whose life is insured lives for a certain term or past a certain age.
7. The period during which paying a delinquent premium can keep a life insurance policy in force is called the ____?____.
8. A(n) ____?____ term in a life insurance policy requires that the insurer pay twice the face value upon the accidental death of the person whose life is insured.
9. A term in a life insurance policy that disallows the insurer from voiding the policy because of inaccurate statements made in the application is referred to as a(n) ____?____.
10. The accumulated funds under a whole life insurance policy that are payable along with the face value of the policy are referred to as the ____?____ of the policy.

TEST YOUR READING

11. Why does the government provide social insurance?
12. Why can't private companies provide social insurance?
13. Name five exclusions typically found in life insurance policies.
14. What is insurance of insurability?
15. Name three types of term insurance commonly available.
16. Why should a person pay interest on money borrowed against the cash value of a whole life policy?
17. When does a contingent beneficiary get paid?
18. Name five types of social insurance.

THINK CRITICALLY ABOUT EVIDENCE

19. Some people, notably extremely rich individuals and individuals without dependents, maintain that they do not need life insurance coverage. Evaluate the positions taken by such people. Are there other people who might make this claim?
20. Assume that Andrew Jackson Borden's life insurance policy contains all of the exclusions from coverage discussed in the chapter. Would the insurance company be allowed to avoid paying if he died in any of the following ways?
     a. He was hatcheted to death by his beneficiary, Lisbeth Andrews Borden.
     b. He died in combat in Eastern Europe.
     c. He died in an auto accident caused by his being intoxicated.
     d. He committed suicide barely a month after taking out the policy. (Would your answer change if the suicide occurred three years after he took out the policy? Why?)
21. On December 13, 20**, while returning home from a long sales trip, Blame Thomas died in an automobile accident. He was buried a few days later. Ten days after his death his wife, Olive, found that the last premium on his life insurance policy was due December 12 but had gone unpaid. The policy was for $250,000 with a triple indemnity clause. What other clause in the policy should Olive look for? If she finds that clause and places the policy back in force, how much should the insurer pay the beneficiary?
22. If you were going to take out a life insurance policy, which would you be more likely to use, term insurance or a fund accumulation policy? State your reasoning.

23. Which of the following facts prevent applicant Herb Hoover from receiving unemployment benefits?
    a. On his application he lied in claiming he was a musician by trade.
    b. He was dismissed from his previous job as a result of an economic downturn.
    c. He was dismissed from his previous job because his employer relocated to Mexico.
    d. Because the pay was only 75 percent of his previous wage, he turned down suitable work arranged for him by the unemployment bureau.
    e. He was dismissed because he participated in a work stoppage at his previous employer's factory.

REAL-WORLD CASE
Lincoln National Life Insurance Company v. *Johnson*
669 F. Supplement 201

Consider the case of a dead insured and the legally insane beneficiary who killed him, yet stood to recover on the deceased's insurance policy.

The insured, Russell Johnson, was allegedly murdered by his son and beneficiary, Kurt Johnson. After Kurt was found not guilty by reason of insanity, the insurance company deposited the proceeds from the policy into a special account to be paid as directed by the court. Kurt's guardian (appointed for him because Kurt was confined to a state mental hospital after the verdict in the murder case) filed a claim for the deposited funds on Kurt's behalf. There is a long-standing policy in Illinois law that someone should not profit from his or her intentionally committed wrongful act.

Think Critically
1. Would it be just for Kurt to recover in this case? Would letting him recover encourage others similarly situated to follow his example? What policy device would prevent this problem?
2. As a matter of law, will Kurt recover in this case? Should a beneficiary who killed the insured in self-defense be able to recover?

CHAPTER  33

Property, Casualty, and Auto Insurance

GOALS

- ◆ Identify the potential losses covered by property and casualty insurance
- ◆ Understand the similarities and differences between property and casualty insurance
- ◆ Know the various auto and fire insurance coverages

Protection Offered by Property and Casualty Insurance

Much can be inferred from the words property and casualty. First, property insurance is obviously intended to protect property, both real and personal, from perils that might befall it. You can insure property against fire, criminal action, earthquake, and storm damage. Casualty insurance, on the other hand, protects the overall worth of the insured person from liability for accidentally or negligently inflicted losses on the property or person of another. Some policies, especially automobile insurance policies, incorporate both property and casualty provisions. In a nutshell, property and casualty insurance afford protection from the harmful and potentially ruinous consequences of the acts of God and people.

Fire Insurance

Fire insurance is a fundamental type of property insurance. The basic fire insurance policy provides indemnification from losses to property resulting from fire, from damage done to property in getting it out of harm's way in a fire, and from lightning strikes. For homeowners, the property covered includes their dwellings, other structures such as garages and storage sheds, and the personal property contained in the buildings.

Basic Policy and Riders

To be certain that the coverage provided by a fire insurance policy is appropriate and fair, each state in the U.S. requires its own standard form for a basic fire insurance policy. Generally, these forms protect property only from the potential losses from fire mentioned above. In each instance however, the basic form can be modified by riders.

Riders (also called *endorsements*) are terms that tailor standard forms to fit specific situations. An **extended coverage rider**, for example, is used in many states to add protection against a variety of perils not covered in a basic policy. High winds, riots, aircraft and vehicle impacts, smoke, explosions, hail damage, and other sources of loss are all covered by this rider.

 # Hypothetical Case

Corrigan lived directly under the approach to Runway 9 at the International Airport in Pennsboro. Concerned about the constant traffic some 2,500 feet above his chimney, he added an extended coverage rider to his fire insurance policy. Less than three weeks later, a very large tire from a jumbo jet's landing gear fell through his roof. Luckily, no one was at home at the time. Because of the added rider, the insurer paid the $28,000 in repair costs for the home. (The insurer then sought to recover its money from the airline. See "subrogated" in the following paragraphs on recovery requirements.)

Recovery Requirements

In most forms of property insurance, a **claim** (an assertion of an insured's right to indemnification) is paid if the insurance company receives proper notice and proof of the loss sustained by the insured person. Depending on the circumstances, the notice must be given immediately or within a reasonable time of the loss. Immediate notice of a fire, for example, enables the insurance company to investigate the occurrence while the embers are still warm.

For many types of losses, written notice is required. Proof of loss, on the other hand, can typically be given within several months of the incident and still be effective. Such "proof" requires a sworn statement providing detailed information, such as the time and cause of the loss and the extent of the loss in both property and personal injuries. It also requires a list of witnesses and of other insurance that may be in force and usable to help indemnify the loss. Proper compliance with the notice and proof of loss requirements greatly increases the chances of a smooth and reasonably quick recovery process.

Under a typical fire insurance policy, the steps necessary to bring about recovery have been augmented somewhat. Proof of loss must show that the fire was actual, hostile, and the proximate cause of the damage. Considering the last step first, you may recall that we dealt with the concept of proximate cause back in Chapter 6. Applying that concept here means that the insured person is required to show that the fire was the indispensable and immediate factor causing the harm. Generally, courts accept without question that the fire was the proximate cause of accompanying losses caused by burning, smoke, scorching, water and other extinguishing efforts, and removal of endangered property as long as it was a "hostile fire."

What then, is a **hostile fire**? It is a fire that erupts someplace where the insured person does not intend burning to occur. A **friendly fire** is a fire that burns where the insured intends it to burn. If your furniture is scorched from being too close to the fire in the fireplace, you cannot recover for that loss under a standard fire insurance policy because the fire is "friendly." However, if a live coal escapes from the fireplace and sets a curtain on fire, you can recover for that loss because the fire has escaped from its friendly confines and become hostile.

Finally, an "actual" fire requires more than just an overabundance of heat. Some flame is necessary to meet this third requirement for recovery.

Once a properly documented claim has been submitted to the insurance company, the insured person can look forward to indemnification. Most property insurance policies however, provide the insurer with a choice as to the form of indemnification. For example, instead of paying for the loss, the insurer can have the damaged property repaired or replaced. If the insurer chooses to pay, the policy may provide that only the **actual cash value** (the original price less a reduction for time in use) of the property is recoverable. Because of inflation, this amount can be far less than the replacement cost of most goods in today's market. Therefore, for additional premiums, insurance companies offer indemnification at replacement cost values.

In situations involving casualty insurance, the insurance company, after having paid, is **subrogated** (substituted for another in pursuing a claim or right)

[**FIGURE 33-1**   Typical Steps in the Recovery of a Fire Insurance Claim]

1. The insured must first give the insurance company prompt notice of loss and later provide the insurance company with proof of loss.

2. Notice and proof allow the insurance company to investigate to establish that the fire was actual, hostile, and the proximate cause of the claimed damage and then to verify the claimed extent of the loss.

3. The insurance company determines whether to repair/replace the damaged property or to pay for the loss.

4. The insurance company settles the insured's claim.

for the insured if some third party is at fault. Then, the insurance company can sue the third party on its own. In the situation described earlier, for example, Corrigan's insurance company pursued recovery against the airline.

Coinsurance

Containing the costs of various forms of insurance has been high on the list of many insured people for some years. A principal means of doing so in the fire insurance area is through coinsurance. In **coinsurance**, the policyholder becomes self-insuring for a certain percentage of the protected property's worth. A typical coinsurance clause requires the insured party to keep a policy in force with a face value of 75 percent of the protected property's worth. If the insured party does so, the insurer pays all losses up to that amount in full. This means that the insured suffers a financial loss only if more than 75 percent of the protected property's worth is destroyed. In the worst possible case, that is, a total loss, the insured loses 25 percent of the worth of the protected property and is compensated by the insurance company for the other 75 percent. However, as fire departments almost always respond quickly enough to prevent a total structural loss, a total loss seldom occurs.

Of course, situations occur where the insured fails to keep up with inflating property values by increasing the face value of the fire insurance accordingly. In such a case, the insurance company determines how much it will pay by multiplying the dollar amount of the losses by a fraction. This fraction's numerator is the current policy face amount, and the denominator is what the policy face amount should have been.

Hypothetical Case

R. A. R. Enterprises owned a large warehouse that it insured against loss by fire. To keep its costs low, it agreed to have a 75 percent coinsurance term placed in the policy. When the policy was taken out, the warehouse was valued at $100,000. Therefore, R. A. R. purchased a policy with a face value of $75,000. In the next seven years, the value of the building doubled, to $200,000. However, R. A. R. did not increase the face value of its policy. Consequently, when a fire caused a $50,000 loss, the fire insurance company paid only $25,000. This equals the $50,000 loss taken multiplied by $75,000/$150,000, that is, the current policy face value divided by the policy face value that R. A. R. should have carried to live up to its end of the coinsurance deal ($150,000 equals 75 percent of $200,000).

If coinsurance terms are complied with, premiums are kept reasonably well below what they would be if the full value of property were insured. If coinsurance terms are not complied with, that is, if the face value of coinsurance policies is not increased as the value of the coinsured property increases, the amount of any consequently uncovered loss usually more than cancels out any short-term savings on premiums.

Marine and Inland Marine Insurance

Marine insurance is another form of property insurance. We discussed it briefly in Chapter 31. It indemnifies for losses resulting from the perils of water transport, and it covers ships and cargoes. **Inland marine insurance** was developed to protect personal property from the perils of land transport. Over the years, several modifications have been made in the basic inland marine policy. The most significant modification offered coverage of personal property, not just in transit, but at any time. Today, an inland marine policy can cover all of the insured's personal property or can be tailored to cover only specific, scheduled property detailed on a list provided by the insured to the insurer. Finally, although originally available only to property owners, a form of inland marine insurance is now offered to such bailees as common carriers and repair shops.

Liability Insurance

It is popularly believed that we live in an extremely litigious (prone to legal disputes) society. Many find confirmation of this belief in the sheer number of lawyers who make a living from courtroom confrontations (or our desire to avoid them). Confirmation is also available in the high premiums that insurance companies charge for providing a certain type of indemnification to professionals and similarly insured people. These insureds are worried about their potential legal responsibility for injuries they may unintentionally inflict on the person or property of others. The insurance they require is termed **liability insurance**. For insureds ranging from doctors to businesspeople to homeowners to operators of motor vehicles, liability insurance (often labeled malpractice insurance when used to cover professionals) and its cost are facts of life.

Hypothetical Case

J.J. Eric turned 16 on the last day of 1990. His parents taught him to drive shortly thereafter. After they were assured of his ability, they gave him primary use of one of the family's three vehicles, a 1988 Mercury Cougar. The state they all lived in required by law that each driver maintain $10,000 of liability coverage in his or her automobile insurance policy. This was because many drivers at fault in accidents were found to be without financial reserves to pay the damages they owed for the harm they had caused. The Erics made a practice of having 10 times the liability coverage that the state required. They did so to avoid being wiped out by a large damage recovery against them for being at fault in an automobile accident. Unfortunately, the driving history of many younger drivers meant that when the Erics placed such liability coverage on J.J., the insurance company more than tripled their premiums.

Advantages of the All-Risk Policy

Instead of contracting for liability, fire, theft, and property insurance separately, many insureds take out one policy for all these coverages. That policy is known as an **all-**

risk policy. It is also known as a "homeowner's policy" or "comprehensive insurance." Such a policy includes not only fire insurance but also the extended coverage provided in many riders to the standard fire policy. The amount of personal property insurance is usually set at a percentage of the amount for which the dwelling is covered. Typically, this insurance provides floating coverage on the household's personal property wherever it is located at the time of the loss (on vacation, at school, etc.).

An all-risk policy is usually more expensive than buying each coverage separately, and the all-risk policy does have exclusions, regardless of its name. For example, the liability coverage usually excludes coverage when the insured is driving an auto, boating, or flying; harms someone intentionally; or faces strictly business losses. However, it covers forms of liability such as that owed to a guest who slips on the rug and fractures a vertebrae. Offsetting the exclusions and the increased cost is the peace of mind that comes with buying a policy tailored to cover the greatest and most significant number of risks to the insured. Also, some provisions are included that may not appear in individually negotiated insurance policies. For example, "living expense coverage," which is used to pay for living quarters while repairs are made to the dwelling (usually up to one-fifth of the face amount), is automatically available with a standard all-risk policy. Also available is "medical expense coverage" for those injured on the insured's premises. This coverage also covers acts of the insured off his or her premises even though the insured is without legal responsibility for the harm done.

Fidelity Insurance

As mentioned in Chapter 31, fidelity insurance makes it possible to insure against embezzlement, fraud, theft, and other criminal conduct by employees that might cause severe harm to an otherwise profitable business. Having such insurance helps in a number of ways that go beyond merely providing the reassurance of promised indemnification. Insurance companies offering fidelity insurance often evaluate the security measures and other safeguards used in a business. This tends to forestall criminal conduct by insiders of the business. If such an evaluation discloses weaknesses, the insurer requires that these be corrected in return for continuing indemnification. Regardless, similar to the other types of coverage we have discussed in this chapter, fidelity insurance can provide an indispensable safety net to those wise enough to employ it.

Typical Automobile Insurance

Now we turn our attention to automobile insurance, a type of insurance that is not only in all likelihood indispensable, but is also legally required in most states in the U.S. As you may have inferred from earlier discussions in this chapter, this particular type of insurance is best obtained in policies that deal with it exclusively. This is mainly because of its complex coverages and the support network necessary to fairly review automobile claims. Each automobile policy can have liability, medical, property, and other coverages specifically tailored to cover the risks of the road and the driver assuming them (see Figure 33-2 on page 464). To properly understand an automobile policy, each of these coverages has to be examined in some detail

Liability Coverage

The most important kind of indemnification in automobile insurance and the one that most states require of licensed drivers is for liability. A typical liability term obligates the insurer to indemnify the insured up to the policy limits "for any bodily injury, death, or property damage claims for which the insured becomes legally responsible to third parties as a result of an auto accident." The bodily injury liability limit is usually stated to indicate the limit that the insurer pays to each bodily injured party and the limit it pays for all bodily injury victims in the accident. The property damage limit is the maximum amount the insurer pays to indemnify the insured for property damage resulting from the accident. Obviously, the higher the liability limits, the higher the premiums are.

Regardless of the amount of liability coverage obtained, the insureds can contract to extend that coverage to household members or drivers operating with the permission of any one of the insureds. This is done by an **omnibus clause**.

Because of potential liability, the insurance company typically contracts for the responsibility of either defending or settling the case. This duty, which includes the payment of attorney's fees, bond premiums, etc., ends at the discretion of the insurer when the limit of liability has been paid or tendered. A settlement negotiated by the insured is invalid unless directly authorized or ratified by the insurer.

Hypothetical Case

While her attention was diverted, Nikki Prince negligently ran a red light and crashed her car into a small van. The van's driver, Bill Washam, was killed. His three passengers were injured. After the impact, the two vehicles' momentum carried them into the front area of a convenience store. Several witnesses at the scene left their names with investigating officers. Their statements all clearly indicated Nikki's fault and Washam's blamelessness. The bodily injury liability limits of Nikki's automotive policy were $200,000 for each injured or deceased person and $500,000 for all such claims stemming from one accident. The policy also indemnified for up to $100,000 in property damage. Because of the evidence, the insurance company entered into negotiations to settle the claims. Washam's family sought $1 million for his wrongful death but agreed to accept $350,000. The claims of the other injured individuals were settled for a total of $150,000. The total property damage equaled $125,000. The insurer paid only $200,000 of the $350,000 because of the per person limit on liability. It also paid all of the other bodily injury claims as each was less than $200,000 and the total of all such claims paid for the accident was less than $500,000. The insurance company paid $100,000 of the $125,000 property damage, again because of the limits set on its indemnification. As Nikki had no other liability insurance protecting her except for an all-risk policy that specifically excluded liability from the operation of automobiles, the unpaid amounts on the property damage and death claims have to be collected from her personal wealth.

Note that if a passenger was riding with Nikki and was injured, that party might have been able to sue her for negligence. Standing in the way of such a suit however, might be one of many **guest statutes**. On the books in many states in the U.S., such statutes prohibit suits by nonpaying passengers unless the driver was grossly negligent or intentionally caused the accident. Gross negligence goes beyond what Nikki displayed in the above incident by negligently running a red light. It is best illustrated by driving while intoxicated or operating a vehicle in a known unsafe condition.

Medical Payments Coverage

The medical claims of the parties in the insured's motor vehicle in an accident such as Nikki's may go uncompensated without **medical payments coverage**. Such coverage indemnifies the insured and any person who is injured while entering, leaving, or riding in or on the insured's vehicle. The guest statutes do not bar collecting on this coverage. Limits are usually expressed in a per person figure ($10,000 per person is a typical coverage), but usually no limit per accident is established.

The breadth of medical payments coverage may surprise you. For example, it covers not only medical costs but funeral expenses as well. Also, it follows the insureds even outside their own vehicles. Therefore, whatever the form of the insured's harmful contact with a motor vehicle, the indemnification is available to them.

Hypothetical Case

As a part of her recovery from the accident, Nikki Prince took up bicycle riding. One day, her brakes failed as she cycled down a long hill. At the bottom she slammed into the side of a parked and unoccupied car. Because she had harmful contact with a motor vehicle, the medical payments coverage of her automobile policy paid for her hospitalization, X-rays, medicines, and doctor and dentist bills.

Collision, Comprehensive, and Uninsured and Underinsured Motorist Coverages

As you have seen, the main focus of an automobile policy is defensive. It is meant, especially through its liability portions, to protect the insured against personally paying for the losses sustained by others as a result of the insured's operation of a motor vehicle. Add-on coverages, such as medical payments coverage, help compensate the insured for his or her personal losses. Similarly, collision and comprehensive coverages are both intended to protect the insured from damage to the insured's own vehicle.

Collision Coverage **Collision coverage** indemnifies the insured for loss to the insured's vehicle due to its running into another object (be it another car, a post, a garage wall, a bridge, or you-name-it) or overturning. The coverage payout is usually based on actual cash value reduced by whatever deductible ($500 is common) the insured may have selected. In return for reduced premiums, the deductible places the burden on the insured for most, if not all, of the losses sustained in minor mishaps.

Comprehensive Coverage   **Comprehensive coverage** indemnifies for damage to the insured's vehicle stemming from causes other than that covered by collision insurance. Theft, hail, vandalism, the chipping or breakage of glass, all and more are covered. Like collision coverage, comprehensive is usually subject to a deductible from the payout based on actual cash value.

Uninsured and Underinsured Motorist Coverage   Despite the various **financial responsibility laws** that require drivers to show proof of insurance or other ability to pay a liability judgment, many drivers are uninsured. **Uninsured motorist coverage**, which is available for an increased premium, allows an insured to collect bodily injury and wrongful death damages (but not property damages) from her or his insurer if the driver causing the harm does not have insurance. The coverage even applies to hit-and-run accidents in which that driver cannot be found. As with liability coverage, per person and per accident limits are set for uninsured motorist coverage.

Underinsured motorist coverage has become available in recent years. Many motorists maintain only the minimum legally required liability coverage (typically $10,000 per person and $25,000 per accident). Therefore, the injured party must look to the negligent driver's personal assets for any substantial recovery. When these are insufficient to cover the loss, **underinsured motorist coverage** allows the insured to collect from her or his own insurer the unrecoverable amount of the damages for bodily injury and wrongful death up to certain per person and per accident limits.

No-Fault Insurance Systems

Although their actual details vary greatly from state to state, **no-fault insurance systems** attempt to cut down on the litigation burden facing our courts. They do this by requiring that, within certain loss limits and regardless of who is at fault, the parties involved in an automobile accident be indemnified by their own insurers. Should the amount of damage exceed the loss limits, the old fault-based rules system comes into play.

FIGURE 33-2 Automobile Insurance Coverages

Liability   For bodily injury, death, or property claims against the insured

Medical payments coverage   For medical treatment of the insured and the insured's passengers for injuries received while riding in or on or getting in or out of the insured's vehicle

Collision coverage   Indemnifies the insured from losses to the insured's vehicle resulting from running into another object or overturning

Comprehensive coverage   Indemnifies for losses to the insured's vehicle resulting from causes other than those covered by collision coverage (such as losses from hail, theft, or vandalism)

Uninsured and underinsured motorist coverages   Allows collection from the insured's insurer of bodily injury and wrongful death damages (but not property damage) inflicted on the insured by an uninsured or underinsured motorist who is at fault in the accident

CHAPTER REVIEW

USE LEGAL TERMS

Fill in the blanks with the appropriate term.

actual cash value
all-risk policy
claim
coinsurance
collision coverage
comprehensive coverage
extended coverage rider
financial responsibility laws
friendly fire
guest statutes

hostile fire
inland marine insurance
liability insurance
medical payments coverage
no-fault insurance system
omnibus clause
riders
subrogated
underinsured motorist coverage
uninsured motorist coverage

1.   ___?___ will not pay as long as the party who is at fault in the auto accident has liability insurance.
2.   A(n) ___?___ indemnifies against fire, theft, windstorm, and other perils often covered in individual policies.
3.   A(n) ___?___ is a legal framework covering automobile insurance under which each insured's insurer indemnifies her or him for losses regardless of who is to blame.
4.   ___?___ indemnifies the insured for losses that occur when his or her own vehicle overturns or runs into another object.
5.   ___?___ prohibit suit by vehicle passengers against drivers unless the drivers are grossly negligent or willfully cause the harm in question.
6.   A(n) ___?___ means something is burning in its intended place.
7.   ___?___ requires that the insured be partially self-insuring for certain indemnifiable losses.

TEST YOUR READING

8.   What is the purpose of property and casualty insurance?
9.   Name five perils typically covered by the extended coverage rider to a fire policy.
10. Who submits a claim and why?
11. Is scorching the same as burning under a standard fire insurance policy? Why or why not?
12. What is the difference between actual cash value and replacement value?
13. What advances have made coinsurance possible?
14. What is the difference between marine and inland marine insurance?

15. What is the purpose of an omnibus clause in an automobile insurance policy?
16. Name five types of coverage typically found in an automobile policy.

THINK CRITICALLY ABOUT EVIDENCE

17. Which of the following losses would not be indemnified under the basic fire insurance policy?
    a. Lightning damage to a main dwelling
    b. Tornado damage to a main dwelling
    c. Lightning damage to a garage or an outbuilding
    d. Damage done to a TV set because it is dropped while being rescued from a hostile fire in the main dwelling
    e. Charring of a coat that has been placed too close to the fireplace
    f. Hail damage to the shingles on a house roof

18. To cover its fire station, the city of Pennsboro bought a fire insurance policy with an 80 percent coinsurance clause. When the insurance was taken out, the building was valued at $100,000 and the required face value was $80,000. As time passed, the value of the building increased to $200,000. Then one day, while the fire department was out fighting a blaze, an unknown arsonist set fire to the station.
    a. Presume that Pennsboro had just increased the face value of the insurance policy to $160,000. If the station were a total loss how much would the insurer pay? How much would the city be responsible for?
    b. If, instead of being a total loss, the damage came to $160,000, how much would the insurer pay if the face value of the policy on the $200,000 station were $160,000? How much would the city be responsible for?
    c. Presume that Pennsboro did not increase the face value of the policy since it was taken out. If the station were at total loss, how much would the insurer pay? How much would the city be responsible for?

19. Which of the following would not be covered by a general (no specific list of insured property required) inland marine insurance policy?
    a. Your watch that is stolen from the repair shop
    b. Your house window that is damaged by an unclaimed baseball
    c. Your television set that is dropped while being moved to the bedroom

20. Which of the following risks would not be covered by the typical all risk (homeowner's) policy described in this chapter?
    a. A fire that destroys much of the family room
    b. The insured's camcorder, which is stolen from her while she is on vacation
    c. The liability incurred by the insured when she playfully pushed a friend off a boat dock while on vacation (The tide was out, the water level lower than she expected. He broke an arm and sustained a concussion.)

21. Bodily injury liability, property damage liability, medical payments, collision, comprehensive, uninsured motorist, and underinsured motorist coverages are often found in automobile insurance policies. Identify which of these coverages would indemnify the following losses:

    a. Hospital and medical costs for injuries sustained in an auto accident by the passenger of the negligent insured

    b. Medical costs for an insured who is hit by a car while roller-skating

    c. The pain, suffering, lost wages, and medical expenses of the vehicle driver who was injured in an auto accident negligently caused by the insured

    d. Damage to the insured's vehicle sustained when the insured failed to make a curve, causing the vehicle to crash into a large oak tree

    e. Damage to the insured's vehicle caused by someone running a sharp metal object along the fender

    f. Damage to the insured's vehicle and injuries to the insured sustained in a crash with a vehicle driven by a person without financial resources or automobile insurance

REAL-WORLD CASE

Hall v. Wilkerson
926 F.2d 311

Consider the potential effect on insurability of alcohol consumption by the driver of a borrowed car.

After having consumed a large quantity of beer, Wayne Wilkerson was involved in a one-vehicle accident in which his passengers, Susan Kilmer and Richard Schoch, were seriously injured. He was driving Gwendolyn Hall's car. Hall's insurance policy read, "WHO IS AN INSURED (under this policy)?" The policy answered its own question as follows: "For YOUR car—YOU, any RELATIVE, and anyone else using YOUR CAR if the use is (or is reasonably believed to be) with YOUR PERMISSION are INSUREDS."

Hall and Wilkerson were not related, and when Hall granted Wilkerson permission to use the car, she specifically told him that there were to be no drugs in the car and that "alcohol is a drug like any other drug."

Hall's insurance company and the injured parties come before the court seeking a declaration of whether Wilkerson was an insured at the time of the accident.

Think Critically

1. Should the policyholder have the power to eliminate insurance coverage by imposing conditions on permission to drive as Hall did here? For example, what if Hall granted Wilkerson permission to drive on the condition that he neither damage the car nor involve it in an accident?

2. If Wilkerson is not an insured, the injured parties lose a major source of funding to pay for the expenses of recovering from their injuries. This may prevent them from receiving treatment that would enable them to engage in gainful employment and/or force them into conditions of financial hardship. On the other hand, holding that they are unable to recover because Wilkerson is not an insured may send a warning to others to be careful about the persons from whom they accept rides under similar circumstances. From a societal standpoint, which alternative do you think is the wiser?

3. How do you think the court held?

GLOSSARY

A

abandoned property   Property whose owner has given up all intention of maintaining rights or interests in it.

acceleration clause   A clause allowing the obligee to declare the full amount of an obligation due and payable upon the occurrence of a particular event, such as a failure to make a payment.

acceptance   A sign by the offeree indicating that she or he will be bound by the terms of the offeror's offer; in sales law, acceptance occurs when the buyer, after a reasonable opportunity to inspect the goods, signifies to the seller that the goods are fine, performs an act inconsistent with the seller's continued ownership of the goods, or simply fails to reject the goods; in commercial paper law, acceptance is an assurance that the drawee will be liable on and pay a draft according to its terms.

accession   The acquisition of property by a natural increase of property already owned, such as by an animal having offspring.

accord and satisfaction   A legal maneuver involving the discharge of a party (satisfaction) from a previous contractual obligation by his or her fulfillment of the terms in a new contract (the accord).

accredited investor   A firm or an individual falling into one of several categories identified by the Securities and Exchange Commission as comprising investors that do not need the protection of registration in a prospective sale of securities.

actual cash value   The amount of indemnification due for property loss: that amount is equal to the original price less a reduction for time in use.

actual cause   The harm-causing factor without which the injury could not have occurred.

actual damages (also referred to as **compensatory damages**)   A monetary amount intended to compensate for the real harm done.

actus reus   The physical behavior that, if it occurs along with the mental state required by statute, constitutes a crime.

adequate assurance of performance   An action satisfactorily indicating intent to fulfill a contract.

administrator, administratrix   An individual selected or endorsed by the court to handle the estate of an individual who died intestate.

affirmative action plans   Plans that specify methods and time frames in which actions will be taken to eliminate the adverse impact on certain subgroups, such as women or racial minorities, of employers' past discriminatory practices.

after-acquired property clause   A term in a security agreement under which property acquired after the agreement has been made can replace the collateral identified in the agreement subject to the lien set up by the agreement.

agency   A legal relationship whereby one party (the principal) gives the power to legally bind him or her to another party (the agent).

agency by estoppel   A court-ordered status whereby individuals are prohibited from denying that an agency existed and thus are responsible for legal obligations created as a result of the agency.

agency coupled with an interest   An agency that is irrevocable by the principal because the agent holds an interest in the subject property above and beyond the expectation of payment for agency services.

agent   A person authorized to bind another legally.

agreement not to compete   Typically, a term in an employment contract that limits a worker's ability to enter into competition with his or her former employer for a reasonable period after termination of the employment relationship.

alienate   To transfer title to property by sale, gift, will, etc.

alien corporation   A corporation organized outside the United States.

all-risk policy (also known as a **homeowner's policy**)   An insurance policy containing coverages for a wide range of risks, including liability, fire, theft, and property loss.

alternative payees   Persons named as payees on a piece of commercial paper, each of whom has a full right to all of the funds to be paid.

annual percentage rate   The interest rate for a loan expressed as a yearly figure.

answer   The defendant's response to a civil complaint.

antedated   An instrument issued bearing a past date.

anticipatory breach   A declaration by a party, made before the actual beginning of performance, that she or he will not perform her or his contractual obligations.

apparent authority   Seeming but not actual authority to legally bind another to contracts.

appeal   A complaint to a higher court of an error of law made during the conduct of a case.

appellate courts   An upper level of courts established to review decisions reached in lower-level courts in order to maintain fairness and uniformity in the application of law.

appellate jurisdiction   The power to review cases for errors of law.

arraignment   A court proceeding at which a person who has been taken into official custody is informed of the charge or charges against her or him and is allowed to plead.

arrest   The taking of a suspect into custody to answer a criminal charge.

arrest warrant   An order that a person be arrested by competent authorities.

arson   The willful and malicious burning of a structure.

articles of incorporation   A written application for corporate status that is filed with the appropriate government entity.

articles of partnership   A partnership agreement (in accordance with Uniform Partnership Act terminology).

artisan   A person skilled in a trade or craft requiring manual dexterity.

artisan's lien   A possessory security interest against personal property for unpaid-for improvements thereon.

assault   An intentional tort that results when the defendant willfully places an individual in reasonable fear of a harmful or offensive touching.

assignee   The party to whom contractual rights are assigned.

assignment   A transfer of rights from the original parties to a contract to others who were not original parties.

assignment of a lease   A transfer by a tenant of all his or her rights and interests in the leased premises to someone else.

assignor   The party who assigns his or her contractual rights to another.

assumption of risk   A defense to tort liability based on the injured party's knowledge and assumption of the specific risk of injury involved.

attach   To seize.

attachment   The point in a loan transaction when the creditor (who may be a lender of money or a seller of the collateral) acquires a legally enforceable right to take the collateral and sell it to satisfy the debt.

auction   An authorized party's public sale of property to the highest bidder.

auction sale without reserve   An auction at which the auctioneer cannot withdraw goods after he or she asks for bids on them.

auction sale with reserve   An auction at which the auctioneer is able to withdraw goods at any time before announcing the completion of the sale.

avoid   To cancel a contract.

B

bail   The property or bond posted with the court to ensure an accused's later appearance.

bailee   Individual to whom goods are bailed.

bailment   The legal relationship created by the acquisition of possession of another's personal property subject to an agreement to return it or deliver it to a third party.

bailor   Individual who bails goods.

bait-and-switch scheme   An illegal sales gimmick whereby a seller lures a buyer with an extremely low price on an understocked, underfeatured item, and then switches the buyer to a far more expensive product.

bankruptcy   A federal statutory procedure by which debtors' eligible assets are utilized to discharge them from some, if not all, of their obligations.

bankruptcy debtor   Any individual or business (except those considered special cases, such as banks, savings and loans, building and loans, railroads, and insurance companies) that claims the protection of the bankruptcy laws.

bankruptcy insider   A person with a close relationship to the bankruptcy debtor, such as a relative or partner.

bankruptcy trustee   An individual selected to administer the debtor's estate in bankruptcy.

barter   The bargained-for exchange of goods and services without the use of money.

battery   An intentional tort that results when the defendant willfully touches someone in a harmful or offensive way.

bearer   A person in possession of a valid legal instrument that does not specifically identify its owner.

bearer paper   Commercial paper payable to its possessor and issued to (1) cash, bearer, or the equivalent and without any endorsements or (2) cash or to the order of someone but with the last endorsement blank.

beneficiary   A party (or parties) for whose benefit a trust is managed in accordance with the settlor's wishes; in insurance law, a party named in an insurance policy to whom compensation for a loss is to be paid.

best evidence rule   A rule that allows only original or firsthand evidence to be placed before the court.

bilateral contract   A contract whose parties assume a mutuality of obligations to fulfill their promises.

bill of exchange   Historically, a paper ordering the transfer of precious metal from one party to another; in current commercial paper law, synonymous with a draft.

bill of lading   A document that states the terms of a shipping contract for consigned goods, contains a description of those goods, and details who has the right to demand them by presenting the document upon their arrival at their destination.

binder   A written voucher of insurance.

blank endorsement   Signature on the reverse of a commercial paper instrument not accompanied by a designation of who is to receive the payoff on the instrument.

blue laws   Laws that regulate the making or performing of contractual obligations on Sunday.

blue-sky law   State laws intended to control intrastate security transactions.

board of directors   The group charged with the management of a corporation.

bonds   A certificate or some other evidence of debt requiring that the issuer/borrower repay the amount borrowed or principal plus interest according to a fixed schedule.

boycott   A refusal to do business with a particular person or firm.

breach of contract   An unexcused failure to perform according to the terms of a contract.

breach of the peace   A violation or disturbance of public tranquility and order.

bribery   Offering, giving, receiving, or soliciting something of value in return for influence on how an official carries out a public or legal duty.

bulk transfer   A trading away of a major part of a commercial enterprise's inventory, supplies, and/or equipment in a transaction that does not occur during the ordinary course of doing business.

business invitees   Those who are impliedly invited onto the premises of another in order to conduct commercial transactions.

business judgment rule   A rule whose effect is to immunize management from liability resulting from business decisions made within the power and authority granted corporate officers in the corporate charter and state statutes.

business law   The relatively specific group of laws that regulate the establishment, operation, and termination of commercial enterprises.

business trust   A business form, popular in some northeastern states, in which selected trustees manage property (signed over to the trust by its owners) so as to provide income or other forms of return to the trust's beneficiaries.

bylaws   The rules governing the internal organization of a corporation and management of the corporation's proceeds.

C

carrier's lien   A possessory security interest in cargo for unpaid shipping charges.

cashier's check   A commercial paper instrument on which a bank is both the drawer and the drawee and which can be issued payable to the purchaser of the instrument or to any party the purchaser desires.

cash value   The interest and principal in the savings fund of a whole life insurance policy or a similar life insurance policy.

causa mortis gift   A gift given in anticipation of death.

certificate of deposit (CD)   A bank's written acknowledgment of the receipt of money coupled with a promise to pay it back, usually with interest, on the due date.

certified check   A check of a depositor in a bank on which the bank has indicated, by the word accepted or certified accompanied by the signature of a bank official and the date, its warranty that sufficient funds are available for payment.

charter   A certificate of incorporation issued by a properly empowered governmental entity that thereby officially creates the separate legal person termed a corporation.

check   An unconditional written directive to a bank to pay deposited funds on demand to the order of an individual named on the instrument or to the bearer.

civil case   A lawsuit to resolve a dispute between private citizens.

claim   The assertion of an insured's right to indemnification.

close corporation   A corporation whose stock-based control is held by a single individual or a tight-knit group of individuals.

codicils   Formal, written, and witnessed alterations of a will.

coinsurance   A contractual means by which a policyholder becomes self-insuring for a certain percentage of the worth of insured property.

collateral   Property subject to a creditor's claims.

collective bargaining   Negotiations over the conditions and terms of employment between representatives of a work force and its employer.

collision coverage   An automobile insurance coverage that indemnifies the insured from losses to the insured's vehicle due to its running into another object or overturning.

co-makers   Two or more promisors on a promissory note.

commercial paper   A written promise or order to pay a sum of money.

common carriers   Businesses that hold themselves out to the general public to transport goods for a fee.

common law   The customary law of a region.

common stock   A type of stock that gives its owner the right to vote in corporate elections and a proportionate share in distributed corporate profits.

comparative negligence   A defense that does not deny all recovery when the party injured in an accident was somewhat negligent but instead allows recovery according to the relative degree of fault of the parties to the accident.

complaint   A document filed in a civil case in which the injured party's version of the facts of the case is stated, the court's jurisdiction over the case is shown, and a request for relief is made.

complete performance   A contractual result whereby all of the parties to a contract perform every promise made in the contract.

comprehensive coverage   An automobile insurance coverage that indemnifies the insured for damage to his or her vehicle stemming from causes other than those covered by collision insurance, such as theft, hail, vandalism, or the chipping or breakage of glass.

concealment   The failure to disclose a material fact when requested to do so by the insurer.

condition concurrent   A contractual term requiring that both parties to a contract perform some or all of its obligations at the same time.

condition precedent   A contractual term specifying an event that must occur before an obligation to perform is placed on one or all the parties to a contract.

condition subsequent   A contractual term specifying an event whose occurrence will extinguish an obligation to perform.

confidential relationships (also termed **fiduciary relationships**)   Relationships that the law recognizes as being founded on trust.

conforming goods   Goods that fulfill the seller's obligations under a contract with the buyer.

confusion   The blending of indistinguishable goods of two or more owners so that each owner's share cannot be identified.

conscious parallelism   A practice followed by the members of oligopolies whereby all of the members follow the pricing policies of the largest member.

consent   A willing and knowledgeable assent.

consequential damages   Damages reasonably foreseeable as being caused by a particular breach of contract.

consideration   What an offeror demands and, in most situations, must receive in return for making his or her offer a promise legally binding against him or her.

consignment   A bailment of goods to a common carrier for shipment.

constitution   The fundamental law of the land.

constitutional law   The text of a constitution and the laws and judicial rulings that interpret and apply it.

constructive delivery   A symbolic act indicating the delivery of a gift.

constructive eviction   A landlord's failure to make necessary repairs or provide necessary services that renders the premises of a lease uninhabitable.

consumer goods   Items purchased primarily for personal, family, or household purposes.

consumer products   Items of tangible personal property that are used for personal, family, or household purposes.

contingent beneficiary   The person named to receive a policy payout should the primary beneficiary die before the insured.

contract   An agreement between two or more parties that creates an obligation.

contract to sell   An agreement involving future goods.

contractual capacity   The ability to appreciate the consequences of entering into a contract.

contributory negligence   A defense that disallows any recovery for an injury if the injured party's negligence contributed to the injury.

convertible bond   A type of bond that is exchangeable for a set amount of stock at the option of the bond's creditor.

copyright   An exclusive right to the publishing, printing, copying, reprinting, and selling of the tangible expression of an author's or artist's creativity.

corporation   A legal entity created through statutory authority to be a separate, artificial person distinct from the operation or project of the business that the entity is organized to conduct.

cost-plus contract   A contract whose terms require the purchaser to pay the developer the amount of money it costs to create a product plus a certain percentage of that amount.

counterclaim   A claim based on the incident at hand that the defendant in a civil case makes against the plaintiff.

counteroffer   A response to an offer that alters the terms of the offer.

course of dealings   Understandings developed by the parties to a contract in their previous transactions.

court of record   A legal forum in which an exact account of what went on at trial is kept so as to allow appeals.

courts of equity   Courts that were empowered to fashion remedies that courts of law could not fashion and then to issue injunctions enforcing those remedies on the parties involved.

courts of law   Courts holding formal proceedings in which they apply powers given them by the political authority in order to resolve disputes of the people.

credit insurance   A term insurance policy that is intended to pay off a particular lender should the debtor die.

creditor beneficiary   A third party to a contract to whom payment of some debt or other obligation is expressly directed by the contractual party owing that debt.

credit rating   An evaluation of a person's ability to repay debts.

crime   A specific behavior that is an offense against the public good, the commission of which is punishable by the government.

criminal case   A prosecution of an individual charged with an offense against society as defined in its law code.

cross-claim   A claim that a defendant in a civil case makes against another defendant.

cross-examination   Examination of a witness concerning the testimony that the witness gave under direct examination by the opposing side.

cumulative preferred stock   A type of preferred stock whose owners must receive all unpaid preferred stock dividends before the owners of common stock receive any dividends.

cumulative voting   A method of voting for directors in corporate elections that increases the likelihood of minority representation on corporate boards.

D

damages   Monetary compensation awarded by the court to the injured party in a lawsuit.

days of grace   A period, usually one month, during which an overdue premium can be paid to keep a life insurance policy in force.

debenture   A bond that is issued without any security.

debt financing   The borrowing of money to capitalize a business.

decreasing term   A term life insurance policy requiring the payment of a constant premium (smaller than the premium paid for level term insurance for the same initial face value) throughout the time that the policy is in force in return for a steadily decreasing face value.

decree   A judgment of a court of equity.

deed   A formal written instrument utilized to transfer title to real property.

de facto corporation   A corporation whose status as such may be challenged by the state in which the corporation's good faith but erroneous attempt to incorporate was made.

defamation   The damaging of another's reputation by the making of false statements.

defamation per se   A category of defamatory statements so obviously harmful that the plaintiff does not have to prove damages to be able to recover for them at law; this category includes statements falsely accusing someone of having a communicable disease, of committing a criminal offense, or of being unable to perform the duties of an office, employment, or profession.

defendant   The person accused of wrongdoing in a criminal case; the person named in a civil complaint as the party causing the injury.

defense of self or others   A defense to criminal charges if the defendant reasonably believed that there was danger of severe bodily harm or death from an unprovoked attack and that the attack could be repelled only if the defendant used enough force.

de jure corporation   A corporation that is considered a separate legal entity by the law and whose status as such cannot be challenged by either private citizens or the state of incorporation.

demand note   A note that becomes due and payable whenever the payee or a subsequent owner presents it for payment.

depository bank   The first bank to which a commercial paper instrument is transferred for collection.

design patent   A statutorily granted monopoly to protect the unique configuration or appearance of the surface or components of an object.

destination term   A sales contract term that requires the seller of goods to be responsible for the delivery of the goods to their destination.

direct examination   The initial examination of a witness by the side that calls him or her.

directors   The stockholder representatives charged with overall responsibility for the management of a corporation.

disability coverage   A life insurance policy term that protects against a potentially devastating consequence of accident and disease, namely a total permanent inability to work.

disaffirm   To avoid.

discharge   To free from a legal obligation.

discounted   In commercial paper law, an instrument sold at less than the face amount.

discrimination in employment   Hiring, promoting, or discharging on the basis of race, color, sex, religion, or national origin; these practices were made illegal by the Civil Rights Act of 1964.

dishonored   A draft on which the drawee refused to pay.

disparagement of reputation   The making of false statements about the reputation of a business or about the quality of its products.

dissolution of partnership   Under the Uniform Partnership Act, a change whereby any partner ceases to be associated with the carrying on of a partnership's business.

dividends   A stockholder's proportionate share in the distribution of corporate profits.

doctrine of incorporation   A contractual doctrine that disregards the legal effect of oral bargains struck before a contract has been reduced to writing.

documents of title   Legal instruments that evidence the power of the person who has them in her or his possession to control the instruments themselves and the goods they cover.

domestic corporation   A corporation doing business in the state under whose laws it was organized.

donee   The intended recipient of a gift.

donee beneficiary   A third party who receives her or his rights under a contract as a gift from a party or parties to the contract.

donor   The person or other entity giving a gift.

dormant partners   Individuals who are actual partners but are not acknowledged publicly as partners and do not actively participate in the management of the partnership.

double indemnity   A term in a life insurance policy that requires the insurer to pay twice (or three or four times for triple or quadruple indemnity, respectively) the face value of the policy upon the accidental death of the person on whose life the insurance is being carried.

draft   An unconditional written order to a person to pay money, usually to a third party.

drawee   The party directed in a draft to pay a sum of money to someone's order.

drawer   The person who issues the order to pay found in a draft.

due process   The right of involved parties to receive notice of the charges or matters to be resolved at an upcoming hearing or trial and to present evidence, confront witnesses, and otherwise represent themselves at that proceeding.

duress   A wrongful threat that denies a person of her or his free will to contract.

ℇ

easement   The right to use the land of another.

egoism   An ethical system under which a person's actions are determined by his or her self-interest (see **psychological egoism** and **hedonism**).

electronic fund transfers   The use of communication and computer technology as a substitute for commercial paper instruments.

embezzlement   The wrongful conversion to his or her personal use of property entrusted to an individual by another.

employee   The party in the employment relationship who is being paid by another to do work.

employer   The party in the employment relationship who is paying another to do work.

employment   A relationship in which one party (the employer) pays another party (the employee) to do work under the control and direction of the paying party.

encumber   To subject property to the legal claim of someone other than the owner.

endorse   To sign the reverse of a piece of commercial paper.

endowment life insurance   A type of accumulation fund policy under which the insured typically pays a very high "premium" for insurance coverage and the right to receive the face value, if still living, at retirement or the end of a certain period.

enjoyment   The exercise of a right.

entrapment   A defense to criminal charges that requires showing that government officers or agents induced the defendant to commit a crime not already contemplated.

equipment   Goods used primarily in an ongoing business.

equity   Basic fairness.

equity financing   The selling of stock of various kinds to individuals who want to become part owners of a business or to increase the amount of their existing ownership in the business.

escheat   The right of the state to property without existing claimants.

estate   The real and personal property interest of a party.

ethical systems   Codes of conduct.

eviction   The act of removing a tenant from the possession of premises.

exclusions   Terms in an insurance contract that eliminate coverage in certain situations.

executed contract   A contract that has been fully performed by all of its parties.

executive branch   The division of government with the power to investigate violations of the law and to prosecute the alleged violators.

executor, executrix   An individual selected or endorsed by the court to handle the estate of a decedent who died testate.

executory contract   A contract in which some performance, regardless of how slight, has yet to be rendered.

exemplary damages (in some jurisdictions, **punitive damages**)   A monetary award arbitrarily set by the jury that bears little, if any, direct relationship to the amount of the plaintiff's actual injuries but is instead aimed at making an example of or punishing (thus punitive) the defendant.

express contract   A contract whose terms are set down in a clear-cut fashion either orally or in writing.

express warranty   An oral or written term or its equivalent in a sales agreement in which a promisor makes some statement of assurance about the good being sold.

extended coverage rider   A policy endorsement used in many states to add protection against a variety of perils not covered in a basic fire policy.

extortion   The use of threats of injury to a victim's person, family, property, or reputation to get consent to take the victim's property.

extreme duress   A real defense to the collection of commercial paper based on the fact that the paper was issued to avert a threat to inflict death or severe bodily harm on the issuer's immediate family or to destroy the issuer's home.

F

face value   The maximum amount that can be paid under a policy if the harm insured against actually occurs.

farm products   Livestock, crops, and supplies used or produced in farming operations that are in the farmer's possession.

felony   A crime severe enough to be punishable by death or imprisonment for a year or longer.

fictitious payee rule   A tenet of commercial paper law providing that, if an employee tricks her or his employer into issuing an instrument in payment of a nonexistent obligation, the loss is to be taken by the employer and not by the payor bank.

fidelity insurance   A type of insurance that provides protection against certain forms of dishonesty and against laxness in fulfilling obligations owed to the insured.

fiduciary duty   In partnership law, a duty requiring that the partner put the partnership's interest above her or his own.

finance charge   The actual cost of a loan expressed in dollars and cents.

financial responsibility laws   Statutes requiring that drivers have insurance or other ability to pay a liability judgment.

financing statement   A brief documentation of the existence of a security interest filed with the appropriate governmental office so as to perfect a creditor's security interest in collateral.

fixtures   Tangible, movable, things that become permanently attached to land or buildings.

forbearance   The refraining by a person from doing something that the person has a legitimate right to do.

foreign corporation   A corporation doing business in any state other than the one in which it was organized.

forgery   The false making or altering of a written document so as to create or change the legal effect of the document with an intent to defraud.

franchise   A business arrangement in which a trademark, trade name, or copyright is licensed to a business for its use in selling goods or services and the business is provided with a detailed and well-tested system for conducting its operations.

franchisee   The recipient and capitalizer of a franchise.

franchisor   The provider of a franchise.

fraud   In contract law, an untrue or reckless statement of a material fact made by one party to induce another party to enter into a contract.

fraud in the execution   A real defense to the collection of commercial paper based on the fact that the issuer did not realize that she or he was issuing commercial paper.

fraud in the inducement   A personal defense to the collection of commercial paper based on the fact that the issuer was deceived or defrauded into issuing the commercial paper.

fraudulent transfer   A shifting of a bankruptcy debtor's assets made with the intent to defraud, hinder, or delay creditors.

friendly fire   A fire burning where it was intended to burn.

fringe benefits   Forms of payment not directly related to work performance, such as pensions, vacation time, and free insurance.

full warranty   The seller's promise to cover the labor and material costs necessary to completely fix a product.

fungible goods   One unit of a good is acknowledged by trade usage to be identical with any other unit.

future goods   Goods not in existence or identified to the contract at the time of the contracting.

G

gambling   Paying something of value to win a prize in a game of pure chance.

garnishment   A court order compelling the payment into the court of an individual's wages or other financial resources held by a third party so as to satisfy a judgment.

general partners   Partners who engage in the management of a partnership and are fully, personally liable for its obligations.

general partnership   An association of two or more persons, each of whom is fully, personally liable for all of the association's financial obligations, to carry on as co-owners a business for profit.

general power of attorney   A written agency authorization that allows the agent to do anything legally necessary to conduct the principal's affairs.

gift   A transfer of property, voluntarily and without consideration, by one party to another.

good faith   Honesty in fact or subjective honesty.

goods   Things that are movable when they are identified as the subject matter of a sales agreement; in secured transactions, things that are tangible and movable when the security interest attaches.

grand jury   A "jury of inquiry" with powers to develop evidence and indict alleged violators of the criminal law.

grantee   A transferee of property.

grantor   A transferor of property.

gratuitous agency   An agency arrangement under which the principal is not obligated to pay for the agent's services.

gratuitous bailment   A bailment for the sole benefit of one of its parties.

group insurance   A term insurance policy offered to each member of a body of people with some common characteristic.

guarantor   A person who agrees to be secondarily liable for the payment of a debt or the performance of an obligation.

guardian   An individual who has been given the responsibility for taking care of a legally incapacitated party.

guest statutes   Laws that prohibit injury suits by nonpaying passengers against the driver of a vehicle in which they were riding unless the injury resulted from the driver's gross negligence or intentional behavior.

H

habitual drunkard   Someone who exhibits an involuntary tendency to become intoxicated as often as the temptation to do so is presented.

hedonism   An ethical system under which persons act to satisfy their senses of taste, touch, smell, sight, and hearing.

historical school   A legal philosophy based on the belief that legal systems develop according to each nation's historical experiences.

holder   A person possessing an instrument issued or endorsed to her or him or made payable to the bearer.

holder in due course   A holder who gives value for a piece of commercial paper in good faith without any notice of defect or dishonor.

holder through a holder in due course   A holder of an instrument who cannot become an HDC on his or her own but who acquires the rights of an HDC by acquiring the instrument after an HDC has held it.

holographic wills   Wills that are written in the decedent's own hand and are typically signed but not witnessed.

hostile fire   A fire that erupts someplace where the insured intends it not to be.

hotelkeeper's lien   A possessory security interest that a hotelkeeper acquires in a guest's property as compensation for unpaid-for lodging.

hung jury   A jury that cannot reach agreement on a verdict.

I

identified to the contract   The selection of specific goods as the subject matter of a deal.

impeachment cases   Trials of government officials for misconduct in office.

implied contract   A contract whose terms have not been stated and must therefore be determined from the surrounding circumstances or a foreign pattern of dealings.

implied warranties   Guarantees imposed on sales agreements by law.

imposter rule   A tenet of commercial paper law stating that if a party has been duped into issuing an instrument to a person whom the issuer has misidentified, the loss from the resulting forgery falls on the careless issuer.

incidental beneficiaries   The unintended recipients of a contract's direct or indirect benefits.

incidental damages   Damages awarded by a court to cover the costs expended by an innocent party to stem the loss from an injury; damages that are foreseeable but indirect losses to the injured party.

incontestable clause   A life insurance contract term that puts a time limit on the insurer's right to void a policy because of fraud or misrepresentations by the insured.

incorporators   The individuals who sign the articles of incorporation.

indemnify   To compensate for loss or damage.

independent contractor   Someone who contracts to do a job for another but performs the work entailed in his or her own way and is not subject to the direction and control of the person with whom he contracted to do the job.

indictment   A grand jury's official accusation of an individual for criminal conduct.

information   An accusation brought by a responsible public officer (the state attorney general or the local prosecutor) against a defendant.

infractions   Minor criminal offenses such as littering or improper parking.

infringement   Violation of the rights of a holder of a patent, copyright, or trademark.

injunction   A court order directing that some action be taken or halted.

inland marine insurance   Insurance of personal property against the perils of land transport.

in pari delicto   A Latin phrase meaning "of equal guilt."

insanity defense   A defense to criminal charges that requires showing that the defendant was suffering from a mental disease or defect that prevented him or her from behaving rationally.

inside directors   Individuals who are employees, officers, or major stockholders of the corporation of which they are directors.

insiders   Officers, directors, major stockholders, and others who are privy to confidential information pertaining to a corporation's activities.

insolvent   The condition of being unable to meet debts when they come due.

installment note   A note that requires a series of payments of principal and interest until a debt has been paid off.

insurable interest   A property right in goods whose potential loss can be indemnified.

insurance   The primary device used to transfer the risk of loss from specific perils from one person to another person or a group.

insurance of insurability   A life insurance policy coverage that allows the purchase of new amounts of life insurance coverage or the continuation of current coverage levels without being required to pass a physical examination or other test.

insured   The party who transfers the risk of loss to the insurer.

insurer   The party who agrees to accept the risk of loss from another.

intentional tort   A personal injury or wrong willfully inflicted by the tortfeasor to harm another's person or property.

interbrand competition   A struggle between firms working against each other to sell distinct competing products from different producers.

interstate commerce   Trade and other commercial activity between or among the citizens of different states or the states themselves.

inter vivos (between the living) *gift*   An absolute, nonconditional gift.

inter vivos trust   A trust created during the lifetime of the settlor.

intestate   The legal condition of a person who dies without leaving a valid will.

intrabrand competition   A struggle between firms working against each other to sell the same product.

intrastate commerce   Trade and other commercial activity conducted wholly within one state.

inventory   Goods bought for sale or lease.

invitation to negotiate   A solicitation of offers.

involuntary bankruptcy   A bankruptcy proceeding initiated with a petition filed by a debtor's creditors.

irresistible impulse (also known as a **temporary mental defect**)   A defense to criminal charges that requires showing that, because of a mental disease or defect, the defendant was temporarily unable to resist an impulse to commit a criminal act.

issuing a bad check   The crime of writing a check on an account knowing that the funds in the account are insufficient to cover it and that the financial institution on which it is written will probably not pay it; doing this becomes a crime when the financial institution does indeed fail to pay it.

J

jointly and severally liable   The status of individuals who may be held responsible individually or as co-obligors for some form of legal liability.

jointly liable   The status of individuals who are held to be co-obligors for some form of legal ability.

joint payees   Payees named on a piece of commercial paper who have equal rights in the funds to be paid.

joint tenancy   A form of property ownership involving two or more parties, each of whom is legally considered to own all of the subject property.

Judeo-Christian ethics   A religion-based ethical system requiring certain behavior regardless of consequences.

judicial branch   The division of government to which the power to conduct trials and pronounce judgment is given.

jurisdiction   The power of a court or other official body to hear and decide cases.

jurisprudence   Legal philosophy.

jury   A panel of citizens whose role is to assess evidence properly introduced in court in order to advise a judge on what the actual facts of a case are.

justice   In jurisprudence, the evenhanded administration of the laws; the title given to judges who sit on state or federal supreme courts.

juveniles   Individuals who are under the age of full responsibility for their criminal acts (generally set at 18 years).

K

Kantian ethical system   A system of ethics that endorses a possible action only if the principle behind it could be made a universal law without producing an illogical or self-defeating situation.

L

landlord   A party renting real property.

lapses   Terminates.

larceny   The unauthorized taking and carrying away of another's goods or money.

law   The rules of conduct that a political authority will enforce.

lease   The agreement under which the exclusive possession of real property or the possession, use, and enjoyment of personal property are temporarily transferred.

leasehold   A legal estate composed of the right to the exclusive possession of the subject premises for a certain term.

legal realism   A school of jurisprudence that holds that the law should reflect the most desirable real-life practices in use in a particular area.

legislative branch   The division of government to which the power to make laws is given.

lessee   A person who rents the real or personal property of another.

lessor   A person from whom real or personal property is being rented.

letter of credit   A promise by a person (typically a financial institution such as a bank) that it will honor and pay drafts drawn in compliance with its terms.

level term   Life insurance policies requiring the payment of a set premium throughout the period that they are in force in return for a constant face value.

liability insurance   Coverage of insureds for their potential legal responsibility for injures that they might unintentionally inflict on the person or property of others.

libel   The communication of false statements in a reasonably permanent form such as in writing or on videotape.

licensees   Persons who are afforded the privilege of entering onto another's real property through the explicit or implied permission of the possessor.

lien   A claim on property for payment of a debt.

life insurance   A contractual means for transferring the potential loss due to the death of a certain individual to an insurer who will pay a prearranged amount of money to a named beneficiary upon that occurrence.

limited liability   Liability for the obligations of a business that extends only to the amount of someone's investment in the business.

limited liability corporation (LLC)   A form of corporate entity available in some states that combines the advantages of the limited partnership and the S corporation while eliminating their usual restrictions (such as the limits set on the number of owners and the prohibition of managing by owners with limited liability).

limited partnership   A partnership composed of one or more general partners with full personal liability and one or more limited partners whose liability for the obligations of the partnership extends only to the amount of their investment in it.

limited power of attorney   A written agency authorization that allows the agent to carry out only specific transactions or to act as agent for only a set period.

limited warranty   A written warranty that meets some but not all of the requirements of a full warranty.

liquidated damages   A realistic approximation of the damages that should be awarded by a court in the event of a breach of contract.

liquidation   A sale for cash.

litigants   The parties who engage in a lawsuit.

lodger   An occupant of premises who has only their use, not their exclusive possession.

lost property   Property that has been involuntarily parted with due to the negligence or inadvertence of its true owner.

M

majority   A legal status afforded to those who are at or beyond a set legal age.

maker   The promisor on a promissory note.

mala in se crime   A crime that is inherently and essentially evil in its nature and consequences.

mala prohibita crime   A crime that is not inherently evil but is considered wrong only because it has been defined as such by a legislature.

malice   A wrong, evil, or corrupt motive.

marine insurance   A form of insurance whose coverage indemnifies for losses due to the perils of water transport.

market share   The percentage of the relevant market under the defendant's control.

material fact   In contract law, a fact crucial to a party's decision as to entering into a contract; in insurance law, a fact that, if correctly known, would have caused the insurer not to issue a policy.

mechanic's lien   An encumbrance against real property for unpaid bills for labor and supplies used in improvements thereon.

medical payments coverage   An automobile policy coverage that indemnifies against medical expenses the insured and any person who is injured while entering, leaving, or riding in or on the insured's vehicle.

Medicare   A social benefit program that helps eligible individuals pay for hospital and doctor expenses.

mens rea   The mental state that, along with the required physical behavior, defines a criminal act.

merchant   A person who deals in goods of the kind involved in a transaction or a person who by his occupation holds himself out as having the knowledge or skill peculiar to the practices or goods involved in a transaction or a person to whom such knowledge or skill may be attributed by his employment of an agent, broker, or other intermediary who by his occupation holds himself out as having such knowledge or skill.

merger   In antitrust law, the absorption of one company by another.

midnight deadline   Midnight of the banking day following the day a commercial paper instrument is received.

minimum wage   A statutorily set floor under hourly wages.

minor   A legal status afforded to those who are under a set age.

misdemeanor   A crime that is punishable by a relatively minor fine and/or imprisonment for less than a year.

mislaid property   Property whose owner consciously laid it aside with the intent to retrieve it later but which now cannot be found.

mistake   A defense to criminal charges when, because of honest error by the defendant, the required criminal mental state is negated.

mitigation   A duty upon the party injured by a breach of contract to minimize the harm done.

money   The medium of exchange that any government has officially adopted as part of its currency.

monogamy   The condition of having only one spouse.

monopolizing conduct   Behavior indicating that a dominant market firm achieved and/or abused its position by improper methods.

monopoly   Control over the production of a good or the provision of a service held by one person or one firm.

monopoly power   The ability to control the marketplace.

mortgage   A device that transfers the right to have the real property subject to it sold to satisfy an unpaid debt.

mortgagee   The creditor in a mortgage transaction.

mortgagor   The debtor in a mortgage transaction.

motion for judgment on the pleadings   A pretrial motion contending that there are no factual issues to be resolved in a full trial and consequently that the judge should just decide which laws to apply to the facts agreed to in the pleadings and enter judgment accordingly.

motive   The reason for acting in a particular manner.

mutual insurance company   An insurance company that is capitalized through the premiums of its insureds.

mutual mistake   A mistake made by both or all parties to a contract.

mutual rescission   A discharge of contractual obligations that is brought about when the parties to a contract agree to return whatever (or the equivalent value of whatever) they have received under the contract.

N

natural law school   A legal philosophy based on the belief that an ideal legal system was implanted in the reason of human beings before they were ruined by passion, greed, and the like.

negligence   Acting in a way that violates the duty of due care that a reasonable person owes to others.

negotiable instrument   A writing signed by its maker or drawer that is unconditionally payable on demand or at a specific time to order or to bearer in a sum certain in money.

negotiation   A transfer of commercial paper as a result of which the transferee becomes a holder, a holder in due course, or a holder through a holder in due course.

no-fault insurance systems   State laws requiring that, within certain loss limits and regardless of who is at fault, the parties involved in an automobile accident be indemnified by their own insurers.

nominal damages   A token monetary award to acknowledge that the rights of the plaintiff have been violated, but with little resultant harm.

nominal partners   Individuals who are not actually partners but hold themselves out as such or allow themselves to be held out as such.

nonconforming goods   Goods that deviate from the specifications of the buyer or are defective in some way.

noncupative wills   Wills that are orally made.

not-for-profit corporation   A corporation created to achieve educational, charitable, or other ends without any return to its investors.

novation   A legal maneuver whereby a contracting party secures a release by substituting someone else to perform her or his contractual obligations.

O

obligee   The person to whom an obligor is obliged.

obligor   The person who is obligated to fulfill a contractual promise.

obvious   Plainly evident to a person with average skill in the particular field involved.

offer   A proposed bargain or exchange.

offeree   The person to whom an offer is made.

offering statement   A document, required to be filed in a Securities and Exchange Commission office for small public offerings, that contains financial statements (not professionally audited) and other information included in a typical prospectus.

offeror   The person who makes an offer.

oligopoly   An economic condition in which only a few companies control most of the market.

omnibus clause   An automobile policy term by which the insured can extend coverage to household members or to drivers operating with the permission of any of the insureds.

open price term   An omission from a sales contract of specification of the consideration due for goods.

option contract   A contract that binds the offeror to his or her promise to keep an offer open for a set period of time.

order of relief   A court declaration that a debtor is in a state of bankruptcy liquidation.

order paper   Commercial paper payable to or at the direction of the party named in the special endorsement at the end of its endorsement chain and found in only one of two forms: (1) either it has been issued to a specific party and has not yet been endorsed, or (2) regardless of whether it was issued to cash or to a specific person, it has a special endorsement at the end of its endorsement chain.

ordinary duress   A personal defense to commercial paper based on the fact that it was issued due to economic threats or legitimate threats of criminal prosecution.

output contract   A contract under which a product maker contracts to sell all of his or her production during a set period to another party to the contract.

outside directors   Individuals without a significant financial interest in the corporation of which they are directors.

overdraft   The amount of a check in excess of the deposited funds.

P

parole   The conditional release of a criminal before the required term of imprisonment has been completed.

parol evidence rule   A contractual doctrine that disallows any oral (parol) testimony contradicting, adding to, or modifying a written contract.

participating preferred stock   A type of stock whose owners are entitled to receive a share of the monies for common stock dividends left over after the dividends on preferred stock have been paid.

partition   The dividing of property held in tenancy or of the value received for such property.

partnership at will   A partnership that any partner may dissolve at any time without incurring any liability for doing so.

partnership by estoppel   Not an actual partnership but a legal device created to make individuals who have alleged nonexistent partnerships or their own nonexistent membership in existing partnerships responsible for the losses that innocent individuals have incurred as a consequence of such allegations.

past consideration   Nonbinding consideration given without expectation of or demand for a binding promise in return.

patent   A nonrenewable legal monopoly over the right to make, use, or sell a device.

payee   The party named in commercial paper to receive the funds or to have the power to order them paid to someone else.

payor bank   The bank by which an item is payable as drawn or accepted.

perfection   In a loan transaction, the next stage after attachment by which a secured party obtains a set priority in relation to other creditors in the collateral.

perfect tender   The tender of delivery of goods and the goods so tendered that conform to the contract in all respects.

periodic tenancy (also known as a **tenancy from year to year**)   A leasehold that continues for successive like intervals of time subject only to termination by proper notice from one of the parties.

personal defenses   Defenses to the collection of commercial paper that are good only against mere holders and assignees.

personal property   All things that are not real property.

piercing the corporate veil   The court-ordered stripping away of the protection of limited liability normally afforded to corporate owners.

plaintiff   A person who initiates a lawsuit by filing a complaint.

plea bargain   An agreement by which the defendant agrees to plead guilty in exchange for a reduced charge or for the prosecutor's recommendation of a lighter sentence.

pleadings   Formal written statements, such as the complaint and answer, exchanged between the parties prior to trial.

pledge   The transfer of possession of a debtor's personal property to a creditor who has the right to sell it upon default to pay off an obligation of its owner.

policy   A written contract of insurance.

possession   The ability to exercise control over something to the exclusion of all others.

postdated   An instrument issued bearing a future date.

power of attorney   A written authorization of agency.

precedent   The rule of law to be applied to a particular legal issue.

preferential transfer   A payment by an insolvent debtor giving the payee creditor more than that person would have received in a Chapter 7 bankruptcy proceeding.

preferred stock   A type of stock whose dividend amount is usually set and whose dividends are paid in full before any dividends are paid on common stock.

preliminary hearing   An official proceeding at which the evidence against the accused is presented so as to allow the court to determine whether the state should be allowed to proceed with a trial.

premises   The real property subject to the legal action at hand.

premium   The amount of consideration that an insurer is paid for assuming a particular risk.

prenuptial agreement   A contract formed in consideration of marriage that specifies the financial rights of both parties in such situations as divorce.

pretrial conference   A conference at which the judge and the attorneys for all parties meet and try to get the parties to settle their problems without a formal trial.

price   The cost in money or value paid for a good or service; in sales law, the consideration required to be transferred in exchange for goods.

prima facie evidence   Proof sufficient on its face to serve as the basis for a factual presumption.

primary beneficiary   The person named first in priority to receive the payout of an insurance policy.

primary liability   The unconditional responsibility to pay a commercial paper instrument whenever the instrument is due.

principal   In commercial paper law, the face amount of a note; in agency law, the person authorizing another to act in her or his stead.

private corporation   A corporate entity set up, funded, and run by private individuals to achieve private ends.

privity   The mutual relationship between buyer and seller based on the establishment of a bargain.

probable cause   Reasonable legal grounds for the action in question.

probate court   A specialized court that is responsible for administering wills and estates.

probation   The release of a party convicted and sentenced for a crime on the condition that the sentence will not be executed as long as the party abides by the terms of the release set by the court.

profit   The right to take from the soil of the land of another.

promisee   The person to whom a contractual promise is made.

promise to perform a preexisting duty   A promise to do something that the promisor is already legally obligated to do.

promisor   The person who makes a contractual promise.

promissory estoppel   A doctrine of contract law that prevents a promisor from stating that he or she did not receive consideration for his or her promise.

promissory note   A written promise by one party to pay money to the order of another party.

promoters   Individuals who advocate a business idea and its corporate form to potential investors.

promotion   The advocacy to potential investors of a business idea and its corporate form.

property   The rights and interests that each of us can have in things.

prospectus   A document on a stock issue (containing information relevant to the purchase of the stock and an invitation to buy it) that must be approved by the Securities and Exchange Commission and be made available to prospective buyers of any portion of the issue.

proximate cause   A harm-causing factor for which the defendant is legally responsible because the harm caused is within the factor's range of foreseeable consequences.

proxy   An authorization by which a shareholder allows someone else to cast his or her vote in a corporate election.

psychological egoism   An ethical system under which an individual acts primarily because of the impact that her or his behavior will have on others.

public corporation   A corporate organization set up by a local or state government or the federal government to accomplish a governmental purpose.

puffing   A salesperson's exaggerated statement of opinion.

punitive damages   See **exemplary damages**.

purchase   The transmittal of property from one person to another by voluntary agreement and action based on consideration.

purchase money security interest   A security interest acquired by a party, be it a lender or a seller, that provides the value needed to purchase specific consumer goods.

Q

qualified endorsement   A signature on the reverse of a piece of commercial paper accompanied by the phrase "without recourse" or another phrase of similar effect.

quarters   A qualifying term for social benefits defined as a period in which a worker earned at least approximately $600.

quasi contract (also referred to as an **implied-at-law contract**)   Not actually a contract, but a remedy that the courts utilize to return value to someone who has enriched another person in the absence of an express or implied contract between them.

quitclaim deed   A deed that merely passes whatever claim or interest the grantor may have or might receive in the real property.

quota   A certain number of employee positions that an employer has set aside to be filled exclusively by a subgroup on which the employer's previous discrimination in employment has had an adverse impact.

R

ratification   The display of a willingness to be bound by a contract's terms.

ratified   In agency law, expressly or impliedly approved by accepting the benefits of an unauthorized act.

ratifies   In commercial paper law, approves or confirms.

reaffirmation agreement   A bankruptcy debtor's agreement made before the completion of the bankruptcy procedure, to pay off a specific debt even after it has been discharged.

real defenses (also called **universal defenses**)   Defenses that will prevent holders, HDCs, HHDCs, and, of course, mere assignees from collecting on a check, draft, or other piece of commercial paper.

real estate   Land and the things permanently attached to land.

real property   Land, buildings, and items permanently attached to the land and buildings.

reference to standard form contract   A contract composed solely of a list of items signed by the contracting parties that is used to fill in the blanks of a predetermined proto-type contract.

registered agent   A person named to represent a corporation in receiving binding service of process.

registration statement   A document that consists of detailed information on the financial status of a company, its history, its management's experience, the reasons for and risks of a particular offering, and a variety of other information; the document must be filed with the Securities and Exchange Commission before a single share of the offering can be sold.

rejection   The expression of a lack of interest in an offer.

relevant market   The total demand for the product or service allegedly being monopolized and those products or services interchangeable with it as determined within the effective geographic area in question.

rent   To pay consideration for the right to use or occupy premises; in addition, the consideration paid for this right.

representations   Statements that the applicant for insurance makes in her or his offer but that are not included in the policy.

repudiation   An express statement or clear implication that a party to a contract is not going to perform.

requirements contract   A contract that obligates one party to the contract to buy all it needs of a particular good from another party to the contract during a set period.

resale price maintenance   The efforts of a manufacturer or distributor to control the price at which a good is marketed at a commercial level other than its own.

rescind   To cancel any current or future effect of a contract and to take all possible steps to return the contract's parties to their precontractual positions.

respondeat superior (let the master answer)   The rule of law placing vicarious liability on the employer or principal.

restricted securities   A designation meaning that the subject shares cannot be resold without registration unless the resale is an exempt transaction.

restrictive endorsement   A signature on the reverse of a piece of commercial paper accompanied by wording that curtails or restricts the transferee's rights.

reverse discrimination Government-endorsed favorable hiring, promoting, or discharging based on the otherwise prohibited categories of sex, race, color, etc.

revocation The recalling or taking back of an offer by the offeror prior to acceptance.

riders (also called **endorsements**) Terms that modify or tailor standard insurance forms to fit specific situations.

right-to-work laws Laws prohibiting collective bargaining agreements from requiring union membership as a condition of employment.

robbery The taking of goods or money in the possession of another, from his person or his immediate presence, by the use of force or fear.

royalty Compensation for the use of property.

rule of reason A Supreme Court decree that certain prosecutions brought under the Sherman Act had to be judged by the courts from a reasonability standpoint to see whether alleged illegal acts eliminated or promoted competition.

S

sale The passing of title to goods from a seller to a buyer for a price.

sale on approval A transaction in which the buyer is allowed to return the goods purchased within a reasonable period even if they conform to the contract.

sale or return A transaction in which goods sold primarily for resale may be returned even if they conform to the contract.

satisfactory performance A contractual result that requires the obligor to satisfy the obligee's personal tastes in order to render a proper performance.

scope of authority The parameters of power that a principal grants an agent.

S corporation A corporation that is organized in the same manner as a normal corporation except for the fact that its profits and losses are taxed directly to its stockholders.

secondary boycott A boycott by third parties who agree to cease doing business with a firm with which a union is involved in a dispute.

secondary liability The legal responsibility to pay a commercial paper instrument whenever the party primarily liable does not do so.

secondary standards Standards of air quality that must be met to preserve the welfare of the public in the form of animal and plant life and visibility.

secret partners Individuals who are working general partners but are not publicly known as such.

secured loan A debt transaction in which the creditor is given a security interest in specific property of the debtor for utilization in the event of the debtor's default.

security Sufficient assurance that a loan will be repaid; in security regulation law, an investment contract whereby investors provide the necessary capital and share in the earnings generated through the promoters' management and control.

security agreement The written agreement by which the owner of collateral creates a creditor's security interest in the collateral.

security interest A property right that allows its holder legal recourse against specific property.

separated The condition of marital partners who live in separate quarters.

service of process An official presentation of the summons and complaint to a defendant.

severally liable The status of a person who is individually responsible for a legal obligation.

severalty Ownership by only one person, the simplest and most common form of ownership.

shareholders The owners of a corporation.

shipment term A sales contract term that requires the seller to turn over the goods sold to a carrier for delivery to the buyer.

sight draft   A draft payable on demand or "at sight."

silent partners   Individuals who are properly and publicly acknowledged as partners but who do not participate actively in management of the partnership.

slander   The communication of false statements in a temporary form (typically, this is done orally).

social insurance   A form of insurance that provides protection against the realities of forced retirement, disability, severe illness, unemployment, and other risks.

sole proprietorship   A business owned by one person who is fully, personally liable for all of its obligations.

special endorsement   A signature on the reverse of a commercial paper instrument along with a statement naming the endorsee and directing payment of the instrument to that party.

specific performance   A contractual remedy by which the court orders that a contract be fulfilled by a particular party.

stale check   A check that is presented for payment over six months after the date of issue indicated on its face.

stare decisis   The policy of enforcing established precedents so as to ensure fairness to all similarly situated parties.

statute   Legislatively created law.

statute of frauds   A statute requiring that, in order to be enforceable, a written version of an alleged contract, signed by the party against whom enforcement is sought, be produced in court.

statute of limitations   A statute that limits the time available to bring suit or to initiate a prosecution.

stay   A suspension or halt.

stock   Certificates or shares of ownership in a corporation.

stock insurance company   A firm that has been capitalized by investors who expect a return on their money from its profits.

stop-payment order   A directive to the drawee institution not to transfer funds in accordance with the terms of a previously issued draft.

strict liability   A legal doctrine that holds the defendant liable for harm resulting from certain types of conduct or activity regardless of how much care the defendant took to prevent the harm from occurring.

strike   A concerted employee refusal to work for an employer.

subletting   A transfer by a tenant of some of her or his rights and interests under a lease.

subrogated   Substituted for another in the pursuit of a claim or right against a third party.

subscription agreement   A written contract by which a potential investor agrees to buy a certain amount of a corporation's stock if and when the stock is issued.

substantial performance   A contractual result whereby a party exhibits a good faith effort that meets contractual expectations except for minor details.

sum certain   An amount clearly ascertainable from the face of a piece of commercial paper.

summons   A court order that the defendant appear and respond to a civil complaint or criminal charge within a given period.

surety   A person who agrees to be primarily liable for the payment of a debt (or the performance of an obligation) of another.

T

tax lien   An encumbrance against property subject to taxation for an unpaid levy.

tenancy at sufferance   A leasehold terminable without notice, that is created by law whenever a periodic tenant or a tenant for years wrongfully retains possession of the premises after the lease has expired.

tenancy at will   A leasehold that permits the exclusive possession of real property for an indefinite duration.

tenancy for years   A leasehold for any fixed duration, such as days, weeks, months, or years.

tenancy in partnership   A co-ownership in partnership property set up in Section 24 of the Uniform Partnership Act by which each partner is given an equal right with the other partners to possess specific partnership property for partnership purposes.

tenant   A renter of real property.

tenant in common   A co-owner of undivided property who may transfer her or his ownership interest without the permission of the other co-owners.

tenants by the entirety   A husband and wife whom the common law treats as tenants who each own all of the subject property in the same manner as joint tenants with the right of survivorship but with the additional proviso that the creditors of one spouse cannot satisfy their claims by reaching the property held by both spouses in this tenancy.

tender of delivery   An offer to turn over goods to a buyer.

tender of performance   A ready, willing, and able offer to perform in accordance with the terms of a contract.

terminable at will   In labor law, a relationship that may be ended by either party at any time without notice and without producing a litigable cause of action unless a fixed term is contracted for.

termination statement   A document filed in the same governmental office as the foregoing financing statement giving notice that the property used as collateral is no longer encumbered.

term insurance   A life insurance policy containing only coverage on the life of the insured.

testate   The legal condition of a person who dies leaving a valid will.

testator, testatrix   The maker of a will.

third-party beneficiary   A party outside a contract to whom the parties to the contract may intend benefits to flow.

third-party complaint   A procedural device that makes a party not previously involved a part of a civil suit.

time draft   A draft due after a certain period, such as a number of days or months.

time note   A note payable at a set future date.

title   The formal ultimate legal right to ownership of property.

tortfeasor   The person who commits a tort.

torts   Personal injuries or wrongs for which the law provides remedies.

trade acceptance   A draft drawn by a seller on a buyer as drawee that the buyer accepts upon receipt of a satisfactory shipment of goods.

trade fixtures   Items attached to another's realty by a renter to facilitate a business that the renter is conducting on the realty.

trademark   The identifying symbol, word(s), or design by which a business distinguishes its products to consumers.

trade usage   An understanding or pattern of dealing established in the area of commerce under consideration.

transcript   A verbatim record of what went on during a trial.

traveler's check   A commercial paper instrument, sold to a user by a financial institution acting as both drawer and drawee, that requires the user's signature before the issuer and then again before the payee as authentication to enable cashing.

travel insurance   Term insurance intended to indemnify for the loss of life of the insured on a trip by plane or some other mode of travel.

trespassers   Persons who willfully enter the property of another without consent.

trial court   The court in which a case is fully heard for the first time.

trial jury   A group of persons selected according to law to impartially determine the factual questions of a case from the evidence allowed before them in court.

trials   Formal proceedings for the examination and determination of legal issues.

trust   A separate entity created by law to which the ownership of property can be transferred so that the property can then be managed by designated individuals in accordance with the wishes of the transferor.

trustees   The parties in charge of a trust.

U

ultra vires   Any action taken by a corporation that is outside its legitimate powers.

unconscionable contract   A contract entered into as a result of the greatly unequal bargaining power of its parties; the stronger party makes a take-it-or-leave-it offer to which the weaker party has no viable market alternative.

underinsured motorist coverage   A coverage available under an automobile insurance policy that allows an insured to collect against her or his insurer for the irrecoverable amount of the damages for bodily injury and wrongful death up to certain per person and per accident limits.

underwriting   Insuring various risks.

undisclosed principal   A principal involved in an agency arrangement in which the agent acts under a contract that forbids revealing that he or she is acting for a principal.

undue influence   A condition in which the dominating party in a confidential relationship is able to compel the dominated party to enter into a contract that benefits the former.

unfair labor practices   Certain forms of conduct by a union or an employer that were made illegal by the National Labor Relations Act.

Uniform Commercial Code (UCC)   A set of laws governing areas of trade and business regulated by the states.

unilateral contract   A contract by which one party to a contract is obligated to fulfill a contractual promise only if another party to the contract performs.

unilateral mistake   A mistake made by only one of the parties to a contract.

uninsured motorist coverage   A coverage available under an automobile insurance policy that allows an insured to collect bodily injury and wrongful death damages (not property damages) from her or his insurer if the driver causing the harm does not have insurance.

unsecured loan   A loan transaction that does not provide the creditor with an interest in specific property of the debtor, thereby leaving the creditor, in the event of default, with the sole alternative of proceeding against the debtor's general asset position.

use   The enjoyment of things by their employment.

usury   The charging of an interest rate for the loan of money that exceeds the legal limit.

utilitarianism   An ethical system under which an action is deemed proper if it produces the greatest good for the greatest number of the people affected by it.

V

valid contract   A contract that is legally binding and enforceable.

valid title   A legally enforceable title.

value (under the UCC)   A contractual consideration, a past indebtedness, or a credit extension.

verdict   A statement of whatever conclusions a jury has reached on the questions of fact.

vicarious liability   A legal doctrine that imposes responsibility on one party for the actionable conduct of another party on the basis of an existing relationship between the two parties.

vocational rehabilitation   Training that is provided to injured employees so that they will be able to assume another type of job.

voidable contract   A contract whose legal effect may be canceled by one or more of its parties.

voidable title   A title that may be terminated at the option of one of its parties.

void contract   A contract that has no legal effect.

void title   A nonexistent title.

W

warehouseman's lien   A possessory security interest in stored items for unpaid storage costs.

warranties   Statements made by an applicant for insurance in her or his offer that become a part of the issued policy.

warranty   A guarantee under the law of sales that is used to describe the product, and its quality and performance.

warranty deed   A deed that not only conveys title from the grantor (the transferor of the property) but also contains several warranties for the benefit of the grantee (the transferee of the property).

warranty of fitness for a particular purpose   An implied warranty imposed on any seller who knows or should know the buyer's intended use for the goods sold and upon whose skill or judgment the buyer is relying for the supply of suitable goods.

warranty of good title   An implied warranty imposed on the seller of goods that guarantees that the title transferred to the buyer is valid and that the transfer is rightful.

warranty of merchantability   A guarantee that the goods sold are fit for their ordinary intended use.

whole life insurance policies   Policies that offer a savings feature and pay a moderate interest rate on the funds accumulated from their premiums.

will   A person's expression of how his or her property is to be distributed upon his or her death.

winding up (of partnership)   The concluding of the partnership's business (no new contracts can be entered into except as necessary to fulfill existing obligations) and the selling of the partnership's property.

writ of certiorari   An order compelling a lower court to turn over the record of a case to an appellate court for review.

writ of execution   A court order to compel a party subject to a court judgment to comply with it.

INDEX

496   Index